# American Foreign Policy / A HISTORY

# American

# Foreign Policy
## A History

THOMAS G. PATERSON
*University of Connecticut*

J. GARRY CLIFFORD
*University of Connecticut*

KENNETH J. HAGAN
*United States Naval Academy*

D. C. HEATH AND COMPANY
*Lexington, Massachusetts    Toronto*

Cartography by Norman Clark Adams

The poem by Robert Underwood Johnson on p. 316
is © 1928 by The New York Times Company.
Reprinted by permission.

International Standard Book Number: 0-669-94698-2

Library of Congress Catalog Card Number: 76-52763

# Preface

Writing a survey book is necessarily a learning experience, for the authors must read and synthesize the prolific work of fellow scholars. We have brought our own research in primary sources and our own interpretations to this synthesis, but the scholarship of our friends and colleagues in diplomatic history has proven indispensable. We have cited their contributions in our extensive footnotes and in the bibliographic sections, and we heartily thank them.

We have designed this book to include the tools needed to study American diplomatic history. The illustrations, many of them rare and unusual prints selected from some seventy depositories in the United States and Great Britain, have been closely integrated with the text. The map program is unique, especially for its "perspective" maps. The book also includes charts and graphs to render the historical record precise and complete. Each chapter presents a listing of the Presidents and Secretaries of State, with their terms of office, and an appendix adds Chairmen of the Senate Foreign Relations Committee and the Secretaries of Defense. The footnotes and "further reading" sections, reflecting excellent recent scholarship, will assist the curious in further exploration. A thorough index, in itself an important study tool, is provided.

For continuity, thoroughness, and thematic unity, we have treated in each chapter such basic points as the comparative influence of ideology, economics, and strategy, the importance of personalities and styles, domestic politics, bureaucratic and executive-legislative competition, criticisms of and alternatives to American foreign policy, definitions of the national interest, historical "lessons," measurements of American power, and the impact of American interventions on other cultures. We emphasize the theme of expansionism. "People" are central to history as both victors and victims. Thus we have incorporated a good deal of biography in the diplomatic story and have liberally quoted participants (and scholars), letting them speak for themselves. Each chapter opens with a "diplomatic crossroad," a significant event that helps illustrate the chief characteristics and issues of the era. The opening episode is then placed in its large historical context and the main themes and characters of the period are discussed. Chronological and topical sections follow next. Each chapter closes with a discussion of the legacy of the period—the lessons each generation bequeathed to the next generation of Americans.

Thomas G. Paterson initiated this project and coordinated its development. With Holly Izard Paterson he researched print collections and wrote captions for the illustrations. He held primary writing responsibility for chapters 5, 6, 8, 9, 10, 12, 13, 14, and 15 and shared in writing chapters 4 and 11. J. Garry Clifford held primary writing responsibility for chapters 1, 2, and 3 and shared in writing chapter 11. Kenneth J. Hagan held primary writing responsibility for chapter 7 and shared in writing chapter 4. The authors criticized one another's work, interchanged suggestions and ideas frequently, and worked as a team to insure a unified book.

We acknowledge with sincere gratitude the help of many people. Professor Alan Henrikson suggested many of the maps and Norman Adams skillfully prepared them. Sol Woolman of the University of Connecticut Photo Lab assisted with the illustrations, always reaching for the highest standards. We thank Robert Beisner, R. Christian Berg, Paul Goodwin, Alan Henrikson, George Herring, Burton Kaufman, Jean-Donald Miller, Stephen Rabe, Thomas G. Smith, Edmund S. Wehrle, Joan Hoff Wilson, and Thomas Zoumaras for reading all or parts of the manuscript and for improving it. For other assistance, we thank Richard Baker, Carol Davidge, James Gormly, Edythe and Richard Izard, Robert McMahon, R. Kent Newmyer, Wayne Repeta, Anna Lou Smethurst, and George Turner. With her customary care and craftsmanship, Sondra Astor Stave prepared the index. We wish also to thank the many museums, libraries, picture agencies, archives, and individuals who helped us locate and obtain illustrations. Their contributions are acknowledged in the credit line for each print. Special thanks go to Max Ascoli of *The Reporter* for permission to reprint several striking caricatures.

To Holly Izard Paterson we particularly extend our gratitude. She too often put aside her quilting, reading, plants, swimming, travel, and piano to edit and type the manuscript, conduct research, manage the illustration program, and press us to write with spirit and clarity.

As scholars whose work is in a constant state of revision, we welcome comments and suggestions from readers of *American Foreign Policy: A History.*

Thomas G. Paterson
*Storrs, Connecticut*

John Garry Clifford
~~Eastford~~, *Connecticut*

Kenneth J. Hagan
*Annapolis, Maryland*

# THE AUTHORS

**Thomas G. Paterson,** a native of Oregon born in 1941, graduated from the University of New Hampshire (B.A., 1963) and earned his Ph.D. from the University of California, Berkeley in 1968. At the University of Connecticut, where he has taught since 1967, Paterson studies and teaches twentieth-century American history and diplomatic history. He has written *Soviet-American Confrontation* (1973) on postwar reconstruction and the onset of the Cold War, edited *The Origins of the Cold War* (2nd ed., 1974), edited *American Imperialism and Anti-Imperialism* (1973), and edited and contributed to *Cold War Critics* (1971), a set of original essays on leading dissenters in the Truman period. Paterson's essay on the Marshall Plan is included in Barton J. Bernstein, ed., *Politics and Policies of the Truman Administration* (1974), and another on George F. Kennan is printed in Frank Merli and Theodore Wilson, eds., *Makers of American Diplomacy* (1974). He has edited *Major Problems in American Foreign Policy* (1978). Paterson is completing a study of the containment doctrine and has already edited *Containment and the Cold War* (1973). He has received fellowships from the National Endowment for the Humanities, Harry S Truman Institute, and the Eleanor Roosevelt Institute and has been elected to the governing Council of the Society for Historians of American Foreign Relations.

(Photograph by R. Kent Newmyer)

**J. Garry Clifford,** a native of Massachusetts born in 1942, earned his B.A. from Williams College (1964) and his Ph.D. in history from Indiana University (1969). Before joining the Political Science faculty of the University of Connecticut, where he teaches American diplomacy, he taught at the University of Tennessee. He has also taught at Dartmouth College. Clifford's book, *The Citizen Soldiers* (1972), on the preparedness movement before World War I, won the Frederick Jackson Turner Award from the Organization of American Historians. With Norman Cousins he has edited *Memoirs of a Man: Grenville Clark* (1975) and he is now working on a biography of Clark, a prominent internationalist, as well as on a history of the Selective Service Act. His essay titled "Change and Continuity in American Foreign Policy Since 1930" is published in James T. Patterson, ed., *Paths to the Present* (1975). The National Endowment for the Humanities has awarded him a fellowship for research.

(Photograph by R. Kent Newmyer)

**Kenneth J. Hagan,** a native of California born in 1936, received his Bachelor's degree from the University of California, Berkeley (1958) and his doctorate from Claremont Graduate School (1970). From 1958 to 1963 he was on active duty as an intelligence officer in the United States Naval Reserve. A specialist in naval and diplomatic history, he taught at Claremont Men's College and Kansas State University before becoming a civilian professor at the United States Naval Academy in 1973. He has authored *American Gunboat Diplomacy and the Old Navy, 1877–1889* (1973), an exploration of the Navy's role in American expansion, and is now editing *In Peace and War: American Naval Policies, 1775–1976*, a comprehensive survey of American naval history. He has also written an essay on naval intervention for Robin Higham, ed., *Intervention or Abstention: The Dilemma of American Foreign Policy* (1975), on naval strategy for the U.S. Naval Institute *Proceedings,* and on Alfred Thayer Mahan for Frank Merli and Theodore Wilson, eds., *Makers of American Diplomacy* (1974). In addition, he has contributed a bibliographical essay on the nineteenth-century navy for Robin Higham, ed., *A Guide to the Sources of United States Military History* (1975). Both the Smithsonian Institution and the National Endowment for the Humanities have awarded him fellowships.

(Photograph by U.S. Naval Academy)

# Contents

## 1 An Independent American Foreign Policy: The Beginnings to 1789

## 2 Independence and Expansion in a World at War, 1789–1815

# 3 Making Way for Continental Expansion, 1815–1848

# 4 Sputtering Expansionism, Sectionalism, and Civil War Diplomacy, 1848–1865

# 5 Global Rivalry, Regional Power, 1865–1895

# 6 Imperialist Thrust, 1895–1900

# 7 Managing and Extending the American Empire, 1900–1914

# 8 World Reform Through World War, 1914–1920

# 9 Power Without Punch: Relations with Europe, 1920–1939

# 10

## A Question of Power: Relations with Asia and Latin America, 1920–1939

# 11

## World War II: The Ordeal of Allied Diplomacy, 1939–1945

# 12 The Origins of the Cold War, 1945–1950

# 13 Something Old, Something New: Global Confrontations, 1950–1961

# 14 Bearing the Burden: The Vietnam Years, 1961–1969

# 15 The Diffusion of World Power: American Foreign Policy Since 1969

# Illustrations

# Maps and Charts

# American Foreign Policy / A HISTORY

**French Snuffbox.** Benjamin Franklin's reputation as a representative of frontier America is captured in a contemporary French snuffbox. In this compliment the reverend gentleman from Pennsylvania joins two other philosophers, Rousseau and Voltaire. (The Metropolitan Museum of Art, Gift of William H. Huntington, 1883)

# 1 An Independent American Foreign Policy: The Beginnings to 1789

## Diplomatic Crossroad: Jay, Franklin, and Adams and Independent Negotiations, 1782

Two disgruntled Americans rode the same carriage from Versailles to the Parisian suburb of Passy on the afternoon of August 10, 1782. John Jay and Benjamin Franklin had just spent a frustrating two hours with the French Foreign Minister, the Comte de Vergennes. These American peace commissioners, seeking to end the Revolutionary War for independence waged since 1775, had asked for French advice on two troublesome problems that had arisen in their concurrent negotiations with British and Spanish representatives. Since the Continental Congress had instructed them to make no decisions without the knowledge and counsel of the French, Jay and Franklin had asked Vergennes whether or not the United States should insist on explicit recognition of independence from England *prior* to a final peace treaty with the "mother country," and whether the western boundary of the new American nation should be the Mississippi River. On both points Vergennes and his secretary, Gerard de Rayneval, made suggestions that seemed to deny American interests. Do not worry about technicalities, Vergennes advised. If independence were made an article of the final treaty, as the British were proposing, Americans should not make a fuss about formal titles during the negotiation. Regarding the western boundary, according to Jay, Vergennes and Rayneval made it clear that "we [Americans] claimed more than we had a right to," and that Spain and England had valid claims to territory east of the Mississippi.[1]

Jay and Franklin wondered why their French ally was giving such negative advice. Jay was particularly suspicious, telling his older colleague that Vergennes was plotting to delay negotiations with England so that Spain, already entrenched in Florida, could acquire the whole Gulf Coast and additional territory to the north. Franklin agreed that Spain wanted to "coop us up within the Allegheny Mountains," but he did not think that the French were sacrificing American interests to gratify Spain.[2] The discussion became animated, and when the carriage reached Passy, Franklin invited Jay inside his apartment to continue their conversation. "Have we any reason to doubt the good faith of the King of France?" inquired Franklin. "We can depend on the French," Jay rejoined, "only to see that we are separated from England, but it is not in their interest that we should become a great and formidable people, and therefore they will not help us to become so." Franklin asked on whom the United States should rely. "We have no rational dependence except on God and ourselves," Jay solemnly answered. The Pennsylvanian shot back: "Would you deliberately break Congress' instructions?" "Unless we violate these instructions the dignity of Congress will be in the dust," Jay asserted. The seventy-five-year-old Franklin pressed further: "Then you are prepared to break our instructions if you intend to take an independence course now." Jay stood up. "*If* the instructions conflict with America's honor and dignity I would break them—like this!" The dignified New Yorker threw his long clay pipe hard into Franklin's fireplace. It shattered.[3]

Nothing that occurred in the diplomacy of the next several weeks elevated John Jay's opinion of Europeans in general, or of Frenchmen and Spaniards in particular. In early September, after further discussions about a suitable western boundary, Rayneval gave Jay a memorandum of "personal ideas" to expedite peace negotiations with England as well as a boundary settlement with Spain. Again, arguing from historical precedent, Rayneval urged the Americans not to press for the Mississippi. Jay, despite Rayneval's "personal" disclaimers, correctly assumed that the memorandum also reflected Vergennes' sentiments. A few days later Rayneval disappeared from Paris, having been dispatched on a secret mission to London. Jay was immediately suspicious. Paris was buzzing with rumors. Even the usually unflappable Franklin became worried. Perhaps Rayneval's mission was designed to bring the same arguments to the British that he was making to the Americans; perhaps France sought the role of arbiter in North America, supported British claims north of the Ohio River, and wanted to give Spain full control over the Mississippi. The next day Jay received from a British agent in Paris an intercepted French dispatch, in cipher, which urged a strong stand against American claims to the Newfoundland fisheries. Franklin cautiously pointed out that this dispatch, sent by a French envoy in America, did not necessarily reflect the views of Vergennes or King Louis XVI. It was enough for Jay, however. On September 11, without first informing Franklin, Jay boldly sent his own secret emissary to London with the proposal that secret and separate negotiations for peace begin at once. The British jumped at the chance to split the Franco-American alliance. When he learned what his younger colleague had done, Franklin protested. But he went along.

By the time the third American peace commissioner arrived in Paris, private talks with the British had gone on for several weeks. John Adams had just successfully negotiated a commercial treaty with the Dutch. He had been in Paris earlier in the war and did not like the French; nor did he like Dr. Franklin, whom he thought too cozy with the French. The cantankerous New Englander found it difficult to trust anyone, but he immediately found a kindred spirit in Jay, who apprised him of the state of the negotiations. Adams approved of everything that had been done, while at the same time warning Jay that Franklin was hopelessly subservient to Vergennes. Adams dallied for four days before making a courtesy call on Franklin. "After the usage I have received from him, I cannot bear go near him," Adams grumbled.[4] Once at Passy, he barely observed amenities. Immediately Adams launched into a lecture. Everything Jay had done was correct. Jay was right in his suspicions toward Vergennes. Jay was right to insist on prior independence, access to the fisheries, and extensive western boundaries. Adams waxed enthusiastic about the decision to ignore Vergennes and negotiate separately with the British on these issues. To do otherwise would be leaving "the lamb to the custody of the wolf."[5] His conscience unburdened, Adams returned to his apartment in the Hotel du Roi.

Franklin hardly replied to Adams' outburst. Suffering from the gout, the old philosopher listened patiently and tolerantly to the person he later described as "always an honest man, often a wise one, but sometimes, and in some things, absolutely out of his senses."[6] Franklin agreed that the United States should remain firm on both the fisheries and the Mississippi boundary. Access to the Newfoundland fishing grounds was vital to New England's economy, while the "Father of Waters" stood as an indispensable highway for trans-Allegheny commerce. "A Neighbor might as well ask me to sell my Street Door," he had said to Jay regarding the Mississippi.[7] What bothered Franklin was the failure to consult Vergennes. French loans had kept America solvent through six long years of war, and French ships and troops had contributed mightily to the decisive victory at Yorktown in 1781. Franklin valued the French alliance. "If we were to break our faith with this nation," he wrote, "England would again trample on us and every other nation despise us."[8] Unlike his younger colleagues, Franklin was not convinced that the French were dealing with Spain and England behind American backs. Nevertheless, Franklin realized the importance of a united front in negotiations. Always a pragmatist, he had written in his *Autobiography:* "So convenient a thing it is to be a *reasonable creature,* since it enables one to find or make a reason for everything one has a mind to do."[9] Franklin decided to be reasonable. The next day, October 30, just prior to meeting with the British commissioners, he startled John Jay: "I am of your opinion, and will go with these gentlemen in the business without consulting this court."[10]

Franklin remained true to his word, and on November 30, 1782, England and the United States signed a "preliminary treaty" of peace. The terms, enumerated in a comprehensive treaty some ten months later, guaranteed American independence and provided generous boundaries. It was, in the words of historian Samuel Flagg Bemis, "the greatest victory in the annals of American diplomacy."[11]

The American decision to negotiate separately in 1782 was as symbolic as it was successful. By going to war with England, the colonies had sought to win their independence, enlarge their commerce, and expand their territorial domain. Patriot leaders hoped to attain these goals without getting entangled in European politics. One motive for independence was the desire to escape the constant wars and dynastic intrigues that characterized eighteenth-century Europe. But victory required help. France became America's ally in 1778, and in the next two years Spain and the Netherlands also joined the war against England. The war for American independence hence became part of a world war. The entanglements Americans hoped to avoid inevitably followed. At the critical moment in the peace negotiations, Jay and Adams rightly suspected that their French ally, although committed to American independence, did not share the expansive American vision of that independence. The two commissioners thereupon persuaded Franklin to pursue an *independent* course, take advantage of European rivalries, and extract a generous treaty from the British. In Adams' eyes especially, these American diplomats were

**John Adams (1735–1826).** Native of Braintree (Quincy), Massachusetts, graduate of Harvard, Boston lawyer, colonial rebel, and diplomat, Adams helped negotiate the treaty of peace with England. Introspective, analytical, and courageous, Adams became President in 1797. (The Metropolitan Museum of Art, Purchase, 1960. Harris Brisbane Dick Fund)

Blessed are the PEACE MAKERS

**"Blessed Are the Peacemakers."** In this critical British cartoon of 1783 a Spaniard and Frenchman lead George III by the neck while Lord Shelburne carries the "Preliminaries of Peace." The procession is commanded by an American wielding a whip and tugging a sulking, boorish Dutchman. (British Museum)

maintaining American honor by breaking instructions which French diplomats had forced on a pliant Congress. It was an ironic moment. Americans said they pursued independence and empire not merely for selfish motives, but also for a more civilized mode of international relations, free from the monarchical double-dealing of European power politics. "We are fighting for the dignity and happiness of human nature," Franklin had stated rather grandly in 1777.[12] To gain their ends, however, Franklin, Jay, and Adams employed the same Machiavellian tactics that they despised in Europeans.

## Reaching for Independence: Principle and Reality

The United States could not have won independence from England without assistance from France. This was the inescapable fact of early American diplomacy. However much the patriots of 1776 wanted to isolate themselves from the wars and diplomatic maneuverings of Europe, European events provided them with the opportunity for national liberation.

The century-old rivalry between France and England for pre-eminence in Europe and control of North America provided the immediate backdrop for the American Revolution. Four wars fought between 1688 and 1763 were European in origin, but had profound consequences in the New World. The most recent war, 1756–1763, called the Seven Years War in Europe and the French and Indian War in America, had ensured the virtual elimination of French power from North America. By the Treaty of Paris (1763) the defeated French ceded Canada and the Ohio Valley to the British and relinquished Louisiana to the Spanish. Spain, in turn, gave up the Floridas to England. For the most part colonial leaders cheered the victorious British war for empire. Benjamin Franklin, then a colonial agent in England, urged removal of the French from Canada. "I have long been of opinion," he wrote in 1760, "that the foundations of the future grandeur and stability of the British empire lay in America. . . . All the country from the St. Lawrence to the Mississippi will be in another century filled with British people."[13] A youthful John Adams similarly predicted that with the defeat of "the turbulent Gallicks, our people according to the exactest computations, will in another century become more numerous than England itself."[14]

The euphoria was short-lived. As soon as the French and Indian War ended, London began to tighten the machinery of empire. A standing army of 10,000 men was sent to America for imperial defense. To pay for its upkeep, and to help defray the costs of the recent war with France, Parliament levied new taxes on the American colonies. Old mercantile regulations forbidding direct American trade with foreign ports in the West Indies were now enforced. The British also tried to discourage American settlement across the Alleghenies. The colonials retaliated with petitions, economic boycotts, and sporadic outbreaks of violence. Parliament responded with more taxes. The Tea Act of 1773 led to the Boston Tea Party, which, in turn, triggered the Coercive Acts. Galling to expansionist Americans, the Quebec Act of 1774 made the Ohio Valley an integral part of Canada. Armed resistance exploded at Lexington and Concord in the spring of 1775, followed by battles around Boston. Then came an abortive American invasion of Quebec in December, 1775. By this time John Adams and Benjamin Franklin were both urging ties with the same "turbulent Gallicks" they had hoped to destroy twenty years before.

As American leaders moved cautiously toward independence, the emerging republican ideology, which embraced the "rights of Englishmen" and the principles of representative government, also contained the roots of an independent foreign policy. Historical lessons seemed to point toward independence. "I have but one lamp by which my feet are guided," said Patrick Henry in 1775, "and that is by the lamp of experience. I know of no way of judging the future but by the past."[15] Benjamin Franklin asked the central question: "Have not all Mankind in all Ages had the Right of deserting their Native Country? . . . Did not the Saxons desert their Native Country when they came to Britain?"[16] More specifically, Americans looked to their colonial past. As British mercantile restrictions tightened in the 1760s, colonial leaders began to argue that the imperial connection with England was one-sided, and that Americans were constantly embroiled in England's wars against their will. Attacks by the French and Indians along the northern frontier usually had their origins in European quarrels, yet Americans nevertheless had to pay taxes, raise armies, and fight and die. Britain did not always seem to appreciate colonial sacrifices. The most telling example occurred in 1745 when New Englanders, through good luck and enormous exertion, captured the strategic French fortress of Louisbourg on Cape Breton Island. In the European peace treaty three years later, however, the British handed back Louisbourg in exchange for French conquests in India. Americans had no wish to be pawns in England's colonial wars. Franklin probably exaggerated when he told Parliament in 1766 that the Americans had been in "perfect peace with both French and Indians" and that the recent conflict had been "really a British war."[17] He was nonetheless expressing what one scholar has called "a deep-seated feeling of escape from Europe and a strong tendency, encouraged by European diplomacy, to avoid becoming entangled in European conflict, whenever it was to their interest to do so."[18]

Americans advocating independence also found arguments in recent British history. Many of the same English Whig writers whom Americans quoted in defense of "no taxation without representation" had also taken part in a great debate over the direction of British foreign policy during the first half of the eighteenth century. These Whigs had criticized British involvement in continental European wars. Since the European balance of power was always unstable, they argued that continental entanglements might improve the German territorial interests of the House of Hanover but certainly not those of England. There was suspicion of England's German kings. "This great, this powerful, this formidable kingdom, is considered only as a province to a despicable electorate [Hanover]," William Pitt complained in 1743.[19] England's true interests, these Whigs never ceased to point out, lay in expanding its commerce and empire. Political alliances were taboo; they have not "produced any advantage to us."[20] One pamphleteer posited a general rule in 1744: "A Prince or State ought to avoid all Treaties, except such as tend towards Commerce or Manufactures. . . . All other Alliances may be look'd upon as so many Incumbrances."[21] The similarity between these arguments for British isolation from Europe and the later American rationale for independence is striking. American leaders were quite aware of the British debate. Benjamin Franklin, as a colonial agent in London in the pre-Revolutionary period, knew many of the Whig critics intimately. Merchants, lawyers, and plantation owners visited England or studied in England. In their desire to avoid British wars and British taxes, it was not surprising that Revolutionary leaders would appropriate British precepts.

Another source of American thinking on independence and foreign policy came in the writings of the French *philosophes*. As sons of the Enlightenment and spokesmen for the rising bourgeoisie, the *philosophes* launched an attack on all diplomatic and political practices that thwarted the proper rule of reason in international affairs. Traditional diplomacy was synonymous with double-dealing, they argued, "an obscure art which hides itself in the folds of deceit, which fears to let itself be seen and believes it can succeed only in the darkness of mystery."[22] Like the English Whigs, the *philosophes* emphasized commercial expansion over standard power politics. Political barriers were artificial; commerce tied the "family of nations" together with "threads of silk."[23] Trade should be as free as possible, unfettered by mercantile restrictions. Some *philosophes* hoped that enlightened princes could transform international relations; more radical writers like Condorcet wanted to take diplomacy out of the hands of princes and remove all obstacles to a direct expression of the popular will. "Alliances," wrote Condorcet, "are only means by which the rulers of states precipitate the people into wars from which they benefit either by covering up their mistakes or by carrying out their plots against freedom."[24] Diplomacy should be as simple as possible, consisting largely of commercial interchange between individual persons rather than governments. Such views on foreign affairs made heady wine for Americans. Although never as widely read in America as the English Whigs, the *philosophes* provided Revolutionary leaders with a humanitarian credo as they sought to win empire and independence from England. Like John Winthrop's Puritans, they would not merely be benefiting themselves, but also erecting a model for the rest of the world. John Adams was perfectly sincere when he told Vergennes in 1781 that "the dignity of North America does not consist in diplomatic ceremonials. . . . [It] consists solely in reason, justice, truth, the rights of mankind, and the interests of the nations of Europe."[25]

The movement for an independent foreign policy reached its climax with the convocation of the Second Continental Congress, following Lexington and Concord, in the summer of 1775. "We are between the hawk and the buzzard," said delegate Robert Livingston of New York, and "we puzzle ourselves between the commercial and warlike opposition."[26] Some Americans who still wanted to remain within the British Empire held out hope that continued commercial opposition—no imports, no exports—would force Parliament and the King to negotiate. More radical delegates wanted to continue the war and declare independence. Benjamin Franklin proposed "articles of confederation" that would give Congress full power to make war and peace. John Adams called for construction of an American navy. Other advocates of independence urged the opening of American ports to foreign trade, arguing that only with protection from foreign navies could American merchant ships reach European ports. With their British market no longer available, the thirteen colonies needed commerce to survive. Foreign trade required foreign assistance. This argument for independence, made repeatedly behind the closed doors of Congress, finally became public on January 10, 1776, with the appearance of Thomas Paine's pamphlet *Common Sense*.

Tom Paine was an English Quaker who had come to America in 1774. While in England he had drunk deeply at the well of Whig dissent, and once in Philadelphia he became friends with the faction of Congress aspiring to independence. Their arguments were summarized in Paine's pamphlet. Opposing further petitions to the King, urging construction of a navy and the immediate formation of a confederation, emphasizing the need for foreign assistance, and calling for the opening of American ports to the rest of the world, Paine's celebrated call for independence also spelled out the benefits of an independent foreign policy. Not only was reconciliation with England no longer possible, it was undesirable as well. As Paine put it with some exaggeration, there was not "a single advantage that this continent can reap by being connected with Great Britain." On the contrary, "France and Spain never were, nor perhaps ever will be, our enemies as Americans, but as Our being subjects of Great Britain." For Paine and his American friends, "Our plan is commerce, and that, well attended to, will secure us the Peace and friendship of all Europe; because it is in the interest of all Europe to have America as a free port. . . . As Europe is our market for trade, we ought to form no partial connection with any part of it. It is the true interest of America to steer clear of European contentions."[27] As soon as independence was declared, he predicted, Europe would compete for America's commercial favors. America would benefit, and so would the rest of the world. Of course, part of what Paine wrote was more nonsense than "common sense," particularly his playing down of privileges that Americans enjoyed as part of the British Empire. Americans would miss British naval protection, British credit, and easy access to the British West Indies after independence. The pamphlet was effective propaganda nonetheless. More than 300,000 copies of *Common Sense* were sold, the equivalent of one copy for every ten persons living in the thirteen colonies in 1776. "For a long time," concluded historian Felix Gilbert, "every utterance on foreign policy [in the United States] starts from Paine's words and echoes his thoughts."[28]

Paine emphasized the attraction of American commerce and assumed that a foreign nation would assist America to protect that trade. With the abortive invasion of Canada in the winter of 1775–76 and the arrival of British reinforcements, it became obvious that some foreign help was necessary for survival. Congress opened American ports in April, 1776, but Paine's logic seemed irrefutable: no foreign power would openly aid the American rebels until independence was a declared fact. Virginia's Richard Henry Lee, on June 6, offered a resolution: "These United Colonies are, and of right ought to be, free and independent States."[29] Lee echoed Paine's thoughts. "No State in Europe," he explained to Patrick Henry, "will either Treat or Trade with us so long as we consider ourselves Subjects of G.B. . . . It is not choice . . . but necessity that calls for Independence, as the only means by which foreign Alliances can be obtained."[30] Thomas Jefferson wrote the Declaration of Independence and Congress endorsed it on July 4, 1776.

The next step was to secure foreign support. Congress designated a committee to prepare a "model treaty" to be presented to the French court. The committee's so-called "Plan of 1776," which Congress debated in August, would also serve as the basis for alliances with other countries. A final, amended version then accompanied Benjamin Franklin to France when he was named American minister at the end of the year. John Adams was the principal author of the Model Treaty. Like Paine, the lawyer from Braintree eschewed political entanglements. "I am not for soliciting any political connection, or military assistance, or indeed naval, from France," he told a friend. "I wish for nothing but commerce, a mere marine treaty with them."[31] Adams' imprint on the Model Treaty was obvious, for it was almost

**Tom Paine (1737–1809).** This working-class Englishman found his way to Philadelphia in 1774, where he took a job as a journalist and became caught up in the excitement of the independence movement. He wrote the anti-British *Common Sense* in 1776, a "best-seller" in its day. The irascible Paine joined the Continental Army and later participated in the French Revolution. (Courtesy of The New-York Historical Society, New York City)

purely a treaty of commerce and navigation, which would permit American ships free entry into French ports while French military supplies entered American ports in ever increasing quantities. Included also were elaborate rules protecting neutral commerce in wartime. The Model Treaty suggested that the United States and France grant the nationals of each country the same "Rights, Liberties, Privileges, Immunities and Exemptions" in trade, but that if "his most Christian Majesty shall not consent" to such a novel idea, then the American commissioners should try to obtain a most-favored-nation clause, whereby American merchants would receive the same commercial benefits enjoyed by other nations.[32]

The only political obligation in the Model Treaty came in Article VIII, which stipulated that America would not aid England in any conflict between Britain and France. Some of his closest friends in Congress, Adams later recalled, "thought there was not sufficient temptation to France to join us. They moved for cessions and concessions, which implied warranties and political alliance that I had studiously avoided."[33] The New Englander argued strenuously for the original wording; like most Americans in 1776, he feared that France, if offered political inducements, might demand Canada and access to the Newfoundland fisheries, both of which the new republic sought for itself. Even a motion to offer France concessions in the West Indies was defeated in Congress. Although their expectations proved somewhat naive, Adams and his colleagues were convinced that the ending of England's monopoly over North American commerce, accomplished through American independence, would by itself suffice to gain French support.

The neutral rights provisions of the Model Treaty deserve special attention. Although these commercial articles would not apply to the war against England, in which the United States was already a belligerent, they formed the basis of what later became America's historic policy of "freedom of the seas." Lifted almost word for word from earlier treaties involving powers with small navies, these commercial clauses guaranteed the principles of "free ships, free goods" (that is, the neutral flag protected noncontraband cargoes from capture), the freedom of neutrals to trade in noncontraband between ports of belligerents, a restricted and narrowly defined list of contraband materials exempting naval stores and foodstuffs from seizure, and a generally liberal treatment of neutral shipping. Such principles of neutral rights were becoming increasingly accepted in the late eighteenth century, particularly among enlightened publicists and countries lacking large navies. Although England had accepted liberal provisions in a few individual treaties, British statesmen were understandably reluctant to endorse them as international law. In a war against an inferior naval power, the British believed that the enemy would allow neutral shipping to carry its commerce, thus protecting its own vulnerable vessels from capture. Moreover, if neutrals were permitted to supply an enemy nation freely, especially with naval stores, it would not be long before Britain's maritime supremacy would be undermined. Americans, on the other hand, looking ahead to independence, envisaged future European wars and hoped, in the absence of political entanglements, to expand their commerce at such times. France, in the event of a naval war against the more powerful British, would benefit from American neutrality. Americans could fatten their pocketbooks and at the same time serve mankind by supporting more civilized rules of warfare.

The Model Treaty, then, introduced the main themes of early American foreign policy. It set forth the ideal of commercial expansion and political isolation, or, as

Thomas Jefferson later put it: "Peace, commerce, and honest friendship with all nations, entangling alliances with none."[34] By specifically binding France against acquiring Canada, it also projected a continental domain for America beyond the thirteen coastal settlements. But did the Model Treaty project goals that could be achieved? Historian Walter LaFeber has pointed out a central dilemma of early American diplomacy, namely, "a longing for landed and/or commercial expansion without having to make the requisite political commitments."[35] To Benjamin Franklin fell the mission to determine whether Adams' "mere marine treaty" was sufficient to secure French assistance.

## The French Connection

Patriot leaders did not err in thinking that France would aid American independence. Indeed, in the years following the humiliating peace of 1763, when France had been stripped of its empire, the compelling motive of French foreign policy was *revanche.* The French foreign minister in the 1760s, the Duc de Choiseul, smacked his lips at England's colonial troubles. "There will come in time a revolution in America," he told the French King, "which will put England into a state of weakness where she will no longer be a terror in Europe. . . . The very extent of English possessions in America will bring about their separation from England."[36] Americans knew of this intense French preoccupation. "All Europe is attentive to the dispute," Benjamin Franklin wrote from London in 1770, "and I . . . have a satisfaction in seeing that our part is taken everywhere."[37] Aside from strengthening the Bourbon Family Compact with Spain and sending secret observers to North America, France made no overt moves to intervene before Choiseul left office in 1770.

The decision to succor the Americans fell to Choiseul's successor, Charles Gravier, the Comte de Vergennes. Suave, polished, outwardly unemotional, Vergennes looked every inch the model of a successful diplomat of the ancien régime. In actuality, there was a streak of impetuosity in him (he had risked his diplomatic career by carrying on a secret liaison with a Franco-Turkish widow and then marrying her against the wishes of the French court), and when the American colonies began their armed rebellion, he adopted the motto *Aut nunc aut nunquam* ("now or never").[38] A perfect scheme for aiding the insurrectionaries short of war presented itself early in 1776 in the person of Pierre Augustin Caron de Beaumarchais. The adventurous author of the *Barber of Seville* proposed to set up a dummy trading company, Rodrigue Hortalez and Company, to be headed by himself, through which munitions and other military supplies could be clandestinely shipped to the American colonies. The French court (and perhaps the Spanish as well) could provide secret financing. Vergennes jumped at Beaumarchais' idea and set about persuading a reluctant Louis XVI. In a remarkable memorandum, Vergennes listed the advantages that would accrue to France from American independence:[39]

> First, it will diminish the power of England, and increase in proportion that of France. Second, it will cause irreparable loss to English trade, while it will considerably extend ours. Third, it presents to us as very probable the recovery of a part of the possessions which the English have taken from us in America, such as the fisheries of Newfoundland. . . . We do not speak of Canada.

**The Comte de Vergennes (1719–1787).** Determined to deal a blow to the British, Charles Gravier, the Comte de Vergennes and the French foreign minister under Louis XVI, seized an opportunity when the American colonies rebelled against London. He sponsored the playwright Beaumarchais. (Sketch by Anthony Saris, American Heritage Collection)

**Beaumarchais (1732–1799).** This man of intrigue worked to undermine the British position in the New World by clandestinely aiding the American rebels through a dummy company. (New York Public Library)

By May of 1776, before any American agent reached France and even before the Declaration of Independence, Paris took the plunge. One million livres (about $200,000) was secretly transferred from the French Treasury to Beaumarchais' "company." Charles III of Spain made a similar grant, and the first shipments of muskets, cannon, powder, tents, and clothing soon began to cross the Atlantic. By the time of Franklin's arrival in December, 1776, then, French assistance was an established fact. Whether this assistance could be converted into recognition and a formal treaty remained to be determined.

Franklin took Paris by storm. Plainly dressed and wearing a comfortable fur cap, the seventy-year-old philosopher was already well known to Frenchmen. *Poor Richard's Almanac,* with its catchy aphorisms, had run through several French editions, and Franklin's electrical experiments and philosophical writings had earned him honored membership in the French Academy. Parisians expected Franklin to be the personification of Rousseau's natural man, and he did not disappoint them. Disarmingly modest, soft-spoken, attentive to the ladies of the court, Franklin won friends everywhere. The British Ambassador, Lord Stormont, immediately recognized that he was "a very dangerous engine" and might soon win open French support.[40] Vergennes warmed to him. Franklin's kindly features were soon appearing on medals and snuffbox covers. The ladies of the French court adopted a *coiffure à la Franklin* in imitation of his omnipresent fur cap, and no social affair could be a success without his presence. Not without hyperbole, John Adams noted that the old Philadelphian was "so fond of the fair sex that one was not enough for him, but he must have one on each side, and all the ladies both old and young were ready to eat him up."[41] Franklin explained the intricacies of physics to Queen Marie Antoinette, played chess with the Duchesse de Bourbon, and even proposed marriage to the wealthy Madame Helvetius. The lady in question avoided Franklin's entangling alliance, but her "careless, jaunty air" and the fact that she kissed the "Good Doctor" in public scandalized Abigail Adams. "I was highly disgusted and never wish for an acquaintance with any ladies of this cast," she wrote.[42] It was, withal, a popular triumph unmatched by an American abroad. Thomas Jefferson did not exaggerate when, on becoming minister to France in 1784, he said that he was merely succeeding Franklin, for no one could replace him.

Social popularity did not ensure diplomatic success, however. Vergennes might have recognized American independence prior to Franklin's arrival had not the successful British military campaign in New York in the summer of 1776 made the French court cautious. Recognition meant war with England, and the French were reluctant to proceed without Spanish assistance. Spain was dragging its feet. Although French loans and supplies continued through 1776 and 1777, Vergennes avoided any formal commitment until there was a sure sign of American military success. Then came Saratoga on October 17, 1777, a battle in which 90 percent of American arms and ammunition had come from French merchants. The defeat of "Gentleman Johnny" Burgoyne's troops in the forests of northern New York helped persuade England to send out peace feelers, with terms offering less than complete independence. Franklin was not averse to using the threat of reconciliation with England as a lever on Vergennes. A French diplomat asked Franklin what action was necessary to prevent Congress from coming to an agreement with England short of "full and absolute independence."[43] Franklin replied: "The immediate conclusion of a treaty of commerce and alliance would induce the

**Benjamin Franklin (1706–1790) at the Court of France.** The elderly philosopher-journalist-humorist-politician-diplomat fascinated the snobbish courts of France when he arrived in Paris in 1776. (Courtesy of Kenneth M. Newman, Old Print Shop, New York City)

Deputies to close their ears to any proposal which should not have as its basis entire liberty and independence, both political and commercial."[44] And so, on February 6, 1778, Vergennes and Franklin affixed their signatures to two pacts. The first, a treaty of amity and commerce, gave the United States most-favored-nation privileges (which meant that any commercial rights granted by France to other countries would also be enjoyed by America). The two nations also agreed on a definition of contraband and neutral rights that followed the articles of the Model Treaty.

The second pact, however, was a treaty of alliance, and it contained political commitments that departed from John Adams' original plan. Instead of the meager promise not to aid England if France entered the war for independence, Franklin had to agree not to make peace with the British without first obtaining French consent. Vergennes made a similar promise. Although Franklin managed to retain the prohibition against French territorial gains on the North American continent, the United States agreed to recognize any French conquests in the Caribbean and to guarantee "from the present time and forever" all French possessions in America and any others that might be obtained at the peace table. France paid an equivalent price. According to Article II, "The essential and direct End of the present defensive alliance is to maintain effectually the liberty, Sovereignty, and independence absolute and unlimited of the said United States, as well in matters of Gouvernement as of commerce." Vergennes also guaranteed "from the present time and forever" American "Possessions, and the additions or conquests that their Confederation may obtain during the war, from any of the Dominions now or heretofore possessed by Great Britain in North America."[45] While France made no specific commitment to help the Americans conquer Canada, Vergennes stood ready to guarantee whatever boundaries Franklin and his colleagues could wrest from England.

The French alliance seemed to constitute the kind of political entanglement that Thomas Paine and John Adams had warned against. Certainly the stipulation prohibiting any peace without French consent, as well as the guarantee of territories, "entangled" American interests in the foreign policies of another power. Congress had retreated considerably from the principles of 1776, having instructed Franklin to seek an alliance with Spain in which the United States would assist Spain in conquering Florida and declare war against Portugal in return for diplomatic recognition and outright military assistance. Such a treaty did not materialize, but the instructions indicated the extent to which Congress, after two years without a major victory, was willing to compromise its ideals for military help against Britain. Both Paine and Adams accepted the French alliance, Paine so enthusiastically that he became for a few years a paid propagandist for the French. Adams, after some initial hesitation, was soon calling the treaty "a rock upon which we may safely build."[46] The treaty did fulfill the most important of Adams' original expectations—that the political and economic independence of the United States from England would be too great a prize for France to pass up. French and American interests coincided on the issue of independence. "Take away America," the British secretary of war claimed, "and we should sink into perfect insignificance."[47] Where French interests diverged was on the extent of American independence. Notwithstanding his vows of self-denial regarding Canada, Vergennes had no desire to replace Britain with a great American empire that might eventually chase the French and the Spanish, as well as the English, out of the New World. "I am persuaded that they would not stop here," he said in 1775, "but would in process of time advance to the Southern Continent of America and either subdue the inhabitants or carry them along with them, and in the end not leave a foot of that Hemisphere in the possession of any European power."[48] Committed to securing American independence from England, the French quite naturally did not wish to create a Frankenstein monster.

The French commitment was tested at the very beginning of the alliance. When the Elector Maximilian of Bavaria died, on December 30, 1777, Joseph II of Austria promptly occupied and annexed that German principality. Frederick the Great of Prussia virtuously went to war on behalf of Bavarian independence. Austria urged France, allied to Austria since 1756, to join the War of Bavarian Succession against Prussia. The Austrian Netherlands would be France's reward, the same Flanders that Louis XIV had coveted and for which French soldiers would die again in the twentieth century. Vergennes was not tempted. A war for Flanders would require peace with England just when the opportunity for revenge was greatest. Toward Austria, therefore, Vergennes slyly assumed the role of benevolent mediator, hoping to keep Europe quiet in order to concentrate on the maritime war against England. This mediation of the *Kartoffelkrieg* ("Potato War"), so-called because the starving soldiers of Austria and Prussia spent the winter of 1778–79 eating frozen potatoes, was successfully accomplished in 1779. Ironically enough, Emperor Joseph was not at all pleased with French interference, and when the opportunity

**King George III
(1738–1820).** An implacable foe of any leniency toward the rebellious Americans, he ruled England from 1750 to 1820, progressively going insane. In 1787, for example, he alighted from his carriage in Windsor Park and addressed a venerable oak tree as the King of Prussia. (Courtesy of Her Majesty the Queen. Copyright reserved)

presented itself in the summer of 1781, he returned the French favor and offered to mediate between Britain and France. Russia also joined in the mediation offer. Since it came at a low point in the military struggle in America, Vergennes might have been forced to accept Austro-Russian mediation (the terms of which would *not* have recognized American independence) in 1781 had not English King George III stubbornly resisted any solution short of complete submission by the American colonies. The point is clear: France, whatever the entanglements and temptations of the European continent, was bent on humiliating England. In Vergennes' steadfast opinion, the best way to accomplish that goal was to back American independence. By the end of the war in 1783 France had expended some 48 million livres (9.6 million dollars) in behalf of American independence.

## Cutting Diplomatic Teeth in Europe

Except for the successful alliance with France, there was something comic, even unseemly, about the futile search for treaties in European courts. Franklin himself had argued that "a virgin state should preserve the virgin character, and not go about suitoring after alliances, but wait with decent dignity for the application of others." [49] Congress, needing money and hoping for military assistance, ruled otherwise. Thus did American diplomats scurry to Berlin, Madrid, Vienna, St. Petersburg, Amsterdam, and other capitals in quest of alliances that never quite materialized. Frederick the Great had intimated that Prussia would recognize American independence if France did, but when William Lee arrived in Berlin, Frederick told his chief minister: "Put him off with compliments." [50] It was difficult for Americans to understand European hesitation. Fear of revolutionary principles, the danger of British retaliation, trading opportunities, and territorial ambitions closer to home—all made the European monarchies reluctant to challenge Britain, their jealousy toward British power notwithstanding. What America needed, John Adams concluded, was the shift by one neutral to belligerency. "Without it, all may nibble and piddle and dribble and fribble, waste a long time, immense treasures, and much human blood, and they must come to it at last." [51]

The Dutch were a case in point. With institutions of representative government firmly entrenched in the Dutch Estates General, one might have expected the Netherlands to be the first to recognize American independence. Not so. The burghers of Amsterdam were more interested in making money. Until Britain declared war on the United Provinces, in December, 1780, the Dutch busied themselves by carrying naval stores from the Baltic to France, as well as using their West Indian island of St. Eustatius as an entrepôt for contraband trade with the Americans. These activities, plus a willingness to join Catherine the Great's League of Armed Neutrality in the year 1780, led to war with England, but the Dutch steadfastly refused to sign a treaty with the United States until October, 1782, by which time the war was virtually over. John Adams, who negotiated the treaty of amity and commerce (following the "Plan of 1776"), could agree with a foreign visitor's assessment of Holland as "a land, where the demon of gold, crowned with tobacco, sat on a throne of cheese." [52] It should be noted, however, that while the Dutch treaty came too late to be of any military assistance in the war, Adams was also able to negotiate a loan of 5,000,000 guilders in June, 1782, from a consortium of Amsterdam bankers. This was the first of a series of Dutch loans, totaling some

9,000,000 guilders ($3,600,000), which served to sustain American credit through the 1780s.

American efforts to join the Armed Neutrality of 1780 marked another episode in futile diplomacy. Organized by Catherine II of Russia, the Armed Neutrality also included Denmark, Sweden, Austria, Prussia, Portugal, and the Kingdom of the Two Sicilies. Its purpose was ostensibly to enforce liberal provisions of neutral rights ("free ships, free goods," no paper blockades, narrow definition of contraband) in trading with belligerents. Never very effective (Catherine herself called it *cette nullité armée* [armed nullity]), the league seemed to hold out some hope for the American cause.[53] Because the Armed Neutrality's principles so closely resembled the "Plan of 1776," Congress immediately adopted its rules by resolution and commissioned a plenipotentiary to St. Petersburg to gain formal adherence to the league by treaty. It was an impossible mission. Aside from the obvious incongruity of a belligerent nation attempting to join an alliance of neutrals, it should have been obvious that Catherine, while no enemy of American independence, would not risk war with England by granting recognition prematurely. The American envoy, Francis Dana of Massachusetts, spent two lonely, frigid years in the Russian capital without ever being received in an official capacity. Indeed, formal diplomatic relations with Russia were not established until 1809, when Catherine's grandson, Tsar Alexander I, received as the American minister John Quincy Adams, who as a fourteen-year-old had served as Dana's secretary during the abortive wartime mission.

There was another ironic epilogue. Once peace negotiations in Paris had established American independence in 1783, the Dutch government urged the United States to join the Armed Neutrality through a formal treaty with the Netherlands. At this point, however, with the war all but over, Congress reconsidered. In a resolution on June 12, 1783, Congress admitted that "the liberal principles on which the said confederacy was established, are conceived to be in general favourable to the interests of nations, and particularly to those of the United States," but there could be no formal treaty. The reason? "The true interest of these [United] states requires that they should be as little as possible entangled in the politics and controversies of European nations."[54] Thus, however much Americans desired freedom of trade for reasons of both profit and principle, they did not want to resort to political entanglements to achieve such an objective. The dilemma would have to be faced again and again.

The most frustrating diplomacy of all was with Spain. Despite previous financial support for the embattled colonials, and notwithstanding the outwardly close alliance with France (the Bourbon Family Compact), the government of Charles III was in no hurry to take up arms against England—especially if Spain's principal objective, reclamation of Gibraltar, could be obtained by other means. Moreover, in view of its own extensive colonial empire in the Americas, Spain was understandably less eager than France to encourage overseas revolutions. Not only might colonial rebellion prove to be a contagious disease, but a powerful American republic could threaten Spanish possessions as effectively as an expanding British Empire. Spanish Foreign Minister Count Floridablanca therefore hemmed and hawed, playing a double game by dickering with both France and England in the hope of regaining Gibraltar. Only by the Treaty of Aranjuez, signed on April 12, 1779, did Spain agree on war with England, and even then the alliance was with France, not with the United States. One article held enormous importance for

American diplomacy. Because of Madrid's obsession with Gibraltar, France agreed to keep on fighting until that rocky symbol of Spanish pride was wrested from the British. It will be remembered that, according to the terms of the Franco-American alliance of 1778, the United States and France had pledged not to make a separate peace and to continue the war until England recognized American independence. Now France was promising to fight until Gibraltar fell. In this curious, devious fashion, without being a party to the treaty or even being consulted, the Americans found their independence, in historian Samuel Flagg Bemis' memorable phrase, "chained by European diplomacy to the Rock of Gibraltar."[55] And because the terms of Aranjuez remained secret, American diplomats could only guess at these new political entanglements.

Congress sent John Jay to Madrid in September, 1779 to obtain a formal alliance. The handsome, thirty-four-year-old New Yorker of Huguenot descent did not have an easy time of it. Not once during his two-and-a-half-year stay was Jay officially received by the Spanish court. His mail was opened and read, spies snooped everywhere, and only rarely would Floridablanca deign to communicate with him. Even more galling, Jay ran out of money and was forced to ask the Spanish for funds. There was also the personal tragedy of his infant daughter's dying shortly after Jay and his wife Sarah arrived in Madrid. Floridablanca was unsympathetic. He wrote snidely of Jay's diplomacy: "His two chief points were: Spain, recognize our independence; Spain, give us more money."[56] In fact, Floridablanca did give Jay some $175,000, but only to keep the American dangling while he secretly negotiated with a British agent, Richard Cumberland, in the hope that Britain would accept outside mediation and cede Gibraltar. Fortunately for American diplomacy, George III remained as stubborn about Gibraltar as he did about American independence, and the Cumberland talks collapsed.

At one point in the summer of 1781 Jay received instructions from Congress that permitted him to give up the American demand for navigation of the Mississippi, if only Spain would recognize American independence and make an alliance. Such instructions reflected the dangerous military situation in the autumn of 1780, following the British capture of Charleston and successful invasion of the South. While personally believing it "better for America to have no treaty with Spain than to purchase one on such servile terms," Jay obediently sought an interview with the Spanish foreign minister.[57] After several weeks an audience was granted. The American made his proposal: a treaty relinquishing navigation rights on the Mississippi south of 31° north latitude, a Spanish guarantee to the United States of "all their respective territories," and an American guarantee to the Spanish King of "all his dominions in America."[58] Floridablanca refused. Had he accepted, the navigation of the "Father of Waters" and the boundary of West Florida—both destined to be troublesome issues in Spanish-American diplomacy—would have been settled to Spain's advantage. As it was, Floridablanca preferred to gamble, to put off that evil day of recognition. Already Spanish troops from New Orleans had occupied the Floridas, and possibly they could claim more territory between the Mississippi and the Alleghenies. Rebuffed, Jay withdrew the concession on Mississippi navigation. He explained to Congress that if Spain refused to make an alliance during the war, the United States should be prepared to reassert its Mississippi claims in any final peace treaty. Congress endorsed his actions. Jay, by now, was furious with the Spaniards. "This government has little money, less wisdom, no credit, nor any right to it," he grumbled.[59] Moreover, he had begun to suspect, from conversations with the French ambassador in Madrid, that the French were encouraging Spain in its trans-Appalachian territorial ambitions. Indeed, by the end of his sojourn in Spain, John Jay had become, in historian Lawrence Kaplan's words, "an almost xenophobic American."[60] Jay's suspicious attitude was to have a decisive effect on the peace negotiations of 1782.

## Peace Without Propriety: The Treaty of Paris

The event that precipitated serious peace negotiations was the surrender of Lord Cornwallis' army at Yorktown on October 19, 1781. General Washington's French lieutenant, the Marquis de Lafayette, wrote home: "The play is over. . . . the fifth act has just ended."[61] George III stubbornly tried to fight on, but the burgeoning public debt and war weariness finally caused the ministry of Lord North to fall early in 1782. The King reluctantly accepted a new ministry under the Marquess of Rockingham, committed to a restoration of peace, but undecided as to what the terms should be.

The English sent an agent to Paris in April, 1782, to sound out Benjamin Franklin. The emissary, Richard Oswald, seemed a curious choice, his chief qualifications being a previous friendship with Franklin and first-hand knowledge of America, derived in part from the slave trade. Franklin sized up Oswald quickly. After introducing the British envoy to Vergennes and saying that the United States would make no separate peace without French concurrence, Franklin privately hinted to Oswald that reconciliation was possible if England granted complete independence and generous boundaries. Franklin even mentioned Canada. The American did not demand Canada, for England might find such a stipulation "humiliating." A voluntary cession, however, would have "an excellent effect . . . [on] the mind of the [American] people in general."[62] Oswald was struck by the suggestion and promised to try to persuade his superiors in London. "We parted exceedingly good friends," Franklin wrote in his journal.[63]

Peace talks stalled for the next several weeks, as the British were preoccupied by another Cabinet crisis. Not until Rockingham's death and Lord Shelburne's succession as Prime Minister on July 1 were the British able to agree on a

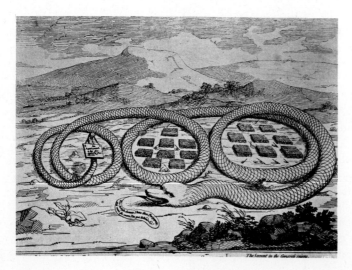

**"The American Rattlesnake."** Coiled around the armies of Burgoyne and Cornwallis, the American snake gloats over triumph in 1782:

> Britons within the Yankeean Plains,
> Mind how ye March & Trench,
> The Serpent in the Congress reigns,
> As well as in the French.

(Library of Congress)

**Cod Fishing, Newfoundland.** In the land of the cod—New England—fishing, curing, and drying the fish was central to the economy. John Adams represented his native region well when he made sure that the treaty of peace preserved an American stake in Newfoundland waters, but the issue constantly disturbed American diplomacy thereafter. (Map Division, New York Public Library, Astor, Lenox and Tilden Foundations)

negotiating position, and even then Shelburne had to proceed cautiously for fear of offending his prickly sovereign. It was during this interval that Franklin summoned his fellow peace commissioners, Jay and Adams, to Paris. Jay, delighted to escape Madrid, arrived by the end of June. Adams continued commercial negotiations in the Netherlands and did not reach the French capital until October 26. In view of the subsequent American decision to disregard Congress's instructions and negotiate separately and secretly with the British, it should be noted that Franklin, in his initial conversation with Oswald, had intimated the possibility of a separate peace. The elderly American never told Vergennes of his suggestions concerning Canada. More trusting of the French than his younger colleagues (and more appreciative of the need for French assistance), Franklin nevertheless always placed American interests first. Whether in matters of the heart or in diplomatic relations, the philosopher from Philadelphia knew when to break the rules.

The success of the separate negotiations, which began in October and ended on November 30, owed much to the conciliatory attitude of Shelburne. A believer in the natural rights of man and a convert to free trade through his friendship with Adam Smith, the Prime Minister wanted very much to wean the United States away from the alliance with France. The peace terms were thus exceedingly generous; as Vergennes later put it: "The English buy the peace more than they make it."[64] Not only was the United States granted complete independence, but also the new nation's extensive boundaries (the Great Lakes and St. Lawrence River to the north, Mississippi River to the west, 31° line across Florida to the south) far surpassed what Americans had won on the battlefield. Any chance of obtaining Canadian territory was probably foreclosed by eleventh-hour British naval victories in the Caribbean and the failure of a combined French-Spanish siege of Gibraltar in September, 1782. With the issues of independence and boundaries easily settled, the most heated dispute occurred over the lesser articles of the treaty. The fisheries question caused much wrangling. The British commissioners argued that access to the fishing grounds off the Grand Banks of Newfoundland, as well as the right to dry and cure fish on Canadian shores, should be limited to citizens of the British Empire. The Americans disagreed. New England, where codfish was king and not George III, had a stubborn spokesman in John Adams. The Americans finally won their point, although the treaty ambiguously granted the "liberty" to fish, not the "right," thus perpetuating a controversy over which succeeding generations of diplomats (and succeeding generations of Adamses) would battle for more than a century.

Sharpest disagreement came over the twin issues of Loyalists and pre-Revolutionary debts. The British, quite understandably, sought generous treatment for the thousands of colonials who had been driven into exile for their loyalty to the Crown. The British negotiators wanted restitution of confiscated property, or at least compensation. The Americans remained adamant, especially Franklin, whose own son William, the former royal governor of New Jersey, had deserted to the British cause. Even the moderate Jay spoke of Loyalists as having "the most dishonourable of human motives" and urged that "every American must set his face and steel his heart" against them.[65] As to the debts, which consisted of some five million pounds owed by Americans (mostly Southern planters) to British merchants, there was a natural reluctance to repay obligations contracted prior to 1775. After considerable argument, Adams found an acceptable compromise. Vowing that he had "no Notion of cheating any Body," the redoubtable New Englander persuaded his colleagues to accept a formula whereby British creditors would "meet with no lawful impediment" in collecting their lawfully incurred debts.[66] This particular clause was instrumental in gaining the support of the British commercial classes for what was an otherwise unpopular treaty; as Adams put it, American concession on the debts prevented the British merchants "from making common Cause with the Refugees [Tories]."[67] The British, for their part, accepted an article in the treaty which forbade all further persecution of Loyalists and "earnestly recommended" to the states that properties seized during the war be restored. Because Congress could not dictate to the states under the Articles of Confederation, both the British and American commissioners understood that the "earnest recommendations" might not be followed.

The preliminary peace terms, because they obtained so much, were received enthusiastically in America. There were some worries that the independent negotiations might strain relations with France. Congress's Secretary for Foreign Affairs, Robert Livingston, informed the commissioners that "it gives me pain that the character for candor and felicity to its engagements which should always characterize a great people should have been impeached thereby."[68] As for Vergennes, the French foreign minister gave no rebuke to the Americans for failing to consult, saying only that they had "managed well."[69] Then, after two weeks of silence, Vergennes wrote plaintively to Franklin: "You are wise and discreet, sir; you perfectly understand what is due to propriety; you have all your life performed your duties. I pray to you to consider how you propose to fulfill those which are due to the [French] King?"[70] Franklin thereupon delivered one of the most beguiling replies in the history of diplomacy. He admitted that the American commissioners had been indiscreet—guilty of a lack of *bienséance* (propriety)—in not keeping the French fully informed, but he hoped that this indiscretion would not harm the alliance. "The English, I just now learn," he told Vergennes, "flatter themselves they have already divided us." Franklin added that he hoped the British would find themselves "totally mistaken."[71] The Frenchman said nothing more. In fact, he even agreed to an additional loan of some 6,000,000 livres, which Franklin had requested.

The mild French response was not difficult to explain. Vergennes, with Paris and Versailles honeycombed with spies, knew all along about the secret negotiations, even if the final terms seem to have startled him. He did not protest because he understood that England was indeed trying to break up the Franco-American alliance. Franklin's hint verified this. Moreover, the separate American peace offered Vergennes a way out of a sticky tangle with Spain. He could now tell the stubborn Spaniards that Gibraltar was no longer a practicable objective with the Americans effectively out of the war. To Vergennes the fact of American independence was more important than Gibraltar, and although he would have preferred a treaty that left the United States more dependent on France, he was not displeased with what Jay, Adams, and Franklin had accomplished. In Lawrence Kaplan's phrase, "even if Vergennes was serving his country first, he served America well."[72]

Peace negotiations between England and France, as well as England and Spain, took several months. The final Treaty of Paris was not signed until September 3,

**"The General P--s, or Peace."** The peace signed, Britain, the Netherlands, the United States, Spain, and France have put down their arms. Who would have thought, read this English cartoon of 1783, "that they'd so soon come to a general P---?" (Library of Congress)

The General P—s, or Peace.

*Say what they will, I call this an honourable P—.*

*I call this a free and Indipendent P—.*

*Such English we confess your exceeding good nature, tho' we have wrangled you out of America you freely make P—, with us.*

Come all who love friendship, and wonder and see,
The belligerent powers, like good neighbours agree,
A little time past Sirs, who would have thought this,
That they'd so soon come to a general P___?

The wise politicians who differ in thought,
Will fret at this friendship, and call it tonought,
And blades that love war will be storming at this,
But storm as they will, it's a general P—.

A hundred hard millions in war we have spent,
And America lost by all patriots consent,
Yet let us be quiet, nor any one hiss,
But rejoice at this hearty and general P—.

'Tis vain for to fret or growl at our lot,
You see they're determin'd to fill us a pot,
So now my brave Britons excuse me in this,
That I for a Peace am oblig'd to write Piss.

1783. Except for some complications regarding Florida (Spain received the Floridas from England in the final treaty), the terms were precisely those of the preliminary treaty between England and the United States. America's diplomats had performed well in overcoming political entanglements and exploiting European rivalries. "Undisciplined marines as we were," said John Adams, "we were better tacticians than we imagined."[73] To obtain both independence and empire was an impressive achievement. In Bemis' estimate, Jay, Franklin, and Adams had taken "the first decisive step to loose a new nation from Europe's bonds and Europe's distresses, so that their people after them might have freedom to expand, and to develop a new continent, to rise to surpassing power."[74]

## Awkward Diplomacy under the Articles of Confederation

Americans were in an exuberant, expansive mood in 1783. "We have the experience of the whole world before our eyes," wrote Noah Webster in the preface to his famous speller. "It is the business of Americans to select the wisdom of all nations . . . [and] to add superior dignity to this infant Empire and to human nature."[75] Nearly half the national territory, some 220 million acres of wilderness, lay across the Appalachian chain, and the flood of emigrants westward, fleeing from heavy taxes to lower ones, from poorer to better lands, was inexorable. More than one hundred thousand Americans settled in Kentucky and Tennessee alone in the years between 1775 and 1790. As Jay put it in 1785, "a rage for emigrating to the western country prevails . . . and the seeds of a great people are daily planting beyond the mountains."[76] Peace also brought trading opportunities. Foreign ships could now enter American ports without fear of British retaliation. Americans could regain British markets for their agricultural exports, trade directly with other European countries, and develop as extensive and free a trade as possible with the rest of the world. One Massachusetts newspaper gave optimistic thanks "to the supreme ruler of the universe by whose beneficence our commerce is freed from those shackles it used to be cramped with, and bids fair to extend to every part of the globe, without passing through the medium of England, that rotten island."[77] The broad Atlantic would serve as both a highway of commerce and a barrier against European predators.

The optimism of 1783 was only partly fulfilled. Trade expanded rapidly in the years after the Revolution. Approximately 72,000 tons of shipping cleared America's busiest port, Philadelphia, in the year 1789, compared to an average of 45,000 tons in 1770–1772. Boston's tonnage increased from 42,506 in 1772 to 55,000 in 1788. Clearances in Maryland and Virginia doubled in volume over the figures from 1769. Tobacco exports brought a favorable balance of more than a million dollars a year in trade with France during the 1780s. By 1788 the Netherlands was importing more than four million dollars annually of tobacco, rice, and naval stores from the United States. Merchants were enterprising in gaining new markets. The *Empress of China,* the first American ship to trade with the Far East, set sail from New York in February, 1784, and reached Canton some six months later. The cargo was ginseng, which the Chinese believed would restore sexual potency to the aged. Another pioneering vessel, the *Columbia,* left Boston in 1787, wintered on the Pacific coast of North America near Vancouver Island, and traded metal trinkets to the Indians for otter furs. The *Columbia* then voyaged to China, exchanged the furs for tea, and returned to Boston—the first American ship to circumnavigate the

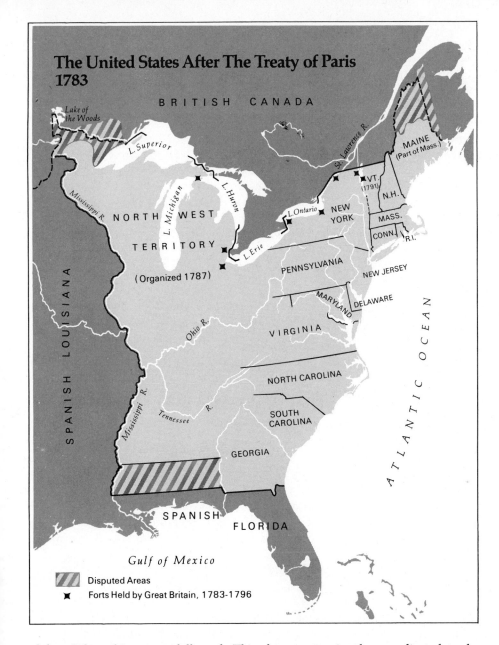

**The United States After The Treaty of Paris 1783**

Lake of the Woods

BRITISH CANADA

L. Superior

Mississippi R.

St. Lawrence R.

MAINE (Part of Mass.)

L. Michigan

L. Huron

VT. (1791)

N.H.

NORTH WEST TERRITORY

L. Ontario

NEW YORK

MASS.

CONN.

R.I.

L. Erie

(Organized 1787)

PENNSYLVANIA

NEW JERSEY

Ohio R.

MARYLAND

DELAWARE

SPANISH LOUISIANA

VIRGINIA

NORTH CAROLINA

Tennessee R.

Mississippi R.

SOUTH CAROLINA

ATLANTIC OCEAN

GEORGIA

SPANISH FLORIDA

Gulf of Mexico

🔲 Disputed Areas

✴ Forts Held by Great Britain, 1783-1796

globe. Other ships soon followed. Thus began a curiously complicated trade, which often included a stop at the Hawaiian (or Sandwich) Islands to pick up sandalwood for Chinese consumers; the trade brought profits to New England merchants for more than thirty years. On her second voyage, in 1792, the *Columbia* entered the mouth of the river named after her and thus helped establish the American claim to Oregon.

Despite the expansion of trade, the instant prosperity that many Americans expected in 1783 did not materialize. Part of the problem was the dual economic adjustment that the United States had to make—the changeover from a wartime to peacetime economy, and from a favored position within the British Empire to independent status in a world dominated by mercantilist restrictions. Because of commercial habits and British credit facilities, the bulk of American trade continued to be with England. In 1790, the earliest year for which full statistics are available, nearly half of all American exports went to England, while 90 percent of American imports originated in England. Fully three-fourths of America's foreign trade remained with the former mother country. Contrary to Paine's *Common Sense,* however, independence brought an end to privileges that had been part of the imperial connection. New England was particularly hard hit when American ships were prohibited from trading with the British West Indies. Even with smuggling, the exports of Massachusetts in 1786 totaled only one-fourth of what they had been in 1774. Moreover, because each of the thirteen states had its own customs service and tariff schedules, American diplomats could not threaten commercial retaliation against England. "It would be idle to think of making commercial regulations on our part," George Washington complained. "One State passes a prohibitory law respecting some article, another State opens wide the avenue for its admission. One Assembly makes a system; another Assembly unmakes it."[78]

Indeed, as peacetime problems multiplied, structural weaknesses under the Articles of Confederation loomed as a major obstacle to successful diplomacy. Not only did the sovereignty of the individual states prevent any uniform commercial policy, but states' rights thwarted national power in other respects as well. Congress had raised a Continental Army and constructed a small Navy during the war, but in peace these "implied" powers collapsed; all naval vessels were sold or scrapped by the end of 1784, and the Army dwindled to a mere regiment. Congress remained nominally in charge of foreign policy. Yet during the war this large body had proven itself so faction-ridden and devoid of responsibility that it had given the French foreign minister veto power over American peace commissioners, and thus, in the words of one scholar, "eliminated itself from any prominent role in foreign affairs for the remainder of the Revolution."[79] The legislative body took a forward step in 1784 by creating a Department of Foreign Affairs and selecting John Jay as secretary. Although Congress retained the basic powers of foreign policy—the right to make war and peace, to send and receive ambassadors, to make treaties and alliances—it lacked the power to enforce its diplomacy. Individual states violated the 1783 peace treaty with impunity. Diplomacy became an awkward, frustrating affair.

Relations with England quickly deteriorated after 1783. In the first flush of peace it had looked like the United States might actually conclude a favorable commercial treaty with the British. Lord Shelburne's grand scheme of rapprochement would have continued the benefits Americans had enjoyed under the Crown, including free access of American goods and ships to British and West Indian ports, and during the negotiations British Commissioner David Hartley had spoken about a common citizenship for the two countries. But Shelburne was soon forced from office for having given the Americans too much, and his successors (even the liberal William Pitt, who became Prime Minister in 1784) found commercial reciprocity with the United States a political impossibility. Mercantilist thinking was still powerful in England. Pamphleteers like the Earl of Sheffield argued that the United States, if allowed to resume the privileges of the British Empire without any of the responsibilities, would eventually outstrip Britain in shipping, trade, and the production of manufactured goods. A restrictive policy, however, would allow England to increase its carrying trade, particularly in the

West Indies, where colonial shipping had long predominated. Canada and Ireland could serve as alternative sources of provisions for the West Indian planters. Such mercantilist precepts became institutionalized in a series of orders in council, according to which American raw materials and foodstuffs, but not manufactures, were permitted to enter the British home islands aboard American vessels, while Canada and the West Indies remained closed to American shipping. Such restrictions, it was believed, would not hurt British exports to America. As Sheffield prophetically observed: "At least four-fifths of the importations from Europe into the American States were at all times made upon credit; and undoubtedly the States are in greater want of credit at this time than at former periods. It can be had only in Great Britain."[80] As for possible commercial retaliation, the British scoffed at the likelihood that all thirteen "dis-united" states could agree on a uniform set of tariff schedules. "Pish! . . . What can Americans do?" boasted one Briton. "They have neither government nor power. Great Britain could shut up all their ports . . . . America take measures against Great Britain indeed!"[81]

The British refusal to evacuate the northwest forts was another serious irritant. These several fortified posts, which ranged from Dutchman's Point on Lake Champlain to Michilimackinac on Lake Michigan, strategically controlled the entire frontier, including the fur trade and Indian tribes between the Great Lakes and the Ohio River. The British had promised, according to Article II of the peace treaty, to relinquish these posts "with all convenient speed." Retention of the forts was later justified on the grounds that the Americans themselves had violated important parts of the treaty, most notably by the failure to repay debts to British creditors and by the shabby treatment accorded Loyalists. Although the United States was admittedly delinquent on these two points, the British had made the decision to keep the forts before the treaty was even ratified. In truth, the British were determined to hold on to the west, retaining the lucrative fur trade and keeping their alliances with the Indians intact. American shipping was thus effectively excluded from the Great Lakes. At the time of Shays' Rebellion in 1786, British officials in Canada, thinking that the United States might soon break up, entered into secret talks with separatist leaders in Vermont, luring them with special trade privileges along the Champlain–St. Lawrence water route. If the breakup did occur, Vermont could easily be attached to Canada, along with the lightly populated territories north of the Ohio. There were further complaints about slaves the British had carried off at the end of the war, as well as a controversy over the Maine–New Brunswick boundary. Americans could only watch, helpless. With no army, no navy, no executive, no power to control the national commerce, the United States under the Articles of Confederation could do little to force British respect for the 1783 peace treaty. As historian Julian P. Boyd has argued, British policies "may well have contributed more to the convoking and to the success of the Federal Convention of 1787 than many who sat in that august body."[82]

The thankless task of enduring humiliation fell to John Adams, who became the first American minister to the Court of St. James's in 1785. King George scarcely concealed his contempt for the young republic, and his ministers were similarly uncordial. When Adams protested the failure of the British to send their own minister to the United States, he was asked whether there should be one envoy or thirteen. "This people cannot look me in the face," Adams wrote. "There is conscious guilt and shame in their countenances when they look at me. They feel they have behaved ill and that I am sensible of it."[83] The New Englander could make no dent in British policy toward trade or toward the forts. The author of the Model Treaty saw the impossibility of free trade. "If we cannot obtain reciprocal liberality," he wrote in 1785, "we must adopt reciprocal prohibitions, exclusions, monopolies, and imposts."[84] British complacency irritated Adams. "If an angel from heaven," he noted sarcastically, "should declare to this nation that our states will unite, retaliate, prohibit, or trade with France, they would not believe it."[85] Indeed, if there was one message that Adams repeated to Congress in dispatch after dispatch during his three frustrating years in England, it was the necessity of giving Congress the power to regulate commerce; otherwise the British would not negotiate. As late as February, 1788, when the new federal Constitution was on the verge of adoption, Adams assured John Jay "that as soon as there shall be one [a national government], the British court will vouchsafe to treat with it."[86]

Diplomacy with Spain after 1783 fared little better. Just as the British refused to evacuate the Ohio Valley after the war, the Spanish tried to retain control over the Southwest. Part of the problem stemmed from ambiguities in the peace treaty. According to Article VII of the Anglo-American treaty, the United States was guaranteed free navigation of the Mississippi "from its source to the ocean" and the northern boundary of Florida was set at 31 degrees. Yet Spain had not agreed to either stipulation. British Florida prior to the war had extended northward to the Yazoo River, and Madrid had no intention of yielding territory or encouraging American settlement by guaranteeing free navigation. Spanish troops continued to hold Natchez on the Mississippi. Like the British north of the Ohio, Spain made alliances with the Creeks and other Indian tribes, and there were occasional attempts to bribe frontier leaders, like General James Wilkinson, into a secessionist connection with the Spanish Crown. The most threatening move came in 1784 when Spain closed the mouth of the Mississippi to American commerce. Westerners exploded in violent protest, for control over the Mississippi meant the difference between a subsistence economy or one of agrarian expansion. George Washington, who visited the frontier territories that summer, reported: "the western settlers . . . stand as it were upon a pivot; the touch of a feather would turn them any way."[87]

Less powerful than the British and unprepared for a war on the frontier, the Spanish preferred to negotiate. Don Diego de Gardoqui arrived in New York in 1785, a crafty, charming envoy, whose instructions were to obtain an American surrender on the Mississippi by dangling trade concessions in Spain and the Canary Islands. Gardoqui also brought a Spanish offer to intercede with the Sultan of Morocco, whose pirates were seizing American merchantmen in the Mediterranean. Since such a treaty would obviously benefit the commercial Northeast at the expense of southern expansionists and western farmers, the Spanish envoy worked hard at flattering Secretary Jay and the other easterners. Gardoqui had a large expense account, and he used it. He gave splendid dinners with the best wines, acquired Spanish jackasses for General Washington, and squired Mrs. Jay to one festivity after another. "I am acting the gallant and accompanying Madame [Jay] to the official entertainments and dances," he reported, "because she likes it and I will do everything which appeals to me for the King's best interest."[88] Jay took the gilded bait. At one point in 1786 he asked Congress for permission to negotiate a treaty whereby the United States would relinquish the *use* of the Mississippi River for twenty-five or thirty years while reserving the *right* to navigate until a time when American power would be sufficient to force Spanish concessions.

Jay's request sparked heated debate in Congress. Dividing geographically, seven northern delegations voted to make the necessary concession, while the five southern delegations stood unanimously opposed. Although negotiations with Gardoqui continued into 1787, it was obvious to Jay that he could never obtain the minimum of nine states necessary to approve a treaty under the Articles. He told Congress that it must decide "either to wage war with Spain or settle all differences by treaty on the best terms available."[89] Congress did neither. Spain resumed its intrigues with western leaders, and in 1788 the Mississippi was temporarily reopened to American shipping after the payment of special duties. A definitive treaty did not come until 1795. The most immediate consequence of the Jay-Gardoqui conversations was to accentuate the political alliance between the South and West and to ensure a clause in the new Constitution that retained a two-thirds majority for senatorial approval of treaties.

Relations with France were equally frustrating. Since the alliance of 1778 contained a mutual guarantee of territories, one might have expected the French to support American claims in the West. France did nothing, however, holding true to Vergennes' view that a United States of limited territorial strength would remain a weak and dependent French client. Thomas Jefferson, who succeeded Franklin as minister to France in 1784, did what he could. He genuinely liked the French and continued the tradition of the cultivated citizen of the world so well set by his predecessor. Jefferson hoped that France could replace England as America's principal trading partner, and he worked very hard to convert the French to liberal commercial theories. Except for the opening of a limited number of French West Indian ports in 1784 and the negotiation of a consular treaty four years later, he ran into the same kind of mercantilist restrictions John Adams faced in England. Whenever Jefferson pressed for commercial concessions, he was usually reminded of the outstanding Revolutionary debt of 35 million livres. The inability of Congress to retaliate distressed Jefferson. He momentarily thought of abandoning commerce and diplomacy and having the United States "stand, with respect to Europe, precisely on the footing of China."[90] Given political and economic realities in America, however, Jefferson understood that such rigid isolation was impossible, so he advocated constitutional reform. "My primary object in the formation of treaties," he wrote in 1785, "is to take the commerce of the states out of the hands of the states, and to place it under the superintendence of Congress, so far as the imperfect provisions of our constitution will admit, and until the states by new compact make them more perfect."[91]

Another impetus to constitutional reform grew out of the dreary record of dealings with the Barbary pirates in the 1780s. The rulers of the North African states—Algiers, Tunis, Tripoli, and Morocco—had transformed piracy into a national industry. By capturing merchantmen, holding sailors and cargoes for ransom, extorting protection money from nations willing to pay, the petty sultans nearly drove American shipping out of the Mediterranean. Through a fortuitous set of circumstances, the United States was able to negotiate a satisfactory treaty with Morocco in 1787, at the bargain price of only $10,000, but other negotiations proved fruitless. The young republic had neither the revenue to pay for protection nor the armed force to coerce the North African pirates. Thomas Jefferson asked for a "fleet of one hundred and fifty guns" to wipe out the pirates, but no steps were taken toward constructing a navy.[92] Americans faced humiliation and tight pocketbooks. For John Jay such awkward diplomacy was a blessing in disguise: "The more we are ill-treated abroad the more we shall unite and consolidate at home."[93]

## The New Constitution and the Legacy of the Founding Fathers

It was amidst this troubled international setting that fifty-five delegates attended the Federal Convention in Philadelphia from May to September, 1787. Although economic woes and Shays' Rebellion in Massachusetts provided the immediate impetus for reform, the "Founding Fathers" had foreign policy in mind too. When Edmund Randolph introduced the Virginia plan to the convention, he cited the need for a stronger foreign policy first among his arguments for increasing federal power. The federal Constitution, approved by the Philadelphia assembly and ratified by the states over the next two years, eliminated most of the weaknesses that had plagued diplomacy under the Articles of Confederation. A central government consisting of an executive, a bicameral legislature, and a judiciary—all designed to balance one another—replaced the weak confederation of sovereign states. Responsibility for negotiations rested with the President, who would make treaties "by and with the advice and consent of the Senate . . . provided two-thirds of the Senators present concur." The impunity with which the individual states had violated the 1783 treaty with England was responsible for Benjamin Franklin's proposal that treaties shall be "the Supreme Law of the land . . . any thing in the Constitution or laws of any State to the contrary notwithstanding."[94] Southerners, remembering the Jay-Gardoqui negotiations, were wary of giving Congress too much power over commerce. Nevertheless, in return for a constitutional prohibition against taxes on exports and a twenty-year moratorium on interference with the slave trade, southern delegates granted Congress the right to regulate imports by a simple majority. The option was open now for commercial retaliation against England. The Constitution also provided for a standing army and navy, thus freeing national defense from dependence on requisitions from the various states. In every respect the United States had strengthened itself. "'Tis done!" Benjamin Rush of Pennsylvania exclaimed. "We have become a nation. . . . We are no longer the scoff of our enemies."[95]

An interesting discussion at Philadelphia, particularly in view of subsequent developments, concerned the warmaking power. The early drafts of the Constitution granted Congress the power to "make" war. Delegates soon perceived, however, that both houses might lack sufficient knowledge and unity to act quickly in the event of attack. Congress might not even be in session. When it was suggested that the President be responsible, the evil memories of Julius Caesar and George III intruded. As delegate Elbridge Gerry of Massachusetts put it, he "never expected to hear in a republic a motion to empower the Executive alone to declare war."[96] Virginia's George Mason, in a telling phrase, was for "clogging rather than facilitating war; but for facilitating peace." Fearful of executive tyranny, but not wanting to leave the country defenseless, Gerry and James Madison of Virginia proposed a compromise whereby Congress retained the power to "declare" war, while the President, as Commander-in-Chief, would still be able to "repel sudden attacks."[97] Since Congress was granted authority to raise and support armies and navies, call out the militia, make rules and regulations for all the armed forces, and control all policy functions associated with national defense, it seems evident that the Philadelphia delegates intended the executive to be subordinate.

The size of the federal republic also aroused debate at Philadelphia. According to classic political theory, particularly the writings of Montesquieu, republics stood the best chance of survival if territorial limits remained small. If the theory were accurate, a real disparity existed between the thirteen coastal states and the vast trans-Allegheny expanse stretching to the Mississippi. It took the thirty-five-year-old Virginia lawyer James Madison to articulate the philosophy of a growing republican empire. Not only did Madison draft much of the handiwork at Philadelphia, he also (along with John Jay and Alexander Hamilton) wrote the *Federalist Papers*, which were so influential in the campaign for ratification of the new Constitution in 1787 and 1788. According to Madison, the greatest danger to republican survival came from factional struggle. Factions derived mainly from economic differences. The size of a republic did not pose the main threat. On the contrary, as Madison argued in *Federalist 10*, once you "extend the sphere" of government, "you take in a greater variety of parties and interests; you make it less probable that a majority of the whole will have a common motive to invade the right of other citizens; or, if such a common motive exists, it will be more difficult for all who feel it to discover their own strength and to act in unison with each other."[98] Although Madison's republican theories may not have necessitated continual expansion to ensure survival, the man who later as secretary of state presided over the huge Louisiana Purchase in 1803 welcomed westward expansion from the outset. Most delegates at Philadelphia did.

It was no coincidence that Congress's last official measure under the Articles of Confederation during the same summer of 1787 dealt with this very issue of westward expansion. With a bare quorum of eight states represented, the dying Congress enacted the Northwest Ordinance of 1787, which set up guidelines for governing the territories of the Old Northwest until they were ready for statehood. Its terms called for Congress to appoint a governor, secretary, and three judges, who would govern until the population of a territory reached 5,000, at which time the settlers would elect a legislature. The territorial legislature would then rule in conjunction with a council of five selected by the governor and by Congress. The governor retained veto power. As soon as the population grew to 60,000, inhabitants could write a constitution and apply for statehood on terms of equality with the original thirteen. Slavery was forbidden. The Founding Fathers at Philadelphia took cognizance of the new law, and stipulated, according to Article IV, Section 3 of the new Constitution, that "Congress shall have Power to dispose of and make all needful Rules and Regulations respecting the territory or other property belonging to the United States." A blueprint for an American colonial system was thus laid down. The same process that led to statehood for Ohio, Indiana, Michigan, Illinois, and Wisconsin continued into the twentieth century, including the admission of Hawaii and Alaska as states in the 1950s.

When George Washington took the oath of office as President on the balcony of Federal Hall in New York on April 30, 1789, he could look optimistically at the international prospects of the federal republic. Not only could Washington employ the new diplomatic tools fashioned at Philadelphia, but he and his countrymen

**George Washington (1732–1799).** A delegate to the Continental Congresses, soldier, politician, farmer on the Potomac, a towering figure among the founding fathers, George Washington commanded the Continental Army during the Revolution and became the first President of the United States. (Library of Congress)

could also make good use of the foreign policy experiences of the past thirteen years. Indeed, if the American Revolution and its aftermath produced nothing else, it provided the United States with a remarkable reservoir of leaders who were sophisticated in world affairs. Diplomats like Jefferson, Jay, and Adams were soon contributing their expertise to the new Administration. Washington himself, as his wartime collaboration with the French attested, understood the intricacies of alliance politics, as did his wartime aide, Alexander Hamilton. Other "demigods" at the Philadelphia convention—Gouverneur Morris, Edmund Randolph, Rufus King, James Madison, to name but a few—would occupy important diplomatic posts in the new government.[99] Because intellectual and political leaders were often the same men in this era, and because domestic, economic, and foreign policies were inextricably related, the Revolutionary generation gave rise to a foreign policy elite of exceptional skills.

The diplomatic goals of independence and expansion were both practical and idealistic. Adams' Model Treaty in 1776 had projected a vision whereby American commerce would be open to the entire world, thus diminishing one of the major causes of war and increasing American profits. Independence and extensive boundaries would protect a republican experiment which, in turn, could serve as a countervailing model for a world of monarchies. The Mississippi River, it seems, even had divine sanction. John Jay told the Spanish in 1780 that "Americans, almost to a man, believed that God Almighty had made that river a highway for the people of the upper country to go to the sea by."[100] For some the vision was even more expansive. The American geographer Jedidiah Morse wrote in 1789: "It is well known that empire has been travelling from east to west. Probably her last and broadest seat will be America. . . . We cannot but anticipate the period, as not far distant, when the AMERICAN EMPIRE will comprehend millions of souls, west of the Mississippi."[101] Of course, before Americans could move beyond the Mississippi, the boundaries of 1783 had to be made secure.

Americans wanted to obtain independence and empire without resort to European-style power politics. The attractions of American commerce proved insufficient to bring automatic aid and recognition; so Franklin in 1778 negotiated the alliance with France. The American preference for commercial treaties instead of political alliances did not diminish after 1778, however, and the commercial and neutral rights provisions of the Model Treaty remained essential to American diplomacy. Commercial treaties in the 1780s with Sweden, Prussia, and the Netherlands followed those principles. Minister to France Thomas Jefferson, in historian Merrill Peterson's estimation, thought of himself as undertaking "nothing less than a diplomatic mission to convert all Europe to the commercial principles of the American Revolution."[102] Probably more than most Americans of his generation, Jefferson retained this faith in the efficacy of commercial power as a substitute for military power. Americans believed, however, that the emphasis on commerce did not exalt profits over principles. As Jefferson's friend James Monroe later wrote: "People in Europe suppose us to be merchants, occupied exclusively with pepper and ginger. They are much deceived. . . . The immense majority of our citizens . . . are . . . controlled by principles of honor and dignity."[103]

Nevertheless, the United States had been forced to compromise principle—to make the alliance with France to win independence. The value of the French alliance was obvious. Without Comte de Rochambeau's army and Admiral de Grasse's fleet, Washington could not possibly have forced Cornwallis' surrender in 1781. French loans of some 35 million livres had kept an impecunious Congress solvent during the war. To be sure, Vergennes wanted to limit American boundaries; French agents in Philadelphia used their influence with Congress to hamstring American diplomats abroad; and as late as 1787 the French chargé d'affaires predicted that America would break up and urged his government to plan the seizure of New York or Rhode Island before the British could act. Still, the French alliance had secured American independence, and the treaty remained valid in 1789, including the provision guaranteeing French possessions in the New World. Most Americans, according to historian William Stinchcombe, "assumed that the alliance would officially end with the arrival of the definitive treaty of peace."[104] Not so.

The status of the French alliance notwithstanding, the eschewing of foreign entanglements remained a cardinal American tenet in the 1780s. "The more attention we pay to our resources and the less we rely on others," wrote Connecticut's Roger Sherman, "the more surely shall we provide for our own honor and success and retrieve that balance between the contending European powers."[105] George Mason echoed these sentiments: "I wish America would put her trust in God and herself, and have as little to do with the politics of Europe as possible."[106]

American diplomats abroad simply did not trust European countries. Europe had its own set of interests, America another. Even a Francophile like Jefferson could write: "Our interest calls for a perfect equality in our conduct towards [England and France]; but no preferences any where."[107] John Adams concurred. "My system," he wrote in 1785, "is a very simple one; let us preserve the friendship of France, Holland, and Spain, if we can, and in case of a war between France and England, let us preserve our neutrality, if possible. In order to preserve our friendship with France and Holland and Spain, it will be useful for us to avoid a war with England."[108] So wary were American leaders of foreign entanglements, they could contemplate political alliances only in the event of attack.

Americans, in short, sought fulfillment of their diplomatic goals without war or foreign allies. The federal Constitution strengthened national power. With an abundant federal revenue came stronger national credit. A flourishing foreign commerce and the power to regulate that commerce, it was hoped, provided an important diplomatic lever. American military power was insignificant. Europeans who visited America in the 1780s analyzed American speech patterns, described the flora and fauna, admired the landscape, but said little of military matters. The United States with its 3.5 million population seemed a slight threat to 15 million British or 25 million French. The traditional Anglo-Saxon fear of standing armies, and the expense of naval construction, made Americans, even under the Constitution, slow to build a defense establishment. Even Hamilton, the most military-minded member of Washington's government, predicted that it would be fifty years before the United States developed military forces sufficient to tip the balance between competing European powers or between the Old World and the New. Without military power or a foreign ally, the United States might find it difficult to maintain its independence, claim its boundaries, and expand its commerce. No one could foresee that the French Revolution would break out within a few months of Washington's inauguration, thus provoking a series of European wars that carried diplomatic consequences for the United States and a serious testing of the young republic's strength, patience, and foreign policy principles.

## Further Reading for the Period to 1789

For the colonial background to American diplomacy, see Felix Gilbert, *The Beginnings of American Diplomacy: To the Farewell Address* (1965), Lawrence S. Kaplan, *Colonies into Nation* (1972), Walter LaFeber, "Foreign Policies of a New Nation," in William A. Williams, ed., *From Colony to Empire* (1972), Max Savelle, *The Origins of American Diplomacy: The International History of Anglo-America, 1492–1763* (1967), and Richard Van Alstyne, *The Rising American Empire* (1960).

The diplomacy of the Revolutionary era is treated in Samuel Flagg Bemis, *The Diplomacy of the American Revolution* (1957), Isabel de Madariaga, *Britain, Russia, and the Armed Neutrality of 1780* (1962), Richard B. Morris, *The Peacemakers* (1965), David Schoenbrun, *Triumph in Paris: The Exploits of Benjamin Franklin* (1976), William Stinchcombe, *The American Revolution and the French Alliance* (1969), and Richard Van Alstyne, *Empire and Independence* (1965).

Foreign policy under the Articles of Confederation is recounted in Arthur B. Darling, *Our Rising Empire* (1940), Merrill Jensen, *The New Nation* (1950),

Frederick W. Marks, *Independence on Trial: Foreign Affairs and the Making of the Constitution* (1973), and Charles R. Ritcheson, *Aftermath of Revolution: British Policy toward the United States, 1783–1795* (1969).

For studies of individual statesmen and their contributions to American foreign policy, see Lawrence A. Kaplan, *Jefferson and France* (1963) and "Thomas Jefferson: The Idealist as Realist," in Frank Merli and Theodore A. Wilson, eds., *Makers of American Diplomacy* (1974), Dumas Malone, *Jefferson and the Ordeal of Liberty* (1962), Frank Monaghan, *John Jay* (1935), Merrill D. Peterson, "Thomas Jefferson and Commercial Policy, 1783–1793," *William and Mary Quarterly* (1965), Page Smith, *John Adams* (1962), Gerald Stourzh, *Benjamin Franklin and American Foreign Policy* (1969), and Carl Van Doren, *Benjamin Franklin* (1938). Brief biographies can be found in John A. Garraty, ed., *Encyclopedia of American Biography* (1974).

Also see for other works Norman Graebner, ed., *American Diplomatic History Before 1900* (1977) and the following notes.

## Notes to Chapter 1

1. Quoted in Richard B. Morris, *The Peacemakers: The Great Powers and American Independence* (New York: Harper and Row, 1965), p. 307.
2. Quoted in Francis Wharton, ed., *The Revolutionary Diplomatic Correspondence of the United States* (Washington: Government Printing Office, 1889; 6 vols.), V, 657.
3. Quoted in Morris, *Peacemakers*, pp. 309–310.
4. Herbert E. Klingelhofer, ed., "Matthew Ridley's Diary During the Peace Negotiations of 1782," *William and Mary Quarterly*, XX (January, 1963), 123.
5. Quoted in Morris, *Peacemakers*, p. 357.
6. Quoted in Albert H. Smyth, ed., *The Writings of Benjamin Franklin* (New York: Macmillan, 1905–1907; 10 vols.), IX, 62.
7. Quoted in Wharton, ed., *Revolutionary Diplomatic Correspondence*, IV, 75.
8. *Ibid.*, VI, 169.
9. Quoted in Richard B. Morris, *Seven Who Shaped Our Destiny* (New York: Harper and Row, 1973), p. 9.
10. Quoted in L. H. Butterfield, ed., *Diary and Autobiography of John Adams* (Cambridge: Harvard University Press, 1961; 4 vols.), III, 82.
11. Samuel Flagg Bemis, *The Diplomacy of the American Revolution* (Bloomington, Ind.: Indiana University Press, 1957), p. 256.
12. Quoted in Paul A. Varg, *Foreign Policies of the Founding Fathers* (Baltimore: Penguin Books, 1970), p. 3.
13. Quoted in Richard Van Alstyne, *The Rising American Empire* (Chicago: Quadrangle Books, 1965), p. 26.
14. Quoted in Richard Van Alstyne, *Empire and Independence: The International History of the American Revolution* (New York: John Wiley & Sons, 1965), p. 1.
15. Quoted in H. Trevor Colbourn, *The Lamp of Experience: Whig History and the Intellectual Origins of the American Revolution* (Chapel Hill: University of North Carolina Press, 1965), Frontispiece.
16. Quoted *ibid.*, p. 129.
17. Quoted in Gerald Stourzh, *Benjamin Franklin and American Foreign Policy* (Chicago: University of Chicago Press, 1969; 2nd ed.), p. 92.
18. Max Savelle, "Colonial Origins of American Diplomatic Principles," *Pacific Historical Review*, III (1934), 337.
19. Quoted in Felix Gilbert, *The Beginnings of American Diplomacy: To the Farewell Address* (New York: Harper Torchbook, 1965), p. 25.
20. Quoted *ibid.*, p. 28.
21. *Ibid.*
22. Quoted *ibid.*, p. 61.
23. Quoted *ibid.*, p. 57.
24. Quoted *ibid.*, p. 65.
25. Wharton, ed., *Revolutionary Diplomatic Correspondence*, IV, 590.
26. Worthington C. Ford, ed., *Journals of the Continental Congress* (Washington: Government Printing Office, 1904–37; 34 vols.), III, 484.
27. Thomas Paine, *Common Sense* (New York: Wiley, 1942), pp. 26–32.
28. Gilbert, *Beginnings of American Diplomacy*, p. 43.
29. Ford, ed., *Journals of the Continental Congress*, V, 425.
30. Quoted in Van Alstyne, *Empire and Independence*, p. 106.
31. Edmund C. Burnett, ed., *Letters of Members of the Continental Congress* (Washington: Carnegie Institution, 1921–36; 8 vols.), I, 502.
32. Ford, ed., *Journals of the Continental Congress*, V, 768–769.
33. Charles Francis Adams, ed., *The Works of John Adams* (Boston: Little, Brown, 1850–1865; 10 vols.), X, 269.
34. James D. Richardson, ed., *A Compilation of the Messages and Papers of the Presidents 1789–1897* (Washington: Government Printing Office, 1897–1900; 9 vols.), I, 323.
35. Walter LaFeber, "Foreign Policies of a New Nation: Franklin, Madison, and the 'Dream of a New Land to Fulfill with People in Self-Control,' 1750–1804," in William Appleman Williams, ed., *From Colony to Empire* (New York: John Wiley & Sons, 1972), p. 19.

36. Quoted in Claude H. Van Tyne, "French Aid Before the Alliance of 1778," *American Historical Review*, XXXI (October, 1925), 27.

37. Quoted in Van Alstyne, *Empire and Independence*, p. 43.

38. Quoted in Morris, *Peacemakers*, p. 113.

39. Quoted in Bemis, *Diplomacy of the American Revolution*, p. 27.

40. Quoted in Van Alstyne, *Empire and Independence*, p. 116.

41. Quoted *ibid.*, p. 163.

42. Quoted in Claude-Anne Lopez, *Mon Cher Papa: Franklin and the Ladies of Paris* (New Haven: Yale University Press, 1966), pp. 257–258.

43. Quoted in Stourzh, *Franklin and Foreign Policy*, p. 139.

44. *Ibid.*, p. 140.

45. Gilbert Chinard, ed., *The Treaties of 1778 and Allied Documents* (Baltimore: The Johns Hopkins Press, 1928), pp. 51–55.

46. Wharton, ed., *Revolutionary Diplomatic Correspondence*, II, 676.

47. Quoted in Van Alstyne, *Empire and Independence*, p. 204.

48. *Ibid.*, p. 93n.

49. Wharton, ed., *Revolutionary Diplomatic Correspondence*, II, 298.

50. Quoted in P. L. Haworth, "Frederick the Great and the American Revolution," *American Historical Review*, IX (April, 1904), 468.

51. Wharton, ed., *Revolutionary Diplomatic Correspondence*, V, 415.

52. Quoted in Morris, *Peacemakers*, p. 200.

53. Quoted in Isabel de Madariaga, *Britain, Russia, and the Armed Neutrality of 1780* (New Haven: Yale University Press, 1962), p. 255.

54. Ford, ed., *Journals of the Continental Congress*, XXIV, 394.

55. Samuel Flagg Bemis, *A Diplomatic History of the United States* (New York: Holt, Rinehart and Winston, 1965; 5th ed.), p. 34.

56. Quoted in Morris, *Peacemakers*, p. 246.

57. Quoted in Frank Monaghan, *John Jay* (Indianapolis: Bobbs-Merrill, 1935), p. 136.

58. Quoted in Morris, *Peacemakers*, p. 242.

59. Quoted *ibid.*, p. 243.

60. Lawrence S. Kaplan, *Colonies into Nation: American Diplomacy, 1763–1801* (New York: Macmillan, 1972), p. 135.

61. Quoted in Louis Gottschalk, *LaFayette and the Close of the American Revolution* (Chicago: University of Chicago Press, 1942), p. 331.

62. Quoted in Morris, *Peacemakers*, p. 263.

63. Quoted in Carl Van Doren, *Benjamin Franklin* (New York: The Viking Press, 1938), p. 671.

64. Quoted in Morris, *Peacemakers*, p. 383.

65. H. P. Johnston, ed., *Correspondence and Public Papers of John Jay* (New York: G. P. Putnam's Sons, 1890–93; 4 vols.), II, 344.

66. Quoted in Mary Beth Norton, *The British-Americans: The Loyalist Exiles in England, 1774–1789* (Boston: Little, Brown, 1972), pp. 175–176.

67. Quoted *ibid.*, p. 176.

68. Quoted in Kaplan, *Colonies into Nation*, p. 143.

69. Quoted in Van Doren, *Benjamin Franklin*, p. 695.

70. Wharton, ed., *Revolutionary Diplomatic Correspondence*, VI, 140.

71. Quoted in David Schoenbrun, *Triumph in Paris: The Exploits of Benjamin Franklin* (New York: Harper and Row, 1976), p. 383.

72. Kaplan, *Colonies into Nation*, p. 144.

73. Quoted in Morris, *Peacemakers*, p. 459.

74. Bemis, *Diplomacy of the American Revolution*, p. 256.

75. Quoted in Merrill Jensen, *The New Nation: A History of the United States During the Confederation, 1781–1789* (New York: Alfred A. Knopf, 1950), p. 105.

76. Johnston, ed., *Correspondence of John Jay*, III, 154.

77. Quoted in Jensen, *The New Nation*, p. 154.

78. Quoted in Samuel Flagg Bemis, *Jay's Treaty: A Study in Commerce and Diplomacy* (New Haven: Yale University Press, 1962), p. 34.

79. William C. Stinchcombe, *The American Revolution and the French Alliance* (Syracuse: Syracuse University Press, 1969), p. 169.

80. Quoted in Kaplan, *Colonies into Nation*, pp. 160–161.

81. Quoted in Frederick W. Marks, III, *Independence on Trial: Foreign Affairs and the Making of the Constitution* (Baton Rouge: Louisiana State University Press, 1973), p. 135.

82. Julian P. Boyd, *Number Seven: Alexander Hamilton's Secret Attempts to Control American Foreign Policy* (Princeton: Princeton University Press, 1964), p. xi.

83. Quoted in Catherine Drinker Bowen, *Miracle at Philadelphia* (Boston: Little, Brown, 1966), p. 137.

84. Quoted in Jerald A. Combs, *The Jay Treaty: Political Battleground of the Founding Fathers* (Berkeley: University of California Press, 1970), p. 24.

85. Quoted in Charles R. Ritcheson, *Aftermath of Revolution: British Policy toward the United States, 1783–1795* (Dallas: Southern Methodist University Press, 1969), p. 44.

86. Quoted in Marks, *Independence on Trial*, p. 68.

87. John C. Fitzpatrick, ed., *The Writings of George Washington* (Washington: Government Printing Office, 1931–1944; 39 vols.), XXVII, 475.

88. Samuel Flagg Bemis, *Pinckney's Treaty: A Study of America's Advantage from Europe's Distress, 1783–1800* (Baltimore: The Johns Hopkins University Press, 1926), p. 84.

89. Quoted in Marks, *Independence on Trial*, p. 31.

90. Quoted in Lawrence S. Kaplan, *Jefferson and France: An Essay on Politics and Political Ideas* (New Haven: Yale University Press, 1963), p. 23.

91. Quoted in Kaplan, *Colonies into Nation*, p. 180.

92. *Diplomatic Correspondence of the United States of America, from the Signing of the Definitive Treaty of Peace, September 10, 1783, to the Adoption of the Constitution, March 4, 1789* (Washington: Blair and Ives, 1837; 3 vols.), I, 792.

93. Quoted in Marks, *Independence on Trial*, p. 48.

94. Article VI of the Constitution.

95. Lyman H. Butterfield, ed., *Letters of Benjamin Rush* (Princeton: Princeton University Press, 1951; 2 vols.), I, 475.

96. Quoted in Jacob Javits, *Who Makes War: The President Versus Congress* (New York: William Morrow, 1973), p. 13.

97. Quoted in Arthur M. Schlesinger, Jr., *The Imperial Presidency* (Boston: Houghton Mifflin, 1973), p. 4.

98. Jacob E. Cooke, ed., *The Federalist* (Middletown, Conn.: Wesleyan University Press, 1961), p. 64.

99. Quoted in Clinton Rossiter, *1787: The Grand Convention* (New York: Macmillan, 1966), p. 138.

100. Quoted in Varg, *Foreign Policies of the Founding Fathers*, p. 41.

101. Quoted in Van Alstyne, *Rising American Empire,* p. 69.

102. Merrill D. Peterson, "Thomas Jefferson and Commercial Policy, 1783–1793," *William and Mary Quarterly, XXII* (October, 1965), 592.

103. Quoted in Ernest R. May, *The Making of the Monroe Doctrine* (Cambridge, Mass.: Harvard University Press, 1975), p. 19.

104. Stinchcombe, *American Revolution and French Alliance,* p. 200.

105. Quoted *ibid.,* p. 205.

106. Quoted in Kate Mason Rowland, *The Life of George Mason* (New York: G. P. Putnam's Sons, 1892; 2 vols.), II, 47.

107. Julian Boyd, ed., *The Papers of Thomas Jefferson* (Princeton: Princeton University Press, 1950–1974; 19 vols.), *VIII,* 545.

108. Adams, *Works, VIII,* 235–236.

***Chesapeake*** versus ***Leopard,*** **1807.** This naval encounter highlighted once again the impressment issue in Anglo-American relations and nearly caused war. The *Chesapeake* got off only one shot against the 50-gun British vessel. After the incident President Thomas Jefferson closed American ports to the Royal Navy, only to find that the British commanders haughtily anchored in Chesapeake Bay. (U.S. Navy)

# 2 Independence and Expansion in a World at War, 1789–1815

## Diplomatic Crossroad: The *Chesapeake* Affair, 1807

At 7:15 A.M. on the morning of June 22, 1807, the 40-gun American frigate *Chesapeake* weighed anchor from Hampton Roads, Virginia, and made sail under a pleasant south-westerly breeze. Commanded by Commodore James Barron, the *Chesapeake* was bound for the Mediterranean, where it would replace its sister vessel, the U.S.S. *Constitution,* as flagship of a small naval squadron that protected American merchantmen from the Barbary pirates. No one expected trouble. The ship's crew numbered 375, several of whom, it was rumored, were deserters from the British Navy who had enlisted on the *Chesapeake* under assumed names. A number of sick sailors, recovering from a drinking bout of the night before, were allowed by the ship's doctor to lie in the sunny air on the upper deck. The gun deck was cluttered with loose lumber. Cables were not stowed away. Four of the guns did not fit perfectly into their carriages. Only five of the powder horns used in priming the guns were actually filled. In fact, the crew had not been exercised at the guns during the ship's fitting out in Hampton Roads. Barron set sail anyway. His ship was already four months behind schedule and there would be ample opportunity for gunnery practice during the long sea voyage.

At 9:00 the *Chesapeake* passed Lynnhaven Bay, where two 74-gun British ships of the line, *Bellona* and *Melampus,* lay anchored. A rumor had circulated in Norfolk that the captain of the *Melampus* was threatening to seize from the *Chesapeake* three alleged deserters, but if Commodore Barron had heard the story, he took no special precautions. Neither British ship stirred. Soon after midday the *Chesapeake* sighted another ship off Cape Henry, the 50-gun frigate H.M.S. *Leopard.* At approximately 3:30 P.M., when both vessels were some ten miles southeast of Cape Henry, the *Leopard* came about and hailed that the British captain wanted to send dispatches to the Mediterranean through the courtesy of the American commodore. The *Chesapeake* hailed back: "We will heave to you and you can send your boat on board of us."[1] At this point Barron made a serious mistake.

**James Barron (1769–1851).** The commander of the *Chesapeake,* according to court-martial proceedings conducted in early 1808, had not prepared his ship properly for battle with the *Leopard.* Many of his fellow officers thought Barron had prematurely surrendered. The Navy suspended Barron for five years without pay. He returned to service but was given only shore duty. Years later he killed his chief nemesis, naval officer Stephen Decatur, in a duel, further bespoiling the reprimanded commander's career. (Library of Congress)

According to naval custom, a captain should never permit a foreign warship to approach alongside without first calling his crew to battle stations. The disorderly conditions on the *Chesapeake,* however, made it difficult to clear the guns quickly, and to Barron, the idea of a British naval attack in home waters seemed preposterous.

British Lieutenant John Meade came aboard at precisely 3:45. He handed Barron a copy of orders from Captain S. P. Humphreys, instructing him to search the *Chesapeake* for British deserters. Humphreys did not elaborate on his orders, except to "express a hope that every circumstance respecting them may be adjusted in a manner that the harmony subsisting between the two countries may remain undisturbed."[2] Barron replied correctly; he could never allow his crew to be mustered "by any other but their own officers. It is my disposition to preserve harmony, and I hope this answer . . . will prove satisfactory."[3] Meade returned to the *Leopard* by longboat. Barron now ordered the gun deck cleared for action.

The time was nearly 4:30. To prepare the frigate for battle required a full half hour. The sea was calm. The *Leopard,* less than a pistol shot away, moved closer. Captain Humphreys again used the hailing pipe: "Commodore Barron, you must be aware of the necessity I am under of complying with the orders of my commander-in-chief." Barron, now on deck where he could plainly see the *Leopard*'s guns, tried to gain time by shouting: "I do not hear what you say."[4] He ordered the men to their stations without the drumbeat. The *Leopard* fired a shot across the *Chesapeake*'s bow. Another shot followed a minute later. Then, from a distance of less than two hundred feet, the helpless *Chesapeake* was raked by an entire broadside of solid shot and canister. The Americans could not fire back. The guns were loaded, but they could not discharge without lighted matches or heated loggerheads from the galley fires. Ammunition had to be brought by hand from the magazine. The *Leopard* poured in more broadsides at point-blank range. In ten minutes of barrage the *Chesapeake* was hulled twenty-two times. Its three masts were badly damaged. The American ship suffered three men killed, eight severely and ten slightly wounded, including Commodore Barron, who stood exposed on the quarterdeck throughout the cannonade. Finally, not wanting to sacrifice lives needlessly, Barron ordered the flag struck. The Americans salvaged a modicum of honor by firing a lone shot at the *Leopard.* A lieutenant had managed to discharge the gun by carrying a live coal in his fingers all the way from the galley. The eighteen-pound shot penetrated the *Leopard*'s hull, but fell harmlessly into the wardroom. The battle was over.

British boats again came alongside. The officers mustered the American crew. Captain Humphreys executed his orders moderately, taking only four sailors from the scores of deserters and identifiable Englishmen aboard the *Chesapeake.* Of the four, three were undeniably Americans, deserters from the *Melampus* the previous March. Two of these, it turned out, both blacks, had previously deserted from an American merchantman and had voluntarily enlisted in the Royal Navy in 1806. The fourth deserter was a surly Londoner, Jenkin Ratford (alias John Wilson), who had openly insulted his former British officers on the streets of Norfolk. Ratford hid deep in the *Chesapeake*'s coal hole, but the British dragged him out. (Ratford was later hanged from a Halifax yardarm, while the three Americans received lesser punishment.) Battered and humiliated, the *Chesapeake* then limped back toward Hampton Roads.

Americans were angry when they heard the news. Heretofore the Royal Navy's practice of impressing alleged British sailors from American merchant ships had caused much diplomatic wrangling. Just a few months earlier, President Thomas Jefferson and Secretary of State James Madison had rejected a treaty with England largely because it failed to disavow "this authorized system of kidnapping upon the ocean."[5] British warships, skippered by arrogant officers, constantly stopped and searched merchantmen in American waters, and once the previous year H.M.S. *Leander* had killed an American when firing a shot across a merchantman's bow. But the *Chesapeake* affair was unprecedented. The British had deliberately attacked an American *naval* vessel, a virtual act of war.

Federalists and Republicans alike were shocked. In historian Henry Adams' words, "the brand seethed and hissed like the glowing olive-stake of Ulysses in the Cyclops' eye, until the whole American people, like Cyclops, roared with pain and stood frantic on the shore, hurling abuse at their enemy, who taunted them from his safe ships."[6] The citizens of Hampton Roads expressed their resentment by destroying some two hundred water casks that were ready for delivery to the thirsty British squadron in Lynnhaven Bay. The British threatened retaliation. At a meeting of citizens in Baltimore, according to Senator Samuel Smith, "there appeared but one opinion—War—in case that satisfaction is not given."[7] Even in Boston, the stronghold of pro-British sentiment, a crowd of two thousand pledged resolutions in support of whatever action the federal government might take. President Jefferson's first step, on July 2, was to issue a proclamation closing American waters to British warships. Two weeks later he told the French minister:

"If the English do not give us the satisfaction we demand, we will take Canada."[8] Secretary of the Treasury Albert Gallatin believed that war would bring increased taxes, debts, and destruction, but that "all these evils" should not be "put in competition with the independence and honor of the nation." War with England, thought Gallatin, might "prevent our degenerating, like the Hollanders, into a nation of mere calculators."[9]

The *Chesapeake* affair did not lead to war—at least not immediately. Jefferson chose, in historian Bradford Perkins' phrase, "to play the part of a damper rather than a bellows."[10] Military preparations and diplomatic alternatives had to be tried first. Even before Congress convened late in the year, Jefferson moved energetically to strengthen American defenses. Without public fanfare, the President called all naval and merchant vessels home, ordered naval gunboats to be readied, armed seven coastal fortresses, sent field guns to various state militia, gave war warnings to all frontier posts, and informed state governors that he might call 100,000 militia members to federal service. In readying American ramparts, however, the Jefferson Administration discovered just how inadequate its defenses were. The Navy Department, it turned out, could not send a ship to the East Indies recalling American merchant ships because there were no funds for such a voyage. Even Washington seemed vulnerable to attack. Gallatin warned prophetically that the British could "land at Annapolis, march to the city, and re-embark before the militia could be collected to repel [them]."[11] When Congress met in December, 1807, however, Jefferson's republican ideology precluded any request for a large standing army, and the President asked for inexpensive coastal gunboats in preference to oceangoing frigates.

Jefferson's diplomacy also proved inadequate. The British government might have settled the matter amicably if the Americans had asked only for an apology and reparations for the *Chesapeake.* Foreign Minister George Canning told American Minister James Monroe exactly that, in late July, 1807, but Jefferson's subsequent instructions insisted that England disavow impressment in all instances, as well as apologize for the attack on an American naval vessel. Canning was willing to disavow the incident but not the practice. As it turned out, a formal apology for the *Chesapeake* was not delivered and accepted until 1811, by which time America's wounded sense of honor and England's stubbornness made war almost impossible to avoid. Indeed, the *Chesapeake* affair had set in motion American thoughts about invading Canada, and the British, in turn, began to repair their alliances with the Indian tribes in the Ohio Valley. In this way were maritime grievances linked to frontier friction. By 1812, most Americans could agree with Andrew Jackson's boast that "we are going to fight for the re-establishment of our national character . . . ; for the protection of our maritime citizens . . . ; [and] to seek some indemnity for past injuries . . . by the conquest of all the British dominions . . . of North America."[12]

## Europe's Wars, America's Crises

The *Chesapeake* affair came during the series of wars that engulfed Europe after 1789. These wars were initially advantageous to the United States. The economic prosperity of the young republic depended on the disposing of agricultural surpluses abroad on favorable terms, and war in Europe automatically created

## Makers of American Foreign Policy from 1789 to 1815

| *Presidents* | *Secretaries of State* |
|---|---|
| George Washington, 1789–1797 | Thomas Jefferson, 1790–1793 |
| | Edmund Randolph, 1794–1795 |
| John Adams, 1797–1801 | Timothy Pickering, 1795–1800 |
| | John Marshall, 1800–1801 |
| Thomas Jefferson, 1801–1809 | James Madison, 1801–1809 |
| James Madison, 1809–1817 | Robert Smith, 1809–1811 |
| | James Monroe, 1811–1817 |

trading opportunities for neutral carriers. American exports amounted to $20,750,000 in 1792, the last year of peace between France and England; by 1796 exports had jumped to $67,060,000. Europe's wars also gave the United States more diplomatic leverage with respect to territorial disputes in North America. Since England and Spain were embroiled with France, and both sets of belligerents desired American trade, the Administration of George Washington could proceed more forcefully in negotiating with Spain over the Mississippi and Florida, and with Great Britain over the still occupied northwest forts. Yet Europe's wars also posed the danger that the United States might get sucked in. France might demand American assistance under the terms of the 1778 alliance. England and Spain might fight rather than concede territorial claims in North America. Even if the United States maintained neutrality, belligerent nations might still disrupt America's neutral commerce. Americans differed over the proper response to Europe's wars, and the ensuing debate over foreign policy coincided with the rise of national political parties. The political and economic stakes were high indeed.

George Washington, whether as plantation manager, military commander, or president, always sought the best counsel before making decisions. Although Vice-President John Adams, Chief Justice John Jay, and Attorney General Edmund Randolph sometimes contributed recommendations, the making of foreign policy during Washington's first Administration often resembled an essay contest between Secretary of State Thomas Jefferson and Secretary of the Treasury Alexander Hamilton. Hamilton usually won, sometimes by using unscrupulous tactics, and around his successful policies coalesced the first national political party in the United States, the Federalist party. Although historians correctly use the term "Hamiltonian" foreign policy, Washington tried to remain above partisanship and accepted Hamilton's advice because he thought it in the national interest. However, the popular father of his country "was an *Aegis very essential to me,*" Hamilton later admitted.[13]

Hamilton dominated diplomacy because early in the Washington Administration he had, as treasury secretary, formulated and won congressional approval for a fiscal program with foreign policy implications. By funding the national debt at par, assuming the Revolutionary debts of several of the states, and paying the arrears on the national debt owed abroad, Hamilton hoped to attract financial support for the federal experiment from wealthier commercial interests. Such a program required revenue. Hamilton provided the necessary monies through a tariff on imports and a tax on shipping tonnage. The revenue laws, passed in July,

1789, levied a tax of fifty cents a ton on foreign vessels in American ports and attached a 10 percent higher tariff on imports in foreign bottoms. Such navigation laws served to stimulate American shipping by discriminating moderately against foreigners, but not enough to curtail trade. Hamilton particularly opposed discriminatory measures against England, such as the bill sponsored by James Madison in 1791 that would have prohibited imports from countries that forbade American imports in American bottoms (as England did with respect to Canada and the British West Indies). In Hamilton's eyes, any interference with Anglo-American commerce spelled disaster. Fully 90 percent of American imports came from England, more than half in British ships; nearly 50 percent of American exports went to British ports. Revenue would dry up if trade were curtailed. National credit, said Hamilton, would be "cut up . . . by the roots."[14] Accordingly, this brilliant bastard son of a West Indian planter spent the better part of his tenure at the Treasury Department defending the sanctity of Anglo-American trade, and hence, Anglo-American diplomatic cooperation.

Opposition to Hamilton's definition of the national interest quickly developed, particularly among Southern agrarian interests hoping to develop new markets on the European continent for grain, cotton, and tobacco. As an echo of Secretary of State Jefferson, who resented Hamilton's encroachment on his prerogatives, James Madison, formerly one of Hamilton's fellow authors of the *Federalist Papers,* raised questions in Congress. Unlike the Federalists, Madison wanted to use commercial discrimination as a lever to obtain trade and territorial concessions from England. As spokesmen for Southern planters whose crops had long been shackled to British markets and British credit, Madison and Jefferson wanted to loosen Anglo-American patterns through favorable commercial treaties with other European states and by legislation favoring non-British shipping. Britain might retaliate, but, as Madison put it with some exaggeration: "The produce of this country is more necessary to the rest of the world than that of other countries is to America. . . . [England's] interests can be wounded almost mortally, while ours are invulnerable."[15] Even though Hamilton blocked Madison's navigation bill in the Senate, the mere threat of commercial reprisals induced the British to send their first formal minister, George Hammond, to the United States in October, 1791. Washington thereupon returned the compliment by sending former Governor of South Carolina Thomas Pinckney to the Court of St. James's.

The American split over commercial policy was exacerbated further by the French Revolution. The initial phase of the French upheaval, with familiar figures like Thomas Paine and the Marquis de Lafayette in positions of leadership, elicited almost universal approbation in America. Then came the spring of 1793 and news that King Louis XVI had been guillotined and France had declared war on England and Spain. While conservative Federalists recoiled at the republican terror in France, Jeffersonian Republicans cheered and began organizing popular societies in apparent imitation of the French Jacobin clubs. Caught up in the enthusiasm, Jefferson himself wrote: "My own affections have been deeply wounded by some of the martyrs to this cause [the executed victims in Paris], but rather than it should have failed I would have seen half the earth desolated; were there but an Adam and an Eve left in every country, and left free, it would be better than it now is."[16] Frightened Federalists began to suspect that the Jeffersonians sought to plunge the country into war on the side of France. The Jeffersonians, in turn, conjured up visions of plots by Federalists, and thought they wanted "to make a party in the confederacy against human liberty."[17] In actuality, the rising political passions in 1793 obscured the fact that neither party placed the interests of France or England above those of the United States. Although Hamilton sometimes talked indiscreetly to British diplomats, he did so in the belief that the twin American goals of commercial and territorial expansion could be best achieved in close relationship with Great Britain. As for Jefferson's celebrated Francophilism, French Minister Pierre Adet commented in 1796: "Jefferson I say is American and as such, he cannot be sincerely our friend. An American is the born enemy of all the European peoples."[18] Even though the country remained officially neutral, it seemed inevitable that Americans would favor one side or the other in the symbolic struggle between England and France, between monarchy and republicanism.

President Washington's proclamation of neutrality on April 22, 1793 received the unanimous backing of his Cabinet advisers. How to reconcile neutrality with the French alliance was another matter. In receiving France's new republican minister, Citizen Edmond Charles Genêt, Jefferson refuted Hamilton's arguments that the 1778 treaties had lapsed with the death of Louis XVI. Jefferson thereby set two important diplomatic precedents: American respect for the sanctity of treaties and quick diplomatic recognition of regimes that had de facto control over a country. The thirty-year-old Genêt eased his reception by not asking the United States to become a belligerent; he even offered new commercial concessions if American merchants would take over France's colonial trade with the West Indies. Exultant, Jefferson innocently noted: "He offers everything & asks nothing."[19]

. Obstacles to Franco-American harmony quickly materialized. Genêt outfitted some fourteen privateers—privately owned American ships, equipped in American ports for war under French commission. Before long they had captured more than eighty British merchant ships, some of them taken within the American three-mile coastal limit. Such activities contravened Washington's proclamation of neutrality. British Minister Hammond protested and Jefferson warned Genêt, but pro-French juries often acquitted those Americans who were arrested. Genêt infuriated Jefferson by promising that a captured British prize, *Little Sarah*, would not be sent to sea as a privateer only a few hours before the vessel (renamed *Petite Democrate*) slipped down the Delaware River to embark on a career of destroying commerce. Not content with these embarrassments, Genêt also scurried about with plans for capturing Spanish-controlled Louisiana, an expedition comprised mostly of American volunteers and led by the drunken Revolutionary hero George Rogers Clark. Although the plan never reached fruition, the French envoy dramatically informed Paris: "I am arming the Canadians to throw off the yoke of England; I am arming the Kentuckians, and I am preparing an expedition by sea to support the descent on New Orleans."[20] Genêt also encouraged pro-French editorials in the press of the nation's capital, Philadelphia, hobnobbed with Republican leaders, and at one point addressed an appeal to the American people over the head of the President. President Washington grew furious, and even Madison admitted that Genêt's "conduct has been that of a madman."[21]

The furor over Genêt abated somewhat by late summer of 1793, when an outbreak of yellow fever caused most government officials to leave Philadelphia. By this time Genêt had made himself so obnoxious that the Washington Administration, Jefferson included, agreed unanimously to ask the French government to recall its envoy. Meanwhile, Washington replaced Gouverneur Morris as American

The Cannibals are landing

Volunteers

Stop de wheels of

de gouvernement

**Factionalism and Foreign Policy.** In this Federalist cartoon of the 1790s, President George Washington attempts to advance toward the invading French ("Cannibals") at the left, but Thomas Jefferson, among others, restrains him. Differences over questions of foreign policy helped propel American leaders into the Federalist and Republican parties. (Courtesy of the New-York Historical Society, New York City)

minister in Paris. The wooden-legged Morris had proven himself a shrewd judge of the French Revolution, but had alienated his hosts by befriending French aristocrats, at one point even aiding in an abortive attempt to spirit the King and Queen out of France. The nomination of James Monroe, a firm Virginia Republican, to replace Morris temporarily patched up quarrels, as did the arrival of Genêt's successor, Joseph Fauchet, in February, 1794. As for Genêt, he never returned to France. By the time of his recall the French Revolution had moved inexorably to the left, the Girondins having been replaced by the Jacobins, and young Genêt was in danger of literally losing his head as well as his reputation. Washington relented and allowed Genêt to remain in America as a private citizen, whereupon the once stormy Frenchman moved to New York, married the daughter of Governor George Clinton, and lived quietly until his death in 1834.

## Commerce, Politics, and Diplomacy: Jay's Treaty

No sooner had the crisis with France eased than the country found itself on the edge of war with England. Seizure of American commerce on the high seas and threats of Indian attacks from Canada touched off a war scare in the winter and early spring of 1794. Indignation raged in Congress when it learned in late February that British cruisers, under a secret order in council (Admiralty decree) declaring foodstuffs contraband, had seized more than 250 American merchantmen trading with the French West Indies. These maritime acts, coupled with an inflammatory speech to the western Indians by Lord Dorchester, governor general of Canada, posed a direct threat to the young republic. Congress responded, on March 26, 1794, by imposing a thirty-day embargo (later extended to sixty days) on all shipping in American ports bound for foreign destinations. Although ostensibly impartial, the legislation was aimed at England.

Cool heads sought to prevent a rupture. Fearful that the Republican majority in the House of Representatives would destroy trade and credit through permanent embargoes and thus cause war with England, Hamilton and other Federalists suggested a special mission to London. By a vote of 18 to 8, the Senate, on April 18, confirmed the appointment of John Jay. Historian Samuel Flagg Bemis has entitled Jay's subsequent agreement "Hamilton's Treaty."[22] Not only did the treasury secretary conceive the special mission, but he also drafted the bulk of Jay's instructions. Only after strenuous argument from Edmund Randolph, who had replaced Jefferson as secretary of state, was a reference inserted to "the possibility of sounding Russia, Sweden, or Denmark as to an alliance on the principles of the Armed Neutrality."[23] The Anglophilic Hamilton deliberately defused this menacing diplomatic weapon, which might have induced England to make concessions on neutral rights, when he leaked to British Minister Hammond the information that Washington's Cabinet, ever wary of entanglements, had actually decided not to join a neutral alliance. Aside from the stipulations forbidding any agreement that contradicted obligations under the 1778 alliance with France, and prohibiting any commercial treaty that failed to open the British West Indies to American shipping, the special minister's instructions afforded him considerable discretion. Moreover, Jay's concern for maintaining peace and commerce with Great Britain was almost as great as Hamilton's.

Amidst wine, dining, and British flattery, the envoy extraordinary negotiated a Treaty of Amity, Commerce, and Navigation, signed on November 19, 1794. England, locked in deadly combat with France, found it prudent to conciliate the United States on North American issues, but generally did not yield on questions involving its maritime supremacy. Jay's most important accomplishment was the British surrender of the northwest forts, which London had already promised to relinquish in the 1783 peace treaty. This time the redcoats actually left. (Meanwhile, General Anthony Wayne had defeated the western Indians in the Battle of Fallen Timbers on August 20, 1794, and the subsequent Treaty of Greenville pacified the northwest frontier for approximately fifteen years.) Another British concession, the opening of the British East Indies to American commerce, held great promise for future trade with Asia. Jay also obtained trade with the British Isles on a most-favored-nation basis. As for the British West Indies, however, American shipping would be limited to vessels of less than seventy tons, and American export of certain staples, like cotton and sugar, was forbidden. Other controversial matters, including compensation for recent maritime seizures, pre-Revolutionary debts still owed by Americans, and the disputed northeast boundary of Maine, were to be decided by mixed commissions of arbitration. In regard to neutral rights, Jay was forced to make concessions that violated the spirit, if not the letter, of America's treaty obligations to France. His treaty stipulated that under certain circumstances American foodstuffs bound for France might be seized and compensation offered and that French property on American ships constituted a fair prize. In other words, "free ships" no longer meant "free goods"—at least insofar as the United States now permitted England to treat its commerce. The commercial clauses were to remain in effect for twelve years, thus making it impossible for Republicans to discriminate against the British. Finally, the treaty said nothing about impressment and abducted slaves. "A bolder party stroke was never struck," Jefferson grumbled. "For it certainly is an attempt of a party, which . . . lost their majority in one branch of the legislature, to make a law by the other branch of the executive, under color of a treaty, which shall bind up the hands of the adverse branch from ever restraining the commerce of their patron nation."[24]

Jefferson's discontent notwithstanding, Jay's Treaty was a milestone on the road to mature national sovereignty. Faced with the loss of American trade, England had compromised on territorial issues in North America. However, London would no more surrender maritime supremacy in 1794 than it would in 1807. Nonetheless, in view of the contempt England had shown American diplomacy since 1783, any concession by treaty constituted real proof that the United States could maintain its independence in a hostile world. By inaugurating a ten-year period of relatively amicable relations between England and the United States, Jay's Treaty gave the United States time in which to grow in territory, population, and national consciousness. When war came in 1812 the United States was able to fight more effectively than in 1794.

The treaty signed in November, 1794 arrived in Philadelphia on March 7, 1795. The Senate had just dispersed, so Washington did not actually submit the treaty for approval until early June. The senators debated in executive session, and only by eliminating Article XII (dealing with the West Indian trade restrictions) were the Federalists able to secure a bare two-thirds vote of endorsement on June 24. Complications prevented the President's immediate signature. Washington was not sure whether he needed to resubmit the treaty to England (without Article XII) before formally ratifying it. While he considered this dilemma Jay's Treaty was leaked to the press. Critics quickly charged that Jay had surrendered American maritime rights for minor British concessions, and that the French alliance had been betrayed. Antitreaty manifestos and protest parades materialized in many towns and cities. In Philadelphia a mob hanged John Jay in effigy and stoned the residence of the British minister. A crowd also stoned Hamilton when he spoke in favor of the treaty in New York. In retreat he shouted: "If you use such striking arguments, I must retire."[25]

Federalist leaders quailed at the onslaught. Washington had to take action to put an end to the clamor and to protect his reputation. "If the President decides wrong, or does not decide *soon*," wrote Oliver Ellsworth of Connecticut, "his good fortune will forsake him."[26] While Washington pondered a decision at Mount Vernon during the summer of 1795, according to historian Joseph Charles, it seemed that the entire "inner circle of the Federalist Party fairly held its breath."[27] Yet the President withheld formal ratification—in part, because he was irked that the British had resumed seizures of American vessels carrying foodstuffs to France. Conferring almost exclusively with Randolph, he decided to wait for adequate British explanations.

Always a deliberate man, Washington might have avoided ratification indefinitely had not suspicions of treason intervened and thereby removed Edmund Randolph, an obstacle to peaceful relations with England. In March, 1795, a British man-of-war had captured a French corvette carrying dispatches from Minister Joseph Fauchet to Paris. Dispatch Number Ten recounted conversations in which Randolph had allegedly sought from Fauchet money for Republican leaders in Pennsylvania during the Whiskey Rebellion of 1794. The report of the conversation was confused and remains puzzling to scholars, but Foreign Minister William Grenville sensed his opportunity and sent Dispatch Number Ten to Minister Hammond with the instruction that "the communication of some of [the information] to well disposed persons in America may possibly be helpful to the King's service."[28] Hammond showed the dispatch to Secretary of War Timothy Pickering, a tall, pinch-faced New Englander and diehard Federalist who seemed convinced of Randolph's treason and who deliberately but subtly mistranslated certain French passages in Number Ten to make the evidence look more incriminating. Then he wrote carefully to Mount Vernon. "On the subject of the treaty," he informed Washington, "I confess that I feel extreme solicitude; and for a *special reason* which can be communicated to you only in person, I entreat that you return with all possible speed."[29]

Washington arrived in Philadelphia in August, read Pickering's translation of Number Ten, and apparently pronounced his secretary of state guilty without trial. He also decided to ratify Jay's Treaty. On August 18, 1795, the President put his official signature on the document. The next day he confronted Randolph. Pickering was in attendance, eyeing the victim like a hawk. Washington handed him Fauchet's dispatch, pronouncing coldly, "Mr. Randolph! here is a letter which I desire you to read, and make such explanations as you choose."[30] The young Virginian's defense was valiant, but foredoomed. Randolph then wrote a voluminous *Vindication,* which he hoped would redeem his name. Even though most modern scholars accept Randolph's innocence, he made the mistake of quarreling openly with the revered President Washington, and in the heated political atmosphere of 1795–1796 neither the Republicans nor the Federalists would take up his cause. Randolph resigned and returned to Virginia embittered.

The Republicans, while avoiding any identification with the fallen Randolph, made one last effort in the House of Representatives to negate Jay's Treaty by trying to block appropriations for its implementation. During the House debates in March, 1796, Republican leaders asked the President to release all official documents and correspondence relating to the treaty. In a precedent-setting decision, Washington categorically refused, citing the need for secrecy and the fact that the treatymaking power lay exclusively with the executive and Senate. The debate raged on. Federalist Fisher Ames of Massachusetts evoked the fear of Indian warfare in the Northwest if appropriations were rejected and British troops did not leave: "In the day time, your path through the woods will be ambushed; the darkness of midnight will glitter with the blaze of your dwellings. You are a father; the blood of your sons shall fatten your cornfield! You are a mother: the war-whoop shall wake the sleep of the cradle! . . . By rejecting the posts, we light the savage fires—we bind the victims."[31] Another Federalist wrote to his congressman: "If you do not give us your vote, your son shall not have my Polly."[32] A bare majority (51 to 48) of the House voted the necessary funds on April 30.

## Pinckney's Treaty, France, and Washington's Farewell

One reason why the House, despite a Republican majority, voted appropriations for Jay's Treaty was the fear that its negation might jeopardize the more popular Pinckney's Treaty with Spain. This treaty (sometimes called the Treaty of San Lorenzo) obtained everything that the United States had sought from Spain since the Revolution, and was especially pleasing to the South and West. Signed by Thomas Pinckney in Madrid on October 27, 1795, the treaty secured for American farmers free navigation of the Mississippi River and the right of depositing goods at New Orleans for transshipment. This privilege of deposit was stipulated to last for three years, renewable either at New Orleans or some other suitable place on the Mississippi. Spain also set the northern boundary of Florida at 31 degrees north latitude. The Senate approved the accord unanimously on March 3, 1796. With America's southeastern frontier now settled with Spain, a number of Republicans in the House did not want to risk losing a similarly favorable settlement in the Northwest by voting against the Jay Treaty. In the sense that they redeemed America's borderlands from foreign control, Jay's Treaty and Pinckney's Treaty were thought to stand together.

In actuality, the popular treaty with Spain seems to have been a by-product of Jay's handiwork in England. When Thomas Pinckney arrived in Spain in June, 1795, the Spanish knew of Jay's Treaty, but no one had yet seen the actual text. The Spanish Foreign Minister, Don Manuel de Godoy, feared that a military alliance had been signed between England and the United States. Spain's lightly garrisoned outposts in North America were already vulnerable to American settlers moving across the Alleghenies, and so an Anglo-American alliance would make Spanish territory indefensible. Better to make concessions to the grasping Americans and keep the peace. Godoy was in the process of extricating Spain from the war against France (effected in July, 1795), and he hoped to renew the old alliance with France. He feared England's wrath when Madrid switched sides: hence his willingness to appease the Americans. Historians have debated whether Godoy actually saw a copy of Jay's Treaty (and therefore knew that it was not a military alliance) before signing Pinckney's Treaty in October. Arthur P. Whitaker argues that Godoy did have an accurate text and thus Spain made a favorable treaty with the United States because it "had no stomach for dealing with the American frontiersman."[33] Samuel Flagg Bemis thinks Godoy did not know, thereby making European diplomatic pressure the major factor. Whatever the main reason, it is clear that Spain's power and attention were diverted from North America by the war in Europe; to use Bemis' famous phrase, it was a classic case of "America's advantage from Europe's distress."[34] European wars permitted American expansion.

If diplomatic advantages from Spain followed logically from the Jay Treaty, the pact generated only trouble with France. James Monroe, who had assured the French that Jay's instructions precluded any pact that violated American obligations to the 1778 alliance, had to bear the brunt of French outrage over the surrender of "free ships, free goods." Monroe had ingratiated himself with the French by hailing France's contributions to human liberty in a speech before the National Convention; he had been the only foreign diplomat to remain in Paris during the Reign of Terror. When news of Jay's Treaty reached Paris, however, poor Monroe made the mistake of predicting that the treaty would never be ratified. In July, 1796, the angry French government announced that American ships would no longer be protected under the neutral rights provisions of the 1778 treaty. To make matters worse, a disgruntled Washington ordered Monroe home on August 22. French agents in America, meanwhile, stepped up their efforts to wean American policy from its pro-British orientation. Minister Pierre Adet, imitating his predecessors Genêt and Fauchet, did his best to bring about "the right kind of revolution" by lobbying unsuccessfully in the House of Representatives against Jay's Treaty and openly backing Thomas Jefferson for the presidency.[35] Adet's electioneering efforts came to naught, however, and John Adams defeated Jefferson by an electoral vote of 71 to 68.

One of the reasons for Adams' victory over Jefferson was the publication of Washington's Farewell Address on September 19, 1796. It was timed for its political impact. To be sure, Washington, ever conscious of history's verdict, was setting down a political testament that he hoped would have lasting effect on posterity. At the same time, the first President and Hamilton, who wrote much of the speech, had French intrigues very much in mind in making the famous warning: "Against the insidious wiles of foreign influence . . . the jealousy of a free people ought to be *constantly* awake."

Read as a whole, Washington's valedictory stands as an eloquent statement of American diplomatic principles. It reiterated the "Great Rule" that "in extending our commercial relations" the United States should have "as little *political* connection as possible" with foreign nations. Like Thomas Paine, he posited the idea of American uniqueness. "Europe," said Washington, "has a set of primary interests which to us have none or a very remote relation. . . . Our detached and distant situation invites and enables us to pursue a different course." Then came perhaps his most memorable words: "'Tis our true policy to steer clear of permanent alliances with any portion of the foreign world. . . . Taking care always to keep ourselves . . . on a respectable defensive posture, we may safely trust to temporary

**George Washington (1732–1799).** The Virginia gentleman farmer and first President always maintained a regal, if not cold, countenance. His Farewell Address of 1796 proved once again that he was a supreme nationalist. (The Cleveland Museum of Art, Hinman B. Hurlbut Collection)

alliances for extraordinary emergencies." Significantly, Washington did not say "no entangling alliances ever," as later politicians sometimes mistakenly claimed.[36] Nor did he preclude westward expansion. Even though Washington seemed to fear a French connection more than a British involvement in 1796, the evenhandedness of his phraseology gave the Farewell Address an enduring quality. "Our countrymen," Jefferson noted in agreement, "have divided themselves by such strong affections to the French and the English that nothing will secure us internally but a divorce from both nations."[37] The next four years would test the assumptions underlying Washington's advice.

## The XYZ Affair and the Quasi-War with France

"My entrance into office," John Adams wrote, "is marked by a misunderstanding with France, which I shall endeavor to reconcile, provided that no violation of faith, no stain upon honor, is exacted. . . . America is not SCARED."[38] In July, 1796, some four months after Jay's Treaty had officially gone into effect, the French decreed that they would treat neutral vessels the way neutrals permitted England to treat them—that is, "free ships" would not guarantee "free goods." Shortly thereafter, French privateers and warships began seizing American merchantmen in the West Indies. There were 316 seizures by June, 1797. In addition, the five-man Directory, which now ruled France, had refused to receive Charles C. Pinckney, the South Carolina Federalist whom Washington had sent to replace James Monroe as American minister. Threatened with arrest, Pinckney had stalked off to the Netherlands, thus presenting Adams with a complete diplomatic rupture. Rejecting suggestions of war from bellicose Federalists, the new President dispatched a special commission to negotiate all outstanding differences with the French. To accomplish this delicate task, Adams named Pinckney, Federalist John Marshall of Virginia, and Massachusetts Republican Elbridge Gerry. Adams displayed his nonpartisanship by selecting Gerry, an old friend, only after Thomas Jefferson and James Madison had declined to serve.

The three American envoys arrived in Paris in October, 1797, whereupon they encountered perhaps the most fascinating, most unscrupulous diplomat of all time. The wily (the word was invented to describe him) Charles Maurice de Talleyrand-Périgord, formerly a bishop in the ancien régime, recently an exile for two years in the United States, had become French foreign minister that summer. Despite his firsthand acquaintance with Americans (indeed, he and Gouverneur Morris had once shared the same mistress in Paris), Talleyrand evinced little affection for France's sister republic. The United States, he once wrote, should not be treated "with greater respect than Geneva or Genoa."[39] Maritime pressure seemed a convenient way to persuade the Americans to acknowledge their commercial obligations to France under the treaty of 1778. The French still wanted the Americans to take over their carrying trade with the French West Indies, an impossible undertaking if the Americans refused to defend such commerce against the British. Talleyrand did not want open war, but as one of his diplomatic agents put it: "A little clandestine war, like England made on America for three years, would produce a constructive effect."[40] The war in Europe had begun to go well again for France under the young Corsican General Napoleon Bonaparte. American questions were not deemed urgent. If Talleyrand could string out negotiations with the American commission, party divisions would reappear in the United

**Talleyrand (1734–1838).** The wily bishop and French minister of foreign relations majored in survival during the stormy years of the French Revolution, but his manipulative skills in politics were not matched in diplomacy, at least not in the XYZ Affair. (Prints Division, New York Public Library, Astor, Lenox and Tilden Foundations)

States, and France could easily make a favorable settlement. Or so Talleyrand thought.

Three French agents, later identified in the American dispatches as X, Y, and Z, soon approached the American commissioners as spokesmen for Talleyrand. The message, though indirect, was unmistakable. If the Americans expected serious and favorable negotiations, they should pay a bribe to the French foreign minister and arrange for a large loan to the French government. To the first request, Pinckney made his celebrated reply: "No; no; not a sixpence."[41] Contrary to legend, this initial attempt at bribery did not terminate negotiations. Conversations continued throughout the autumn and into the new year. Talleyrand even employed a beautiful woman to work her charms on bachelors Gerry and Marshall. "Why will you not lend us money?" she asked at one point. "If you were to make us a loan, all matters will be adjusted. When you were contending your Revolution we lent you money."[42]

Talleyrand's methods were common enough in European chancelleries. The Americans refused to pay because they had no instructions, not solely because they were indignant. Gradually, however, they lost patience. Marshall correctly observed that "this haughty, ambitious government is not willing to come to an absolute rupture with America during the present state of the war with England but will not condescend to act with justice or to treat us as a free and independent nation."[43] In January, 1798, Marshall drew up a memorial, signed by Gerry and Pinckney, which recounted all American grievances against France, including the personal indignities gratuitously inflicted on the American commissioners. Talleyrand made no reply. The French issued new and harsher decrees that made a neutral cargo liable to capture if any part of it—a jug of rum, even an English-made compass or sextant—had British origins. Angry and frustrated, Marshall and Pinckney asked for their passports, although Gerry stayed another three months in a futile attempt to negotiate.

Rumors of French insolence began to filter back to the United States in early 1798. After receiving the first official dispatches from his three emissaries, Adams went before Congress on May 19. Pointing out that his peace overtures had been refused, the President asked for authority to arm merchant ships and for other defensive measures. Jeffersonian Republicans smelled a Federalist trap. The House of Representatives demanded that the President send it all relevant diplomatic correspondence. Adams, ignoring the precedent of Washington's refusal in the case of Jay's Treaty, sent all dispatches to the House, substituting the letters X, Y, and Z for the real names of Talleyrand's highwaymen. The country was soon aflame with the news. "Millions for defense but not one cent for tribute" (a phrase mistakenly attributed to Charles C. Pinckney) became a popular slogan, and John Marshall was hailed as a triumphant hero on his return to New York. Even the dour Adams aroused cheers when he promised Congress in June that he would never "send another minister to France without assurances that he will be received, respected, and honored as the representative of a great, free, powerful, and independent nation."[44] A frightened Jefferson observed: "All the passions are boiling over, and one who keeps himself cool and clear of the contagion, is so far below the point of ordinary conversation, that he finds himself insulted in every society."[45]

The young republic nearly went to war with France. In the summer of 1798 Congress passed a series of measures that amounted to "quasi-war." It declared all French treaties null and void, created a Navy Department, funded the construction of new warships, and authorized increases for the regular Army. George Washington came out of retirement to lead this new body of 50,000 men, although effective command remained in the hands of Washington's Inspector General, Alexander Hamilton. Jeffersonians saw the Army, in conjunction with the new Alien and Sedition Laws directed at pro-French radicals, as suppression of political opposition; the Administration meant "to arm one half the people, for the purpose of keeping the other in awe."[46] As it was, Adams did not request, nor did Congress authorize, a declaration of war. The American Navy was ordered to retaliate against French warships and privateers, but offensive operations and the capture of merchant prizes were forbidden. The quasi-war lasted more than two years, during which time the Navy captured some eighty-five French armed vessels. The new frigates performed brilliantly, and such spectacular victories as that of the *Constellation* over the *Insurgente* helped to deter the French from widening hostilities. Adams was content with naval retaliation. He correctly perceived that France was too bogged down against Britain (Lord Horatio Nelson defeated the French in the battle of the Nile in August, 1798) to respond with full-scale war or invasion.

Federalist partisans, including a majority of Adams' Cabinet, were more warlike. Hamilton became particularly fascinated by a grand scheme promoted by Venezuelan revolutionary Francisco de Miranda, whereby the Americans would undertake a joint expedition with the British against both Spain and France in the Americas, thus securing the liberation of all Latin America, the acquisition of Florida and Louisiana for the United States, and military glory for Inspector General Hamilton. The idea of a British alliance intrigued Secretary Pickering, Treasury Secretary Oliver Wolcott, and other high Federalists, and Miranda hurried to London in the autumn of 1798 to elicit British cooperation.

The scheme failed. Adams, always suspicious of British wiles anyway, thought Miranda a "knight errant, as delirious as his immortal countryman, the ancient

**John Adams (1735–1826).** The second President wanted to be remembered for having defused the XYZ Affair, thereby smoothing relations with France. (The Metropolitan Museum of Art, Gift of William H. Huntington, 1883)

hero of La Manche."[47] The British, too, balked at aiding a new revolution, even one aimed at reducing French and Spanish power in the New World. Enough Anglo-American cooperation did occur during the quasi-war (British naval convoys for American merchantmen, a temporary softening of British maritime practices, cordial personal relations between Minister Rufus King and Foreign Secretary Lord Grenville) for historian Bradford Perkins to dub this period the "first rapprochement."[48] The point is clear, however: the Adams Administration followed Washington's "Great Rule" by avoiding war with France or alliance with England.

Ironically enough, the individual most responsible for stopping full-scale war was the person who had initiated the crisis, Talleyrand. Throughout the summer and fall of 1798, first through the departing Elbridge Gerry, then through assurances to the American minister in the Netherlands, William Vans Murray, Talleyrand let it be known that France wanted peace. He promised Murray that any new envoy sent to make peace would "undoubtedly be received with the respect due to the representative of a free, independent, and powerful nation."[49] These were the same words Adams had used before Congress in June, 1798. To emphasize such assurances, the French repealed their decrees against American shipping and reined in their privateers.

Adams took the chance for peace. The President had received reports from his son John Quincy Adams, now American minister to Prussia, fully corroborating Murray's opinion that France was not bluffing and "a negotiation might be risked."[50] Always a solitary person, President Adams deliberated in private, shunned his Cabinet, and, on February 18, 1799, sent a message to the Senate nominating William Vans Murray as minister plenipotentiary to France. Abigail Adams wrote from Massachusetts: "It comes so sudden, was a measure so unexpected, that the whole community were [sic] like a flock of frightened pigeons." She correctly ranked it as "a master stroke of policy."[51]

Federalist partisans, their appetites whetted for war with France, reacted mindlessly, even threatening to delay Murray's confirmation until Adams nominated Oliver Ellsworth and William R. Davie, both Federalists, as additional plenipotentiaries. Secretary of State Pickering dragged his feet and managed to delay departure of the mission for several months. Adams eventually fired him. The President understood that his decision for peace meant political suicide, but he persisted anyway. Abigail wrote of her husband: "He has sustained the whole force of an unpopular measure which he knew would excite the passions of many, thwart the views of some, and showered down upon his head a torrent of invective produced by ignorance and malevolence and jealousy."[52] Years later Adams himself declared: "I desire no other inscription over my gravestone than: 'Here lies John Adams, who took upon himself the responsibility of the peace with France in the year 1800.'"[53]

The American commissioners arrived in Paris in March, 1800, and negotiations continued until the following autumn. Politics had again shifted in France. Napoleon Bonaparte had returned from Egypt, seized power in the coup d'état of 18 Brumaire, and was now first consul. Joseph Bonaparte, the future king of Spain, took charge of talks with the Americans. Although the war in Europe still raged fiercely, the new leadership had begun to think seriously of reconstituting France's empire in North America. Talleyrand, who had earlier approached the Spanish about Louisiana, encouraged Napoleon in this direction. The rebuilding of a French Empire required peace with Europe, and especially reconciliation with the United States. Napoleon's great victory at Marengo in June, 1800 made a European settlement possible by assuring French control of territory in Italy, which Spain might accept in lieu of Louisiana. One day after the Franco-American Treaty of Mortefontaine was signed, at Joseph Bonaparte's estate outside Paris, the French and Spanish, on October 1, 1800, concluded secret arrangements whereby Napoleon promised Spain the Italian Kingdom of Tuscany, or its equivalent, in exchange for Louisiana. Although American plenipotentiaries did not know about this so-called treaty of San Ildefonso, the French desire for Louisiana played an important, if silent, role nonetheless in the Franco-American accord.

The Treaty of Mortefontaine, or Convention of 1800, amounted to a horse trade. The American negotiators had presented two basic demands: the French were to nullify the 1778 treaties, and pay some $20,000,000 in compensation for illegal seizures of American cargoes. America, the French retorted, had itself invalidated the 1778 treaties by conceding maritime rights to the British in Jay's Treaty; thus French spoliations after 1795 were not illegal. The logjam broke when the Americans agreed to assume the claims of their own citizens, whereupon the French abrogated all previous treaties. Napoleon then suggested the insertion of a statement reaffirming American principles of neutral rights as enumerated in the Model Treaty and in the 1778 alliance. The Americans, seeing no entangling commitments, agreed. The formal signing of the treaty, on September 30, 1800, came amidst much splendor and pageantry. Nearly two hundred diplomats were treated to a deer hunt and huge banquet echoing with toasts to Franco-American harmony.

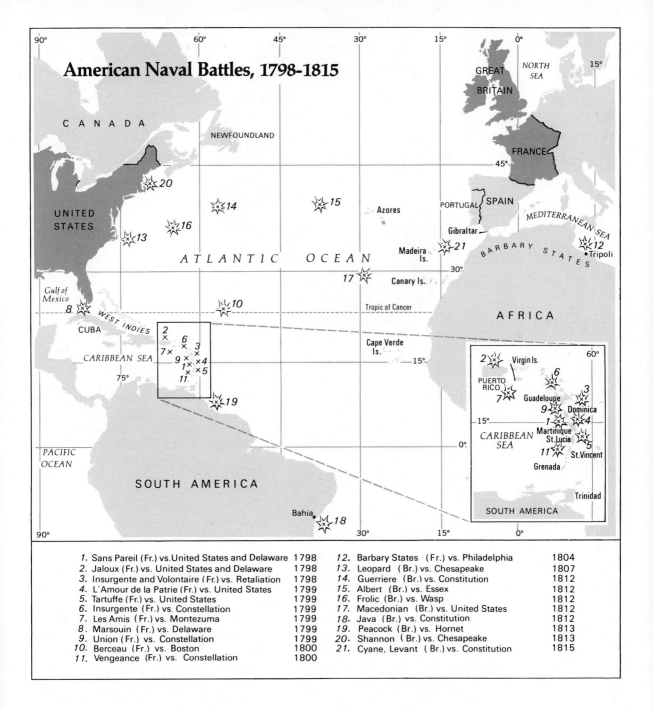

# American Naval Battles, 1798-1815

| | | | |
|---|---|---|---|
| *1.* Sans Pareil (Fr.) vs.United States and Delaware | 1798 | *12.* Barbary States (Fr.) vs. Philadelphia | 1804 |
| *2.* Jaloux (Fr.) vs. United States and Delaware | 1798 | *13.* Leopard (Br.) vs. Chesapeake | 1807 |
| *3.* Insurgente and Volontaire (Fr.) vs. Retaliation | 1798 | *14.* Guerriere (Br.) vs. Constitution | 1812 |
| *4.* L'Amour de la Patrie (Fr.) vs. United States | 1799 | *15.* Albert (Br.) vs. Essex | 1812 |
| *5.* Tartuffe (Fr.) vs. United States | 1799 | *16.* Frolic (Br.) vs. Wasp | 1812 |
| *6.* Insurgente (Fr.) vs. Constellation | 1799 | *17.* Macedonian (Br.) vs. United States | 1812 |
| *7.* Les Amis (Fr.) vs. Montezuma | 1799 | *18.* Java (Br.) vs. Constitution | 1812 |
| *8.* Marsouin (Fr.) vs. Delaware | 1799 | *19.* Peacock (Br.) vs. Hornet | 1813 |
| *9.* Union (Fr.) vs. Constellation | 1799 | *20.* Shannon (Br.) vs. Chesapeake | 1813 |
| *10.* Berceau (Fr.) vs. Boston | 1800 | *21.* Cyane, Levant (Br.) vs. Constitution | 1815 |
| *11.* Vengeance (Fr.) vs. Constellation | 1800 | | |

Napoleon, that "most skillful self possest [sic] Fencing master," as Murray called him, was trying to lull the Americans until his plans for Louisiana jelled.[54]

The peace of Mortefontaine, followed by Thomas Jefferson's victory in the presidential election of 1800, ended the Federalist era in American diplomacy. The administrations of George Washington and John Adams, despite internal debate and external pressures, pursued a consistent foreign policy. Seeking to maintain

**Thomas Jefferson (1743–1826).**
Before he became President in 1801
Jefferson had served as secretary
of state. His presidency was plagued
by the neutral rights question and
distinguished by the Louisiana
Purchase. This idealized view of the
Virginian by Thaddeus Kosciuszko
is titled "A Philosopher—A Patriot
—and a Friend." (Courtesy, The
Henry Francis du Pont Winterthur
Museum)

independence and honor and to expand trade and territorial boundaries, the young
republic at times seemed to veer in a pro-French direction and on other occasions
tilted toward the British. At every juncture, however, Washington and Adams
escaped being pulled into the European maelstrom in alliance with either France
or Britain. Like Jay's Treaty before it, the peace of Mortefontaine avoided a war
that hotheaded partisans had advocated. Jefferson's Inaugural Address seemed to
promise continuity. "We are all Federalists; we are all Republicans," he said.
Slightly amending Washington's advice, the former Francophile pledged "peace,
commerce, and honest friendship with all nations, entangling alliances with
none."[55]

## The Louisiana Purchase and Empire for Liberty

For one who never traveled more than a hundred miles west of his beloved
Monticello, the new President showed an intense interest in American expansion.
A few months after his inauguration Jefferson told Monroe: "However our present
interests may restrain us within our limits, it is impossible not to look forward to
distant times when our rapid multiplication will expand it beyond those limits, &
cover the whole northern if not the southern continent."[56] Jefferson primarily eyed
the Mississippi Valley, but his vision also embraced the Pacific Coast, the Floridas,
Cuba, and a Central American canal. So long as Spain occupied America's borderlands, standing, in Henry Adams' phrase, like a "huge, helpless, and profitable
whale," Jefferson was in no hurry.[57] The rapid expansion of the American frontier
population, hungry for new land and numbering some 900,000 inhabitants beyond
the Alleghenies by 1800, would enable the United States to take over Spanish
lands peacefully, "peice by peice [sic]."[58]

Then came rumors in the summer of 1801 about Spain's retrocession of Louisiana to France, along with news that England and France had made peace. Soon
French ships were carrying an army to the New World, commanded by Napoleon's

brother-in-law, Victor Emmanuel Leclerc, with orders to put down the black rebellion led by Toussaint L'Ouverture on Santo Domingo, and then, presumably, to occupy New Orleans, Louisiana, and perhaps the Floridas as well. American leaders grew alarmed. With Spain no longer controlling the Mississippi, Pinckney's Treaty would become obsolete. Even if the French did not encroach on American territory, their control of New Orleans and commerce on the Mississippi might provoke western farmers to either wage war or secede from the Union. As Madison put it: "The Mississippi is to them [the westerners] everything. It is the Hudson, the Delaware, the Potomac and all the navigable rivers of the Atlantic States formed into one stream."[59] Jefferson seemed willing to consider a veritable revolution in American foreign policy. In a letter of April, 1802 to Minister Robert Livingston in Paris, Jefferson warned that the day France took possession of New Orleans "we must marry ourselves to the British fleet and nation."[60] The President made sure that the warning became public knowledge in France.

Even the threat of an Anglo-American alliance made little impact on France during 1802. Livingston, who was himself hard of hearing, found Talleyrand deaf, dumb, and blind on the subject of Louisiana. The French foreign minister baldly denied the existence of a retrocession treaty for several months (the Spanish King did not actually sign the order of transfer until October, 1802), and then he refused to consider Livingston's offer to purchase New Orleans and West Florida. Napoleon, bent on reviving a grand French empire in America, redoubled his efforts to acquire the Floridas from Spain.

Tension in America nearly reached the snapping point when, on October 16, 1802, the Spanish intendant of Louisiana suddenly withdrew the American right of deposit at New Orleans, in direct violation of Pinckney's Treaty. Most Americans suspected Napoleon's hand in the plot. The riflemen of Tennessee and Kentucky talked of seizing New Orleans before the French could take formal possession. Some Federalists suddenly found themselves supporting the West and urging war to embarrass Jefferson. Alexander Hamilton exhorted the Administration "to seize at once on the Floridas and New Orleans, and then negotiate."[61] To calm the growing clamor and buy time for diplomacy, Jefferson, in January, 1803, nominated James Monroe as a special envoy to France and Spain, empowered to assist Livingston in purchasing New Orleans and Florida for $10 million. As the French minister reported to Talleyrand, the former governor of Virginia had *"carte blanche and . . . he goes to London if badly received in Paris."*[62] Congress provided more diplomatic muscle by authorizing the President to call some 80,000 militia members into federal service in case France proved unreasonable. Monroe finally embarked on March 8, arriving in Paris on April 12. The previous day Talleyrand had astonished Robert Livingston by offering to sell all Louisiana to the United States for $15 million.

The decision to relinquish Louisiana was solely Napoleon's. His motives were mixed. The French failure in Santo Domingo probably loomed largest, an especially distressing defeat for Napoleon as Leclerc's 30,000-man army melted away, victims of guerrilla attacks and yellow fever. When Bonaparte learned in January that his brother-in-law had also succumbed to fever, he burst out: "Damn sugar, damn coffee, damn colonies."[63] In the Napoleonic scheme of empire, Louisiana was to have been the source of supply for the sugar and coffee plantations of Santo Domingo, but without Santo Domingo, Louisiana became a liability. In the event of war with England Louisiana could be easily overrun, and Napoleon was already thinking of war. In historian Marshall Smelser's words, "he wished to get back to his glorious drums and trumpets, his drilling and killing of the fittest youth in Europe."[64] Hence, it made sense to sell Louisiana to the Americans rather than return it to Spain. The sale price would fill French coffers in preparation for the next campaigns, while at the same time eliminating American hostility.

The negotiations did not take long. Napoleon was eager to sell and the Americans eager to buy. Monroe and Livingston had no compunction about violating their instructions; instead of paying $10 million for New Orleans, they pledged $15 million for New Orleans and an undefined empire that lay entirely to the west of the Mississippi, including 50,000 new citizens of French-Spanish descent and about 150,000 Indians. The treaty, signed on April 30, 1803, stipulated that the United States was to receive Louisiana on the same terms that Spain had retroceded the territory to France. Livingston, wondering if any of West Florida came with the purchase, asked Talleyrand what the precise boundaries were. The Frenchman replied vaguely: "You have made a noble bargain for yourselves, and I suppose you will make the most of it."[65] This enigmatic remark provided the basis for future American claims to Spanish territory in Florida and Texas. As it was, acquiring some 828,000 square miles of territory at 3 cents an acre seemed an enormous achievement. Livingston observed, "from this day the United States take their place among the powers of the first rank."[66] Bonaparte himself remarked: "This accession of territory affirms forever the power of the United States, and I have just given England a maritime rival that sooner or later will lay low her pride."[67]

The treaty still had to be approved and ratified in Washington. Some Federalists, thinking that the addition of trans-Mississippi lands would tip the political balance

**New Orleans, 1803.** The American eagle spreads its wings over the port of New Orleans at the mouth of the Mississippi River—a prize acquisition in the Louisiana Purchase. (Chicago Historical Society)

UNDER MY WINGS EVERY THING PROSPERS

toward agrarians, attacked the treaty. "We are to give money of which we have too little for land of which we already have too much," bewailed one Bostonian.[68] Others accused Jefferson of being in cahoots with Napoleon. There was also the problem, particularly bothersome to Federalist Senator John Quincy Adams, of whether the Constitution, under the treaty power, permitted the incorporation of 50,000 Creoles into the Union without their consent. The President, however, shedding his reputation as a strict constitutionalist, told Madison "that the less we say about constitutional difficulties respecting Louisiana the better, and that what is necessary for surmounting them must be done sub silentio."[69] With the support of such prominent Federalists as Alexander Hamilton, Rufus King, and John Adams, the purchase passed the Senate 24 to 7 in October. The formal transfer of territory came at noon on December 20, 1803, in the Place d'Armée in New Orleans. As the French flag was hauled down and the Stars and Stripes climbed upward, the United States officially doubled its territorial domain.

The Spanish borderlands continued to attract American diplomatic interest for the next several years. Taking advantage of the ambiguous terms of the Louisiana Purchase, Jefferson hoped to harness French support to American agrarian migration and obtain West Florida and Texas from Spain. But Napoleon refused to help, and before long the maritime crisis with England forced Jefferson to defer expansion, although other Americans probed Spanish lands. In 1806–1807 an American military officer, Lieutenant Zebulon M. Pike, led a cartographic expedition up the Arkansas River into Spanish territory, failed to climb the mountain peak which bears his name, and was temporarily detained by Spanish troops for violating Spanish sovereignty. At this time, too, Aaron Burr and sixty followers went down the Mississippi on flatboats, ostensibly to capture Texas from the Spanish, but more likely to set Burr up as the emperor of a secessionist Louisiana. Whatever the purpose of Burr's conspiracy, Jefferson had his former vice-president arrested and took special care to keep the peace with Spain.

The most enduring example of Jefferson's interest in westward expansion during these years was his sponsorship of the Lewis and Clark Expedition. Conceived by Jefferson even before he considered the acquisition of Louisiana, the expedition was designed to find a useful route to the Pacific, to study geography, and to develop fur trade with the Indians. Leaving St. Louis in May, 1804, the "Corps of Discovery" went up the Missouri, crossed the Continental Divide, and followed the Snake and Columbia rivers to the Pacific (Seaside, Oregon today claims the "end of the trail"). Lewis and Clark returned along the same route, arriving at St. Louis in September, 1806. This epic exploration, which Jefferson took pains to publicize, stimulated interest in the rich furs and abundant fauna of the Rocky Mountains and suggested wrongly that the Missouri-Columbia route was a convenient waterway for trade with China. John Jacob Astor's American Fur Company was chartered in 1808, and, with Jefferson's encouragement, Astor projected a line of fortified posts from St. Louis to the Pacific. Only Astoria, at the mouth of the Columbia River, was completed by the outbreak of war in 1812.

Jefferson's efforts at territorial expansion were cut short by a growing crisis with England after 1805, but his optimism remained undimmed. He told Madison, shortly after leaving the White House in 1809, that the United States would become "such an empire for liberty as she has never surveyed since the creation; and I am persuaded that no constitution was ever so well calculated as ours for extensive empire and self-government."[70]

**Canton, China, 1800.** This Chinese painting of the wharf at the busy commercial port of Canton about 1800 shows the American flag, third from left, flying over *hongs,* or warehouses. Thirty-four American or "barbarian" vessels visited Canton in 1801 alone. (Peabody Museum of Salem)

If Jefferson sought to expand American institutions on land, he also attempted to maintain free American commerce on the high seas. Until the Anglo-French war riveted all attention on the Atlantic, Jefferson eagerly employed the American Navy in the Mediterranean to protect trade against the depradations of the Barbary pirates. The war with Tripoli was especially satisfying to young America. A squadron consisting of the frigates *Constitution* and *Philadelphia* and six smaller vessels performed creditably under the command of Commodore Edward Preble in 1803 and 1804. The *Philadelphia,* however, ran aground while chasing pirates, and the ship and crew were captured. Lieutenant Stephen Decatur heroically slipped into Tripoli Harbor and burned the American vessel at night. In 1805 a contingent of Marines (seven in all) marched overland from Egypt and seized the port of Derna on the shores of Tripoli. The Sultan of Tripoli made peace shortly thereafter, but not until he was paid some $60,000 in tribute. The remainder of the Barbary pirates had to wait until the end of the War of 1812 for American retribution. Jefferson, at least in the Mediterranean, proved no less a defender of American commercial rights than the Federalist merchants of Boston.

## Blockades and Impressment: The Perils of Neutral Trade, 1803–1807

Some two weeks after unloading Louisiana on the Americans in the spring of 1803, Napoleon picked a quarrel with England over the insignificant island of Malta. War raged for twelve years, spreading over much of the world, and ending only with Bonaparte's lonely exile to St. Helena in 1815. The war transformed the

United States into the world's largest neutral carrier. Shipping boomed in America, expanding at a rate of seventy thousand tons annually. Particularly significant was the trade between French and Spanish ports in the West Indies and French and Spanish ports on the European continent. Because such direct trade violated Britain's arbitrary Rule of 1756 (which decreed that trade not open to a nation in time of peace could not be opened in time of war), American merchants usually "broke" the voyage by stopping at an American port and paying duties on the cargo, thus converting it to "free goods." The voyage would then continue until the "neutralized cargo" reached France or Spain. While direct American exports amounted to a steady $42 million annually in 1803–1805, the lucrative re-export trade soared from $13 million in 1803 to $36 million in 1804 to $53 million in 1805. Most Americans, basking in the war-induced prosperity, did not share John Randolph's fear that "this mushroom, this fungus of war" would bring the United States into the conflagration.[71]

For more than two years neither the British nor the French interfered seriously with American commerce. Indeed, British admiralty courts in the case of the American ship *Polly* (1800) had not disputed the legality of the "broken voyage." But on October 21, 1805, Lord Horatio Nelson's black-hulled ships smashed the combined French and Spanish fleets off Trafalgar, thus establishing England's overwhelming control of the seas. Less than two months later Napoleon crushed the Russian and Austrian armies at Austerlitz, making him master of Europe. Neither the Tiger nor the Shark, each supreme in its own element, could fight the other directly. For the next several years commercial warfare dominated the struggle between England and France. In the ensuing web of blockades and counterblockades, America's neutral trade became inextricably ensnared.

The British decision in the *Essex* case, in May, 1805, signaled trouble. The American merchant brig *Essex* had been captured en route to Havana from Barcelona after having stopped (the "break" in the voyage) in Salem, Massachusetts. The British admiralty judge reversed the *Polly* decision, claiming that the *Essex* had not paid bona fide duties on its cargo. Thereafter American shippers had to prove that importation of enemy goods into the United States was in good faith, not merely a legal subterfuge to bypass the Rule of 1756. Under the new doctrine of the "continuous" voyage, trade carried by a neutral between a belligerent colonial port and home port violated British maritime regulations. Soon British cruisers lurked outside American harbors, practically blockading the coastline.

The British followed up the *Essex* decision with the Order in Council of May 16, 1806, calling for a complete blockade of Napoleonic Europe, from Brest to the Elbe River. Americans angrily complained that this was a "paper blockade" because British cruisers ranged far out to sea and did not actually deny access to enemy ports. Napoleon, "fleetless but well supplied with parchment and sealing wax," retaliated in November with his Berlin Decree, which created a paper blockade of the British Isles.[72] The decree declared that any ship that had previously touched at a British port was a lawful prize and its cargo forfeit. The London government struck back with two more orders in council (January and November, 1807), barring all trade with ports under French jurisdiction unless that shipping first passed through a system of British controls and taxes. England was in essence telling neutrals that they could trade with the continent of Europe only if they paid tribute first. Napoleon retaliated again, this time in the Milan Decree of December, 1807, which stated that any ship that paid taxes to the British, that submitted to

**"John Bull Taking A Lunch."** The Englishman enjoys a French warship for lunch. The naval war between England and France meant in fact that many American vessels were munched as well. (Library of Congress)

visit and search by British cruisers, or stopped at a British port, would be treated, ipso facto, as a British ship. The French Emperor was erecting what he called his "Continental System," a gigantic attempt to ruin England's export trade by closing off all European outlets. The Continental System never became fully effective, as Spain, Sweden, and Russia opened their ports to British goods at various intervals after 1807. John Quincy Adams likened the system to excluding "air from a bottle, by sealing up hermetically the mouth, while there was a great hole in the side."[73] Caught in the vise of French decrees and British orders in council, Yankee traders ran the risk of British seizure if they traded directly with French-controlled ports, whereas they incurred Napoleonic displeasure if they first submitted to British trade regulations.

"I consider Europe as a great mad-house," Jefferson lamented, "& in the present deranged state of their moral faculties to be pitied & avoided."[74] In the diplomatic protests that followed, American efforts were directed more at England than at France, because British maritime practices (particularly British warships operating in American waters) more directly jeopardized American commerce. The British, so absorbed in the life-or-death struggle against Napoleon, were hardly humble or apologetic toward Washington, which took offense easily. French seizures, numerous though they were, usually occurred in French ports and in the Caribbean, and were often shrouded in official verbiage that smacked of misunderstanding and promised rectification. With the Americans, Napoleon was tricky and evasive, but seldom arrogant.

Impressment, which rose to alarming proportions after 1803, and which exploded as an issue in the *Chesapeake* affair, helped focus resentment upon England rather than France. With American shipping expanding rapidly during this period, and with life on a British naval vessel resembling life in a British prison, English seamen in increasing numbers jumped ship, took advantage of liberal American naturalization laws, and then enlisted in the American merchant marine. To cite one example, the vessel carrying the new British minister Anthony Merry to America in the autumn of 1803 lost fourteen men to desertion when the ship touched port. By 1812, according to official British claims, some 20,000 English sailors were manning American vessels, approximately one-half of all able-bodied seamen then serving in the merchant marine. Since the British Navy required 10,000 new recruits annually to maintain full strength, the need to impress British deserters from American service became urgent. In carrying out impressment, however, British captains, in historian Paul Varg's phrase, "resorted to the scoop rather than the tweezers," and soon naturalized Americans by the hundreds were manning Royal Navy yardarms.[75] Altogether, according to James Monroe's figures in 1812, some 6,257 Americans were impressed after 1803, probably a more accurate estimate than the 1,600 conceded by the British.

Impressment was an explosive issue. The British could not accept any abridgment of a practice which they saw as vital to maritime supremacy. Americans admitted the British right to search for contraband or enemy personnel, but denied that this right justified the impressment of American citizens. "That an officer from a foreign ship," wrote Secretary of State James Madison in 1807, "should pronounce any person he pleased, on board an American ship on the high seas, not to be an American Citizen, but a British subject, & carry his interested decision on the most important of all subjects to a freeman, into execution on the spot . . . is anomalous in principle, . . . grievous in practice, and . . . abominable in abuse."[76]

Jefferson and Madison missed an opportunity to alleviate some of the controversy when they rejected the Monroe-Pinkney Treaty of December, 1806. Jefferson had sent William Pinkney, an able Maryland lawyer, to join James Monroe in London in an attempt, similar to the Jay mission of 1794, to settle all outstanding differences with England, including impressment and "broken" voyages. Jefferson and Madison attached a *sine qua non* to the instructions: the treaty must contain an explicit British disavowal of impressment. The British would make concessions on broken voyages and the re-export trade, but not on impressment. The most the British Cabinet could concede was a separate note, attached to the final treaty, promising "observance of the greatest caution in the impressing of British seamen; . . . the strictest care . . . to preserve the citizens of the United States from any molestation or injury; and . . . immediate and prompt redress . . . of injury sustained by them."[77] Here was a British promise to mitigate in practice what they would not surrender in principle. Mindful of growing anti-American sentiment in England, and fearful of repercussions from Napoleon's recent Berlin Decree, Pinkney and Monroe opted for half a loaf. Their treaty, signed on December 31, 1806, was probably the best bargain that the United States could have extracted from England during the Napoleonic Wars. Still, Jefferson refused to submit it to the Senate. He and Madison believed that the passage of time, plus the threat of American economic retaliation, would force the British to reconsider. Like John Adams in the Model Treaty of 1776, Jefferson and Madison thought that the attractions of American commerce, not to mention the rightness of American principles, would cause England to mend its ways. In Robert Rutland's apt phrase, they were "old-fashioned men still dreaming that Hobbes was wrong and Locke was right."[78]

## "Peaceable Coercions" and the Coming of the War of 1812

Anglo-American relations deteriorated steadily following the abortive Monroe-Pinkney Treaty. The *Chesapeake* episode of June, 1807 underscored the volatile nature of the impressment issue. "Never since the battle of Lexington," Jefferson wrote in July, "have I seen this country in such a state of exasperation as at present."[79] The President could have obtained a declaration of war from Congress, but, owing partly to the country's lack of military and naval muscle, he sought another alternative. As he once put it, "those peaceable coercions which are in the power of every nation, if undertaken in concert & in time of peace, are more likely to produce the desired effect."[80] On December 22, 1807, he won congressional approval for the Embargo Act.

Evenhanded in principle, the embargo, in combination with a nonimportation measure against England, was aimed primarily at the British. The embargo's rules were simple: the export of goods anywhere, by sea or land, was virtually prohibited. Coastal American trade, however, continued with increasingly elaborate controls. Recorded American exports dropped 80 percent in 1808. American imports from Britain, not strictly enforced under the nonimportation act, decreased by 56 percent. One scholar has succinctly concluded that the embargo "stimulated manufactures, injured agriculture, and prostrated commerce."[81]

Domestic protest was loud and shrill. John Randolph, pointing to the loss of shipping and declining agricultural prices, charged his fellow Virginians with attempting to "cure the corns by cutting off the toes."[82] Numerous vituperative epistles reached the White House, including one of August, 1808:[83]

> Thomas Jefferson
> You are the damdest
> dog that God put life into
> God dam you.

Such dissent, when combined with widespread resistance to enforcement, caused Jeffersonians to despair. "I had rather encounter war itself than to display our impotence to enforce our laws," Secretary of the Treasury Albert Gallatin wrote dejectedly.[84] In New England, where Yankee merchants and sailors had long depended on commerce for their livelihood, the economy suffered badly. Ships rotted in harbor and grass grew on once busy wharves. Paranoid Federalists accused Jefferson of conspiring with Napoleon in initiating the embargo, and in the winter of 1808–1809 there were widespread rumors of secessionist conversations between New Englanders and British agents. "I felt the foundation of government shaken under my feet by the New England townships. . . . We [were] driven by treason from the high and wise ground we had taken," the President said in later years.[85] The choice appeared to be repeal or civil war. On March 1, 1809, three days before Jefferson turned over the presidency to Madison, Congress replaced the embargo with the Non-Intercourse Act, thus freeing American exports to all ports except those controlled by England and France, and promising renewed trade with either belligerent if American neutral rights were respected.

Jefferson's embargo simply did not accomplish the desired diplomatic effect. The British government was initially delighted with the measure, inasmuch as it removed quarrels over neutral rights and gave British shippers a virtual monopoly over trade with Europe. Nonimportation limited trade with Britain, but alternative markets for British goods conveniently appeared in Spain (which revolted against Napoleonic rule in 1808) and Spain's Latin American colonies. As for the French, they continued to seize American ships, even those that evaded the British blockade, using the argument that such ships had to be British in disguise because American law prohibited their presence on the high seas. Rising food prices in England, plus the decline of manufacturing sales, might have caused the British to

By the Virtue, Firmness and Patriotism of

# JEFFERSON & MADISON,

Our Difficulties with England are settled—our Ships have been pre-served, and our Seamen will, hereafter, be respected while sailing under our National Flag.

NEW-YORK, SATURDAY MORNING, APRIL 22, 1809.

## *IMPORTANT.*

### By the President of the United States.—A Proclamation.

WHEREAS it is provided by the 11th section of the act of Congress, entitled "An "act to interdict the commercial intercourse between the United States and Great Bri-"tain and France, and their dependencies; and for other purposes,"—and that " in "case either France or Great Britain shall so revoke or modify her edicts as that they "shall cease to violate the neutral commerce of the United States," the President is au-thorised to declare the same by proclamation, after which the trade suspended by the said act and by an act laying an Embargo, on all ships and vessels in the ports and harbours of the United States and the several acts supplementary thereto may be renewed with the nation so doing. And whereas the Honourable David Montague Erskine, his Britannic Majesty's Envoy Extraordinary and Minister Plenipotentiary, has by the order and in the name of his sovereign declared to this Government, that the British Orders in Council of January and November, 1807, will have been withdrawn, as respects the United States on the 10th day of June next. Now therefore I James Madison, President of the United States, do hereby proclaim that the orders in council aforesaid will have been withdrawn on the tenth day of June next; after which day the trade of the United States with Great Britain, as suspended by the act of Congress above mentioned, and an act laying an embargo on all ships and vessels in the ports and harbors of the United States, and the several acts supplementary thereto, may be renewed.

Given under my hand and the seal of the United States, at Washing-ton, the nineteenth day of April, in the year of our Lord, one (L. S) thousand eight hundred and nine, and of the Independence of the United States, the thirty-third.

JAMES MADISON.

By the President,
RT. SMITH, *Secretary of State.*

appease their best trading partner if the embargo had been maintained another year or so. But this was impossible because of domestic American opinion. "The philosopher-king," historian Bradford Perkins has written, "had asked too much of his people."[86]

Non-intercourse was a face-saving substitute that actually favored the British more than the French: American vessels could now clear port for some neutral destination, such as the Azores or Sweden, and somehow find their way to Liverpool; ships entering French-controlled ports still had to run the gauntlet of British blockade ships. The new President, James Madison, nonetheless hoped to use non-intercourse as a lever for settling accounts with England, and he found a willing collaborator in British Minister David M. Erskine. Married to an American wife, Erskine was the only British envoy in the early national period who developed cordial personal relations with his American hosts. When he came to Washington in 1806, he wanted very much to avoid war with America and, at Madison's urging, Erskine recommended repeal of the orders in council, provided that the United States keep non-intercourse against France. Foreign Minister Canning was agreeable if the United States promised to accept the Rule of 1756. Canning also stipulated that the Royal Navy should be allowed to seize any American vessel that violated the Non-Intercourse Act. Erskine proceeded to negotiate a treaty, although nothing explicit was said about the British Navy or the Rule of 1756. In late April, Madison issued a proclamation lifting non-intercourse against Britain on June 10, the date that England, according to the Erskine agreement, would repeal its orders in council. More than 600 American vessels laden with two years' accumulation of goods promptly set sail for British ports. Huzzas echoed from Maine to Georgia.

The joy soon whimpered away. When Canning learned that Erskine's agreement lacked the stipulations he had set, he repudiated the treaty and the "damned Scotch flunkey" who had negotiated it.[87] The foreign secretary, of course, allowed American ships still at sea to bring supplies to England. News of repudiation stunned Americans and angered Madison, who termed it a "mixture of fraud and folly."[88] The President quickly renewed non-intercourse, but the damage had been done. "We are not so well prepared for resistance as we were one year ago," Gallatin reported. "[Then] all or almost all our mercantile wealth was safe at home, our resources entire, and our finances sufficient. . . . Our property is now afloat; England relieved by our relaxations might stand two years of privations with ease; we have wasted our resources without any national unity."[89]

Canning aggravated matters further by replacing Erskine with Francis James ("Copenhagen") Jackson, a notorious diplomat whose mission to Denmark in 1807 had consisted of a brutal ultimatum followed by the destruction of the Danish capital by the guns of the British fleet.[90] Jackson's instructions, in Henry Adams' phrase, were "to propose nothing whatever."[91] The bumptious Briton managed to offend everyone in Washington, save for a handful of Federalists. Diplomacy got nowhere, as Jackson and Madison soon clashed over British charges that the Americans had consciously connived with Erskine to violate Canning's directions. "God damn Mr. Jackson," shouted one Kentuckian, "the President ought to . . . have him kicked from town to town until he is kicked out of the country. God damn him."[92] Madison finally declared Jackson *persona non grata;* London recalled him in April, 1810, and a replacement did not arrive for nearly two years.

The Non-Intercourse Act expired in the spring of 1810. A complicated piece of legislation known as Macon's Bill Number Two replaced it. The new law ostensibly removed all restrictions on American commerce, including trade with England and France; it also empowered the President to renew non-intercourse against one belligerent if the other gave up its punitive decrees. Madison noted that "public attention is beginning to fix itself on the proof . . . that the original sin agst. Neutrals lies with G.B. & that whilst she acknowledges it, she persists in it."[93] Here was an opportunity for Napoleon. Without actually stopping the seizure of American ships, he promised repeal of the Berlin and Milan decrees against American commerce, provided only that the United States "shall cause their rights to be respected by the English."[94] The French pledged to lift their decrees on

November 1, 1810. Whether or not Madison was trying to outfox Napoleon is a matter of scholarly debate, but the President assumed that the French promises were genuine. On November 2, 1811, without adequate proof that Napoleon had freed American shipping (he had not), the President proclaimed non-intercourse against Britain.

This time Madison's exercise in commercial coercion succeeded, but not quickly enough. The British, quite understandably, refused to be blackmailed into lifting their blockade while Napoleon pretended to revoke his decrees. Not only did the British not repeal their orders in council, they enforced them even more vigorously. (Altogether the French confiscated 558 American vessels in the period 1803–1812, as compared to 917 British seizures. In the years 1811–1812, however, French confiscations dwindled to a mere 34.) "The United States," wrote the new Secretary of State James Monroe, "cannot allow Great Britain to regulate their trade, nor can they be content with a trade to Great Britain only. . . . The United States are, therefore, reduced to the dilemma either of abandoning their commerce, or of resorting to other means more likely to obtain a respect for their rights."[95]

Indian troubles on the frontier also contributed to Anglo-American animosities. Beginning in 1806 two remarkable Shawnee Indians, Tecumseh and the Prophet, began to organize the western tribes against further white expansion. Americans had largely their own land grabbing and treaty breaking to account for Indian hostility, but frontier leaders were quick to attribute conspiratorial designs to the British in Canada, where Tecumseh's tribes received food and shelter (but not guns and ammunition, as Americans alleged). Finally, on November 7, 1811, an armed clash occurred at Tippecanoe Creek in what is now Indiana. American forces under General William Henry Harrison barely defeated a superior Indian concentration. Americans simply assumed that the British were stirring up the tribes, even though the opposite was true. Talk of taking Canada was heard in Congress and in the West. As Henry Clay put it: "Is it nothing to us to extinguish the torch that lights up savage warfare?"[96]

The United States thus moved inexorably, albeit haltingly, toward war in the winter and spring of 1812, not knowing that economic distress was finally causing Britannia to alter course. For, beginning in the autumn of 1810, a depression hit the British, accompanied by poor harvests, bread riots, unemployment, higher taxes, higher prices, and general unrest. British exports to the Continent dropped by one-third from 1809 to 1811, while exports to the United States were reduced by seven-eighths. Manufacturing interests began to put pressure on Parliament. A petition from Birmingham contained some 20,000 signatures on a sheet of paper fifty feet in length. On June 16, 1812, Foreign Minister Lord Castlereagh announced in Parliament that the orders in council would be immediately suspended. Two days later, however, without knowing of Castlereagh's action, the American Congress declared war against England.

## War for Sovereignty by Land and Sea

Because the vote for war was close (79 to 49 in the House, 19 to 13 in the Senate) and came after only two weeks of sharp debate, scholars have noted that had speedier transatlantic communications existed in 1812, war might have been prevented. True enough. But it does not necessarily follow that Americans went to war for imaginary, and therefore frivolous, reasons. The causes of the War of 1812 were numerous and compelling, and Madison gave a reasonably accurate listing in his war message of June 1. The President placed impressment first, spotlighting those hundreds of Americans "dragged on board ships of war of a foreign nation and exposed, under the severities of their discipline, to be exiled to the most distant and deadly climes, to risk their lives in the battles of their oppressors." Second, Madison mentioned British depradations against American commerce within sight of American harbors, as well as "pretended blockades" that disregarded all principles of international law. Third, he charged that Britain's orders in council waged war on American commerce in order to maintain "the monopoly which she covets for her own commerce and navigation." And last, Madison blamed the English for igniting "the warfare just renewed by the savages on one of our extensive frontiers."[97] Privately, without the need for presidential embellishment, Madison noted that Britain's conduct left the United States "no choice but between that [war] & the greater evil of a surrender of our sovereignty . . . , on which all nations whose agriculture & commerce are so closely allied, have an essential interest."[98]

Historians have speculated about the seeming contradiction between Madison's emphasis on maritime causes and the fact that a majority of war votes came from the agrarian South and West, not from the commercially minded Northeast. Some scholars, echoing John Randolph's contemporary charge that the "war hawks" were motivated by a "whip-poor-will cry" for Canada, have listed land hunger or a desire for territorial expansion as major causes of the war.[99] Part of the apparent paradox can be explained by delineating economic self-interest: the West and South were wracked by depression in 1812; eastern merchants, even with British and French depredations, were still making profits. Jeffersonian farmers and frontiersmen, many dependent on the export trade, blamed falling agricultural prices on the British blockade. As John C. Calhoun of South Carolina argued: "they see in the low price of the produce, the hand of foreign injustice; . . . they are not prepared for the colonial state to which again that Power is endeavoring to reduce us."[100] Westerners, moreover, perhaps imbued with a sense of frontier justice, were quick to protest such affronts to the national honor as impressment and the *Chesapeake* affair. The "war hawks" of the Twelfth Congress did talk of adding Florida and Canada to the American union, sometimes making spread-eagle statements that foreshadowed the Manifest Destiny arguments of the 1840s. Westerners focused on Canada in 1811–1812, in part because of their mistaken belief that England was stirring up the Indian tribes north of the Ohio River, but also because Canada was the only place to retaliate against British maritime practices. Matthew Clay of Virginia proclaimed, "We have the Canadas as much under our command as she [Great Britain] has the ocean; and the way to conquer her on the ocean is to drive her from our land."[101]

National honor served as another unifying force for war. The great bulk of the votes for war came from the same southern Republicans who had earlier supported the Embargo and Non-Intercourse laws. Commercial coercion had not worked. In historian Norman Risjord's words, "submission to the orders in council presaged a return to colonial status; war seemed the only alternative."[102] The real issue, wrote one Virginian in 1812, "has ceased to be a question merely relating to certain rights of commerce . . . —it is now clearly, positively, and directly *a question of independence;* that is to say, whether the U. States are an independent nation."[103]

Scholars have also stressed the importance of contingencies, emotions, and personalities. War might have occurred as early as 1807 over impressment and the *Chesapeake* affair, had not Jefferson and Madison chosen economic coercion rather than military retaliation. Even after the embargo failed, Madison persisted in economic pressure. Unlike later presidents who vigorously guided the nation into war, Madison followed policies that led to war out of frustration. The impetus came from younger men, "war hawks" in Congress like John C. Calhoun and Henry Clay. Frustrated by the failure of the embargo and non-intercourse, many "war hawks" in 1811–1812 pushed for war without understanding the dangers involved. Good Republicans, they talked of conquering Canada but did not vote taxes to expand the Army and Navy. Madison asked Congress to take preparatory measures in November, 1811, but he exercised little leadership in military and naval matters. As biographer Ralph Ketcham has written, "he often spoke loudly while carrying no stick at all."[104] Federalists, unable to believe that the Administration would actually open hostilities after five years of half measures, initially supported preparedness to embarrass their opponents. But, as one Federalist lamented, "jests sometimes become serious & end in earnest."[105]

England also realized too late that the United States might actually fight. Preoccupied by the war against Napoleon and depression at home, the British were poorly served by their Minister, Augustus Foster, who fraternized too much with Federalists and did not take Madison's bellicose hints seriously. Usually inattentive to American relations anyway, British politicians became even more inward-looking at the close of 1810, when the aged George III finally went incurably insane upon the death of his favorite child. Several months were taken up with political debate over the accession of the Prince Regent, who was mistakenly thought to favor repeal of the orders in council. Later, in the spring of 1812, a lunatic assassinated Prime Minister Spencer Percival, thus delaying for another month the decision to lift the orders against American shipping. These distractions notwithstanding, perceptive reporting by American diplomats in England might have shown the signs that pointed to eventual repeal. Unfortunately, the capable William Pinkney had departed England in despair in February, 1811, and chargé d'affaires Jonathan Russell simply discounted the effect of protests and petitions on Parliament. Russell's last dispatches, which reached the United States on May 22, 1812, held out no promise that England would repeal her decrees. Madison and the "war hawks" made their decisions accordingly, in defense of American commerce, honor, and sovereignty.

Why did the United States not declare war against France as well? In a preliminary vote on June 12, a Federalist proposal to place France and England on the same belligerent footing failed of passage by a narrow 17 to 15 margin. The suspicious Federalists, citing Madison's false claim that France had repealed the Berlin and Milan decrees, subsequently charged that the declaration of war against England was made in collusion with Napoleon. Such was not the case. Madison and his Republican colleagues had no love for Napoleonic France; they knew that French cruisers were still seizing American merchantmen. Nevertheless, a triangular war seemed out of the question. "We resist the enterprises of England first," Jefferson observed, "because they first come vitally home to us, and our feelings repel the logic of bearing the lash of George III for fear of that of Bonaparte at some future day."[106] French outrages occurred in European waters. British press gangs roamed just off American shores, and British officers—not French—were thought to be stirring up the Indians in the Northwest. In Marshall Smelser's words: "Britain commanded the Americans as one commands lackeys. Napoleon appeared to treat the Americans as sovereign peers—while picking their pockets on the sly."[107] The United States could deal with Napoleon *after* it captured Canada. "As to France," Henry Clay explained, "we have no complaint . . . but of the past. Of England we have to complain in all the tenses."[108]

Madison was well aware of the potential advantages of co-belligerency with France. Napoleon's forces would keep the British bogged down in Spain. The Franch invasion of Russia, which began a week after the American declaration of war, might bring about the full application of the Continental System, thus putting added pressure on Britain. American cruisers and privateers, meanwhile, could use French ports to refit and sell their prizes. It was a policy dictated by American military weakness, reminiscent of American dependence on France during the Revolutionary War. But Madison shunned any formal alliance with France. Even in going to war with England, he tried to make the most of an independent foreign policy.

## Wartime Diplomacy and the Peace of Ghent

"At the moment of the declaration of war, the President regretted the necessity which produced it, looked to its termination, and provided for it."[109] Thus did Secretary of State Monroe write to the American chargé in London, Jonathan Russell, with instructions to seek an armistice, provided that England agreed to end impressment and revoke its orders in council. Several weeks after the Ameri-

**"Preparation for War to Defend Commerce."** The seas provided a substantial number of Americans with their livelihood and their national pride. When both were challenged, the United States prepared for war and took the serious step against Britain in 1812. (Historical Society of Philadelphia)

can war declaration, news reached Washington of the British repeal of the orders in council. Hopes for a quick peace were dashed, however, when the British held stubbornly to their policy of impressment. "The Government could not consent to suspend the exercise of a right," Foreign Minister Castlereagh told Russell, "upon which the naval strength of the empire mainly depends."[110] The Americans also remained stubborn about impressment. Two years of war followed.

The next hint of peace came from remote St. Petersburg in the winter of 1812–1813. The Russian foreign minister offered mediation to American envoy John Quincy Adams, an offer which President Madison grasped eagerly. Without waiting for formal British agreement, Madison appointed Federalist James Bayard and Treasury Secretary Albert Gallatin to join Adams as peace commissioners in the Russian capital. The British politely put off their Russian ally, however, saying that the Anglo-American war had no bearing on the common struggle against Napoleon. It was not that British statesmen feared peace negotiations, but that they objected to Russian mediation. The flighty Tsar Alexander, in a moment of moral exultation, might find himself supporting the American position on maritime rights. "I fear the Emperor of Russia is half an American," Prime Minister Lord Liverpool complained.[111] The British told the Russians that they had no objection to treating directly with the Americans, but no one bothered to tell the three plenipotentiaries in St. Petersburg. Not until January, 1814 did Castlereagh formally propose direct negotiations to the United States, and even then he remained imprecise as to time and place.

In America during these months the war was not going well. Aside from the naval victory of Commodore Oliver Hazard Perry on Lake Erie in 1813 and the occupation of a small area of Canadian territory opposite Detroit the following year, the Americans found themselves constantly on the defensive. The conquest of Canada, contrary to Jefferson's boast, had not proven "a mere matter of marching."[112] American generals displayed incompetence, state militia units performed erratically, and the Canadians fought loyally under British command. The Madison Administration shuddered at the prospect of British reinforcements, soon to be shipped to North America after the defeat of Napoleon. At sea the Americans fared better, with swift Yankee frigates winning several ship-to-ship duels with British men-of-war, and numerous American privateers waging war against British maritime trade. All told, the Americans captured 1,408 British prizes. But even on the oceans British supremacy began to assert itself by 1814 against the puny American Navy. The British blockade remained strong, and naval convoys kept commerce destruction to a tolerable minimum. The Royal Navy, as the events of 1814 were to prove, could land troops unopposed anywhere on the American coast. Little wonder, then, that Madison jumped at Castlereagh's new offer to negotiate. In a shrewd move, the President added Jonathan Russell and Henry Clay to the triumvirate of peace commissioners already in Europe. The appointment of Clay, the brashest "war hawk" of all, provided excellent insurance with Congress in case the peace treaty could not obtain all the goals for which Americans had gone to war in 1812.

A diplomatic retreat seemed unavoidable. On June 27, 1814, just prior to the embarrassing British burning of Washington and a few weeks before peace negotiations began in Belgium, Secretary Monroe instructed the plenipotentiaries to "omit any stipulation on the subject of impressment," if such action would facilitate a peace settlement.[113] The American peacemakers paced for six weeks in the picturesque Flemish village of Ghent before the British delegation finally arrived on August 8. Castlereagh stalled in selecting and instructing his commissioners. Preoccupied with the more important European peace conference at Vienna (which Castlereagh attended in person), the British foreign secretary also thought that news of British military successes in North America would simplify diplomacy at Ghent. Meanwhile, like thoroughbred horses, the American delegates chafed and snapped at each other. The acerbic John Quincy Adams continually found fault with his colleagues' ideas and habits. Clay's predilection for poker, brandy, and cigars irritated the doughty New Englander, whose stoic regimen commenced each dawn with an hour of Bible study. Adams' icy disdain gradually melted, however, warmed by Clay's affability, Gallatin's tactful urbanity, and Bayard's good-humored patriotism. "We appear all to be animated by the same desire of *harmonizing* together," he wrote to his wife.[114]

The British peace proposals sorely tested American unity. By asking for the formation of a separate Indian buffer state in the Old Northwest, some adjustment in the Canadian-American boundary south of the Great Lakes, and a *quid pro quo* for renewing American fishing rights (which London claimed had lapsed during the war), the British nearly ended negotiations at the start. Of the Americans, only Clay, the self-proclaimed expert at the western game of brag, thought the British were bluffing. He was right. After a few weeks the Indian issue gradually disappeared. The British still insisted on boundary changes, direct access to the Mississippi, and compensation for fishing privileges. Adams experienced a sense of *déjà vu.* "The situation in which I am placed," he wrote to his father in Massachusetts, "often brings to mind that in which you were situated in the year 1782. . . . I am called upon to support the same interests, and in many respects, the same identical points and questions. . . . It is the boundary, the fisheries, and the Indian savages."[115] Next came a British demand for *uti possidetis,* or peace based upon the war map of the moment, meaning that the English would continue to hold eastern Maine and portions of American territory south of the Great Lakes. The Americans insisted on the 1783 boundary. News finally reached Ghent in late October that the British invasion of the Hudson Valley had been stopped dead at Plattsburgh, New York, and the amphibious attack on Baltimore had been repelled with the loss of one of England's best generals. Worse yet, President Madison had rallied support (even among New England Federalists) by violating diplomatic etiquette and publishing the initial British peace demands. "Mr. Madison has acted most scandalously," sniffed the Prime Minister, Lord Liverpool.[116]

Great Britain had a choice—either continue the war or accept a peace without territorial gain. Castlereagh was having a difficult time in Vienna, where the Prussians were hungrily eyeing Saxony and the Russians demanding all of Poland. The British Cabinet thereupon turned for advice to the Duke of Wellington, then in command of occupied and unruly Paris. The Iron Duke said that he would lead His Majesty's troops in America, if ordered, but it would be better, after the defeat at Plattsburgh, to negotiate peace on the terms *status quo ante bellum.* Lord Liverpool agreed, advising Castlereagh on November 18, 1814, to seek peace without any territorial additions.

European trouble once again proved an American blessing. Another month of speedy negotiations settled all remaining questions. Ironically enough, it was during this last phase that the one serious disagreement arose among the American delegates. The British, still hoping for a *quid pro quo* in return for American fishing rights, asked for access to the Mississippi River. When Adams, ever the protector of Yankee fishermen, seemed disposed to accept such a bargain, Jonathan Russell accused him of trying to "barter the patriotic blood of the West for blubber, and exchange ultra-Allegheny scalps for codfish."[117] Gallatin smoothed over the contretemps, however, by suggesting that any reference to the Mississippi and the fisheries be omitted from the final treaty. The British delegation agreed. And so, on the night before Christmas, 1814, in the residence of the British commissioners at Ghent, the treaty of peace was signed. "I hope," said Adams, "it will be the last treaty of peace between Great Britain and the United States."[118]

The pact was received with great rejoicing when it reached Washington in early February, 1815. The Senate voted approval 35–0, despite the fact that none of the ostensible causes of the war were mentioned in the treaty. Partly responsible for the euphoric atmosphere was the *previous* arrival of news concerning Andrew Jackson's smashing victory over the British at New Orleans on January 8, 1815. Many Americans believed erroneously that Jackson's achievement influenced the Ghent Treaty, and the Madison Administration was not averse to ending what had been an unpopular war in a blaze of military glory. News of Ghent and New Orleans also undermined any impact that delegates from the Hartford Convention might have had on American diplomacy. Composed of New England Federalists who opposed Madison's war against England, the Hartford Convention had sent delegates to Washington with proposals to amend the Constitution (among the suggestions was a sixty-day limit on embargoes and a two-thirds vote of Congress for war). Madison ignored the New Englanders, who slunk home in disgrace.

## Europe's Wars and American Independence, 1789–1815: The Legacy

The Peace of Ghent, coinciding with the end of the Napoleonic wars in Europe, marked the culmination of an important phase of American foreign policy. The United States, after 1793, had reacted to Europe's wars by trying to expand its commerce as a neutral carrier and enlarge its territory by playing upon European rivalries. American statesmen sought these goals without war or European entanglements until 1812, when the accumulation of grievances against America's neutral rights and a traditional interest in territorial gains catapulted an unprepared country into a second war of independence against Great Britain. The end of that Anglo-American conflict, combined with peace in Europe, made all questions of maritime rights academic. Thereafter, for the next thirty years or so, American relations with Europe focused almost exclusively on the matter of territorial expansion in the western hemisphere. A biographer of Madison has written, "the red sea of British dead created by the fire of Jackson's men [at New Orleans] dramatically and finally underscored American possession of the Western empire."[119]

By twentieth-century standards the War of 1812 seems inexpensive—only 2,260 battle deaths and $105 million in direct costs. Yet its consequences were large. Henry Clay thought that the country had gained "respectability and character abroad—security and confidence at home. . . . [O]ur character and Constitution are placed on a solid basis, never to be shaken."[120] Albert Gallatin's estimate was more balanced. "The War has been productive of evil & good," he wrote, "but I think the good preponderates. . . . Under our former system we were become too selfish. . . . The people . . . are more Americans: they feel & act more as a Nation, and I hope that the permanency of the Union is thereby better secured."[121] So impressed was the French minister in Washington that he characterized the naval victories of the Americans as "a prelude to the lofty destiny to which they are called," and concluded that "the war has given the Americans what they so essentially lacked, a national character founded on a glory common to all."[122]

This sense of national confidence and glory rested partly upon illusion. Jackson's heroics at New Orleans caused people to forget the burning of Washington, to forget that the war was a draw at best, hardly a spectacular success. The myth arose, not easily dispelled, that "citizen soldiers" were a sufficient defense against European professionals, and that frontier captains were superior to West Point graduates. The lack of preparedness was forgotten. John Quincy Adams spoke only for himself in hoping that the United States would learn "caution against commencing War without a fair prospect of attaining its objects."[123] Forgotten, too, was the probability that, with more patience on the part of the Madison Administration, and less haughtiness and more attentiveness to American issues on the part of the British, the War of 1812 need never have been fought. The legitimate, if limited, naval successes of the war had a more enduring effect, as much of the wartime navy was maintained after 1815. Less than a year after Ghent a squadron of ten vessels under Captain Stephen Decatur extracted favorable treaties from the Barbary sultans of Tripoli, Algiers, and Tunis, and in the ensuing decades naval officers continued to serve as advance agents of American empire. But even in naval matters the limits of American power were less remembered than the superpatriotism of Decatur's famous toast: "Our country! In her intercourse with foreign nations may she always be in the right; but our country, right or wrong."[124] The revulsion against the Federalists, furthermore, for their apparent lack of patriotic fervor, provided an ominous precedent for future opponents of American wars.

American gains were substantial nonetheless. Even if the British refused to revoke impressment in theory, the end of the war brought the release of hundreds of American citizens from British ships and British prisons. The defeat of Napoleon would have meant the end of impressment anyway, but at least the Americans had the satisfaction of vindicating their honor. Never again would the forceful abduction of American citizens on the high seas be a problem in Anglo-American relations. No longer could the northwest Indians rely on British support to oppose American expansion. Even if the peace settled no major issues by treaty, the United States, with its population doubling every 23 years, profited. In Henry Adams' words, "they gained their greatest triumph in referring all their disputes to be settled by time, the final negotiator, whose decision they could safely trust."[125] America's economic independence was thus established and its territorial integrity defended. However much the United States risked its diplomatic goals by going to war in 1812, the paradoxical effect of that war was to increase American self-confidence and to ensure European respect. The young republic still had not reached the rank of a great power by Europe's standards, but the war with England had shown that in North America the United States could not be treated like Geneva or Genoa.

The legacy of 1812 was most evident in Anglo-American relations. Britain, engaged in a life-or-death struggle with Napoleon, found the United States a tough adversary. As the Duke of Wellington recognized, Canada was useless as an offensive base and could be defended only with the greatest difficulty. There was also the matter of Anglo-American trade, as British exports to America rose substantially, thus presaging a commercial interdependence which, like Canada, served as a hostage to peaceful Anglo-American relations. Rivalry between the two English-speaking nations did not end in 1815, of course, and Great Britain still stood as the chief barrier to American expansion. But after 1815 the former mother country chose to settle differences with the United States at the negotiating table, not on the battlefield. Many Britons came to share the prophetic words of French envoy Hyde de Neuville in 1808: "In thirty or forty years the dynamic American giant will exercise great influence in the Old World and the New. He is destined to be the balance among the great powers."[126]

## Further Reading for the Period 1789–1815

General histories of American diplomacy after 1789 include Henry Adams, *History of the United States During the Administrations of Jefferson and Madison* (1889–1891), Lawrence S. Kaplan, *Colonies into Nation* (1972), Marshall Smelser, *The Democratic Republic, 1801–1815* (1968), and Paul A. Varg, *Foreign Policies of the Founding Fathers* (1970).

The diplomacy of George Washington's Administration is recounted in Harry Ammon, *The Genet Mission* (1973), Samuel Flagg Bemis, *Jay's Treaty* (1962) and *Pinckney's Treaty* (1960), Julian P. Boyd, *Number 7: Alexander Hamilton's Secret Attempts to Control American Foreign Policy* (1964), Joseph Charles, *The Origins of the American Party System* (1956), Jerald A. Combs, *The Jay Treaty* (1970), Alexander DeConde, *Entangling Alliance* (1958), Gilbert Lycan, *Alexander Hamilton and American Foreign Policy* (1970), Charles R. Ritcheson, *Aftermath of Revolution* (1969), and Arthur P. Whitaker, *The Spanish-American Frontier, 1783–1795* (1927).

The XYZ Affair and John Adams' diplomacy are treated in Albert H. Bowman, *The Struggle for Neutrality: Franco-American Diplomacy During the Federalist Era* (1974), Alexander DeConde, *The Quasi-War: The Politics and Diplomacy of the Undeclared War with France, 1797–1801* (1966), Stephen Kurtz, *The Presidency of John Adams* (1957), and William Stinchcombe, "Talleyrand and the American Negotiations of 1797–1798," *Journal of American History* (1975).

The Louisiana Purchase and Jeffersonian expansion are studied in Alexander DeConde, *This Affair of Louisiana* (1976), E. Wilson Lyon, *Louisiana in French Diplomacy, 1759–1804* (1934), Dumas Malone, *Jefferson the President* (1970), and Arthur P. Whitaker, *The Mississippi Question, 1795–1803* (1934).

Diplomatic issues leading to the War of 1812 are traced in Roger Brown, *The Republic in Peril: 1812* (1964), A. L. Burt, *The United States, Great Britain, and British North America* (1940), Reginald Horsman, *The Causes of the War of 1812* (1962), Walter W. Jennings, *The American Embargo, 1807–1809* (1921), Julius Pratt, *Expansionists of 1812* (1925), Bradford Perkins, *The First Rapprochement* (1955) and *Prologue to War* (1961), Norman K. Risjord, "1812: Conservatives, War Hawks, and the Nation's Honor," *William and Mary Quarterly* (1961), Robert A. Rutland, *Madison's Alternatives* (1975), and Louis M. Sears, *Jefferson and the Embargo* (1927).

Wartime questions and the peacemaking at Ghent appear in James Banner, *To the Hartford Convention* (1970), Fred L. Engelman, *The Peace of Christmas Eve* (1962), Bradford Perkins, *Castlereagh and Adams: England and the United States, 1812–1823* (1964), and Patrick C. T. White, *A Nation on Trial* (1965).

Biographical studies of leading statesmen include Harry Ammon, *James Monroe* (1971), Samuel Flagg Bemis, *John Quincy Adams and the Foundations of American Foreign Policy* (1949), Irving Brant, *James Madison* (1956, 1961), John Garry Clifford, "A Muddy Middle of the Road: The Politics of Edmund Randolph, 1790–1795,"

*Virginia Magazine of History and Biography* (1972), Peter P. Hill, *William Vans Murray, Federalist Diplomat* (1971), Ralph Ketcham, *James Madison: A Biography* (1971), Page Smith, *John Adams* (1962), and Raymond Walters, Jr., *Albert Gallatin: Jeffersonian Financier and Diplomat* (1957). Short biographies are located in John A. Garraty, ed., *Encyclopedia of American Biography* (1974).

For other studies, see Norman Graebner, ed., *American Diplomatic History Before 1900* (1977) and the following notes.

## Notes to Chapter 2

1. Quoted in Henry Adams, *History of the United States During the Administrations of Jefferson and Madison* (New York: Charles Scribner's Sons, 1889–1891; 9 vols.), IV, 11.

2. *Ibid.*, p. 13.

3. *Ibid.*, p. 14.

4. *Ibid.*, pp. 15–16.

5. Quoted in Dumas Malone, *Jefferson and His Time* (Boston: Little, Brown, 1948–1974; 5 vols.), V, 401.

6. Adams, *History of Jefferson and Madison*, IV, 27.

7. Quoted in Malone, *Jefferson*, V, 425.

8. Quoted in Reginald Horsman, *The Causes of the War of 1812* (Philadelphia: University of Pennsylvania Press, 1962), p. 169.

9. Quoted in Adams, *History of Jefferson and Madison*, IV, 33.

10. Bradford Perkins, *Prologue to War: England and the United States, 1805–1812* (Berkeley: University of California Press, 1961), p. 144.

11. Quoted in Paul A. Varg, *Foreign Policies of the Founding Fathers* (Baltimore: Penguin Books, 1970), p. 192.

12. Quoted in Horsman, *Causes of the War of 1812*, p. 235.

13. Henry Cabot Lodge, ed., *The Works of Alexander Hamilton* (New York: G. P. Putnam's Sons, 1904; 12 vols.), X, 357.

14. Quoted in Samuel Flagg Bemis, *Jay's Treaty: A Study in Commerce and Diplomacy* (New Haven: Yale University Press, 1962; rev. ed.), p. 372.

15. Quoted in Jerald A. Combs, *The Jay Treaty: Political Battleground of the Founding Fathers* (Berkeley: University of California Press, 1970), p. 76.

16. A. A. Lipscomb, ed., *The Writings of Thomas Jefferson* (Washington: Thomas Jefferson Memorial Association, 1903–1904; 19 vols.), IX, 10.

17. Worthington C. Ford, ed., *Writings of Thomas Jefferson* (New York: G. P. Putnam's Sons, 1892–1899; 10 vols.), VI, 278.

18. Quoted in Lawrence S. Kaplan, *Colonies into Nation: American Diplomacy, 1763–1801* (New York: Macmillan, 1972), p. 219.

19. Lipscomb, *Writings of Jefferson*, IX, p. 97.

20. Quoted in Harry Ammon, *The Genet Mission* (New York: W. W. Norton, 1973), p. 86.

21. Quoted in Claude G. Bowers, *Jefferson and Hamilton: The Struggle for Democracy in America* (Boston: Houghton Mifflin, 1925), p. 229.

22. Bemis, *Jay's Treaty*, p. 373.

23. Quoted in John Garry Clifford, "A Muddy Middle of the Road: The Politics of Edmund Randolph, 1790–1795," *Virginia Magazine of History and Biography*, LXXX (July, 1972), 298.

24. Paul Leicester Ford, ed., *The Works of Thomas Jefferson* (New York: G. P. Putnam's Sons, 1904; 12 vols.), VIII, 193.

25. Quoted in Kaplan, *Colonies into Nation*, p. 243.

26. Quoted in Clifford, "Edmund Randolph," p. 306.

27. Joseph Charles, *The Origins of the American Party System* (Williamsburg: Institute of Early American History and Culture, 1956), p. 106.

28. Bernard Mayo, ed., "Instructions to the British Ministers to the United States, 1791–1812," *Annual Report of the American Historical Association for 1936* (Washington: Government Printing Office, 1941; 3 vols.), III, 83.

29. Quoted in John A. Carroll and Mary W. Ashworth, *George Washington: First in Peace* (New York: Charles Scribner's Sons, 1957), p. 278.

30. Quoted *ibid.*, p. 294.

31. Quoted in Combs, *The Jay Treaty*, p. 184.

32. *Ibid.*

33. Arthur P. Whitaker, *The Spanish-American Frontier, 1783–1795* (Boston: Houghton Mifflin, 1927), p. 220.

34. Samuel Flagg Bemis, *Pinckney's Treaty: A Study of America's Advantage from Europe's Distress* (New Haven: Yale University Press, 1962; rev. ed.).

35. Quoted in Henry Blumenthal, *France and the United States, Their Diplomatic Relations, 1789–1914* (Chapel Hill: The University of North Carolina Press, 1970), p. 14.

36. James D. Richardson, ed., *A Compilation of the Messages and Papers of the Presidents, 1789–1901* (Washington: Government Printing Office, 1896–1914; 10 vols.), I, 221–223.

37. Quoted in Albert H. Bowman, *The Struggle for Neutrality* (Knoxville: University of Tennessee Press, 1974), pp. 268–269.

38. Quoted in Alexander DeConde, *The Quasi-War: The Politics and Diplomacy of the Undeclared War with France, 1797–1801* (New York: Charles Scribner's Sons, 1966), p. 3.

39. Quoted in William Stinchcombe, "Talleyrand and the American Negotiations of 1797–1798," *Journal of American History*, LXII (December, 1975), 578.

40. Quoted in Bowman, *The Struggle for Neutrality*, p. 277.

41. Walter Lowrie and Matthew St. Clair Clarke, eds., *American State Papers* (Class I) *Foreign Relations* (Washington: Government Printing Office, 1832–1859; 6 vols.), II, 161.

42. Quoted in DeConde, *Quasi-War*, p. 52.

43. Quoted in Kaplan, *Colonies into Nation*, p. 276.

44. Richardson, ed., *Messages of the Presidents*, I, 256.

45. Quoted in Varg, *Foreign Policies of the Founding Fathers*, p. 135.

46. Quoted in DeConde, *Quasi-War*, p. 99.

47. Quoted in Kaplan, *Colonies into Nation*, p. 282.
48. Bradford Perkins, *The First Rapprochement: England and the United States, 1795–1805* (Philadelphia: University of Pennsylvania Press, 1955).
49. Lowrie and Clarke, eds., *American State Papers, Foreign Relations*, II, 242.
50. Quoted in Page Smith, *John Adams* (Garden City: Doubleday, 1962; 2 vols.), II, 995.
51. Quoted *ibid.*, II, 1000.
52. Quoted *ibid.*, II, 1002.
53. Charles Francis Adams, ed., *The Works of John Adams* (Boston: Little, Brown, 1856; 10 vols.), X, 113.
54. Quoted in Peter P. Hill, *William Vans Murray, Federalist Diplomat: The Shaping of Peace with France, 1797–1801* (Syracuse: Syracuse University Press, 1971), p. 196.
55. Richardson, ed., *Messages of the Presidents*, I, 309–312.
56. Lipscomb, *Writings of Jefferson*, X, 296.
57. Adams, *History of Jefferson and Madison*, I, 340.
58. Quoted in Marshall Smelser, *The Democratic Republic, 1801–1815* (New York: Harper and Row, 1968), p. 87.
59. Gaillard Hunt, ed., *The Writings of James Madison* (New York: G. P. Putnam's Sons, 1900–1910; 9 vols.), VI, 462.
60. Quoted in Malone, *Jefferson and His Time*, IV, 256.
61. Quoted *ibid.*, IV, 277.
62. Quoted in Harry Ammon, *James Monroe: The Quest for National Identity* (New York: McGraw-Hill, 1971), p. 206.
63. Quoted in E. Wilson Lyon, *Louisiana in French Diplomacy, 1759–1804* (Norman: University of Oklahoma Press, 1934), p. 194.
64. Smelser, *Democratic Republic*, p. 94.
65. Quoted in Alexander DeConde, *This Affair of Louisiana* (New York: Charles Scribner's Sons, 1976), p. 174.
66. Quoted in François de Barbé-Marbois, *History of Louisiana* (Philadelphia: J. B. Lippincott, 1830), pp. 310–311.
67. Quoted in Lyon, *Louisiana in French Diplomacy*, p. 206.
68. Quoted in Malone, *Jefferson and His Time*, IV, 297.
69. Quoted *ibid.*, p. 316.
70. Lipscomb, *Writings of Jefferson*, XII, 277.
71. *Annals of Congress*, 9 Cong., 1 Sess. (March 5, 1806), p. 557.
72. Smelser, *Democratic Republic*, p. 148.
73. Charles F. Adams, ed., *Memoirs of John Quincy Adams* (Philadelphia: J. B. Lippincott, 1874–1877; 12 vols.), II, 92.
74. Quoted in Perkins, *Prologue to War*, p. 41.
75. Varg, *Foreign Policies of the Founding Fathers*, p. 173.
76. Quoted in Perkins, *Prologue to War*, p. 89.
77. Quoted in Varg, *Foreign Policies of the Founding Fathers*, p. 182.
78. Robert A. Rutland, *Madison's Alternatives: The Jeffersonian Republicans and the Coming of War, 1805–1812* (Philadelphia: J. B. Lippincott, 1975), p. 5.
79. Lipscomb, *Writings of Jefferson*, XI, 274.
80. Quoted in Horsman, *Causes of the War of 1812*, p. 59.
81. Walter W. Jennings, *The American Embargo, 1807–1809* (Iowa City: University of Iowa Studies in the Social Sciences, 1921), p. 231.
82. Quoted in Perkins, *Prologue to War*, p. 163.
83. Quoted in Robert H. Ferrell, ed., *Foundations of American Diplomacy, 1775–1872* (New York: Harper and Row, 1968), p. 6.
84. Quoted in Perkins, *Prologue to War*, p. 161.
85. Quoted in Jennings, *American Embargo*, p. 93.
86. Perkins, *Prologue to War*, p. 183.
87. Quoted *ibid.*, p. 220.
88. Quoted in Smelser, *Democratic Republic*, p. 194.
89. Quoted in Ralph Ketcham, *James Madison: A Biography* (New York: Macmillan, 1971), p. 496.
90. Rutland, *Madison's Alternatives*, p. 25.
91. Adams, *History of Jefferson and Madison*, V, 103.
92. Quoted in Horsman, *Causes of the War of 1812*, p. 155.
93. Quoted in Rutland, *Madison's Alternatives*, p. 27.
94. Quoted in Roger H. Brown, *The Republic in Peril: 1812* (New York: Columbia University Press, 1964), p. 23.
95. Quoted in Varg, *Foreign Policies of the Founding Fathers*, p. 286.
96. Quoted in Perkins, *Prologue to War*, p. 283.
97. Richardson, ed., *Messages of the Presidents*, II, 484–490.
98. Quoted in Varg, *Foreign Policies of the Founding Fathers*, p. 292.
99. Quoted in Perkins, *Prologue to War*, p. 359.
100. *Annals of Congress*, 12 Cong., 1 Sess. (December 12, 1811), p. 482.
101. Quoted in Horsman, *Causes of the War of 1812*, p. 182.
102. Norman K. Risjord, "1812: Conservatives, War Hawks, and the Nation's Honor," *William and Mary Quarterly*, XVII (April, 1961), 200.
103. Quoted *ibid.*, p. 205.
104. Ketcham, *James Madison*, p. 532.
105. Quoted in Perkins, *Prologue to War*, p. 434.
106. Quoted in Lawrence S. Kaplan, "France and Madison's Decision for War," *Mississippi Valley Historical Review*, L (March, 1964), 658.
107. Smelser, *Democratic Republic*, p. 223.
108. James F. Hopkins, ed., *The Papers of Henry Clay* (Lexington, Ky.: University of Kentucky Press, 1959–1973; 5 vols.), I, 674.
109. Lowrie and Clarke, eds. *American State Papers, Foreign Relations*, III, 585–586.
110. *Ibid.*, III, 589–590.
111. Quoted in Bradford Perkins, *Castlereagh and Adams: England and the United States, 1812–1823* (Berkeley: University of California Press, 1965), p. 14.
112. Quoted in Adams, *History of Jefferson and Madison*, VI, 337.
113. Lowrie and Clarke, eds., *American State Papers, Foreign Relations*, III, 704.
114. Quoted in Perkins, *Castlereagh and Adams*, p. 49.
115. Quoted in Samuel Flagg Bemis, *John Quincy Adams and the Foundations of American Foreign Policy* (New York: Alfred A. Knopf, 1949), p. 196.
116. Quoted in Perkins, *Castlereagh and Adams*, p. 113.
117. Quoted *ibid.*, p. 124.
118. Quoted in Bemis, *John Quincy Adams*, p. 218.
119. Ketcham, *James Madison*, p. 596.
120. Quoted in Perkins, *Castlereagh and Adams*, p. 150.
121. Quoted in Raymond Walters, Jr., *Albert Gallatin: Jeffersonian Financier and Diplomat* (New York: Macmillan, 1957), p. 288.
122. Quoted in Ketcham, *James Madison*, pp. 397–398.
123. Quoted in Perkins, *Castlereagh and Adams*, p. 151.
124. Quoted in Charles J. Peterson, *The American Navy* (Philadelphia: James B. Smith, 1858), p. 287.
125. Adams, *History of Jefferson and Adams*, IX, 53.
126. Quoted in Blumenthal, *France and the United States*, p. 38.

**AN AVAILABLE CANDIDATE.**
THE ONE QUALIFICATION FOR A WHIG PRESIDENT.

"An Available Candidate. The One Qualification for a Whig President." This unflattering cartoon castigates the Mexican War exploits of General Zachary Taylor (1784–1850) during the presidential campaign of 1848. "Old Rough and Ready," a professional military man who spent much of his career battling Western Indians, overcame his detractors and won the election. Although a slaveholder, Taylor opposed the extension of slavery into the territories taken from Mexico, unless the people of California and New Mexico voted for the "peculiar institution." (Library of Congress)

# 3 Making Way for Continental Expansion, 1815–1848

## Diplomatic Crossroad: Mexican-American War on the Rio Grande, 1846

The momentous order to march to the Rio Grande reached "Old Rough and Ready" General Zachary Taylor on February 3, 1846. Planning and reconnoitering took several weeks, so the first infantry brigades did not tramp out single file from Corpus Christi until March 9. The army averaged ten miles a day, through suffocating dust, across sunbaked soil, through ankle-deep sands, past occasional holes of brackish water, into areas that gradually became grasslands capable of supporting trees and other vegetation. Near a wide, marshy stream called the Arroyo Colorado, American troops nearly tangled with a Mexican cavalry force, but the numerically superior "gringoes" managed to cross unmolested. Late in the morning of March 28 Taylor's army reached its goal, an expansive area of plowed field on the north bank of the Rio Grande some 150 miles south of Corpus Christi. Across the 200 yards of mud-colored river was the Mexican town of Matamoros and its well-armed garrison of nearly 3,000 men. Taylor encamped, set up earthworks (later called Fort Texas), and waited.

The next three weeks were nervous, but peaceful. The initial parley between Taylor and the Mexicans had to be conducted in French because no American could speak Spanish and none of the Mexicans present had mastered English. Taylor assured the Mexicans that his advance to the Rio Grande was neither an invasion of Mexican soil nor a hostile act. The suspicious Mexicans reinforced their garrison with some 2,000 additional troops. Then, on April 24, Major General Mariano Arista arrived to assume command of the Division of the North and immediately notified Taylor that hostilities had begun. A force of Mexican cavalry, 1,600 strong, crossed the river at La Palangana, fourteen miles upstream from Matamoros. Taylor sent a detachment of dragoons to investigate, but they returned somehow having seen nothing. That same evening, April 24, Taylor ordered out another cavalry force under Captain Seth B. Thornton. This time the Americans rode into a deadly ambush. Thornton tried to fight his way free but lost 11 men killed.

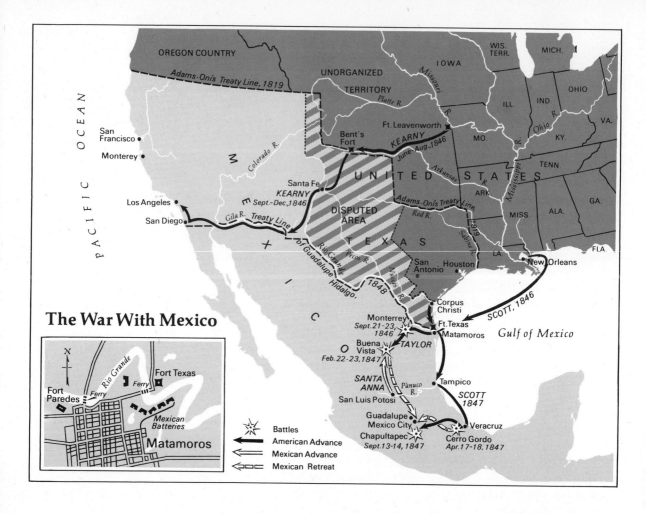

## The War With Mexico

Battles
American Advance
Mexican Advance
Mexican Retreat

The rest of his 63-man contingent was captured. News of the fight reached Taylor at reveille on April 26 when Thornton's guide returned to Fort Texas. "Hostilities may now be considered as commenced," an agitated Taylor immediately wrote to Washington.[1] His dispatch, which had to travel overland, took two weeks to reach the capital.

President James K. Polk was a stiff, angular man, with sharp grey eyes set in a sad, thin face. This hardworking, unhumorous chief executive had called a Cabinet meeting on Saturday, May 9. He was looking for an excuse to declare war on Mexico. Reviewing the diplomacy of the past year, which included the annexation of Texas, suspension of relations with Mexico, and abortive attempts to solve boundary disputes and to purchase California and New Mexico, Polk self-righteously told his Cabinet that "in my opinion we had ample cause of war, and that it was impossible that we could stand in *statu quo,* or that I could remain silent much longer; that I thought it was my duty to send a message to Congress very soon and recommend definitive measures."[2] He hoped that the Mexicans would commit an act of "aggression" against Taylor's army, but as yet nothing had happened. The Cabinet was polled. All agreed that a declaration of war should be sent to Congress by the following Tuesday, although Secretary of the Navy George Bancroft thought it would be better if some hostile act on the border had occurred. The Cabinet adjourned around 2:00 P.M., and Polk began to compose the war message.

At six o'clock that evening the news about the Rio Grande skirmish reached the White House. The Cabinet hastily reconvened. It reached a unanimous decision: submit a war message as quickly as possible. All day Sunday, except for two hours at church, Polk labored over his message, conferring with Cabinet colleagues, military advisers, and congressional leaders. "It was a day of great anxiety to me," the President wrote in his diary.[3] At noon on Monday he sent the message to Congress. "The cup of forbearance has been exhausted," Polk declared. "After reiterated menaces, Mexico has passed the boundary of the United States, has invaded our territory and shed American blood upon American soil." War exists, and "notwithstanding all our efforts to avoid it, exists by the act of Mexico herself." Accompanying the war message was a bill authorizing the President to accept militia and volunteers for military duty. The bill did not specifically declare war, but rather asked Congress to recognize that "by the act of . . . Mexico, a state of war exists between the government and the United States."[4]

A disciplined Democratic majority responded swiftly and efficiently to Polk's recommendations. Debate in the House was limited to two hours. Angry Whigs asked for time to examine documents that Polk sent with his message. Denied. The Speaker of the House repeatedly failed to recognize representatives who wanted to ask detailed questions about how the war started. Only by resorting to a parliamentary trick—by demanding permission to explain why they wanted to be excused from voting—did two dissenters gain the floor and proclaim Polk's war message an "utter falsehood." The House vote of 174 to 14 was a victory for stampede tactics. In the Senate the following day, notwithstanding a more prolonged debate, the vote was even more decisive in favor of the war bill, 40 to 2. The "haughty and dominating" majority again refused members time to study controversial questions.[5] Whigs and dissident Democrats, remembering the political fate of Federalists who had opposed the War of 1812, either voted aye or did not vote. Democratic Senator John C. Calhoun of South Carolina, who did not accept Polk's version of the Rio Grande as the Texas boundary, later insisted that fewer than 10 percent of his colleagues would have voted for the war bill if the issue had been fairly presented. Nonetheless, Calhoun sat silently in his seat when his name was called.

Thus began the Mexican War, a conflict that lasted nearly two years and added to the United States a vast domain, which included the present-day states of New Mexico, Arizona, California, Nevada, and Utah. Contemporaries called it "Mr. Polk's War," a most appropriate appellation. Despite backing from a unanimous Cabinet and an overwhelming congressional declaration, it was the plodding, secretive man from Tennessee who made the crucial decisions for war. It was Polk who unilaterally defined the geographic limits of Texas as including disputed land between the Nueces River and the Rio Grande. It was Polk who, as Commander-in-Chief, ordered General Taylor to the Rio Grande. It was Polk who decided that Mexico had fired the first shot. It was Polk who presented Congress with an accomplished fact. Despite congressional authorization, the rise of presidential war did not go unchallenged. Congressman John Quincy Adams, then in the last year of his distinguished life and himself once an advocate of expansion, was one of the few who voted against war. "It is now established as an irreversible precedent," Adams lamented, "that the President of the United States has but to

**James K. Polk (1795–1849).** Tennessean, graduate of the University of North Carolina, and eleventh President of the United States, this vigorous Democratic expansionist and admirer of Andrew Jackson fixed his gaze on Mexican lands and helped spark war in 1846 to obtain them. (Library of Congress)

declare that War exists, with any Nation upon Earth and the War is essentially declared. . . . It is not difficult to foresee what the ultimate issue will be to the people of Mexico, but what it will be to the People of the United States is beyond my foresight, and I turn my eyes away from it."[6] It was "Mr. Polk's War," but he could bring it off successfully because his aims reflected the grand hopes of expansionist America.

## Manifest Destiny: The Roots of Expansionism

"Mr. Polk's War" on the Rio Grande came at a critical juncture and dramatized, in microcosm, some of the expansionist themes that dominated American foreign policy after the War of 1812. At the very time Taylor's troops were killing Mexicans in the Southwest, Polk was quietly settling a dispute with England over control of the Pacific Northwest. By dividing Oregon at 49 degrees north latitude in June, 1846, Polk temporarily abated the rivalry with England over the territory and commerce of North America. The anti-British fervor of the Revolutionary era remained strong in the 1830s and 1840s, and the fear of British encroachment in Texas and California contributed to the outbreak of war against Mexico. That the United States fought Mexico and not Britain in 1846 illustrated another theme, namely, American expansionists were more aggressive against weaker peoples like Spaniards, Mexicans, and Indians than against the stronger Britishers. According to the expansionist ideology, those peoples who neither improved the land they held nor developed effective political institutions had to make way for those who could. The lands Polk wanted from Mexico were lightly populated, and he assumed that American institutions could be easily assimilated. England, with greater power and similar traditions, could be a rival, but not a victim. Indeed, as Polk moved toward war in the winter of 1845–46 he invoked the precedent of the Monroe Doctrine in warning England against further expansion in North America, thus making explicit what had been implicit in 1823—that Europeans could not seize territory in the western hemisphere, but the United States could. Polk sincerely believed that Mexico fired the first shot on the Rio Grande, just as many Americans sincerely believed that God had destined the United States to control the entire continent. The sincerity of such beliefs did not stop expansionism from being both racist and imperialistic.

Continental expansion became the watchword in the three decades after 1815. Having defended their territorial integrity during the second war with Great Britain, American statesmen proceeded to acquire Florida, Texas, Oregon, and the Mexican cession, some 1,263,301 square miles. Population nearly trebled, from 8,419,000 in 1815 to 22,018,000 in 1848. American commerce expanded into new channels, notably Latin America and the Far East, with total exports climbing from $53 million in 1815 to $157 million in 1847. The gross output of farm production increased from $338 million in 1820 to $904 million thirty years later. The production of cotton, a vital ingredient in Anglo-American relations, rose from 209,000 bales in 1815 to 2,615,000 bales in 1847. The construction of canals and railroads created a transportation revolution that served to quicken American growth. It became the purpose of American diplomacy during these years to facilitate this expansion. *"On s'agrandit toujours un peu, dans ce monde"* ("Everyone always grows a little in this world"), said Tsar Alexander I of Russia after John

South Street, New York City, 1828. This bustling port became pre-eminent in the growth of American foreign trade. (Museum of the City of New York)

Quincy Adams told him of the American acquisition of Florida.[7] Americans were out to grow.

It is difficult to isolate the tangled roots of expansion—historical, economic, demographic, intellectual, strategic. Nor does it suffice to say that the United States, like Topsy, "just growed." To be sure, "extending the sphere" (in Madison's phrase) was nothing new, and much that occurred after 1815 derived from earlier precedents. Part of the rationale for acquiring Florida in 1819 followed the example of Louisiana: just as New Orleans under foreign control had blocked navigation of the Mississippi, so too did Spanish sovereignty over the mouths of the Pearl, Perdido, and Chattahoochee rivers make it difficult for American farmers upstream to get their produce to market. Moreover, Florida, just like New Orleans, might be ceded by Spain to a more dangerous power, hence the argument for possessing it before England or France could grab it. Memories of the Revolution of 1776, combined with opportunities for Latin American markets, helped bring about the Monroe Doctrine of 1823. By stipulating that Europe and the Americas had distinctly different political systems, Monroe's message recalled the isolationist principles of Paine's *Common Sense* and Washington's Farewell Address. There were echoes from the past in the Anglo-American trade rivalry in Latin America and in the attempts to gain equal access to the British West Indian trade in the 1820s. A more explicit reference to earlier concerns about neutral rights came in 1831 when President Andrew Jackson negotiated an agreement whereby France promised to pay an indemnity of 25 million francs for illegal seizures of American shipping in the years 1805–1812. When the French defaulted on an installment in 1834, Jackson is reported to have shouted: "I know them French. They won't pay unless they are made to."[8] The French paid. Undoubtedly, Jackson's pugnacity reflected good electioneering instincts, but it also served notice that the United States would insist on the right to expand its carrying trade in the event of another European conflagration.

Perhaps the most important element in expansion after 1815 was the growing vision of what was possible. As early as 1813 Jefferson himself envisioned *"American* governments, no longer to be involved in the never-ceasing broils of Europe. . . . America has a hemisphere to itself. It must have a separate system of interest which must not be subordinated to those of Europe."[9] But Jefferson thought in terms of separate and independent republics, not a grand republican empire ruled from Washington. Despite treaties in 1818 and 1819 that established a firm claim to the Pacific Coast, most Americans still thought of the Rocky Mountains as a "natural" boundary. Oregon was far away. It had taken Lewis and Clark eighteen months to travel to the Pacific from St. Louis. A sea voyage from Boston to the Pacific Coast lasted six to eight months, depending on the weather. Even Senator Thomas Hart Benton of Missouri, who would catch the Oregon "fever" with a vengeance in the 1840s, went on record in 1825 in favor of the Rocky Mountain limitation. "Along the back of this ridge," he intoned, "the Western limit of the republic should be drawn, and the statue of the fabled god, Terminus, should be raised upon its highest peak, never to be thrown down."[10]

**"Manifest Destiny."** John Gast's painting captures the ebullient spirit of the trek westward. Pioneers relentlessly move on, attracting railroads and driving out Native Americans, as "Columbia" majestically pulls telegraph wires across America. (Collection of Harry T. Peters, Jr.)

Technology shrank geography and expanded horizons. Steamboats, canals, and railroads stimulated imaginations as well as commerce. Although there were still fewer than 5,000 miles of railroad track in the United States in 1845, plans for constructing transcontinental lines had already reached the drawing boards. The development of high-speed printing presses gave rise in the early 1840s to mass circulation newspapers, which in turn trumpeted expansionist rhetoric to a larger foreign policy public. Samuel Morse's invention of the telegraph, first put into operation in 1844, came at an opportune time. "The magnetic telegraph," boasted editor John L. O'Sullivan in 1845, "will enable the editors of the 'San Francisco Union,' the 'Astoria Evening Post,' or the 'Nootka Morning News,' to set up in type the first half of the President's Inaugural before the echoes of the latter half shall have died away beneath the lofty porch of the Capitol, as spoken from his lips."[11]

The same O'Sullivan, editor of the *Democratic Review*, gave the expansionist process a name in the summer of 1845. The United States, according to O'Sullivan, had the "manifest destiny to overspread the continent allotted by Providence to the free development of our yearly multiplying millions."[12] Although the geographical limits of the Temple of Freedom were not always clear—the Pacific? the continent? the hemisphere?—most believers in Manifest Destiny followed John Quincy Adams' notion, expressed in 1819, that "the United States and North America are identical."[13] Manifest Destiny meant republicanism, religious freedom, states' rights, free trade, cheap land. Manifest Destiny in its purest form did not envisage acquisition of territory by force. Peaceful occupation of uninhabited wilderness, followed by self-government on the American model and eventual annexation by mutual consent—this was the ideal. Neighboring peoples of Spanish and Indian heritage, given time and the American example, might qualify. The process was supposed to be almost automatic. "Go to the West," said an Indiana congressman in 1846,[14]

> and see a young man with his mate of eighteen; and [after] a lapse of thirty years, visit him again, and instead of two, you will find twenty-two. That is what I call the American multiplication table. We are now twenty millions strong; and how long, under this process of multiplication, will it take to cover the continent with our posterity, from the Isthmus of Darien to Behring's straits?

Unfortunately, reality did not match the ideal, as "Polk's War" on the Rio Grande sadly attested. Expanding the area of freedom meant expanding also the institution of slavery, and so Southerners tended to favor expansion into different regions (Texas? Cuba?) than did Northerners (Oregon? California?). Some expansionists wanted to hurry the process, to steal a jump on destiny by purchasing territory, urging "spontaneous" revolutions, or threatening war. Indian tribes had to be moved, often with high loss of life. There was also the problem, never squarely faced until General Winfield Scott occupied Mexico City in the autumn of 1847, of accommodating large numbers of alien inhabitants within American institutions and processes. As Secretary of State James Buchanan asked about Mexico, "How should we govern the mongrel race which inhabit it?"[15] It was one thing to acquire territory where Yankee settlers outnumbered Indians or Mexicans by more than twenty to one, quite another to force American rule on eight million souls. To impose Manifest Destiny by bayonet seemed a contradiction in terms. Yet contradictions occurred.

In some ways American expansion was a natural, almost organic process.

Americans always sought greater productivity through the cultivation of new lands. Problems generating from increased population, inadequate transportation, depressed agricultural prices, and general hard times also caused periodic migrations into new areas. Whether this movement was into American territory beyond the Alleghenies or into fertile lands under alien rule, the causes and results were similar. Once established, American settlers retained their distinctly Yankee customs and institutions; if under foreign rule, they rejected alien processes and virtually established American "colonies." Friends, relatives, and politicians at home directed American foreign policy toward the "protection" of their fellow countrymen, perhaps even incorporating them into the Temple of Freedom. Thus came the rhetoric of Manifest Destiny—the spread-eagle appeals to national prestige, the glittering description of natural resources and fertile lands. As the American "colonies" grew in size, so too did fears increase that some European power, probably perfidious England, would snatch the potential prize. If politicians sometimes exaggerated the extent to which England meddled in such places as California, Oregon, and Texas, the fact that British involvement did exist contributed to the expansionist momentum.

Population movements tended to come on the heels of economic downturns. The Panic of 1819, combined with Mexico's generous land policies, encouraged the first flood of immigration into Texas in the 1820s. Similarly, the severe economic depression in 1837–1842 stimulated more western farmers and southern planters to migrate westward. The population of Texas ballooned to 100,000 by 1845, and in far-off Oregon some 5,000 Americans had crossed the Rockies. Actually, settlement in California was still miniscule in 1845, but as one resident put it: "Once let the tide of emigration flow toward California, and the American population will soon be sufficiently numerous to play the Texas game."[16] It was this organic, seemingly inevitable process of agrarian migration that prompted John C. Calhoun in 1843 to advocate a "wise and masterly inactivity" on the part of the American government.[17] God and the passage of time seemed to smile benevolently upon American expansion. Force did not seem necessary—at least not in theory.

## Makers of American Foreign Policy from 1815 to 1848

| Presidents | Secretaries of State |
| --- | --- |
| James Madison, 1809–1817 | James Monroe, 1811–1817 |
| James Monroe, 1817–1825 | John Quincy Adams, 1817–1825 |
| John Quincy Adams, 1825–1829 | Henry Clay, 1825–1829 |
| Andrew Jackson, 1829–1837 | Martin Van Buren, 1829–1831 |
| | Edward Livingston, 1831–1833 |
| | Louis McLane, 1833–1834 |
| Martin Van Buren, 1837–1841 | John Forsyth, 1834–1841 |
| William H. Harrison, 1841 | Daniel Webster, 1841–1843 |
| John Tyler, 1841–1845 | Abel P. Upshur, 1843–1844 |
| | John C. Calhoun, 1844–1845 |
| James K. Polk, 1845–1849 | James Buchanan, 1845–1849 |

A heightened interest in the commercial potential of the Pacific during the 1840s also fueled expansion. Trade with Latin America reached a peak in the early 1830s, and merchants trading on the west coast of South America made easy profits that could in turn be used to purchase the products of East Asia. "The North American road to India" was Senator Benton's colorful description of the Columbia River Valley during the 1840s.[18] Whaling, salmon fisheries, furs, the fabled China trade, commercial rivalry with Britain and Russia—all were stressed from the 1820s onward by publicists seeking to colonize Oregon as a means to commercial empire. The Columbia and Missouri rivers would link with the Mississippi in an ever expanding economic network. In historian Frederick Merk's words: "Furs from the Oregon Country would flow to China. In return teas, silks, and spices would move to St. Louis. St. Louis would become the Venice of the New World. A modern Tyre would rise at the mouth of the Columbia."[19]

Coincidentally, just as the first wave of settlers reached Oregon in 1843, the British, victorious in the Opium War, were breaking down Chinese trade barriers. By the Treaty of Nanking in 1842, Britain forced China to open five new coastal ports (Canton, Amoy, Ningpo, Foochow, and Shanghai) and grant broad rights of extraterritoriality (legal trials for foreigners in special courts of their own nationality). This was a signal for Americans to obtain their own treaty. President John Tyler, in what has been described as the "me-heap-big-paleface style" of diplomacy, entrusted Massachusetts Whig Caleb Cushing with the mission.[20] Cushing, whose friends and family were involved in the China trade, bought a special uniform consisting of white pantaloons with gold stripes, white vest, blue coat with gilt buttons, and plumed headpiece, all presumably calculated to overawe the Chinese. The uniform was unfortunately destroyed in a fire, but Cushing successfully negotiated the Treaty of Wanghia (1844) without sartorial persuasion. It secured for the United States the same rights, on an unconditional most-favored-nation basis, that England had won in the Opium War.

The American Navy, although ranking only eighth in the world in 1836, also aided expansion. Its contribution came primarily in the cartographic and exploratory expeditions of such officers as Matthew Perry, Matthew Maury, and Charles Wilkes. Charting coastlines, publicizing points of commercial and strategic interest, recommending steps to Washington for increasing American commerce in the Pacific, these naval explorers became, in historian Geoffrey Smith's phrase, "'maritime frontiersmen,' mirror images of the thousands of mountain men, traders, pioneers, adventurers, and army surveyors who trekked westward to the Pacific."[21] Important in stimulating expansion was the publication of Lieutenant Wilkes's *Narrative of the United States Exploring Expedition during the Years 1838, 1839, 1840, 1841, 1842,* five weighty volumes containing accurate information about the Pacific Coast from Vancouver Island to Lower California. Wilkes's unqualified praise for San Francisco and the Strait of Juan de Fuca ("two of the finest ports in the world") sharply contrasted with his pessimistic dismissal of the Columbia River, with its shifting sandbars, as a viable commercial entrepôt. Once Wilkes's findings became known in 1842, American diplomats—particularly Daniel Webster—stepped up efforts to acquire either or both of these harbors. The main reason that American diplomacy pressed hard for the triangle of Oregon between

**San Francisco in the 1840s.** Ships at port attested to the trading activities that drew Americans to the Pacific before the frantic gold rush of 1849. (Courtesy, The Bancroft Library, University of California, Berkeley)

the Columbia and Fuca Strait was the need for a deep water port. Only seven Americans lived north of the Columbia River in 1845.

Commercial empire was even more exclusively the object in California. When a British naval officer entered San Francisco Bay in 1845, he exclaimed: "D–n it! is there nothing but Yankees here?"[22] The Americans were connected primarily with the Boston trading company of Bryant & Sturgis. Having pioneered the otter trade in the Pacific and opened an office in Portuguese Macao, Bryant & Sturgis began in the 1820s to shift from furs to hides, which it bought cheaply from Spanish missions and rancheros. The firm established an office in Santa Barbara in 1829, moving a few years later to Monterey. Thomas O. Larkin, later appointed the first American consul to California and a crucial figure in the diplomacy of 1845–1846, was associated with Bryant & Sturgis, as was Richard Henry Dana, the author of the epic narrative *Two Years Before the Mast*, depicting a voyage to California around Cape Horn. Altogether, there were some 25,000 persons in California in 1845, including 800 Americans. Its link with Mexico City, more than 1,500 miles away, was weak. Overland communications were extremely difficult, and courts, police, schools, and newspapers scarcely existed. American merchants, whalers, and sailors competed with their British counterparts. As the American minister to Mexico put it in 1842, California was "the richest, the most beautiful, the healthiest country in the world. . . . The harbor of St. [sic] Francisco is capacious enough to receive all the navies of the world, and the neighborhood furnishes live oak enough to build all the ships of those navies."[23] Daniel Webster, equally impressed, thought the port of San Francisco "twenty times as valuable to us as all Texas."[24]

Commercial opportunities also beckoned in Hawaii, which by the 1840s had become a piece of New England in the mid-Pacific. "Honolulu," Samuel Eliot Morison has written, "with merchant sailors rolling through its streets, shops fitted with Lowell shirtings, New England rum and Yankee notions, orthodox missionaries living in frame houses brought around the Horn, and a neo-classic meeting house built out of coral rocks, was becoming as Yankee as New Bedford."[25] While the Hawaiian archipelago did not become a formal part of the American empire until the 1890s, the absorption process was well underway several decades earlier.

Mercantile interest in the Pacific Coast was confined largely to New England and the Atlantic seaboard, but there were growing commercial interests in the Midwest which sought to link maritime trade to agrarian migrations. Farmers moving to Oregon had in mind an expanded market for their products in Asia, as did some Southerners, who saw the Chinese as potential buyers of cotton and tobacco. Politicians like Stephen Douglas, an agrarian spokesman, embraced projects linking the Mississippi Valley with the Pacific via a transcontinental railroad. Indeed, it was in January, 1845 that Asa Whitney, a New York merchant involved in the China trade, first proposed the idea of government land grants to any group undertaking to build a railroad from the Great Lakes to Oregon. Such schemes did not reach fruition until after the Civil War, but their existence in the era of Manifest Destiny testifies to the dual nature (maritime and agrarian) of continental expansion.

## Nibbling and Swallowing Florida

Following the Louisiana Purchase of 1803, American diplomats had tried to obtain part of the large tropical peninsula of Florida by arguing that it had always been a part of Louisiana. The Spanish rejected such notions. The first bite out of the territory did not come until September, 1810, when a group of American settlers revolted against Spanish rule, captured the fortress at Baton Rouge, and proclaimed the "Republic of West Florida." The Bourbon banner was replaced by a blue woolen flag with a single silver star. President James Madison immediately proclaimed West Florida part of the United States, although he actually sent troops to occupy an area only to the Pearl River. During the War of 1812 American soldiers occupied Mobile and all of West Florida to the Perdido River—the only tangible addition of territory resulting from that war.

It fell to the Monroe Administration (1817–1825) and Secretary of State John Quincy Adams to complete the absorption. Spanish Minister Don Luis de Onís proved himself a dogged, skillful advocate of a hopeless cause. Adams took the diplomatic offensive, arguing that Spain should cede East Florida to the United States because Spanish authorities had not prevented Indians from raiding into American territory (as stipulated in Pinckney's Treaty of 1795). Adams also blamed the Spanish for not returning thousands of escaped slaves and accused them of cooperating with British forces during the War of 1812. Onís was prepared to cede East Florida, but not without a *quid pro quo*. Faced with revolts in its South American empire, Spain wanted a promise from the United States neither to assist the revolutionaries nor to recognize their declared independence. Furthermore, Madrid instructed Onís to settle the disputed western boundary of Louisiana, and only to cede Florida in exchange for the best frontier that circumstances would admit. Adams, delighted to negotiate this second issue, urged that the boundary be set deep in the south at the Rio Grande, or at least the Colorado River of Texas. Onís, after first insisting on the Mississippi, moved grudgingly to the Mermentau and Calcasieu rivers in the middle of present-day Louisiana. The negotiators were far apart. "I have seen slippery diplomatists," Adams later observed, "but Onís is the first man I ever met who made it a point of honor to pass for more of a swindler than he was."[26]

The man who would break the impasse was in early 1818 bivouacked with three thousand troops at Big Creek, near the Georgia–Florida boundary. This was General Andrew Jackson, the hero of New Orleans, a volatile mixture of frontier passion and calculating ambition. Ostensibly under orders to pursue and punish Seminole Indians who had been using Spanish Florida as a base from which to raid American settlements, Jackson had suggested in a secret letter to Monroe that "the whole of East Florida [be] seized and held as indemnity for the outrages of Spain upon the property of our Citizens."[27] Whether or not Monroe or Secretary of War John C. Calhoun explicitly approved Jackson's proposal has never been determined. Jackson claimed they had; both denied it. What is known is that neither Monroe nor Calhoun ever told Jackson *not* to cross the border. To the pugnacious Tennessean, this silence from Washington constituted tacit agreement that the Spanish were every bit as much the enemy as were the Seminoles.

"Old Hickory" burst across the border in late March, 1818. On April 6 the Spanish garrison at St. Marks meekly surrendered. "My love," Jackson wrote to his wife, "I entered the Town of St. Marks on yesterday. . . . I found in St. Marks the noted Scotch villain Arbuthnot. . . . I hold him for trial."[28] Alexander Arbuthnot, in actuality, was a kindly, seventy-year-old British subject whose commercial dealings with the Indians were so scrupulously honest that his profit-minded superiors in England were annoyed with him. Convinced that Arbuthnot was in cahoots with the Seminoles, Jackson plunged into the jungle swamps looking for the main Indian camp. He found the camp, but not the Indians. He seized another Englishman lurking nearby, one Lieutenant Robert C. Ambrister, formerly of the British Royal Colonial Marines. Returning to St. Marks, Jackson convened a court martial, hanged Arbuthnot, and shot Ambrister, not at all perturbed that he was administering American "justice" on Spanish soil to two British citizens. "Old Hickory" next turned west toward Pensacola, where he felt certain that the "Red Sticks" were being fed and supplied by the Spanish governor. Pensacola capitulated quickly on May 28 and Jackson promptly took over the royal archives, replaced the governor with one of his own colonels, and declared in force the revenue laws of the United States. In two short months, although he killed or captured very few Indians, Jackson had occupied every important Spanish post in Florida except St. Augustine.

When news of Jackson's deeds reached Washington in early July, there was considerable embarrassment. Minister Onís roused John Quincy Adams from his early morning Bible study and demanded an indemnity, as well as punishment of Jackson. Calhoun and other Cabinet members suggested a court martial for the rambunctious general. Monroe, who disapproved less of what Jackson had done than the way he did it, quietly agreed to return the captured posts to Spain. But he did not censure Jackson and even offered to falsify some of the general's dispatches so that the invasion would appear in a more favorable light. Congress, led by Henry Clay, launched an investigation into the entire Florida undertaking. Only Adams stoutly defended Jackson.

When the British did not protest the murder of Arbuthnot and Ambrister, Monroe gave his secretary of state full backing. As usual, Adams thought that the best defense was a good offense, and thereupon drew up a memorable reply to Onís' demands for censure and indemnity. Self-defense was the motif. If Spain could not restrain her Indians, the United States would. A bit embarrassed by the lack of precedents in international law, Adams boldly claimed that the right of defensive invasion was "engraved in adamant on the common sense of mankind." Charging the Spanish with "impotence" rather than perfidy, the secretary demanded that "Spain must immediately make her election, either to place a force in Florida adequate at once to the protection of her territory and to the fulfillment of her engagements, or cede to the United States a province, of which she retains nothing but the nominal possession, but which is, in fact, a derelict, open to the occupancy of every enemy, civilized or savage, of the United States, and serving no other earthly purpose than as a post of annoyance to them."[29] This chauvinistic proclamation, which was presently published, impressed Thomas Jefferson as the greatest state paper in American history. Onís could make no effective rejoinder. Even worse, his superiors in Madrid reacted to Jackson's forays with instructions to cede Florida quickly and retreat to the best possible boundary between Louisiana and Mexico.

More negotiations followed, finally culminating in the Adams-Onís Treaty, signed in Washington on February 22, 1819. The United States acquired East Florida, tacit recognition that previously occupied West Florida was part of the Louisiana Purchase, and a new boundary line that began at the mouth of the Sabine River, moved stairstep fashion along various rivers in a northwesterly direction to the forty-second parallel, and then went straight west to the Pacific. Adams' initiative in running the boundary to the Pacific was entirely his own. While contemporaries considered the Rocky Mountains the natural boundary and dreamed of the Pacific Northwest as some future and separate American republic, Adams had his eyes fixed on the Columbia River Basin. It was a grand vision and a masterful diplomatic victory.

In return for these lucrative gains, Adams surrendered the vague claims for Texas arising from the Louisiana Purchase. As it turned out, Onís had instructions to retreat even on the Sabine boundary, but Monroe and the Cabinet thought that Florida was more important than Texas and did not press the matter. The United States also agreed to assume the claims of its own citizens against Spain, some five million dollars resulting from Franco-Spanish seizures of American shipping during the undeclared war of 1798–1800. The Transcontinental Treaty said nothing about American recognition of Spain's rebellious colonies. Partly because of this silence, and partly because of personal intrigues over royal land grants in Florida, Madrid dragged its feet over ratification. Adams staunchly resisted any hand-tying nonrecognition pledge. Two years passed before ratifications were exchanged in 1821.

Perhaps the importance of the Adams-Onís Treaty lay not in what was acquired in 1819, but in what it foreshadowed. Just as in his diplomacy with England in the Convention of 1818 (discussed below), Adams was projecting a continental vision. It did not matter if he and Onís were drawing lines across deserts that did not exist or around mountains that were not where maps said they should be. "It was . . . a battle between two kinds of imagination," historian George Dangerfield has written. "Onís was defending . . . a moribund, revolted, and helpless empire; Adams . . . was thinking and dreaming of an America of the future whose westward movement, in those days before the railroad, was hardly calculable."[30] Although the actual phrase was not coined until the 1840s, John Quincy Adams was the first to speak the language of Manifest Destiny. "The remainder of the continent shall ultimately be ours," he wrote at the time.[31]

A second, more disturbing precedent was the way in which Jackson's invasion of Florida had buttressed diplomacy. Spain's willingness to yield Florida, combined

John Quincy Adams (1767–1848). This daguerreotype photograph taken in 1843, near the end of Adams' distinguished career as diplomat, secretary of state, President, and congressman from Massachusetts, demonstrates well that his countenance was austere and gloomy indeed. (The Metropolitan Museum of Art, Gift of I. N. Phelps Stokes, Edward S. Hawes, Alice Mary Hawes, Marion Augusta Hawes, 1937)

with Britain's refusal to question the execution of Ambrister and Arbuthnot, minimized diplomatic repercussions. Nevertheless, as the congressional investigation into the affair revealed, Monroe and Jackson had virtually waged war without the sanction of Congress. According to Henry Clay, Monroe had assured the Congress that no Spanish forts would be seized if Jackson crossed the border in pursuit of Seminoles, but this was precisely what had occurred. It was, said Clay, "dangerous to permit this type of conduct to pass without comment by the House. Precedents, if bad, are fraught with the most dangerous consequences."[32] Clay may have been right in this instance, but he also wanted to become President. Contemporaries viewed the investigation as an attack on Clay's chief rival, Jackson. They also liked what the general had done. Thus, on February 8, 1819, after a twenty-seven-day debate, the four congressional resolutions condemning Jackson were defeated by comfortable margins. Jackson's popularity, of course, later carried him to the White House. Congress—not for the last time—voted to acquiesce in its own subordination.

## The Monroe Doctrine Clears the Way

The next notable milestone for expansion came with the Monroe Doctrine of 1823. At first glance, that remarkable statement of American diplomatic principles appears entirely anti-imperialist in intent—a stern warning to reactionary Europe not to interfere with revolutions in the New World, a gesture of solidarity and sympathy with the newly independent republics to the south. It was indeed a warning and a gesture, but motives more selfishly American were also involved. In saying "Thou Shalt Not" to Europe, James Monroe and John Quincy Adams were careful to exempt the United States. By facilitating commercial expansion into Latin America and landed expansion across the North American continent, the Monroe Doctrine became, in historian Richard Van Alstyne's words, "an official declaration fencing in the 'western hemisphere' as a United States sphere of influence."[33]

The Latin American revolutions (1808–1822) had a magnetic effect on the United States. The exploits of such Latin American leaders as Bolívar, San Martín, and O'Higgins rekindled memories of 1776. Henry Clay, in a famous oration in 1818, proclaimed that the Latin leaders "adopted our principles, copied our institutions and . . . employed the very language and sentiments of our revolutionary papers."[34] That the United States did not heed popular enthusiasms and immediately recognize the Latin American republics was due primarily to the calculating diplomacy of John Quincy Adams. Cynical and cautious, Adams "wished well" to the emerging Latin states, but doubted that they could "establish free or liberal institutions of government. . . . Arbitrary power, military and ecclesiastical, was stamped upon their education, upon their habits, and upon all their institutions. Civil dissension was infused into all their seminal principles."[35] So Adams carefully avoided recognition, thereby facilitating negotiations with Spain over the Transcontinental Treaty of 1819. Not until the spring of 1822, after the expulsion of Spanish armies from the New World, and following a sharp rise in United States trade with Latin America, did President Monroe extend formal recognition to the new governments of La Plata, Chile, Peru, Colombia, and Mexico. Adams instructed American diplomats to focus their energies on obtaining favorable trading rights. He did not want the new "republics" to exchange Spanish political domination for British commercial domination.

There were additional European threats. Following Napoleon's final defeat, European statesmen had endeavored to restore order and legitimacy to an international system thrown out of kilter by the French Revolution and the conquests of the Corsican usurper. Conservatism became the watchword, and by the Treaty of Paris of 1815 the members of the Quadruple Alliance (Austria, Prussia, Russia, and Britain) bound themselves to future diplomatic congresses for the maintenance of peace and the status quo. A penitent France formally joined the "Concert of Europe" in 1818, and the Quadruple Alliance turned into the Quintuple Alliance. The allies also signed in 1815 a vague agreement called the Holy Alliance. By 1819–1820 the Austrian Foreign Minister, Prince Klemens von Metternich, enthusiastically supported by Tsar Alexander I of Russia, had transformed both alliances into instruments for suppressing revolutions. At the Congress of Troppau in 1820 the Holy Allies agreed that if internal revolutions posed threats to neighboring states, "the powers bind themselves, by peaceful means, or if need be by arms, to bring back the guilty State into the bosom of the Great Alliance."[36] Thus, in due course, Austrian armies were sent to put down uprisings in Naples and Piedmont in 1821. The following year a French army marched across the Pyrenees in support of Spain's imbecilic Ferdinand VII, who was then being embarrassed by a liberal Constitutionalist government. Similarly, the Holy Allies gave diplomatic support to Ottoman Turkey in attempting to snuff out national revolutions in Greece and the Danubian principalities. Americans were particularly incensed at the betrayal of freedom in Greece. Would the Holy Alliance's zeal for putting down revolutions everywhere lead to the restoration of legitimate rule over the insurrectionist colonies of Spain in the New World?

British diplomacy during these years played an ambivalent and tortuous role. Foreign Secretary Castlereagh wanted very much to support the system devised at the Congress of Vienna and to preserve the grand coalition that had defeated Napoleon. The British had little sympathy for revolution per se. Nevertheless, confident of the stability of their own political institutions, and guarded by the English Channel and the Royal Navy, many Britons came to see the use of French and Austrian troops to suppress foreign revolts as upsetting the balance of power. When the Congress of Verona (1822) sanctioned the deployment of French military forces in Spain, something the British had fought the long and bitter Peninsular War (1809–1814) to prevent, England's withdrawal from the Holy Alliance became inevitable. The distraught Castlereagh committed suicide, and his successor, George Canning, promised a return to splendid isolation. Economic factors also influenced the British. Since 1808 British merchants had captured the lion's share of trade with Spanish ports in the New World. These lucrative commercial dealings had not sufficiently overcome London's antipathy to revolution so as to bring about formal recognition. The British, however, did fear that restoration of the Spanish colonies to Ferdinand VII might result in the elimination of British trade. As Canning later boasted, "I resolved that if France had Spain, it should not be Spain 'with the Indies.' I called the New World into existence to redress the balance of the old."[37]

Canning's determination to prevent any restoration in Spanish America led, in August, 1823, to a remarkable conversation with American Minister Richard Rush.

The two men were talking about the progress of French armies in Spain. Rush casually mentioned how confident he was that the British would never permit France to interfere with the independence of Latin America or to gain territory there by conquest or cession. Canning listened intently. What, he asked Rush, would the American government say to going hand in hand with England in such a policy? No concerted action would be necessary; if the French were simply told that the United States and Britain held the same opinions, would that not deter them? Both nations would also disavow any intention of obtaining territories for themselves. Four days later, Canning wrote Rush, "nothing would be more gratifying to me than to join you in such a work, and I am persuaded, there has seldom, in the history of the world, occurred an opportunity, when so small an effort of two friendly Governments, might produce so unequivocal a good and prevent such extensive calamities."[38] Rush was admirably cool. One of the most able diplomats of his generation, Rush told Canning that he lacked instructions to conclude such an agreement; nevertheless, if the foreign secretary agreed to recognize the independence of the new Latin republics, Rush would initial such a joint statement without specific authorization. A cautious Canning talked vaguely of future recognition, so Rush referred the matter to Washington.

Rush's dispatch arrived in early October and sparked one of the most momentous discussions in American history. Monroe sought the advice of Thomas Jefferson and James Madison. These two elder Virginians agreed with the President that the British proposal should be accepted. Jefferson's reply recalled memories of 1803, when the French seemed ready to take New Orleans. "Great Britain," he wrote, "is the nation which can do us the most harm of any one, or all on earth; and with her on our side we need not fear the whole world."[39] Madison also counseled that "with British cooperation we have nothing to fear from the rest of Europe."[40] Madison even suggested a joint statement with the British on behalf of Greek independence. Armed with these opinions, Monroe called a Cabinet meeting on November 7, fully prepared to embrace British cooperation.

John Quincy Adams, however, fought vigorously for a unilateral course. Adams did not trust the British. Hoping to compete successfully for Latin American markets, and not wanting to tie American hands in some future acquisition of, say, Texas or Cuba, the secretary of state argued that it would be more dignified and candid to make an independent declaration of principles to the Holy Alliance than "to come in as a cockboat in the wake of the British man-of-war."[41] In this and subsequent meetings Adams gradually won Monroe over. Complications arose when another dispatch from Rush reported that Canning had mysteriously lost interest in a joint declaration. (Rush did not know that Canning, on October 9, had made an agreement with the French, the so-called Polignac Memorandum, whereby the French "abjured any design" of acting against the former Spanish colonies in Latin America.[42]) News also arrived of the French capture of Cadiz, along with rumors that a French fleet might soon embark for the New World. Secretary of War Calhoun was "perfectly moonstruck" by the French threat and, according to Adams, "has so affected the President that he appeared entirely to despair of the cause of South America." Adams remained optimistic. He pointed out the competing national interests within the Holy Alliance, noted England's stake in Latin America, and sarcastically told Calhoun that "I no more believe that the Holy Allies will restore the Spanish dominion on the American continent than that the Chimborazo will sink beneath the ocean."[43] Adams won his point, although President Monroe could never completely dismiss the possibility of European intervention.

The next step was the declaration. Monroe's original draft followed Adams' previous arguments in the Cabinet, but it also included a ringing indictment of the French intervention in Spain and a statement favoring the independence of revolutionary Greece. Adams opposed both points. However much he deplored events in Spain and Greece, the secretary of state advocated isolation from European embroilments. He urged the President "to make an American cause and adhere inflexibly to that."[44] The offending passages were excised. The now famous Monroe Doctrine thus became part of the President's message to Congress of December 2, 1823. It contained three essential points: noncolonization, "hands off" the New World, and American noninvolvement in European quarrels.

The first point, noncolonization, was aimed specifically at Russia, and was a response to an announcement by the Tsar in 1821 that Russian dominion extended southward from Alaska along the Pacific to the fifty-first parallel. Adams had opposed this aggrandizement in a note to the Russian minister in the summer of 1823, so Monroe simply reiterated the axiom that "the American continents, by the free and independent condition which they have assumed and maintain, are henceforth not to be considered as subjects for future colonization by any Euro-

**James Monroe (1758–1831).** Before becoming President in 1817, the distinguished Virginian served as secretary of state (1811–1817). Sharing John Quincy Adams' nationalist perspective, Monroe helped shape the doctrine against European intrusions into Latin America. (The Metropolitan Museum of Art, Bequest of Seth Low, 1929)

pean powers." By implication, the noncolonization principle applied to England and the Holy Alliance, as well as to Russia.

Monroe's second principle, "hands off," was revealed in a lengthy discussion of possible intervention by the Holy Allies. Positing the notion of two different worlds, he observed that the monarchical system of the Old World "is essentially different from that of America." Monroe warned that "any attempt" by the Holy Alliance to "extend their system to any portion of this hemisphere" would be regarded as "dangerous to our peace and safety." In convoluted but striking language, the President declared:

> With the existing colonies or dependencies of any European power we have not interfered and shall not interfere. But with the Governments who have declared their independence . . . we could not view any interposition for the purpose of oppressing them, or controlling in any other manner their destiny, by any European power in any other light than as the manifestation of an unfriendly disposition toward the United States.

As for the final principle, abstention, Monroe echoed Washington's Farewell Address: "In the wars of the European powers in matters relating to themselves we have never taken any part, nor does it comport with our policy to do so."[45]

An implicit corollary to the Monroe Doctrine, though not mentioned in the address, was the principle of "no transfer." Earlier that same year, in response to reports that Britain might try to negotiate the cession of Cuba from Spain, Adams had informed both Spain and the Cubans that the United States opposed British annexation. "Cuba," Adams wrote in April, 1823, "forcibly disjoined from its own unnatural connection with Spain, and incapable of self-support, can only gravitate towards the North American Union, which by the same law of nature cannot cast her off from its bosom."[46] Thus, when read in the context of Adams' concern with Cuba, the noncolonization principle in the Monroe Doctrine also warned Spain against transferring its colony to England or to any other European power.

The immediate effect of the pronouncement was hardly earthshaking. Brave words, after all, would not prevent the dismemberment of Latin America. The Polignac Memorandum and the British Navy actually took care of such a contingency. The Holy Allies sniffed in contempt, calling Monroe's principles "haughty," "arrogant," "blustering," and "monstrous." Metternich ignored the "indecent declarations," as did the Tsar, who thought "the document in question . . . merits only the most profound contempt."[47] Canning was pleased at first, but soon realized that Monroe and Adams might steal his thunder and turn Latin gratitude into Yankee trade opportunities. Canning thereupon rushed copies of the Polignac Memorandum to Latin American capitals, where it was quickly learned that England, not the upstart Americans, had warned off the Holy Allies. Latin Americans at first received the Monroe Doctrine cordially. When Washington refused to negotiate military alliances with Colombia and Brazil, however, disillusionment quickly set in.

At home the response was enthusiastic. "The explicit and manly tone," reported the British chargé, "has evidently found in every bosom a chord which vibrates in strict unison with the sentiments so conveyed. It would, indeed, be difficult . . . to find a more perfect unanimity."[48] Such unanimous response derived from the anti-British, anti-European thrust of Monroe's warning. As Adams knew, it was fortunate that the United States did not have to back up words with deeds. The irony of Monroe's message, despite its anti-imperialist intent, was that later generations remembered the words in ways that justified American expansion in the name of hemispheric solidarity and republican principles. It was one thing to defend one's own territory, even to expand at the expense of Spaniards and Indians in North America, quite another to guarantee republican governments in other countries, including Latin America. The Boston *Advertiser* seemed a lone prophetic voice in 1823: "Is there anything in the Constitution which makes our Government the Guarantors of the Liberties of the World? Of the Wahabees? The Peruvians? The Chilese? The Mexicans or Colombians?"[49]

## Anglo-American Accommodations and Tensions

In the decades following the Monroe Doctrine, because of commercial rivalry in Latin America, squabbles over West Indian trade, political troubles in Canada, boundary disputes, and British attempts to suppress the international slave trade, most Americans continued to regard Britain as *the* principal threat to the national interest. As co-occupant of the North American continent, the strongest naval power in the world, and a commercial giant, only England could block American expansion.

Fortunately, just as in the 1790s, the intertwining of the two economies helped to countervail any impulse toward war. In 1825, for example, the United States exported $37 million in goods to England, out of total exports valued at $91 million; by 1836 the figures rose to $58 million and $124 million; in 1839 they stood at $57 million and $112 million. As for imports, the United States bought $37 million in goods from Britain in 1825, out of total imports of $90 million. In 1840 the figures were $33 million and $98 million. Imports from Britain during this period fluctuated between one-half and one-third of total American imports. While Britain was less dependent on the United States, its trade with America was still highly significant, especially as the burgeoning British textile industry came to depend on American cotton. In 1825, 18 percent of total British exports went to the United States; in 1840, 10 percent. In those same years England received 13 percent and 27 percent of her total imports from America. These figures, combined with the British decision in 1830 to open the West Indies to direct trade with the United States, reflected a growing British trend toward free trade, which in the 1840s resulted in the dismantling of imperial preference, repeal of the Corn Laws, and concentration on manufactured exports. American grain exports to England would grow considerably in the 1850s and 1860s. This economic interdependence, while hardly a guarantee against war, certainly acted as a brake against military hostilities. At the same time, expanding foreign trade created an intense commercial rivalry.

Ironically, the years immediately following the War of 1812 marked a high point in Anglo-American relations, thanks largely to the conciliatory diplomacy of John Quincy Adams and Lord Castlereagh. After signing the Treaty of Ghent, Adams, Albert Gallatin, and Henry Clay went directly to London and negotiated a commercial treaty with the British Board of Trade in 1815. It was a simple reciprocal trade agreement that repeated the terms of Jay's Treaty with respect to commercial intercourse between America and Great Britain. The British West Indies remained closed to American ships. The treaty also forbade discriminatory duties by either country against the ships or commerce of the other, thus tacitly conceding the failure of Jefferson's earlier attempts at "peaceable coercions." Nothing was said about impressment or neutral rights. This commercial convention was renewed in 1818 for ten more years.

War's end also found the British and Americans engaged in feverish warship construction on the Great Lakes, the beginnings of a naval race that neither London nor Washington could afford. Concerned about postwar finances and confident that the United States could build vessels quickly in a crisis, the Monroe Administration proposed a standstill agreement to the British. Much to the disappointment of the Canadians, Castlereagh agreed. By the Rush-Bagot agreement, negotiated in Washington in April, 1817, each country pledged to maintain not more than one armed ship on Lake Champlain, another on Lake Ontario, and two on all the other Great Lakes. The Rush-Bagot accord applied only to warships and left land fortifications intact. Not until the Treaty of Washington in 1871 did relations between Canada and the United States become amicable enough for the myth of the "unguarded frontier" to become reality.

The Convention of 1818, negotiated in London by Richard Rush and Albert Gallatin, dealt with the fisheries and the northwestern boundary. In an effort to settle the vaguely defined limits of the Louisiana Purchase, the Americans initially proposed to extend the Canadian-American boundary westward from the Lake of the Woods to the Pacific Ocean along the line of 49 degrees north latitude. Because Britain refused to abandon its claims to the Columbia River Basin, the convention stipulated that the boundary should run from Lake of the Woods to the "Stony Mountains" along the forty-ninth parallel. Beyond the Rockies, for a period of ten years, subject to renewal, the Oregon territory should remain "free and open" to both British and American citizens. As for the vexatious matter of the Atlantic fisheries, Gallatin and Rush won confirmation of the "liberty" to fish "for ever" along specific stretches of the Newfoundland and Labrador coasts, as well as to dry and cure fish along less extensive areas of the same coastline. Although the phrasing was vague enough to cause controversy in later decades, Secretary John Quincy Adams accepted the agreement as vindication of his family's honor. Not for nothing was the motto on the Adams family seal *Piscemur, venemur ut olim* ("We will fish and hunt as heretofore").

The fisheries question, one should hasten to add, was not definitively settled until 1910 in an arbitration before the Hague Court. Technically, the issue was probably the most complicated in nineteenth-century American diplomatic history. According to a story at Harvard University, the humorist Robert Benchley was once forced to answer an examination question on the North Atlantic fisheries in a course on American foreign policy. Benchley knew nothing about the fisheries. Undaunted, he wrote: "This question has long been discussed from the American and British points of view, but has anyone considered the viewpoint of the fish?"[50] Benchley proceeded to analyze the codfish question and was awarded, appropriately enough, the grade of "C".

Following Castlereagh's death in 1822 and the cautious fencing that characterized the unilateral announcement of the Monroe Doctrine, George Canning hoped to avoid unnecessary friction with Washington. "Let us hasten settlement, if we can," he wrote, "but let us postpone the day of difference, if it must come; which however I trust it need not."[51] Then a series of crises disrupted relations in the

1830s. Most important was the Canadian rebellion of 1837, led by William Lyon Mackenzie. Many American volunteers joined the tumult. Coming a year after the Texas war for independence, the Canadian rebellion revived expansionist visions of 1812, particularly in areas along the Canadian-American border. Rensselaer Van Rensselaer, the drunken son of an American general, tried to become a Canadian version of Sam Houston, leading a motley group of Canadian patriots and American sympathizers on raids into Canada from New York. It was after one of these forays that Canadian soldiers, on December 29, 1837, struck Van Rensselaer's stronghold on Navy Island in the Niagara River, hoping to capture the rebel supply ship *Caroline.* The troops crossed to the American shore, found the 45-ton *Caroline,* set her afire, and cast her adrift to sink a short distance above the great falls. During the fracas an American, one Amos Durfee, was killed. Outrage gripped Americans along the border. Durfee's body was displayed before 3,000 mourners on the porch of the Buffalo city hall. The good citizens of Lewiston, New York made a bonfire of books by British authors. In May of 1838 some Americans boarded the Canadian steamboat *Sir Robert Peel,* plying the St. Lawrence River. They burned and looted the vessel, all the while shouting "Remember the Caroline!" Raids and counterraids continued through 1838. Fortunately, the authorities in Washington maintained their equilibrium. President Martin Van Buren warned Americans against joining the rebellion and sent General Winfield Scott to the New York-Ontario border to restore quiet. Scott brooked no nonsense. "Except if it be over my body," he shouted to an unruly crowd, "you shall not pass this line—you shall not embark."[52] When Mackenzie and Van Rensselaer fled to the American border, they were quickly arrested, and the rebellion petered out.

A new crisis flared up in February, 1839 in northern Maine. The vast timberlands spanning the Maine–New Brunswick border had long been a subject of diplomatic dispute because of cartographic errors contained in the 1783 peace treaty. The matter had not seemed urgent until the mid-1830s, when the discovery of fertile soil in the Aroostook Valley brought an influx of settlers, rival claims, and occasional brawls. Soon axe-wielding lumberjacks were embroiled in the bizarre "Aroostook War." Maine mobilized its militia that winter, as did New Brunswick, and Congress appropriated some $10 million for defense. It seemed an opportunity to whip the "Warriors of Waterloo."[53] As the "Maine Battle Song" had it:[54]

> Britannia shall not rule the Maine,
> Nor shall she rule the water;
> They've sung that song full long enough,
> Much longer than they oughter.

The "war" did not last long. General Scott again rushed to the scene, and after a few tense weeks the British minister and Secretary of State John Forsyth negotiated a temporary armistice pending a final boundary settlement. The only American death in the affair occurred at the very end when a Maine militiaman accidentally killed a comrade while firing his musket in celebration of peace.

Any possibility that the *Caroline* affair would be forgotten soon disappeared in November, 1840, when a Canadian named Alexander McLeod bragged in a Utica, New York saloon that he had personally killed Amos Durfee. McLeod was quickly arrested and charged with murder and arson. While this development brought huzzas from Americans remembering the *Caroline,* it aroused apoplectic roars from the British Foreign Secretary Lord Palmerston, who let it be known that McLeod's execution "would produce war, war immediate and frightful in its character, because it would be a war of retaliation and vengeance."[55] Daniel Webster was then secretary of state and anxious to avoid trouble, but the federal government did not have jurisdiction in the case. Fortunately for Anglo-American amity, McLeod told a different story sober than he had while drunk, the jury believed him, and he was acquitted.

Within a month of McLeod's acquittal, however, another crisis erupted. In November, 1841, a cargo of slaves being transported from Hampton Roads to New Orleans mutinied and took control of the American vessel *Creole*, killing one white man in the process. The slaves sought refuge at Nassau in the Bahamas, where British authorities liberated all but the actual murderers. Southerners were incensed. This was not the first time the British had refused to return escaped slaves. Moreover, the British efforts to suppress the international slave trade were constantly hampered by the unwillingness of the United States to allow its ships to be searched. This refusal to permit search stemmed in part from memories of impressment, but to the British, Uncle Sam was a crude and brutal defender of the inhumane traffic in human souls.

Thus, as the year 1842 approached, Anglo-American relations were beset with troubles. The northeastern boundary remained in contest. Britain had not apologized for the *Caroline* affair. There were rumblings over British interest in Oregon and Texas. Americans disliked British snobbery. British visitors, most notably Charles Dickens, wrote scathingly of American manners and morals. Britons were incensed over America's inadequate copyright laws. But the time seemed ripe for the settlement of many of these issues. A new Tory government took office in September, 1841, and Lord Aberdeen, a conciliatory man who had been a protégé of Castlereagh, replaced the cantankerous Palmerston at the Foreign Office. Aberdeen appointed as the new British minister to Washington the equally conciliatory Lord Ashburton. Ashburton, only recently retired from the great financial house of Baring Brothers, had married an American, and it was said that he was so friendly to the United States that he had openly supported the American side during the War of 1812. Ashburton's fellow negotiator, beetle-browed Daniel Webster, reciprocated the Briton's amicability. He had known Ashburton for years. Indeed, despite service in Congress, Webster had been for many years the American legal agent for the Baring firm, often earning several times his government salary through British commissions. Three years earlier the "godlike Daniel," an erudite and eloquent orator then at the peak of his political career, had toured England and was lionized as few American visitors were. Nothing would have pleased Webster more than to be appointed minister to the Court of St. James's. If he could negotiate a reasonable compromise with Ashburton, both countries (and Webster) might profit. The two men therefore met leisurely for several weeks in the summer of 1842. There was little interchange of diplomatic notes, but much consumption of good food and drink. The result was the Webster-Ashburton Treaty, signed and approved in August, 1842.

The Anglo-American agreement drew a new Maine boundary. Far enough south not to block a military road the British wanted to build between New Brunswick and Quebec, the border was still considerably north of Britain's maximum demand. The United States received approximately 7,000 of the 12,000 square miles under dispute, although this was some 893 square miles less than had been awarded by the King of the Netherlands in 1831 in his abortive attempt to arbitrate the controversy. Farther west Webster won most of the disputed territory near the headwaters of the Connecticut River, as well as a favorable boundary from Lake Superior to the Lake of the Woods. Included in the latter award, but largely unbeknownst at the time to the negotiators, was the valuable iron ore of the Mesabi Range in Minnesota. Although not part of the treaty per se, two inconclusive notes on the *Creole* and *Caroline* affairs were exchanged, burying the issues.

Characterized by compromise and cordial personal relations, Webster's discussions with Ashburton were simple compared to his diplomacy with Maine and Massachusetts. The Bay State had retained half ownership in Maine's public domain after the latter had become a separate state in 1820, and so Webster had to persuade both states to approve the new boundary with Canada. For this difficult task, the secretary of state resorted to a bit of skullduggery. One of Webster's friends was Jared Sparks, an historian and scholar who later became president of Harvard. Sparks had been researching the diplomacy of the American Revolution in British and French archives, and he told Webster that he had seen the original map on which Benjamin Franklin had drawn a strong red line delineating the northeast boundary. Sparks reproduced such a line from memory on a nineteenth-century map, and it corresponded closely to British claims. A second map turned up, older but still not genuine, also supporting the British position. Webster thereupon sent Sparks with these two spurious maps to persuade officials in Boston and Augusta to accept the treaty before the British could discover the incriminating evidence and back out of their bargain. Webster also agreed to pay each state $150,000. Maine and Massachusetts then endorsed the Webster-Ashburton Treaty. In point of fact, the original maps used in the 1783 peace negotiations (four copies were later discovered) actually supported the American boundary claims. The British had found one of the maps in 1839, but said nothing. With a little effort Webster could have acquired an accurate map; indeed, one turned up in the Jay family papers in 1843. Instead, it seems that 3,207,680 acres of piny woodland that belonged to the United States became a part of Canada.

## Contest over Oregon

The Webster-Ashburton negotiations did not settle the question of Oregon. Webster proposed yielding Oregon north of the Columbia, if the British in return would persuade Mexico to sell California. Ashburton declined. That same year, 1842, saw the beginning of "Oregon fever," as farmers by the hundreds began to arrive in the lush valley of the Willamette River. Oregon suddenly became controversial. In 1843 the Senate passed a bill calling for the construction of forts along the Oregon route, but the House demurred. When rumors leaked of Webster's offer to surrender the territory north of the Columbia, numerous "Oregon conventions" met, especially in the Midwest, to reassert America's claim to 54° 40'. When Secretary of State John C. Calhoun again proposed to the British, in 1844, that Oregon be divided at the forty-ninth parallel, this too was considered betrayal by the vociferous expansionists. The Democratic platform in 1844 called for the "reoccupation" of Oregon, and "Fifty-four forty or fight" seemed more than a hollow slogan.

In actuality, war over Oregon was not as close as it appeared. The American population in Oregon, while increasing every year, still numbered only 5,000 persons in 1845, and all but a handful lived south of the Columbia River. In contrast, the 700-odd trappers and traders associated with the Hudson's Bay Company all lived north of the river. Four times, in 1818, 1824, 1826, and 1844, the British had proposed the Columbia as the boundary. Each time the United States had countered with 49 degrees. The dispute, by any dispassionate analysis, centered on the triangle northwest of the Columbia, including the deep water Strait of Juan de Fuca. Notwithstanding shouts of "Fifty-four forty or fight" from such ultras as Benton, only a minority of the Democratic party, mainly midwesterners, were ready to challenge England. Southern Democrats cared more for Texas than Oregon. A few Whigs, like Webster, wanted Pacific ports, but not at the risk of war. Even though Polk had been elected on an expansionist platform, the new President had ample opportunity to settle the Oregon boundary through diplomacy.

Polk began badly. Bound by the Democratic platform to assert full American claims, he announced in his inaugural address (March 4, 1845) that the American title to the whole of Oregon was "clear and unquestionable."[56] This claim, coming in an official state paper, raised British hackles. Polk, it seems, was talking more for domestic consumption, for in July he had Secretary of State James Buchanan propose the forty-ninth parallel (including the southern tip of Vancouver Island) as a fair compromise. Buchanan explained that the President "found himself embarrassed, if not committed, by the acts of his predecessors."[57] Buchanan's offer, however, did not include free navigation of the Columbia River, and this omission, coupled with Polk's earlier blustering about 54° 40', unfortunately caused the British Minister, Richard Pakenham, to reject the proposal without referring it to London. Polk waited several weeks. Then, on August 30, after rejecting the advice of Buchanan—who wanted to temporize because of tensions with Mexico over Texas—the President withdrew his offer and reasserted American claims to 54° 40'.

Polk increased the pressure further in his annual message to Congress of December, 1845. Laying claim again to all of Oregon, Polk recommended giving Britain the necessary year's notice for ending joint occupation. This was a virtual ultimatum, and he hinted at military measures to protect Americans in Oregon. Polk also made specific reference to the Monroe Doctrine. "The United States," he said, "cannot in silence permit any European interference on the North American continent, and should any such interference be attempted [the United States] will be ready to resist it at any and all hazards."[58] Polk had Texas and California in mind, in addition to Oregon, but the "European" power being warned was clearly Britain.

For the next five months, while Congress debated the ending of joint occupation, Polk remained publicly adamant for 54° 40'. Twice the British offered to arbitrate; each time the United States refused. Privately, however, perhaps influenced by the growing likelihood of war with Mexico, Polk began to drop hints that the United States would resume negotiations if the British made a reasonable counterproposal. Lord Aberdeen sincerely wanted a settlement, but he could not afford to retreat in the face of Yankee braggadocio. Moving carefully, the foreign secretary already had begun a propaganda campaign in the London *Times* and other journals

**Thomas Hart Benton (1782–1858).** Bullnecked and belligerent, a Missouri senator from 1821 to 1851, this splashy orator championed westward expansion with seldom equaled intensity. He accepted the compromise boundary of the forty-ninth parallel for the Oregon Territory in 1846. (Sketch by Marshall Davis, American Heritage Collection)

designed to prepare public opinion for the loss of the Columbia River triangle. He was greatly aided in this effort when the Hudson's Bay Company, faced with the flood of American settlers into the Willamette Valley, decided in 1845 to abandon the "trapped-out" southern part of Oregon and move its main depot from Port Vancouver on the Columbia River north to Vancouver Island. Still, the British statesman told the United States government that he would no longer oppose offensive military preparations in Canada, including the immediate dispatch of "thirty sail of the line. . . ." When this news reached Washington in late February, 1846, Polk replied that if the British proposed "extending the boundary to the Pacific by the forty-ninth parallel and the Strait of Fuca," he would send the proposition to the Senate, "though with reluctance."[59]

The British proposal came on June 6, 1846, but because it guaranteed free navigation of the Columbia to the Hudson's Bay Company, Polk found it distasteful. Nevertheless, on the advice of his Cabinet, he decided on an unusual procedure. Before signing or rejecting the treaty, he submitted it to the Senate for *previous* advice. This procedure placed responsibility for the settlement squarely on the Senate and absolved Polk from his ignominious retreat from 54° 40'. On June 12, the Senate advised Polk, by a vote of 38 to 12, to accept the British offer. On June 15 the President formally signed the treaty, which the Senate then approved, 41–14, three days later. Of course, one major reason Polk and the Senate were so willing to compromise was the fact that war with Mexico had begun some six weeks earlier.

## Taking Texas

It was the acquisition of Texas that brought about the Mexican War. The United States had confirmed Spanish claims to this northernmost province of Mexico in the Adams-Onís Treaty of 1819, but the self-denial was only temporary. After Mexico won independence from Spain in 1821, two American ministers attempted to purchase the area. The first, South Carolinian Joel Poinsett, involved himself in local politics in the late 1820s and tried to work through friendly liberals in the Mexican Congress. His successor, Anthony ("What a scamp!") Butler, an unscrupulous crony of Andrew Jackson, tried bribery. Both efforts came to naught. As in the case of Oregon and Florida, transborder migration became the chief engine of American expansion.

Large-scale American settlement did not begin until the 1820s. Spanish authorities, in 1821, hoping to build up Texas as a buffer against American expansion, had foolishly encouraged immigration through generous grants of land. Moses Austin, a Connecticut Yankee from Missouri, and his son Stephen undertook to become the first "empressarios" by pledging to bring in 300 families, who, in turn, were required to swear an oath to defend the Spanish King and the Catholic faith. Successive Mexican governments after 1822 confirmed these grants and issued others. Within a decade more than 20,000 Americans had crossed into Texas seeking homesteads—more people than had settled in the previous three centuries. Most were God-fearing, hardworking farmers seeking the fertile delta soil along the Gulf Coast. In historian Marquis James's phrase, however, some crossed the Sabine "with schemes in their heads and guns in their hands—fleeing justice, fleecing Indians, gambling in land and promoting shooting scrapes called revolutions."[60]

Friction was inevitable. The newcomers, required by law to become Roman Catholics and Mexican citizens, were predominantly Protestants who never ceased to think of themselves as Americans. There was sporadic trouble over immigration, tariffs, slavery, and Mexican army garrisons. Finally, General Antonio Lopez de Santa Anna seized dictatorial power in 1834 and attempted to establish a strong centralized government in Mexico City. Regarding this as a violation of their rights under the Mexican Constitution of 1824, Texans submitted a "Declaration of Causes" that resembled the "Declaration of Rights and Grievances" of 1775. By the autumn of 1835, Texans had skirmished with local Mexican soldiers, set up a provisional government, and begun raising an army under the leadership of Sam Houston.

Santa Anna responded by leading a huge force north across the Rio Grande. At the old Alamo mission in San Antonio, some 200 Texans stood off 5,000 Mexicans for nearly two weeks. Then, on March 6, 1836, with the Mexican bugles sounding "no quarter," Santa Anna's forces broke through the Alamo's defenses and killed every one of the resisters, including the legendary Davy Crockett and James Bowie. Three weeks later another Texan force, numbering some 400 recent volunteers from the United States, surrendered at Goliad. More than 300 were promptly shot. These atrocities enraged the North Americans and hundreds of volunteers flocked to Sam Houston's army, which continued to retreat eastward. The showdown came on April 21, 1836, when Houston's army, now numbering 800 men, turned and attacked the Mexican main force near the ferry of the San Jacinto River, not far from the present-day site of Houston, Texas. With a makeshift band playing the ballad "Will You Come to the Bower I Have Shaded for You," the Texans charged across an open field, yelling "Remember the Alamo," and routed the Mexicans, killing about 630. Taken by surprise when the Texans attacked during afternoon siesta, Santa Anna was found hiding in a clump of long grass, dressed in a blue shirt, white pants, and red carpet slippers. Instead of hanging Santa Anna from the nearest tree, Houston extracted a treaty from the Mexican leader that recognized Texas' independence and set a southern and western boundary at the Rio Grande. Mexico repudiated this agreement after Santa Anna's release, but for all practical purposes the battle of San Jacinto ensured Texas' independence.

Texas sought immediate annexation to the United States. Houston's good friend President Andrew Jackson certainly wanted Texas and had tried to purchase the territory from Mexico, but by 1836 Texas had become a hot potato politically. The problem was slavery. Even a fervent continentalist like John Quincy Adams was beginning to see that expansion westward meant the expansion of slavery as well as free institutions. The balance in 1836 stood at thirteen slave states and thirteen free states. No one ever accused Andrew Jackson of being a poor politician, and so "Old Hickory" tiptoed quietly. Not until the last days of his Administration, some eleven months after San Jacinto, did Jackson even recognize Texas' independence. Jackson's chosen successor, Martin Van Buren, also refused to consider annexation for fear of rousing abolitionist zealots. The annexation issue slumbered until 1843, when unpopular President John Tyler, having everything to gain and nothing to lose, seized upon Texas as a vehicle for lifting his political fortunes. Tyler successfully negotiated an annexation treaty with the Texans and submitted it to the Senate in April, 1844, just prior to the presidential nominating conventions.

Tyler, and later Polk, hoped to gain support for the absorption of Texas by playing on fears of British intrusion. Having recognized Texan independence in 1840, Britain had developed a clear interest in maintaining that independence. Motives in London were mixed. Paramount was the hope that an independent Texas would block American expansion, perhaps in time to serve as a balance in the classic European model. Further, Texas could offer an alternative supply of cotton for England's textile factories. A low-tariff Lone Star Republic might grow into a large British market and, by example, stimulate Southern states to push harder in Washington for tariff reduction. Certain Britishers also hoped that Texas might be persuaded to abolish slavery, an illusion that Texan leaders manipulated to gain British support against Mexico. Such help was forthcoming, as England in 1842 arranged a truce between Texas and Mexico. Later, in the spring of 1844, Lord Aberdeen toyed with the idea of an international agreement whereby Mexico would recognize Texas; and England, France, and, he hoped, the United States would guarantee the independence and existing borders of both Texas and Mexico. The scheme collapsed when Mexico stubbornly refused any dealings with Texas. Not until May, 1845, after a resolution for annexation had already passed the United States Congress, did Mexico agree to recognize Texas, but by then it was too late.

Those foreign maneuvers, however legal and aboveboard, alarmed American expansionists. By nurturing such anxieties, the Tyler Administration might have achieved annexation in 1844 had not Calhoun injudiciously boasted that annexation was "the most effectual, if not the only means of guarding against the threatened danger" of abolition under British tutelage.[61] Calhoun went on to defend slavery with pseudo-scientific arguments that offended the British far less than they antagonized abolitionists and free soilers in the North. Accordingly, when the Senate took its final vote on June 8, 1844, the tally was 35 to 16, a two-thirds majority *against* annexation. The hapless Tyler won neither the Whig nor Democratic nomination that summer.

Texas and annexation did, however, become a central feature of the 1844 presidential campaign. Nominating James K. Polk of Tennessee, a disciple of Jackson, the Democrats fervently embraced expansion. The party platform promised the "reoccupation of Oregon and the re-annexation of Texas," giving rise to the myth that somehow the United States once owned Texas and perhaps John Quincy Adams had given it back to Spain in 1819. The Whigs chose Henry Clay, who opposed taking Texas if it meant war. It was a fierce campaign, full of expansive oratory, and Texas loomed as the central issue. Polk won by a close margin: 1,337,000 to 1,299,000 in the popular vote and 170 to 105 in the electoral college. Although people at the time considered the Democratic victory a mandate for expansion, other factors, including an abolitionist third-party candidate who took key votes from Clay in the decisive state of New York, explain Polk's victory. Whatever the reasons for their choice, the voters, in one of the rare presidential elections in which foreign policy issues predominated, had elected the candidate who would bring war. If Clay had won in 1844, he almost certainly would have kept peace with Mexico.

Even before Polk took office, the annexationists acted. Unable to win a two-thirds Senate majority for a treaty, lame-duck Tyler suggested annexation by joint resolution (simple majorities of both houses). Opponents howled. Albert Gallatin called it "an undisguised usurpation of power," and John Quincy Adams grumbled about the "apoplexy of the Constitution."[62] But the annexationists had the votes—120–98 in the House, 27–25 in the Senate—and on March 1, 1845, three days before leaving office, Tyler signed the fateful measure. Five days later the Mexican minister in Washington asked for his passports and went home.

Polk did not inherit an inevitable conflict with Mexico. Rather, the President made decisions and carried them out in ways that exacerbated already existing tension and made war difficult to avoid. Mexico had stated unequivocally that it would sever diplomatic relations if Texas were annexed to the United States, but Polk compounded the problem by supporting Texas' flimsy claim to the Rio Grande as its southern and western boundary. Except for the treaty extracted from Santa Anna in 1836, the Nueces River had always stood as the accepted boundary, and during the nine years of Texas' independence no move had been made to occupy the disputed territory south of Corpus Christi. Nevertheless, during the negotiations to complete annexation in the summer of 1845, Polk's emissaries apparently urged Texas President Anson Jones to seize all territory to the Rio Grande. Polk's orders to American military and naval forces, though couched in defensive terms, were aimed at preventing any Mexican retaliation. At this time, too, the President sent secret orders to Commodore John D. Sloat, commander of the Pacific Squadron, to capture the main ports of California in the event that Mexico attacked Texas. Whether Polk actively sought to provoke war, or was merely using force to buttress diplomacy, he was making unilateral decisions that disregarded Mexican sensibilities and ignored congressional prerogatives.

When Mexico failed to retaliate, Polk again turned to diplomacy. He had received word from the American consul in Mexico City that the government, while furious at annexation, was unprepared for war and would receive a special emissary to discuss Texas. Polk sent John Slidell, a Louisiana Democrat, as a full Minister Plenipotentiary empowered to re-establish formal relations and to negotiate on issues other than Texas. California now loomed large in Polk's mind, even larger than Texas. No sooner had the President instructed Slidell to purchase New Mexico and California for $25 million (Slidell could go as high as $40 million) than a report arrived from Consul Thomas Larkin in Monterey describing in lurid terms British machinations to turn California into a protectorate. Since Polk had no way of knowing that Larkin was reporting false rumors and exaggerating local British activities, this information only increased his resolve to obtain California. He ordered Larkin to propagandize among the Californians for annexation to the United States and for resistance against the British. Similar orders went to Lieutenant John C. Frémont, head of a United States Army exploring party in eastern California. Frémont, the son-in-law of expansionist Senator Thomas Hart Benton, interpreted his instructions as a command to foment insurrection among American settlers, and this he proceeded to do in the summer of 1846.

Slidell's mission, meanwhile, was a complete failure. When he reached Mexico City in early December, 1845, officials refused to receive him because, they said, his title of Minister Plenipotentiary suggested prior acceptance of Texas' annexation. Actually, even if Slidell had made the monetary offer for California, no Mexican government would sell territory to the United States in the highly charged atmosphere of 1845–1846. Too many Mexicans remembered the bizarre incident in 1842, when Commodore Thomas ap Catesby Jones, mistakenly believing that war had broken out, sailed into Monterey harbor and forced the astonished authorities to surrender. Jones discovered his error, apologized, and sailed away, leaving the Mexicans understandably angry. Any offer to purchase California, coming so closely on the heels of Texas' annexation, was out of the question. War seemed preferable. Some Mexican leaders thought that their large professional army stood an excellent chance of beating the corrupt, land-grabbing Yankees. "Depend upon it," Slidell arrogantly reported, "we can never get along well with them, until we have given them a good drubbing."[63]

Polk responded on January 13, 1846, as we have seen, by ordering General Taylor to move south from Corpus Christi and occupy the left bank of the Rio Grande. Even though Polk initially regarded this action as added pressure on Mexico to negotiate, Mexicans interpreted it as heralding a war of aggression. Taylor blockaded Matamoros, itself an act of war under international law. The Mexicans retaliated. The first clash occurred on April 24, and Polk was able to present Congress with a fait accompli.

## Wartime Diplomacy and the Peace

Polk never wanted a long war. California and the Rio Grande boundary were his principal objectives, and he was willing to explore diplomatic alternatives. Shortly after hostilities broke out, the President was approached by an emissary of Santa Anna, then living in exile in Havana. The former dictator promised Polk that if the United States helped him to return to Mexico he would undertake to give Polk the territory he desired. Terms were worked out, and in August, 1846 Santa Anna was permitted to slip through the American naval blockade and land at Veracruz. A revolution conveniently occurred in Mexico City and Santa Anna was named President. Instead of making peace, however, the self-proclaimed Napoleon of the West organized an army and marched north to fight General Taylor. More than a year passed before Polk understood that he had been doublecrossed. As late as General Scott's campaign to capture Mexico City in the autumn of 1847, Polk was still hoping to bribe Santa Anna into a settlement. The wily Mexican took the money, but kept fighting.

An even more bizarre diplomatic opportunity presented itself in November, 1846 in the persons of Moses Y. Beach and Jane McManus Storms. Beach, the Democratic editor of the *New York Sun* and a chief drum-beater for Manifest Destiny, had contacts in the Mexican army and the Catholic hierarchy in Mexico City. He suggested to Polk that he be sent as a confidential agent to Mexico, empowered to negotiate a suitable peace which would include, in addition to Texas and California, the right to build a canal across the Isthmus of Tehuantepec. Polk agreed, thinking that it would be a "good joke" if Beach were to succeed.[64] Beach then journeyed to Veracruz and Mexico City, accompanied by Mrs. Storms, a beautiful and adventuresome journalist whose greatest notoriety had come some twelve years before when she was named co-respondent in the divorce trial of seventy-seven-year-old Aaron Burr. Once in the Mexican capital, the two Americans rashly joined a clerical uprising against Santa Anna, only to have the dictator suddenly arrive on the scene, claiming to have beaten back Taylor's army at Buena Vista. The revolution collapsed, along with hopes for a quick peace. Beach and Storms fled.

The President finally decided in the spring of 1847 to send an accredited State Department representative along with Scott's army. At first he thought of Secretary Buchanan, but negotiations might take months and such an important Cabinet member could not be spared. He settled on Nicholas P. Trist, the chief clerk of the State Department, a man of impeccable Democratic credentials (he had once been Andrew Jackson's private secretary and had married a granddaughter of Thomas Jefferson). Trist, Polk thought, could be easily managed and would keep a watchful eye on the politically ambitious Scott, a Whig. The President immediately regretted his choice. In May Trist reached the American Army, then marching toward the plain of Central Mexico. He soon quarrelled furiously with General Scott, who resented Trist's power to decide when hostilities should cease. The two men did not speak to one another for six weeks, communicating only through vituperative letters, some up to thirty pages in length. Then Trist fell ill, and Scott chivalrously sent a special jar of guava marmalade to speed his recovery. Overnight the two prickly prima donnas resolved to work together.

By this time, September, 1847, Scott's troops had battered their way to Mexico City, and the diplomat and warrior were trying to conclude peace with any Mexican faction that would treat. Polk, suspicious at the political implications of the Scott-Trist entente and angry that Trist had forwarded to Washington a Mexican peace proposal that still insisted on the Nueces as the Texas boundary, summarily recalled his unruly representative. The President now seemed in no hurry to conclude peace. Military successes had made it possible to obtain more

**Americans Enter Mexico City, 1847.** General Winfield Scott triumphantly parades in the plaza as an American flag flies over the palace at the right. One Mexican, at the left with stone in hand, did not appreciate the ceremonies. (Library of Congress)

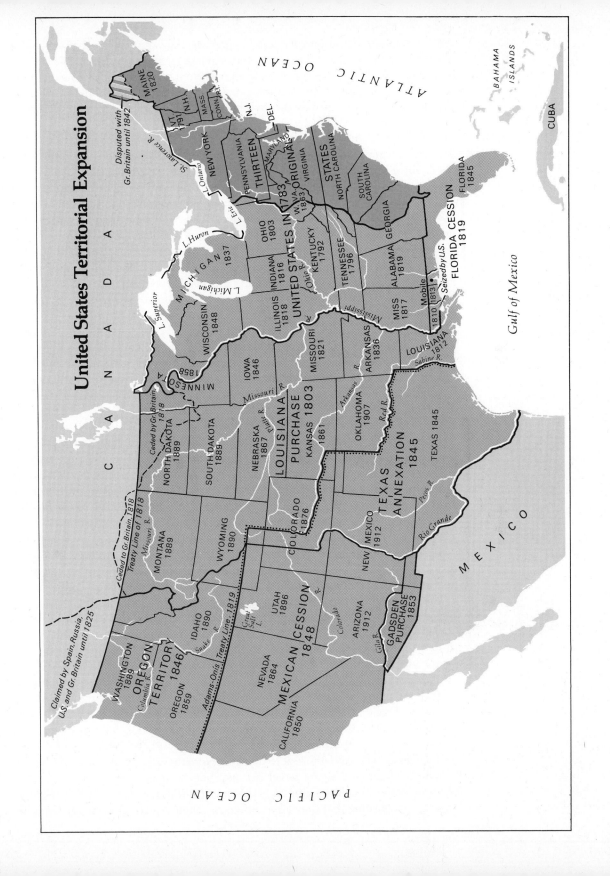

# United States Territorial Expansion

**ATLANTIC OCEAN**

**PACIFIC OCEAN**

**Gulf of Mexico**

**CANADA**

**MEXICO**

*BAHAMA ISLANDS*

*CUBA*

Disputed with Gr. Britain until 1842

MAINE 1820

VT. 1791

N.H.

MASS.

CONN. R.I.

NEW YORK

N.J.

DEL.

PENNSYLVANIA

MARYLAND

THIRTEEN

W. VA. 1863

VIRGINIA

UNITED STATES IN 1783

ORIGINAL

STATES

NORTH CAROLINA

SOUTH CAROLINA

GEORGIA

FLORIDA CESSION 1819

FLORIDA 1845

St. Lawrence R.

L. Ontario

L. Erie

L. Huron

L. Superior

L. Michigan

MICHIGAN 1837

OHIO 1803

Ohio R.

KENTUCKY 1792

TENNESSEE 1796

ALABAMA 1819

Mobile 1813

Seized by U.S. 1810

WISCONSIN 1848

ILLINOIS 1818

INDIANA 1816

Mississippi R.

MISS 1817

MINNESOTA 1858

IOWA 1846

Missouri R.

MISSOURI 1821

ARKANSAS 1836

LOUISIANA 1812

Sabine R.

Ceded by Gr. Britain 1818

Ceded by Gr. Britain 1818

Treaty Line of 1818

NORTH DAKOTA 1889

SOUTH DAKOTA 1889

NEBRASKA 1867

Platte R.

LOUISIANA PURCHASE 1803

KANSAS 1861

OKLAHOMA 1907

Arkansas R.

Red R.

TEXAS 1845

TEXAS ANNEXATION 1845

Ceded to Gr. Britain 1818

Treaty Line of 1818

MONTANA 1889

Missouri R.

WYOMING 1890

COLORADO 1876

NEW MEXICO 1912

Pecos R.

Rio Grande

Claimed by Spain, Russia, U.S. and Gr. Britain until 1825

WASHINGTON 1889

OREGON TERRITORY 1846

Columbia R.

IDAHO 1890

Snake R.

Treaty Line 1819

Adams-Onis Treaty Line 1819

UTAH 1896

Great Salt L.

MEXICAN CESSION 1848

ARIZONA 1912

Colorado R.

Gila R.

GADSDEN PURCHASE 1853

OREGON 1859

NEVADA 1864

CALIFORNIA 1850

territory than he had originally sought—perhaps Lower as well as Upper California, the Isthmus of Tehuantepec, and the provinces north of the Sierra Madre. Polk even contemplated the absorption of all Mexico. Lewis Cass, a Michigan Democrat, grandly declared: "To attempt to prevent the American people from taking possession of Mexico, if they demand it, would be as futile . . . as to undertake to stop the rushing of the cataract of Niagara."[65]

Nicholas Trist thereupon did an extraordinary thing. He refused to be recalled. Trist, as historian Frederick Merk has pointed out, was a true believer in the vision of Manifest Destiny, "confident that Mexico, left to herself, would someday enter the temple of freedom."[66] But such a process could not be forced. Reconciliation had to come first. Any peace that demanded too much would violate this canon. Even before he received his recall notice, Trist had begun negotiations with a moderate faction that had come to power. These Mexicans urged him to remain. Scott concurred. His mind made up, Trist informed Polk, in a bristling sixty-five-page letter, that he was continuing peace talks under his original instructions. Polk was apoplectic. "I have never in my life felt so indignant," he told his diary.[67]

In due course Trist negotiated his peace treaty, signed on February 2, 1848, at Guadalupe Hidalgo, near Mexico City. According to its terms Mexico ceded California and New Mexico to the United States and confirmed the annexation of Texas with the Rio Grande as the boundary. In return, the United States was to pay $15 million and assume the claims of American citizens totaling another $3.25 million. When the treaty arrived in Washington, the President reluctantly decided to submit it to the Senate, notwithstanding that "Mr. Trist has acted very badly." The territorial gains were all that Slidell had been empowered to obtain in his 1845–1846 mission. "If I were now to reject a treaty," Polk explained to the Cabinet, "made upon my own terms, as authorized in April last, with the unanimous approbation of the Cabinet, the probability is that Congress would not grant either men or money to prosecute the war."[68] The Whig-dominated Senate had just passed a resolution praising General Taylor's victories in "a war unnecessarily and unconstitutionally begun by the President of the United States." Congress had repeatedly voted men and supplies for the army, but Polk did not want to risk his gains. The treaty passed the Senate, 38 to 14, on March 10, 1848. A Whig critic cynically commented that the peace "negotiated by an unauthorized agent, with an unacknowledged government, submitted by an accidental President, to a dissatisfied Senate, has, notwithstanding these objections in form, been confirmed."[69]

The antiwar movement had made little impact. In Congress this opposition consisted largely of Whigs and Calhoun Democrats. The target of criticism at the outset was the questionable way in which Polk had begun the war, but it soon shifted to attempts to bar slavery from any territorial gains, and, finally, after Scott's victorious march to the Halls of Montezuma, opposition to any Administration effort to take "All Mexico." The Wilmot Proviso was the most ominous war protest. Attached as a rider to the war appropriation bill of August, 1846 by Democrat David Wilmot of Pennsylvania, the proviso held that none of the territory acquired from Mexico should be open to slavery. Its supporters were almost exclusively Northerners, and a coalition of Southern Whigs and Administration Democrats was sufficient to defeat it. Nonetheless, the Wilmot Proviso was introduced again and again, never passing, but sparking ever increasing debate, causing Southerners like Calhoun to despair of the Union. Polk struck back at his critics by suggesting that they were aiding the enemy, a stinging charge using the

**Ralph Waldo Emerson (1803–1882).** This talented writer and lecturer from Massachusetts was an outspoken critic of slavery and the Mexican War. Conquering Mexico, this abolitionist said, was like taking poisonous arsenic, because it exacerbated the issue of slave expansion and deeply divided the nation. (Harvard University Archives)

Constitution's definition of treason. Few critics chose to risk voting against military supplies. Americans believed that a war, right or wrong, which Congress had voted, must be upheld.

### The Lessons and Costs of Continental Expansion, 1815–1848

The United States acquired more than 500,000 square miles of territory in the war against Mexico, which young Congressman Abraham Lincoln labeled "a war of conquest."[70] This accession, combined with the Oregon settlement with England, completed the continental expansion of the 1840s. Polk did not obtain "All Mexico," nor did he fight for "Fifty-four forty," but he had taken what he wanted: Texas and California. The casualties: 1,721 Americans killed in battle and 11,550 deaths from other causes, mainly disease. About 50,000 Mexicans died.

The war brought other ugly consequences that could not be easily quantified. The arrogant rationalizations for expansion appalled an old Jeffersonian like Albert Gallatin, who noted in 1848: "All these allegations of superiority of race and destiny neither require nor deserve any answer; they are pretences [sic] . . . to disguise ambitions, cupidity, or silly vanity."[71] Ralph Waldo Emerson had pre-

**"The Trail of Tears."** Robert Lindneux's poignant painting of Indian removal illustrates one of the tragic consequences of American expansion. (From the original oil painting at Woolaroc Museum, Bartlesville, Oklahoma)

dicted in 1847 that the United States would gobble Mexican territory "as the man swallows arsenic, which brings him down in turn."[72] Indeed, debates over the Wilmot Proviso raised the all-important question whether the new territories would be free or slave. It took two more decades and a bloody civil war to answer the question. In fact, the issue of race in the 1850s blocked any possibility that the United States might acquire additional territories in the Caribbean or Pacific. Such potential prizes as Cuba or Hawaii had racially mixed populations, and thus seemed less adaptable to American settlers and institutions than did the lightly populated prairies of North America. Opponents of slavery became opponents of expansion.

The American Indian was another hidden victim of expansion. "Land enough—Land enough! Make way, I say, for the young American Buffalo!" shouted one fervent orator for Manifest Destiny in 1844.[73] It was the Indian who had to give way. While Americans in the 1820s and 1830s sought fertile lands in Texas and Oregon, other farmers were encroaching on Indian lands east of the Mississippi. Despite solemn treaty commitments, those years saw the removal of most of the tribes in the Old Northwest and Southwest to new reservations in

Missouri and Oklahoma. It was a brutal process—a "trail of tears." Indians were uprooted, forced to march thousands of miles, robbed by federal and state officials, ravaged by disease. Some tribes resisted, as evidenced by the Black Hawk War of 1832 and the guerrilla warfare waged by the Seminoles in the Everglades for nearly a decade. In the case of the Creeks, the population in 1860 was only 40 percent of what it had been 30 years earlier. Other tribes suffered similar losses. Native Americans beyond the Mississippi and Missouri rivers would feel the pinch of empire after 1848.

The costs of American expansion for Mexico were also easily overlooked at the time. The loser in a disastrous war, Mexico suffered 50,000 dead, relinquished more than half its national territory, and saw large amounts of real estate, food-stuffs, art treasures, and livestock destroyed by the invading armies. The American invaders treated Mexicans as they did the Indians—as racial inferiors. General John Quitman, temporarily the governor of Mexico City, called Mexico's 8,000,000 inhabitants "beasts of burden, with as little intellect as the asses whose burdens they share."[74] Then, too, Mexican politics, stormy since independence, grew even more tumultuous, and the country had to endure another 25 years of rebellion, civil war, and foreign intervention before a degree of national unity could be attained under the authoritarian regime of Porfirio Díaz. The war increased the disparity in size, power, and population between the United States and Mexico, thus creating a set of national attitudes that would bring mixed results in the twentieth century.

The success of continental expansion left one obvious imprint on the United States—that of increased power. To be sure, the Mexican War did not propel the United States into great power status; it would take another half-century, indus-trialization, and a war with Spain to achieve such ranking. Nonetheless, the nation had grown from a third-rate to a second-rate power, capable of challenging any of the European giants within its own hemisphere. The evolution of the Monroe Doctrine mirrored this growth. President Monroe had hurled his defiant message in 1823 without the power to enforce it. When Britain seized the Falkland Islands in 1833 and the French bombarded Mexican ports in 1838, American statesmen did nothing. In 1842, however, President Tyler specifically warned England and France against annexing Hawaii. Three years later Polk arrogantly invoked the Monroe Doctrine in proclaiming American rights to Texas, California, and Oregon. As American power continued to increase after 1848, as economic interests began to focus on the Caribbean and the possibility of an isthmian canal, American statesmen would also invoke the Monroe Doctrine. The same mixture of motive that operated in the 1820s would continue—namely, a genuine desire to forestall European intervention, combined with a wish to extend American influence, political and economic, throughout the hemisphere.

Few persons would deny that continental expansion served American interests. One opponent of the Mexican War suggested: "If just men should ever again come into power, I believe they ought not to hesitate to retrocede to Mexico the country of which we have most unjustly despoiled her."[75] Just or not, no American President has ever offered to return Mexican lands. The attitude of the Whig party was indicative. Approximately 90 percent of the Whigs in Congress in 1845 opposed territorial expansion. Once war with Mexico was declared, however, with Whig generals Scott and Taylor gaining popular laurels, Whigs voted for war supplies and eventually accepted the Treaty of Guadalupe Hidalgo. The commercial attractions of the Pacific Coast salved many Whig consciences. The real debate was not over the fact of continental expansion, but the way it was accomplished. The rhetoric of Manifest Destiny envisioned a peaceful extension of American institutions across the continent—yet war had occurred. Many still asked if it was necessary to resort to force.

Polk told one congressman in 1846 that "the only way to treat John Bull was to look him straight in the eye."[76] This was the diplomacy of eyeball-to-eyeball confrontation. Polk's resolute style seemed successful with both Britain and Mexico. The Tennessean's "lessons" for later American diplomats take on added importance when one considers his high reputation in the twentieth century. Theodore Roosevelt saw in Polk a model for reasserting strong executive leadership in foreign policy. In 1919 Justin H. Smith published his Pulitzer prize-winning history of the Mexican War, defending Polk at every turn. A poll of historians in the early 1960s ranked him eighth in importance among American Presidents, just ahead of Harry Truman.

In point of fact, Polk was probably lucky. Unlike John Quincy Adams, whose forceful diplomacy against Spain and the Holy Allies was based on a shrewd understanding of international power realities, Polk moved against Mexico and Britain without careful thought of consequences. Regarding Oregon, his initial call for 54° 40′ unnecessarily heightened jingo fevers on both sides of the Atlantic and postponed any settlement until the spring of 1846. In view of the concurrent crisis with Mexico, such a delay invited the disastrous possibility of a war on two fronts. Nor was England's decision to settle at the forty-ninth parallel the beneficent result of "looking John Bull straight in the eye." British conciliation was due more to troubles at home—the potato famine in Ireland, tensions with France, political turmoil over repeal of the Corn Laws. Aberdeen's sobering presence also helped. Had Palmerston become foreign secretary (as he very nearly did, in January, 1846), Polk's "eyeball" tactics might have meant war. Given the flood of American immigration into the Pacific Northwest in 1844–1846, Calhoun's policy of "masterly inactivity" would almost certainly have produced a favorable settlement without risking war. Polk apparently had not heard what Castlereagh said a generation earlier: "You need not trouble yourselves about Oregon, you will conquer Oregon in your bedchambers."[77]

"Masterly inactivity" might have worked with Mexico as well. Polk did not want war so much as he desired the fruits of war. He wanted California, New Mexico, and the Rio Grande boundary, and, suspicious of British intrigues, he was in a hurry. Slidell's offer to purchase the territory was genuine and, in Polk's narrow mind, generous, but it completely disregarded Mexican nationalist sensibilities. Keeping Taylor's army at Corpus Christi would have protected Texas with little provocation to Mexico. Negotiations could resume when tempers cooled. Whether Mexico would have ever released the territories is, of course, an open question. As for California, Polk should have understood, after a careful reading of all diplomatic correspondence, that England had no serious intention of seizing that lucrative prize. The obvious alternative was to wait, and see if the influx of American settlers would make California another Texas or Oregon. Annexation might have come peacefully—perhaps, as historian David Pletcher has suggested, during some subsequent European crisis like the Crimean War. As it turned out,

Polk's decision for war in the spring of 1846 was reckless, coming as it did while tensions with England were still acute. War risked all the expansionist goals. A major Mexican victory (and Santa Anna nearly won the battle of Buena Vista) might have brought a European loan to Mexico, military stalemate, and possible British mediation. California might have been lost. If Polk truly believed in Manifest Destiny, after all, it seems strange that he should have tried to hurry what Americans thought was inevitable. Because Polk ultimately succeeded in pushing American borders to the Pacific, however, the blemishes in his diplomatic record will probably continue to be covered with the cosmetic cream of national celebration.

## Further Reading for the Period 1815–1848

For studies of American expansion and Manifest Destiny in the nineteenth century, see William H. Goetzmann, *When the Eagle Screamed: The Romantic Horizon in American Diplomacy, 1800–1860* (1966), Norman A. Graebner, ed., *Manifest Destiny* (1968), Walter LaFeber, ed., *John Quincy Adams and American Continental Empire* (1965), Frederick Merk, *Manifest Destiny and Mission in American History* (1963) and *The Monroe Doctrine and American Expansionism, 1843–1849* (1966), Vincent Ponko, *Ships, Seas, and Scientists: U.S. Naval Exploration and Discovery in the Nineteenth Century* (1974), Geoffrey S. Smith, "Charles Wilkes and the Growth of American Naval Diplomacy," in Frank Merli and Theodore A. Wilson, eds., *Makers of American Diplomacy* (1974), William Stanton, *The Great United States Exploring Expedition of 1838–1842* (1975), Richard W. Van Alstyne, *The Rising American Empire* (1960), Charles Vevier, "American Continentalism: An Idea of Expansion, 1845–1910," *American Historical Review* (1960), and Albert Weinberg, *Manifest Destiny* (1935).

The acquisition of Florida, Latin American issues, and the formulation of the Monroe Doctrine are studied in Samuel Flagg Bemis, *John Quincy Adams and the Foundations of American Foreign Policy* (1949), Philip C. Brooks, *Diplomacy and the Borderlands: The Adams-Onís Treaty of 1819* (1939), George Dangerfield, *The Awakening of American Nationalism, 1815–1828* (1965) and *The Era of Good Feelings* (1952), Ernest May, *The Making of the Monroe Doctrine* (1975), Bradford Perkins, *Castlereagh and Adams* (1964), Dexter Perkins, *The Monroe Doctrine, 1823–1826* (1927) and *A History of the Monroe Doctrine* (1955), and Arthur P. Whitaker, *The United States and the Independence of Latin America 1800–1830* (1941).

Anglo-American crises, including the Oregon question, appear in Ray A. Billington, *The Far Western Frontier* (1956), Charles C. Campbell, *From Revolution to Rapprochement: The United States and Great Britain, 1783–1900* (1974), Norman A. Graebner, *Empire on the Pacific* (1955), Wilbur D. Jones, *Lord Aberdeen and the Americas* (1958) and *The American Problem in British Diplomacy, 1841–1861* (1974), and Frederick Merk, *Albert Gallatin and the Oregon Problem* (1950) and *The Oregon Question* (1967). Also see Howard Kushner, *Conflict on the Northwest Coast: American-Russian Rivalry in the Pacific Northwest, 1790–1867* (1975).

Texas and the Mexican War receive scrutiny in Ephraim D. Adams, *British Interests and Activities in Texas, 1838–1846* (1910), William C. Binkley, *The Texas Revolution* (1952), Gene Brack, *Mexico Views Manifest Destiny, 1821–1846* (1975), J. D. P. Fuller, *The Movement for the Acquisition of All Mexico, 1846–1848* (1936),

David M. Pletcher, *The Diplomacy of Annexation: Texas, Oregon, and the Mexican War* (1973), Glenn W. Price, *Origins of the War with Mexico: The Polk-Stockton Intrigue* (1967), John H. Schroeder, *Mr. Polk's War: American Opposition and Dissent, 1846–1848* (1973), and Charles G. Sellers, *James K. Polk: Continentalist, 1843–1846* (1966).

For representative essays on the coming of the Mexican War, see Archie P. McDonald, ed., *The Mexican War* (1969), and Ramon Ruiz, ed., *The Mexican War* (1963). Also see the list of works in Don E. Fehrenbacher, ed., *Manifest Destiny and the Coming of the Civil War, 1841–1860* (1970), and Norman A. Graebner, ed., *American Diplomatic History Before 1900* (1977). For short biographies use John A. Garraty, ed., *Encyclopedia of American Biography* (1974).

See also the following notes.

## Notes to Chapter 3

1. Quoted in David M. Pletcher, *The Diplomacy of Annexation: Texas, Oregon, and the Mexican War* (Columbia: University of Missouri Press, 1973), p. 377.

2. Milo M. Quaife, ed., *The Diary of James K. Polk, 1845–1849* (Chicago: A. C. McClurg, 1919; 4 vols.), I, 384.

3. *Ibid.*, I, 389–390.

4. James D. Richardson, ed., *A Compilation of the Messages and Papers of the Presidents, 1789–1897* (Washington: Government Printing Office, 1897–1900; 9 vols.), IV, 442.

5. Quoted in Frederick Merk, *Manifest Destiny and Mission in American History* (New York: Vintage Books, 1963), p. 90.

6. Quoted in Arthur M. Schlesinger, Jr., *The Imperial Presidency* (Boston: Houghton Mifflin, 1973), pp. 41–42.

7. Quoted in Charles F. Adams, ed., *Memoirs of John Quincy Adams* (Philadelphia: J. B. Lippincott & Company, 1874–1877; 12 vols.), II, 261.

8. Quoted in Marvin R. Zahniser, *Uncertain Friendship: American-French Relations Through the Cold War* (New York: John Wiley and Sons, 1975), p. 102.

9. Quoted in Arthur P. Whitaker, *The Western Hemisphere Idea: Its Rise and Decline* (Ithaca: Cornell University Press, 1954), p. 29.

10. Quoted in Frederick Merk, *Albert Gallatin and the Oregon Problem* (Cambridge: Harvard University Press, 1950), p. 13.

11. *Democratic Review*, XVII (July–August, 1845), 9.

12. *Ibid.*, p. 5.

13. Adams, *Memoirs of John Quincy Adams*, IV, 439.

14. *Congressional Globe*, 29 Cong., 1 Sess. (January 10, 1846), p. 180.

15. Quoted in Norman Graebner, ed., *Manifest Destiny* (Indianapolis: Bobbs-Merrill, 1968), p. lii.

16. Quoted *ibid.*, p. xxxvii.

17. *Congressional Globe*, 27 Cong., 3 Sess. (January 4, 1843), p. 139.

18. Quoted in William H. Goetzmann, *When the Eagle Screamed: The Romantic Horizon in American Diplomacy, 1800–1860* (New York: John Wiley & Sons, 1966), pp. xvii, 43.

19. Merk, *Gallatin and the Oregon Problem*, pp. 15–16.

20. John Paton Davies, *Dragon by the Tail* (New York: W. W. Norton, 1972), p. 70.

21. Geoffrey S. Smith, "Charles Wilkes and the Growth of American Naval Diplomacy," in Frank J. Merli and Theodore A. Wilson, eds., *Makers of American Diplomacy* (New York: Charles Scribner's Sons, 1974), p. 143.

22. Quoted in Norman A. Graebner, *Empire on the Pacific: A Study in American Continental Expansion* (New York: Ronald Press, 1955), p. 79.

23. Quoted in Sidney Lens, *The Forging of the American Empire* (New York: Thomas Y. Crowell, 1971), p. 121.

24. Fletcher Webster, ed., *The Private Correspondence of Daniel Webster* (Boston: Little, Brown, 1857; 2 vols.), II, 204.

25. Samuel Eliot Morison, *Maritime History of Massachusetts, 1783–1860* (Boston: Houghton Mifflin, 1923), p. 264.

26. Worthington C. Ford, ed., *The Writings of John Quincy Adams* (New York: Macmillan, 1913–1917; 7 vols.), VII, 167.

27. John S. Bassett, ed., *Correspondence of Andrew Jackson* (Washington: Carnegie Institution of Washington, 1926–35; 6 vols.), II, 346.

28. Quoted in Marquis James, *The Life of Andrew Jackson* (Indianapolis: Bobbs-Merrill, 1938; 2 vols. in one), p. 288.

29. Quoted in Samuel Flagg Bemis, *John Quincy Adams and the Foundations of American Foreign Policy* (New York: A. A. Knopf, 1949), p. 327.

30. George Dangerfield, *The Awakening of American Nationalism, 1815–1828* (New York: Harper and Row, 1965), p. 66.

31. Quoted in Graebner, *Manifest Destiny*, p. xxiv.

32. Quoted in Jacob K. Javits, *Who Makes War: The President Versus Congress* (New York: William Morrow, 1973), p. 74.

33. Richard Van Alstyne, *The Rising American Empire* (Chicago: Quadrangle Books, 1965), p. 99.

34. *Annals of Congress*, 15 Cong., 1 Sess. (March, 1818), II, 1482.

35. Adams, *Memoirs of John Quincy Adams*, V, 325.

36. Quoted in Charles K. Webster, *The Foreign Policy of Castlereagh: 1815–1822* (London: G. Bell and Sons, 1963), p. 295.

37. Quoted in Harold W. V. Temperley, *The Foreign Policy of Canning, 1822–1827* (London: G. Bell and Sons, 1925), pp. 380–381.

38. Quoted in Dangerfield, *Awakening of American Nationalism*, p. 177.

39. Paul L. Ford, ed., *The Works of Thomas Jefferson* (New York: G. P. Putnam's Sons, 1904–1905; 12 vols.), XII, 319.

40. *Letters and Other Writings of James Madison* (Philadelphia: J. B. Lippincott, 1865; 4 vols.), III, 339.

41. Quoted in Ernest A. May, *The Making of the Monroe Doctrine* (Cambridge, Mass.: Harvard University Press, 1975), p. 199.

42. Quoted in Dexter Perkins, *The Monroe Doctrine, 1823–1826* (Cambridge: Harvard University Press, 1927), p. 118.

43. Adams, *Memoirs of John Quincy Adams*, VI, 186.

44. *Ibid.*, VI, 198.

45. Richardson, ed., *Messages of the Presidents*, II, 209, 217–219.

46. Ford, *Writings of John Quincy Adams*, VI, 371–372.

47. Quoted in Perkins, *The Monroe Doctrine*, pp. 166–168.

48. Quoted in Charles K. Webster, ed., *Great Britain and the Independence of Latin America, 1812–1830* (London: Oxford University Press, 1938), II, 508.

49. Quoted in Perkins, *The Monroe Doctrine*, p. 146.

50. Quoted in Richard M. Dorson, *American Folklore* (Chicago: University of Chicago Press, 1959), pp. 256–257.

51. Quoted in Bradford Perkins, *Castlereagh and Adams: England and the United States, 1812–1823* (Berkeley: University of California Press, 1964), p. 346.

52. Quoted in Howard Jones, "The *Caroline* Affair," *The Historian*, XXXVIII (May, 1976), 498.

53. Quoted in Howard Jones, "Anglophobia and the Aroostook War," *New England Quarterly*, XLVII (December, 1975), 527.

54. Quoted in John F. Sprague, *The Northeastern Boundary Controversy and the Aroostook War* (Dover, Maine: The Observer Press, 1910), pp. 110–111.

55. Quoted in Charles S. Campbell, *From Revolution to Rapprochement: The United States and Great Britain, 1783–1900* (New York: John Wiley and Sons, 1974), pp. 56–57.

56. Richardson, ed., *Messages of the Presidents*, IV, 381.

57. Quoted in Campbell, *Revolution to Rapprochement*, p. 66.

58. Richardson, ed., *Messages of the Presidents*, IV, 398.

59. Quoted in Campbell, *From Revolution to Rapprochement*, p. 70.

60. Quoted in Lens, *Forging of American Empire*, p. 103.

61. Quoted in Charles M. Wiltse, *John C. Calhoun: Sectionalist, 1840–1850* (Indianapolis: Bobbs-Merrill, 1951), pp. 169–70.

62. Quoted in Schlesinger, *Imperial Presidency*, pp. 40–41.

63. Quoted in Charles G. Sellers, *James K. Polk: Continentalist, 1843–1846* (Princeton: Princeton University Press, 1966), p. 404.

64. Quaife, *Diary of James K. Polk*, II, 477.

65. *Congressional Globe*, 30 Cong., 1 Sess. (December 30, 1847), p. 79.

66. Merk, *Manifest Destiny and Mission*, p. 181.

67. Quaife, *Diary of James K. Polk*, III, 201.

68. *Ibid.*, III, 346–351.

69. Bayard Tuckerman, ed., *The Diary of Philip Hone, 1828–1851* (New York: Dodd, Mead, 1889; 2 vols.), II, 347.

70. Quoted in Ramon E. Ruiz, "A Commentary on Morality: Lincoln, Justin H. Smith, and the Mexican War," *Journal of the Illinois State Historical Society*, LXIX (February, 1976), 29.

71. Quoted in Reginald Horsman, "Scientific Racism and the American Indian in the Mid-Nineteenth Century," *American Quarterly*, XXVII (May, 1975), 168.

72. Quoted in John H. Schroeder, *Mr. Polk's War: American Opposition and Dissent, 1846–1848* (Madison: University of Wisconsin Press, 1973), p. 117.

73. Quoted in Albert K. Weinberg, *Manifest Destiny* (Baltimore: The Johns Hopkins University Press, 1935), p. 119.

74. Quoted in Blanche Wiesen Cook, "American Justification for Military Massacres from the Pequot War to Mylai," *Peace and Change*, III (Summer–Fall, 1975), 9.

75. Quoted in Schroeder, *Mr. Polk's War*, p. 159.

76. Quaife, *Diary of James K. Polk*, I, 155.

77. Quoted in Pletcher, *Diplomacy of Annexation*, p. 103.

**"Black Ship."** This smoke-belching, dragonlike steamship represented in the Japanese mind the threatening "black ships" Commodore Matthew Perry sailed into Tokyo Bay in 1853–1854. (Courtesy, The Mariner's Museum, Newport News, Virginia)

# 4 Sputtering Expansionism, Sectionalism, and Civil War Diplomacy, 1848–1865

## Diplomatic Crossroad: Commodore Perry's "Opening" of Japan, 1853–1854

On July 14, 1853, as the early morning sun burned the summer haze off the Bay of Yedo (Tokyo), Commodore Matthew C. Perry paid careful attention to combing his dark, curly hair. An unsmiling person with scowling, bushy eyebrows, Perry grew anxious as he pulled on his uncomfortable full dress uniform. On the beach, five to seven thousand Japanese troops awaited him. Perry armed every man in his landing party, including the forty musicians, with swords, pistols, or muskets. The flag bearer was sternly warned not to let the Japanese capture the American ensign. Perry had already positioned his ships across the bay with loaded guns aimed at surrounding forts. With all precautions taken and spirits running high, Perry, accompanied by fifteen launches and cutters, began the short journey in his official barge over smooth water to the shore. Dour as always, the commodore was nonetheless resplendent in gold braid, bright buttons, and ceremonial sword. All the trappings were "but for effect," he noted.[1]

For Perry, appearances counted. He came from a long line of successful naval officers. His older brother, Oliver Hazard Perry, had gained a national reputation during the War of 1812. Matthew was noted for spending hours grooming himself and surrounding himself with bodyguards, secretaries, and aides. An unrelenting disciplinarian, he thought lashings a proper punishment. On one occasion he slugged a sailor to make his point stick. "Old Bruin," like most seasoned officers, had wanted to command the prestigious and salubrious Mediterranean Squadron. In early 1852, however, he was ordered to command the distant East India Squadron. Disappointed but loyal, Perry took the command seriously. He was an expansionist, and expansion into Asia came logically on the heels of the victory over Mexico, the absorption of California, and the Oregon settlement. The Orient was nearer to America than ever before, and it seemed inevitable that Americans would penetrate it. "Our people must naturally be drawn into the contest for empire," Perry wrote in the spring of 1852.[2]

The fifty-seven-year-old officer's special assignment was the "opening" of Japan to Westerners. Washington sought trading and coaling ports and the protection of American sailors, often shipwrecked from whaling vessels. Congressional backing for the venture was stimulated by the New England whaling industry and by some American manufacturers. Perry read everything he could about Japan. Like most Americans, he thought the Japanese "a weak and semi-barbarous people" who might have to be "severely chastised" if they did not accede to American requests.[3] Except for a single port, Nagasaki, where the Dutch traded, few Westerners were welcome in a Japan governed by feudal lords bent on maintaining their isolation from "barbarian" whites. Herman Melville in *Moby Dick* called Japan the "double-bolted land."[4] American Commodore James Biddle had visited Japan in 1846 and had been rudely shoved by a Japanese official and his ship unceremoniously towed out to sea. Perry would tolerate no such indignities. Unlike Biddle, Perry would not permit Japanese "sightseers" aboard or Japanese guard boats around his ships.

Perry had a distinct psychological advantage. Two of his four warships were steam-powered, belching clouds of black smoke. The Japanese had never seen such vessels before, and when the two steamers appeared on the horizon, in July, 1853, the Japanese thought them afire, "a conflagration on the sea."[5] One feared that Japan was being invaded by "barbarians . . . in floating volcanoes."[6] For a week, in early July, the terrifying "black fleet" rested in the Bay of Yedo. The commodore, as if to illustrate his exalted importance, remained secluded on his flagship, the U.S.S. *Susquehanna,* allowing no Japanese on board. He sent word that he would meet only with the highest officials and threatened to sail directly to Tokyo. Also admirers of pomp and ceremony, the Japanese decided upon a polite and cool reception for the imposing American. On July 14, accompanied by a thirteen-gun salute, about four hundred armed personnel, two heavily armed black bodyguards, and a band playing "Hail, Columbia!" Perry landed from his barge and handed the Japanese officials a letter from President Millard Fillmore. "Our steamships can go from California to Japan in eighteen days," Fillmore boasted. "I am desirous that our two countries should trade with each other, for the benefit both of Japan and the United States." He told the Japanese to revise their laws to permit American trade and to treat shipwrecked American seamen "with kindness," adding, "we are very much in earnest in this." Finally, he asked for coaling stations for American ships. The Japanese sternly replied that the impertinent letter was received "in opposition to Japanese law" and that Perry could now "depart." Jilted and apparently deflated, Perry remarked that his fleet would leave in a few days. But, he warned, he would return next year for an answer to the President's letter. When asked if he would bring all four vessels, he replied, "all of them and probably more."[7] Although he accomplished little by his bluff, Perry was satisfied that he had not suffered any indignities.

Perry's second ceremonial landing of March 8, 1854 was more impressive. This time three steamers in a total of nine warships anchored at bay. One crew member described the "long line of boats crowded with men glittering with bayonets, the brass . . . guns blazing in the sun ready to vomit forth death and destruction."[8] Perry disembarked to a seventeen-gun salute and the playing of "The Star Spangled Banner" by three fully armed bands. Five hundred seamen marched with him. Although the Japanese had resisted negotiations (Perry sat in the harbor for two weeks before the March 8 event), they received the commodore

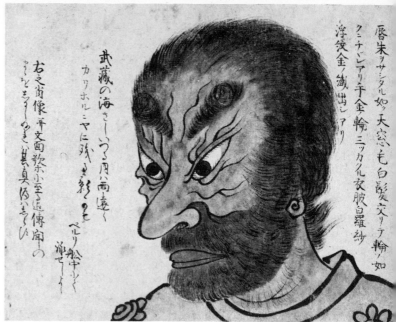

**Matthew C. Perry (1794–1858).** The career naval officer, born in Newport, Rhode Island, is seen here in sharply contrasting portraits. The exaggerated Japanese depiction does not convey the majesty Perry himself surely admired in the American painting by John Beaufain Irving. Perry was not a distinguished navalist, but he did help open Japan and did help initiate the steam Navy. (Honolulu Academy of Arts, Gift of Mrs. Walter F. Dillingham in memory of Alice Perry Grew, 1960; and U.S. Naval Academy Museum)

courteously. Banquets, *sumo* wrestling, and an American minstrel entertained guests and hosts. Gifts were exchanged. The Japanese offered precious art objects; the Americans, reflecting their burgeoning industrial economy at home, provided the curious Japanese with a quarter-scale railroad train and a telegraph system. Both were conspicuously set up on shore. The berobed Japanese enjoyed themselves immensely. The commodore also handed over a copy of a history of the war with Mexico, which included dramatic sketches of the American fleet bombarding Veracruz. Perry complained privately that the American gifts were worth more than the Japanese offerings.

Although instructed to negotiate an expansion of commercial relations between the two countries, Perry settled for less. The Japanese protested that they did not need foreign products. "You are right," said Perry. "Commerce brings profits to a country, but it does not concern human life. I shall not insist upon it."[9] The Treaty of Kanagawa, signed on March 31, 1854, guaranteed protection for shipwrecked American crews, opened up two ports for obtaining coal and other supplies, and established consular privileges at these ports. But the treaty had shortcomings. The two ports, Shimoda and Hakodate, were relatively inaccessible and unimportant. And, although Japan granted the United States most-favored-nation treatment, there was no binding provision for beginning trade. Perry had fallen short of his instructions; he had "opened up" Japan only slightly.

One member of the expedition wrote that the Perry mission was "the beginning of American interference in Asia,"[10] and another began his diary with these pompous words: "The American Eagle allows little birds to sing."[11] Similar chauvinism was expressed in the hero's welcome accorded Perry in the United States, in April, 1855. The New York Chamber of Commerce presented him with a 381-piece silver dinner service, Boston merchants pinned a medal on him, and Congress voted him a bonus of $20,000. There was even talk about a presidential candidacy. The Senate ratified the treaty unanimously. Apparently everybody thought Perry had opened Japan to trade. Secretary of the Navy James C. Dobbin had earlier congratulated the commodore for having "secured for your country, for commerce, and for civilization, a triumph the blessings of which may be enjoyed by generations yet unborn."[12] Surely, his admirers thought, "Old Bruin" had accomplished more than appeared on paper. Perry himself later admitted that his treaty was not a "commercial compact." Commerce would result, he said, if the United States followed up with "corresponding acts . . . of national probity." Nonetheless, he envisioned "that the people of America will, in some form or other, extend their dominion and their power, until they shall have brought within their mighty embrace the Islands of the great Pacific, and place the Saxon race upon the eastern shores of Asia."[13]

## Sputtering Expansionism and Sectionalism

Perry's excursion to Japan grew out of the 1840s spirit of expansionism that had generated the Oregon settlement, the Mexican War, and visions of a Pacific empire. After that successful war, with California firmly a part of the Union and with a long, unbroken Pacific coastline, expansionists dreamed of strengthening links with Asia. With new and faster steamships, with the valuable ports of San Diego and San Francisco, with already existing commercial and missionary ties, with the possibility of a canal across Central America and a transcontinental railroad to reduce the travel time between New York City and San Francisco, with the population of San Francisco ballooning (in part because of the gold rush of 1849)—with all of these changes and aspirations, American interest in Asia flamed anew after 1848. Lieutenant John Rodgers, who headed the United States Survey-ing Expedition to the North Pacific Ocean in 1853–1856, predicted great trade with the Chinese: "We shall carry to Europe their teas and silks. . . . The results are so vast as to dazzle sober calculation."[14]

This interest in Asia was nothing new. The first American ship to China sailed in the 1780s and American businessmen were trading in Canton at the turn of the century. Caleb Cushing, the first American commissioner to China, secured trading privileges in five ports from China by the Treaty of 1844. The "aim of the Western trading powers in China," according to historian John K. Fairbank, "was to trade but not to govern."[15] By the early 1850s Americans carried about one-third of China's trade with the West. The United States was not a major player in Asian politics, however. As junior partners, Americans usually trailed behind the British, who were not averse to using military force to build up imperial privileges: for

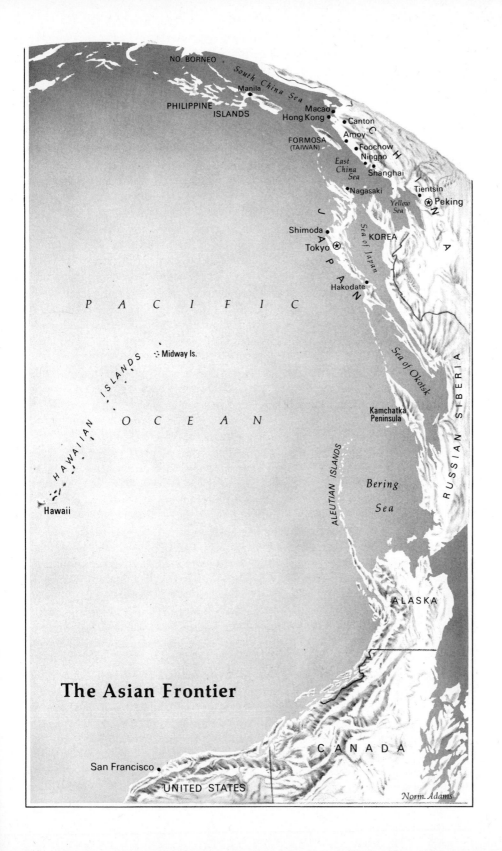

The Asian Frontier

*Norm. Adams*

example, the Opium War enabled Cushing to negotiate the Treaty of Wanghia. The Americans, complained a Chinese official in Shanghai, "do no more than follow in England's wake and utilize her strength."[16] Although the United States proved much less warlike than the other Western powers in Asia, and did not gobble up territory as had Britain (India), the Netherlands (East Indies), and Portugal (Macao), Asians could only view America as another nation of grasping white foreigners wishing to deny them their sovereignty and dignity.

In 1858, during a civil war called the Taiping Rebellion, France and Britain further gouged China by opening ten new treaty ports. Once again practicing what some historians call "hitchhiking imperialism," the United States gained access to eleven more ports and low tariffs in the dictated Treaty of Tientsin. In Japan, where the United States in 1856 sent Townsend Harris as consul to capitalize on Perry's expedition, the gains were less impressive, but nonetheless important. Isolated at the port of Shimoda, Harris patiently waited for an opportunity to negotiate a commercial treaty. Lacking the naval power exerted by the Westerners in China and displayed by Perry in 1854, Harris could not threaten Japanese leaders, who resented his very presence; but he pressed his case in a prime early example of what would later become known as "personal diplomacy." In 1858 his tenacity paid off in a treaty wherein Japan opened other ports, provided for freedom of trade, and created a tariff schedule. The next year Harris became minister to Japan and established an American legation in Tokyo.

Despite these evidences of American expansion in the Orient in the 1850s, for statesmen and Americans generally, writes historian Charles E. Neu, "Asia remained an abstract idea, a distant area that was only one part of a worldwide commercial empire."[17] The euphoria following Perry's drama soon evaporated. The State Department gave little guidance to its representatives in the Far East, who therefore often acted on their own: in 1856, for example, Commodore James Armstrong's ships destroyed five Chinese forts near Canton after a cannon fired on an American vessel. President Franklin Pierce thereupon reprimanded the naval officer. As another example of America's secondary interest in Asia, Rodgers of the North Pacific Surveying Expedition found upon returning to San Francisco in 1856 that he could not complete his survey of trade routes because his funds had run out and he could obtain no more. Even Perry, who had requested twelve warships for his presidentially authorized expedition to Japan in 1854, was given only four.

America's relative inattention to Asian affairs reflected the general waning of American expansionism and Manifest Destiny after the Mexican War. Talk of annexing Canada subsided. Even in Latin America, an area of prime focus, expansionist ventures sputtered and imperial ambitions dissipated. Attempts to grab Cuba collapsed and cries for grabbing more territory from Mexico were muffled. Notions of planting an American colony in slaveholding Brazil enjoyed some currency, after an exploration directed by Lieutenant Matthew F. Maury, but nothing came of the hopes. Washington did persuade Mexico to negotiate the Gadsden Purchase of 1853, which added 54,000 acres of land to the United States at a cost of $10 million for a potential railroad route to the Pacific Coast—the only land acquired by the United States in the period from the Mexican War to the end of the Civil War. Only trade continued to expand abroad, sustaining faltering hopes for an ever growing empire. "There is not in the history of the Roman Empire," asserted Senator William H. Seward of New York in 1850, "an ambition for aggrandizement so marked as that which has characterized the American people."[18] Yet that ambition sputtered in the 1850s and early 1860s. The reason lay at home, in the heated sectional debates over chattel slavery that led to the Civil War.

The divisive issue of slavery curbed Northern appetites for ventures into Latin America, where the "peculiar institution" might flourish and slave states might arise to vote with the South. Many residents of the latter, having beaten back restrictions like the Wilmot Proviso, continued the cry for empire, hoping to enhance their declining political status and mollify the threat to slavery, "the cornerstone of their way of life."[19] Northern leaders regretted that Manifest Destiny had fallen victim to the crude aspirations of slavemasters. Slavery, said Abraham Lincoln in 1854, "deprives our republican example of its just influence in the world—enables the enemies of free institutions to taunt us as hypocrites."[20] Badly divided at home by insistent Northern abolitionists and Southern "fire-eaters," the United States could not successfully undertake further bold schemes in international affairs, because it could not reach a foreign policy consensus. Intensely preoccupied as Americans were by the Compromise of 1850, the Fugitive Slave Act, "bleeding Kansas," the Dred Scott decision, the commercial and financial panic of 1857, the Lincoln-Douglas debates, John Brown's raid, the formation of the new Republican party, and the 1860 election of Abraham Lincoln, they gave less and less attention to foreign policy questions.

Some Americans, however, at the very time their own nation was being torn apart by sectional differences after the Mexican War, joined the nationalistic "Young America" movement. They identified the revolutions of 1848 in Europe as evidence of New World, republican influences on the Old, and applauded Camillo Bensi di Cavour, Giuseppe Mazzini, and Giuseppe Garibaldi of Italy and Lajos Kossuth of Hungary. Their short-lived rebellions against entrenched conservatism and monarchy kindled American sympathies. In late 1850 Whig Secretary of State Daniel Webster, for example, lectured the Hapsburg government, claiming that, compared to the mighty United States, Austria was "but a patch on the earth's surface."[21] Concerned about bitter division at home over the expansion of slavery, he hoped his public rebuke to the government that had crushed the Hungarian revolution would "touch the national pride, and make a man feel *sheepish* and look *silly* who should speak of disunion."[22] In other words, Webster sought to use a nationalist movement abroad to generate nationalism at home. When Kossuth excited the United States in 1851–1852 during a rousing visit, Webster once again applied his exceptional oratorical abilities on behalf of liberty and American nationalism. In the 1852 Democratic party platform, the rallying cry was "Young America." The following year, "Young America" advocate and Democratic Secretary of State William Marcy ordered a new dress code for American diplomats; they were to wear the "simple dress of an American citizen" to reflect America's "republican institutions."[23] But the "Young America" movement was no formula for perpetuating the ebullient nationalism and Manifest Destiny of the 1840s. "Young America" fell into the hands of Democratic party expansionists, many of whom favored the extension of slavery. An incongruity impressed some observers: "Young America" advocates championed liberty abroad, while at home they denied it to black human beings under the repressive system of slavery.

Scholars generally agree that political leadership in the United States between the Mexican War and Civil War was undistinguished, quite mediocre and unimaginative. Contemporary historian George Bancroft thought it "feeble and

## Makers of American Foreign Policy from 1848 to 1865

| Presidents | Secretaries of State |
| --- | --- |
| James K. Polk, 1845–1849 | James Buchanan, 1845–1849 |
| Zachary Taylor, 1849–1850 | John M. Clayton, 1849–1850 |
| Millard Fillmore, 1850–1853 | Daniel Webster, 1850–1852 |
| | Edward Everett, 1852–1853 |
| Franklin Pierce, 1853–1857 | William L. Marcy, 1853–1857 |
| James Buchanan, 1857–1861 | Lewis Cass, 1857–1860 |
| | Jeremiah S. Black, 1860–1861 |
| Abraham Lincoln, 1861–1865 | William H. Seward, 1861–1869 |

incompetent."[24] Allan Nevins later identified a "special weakness" of Democratic President Franklin Pierce: "a tendency to rash pyrotechnics."[25] The presidents and secretaries of state conducted a blustering foreign policy, often playing to domestic political currents through bombastic rhetoric. Few had diplomatic experience. One writer in 1853 was satisfied that whether American foreign affairs were "directed by a sot or a simpleton, they will continue to grow and expand by a law of nature and a decree of Providence."[26] But inept leaders muddled relations with Spain, crudely grasped at an elusive Cuba, permitted filibusters to alienate Latin America, squabbled clumsily with Britain in Central America, meddled with emotion but without power in European revolutions, followed the British in humiliating the Chinese, and gave halfhearted attention to Japan after "opening" it. President Abraham Lincoln and his inveterately expansionistic secretary of state, William H. Seward, certainly raised the level of competence in Washington, despite Seward's suggestion in 1861 that the United States provoke a foreign dispute to galvanize nationalism at home and forestall Southern secession. The two managed to win the Civil War and contain it as a "localized" conflict, avoiding the world war it might have become. In doing so they preserved American power, thereby permitting the United States to resume its expansionist course after the fratricidal conflict.

## The South's Dream of Empire: Filibustering and Slave Expansion

Many Southern leaders tried to exploit Manifest Destiny for territorial conquest in the Caribbean. They failed largely because they aroused domestic opposition by insisting that slavery be permitted to expand into new lands. They failed because they dressed expansionism in sectional garb. In the 1850s Northern expansionists parted company with Southern sectionalists and steadfastly opposed ventures into Latin America that might add slave territories to the Union. At the same time, some Northern expansionists, like Seward—then senator from New York—hoped that the abolition of slavery would eliminate Northern opposition to expansion into the Caribbean and Mexico. The paradox was striking: Southern expansionists sought a larger empire for the United States while at the same time they denigrated the supremacy of the federal government itself, during the heated debates of the 1850s that led to the Civil War. "You are looking toward Mexico, Nicaragua, and Brazil," Congressman Thomas Corwin of Ohio lectured his Southern colleagues, "while you are not sure you will have a government to which these could be ceded."[27]

For Southerners, expansion seemed essential. Since the Missouri Compromise of 1820, they had witnessed a profound shift in both the political and economic balance to the North, the free states. Under the Compromise of 1850, the territories seized from Mexico were given instructions: California would enter the Union as a free state, and the rest of the Mexican cession could determine whether it wished to be slave or free (the concept of "popular sovereignty"). A strong majority of Southern congressmen voted against the compromise bill and looked upon its

# The Southern Perspective on Expansion

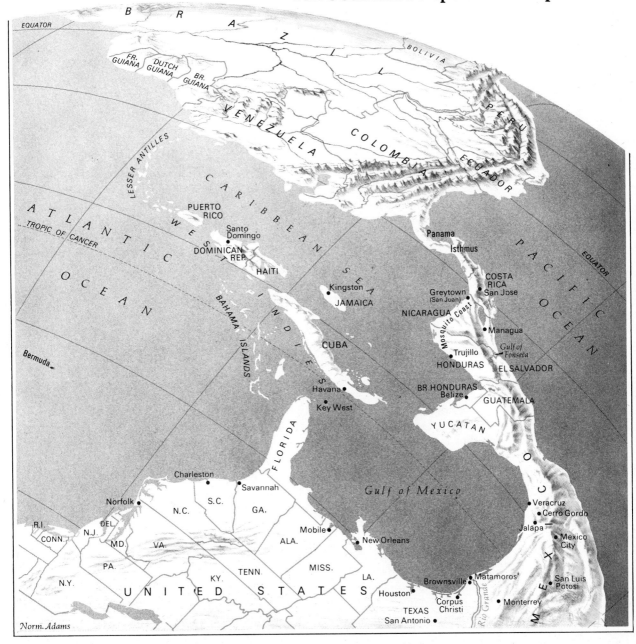

Norm. Adams

passage as further evidence of their diminishing political power. Potential slave states had to be found to right the balance. Tropical states where black slaves could toil under white mastery had long been part of the Southern imagination, but now, in the 1850s, the matter became urgent. The message was sent out by belligerent voices like those of James D. E. B. DeBow, in his widely read *DeBow's Review,* and the Knights of the Golden Circle, a secret society of several thousand members, many of them prominent politicians pledged to tropical expansion. The Gulf of Mexico, DeBow opined, was the "great *Southern sea.*"[28] The vision of expanded slavery took in Cuba, Mexico, and Central America. "With swelling hearts and suppressed impatience they await our coming," proclaimed a Southern congressman, "and with joyous shouts of 'Welcome! Welcome!' will they receive us."[29]

Yet Southern expansionists could not realize their dreams through diplomacy. Stymied by the Northern rejection of their proslave imperialist aspirations, many Southerners supported the filibusters, those dramatic warriors who attempted to grab territories through unauthorized and illegal attacks upon sovereign nations recognized by the United States. Most of the filibustering bands originated in New Orleans, were "Southern" in goals and personnel, and employed the rhetoric of Manifest Destiny for sectional purposes. Narciso López, John A. Quitman, and William Walker led the ill-fated ventures.

Venezuelan by birth, General Narciso López had been a Spanish military officer and Cuban businessman before his attempted invasion of Cuba in 1849. Married into a proslave aristocratic Cuban family, he came to believe he was the island's savior from the perfidies of mother Spain. He wished to free Cuba and annex it to the United States. Using New York City and New Orleans as bases, López sought supporters. He hired some desperate-looking veterans from the Mexican War, promising them "plunder, women, drink, and tobacco"; each soldier would receive a $1000 bonus and 160 acres of Cuban land if the expedition succeeded.[30] López gathered his several hundred mercenaries at Round Island, off the Louisiana coast, but in September, 1849 the United States Navy blockaded the isle and foiled his plans.

López reached for support elsewhere in the South. He won over Southern expansionists like John A. Quitman, a wealthy sugar and cotton planter, former general in the Mexican War, and governor of Mississippi (1850–1851); the editor of the *New Orleans Delta,* Laurence J. Sigur; a former senator and cotton planter from Mississippi, John Henderson; and editor John L. O'Sullivan of Manifest Destiny fame. In May, 1850, disguised as emigrants to California, the filibusters of the López expedition departed New Orleans. On May 19 they landed at Cárdenas, but beat a hasty retreat when superior Spanish forces confronted them. López hurriedly charted a course to the United States, where American officials prosecuted him for violating the Neutrality Act of 1818, which forbade military expeditions from American soil against nations at peace with the United States. In New Orleans, López, Quitman, Henderson, Sigur, and O'Sullivan, among others, were put on trial. After three mistrials for Henderson, the federal government dropped charges against the others. Ever adventuresome, López in August, 1851 launched another attack against Cuba with 500 followers, called by black abolitionist leader Frederick Douglass "freebooters, pirates, and plunderers."[31] Federal officials in New Orleans obligingly looked the other way. The flamboyant filibuster carried a proclamation: "The star of Cuba . . . will rise beautiful and shining perchance to be admitted gloriously into the splendid North American constellation according to its inevitable destiny."[32] López himself was denied glory. Having garnered little Cuban backing, he and his half-starved and undermanned contingent were captured. Among them was Colonel William Crittenden of Kentucky, nephew of the attorney general of the United States. López, Crittenden, and fifty of the mercenaries were executed.

Undeterred by the debacle of the López expedition, DeBow proclaimed that the American "lust for dominion" over Cuba remained an American sentiment.[33] And riots against Spanish property broke out in New Orleans. Secretary of State Daniel Webster apologized in early 1852 and paid $25,000 to Spain for damage to its consulate in New Orleans. Quitman, who had resigned his governorship in 1851 because of the filibustering flap, grew angry. He detested the Compromise of 1850 and feared that Spain might free slaves in Cuba, constituting a "fatal stab" at Southern institutions.[34] Indeed, he thought a "strong negro or mongrel empire" might arise in Cuba to thwart Southern expansion.[35] Quitman plotted a new journey. In 1854 he agreed to command an expedition of 3,000 men, but financial shortages, lack of support in Cuba, and hostility from Washington persuaded him to scotch his mission in early 1855. Quitman thereupon retired from filibustering, futilely complaining about the "humbug administration" in Washington.[36]

Then came William Walker, the "grey-eyed man of destiny."[37] Restless and reckless, Tennessean Walker earned a physician's degree from the University of Pennsylvania, studied medicine in Paris, practiced law in Louisiana, and edited a Southern journal before he embarked on schemes in Mexico and Nicaragua. Attracted to California in 1850 by the euphoric gold rush, Walker hatched plans for an invasion of Lower California, which was indisputably Mexican territory. At age twenty-nine, in 1853, this man of small figure and simple dress marched into Mexican lands and captured the territorial capital of La Paz. In early 1853, however, the expedition collapsed from discontent among his followers and faulty organization. Tried for violating the Neutrality Act, Walker was acquitted by an admiring San Francisco jury.

"Once more aiding the stars," the man of destiny next eyed Nicaragua, then a country of some mention as a route for an isthmian canal.[38] Hardly the agent of benevolent, democratic Manifest Destiny that his admirers attempted to portray, the persevering Walker became a petty tyrant who "ruled with a rod of iron."[39] He sought to subjugate Nicaragua in 1855, 1857, 1858, and 1860. He plundered and killed. In the first expedition, leading men whom he described as "tired of the humdrum of common life," he proclaimed himself president of the country.[40] Apparently under the influence of Pierre Soulé, he then instituted slavery. The American minister in Nicaragua, North Carolinian plantation owner and slaveholder John Hill Wheeler, abetted Walker in this adventure, since he was convinced that the "rich soil so well adapted to the culture of cotton, sugar, rice, corn, cocoa, indigo, etc. can never be developed without slave labor."[41] Walker dreamed beyond Nicaragua; he wanted to build a Central American federation and then attack Cuba. Thinking that the decision would be politically popular, and finding no other Nicaraguan government in existence, the Pierce Administration recognized Walker's regime in 1856. But the filibuster soon wobbled. Walker alienated the native population through pillaging and dictatorial orders, and his soldiers fell victim to frequent drunkenness and disease. He then alienated transportation magnate Cornelius Vanderbilt, who had interests in Nicaragua; the influential "Commodore" backed Honduras, Guatemala, San Salvador, and Costa

**William Walker (1824–1860).** The "grey-eyed man of destiny" flouted American laws, invaded Latin American countries, ruled Nicaragua for a short time, and established himself as the United States' supreme filibuster, a dubious distinction. He fell before a Honduran firing squad. (Smithsonian Institution)

Rica when they took up arms against the intruding adventurer. In May of 1857 Walker fled to the United States.

The famed filibuster tried to return to Nicaragua in November, 1857, but United States naval officers arrested him near Greytown. He escaped prosecution. Walker's third futile effort, in 1858, ended ingloriously on a coral reef near British Honduras, where his ship went aground. Still claiming to be the legitimate president of Nicaragua, the irrepressible Walker headed for his adopted country once again in the spring of 1860. This time he attacked Honduras first. Honduran troops inflicted heavy casualties, and Walker soon surrendered to an unsympathetic British official, who turned him over to Honduran officers. "Will the South stand by and permit him to be shot down like a dog?" exhorted one Southern woman. "If so, let her renounce forever her reputation for chivalry, valor, policy, or pride!"[42] Such appeals went unheeded, and Walker was executed by a firing squad on September 12, 1860.

William Walker, like the other filibusters, aroused considerable enthusiasm in the South among prominent politicians, planters, and editors. He symbolized for many the survival of slavery and hence the Southern way of life. Although Southerners came to adopt Walker as a tool of expansion, it does not appear that he was committed to either Southern expansion or slavery. His was a story of personal ambition, from which sectionalists hoped to benefit. Hindered by Northern opponents from territorial gains through diplomacy or war, the ardent defenders of the "peculiar institution" turned to the illegal machinations and drama of the filibusters. They would also turn to civil war in 1861. "As dream and reality met," historian Robert E. May has written, "the South's grandiose vision of empire dissolved in the blood of war."[43]

## Cuba by Hook or by Crook

Cuba, the Pearl of the Antilles, lay too close to the United States to escape the latter's expansionist urges. Spain once called it the "Ever Faithful Isle" because, unlike other Spanish possessions in the New World, Cuba did not revolt against Madrid in the stormy decades of the early nineteenth century. Like a "coy temptress," to use historian William H. Goetzmann's words, Cuba attracted American attention.[44] A rich producer of sugar, Cuba drew American businessmen and traders as the United States became the island's largest commercial partner. Slave revolts in the 1830s and 1840s, as well as anticolonial rebellions in the following decade, aroused Americans, especially those who wished to abolish slavery. Slaveholders in Cuba had a notorious reputation as cruel masters. A corrupt and inept Spanish administration heightened Cuba's plight and gained American sympathies. One prominent twentieth-century historian, Allan Nevins, has described Spanish rule in Cuba as "an outrage upon the name of Christian civilization."[45] Caught up in the ideology of Manifest Destiny, Americans believed that inevitably, by "natural growth," Cuba would be taken under their eagle's outstretched wings.[46] Or, to use a metaphor of the times: "The fruit will fall into our hands when it is ripe, without an officious shaking of the tree. Cuba will be ours, and Canada and Mexico, too—if we want them—in due season, and without the wicked imperative of a war."[47]

Some Americans tried to hurry the ripening process. In 1848 President James K. Polk, looking for other fruits to match Oregon and the Mexican cession, contemplated purchasing Cuba from Spain for $100 million. But Spanish resistance and the ardent opposition of France and Britain blocked him. In the late 1840s and early 1850s the question of the annexation of Cuba to the United States became ensnarled in the debate over slavery and its expansion. Southern defenders of the "peculiar institution" increasingly included Cuba in their dreams of a Caribbean empire wherein slavery might flourish. Filibustering expeditions like those of Narciso López fired Southern hopes for the absorption of Cuba.

In 1852 Britain and France asked the United States to join them in a three-power statement to disavow "all intention of obtaining possession" of Cuba.[48] Unwilling to be bound by such a self-denying agreement, Washington rejected the overture. President Millard Fillmore told the French and British ministers that "this question would fall like a bomb in the midst of the electoral agitation for the presidency" and divide North from South.[49] Secretary of State Edward Everett, who seemed to be "hunting larks with an elephant rifle," informed London and Paris that the United States did not "covet" Cuba, but the status of the island was "mainly an American question."[50] He went on to extoll the island's strategic and commercial value, deprecating at the same time the Cuban slave trade. By quoting Washington's Farewell Address and Jefferson's aversion to "entangling alliances," Everett shunned any hint of a pact with European nations. One thing was evident: the United States would not permit the transfer of Cuba to any other power. European capitals thought Everett's statements pompous and alarming, with their allusions to United States pre-eminence in the Caribbean. Lord Palmerston, ever mindful that British colonies in the West Indies lay in the path of American growth, angrily berated officials in his government who argued that Britain should concede Cuba to the United States. No, that "would be like propitiating an animal of Prey by giving him one of one's Travelling Companions. It would increase his desire for similar food and spur him on to obtain it."[51]

Fillmore's successor coveted Cuba. In his inaugural address, Franklin Pierce asserted that he would not be "controlled by any timid forebodings of evil from Cuba."[52] Backed by expansionists Secretary of State William L. Marcy (secretary of war under Polk), Minister to Britain James Buchanan (secretary of state under Polk), Minister to Spain Pierre Soulé (ardent defender of slavery from Louisiana), and Minister to France John Y. Mason (attorney general under Polk), Pierce played to the desire for Cuba of the Southern wing of the Democratic party. Soulé was impetuous, stubborn, and vain, "of swarthy complexion, black flashing eyes, and Frenchified dress and speech."[53] Born in France, schooled as a lawyer, and elected United States senator from Louisiana, the hotheaded minister became a central figure in the American quest for Cuba. Within weeks of his arrival in Madrid, Soulé wounded the French ambassador in a duel. Convinced that the United States could satisfy its "lusty appetite" for expansion by taking Cuba, this misplaced "diplomat" seemed to take every opportunity to make himself irritable to the Spanish, thereby thwarting the American goal of obtaining Cuba.[54]

Secretary Marcy believed that decrepit Spain would perceive the wisdom of selling its rebellious colony. He instructed Soulé to inquire discreetly about sale. "Discreetly," however, was not a word in Soulé's vocabulary. In February of 1854, an American merchant ship, the *Black Warrior*, was seized at Havana for violating port regulations. Apparently seeing an opportunity to force Cuba from Spain through a threat of war, President Pierce demanded a $100,000 indemnity (raised to $300,000 soon after) for the vessel's owners and heated up American fevers for

**"Master Jonathan Tries To Smoke a Cuba, But It Doesn't Agree With Him!"** America's trouble with Spanish-controlled, slavery-plagued Cuba was depicted in this mocking British cartoon. The Ostend Manifesto debacle of 1854 was particularly discomforting to the United States. (*Punch*, 1850)

revenge by sending a belligerent anti-Spanish message to Congress. Pierce thus fed Soulé's intemperance. The haughty minister thereupon demanded an apology from the Spanish government for an affront to the American flag. The Spanish agreed to restore the ship to its owner and pay a smaller indemnity, but Marcy found the Spanish reply full of "evasions" and called it a "disingenuous perversion of language."[55]

The much inflated *Black Warrior* affair was soon overshadowed by a new, rash attempt to annex Cuba. Marcy instructed Soulé in April of 1854 to try to buy Cuba for $130 million or less. Failing that, "you will then direct your efforts to the next desirable object which is to detach that island from the Spanish dominion and from all dependence on any European power."[56] Then, in August, the secretary told Soulé to meet with ministers Buchanan and Mason to discuss the question of annexation. The three expansionists relished the chance; they met in October at Ostend, Belgium, and then at Aix-la-Chapelle in Rhenish Prussia, where they created the remarkable confidential document known as the Ostend Manifesto. The three emissaries agreed that Cuba should be purchased for no more than $120 million. But if Madrid refused to sell, "by every law, human and divine, we shall be justified in wresting it from Spain if we possess the power."[57] The manifesto found its way into the press and the Pierce Administration was soon accused of propagating a Southern slave conspiracy. The Free Soil party thought the document "the highwayman's plea, that might makes right."[58] Reeling from the loud criticism hurled by antislavery forces, the Pierce Administration tried to place blame on Soulé. Fearing that Soulé would "break" more "ground" on behalf of the "robber doctrine," a relieved President Pierce accepted his resignation.[59] The "gasconading" Soulé returned home ignobly in early 1855.[60]

One author of the Ostend Manifesto, James Buchanan, became President in 1857. After his nomination as the Democratic candidate, he remarked that "if I can be instrumental in settling the slavery question . . . , and then add Cuba to the Union, I shall be willing to give up the ghost."[61] He appointed a Wall Street banker, the American representative of the Rothschilds, August Belmont, as minister to Spain. Belmont was a noted advocate of bribing Spanish officials to acquire Cuba and the Senate rejected him. Thereupon, in his annual message to

Congress in December, 1858, the President praised the commercial and strategic virtues of Cuba, urged its purchase, and asked Congress to appropriate a large sum to be put at his own disposal for this purpose. The Senate Foreign Relations Committee then issued a favorable report that declared the "law of our national existence is growth. We cannot if we would, disobey it."[62] The fruit was ripe for plucking. If the United States did not act, a European power might. The report also recommended an appropriation of $30 million—some of it no doubt for bribes of Spanish public officials. But Republican abolitionists who opposed annexation would have none of it and delayed action until Congress adjourned.

A slow learner, Buchanan appealed to Congress to pass the "Thirty Million Dollar Bill" again in his annual messages of 1859 and 1860. In the presidential election of 1860, however, Abraham Lincoln, a firm opponent of slave expansion, was elected, thus killing possibilities of annexing Cuba. By then the acquisition of Cuba had become solely the pet project of the South. One Southerner waxed erotic: "Who can object if he throws his arms around the Queen of the Antilles, as she sits, like Cleopatra's burning throne, upon the silver waves, breathing her spicy, tropic breath, and pouting her rosy, sugared lips. Who can object? None. She is of age—take her Uncle Sam."[63] But the objections were vociferous, Uncle Sam spurned an embrace, and the South learned by 1860 that its expansionist passions were frustrated.

## Nudging the British out of Central America

Great Britain kept a worried and watchful eye on United States attempts, official and unofficial, to expand in the Caribbean and Central America. At the close of the Mexican War, Anglo-American relations seemed on the eve of improvement. In 1842 Webster and Ashburton had drawn the Maine boundary and a line from Lake Superior to Lake of the Woods, and in 1846 President Polk had compromised on Oregon. As the danger of war over the Canadian-American border declined, the "Atlantic economy" revived.[64] In the mid-1840s the growth of trade between the United States and Britain had resumed, after a decade of sluggishness; by the 1850s the United States supplied Britain with 50 percent of its imports and 80 percent of its raw cotton, the basis of England's largest export industry. Forty percent of all American imports originated in Great Britain, and America's expanding economy attracted surplus British capital, especially during the railroad building boom of the 1840s. "Increased Commercial Intercourse may add to the Links of mutual Interest," Britain's Viscount Henry John Palmerston observed. But he also warned acidly that "commercial Interest is a Link that snaps under the Pressure of National Passions."[65]

In the 1840s and 1850s, as we have seen, American passions were aroused by dreams of expansion into Central America and the Caribbean. A treaty negotiated with New Granada (later Colombia) in 1846 and ratified in 1848 granted the United States extensive transit rights across the Isthmus of Panama, one of the more promising railroad and canal routes in Central America. Alarmed by this intrusion upon their maritime supremacy in the Caribbean, the British struck back. In January, 1848, they seized a Nicaraguan town at the mouth of the San Juan River. Renamed Greytown, this port controlled the most feasible transisthmian canal route, given the technology of the time. When added to the British protectorate over the Mosquito Indians inhabiting Nicaragua's eastern coast, possession of Belize (later British Honduras) and the Bay Islands, and the Royal Naval base at nearby Jamaica, Greytown accorded Great Britain a substantial position in Central America.

In the same month that the British took Greytown, John Marshall discovered gold at Sutter's mill in California. The great gold rush soon swelled California's population by 100,000 and led to admission of the Golden State to the Union in 1850. Most of the "Forty-niners" reached San Francisco by steamship. The trek included arduous overland travel through Nicaragua or Panama. For many Americans, construction of an efficient isthmian canal or railway suddenly became a matter of domestic urgency. But the conspicuous British presence in Central America precluded unilateral United States action. Whig Secretary of State John M. Clayton therefore proposed "a great highway" across the isthmus, "to be dedicated especially by Great Britain and the United States, to the equal benefit and advantage of all the nations of the world."[66]

Acerbic Foreign Secretary Palmerston, or Lord "Pumicestone," who thought "these Yankees are most disagreeable Fellows to have to do with about any American Question," respected the ability of the "ingenious Rogues" to deny to his Canadian provinces their much desired commercial reciprocity.[67] Thus he graciously told Clayton that Britain had "no selfish or exclusive views" about the isthmus. Like Clayton, he hoped "that any undertaking of this sort . . . should be generally open to and available to all the nations of the world."[68] To confirm this understanding, he sent Sir Henry Bulwer to Washington in December, 1849. Both Bulwer and Clayton wanted to neutralize isthmian transit. But Zachary Taylor's Administration also wanted British abandonment of Greytown and the Mosquito Coast. What followed was, as the *Times* of London put it, a struggle "for generalship in the use of terms"—what historian Charles S. Campbell has called "a treaty in obscure language."[69] The Clayton-Bulwer Pact of April 19, 1850 stipulated that neither Great Britain nor the United States alone would ever monopolize or fortify a canal in Central America, and that neither would "colonize, or assume, or exercise any dominion over . . . any part of Central America."[70]

This superficial, self-denying clause invited conflicting interpretations, as became apparent during the exchange of ratifications. On July 4, 1850, Bulwer informed Clayton that Britain did not believe the treaty included "whatever is Her Majesty's settlement at Honduras, nor whatever are the Dependencies of that settlement."[71] Having deftly exempted Belize and the Bay Islands from the terms of the Clayton-Bulwer Treaty, Britain thereafter excluded the Mosquito protectorate and Greytown, arguing that the treaty referred only to the acquisition of *new* territory. Despite London's verbal agility, the treaty in effect meant that "Britain could hardly turn around in Central America without being charged by Americans with violating its provisions."[72] Nonetheless, as Bulwer accurately perceived, the agreement defused Anglo-American tension and seemed "to bind the United States against further annexation."[73] As British historian Kenneth Bourne concludes, "considering that the American administration was . . . tackling the British in an area where they were already well entrenched, the Americans appeared to have scored a considerable success in facilitating the construction of a canal free from the threat of British control."[74]

That canal would await the twentieth century, but American enterprise soon began to saturate Central America. Cornelius Vanderbilt organized an interoceanic steamship and railroad connection through Nicaragua, and other entrepreneurs completed a railroad across Panama in 1855. However, the flag did not follow investors into Central America. The deepening domestic crisis over the expansion of slavery prevented President Franklin Pierce and his successor, James Buchanan, from doing much more than nipping verbally at the heels of the gradually retreating British. For his part, Lord Palmerston continued to berate the "vulgar minded Bullies" of North America, from whom "nothing is gained by submission to Insult & wrong."[75] But in 1854, when the U.S.S. *Cyane* bombarded Greytown in an excessive reprisal for an insult to an American diplomat and President Pierce refused to disavow the attack, London quietly let the matter drop.

The costly Crimean War (1854–1856), which pitted England and France against Russia, drained London's political and military energy and made a showdown with the United States over Central America unthinkable. As British soldiers fell like flies before Sebastopol in the Crimea, the desperate English government sent agents to the United States to recruit replacements, leading Secretary of State William Marcy to dismiss the British minister. Even Palmerston recognized his country's precarious position and recommended "some little Flourish" addressed to the "free, enlightened and Generous Race . . . of the great North American Union" as a means of dampening Marcy's "Bunkum vapouring" against Great Britain.[76]

Marcy had helped induce Palmerston's restraint by negotiating a long-desired reciprocity treaty in 1854. In 1852 the British had begun to interpret the Convention of 1818 very strictly and along the maritime provinces of British North America had seized some American fishing vessels. While hotheads in Massachusetts called for war and Matthew C. Perry steamed north in the *Mississippi,* President Millard Fillmore announced his willingness to settle the outstanding issues of fishing rights, free navigation of the St. Lawrence, and reciprocity with Canada. In May, 1854, London sent the Governor-General of Canada, Lord Elgin, to negotiate with Marcy. His lordship was shrewd and the environment highly congenial. "Lord Elgin pretends to drink immensely," his secretary recorded, "but I watched him [at a party], and I don't believe he drank a glass between two and twelve. He is the most thorough *diplomat* possible,—never loses sight for a moment of his object, and while he is chaffing the Yankees and slapping them on the back, he is systematically pursuing that object."[77] The "objects" of the two diplomats meshed and they signed the Marcy-Elgin Treaty on June 5, 1854. Americans could now navigate the St. Lawrence without restriction and fish within three miles of British North America, while Canadians could send duty-free a wide variety of agricultural products into the United States. The Marcy-Elgin Treaty, like the Webster-Ashburton Treaty and the Oregon settlement, contributed to tranquillity along the great northern border of the United States.

That Anglo-American relations in the 1850s ended with a whimper and not a bang was in large measure due to the deepening American crisis over the expansion of slavery. But a British reappraisal following the Crimean War also facilitated Anglo-American détente. Always the bellwether of official British opinion, Lord Palmerston wrote in December, 1857, in regard to Central America, that the Americans "are on the Spot, strongly, deeply interested in the matter, totally unscrupulous and dishonest and determined somehow or other to carry their Point. We are far away, weak from Distance, controlled by the Indifference of the Nation . . . and by its Strong commercial Interest in maintaining Peace with the completed a railroad across Panama in 1855. However, the flag did not follow relinquished the Bay Islands to Honduras and the Mosquito Coast to Nicaragua. According to historian Kenneth Bourne, this retreat held great symbolic importance: "Had not the Civil War intervened, the era of 1895–1902 [rapprochement] might in many respects have been anticipated by some thirty years. Even as it was, Great Britain was never again seriously to challenge American expansion."[79] Without war the United States had gradually nudged Britain out of Central America. The Civil War, however, was to raise new issues in Anglo-American relations.

## 1861: Year of Crises

**William H. Seward (1801–1872).** Graduate of Union College, New York state politician, lawyer, United States senator (1849–1861), and secretary of state (1861–1869), Seward had wanted to be President but lost the Republican nomination to Abraham Lincoln in 1860. He spent the Civil War years trying to preserve the Union by keeping the European powers neutral.

On April 12, 1861, at Charleston, South Carolina, Brigadier General Pierre G. T. Beauregard's Provisional Forces of the Confederate States opened fire on the federal garrison barricaded in Fort Sumter. With this defiant act the rebellious South forced Abraham Lincoln to choose between secession and civil war. Sworn to defend the Constitution, and conscious that his task was "greater than that which rested upon Washington," the new Republican President called for 75,000 militiamen to suppress the insurrection.[80]

For support, Lincoln leaned upon a factious Cabinet of politically ambitious men, headed by a secretary of state who thought himself far abler and more sophisticated than his chief. Convinced that his superior wisdom entitled him to act as prime minister to a hesitant President, William Henry Seward concocted plans to "wrap the world in flames" in order to melt domestic disunity in the furnace of foreign war.[81] On April 1, he sent Lincoln a memorandum titled "Some Thoughts for the President's Consideration." He criticized Lincoln for being "without a policy either domestic or foreign" and proposed hostility or war against Britain, France, Russia, and Spain. The next day Seward responded to Spain's reannexation of Santo Domingo with a threat of war. Spain ignored the bombastic secretary of state and Lincoln cautioned him that he himself would formulate policy with "the advice of all the Cabinet."[82]

Scarcely deterred, Seward challenged Great Britain's interpretation of international maritime law. He successfully urged Lincoln to proclaim a blockade of the Southern ports as a matter of domestic policy. Britain quite properly interpreted the Union blockade as the act of a nation at war, insisted that the blockade must effectively close Southern harbors to be legally binding upon neutral shippers, and recognized the belligerent status of the Confederacy. With equal logic, Confederate President Jefferson Davis met Lincoln's blockade with a call for privateers, an historic mode of American naval warfare.

In the 1856 Declaration of Paris following the Crimean War, Great Britain and France had codified the rules of maritime warfare and outlawed privateering. The United States had refused to sign away its favorite naval strategy, but the Confederacy's resort to privateering impelled Seward to inform the British Minister, Lord Richard Lyons, that he wished belatedly to initial the covenant. Lyons welcomed United States adherence, but noted Washington's lack of authority to obligate the South. When Seward remonstrated that the Confederate States were not independent, Lyons coolly exposed the fatal political inconsistency of Lincoln's maritime strategy: "Very well. If they are not independent then the President's proclamation of blockade is not binding. A blockade, according to the convention, applies only to two nations at war." Seward went into a lather: "Europe must

**"King Cotton Bound."** The Northern eagle attacks the Confederate "King Cotton," here rendered impotent by the naval blockade. (*Punch,* 1861)

interpret the law our way or we'll declare war, [and] commission enough privateers to prey on English commerce on every sea."[83]

Seward spoke from weakness and the British knew it. The Union had twice the population of the South and produced 92 percent of all goods manufactured in the United States. But the North faced the difficult military challenge of subduing 9,000,000 hostile people and sealing off innumerable harbors strung along 3,500 miles of coastline. To blockade this coast, Secretary of the Navy Gideon Welles could muster only 42 operational warships, and of these only 8 were in home waters. British statesmen thought it implausible that Lincoln could reconstruct the Union against such odds.

The economic balance sheet also seemed to work against the North. Prior to the Civil War, British subjects invested widely in American securities, sent at least 25 percent of their annual exports to the United States, and depended on America for 55 percent of all foodstuffs imported each year. But these economic ties favoring the industrial North and farming West paled beside the South's share of over 70 percent of the British market for raw cotton, the staple undergirding an industrial and commercial empire employing between 4 and 5 million people. Were the cotton trade interrupted, worried Britishers predicted, England would become economically prostrate. As a Southern planter and politician bragged, cotton was "the king who can shake the jewels in the crown of Queen Victoria."[84]

Jefferson Davis moved quickly to convert economic advantage into political impregnability. In March he despatched three ministers to Europe to seek full

**Charleston, South Carolina.** Its wharves piled with cotton for export, this Southern city governed by wealthy planters and gentlemen relied heavily on the cotton trade for prosperity. In 1860 Charleston ranked third behind New Orleans and Mobile as a cotton-exporting port. (Library of Congress)

diplomatic recognition, or even intervention, in exchange for an uninterrupted supply of cotton, free trade with the Confederacy, and expansion of European power throughout the western hemisphere. From Washington, Lyons counseled the British foreign secretary to receive the Southern commissioners informally, and a worried Lord John Russell replied, "I shall see the Southerners when they come, but not officially, and keep them at a proper distance."[85]

To parry this diplomatic thrust, Seward sped Charles Francis Adams to the Court of St. James's. Described by a contemporary Northern diplomat as "the Archbishop of antislavery," Adams was the son of the author of the Monroe Doctrine and grandson of the diplomat who had helped make peace with England in 1783.[86] Aloof, cool, steeped in the traditions of diplomacy, and serenely confident that his appointment would lead him to the presidency, Adams ultimately insulated London from Seward's highly charged flashes without deviating from the secretary's goals. Historian Jay Monaghan has compared Adams to his adversary, British Foreign Secretary Russell: "The two men were equally cold, formal, diplomatic, and almost equally British. A diamond come to cut a diamond."[87]

Adams arrived in London on May 14, 1861, dismayed to learn that England had proclaimed itself neutral and had recognized Confederate belligerency. Fortunately, the British government had also forbidden its subjects to supply ammunition or privateers to either side. Adams sought an early audience with Lord Russell to determine the extent of British recognition of the Southern commissioners. The foreign secretary vaguely admitted that he had received them "some time ago" and "once more sometime since," but he concluded, "I have no intention of seeing them any more." For the time being, Adams had to content himself with this "provokingly diplomatic" reassurance.[88] His secretary and son, Henry Adams, thought there were sufficient grounds for severing diplomatic relations, but he and his father rejected such action as the "extreme of shallowness and folly," because a war with England, added to the Civil War, "would grind us all into rags in America."[89]

A process of amelioration then began on both sides of the Atlantic. On May 21, Seward drafted a hostile dispatch for Adams, threatening to declare war if Britain recognized Confederate independence, only to have Lincoln pencil out the most warlike phrases and insist that the message be sent for Adams' guidance rather than as an ultimatum to Lord Russell. Even when toned down, Dispatch No. 10 struck Adams' son Henry as "so arrogant in tone and so extraordinary and unparalleled in its demands that it leaves no doubt in my mind that our Government wishes to face a war with all Europe."[90] As Adams quietly pocketed the diplomatic bombshell, reverses at the front rendered the secretary's threats of war with Europe ridiculous. On July 21, 1861, at Manassas Junction, Virginia, Confederate troops stampeded a Union army into full retreat north.

The summer and fall of 1861 brought further encouragement to Confederate statesmen. In England James D. Bulloch, head of the Confederacy's overseas secret service, contracted for the construction of two sloops. Disguised as merchant ships until their departure from British waters, in order to circumvent the neutrality proclamation, the *Florida* and *Alabama* promised to play havoc with Northern commerce. In August the *Bermuda,* a blockade runner laden with war material for Savannah, dashed from the Thames. Russell snidely deflected Adams' protest with an invitation to sign the Declaration of Paris. To exploit this favorable drift of events, President Davis sent two fresh and aggressive ministers to Europe, the aristocratic James M. Mason of Virginia and John Slidell, the political boss of Louisiana and Polk's emissary to Mexico in 1845. On October 11, they boarded the Confederate steamer *Nashville* at Charleston to begin the first leg of their journey.

Hoping to avoid capture by crossing the Atlantic under a neutral flag, Mason and Slidell transferred to the British mail steamer *Trent* in Havana. Captain Charles Wilkes, one of the United States Navy's most audacious officers, learned of their plans and intercepted the *Trent* as it left Cuban waters on November 8, 1861. Since the British vessel carried Confederate mail, Wilkes could have seized it as a prize. But instead, he hauled Mason and Slidell aboard the U.S.S. *San Jacinto* and allowed the *Trent* to continue its voyage, an act reminiscent of the British practice of impressment before the War of 1812. When Washington learned of this bold stroke, crowds cheered the hero of the *Trent* and Congress passed a resolution of thanks for Wilkes, but diplomats and senators worried that the capture of Mason and Slidell might spark war with Great Britain. European ministers in the capital city unanimously decried the illegality of the seizure, and the Chairman of the Senate Foreign Relations Committee, Charles Sumner, urged immediate release of the two Confederates. Lincoln himself feared Mason and Slidell might become "white elephants," but believed he could not free the prisoners without inviting overwhelming popular disapproval.[91]

News of Wilkes's audacity reached London on November 27, igniting a panic on the stock exchange and fanning fears of war. The *Morning Post* echoed Prime Minister Palmerston's typically British confidence in the Royal Navy. "In one month we could sweep all the *San Jacintos* from the seas, blockade the Northern ports, and turn to a direct and speedy issue the tide of the [civil] war now raging."[92] Palmerston began emergency Cabinet meetings on November 29, reportedly opening one of them with the angry expostulation, "I don't know whether you are going to stand this, but I'll be damned if I do!"[93] At a meeting on November 30, the Cabinet called for "ample reparation for this act of violence committed by an officer of the United States Navy against a neutral and friendly nation." Lord Lyons was instructed to demand the release of Mason and Slidell and a formal apology "for the insult offered to the British flag." These instructions were rushed to Windsor Castle for review and approval by Queen Victoria's consort, Prince Albert, a staunch advocate of Anglo-American peace. He devised a loophole allowing the United States government, if it wished, to deny that Wilkes had acted under instructions, "or, if he did, that he misapprehended them." In revised instructions reflecting Albert's determination to maintain pacific relations with the United States, Lord Russell directed Lyons "to abstain from anything like menace" when insisting on freedom for Mason and Slidell and "to be rather easy about the apology."[94]

As the watered-down ultimatum crossed the Atlantic, British merchants profit-

**"Look Out For Squalls."** The British John Bull, knowing full well his naval supremacy and aroused by the *Trent* affair, cautions a rather disreputable looking American: "You do what's right, my son, or I'll blow you out of the water." (*Punch,* 1861)

ing from trade with the Union joined Manchester liberals in an effort to quiet popular indignation. Some tough realists in the War Office and Admiralty tempered their enthusiasm for war with concern over the vulnerability of Canada and invulnerability of Boston and New York. They also feared marauding Yankee cruisers that might elude a British "blockade and prowl about the ocean in quest of prey." Albert's death from typhoid on December 14 further sobered the national mood. Two days later, Russell advised the Prime Minister to be restrained: "I incline more and more to the opinion that if the [American] answer is a reasoning, and not a blunt offensive answer, we should send once more across the Atlantic to ask compliance. . . . I do not think the country would approve an immediate declaration of war."[95]

Lyons informally delivered the ultimatum to Seward on December 19. While the President and secretary of state debated their response, pressure mounted for capitulation. From London, Charles Francis Adams warned of implacable British determination to see Mason and Slidell free. The French minister in Washington advised that the Franco-American tradition of neutrality prescribed safe passage for enemy civilians aboard neutral vessels. Charles Sumner chastised irresponsible war hawks who seemed willing to invite the shelling of American cities by British guns. So unanimous and ominous were the warnings of British resolve that Lincoln and Seward decided to defuse the crisis. In his reply to Lord Lyons, the secretary of state chauvinistically defended Wilkes's right to search the *Trent* "as a simple, legal and customary belligerent proceeding," but he diplomatically concluded that the naval officer erred in not completing the capture of the vessel and carrying her "before a legal tribunal." Seward thus disavowed Wilkes, and the United States "cheerfully liberated" the two Confederate prisoners.[96]

The successful conclusion of the *Trent* affair by no means eliminated all tension with Europe. During the crisis, Britain, France, and Spain had landed troops at Veracruz, Mexico, ostensibly to compel payment of interest on a $65 million foreign debt. Lord Russell had cautiously invited American participation in this intervention, although stipulating that his invitation did not constitute acceptance of "the extravagant pretensions" of the Monroe Doctrine. On December 4, 1861, Seward declined to participate but acknowledged the right of the powers to collect debts forcibly, provided they did not harbor political or territorial ambitions in Mexico. American fears of European plots to implant a monarchical government in Latin America were realistic. In early 1862, Prime Minister Palmerston thought "the monarchy scheme if it could be carried out . . . would be a great blessing for Mexico. . . . It would also stop the North Americans . . . in their absorption of Mexico."[97] However, the foreign office soon perceived the even more enticing opportunity to prevent Napoleon III from tampering with the continental European balance of power by allowing him to become mired down in Mexican affairs.

In April, 1862, Britain and Spain made separate arrangements for Mexican payment of their debts and withdrew from the joint venture. They left French troops to inch their way westward toward Mexico City, where Napoleon hoped to install a puppet government under Archduke Ferdinand Maximilian, an unemployed brother of the Austrian Emperor. Fierce Mexican resistance obliged Napoleon to commit increasingly large numbers of men, delaying occupation of the capital city until June of 1863. This entrapment forced Napoleon to follow Britain's lead in Civil War diplomacy, despite his own romantic predilection toward mediation in favor of the South. As historian David Crook observes, "balance of power considerations dramatized the dangers of playing solitaire in overseas adventures to the neglect of French security in Europe."[98]

## "Lookers On" Across the Atlantic

For the first nine months of 1862 British policymakers warily viewed the bloody contest. Along the Southern coast the Union's tightening blockade locked up Confederate privateers and drove neutral shipping to uneconomical, shallow draft steamers. In Tennessee an unknown general, Ulysses S. Grant, chased the rebels from Forts Donelson and Henry. Admiral David G. Farragut captured New Orleans in April, opening the Mississippi River to a campaign that would finally sever Texas and the West from the Confederacy. However, neither North nor South could score a decisive victory in the critical Eastern theater. General George B. McClellan faltered and retreated outside Richmond in July, 1862, just as Virginia's Robert E. Lee pulled back after the bloodletting at Antietam two months later. Always mindful of the vulnerability of Canada, and confident that the stalemate ultimately would exhaust Northern stamina and lead to a permanent separation of the sections, the British looked to their own interests.

From the beginning Great Britain prudently acquiesced in the Union blockade, accumulating precedents useful for future conflicts when once again England would be a belligerent and the United States neutral. The Crown's law office advised Russell that it was "highly desirable at present to avoid discussions upon abstract principles of International Law," even though the Union appeared "to have acted liberally in regard to this blockade."[99] A spokesman for the government raised the crucial question in Parliament: "how would it have been if . . . we had been the first . . . to say that the United States as a belligerent Power should not exercise all belligerent rights in the ordinary manner, because we wanted cotton?"[100]

During the first year of the blockade, in fact, England did not "want" raw cotton. The bumper American crop of 1860 provided 1.6 million bales for the saturated Lancashire mills in 1861, and production of cotton textiles far exceeded demand. Reflecting the prevalent anticipation of an early end to the Civil War, British cotton manufacturers complacently counted on their stockpiled raw cotton to carry them through a short-term crisis, which they alleviated by laying off workers and curtailing inflated production. As the military deadlock deepened in 1862, the textile producers began to fear future shortages and energetically stimulated development of alternative sources of fiber, notably in Egypt and India. These new fields began to yield amply by 1863. In France, mill owners proved less resourceful, but Napoleon's insistence on following British policy toward the Civil War prevented the Confederacy from capitalizing upon discontent in the French cotton industry. As a close student of Civil War diplomacy has concluded, "King Cotton theory was a washout in the first year of the war, a phony threat to those in the know."[101]

The Confederacy fared better in maritime Liverpool. Contemptuous of the blockade and the Queen's neutrality proclamation, Liverpool shipping interests sought to recoup from the costly disruption of trade with the South by building blockade runners, commerce raiders, and rams for English adventurers and the South's James D. Bulloch. The blockade runners returned high profits to builders, skippers, and crews. Of 2742 runs attempted during the war, steam-driven runners completed 2525, or 92 percent. However, these vessels were of light tonnage, and a substantial percentage of the successful runs occurred during the largely ineffective first year of the blockade. Moreover, greed for profits induced many Southern shippers to import luxury items rather than military materiel, thus wasting precious cargo space and draining off scarce Southern capital.

Commerce raiders presented a greater threat to the Union. James D. Bulloch contracted for these vessels and disguised them as cargo ships during construction in order to circumvent the British neutrality proclamation, which forbade outfitting warships for either belligerent. In March of 1862 the *Oreto*, to be renamed *Florida* once at sea, slipped from Liverpool. Charles Francis Adams protested vainly and pleaded with Lord Russell to detain a larger second vessel, "Number 290," then nearing completion. On July 31, Russell grudgingly concluded the new ship was intended to be a Confederate commerce raider, but his order to seize it arrived a day after the "290," an alias for *Alabama*, had sailed. Under the command of the South's most gifted naval officer, Raphael Semmes, the C.S.S. *Alabama* sank nineteen Union merchantmen in its first three months at sea. Together with the *Florida* and lesser destroyers, it preyed on worldwide Union commerce, driving Northern merchants to flags of foreign registry and sharply accelerating a scarcely noticed prewar decline in the American merchant marine. Adams ultimately obtained redress for the United States, but only after the guns of war had stilled.

Two months after the *Alabama*'s escape, Adams and the Union faced "the very crisis of our fate."[102] Awed by the Second Battle of Bull Run and the endless rivers of blood irrigating North America, Lord Russell proposed to Palmerston an Anglo-French mediation "with a view to the recognition of the independence of the Confederates."[103] Cotton shortages—the worst of the war—and fear of riots by unemployed Lancashire operatives added impetus to Russell's proposal, and at first the Prime Minister, whom Henry Adams considered "as callous as a rhinoceros," seemed receptive.[104] Unfortunately for the foreign secretary, however, France at that moment was caught in a cabinet crisis stemming from Napoleon's Mexican schemes and the Emperor's vacillation toward Italy, where a near civil war erupted in August. The Quai d'Orsay therefore hesitated, and from St. Petersburg came a resounding endorsement of the North and reunion, which the Tsar favored as a check on British supremacy in the Atlantic. News of Lee's reversal at Antietam and retreat south across the Potomac finally inclined the Prime Minister "to change the opinion on which I wrote you when the Confederates seemed to carry all before them." He had now "very much come back to our original view of the matter, that we must continue to be lookers on till the war shall have taken a more decided turn."[105] This repudiation on October 22, 1862, of both mediation and recognition of Confederate independence re-established the policy Great Britain followed for the remainder of the war.

Lincoln did all he could to insure continued European neutrality. Aware of Britain's ingrained hatred of slavery and Palmerston's abhorrence of the "diabolical Slave Trade," he issued the Emancipation Proclamation on September 22.[106] This historic gesture set January 1, 1863, as the date for freedom of slaves in areas not controlled by the Union—in short, only in districts still in rebellion. The Great Emancipator thought "it is a momentous thing to be the instrument under Providence for the liberation of a race."[107] But Palmerston sniffed that the proclamation was "trash," and Lord Russell, by then on the defensive, cynically observed of the limited manumission, "the right of slavery is made the reward of loyalty."[108] Even the workers of Lancashire evinced apathy or opposition to the emancipation. Yet some British publicists could thereafter denounce British mediation or forcible intervention on behalf of the Confederacy as "immoral."[109] As one historian judiciously writes, "much evidence still stands to the effect that the northern image improved, in the long run, after Lincoln adopted a war aim more intelligible to European opinion."[110]

As 1863 opened, Britain's cautious policy of watchful waiting was reinforced by a Polish uprising against Russian rule, which threatened general war and destruction of the critical European balance of power. Charles Francis Adams welcomed the "favorable interlude" of European disorder and waited impatiently for Union victories to give him real diplomatic clout.[111] In March, Henry Adams wrote his brother in the Union army that the diplomats needed encouragement from "military heroes," so that "we should be the cocks of the walk in England. . . . Couldn't some of you give us just one leetle sugar-plum? We are shocking dry."[112] Then in July came the good news; the Northern armies had held at Gettysburg and Grant had won control of the Mississippi River at Vicksburg. As Confederate bonds plummeted thirty-two points on the London market, Minister Adams pressed Lord Russell to seize two ironclad, steam-driven vessels nearing completion at the Laird yards in Liverpool. These shallow draft warships mounted seven-foot iron rams, theoretically an ideal weapon for piercing the wooden hulls of the Union's blockaders. Bulloch had ordered construction of the Laird rams, but he had so cleverly covered his tracks that the Pasha of Egypt appeared to be their legal owner. Since the rams lacked guns and the Crown lacked proof of Confederate ownership, Russell's law officers could not find them in violation of British neutrality. Russell, however, dared not disregard Adams' increasingly shrill warnings, nor the Union's midsummer military victories. On September 3, 1863, he prudently detained the rams. Should the purchasers successfully claim damages in British courts, he wrote Palmerston, "we have satisfied the opinion which prevails here as well as in America that that kind of neutral hostility should not be allowed to go on without some attempt to stop it."[113]

Unaware of the foreign secretary's concession, Adams on September 5 penned a scathing note warning that if the rams were not halted, "it would be superfluous in me to point out to your lordship that this is war!"[114] Palmerston bridled at Adams' "insolent threats of war" and thought Russell should "say to him in civil terms, 'You be damned.'"[115] But the Prime Minister's private irritation did not detract from Adams' successful elimination of the Confederacy's last threat to the blockade, a triumph his son Henry immodestly recorded as a second Vicksburg victory. Indeed, the "American Minister had trumped their [the British] best card and won the game."[116]

Northern morale also received a boost from the visit of the Russian Baltic and Pacific squadrons to New York and San Francisco in September and October of 1863. Fearful of war with England over Poland, Russia sent its ships in the hope that they could operate against the Royal Navy from the ice-free American ports. Northerners, however, wishfully interpreted the visit as a sign of St. Petersburg's support for their cause. Secretary of the Navy Gideon Welles thought "our Russian friends are rendering us a great service."[117]

In 1863, too, the troops of Napoleon III finally fought their way into Mexico City. In July, the victorious French Emperor proclaimed a Mexican monarchy under Austrian Archduke Maximilian. Secretary Seward immediately recalled his

**Charles Francis Adams (1807–1886).** Son of John Quincy Adams, graduate of Harvard, abolitionist, and Republican congressman from Massachusetts before Lincoln appointed him minister to Great Britain (1861–1868), the suave and self-possessed diplomat labored diligently to keep London neutral during the Civil War. (Portrait by William Morris Hunt, Fogg Art Museum, Courtesy of the Harvard University Portrait Collection)

minister, and denied recognition to Maximilian when the hapless claimant to the shaky new throne arrived in Mexico in July, 1864. By then Sherman was marching through Georgia and Grant was creeping bloodily toward Richmond. The apparently inevitable Union triumph would place a huge army and one of the world's largest navies along the border of Napoleon's puppet state. In April the United States Congress passed a resolution condemning the French invasion of Mexico. But Lincoln's Administration, hoping to avoid confrontation with France, disavowed the measure, confident in Seward's words that "those who are most impatient for the defeat of European and monarchical designs in Mexico might well be content to abide the effects which must result from the ever-increasing expansion of the American people westward and southward."[118] Napoleon began to scale down his commitment, intending to remove all but 20,000 French troops from Mexico by 1867. He also curried favor with Washington by directing Maximilian not to receive any Confederate ministers, and to further appease Seward he seized two Confederate rams under construction at Nantes in May, 1864. A month later the U.S.S. *Kearsarge* sank the C.S.S. *Alabama* within sight of Cherbourg. The diplomatic and naval isolation of the Confederacy was complete. "King Cotton" had failed. Confederate diplomacy, lacking decisive support from the battlefield, did not win European capitals to its cause. The "War Between the States" had remained just that.

## "A Power of the First Class": The Expansionist Revival

When the guns of the Civil War quieted at Appomattox in April, 1865, Americans took account of their recent past and their apparently dim future. Over six hundred thousand countrymen lay dead and hundreds of thousands nursed disfiguring wounds. The war cost at least twenty billion dollars in destroyed property and expenditures. The American merchant marine was in a shambles, and commerce was badly disrupted. The eleven Confederate states suffered heavy economic losses, as a dislocated population and labor force, including four million former slaves, looked upon trampled and denuded agricultural fields and burned-out cities. Although the Union was whole once again, regional bitterness persisted. The wrenching Civil War experience and the necessity of postwar reconstruction suggested indeed that sectionalism would continue to impede traditional United States expansion abroad.

Countervailing evidence, however, indicated that the expansionism that had flourished in the 1840s and was muted in the 1850s would enjoy a rebirth. Ideas of Manifest Destiny about the natural growth of the United States into new territories survived. Although trade had been thrown askew, Northern commerce in wheat with England expanded greatly during the war, and prospects for a renewal of the cotton trade were good. Measurable economic changes held foreign policy implications. During the war Northern politicians established high tariffs to protect Northern manufacturers, stabilized the banking system, passed the Homestead Act to settle western lands and the Morrill Act to build land-grant colleges, and provided for the construction of a transcontinental railroad. Although historians differ over the economic impact of the Civil War on the North, it was evident that large federal expenditures of about $2 million a day generated capital accumulation and stimulated some industries. In so doing, the Civil War helped spur the "industrial revolution" of the late nineteenth century in America, which increasingly shifted the character of American foreign trade from agricultural to industrial goods and prompted the sale of surplus production overseas. Conspicuous industrial might was also a component of American power in the eyes of other nations. Because Northern diplomacy and European caution had prevented the Civil War from becoming an international conflict, these economic gains could be registered, insuring opportunities for expansion.

Once freed from the constraints of war, Secretary of State William H. Seward envisioned a larger American empire. Noted as an expansionist before the Civil War, Seward during the war had bristled over the intrusion of domestic affairs in his grand vision for continued expansion of the United States. In 1853 Seward had proclaimed that the boundary of the United States "shall be extended so that it shall greet the sun when he touches the tropics and when he sends his gleaming rays towards the polar circle, and shall include even distant islands in either ocean."[119] In 1865 Seward turned his attention southward, intent upon driving the

French and Maximilian from Mexico, annexing territories, and building naval bases in the Caribbean. Santo Domingo, which Spain had cast off again in July, 1865, became one of Seward's first targets. The British, when they began their retreat from Central America in the late 1850s, had predicted that the United States would eventually "overrun" neighbors just as it had done with Louisiana, Texas, and California.[120] *The Spectator* summed up the postwar reality: "Nobody doubts any more that the Union is a power of the first class, a nation which it is very dangerous to offend and almost impossible to attack."[121]

The British had good reason to be sensitive about the United States. Northern anger toward London was bitter, especially over the depredations of the *Alabama* and the seeming British tolerance of Southern secession. Also, Anglo-American competition in Central America and the Caribbean joined competition in the Pacific and Asia to propel London and Washington along a collision course. Reciprocity with Canada was breaking down, and the Agreement of 1854 was abrogated in 1866. A new generation of American Anglophobes vowed to twist the British lion's tail. Some Americans insisted that Britannia relinquish Canada to the United States as proper repentance for British sins in the Civil War. If the British reaped intense American hostility, they also carried away from the scrape some welcomed precedents in international law. The seafaring British acquiesced in the tortuous American rendering of maritime rights during the Civil War. The Lincoln Administration reversed the traditional American view of neutral rights and adopted what had been the British position. Seward insisted that the war was a *domestic* conflict, yet the United States declared a paper-thin blockade under *international* law. Not only did this behavior constitute a glaring contradiction; it also proved to be a violation of international law, for blockades must be effective. Seward also condemned Confederate privateering and commerce raiding. He even reversed the hallowed American doctrine that neutral shipping was immune to capture when traveling between neutral ports, regardless of the ultimate destination of the cargo: in 1863 he implicitly approved the capture of the *Peterhoff*, a British steamer loaded with Confederate goods en route to Matamoros, Mexico. The United States, it seemed to Britons, had repudiated principles thought worthy to fight over in 1812. During the period of American neutrality in the First World War (1914–1917), the British dusted off their history tomes and reminded Washington of Seward's Civil War policies. The legacy of the Civil War had a long reach indeed.

## Further Reading for the Period 1848–1865

For the muted expansionism of the 1850s, especially in the western hemisphere, see Amos A. Ettinger, *The Mission to Spain of Pierre Soulé, 1853–1855* (1932), Philip Foner, *A History of Cuba and Its Relations with the United States* (1962–1963), Norman A. Graebner, ed., *Manifest Destiny* (1968), Lester D. Langley, *The Cuban Policy of the United States* (1968), Robert E. May, *The Southern Dream of a Caribbean Empire, 1854–1861* (1973), Dexter Perkins, *The Monroe Doctrine, 1826–1867* (1933), Basil Rauch, *American Interest in Cuba, 1848–1855* (1948), William O. Scroggs, *Filibusters and Financiers* (1916) (on Walker), Lester B. Shippee, *Canadian-American Relations, 1849–1874* (1939), and Richard W. Van Alstyne, "Empire in Midpassage, 1845–1867," in William A. Williams, ed., *From Colony to Empire* (1972) and *The Rising American Empire* (1960).

The contributions of principal makers of American diplomacy are examined in Samuel Flagg Bemis, ed., *The American Secretaries of State and Their Diplomacy* (1927–1970), David Donald, *Charles Sumner and the Rights of Man* (1970), Holman Hamilton, *Zachary Taylor* (1941–1951), Philip S. Klein, *President James Buchanan* (1962), Jay Monaghan, *Diplomat in Carpet Slippers* (1945) (on Lincoln), Roy F. Nichols, *Franklin Pierce* (1958), John Niven, *Gideon Welles, Lincoln's Secretary of the Navy* (1973), Ernest N. Paolino, *The Foundations of the American Empire* (1973) (on Seward), Walter G. Sharrow, "William Henry Seward and the Basis for American Empire, 1850–1860," *Pacific Historical Review* (1967), Kenneth E. Shewmaker, "Daniel Webster and the Politics of Foreign Policy, 1850–1852," *Journal of American History* (1976), Ivor D. Spencer, *The Victor and the Spoils* (1959) (on Marcy), and Glyndon G. Van Deusen, *William Henry Seward* (1967). For brief sketches of leaders, consult John A. Garraty, ed., *Encyclopedia of American Biography* (1974).

American contacts with Asia, including Perry's expedition, are discussed in Warren I. Cohen, *America's Response to China* (1971), Tyler Dennett, *Americans in Eastern Asia* (1922), Foster R. Dulles, *China and America* (1946) and *Yankee and Samurai* (1965) (on Japan), John K. Fairbank, *Trade and Diplomacy on the China Coast: The Opening of the Treaty Ports, 1842–1854* (1953) and "'American China Policy' to 1898: A Misconception," *Pacific Historical Review* (1970), Akira Iriye, ed., *Mutual Images: Essays in American-Japanese Relations* (1975), Samuel E. Morison, *"Old Bruin:" Commodore Matthew C. Perry* (1967), Charles Neu, *The Troubled Encounter: The United States and Japan* (1975), William L. Neumann, *America Encounters Japan* (1963), Richard W. Van Alstyne, *The United States and East Asia* (1973), and Arthur Walworth, *Black Ships Off Japan* (1946).

The pivotal Anglo-American relationship is the subject of H. C. Allen, *Great Britain and the United States* (1955), Kenneth Bourne, *Britain and the Balance of Power in North America, 1815–1908* (1967), Charles S. Campbell, *From Revolution to Rapprochement* (1974), Wilbur D. Jones, *The American Problem in British Diplomacy* (1974), Herbert G. Nicholas, *The United States and Britain* (1975), and Mary W. Williams, *Anglo-American Isthmian Diplomacy, 1815–1915* (1916).

For European issues, see Henry M. Adams, *Prussian-American Relations, 1775–1871* (1960), Thomas A. Bailey, *America Faces Russia* (1950), Henry Blumenthal, *A Reappraisal of Franco-American Relations, 1830–1871* (1959) and *France and the United States: Their Diplomatic Relations, 1789–1914* (1970), Merle E. Curti, "Austria and the United States, 1848–1852," *Smith College Studies in History* (1926) and "Young America," *American Historical Review* (1926), Alan Dowty, *The Limits of American Isolation* (1971) (on Crimean War), James A. Field, Jr., *America and the Mediterranean World, 1776–1882* (1969), and William A. Williams, *American-Russian Relations, 1781–1947* (1952).

For the Union and Confederate foreign policies of the Civil War years, especially for questions arising from navies and maritime rights, see some of the works cited above and Ephraim D. Adams, *Great Britain and the American Civil War* (1925), Stuart L. Bernath, *Squall Across the Atlantic: American Civil War Prize Cases and Diplomacy* (1970), Henry Blumenthal, "Confederate Diplomacy," *Journal of Southern History* (1966), Lynn M. Case and Warren F. Spencer, *The United States and France: Civil War Diplomacy* (1970), Adrian Cook, *The Alabama Claims* (1975), David P. Crook, *Diplomacy During the American Civil War* (1974) and *The North, the South, and the Powers, 1861–1865* (1974), Charles P. Cullop, *Confederate Propaganda in Europe*

(1969), Norman A. Graebner, "Northern Diplomacy and European Neutrality," in David Donald, ed., *Why the North Won the Civil War* (1960), Frank J. Merli, *Great Britain and the Confederate Navy* (1970), Frank L. and Harriet Owsley, *King Cotton Diplomacy* (1959), Carlton Savage, *Policy of the United States toward Maritime Commerce in War* (1934), Robin Winks, *Canada and the United States: The Civil War Years* (1960), and Albert A. Woldman, *Lincoln and the Russians* (1952).

For other works, see Norman A. Graebner, ed., *American Diplomatic History Before 1900* (1977) and the following notes.

## Notes to Chapter 4

1. Quoted in Arthur Walworth, *Black Ships Off Japan* (New York: Alfred A. Knopf, 1946), p. 96.
2. Quoted in William L. Neumann, *America Encounters Japan: From Perry to MacArthur* (Baltimore: The Johns Hopkins University Press, 1963), p. 30.
3. Quoted in Henry F. Graff, *Bluejackets with Perry in Japan* (New York: New York Public Library, 1952), p. 68.
4. Quoted in Shunsuke Kamei, "The Sacred Land of Liberty: Images of America in Nineteenth Century Japan," in Akira Iriye, ed., *Mutual Images: Essays in American-Japanese Relations* (Cambridge, Mass.: Harvard University Press, 1975), p. 55.
5. Quoted in Oliver Statler, *The Black Ship Scroll* (Tokyo: John Weatherhill, 1963), p. 8.
6. Quoted in Walworth, *Black Ships Off Japan*, p. 71.
7. Francis L. Hawks, ed., *Narrative of the Expedition of an American Squadron to the China Seas and Japan* (Washington: Beverley Tucker, Senate Printer, 1856; 3 vols.), I, 256–257, 261, 263.
8. Quoted in Graff, *Bluejackets with Perry*, p. 127.
9. Quoted in Samuel Eliot Morison, *"Old Bruin": Commodore Matthew C. Perry, 1794–1858* (Boston: Little Brown, 1967), p. 371.
10. Quoted in Neumann, *America Encounters Japan*, p. 40.
11. Quoted in Graff, *Bluejackets with Perry*, p. 68.
12. Quoted in Morison, *"Old Bruin,"* p. 411.
13. Quoted *ibid.*, pp. 417, 425, 429.
14. Quoted in Richard W. Van Alstyne, *The Rising American Empire* (New York: W. W. Norton, 1974 [1960]), p. 175.
15. John K. Fairbank, *Trade and Diplomacy on the China Coast* (Cambridge, Mass.: Harvard University Press, 1953; 2 vols.), I, 208.
16. Quoted in Warren I. Cohen, *America's Response to China* (New York: John Wiley & Sons, 1971), p. 22.
17. Charles E. Neu, *The Troubled Encounter: The United States and Japan* (New York: John Wiley & Sons, 1975), p. 9.
18. Quoted in Richard W. Van Alstyne, "Empire in Mid-passage, 1845–1867," in William A. Williams, ed., *From Colony to Empire* (New York: John Wiley & Sons, 1972), p. 119.

19. Eugene D. Genovese, *The Political Economy of Slavery* (New York: Vintage Books, 1967), p. 270.
20. Quoted in Eric Foner, *Free Labor, Free Soil, Free Men* (New York: Oxford University Press, 1970), p. 72.
21. Quoted in Kenneth E. Shewmaker, "Daniel Webster and the Politics of Foreign Policy, 1850–1852," *Journal of American History*, LXIII (September, 1976), 308.
22. Quoted in George T. Curtis, *Life of Daniel Webster* (New York: D. Appleton, 1870; 2 vols.), II, 537.
23. Quoted in Robert R. Davis, Jr., "Diplomatic Plumage: American Court Dress in the National Period," *American Quarterly*, XX (Summer, 1968), 173.
24. Quoted in Russell B. Nye, *George Bancroft: Brahmin Rebel* (New York: Alfred A. Knopf, 1944), p. 205.
25. Quoted in Allan Nevins, *Ordeal of the Union* (New York: Charles Scribner's Sons, 1947; 2 vols.), II, 347.
26. Quoted in Albert K. Weinberg, *Manifest Destiny* (Chicago: Quadrangle Books, 1963 [1935]), pp. 201–202.
27. Quoted in David Potter, *The Impending Crisis, 1848–1861* (New York: Harper & Row, 1976), p. 198.
28. Quoted in Robert F. Durden, "J. D. B. DeBow: Convolutions of a Slavery Expansionist," *Journal of Southern History*, XVII (November, 1951), 450.
29. Quoted in Robert E. May, *The Southern Dream of a Caribbean Empire, 1854–1861* (Baton Rouge: Louisiana State University Press, 1973), p. 5.
30. Quoted in Philip S. Foner, *A History of Cuba and Its Relations with the United States* (New York: International Publishers, 1962–1963; 2 vols.), II, 43.
31. Quoted *ibid.*, p. 64.
32. Quoted *ibid.*, p. 59.
33. Quoted in Durden, "J. D. B. DeBow," p. 451.
34. Quoted in C. Stanley Urban, "The Abortive Quitman Filibustering Expedition, 1853–1855," *Journal of Mississippi History*, XVIII (July, 1956), 177.
35. Quoted in C. Stanley Urban, "The Africanization of Cuba Scare, 1853–1855," *Hispanic American Historical Review*, XXXVII (February, 1957), 37.
36. Quoted in May, *Southern Dream*, p. 75.

37. Quoted in William H. Goetzmann, *When the Eagle Screamed: The Romantic Horizon in American Diplomacy, 1800–1860* (New York: John Wiley & Sons, 1966), p. 87.

38. Quoted in Roy F. Nichols, *Franklin Pierce: Young Hickory of the Granite Hills* (Philadelphia: University of Pennsylvania Press, 1931), p. 459.

39. William O. Scroggs, *Filibusters and Financiers: The Story of William Walker and His Associates* (New York: Macmillan, 1916), p. 241.

40. Quoted in May, *Southern Dream*, p. 91.

41. Quoted in Randall O. Hudson, "The Filibuster Minister: The Career of John Hill Wheeler as United States Minister to Nicaragua, 1854–1856," *North Carolina Historical Review*, XLIX (July, 1972), 295.

42. Quoted in May, *Southern Dream*, pp. 131–132.

43. *Ibid.*, p. 244.

44. Goetzmann, *When the Eagle Screamed*, p. 78.

45. Nevins, *Ordeal of the Union*, II, 63.

46. Quoted in Weinberg, *Manifest Destiny*, p. 190.

47. Parke Goodwin, quoted in Norman A. Graebner, ed., *Manifest Destiny* (Indianapolis: Bobbs-Merrill, 1968), p. lxiv.

48. Quoted in John A. Logan, Jr., *No Transfer: An American Security Principle* (New Haven: Yale University Press, 1961), p. 227.

49. Quoted in Basil Rauch, *American Interest in Cuba, 1848–1855* (New York: Columbia University Press, 1948), p. 176.

50. Foster Stearns, "Edward Everett," in Samuel Flagg Bemis, ed., *American Secretaries of State and Their Diplomacy* (New York: Cooper Square Publishers, 1963; 18 vols.), VI, 135, and John Bassett Moore, *A Digest of International Law* (Washington, D.C.: Government Printing Office, 1906; 8 vols.), VI, 462.

51. Quoted in Gavin B. Henderson, "Southern Designs on Cuba, 1854–1857 and Some European Opinions," *Journal of Southern History*, V (August, 1939), 385.

52. Quoted in Lester D. Langley, *The Cuban Policy of the United States* (New York: John Wiley & Sons, 1968), p. 37.

53. Quoted in J. Preston Moore, "Pierre Soulé: Southern Expansionist and Promoter," *Journal of Southern History*, XXI (1955), 205–206.

54. Quoted *ibid.*, p. 207.

55. Quoted in Amos A. Ettinger, *The Mission to Spain of Pierre Soulé, 1853–1855* (New Haven: Yale University Press, 1932), p. 378.

56. Quoted in Henry B. Learned, "William Learned Marcy," in Bemis, ed., *American Secretaries of State*, VI, 193.

57. Quoted in Ruhl J. Bartlett, ed., *The Record of American Diplomacy* (New York: Alfred A. Knopf, 1960; 3rd ed.), p. 241.

58. Quoted in Henderson, "Southern Designs," p. 374.

59. Quoted in Ivor D. Spencer, *The Victor and the Spoils: A Life of William L. Marcy* (Providence: Brown University Press, 1959), pp. 338–339.

60. Nichols, *Franklin Pierce*, p. 371.

61. Quoted in Philip S. Klein, *President James Buchanan: A Biography* (University Park: Pennsylvania State University Press, 1962), p. 324.

62. Quoted in Graebner, *Manifest Destiny*, p. 298.

63. Quoted in May, *Southern Dream*, p. 7.

64. Quoted in H. G. Nicholas, *The United States and Britain* (Chicago: University of Chicago Press, 1975), p. 22.

65. Quoted in Philip Guedalla, ed., *Gladstone and Palmerston* (New York: Kraus Reprint, 1971 [1928]), p. 208.

66. United States Senate, Executive Document 27 [Serial 660], 32 Cong., 2 Sess., p. 30.

67. Quoted in Kenneth Bourne, *The Foreign Policy of Victorian England, 1830–1902* (Oxford: Clarendon Press, 1970), p. 334.

68. Quoted in Wilbur D. Jones, *The American Problem in British Diplomacy, 1841–1861* (Athens: University of Georgia Press, 1974), p. 75.

69. Quoted in Mary W. Williams, *Anglo-American Isthmian Diplomacy, 1815–1915* (Washington: American Historical Association, 1916), p. 92, and Charles S. Campbell, *From Revolution to Rapprochement: The United States and Great Britain, 1783–1900* (New York: John Wiley & Sons, 1974), p. 81.

70. Hunter Miller, ed., *Treaties and Other International Acts of the United States of America* (Washington: Government Printing Office, 1931–1948; 8 vols.), V, 672.

71. *Ibid.*, p. 685.

72. Jones, *American Problem*, p. 88.

73. Quoted in Richard A. Van Alstyne, "The Clayton-Bulwer Treaty, 1850–60," *Journal of Modern History*, XI (June, 1939), 156.

74. Kenneth Bourne, *Britain and the Balance of Power in North America, 1815–1908* (London: Longmans, Green, 1967), p. 177.

75. Quoted *ibid.*, p. 182.

76. Quoted *ibid.*, p. 189.

77. Quoted in Margaret O. W. Oliphant, *Memoir of the Life of Laurence Oliphant and of Alice Oliphant, His Wife* (Edinburgh: William Blackwood and Sons, 1891; 2 vols.), I, 120.

78. Quoted in H. C. Allen, *Great Britain and the United States* (New York: St. Martin's Press, 1955), p. 423.

79. Kenneth Bourne, "The Clayton-Bulwer Treaty and the Decline of British Opposition to the Territorial Expansion of the United States, 1857–60," *Journal of Modern History*, XXXIII (September, 1961), 289.

80. Quoted in Allan Nevins, *The Coming Fury* (Garden City, N.Y.: Doubleday, 1961), p. 217.

81. Jay Monaghan, *Diplomat in Carpet Slippers: Abraham Lincoln Deals with Foreign Affairs* (Indianapolis: Charter Books, 1945), p. 58.

82. Quoted in John G. Nicolay and John Hay, *Abraham Lincoln: A History* (New York: The Century, 1890; 10 vols.), III, 445–449.

83. Quoted in Monaghan, *Diplomat in Carpet Slippers*, p. 82.

84. S. R. Cockerill, quoted in Frank L. Owsley and Harriet C. Owsley, *King Cotton Diplomacy: Foreign Relations of the Confederate States of America* (Chicago: University of Chicago Press, 1959; rev. ed.), p. 19.

85. Quoted in Norman A. Graebner, "Northern Diplomacy and European Neutrality," in David Donald, ed., *Why the North Won the Civil War* (Baton Rouge: Louisiana State University Press, 1960), p. 56.

86. Quoted in Monaghan, *Diplomat in Carpet Slippers*, p. 26.

87. *Ibid.*, p. 100

88. Quoted *ibid.*, p. 102.

89. Worthington C. Ford, ed., *Letters of Henry Adams* (Boston: Houghton Mifflin, 1930-1938; 2 vols.), I, 92.

90. Quoted *ibid.*, p. 93.

91. Quoted in Allan Nevins, *The War for the Union* (New York: Charles Scribner's Sons, 1959-1971; 4 vols.), I, 392.

92. Quoted in David P. Crook, *The North, the South, and the Powers* (New York: John Wiley & Sons, 1974), p. 130.

93. Quoted in Bourne, *Britain and Balance of Power*, p. 219.

94. Quoted in Crook, *The North, the South, and the Powers*, pp. 132, 133-134.

95. Quoted *ibid.*, pp. 147, 140.

96. George E. Baker, ed., *The Works of William H. Seward* (New York: Redfield; and Boston: Houghton Mifflin, 1853-1884; 5 vols.), V, 295-309.

97. Quoted in Crook, *The North, the South, and the Powers*, pp. 93, 184.

98. *Ibid.*, p. 182.

99. *Ibid.*, p. 176.

100. *Ibid.*, p. 179.

101. David P. Crook, *Diplomacy During the American Civil War* (New York: John Wiley & Sons, 1975), p. 74.

102. Quoted in Crook, *Diplomacy*, p. 93.

103. Quoted *ibid.*, pp. 86-87.

104. Ford, *Letters of Henry Adams*, I, 122.

105. Quoted in Norman A. Graebner, "European Interventionism and the Crisis of 1862," *Journal of the Illinois State Historical Society*, LXIX (February, 1976), 43.

106. Quoted in Campbell, *From Revolution to Rapprochement*, p. 79.

107. Quoted in Monaghan, *Diplomat in Carpet Slippers*, p. 273.

108. Quoted in Robert H. Jones, *Disrupted Decades: The Civil War and Reconstruction Years* (New York: Charles Scribner's Sons, 1973), p. 376 and Crook, *Diplomacy*, p. 96.

109. Quoted in Crook, *Diplomacy*, p. 97.

110. Crook, *The North, the South, and the Powers*, p. 237.

111. Quoted in Crook, *Diplomacy*, p. 123.

112. Ford, *Letters of Henry Adams*, I, 96.

113. Quoted in Monaghan, *Diplomat in Carpet Slippers*, p. 328.

114. Quoted in Frank J. Merli, *Great Britain and the Confederate Navy, 1861-1865* (Bloomington: Indiana University Press, 1970), p. 201.

115. Quoted in Owsley and Owsley, *King Cotton Diplomacy*, p. 402.

116. Henry Adams, *The Education of Henry Adams: An Autobiography* (Boston: Houghton Mifflin, 1961 [1918]), p. 174.

117. Quoted in Howard K. Beale, ed., *Diary of Gideon Welles* (New York: W. W. Norton, 1960; 3 vols.), I, 484.

118. Quoted in Crook, *Diplomacy*, p. 164.

119. Quoted in Ernest N. Paolino, *The Foundations of the American Empire: William Henry Seward and U.S. Foreign Policy* (Ithaca: Cornell University Press, 1973), p. 7.

120. Lord Clarendon quoted in Bourne, *The Balance of Power in North America*, p. 202.

121. Quoted in H. C. Allen, "Civil War, Reconstruction, and Great Britain," in Harold Hyman, ed., *Heard Round the World: The Impact Abroad of the Civil War* (New York: Alfred A. Knopf, 1969), p. 35.

**Ulysses S. Grant (1822–1885).** Graduate of the United States Military Academy, soldier in the Mexican War, and Civil War general before becoming President, Grant worked hard but unsuccessfully for the annexation of the Dominican Republic. (Library of Congress)

# 5 Global Rivalry, Regional Power, 1865–1895

## Diplomatic Crossroad: The Foiled Grab of Santo Domingo, 1869–1870

President Ulysses S. Grant was infatuated with his pet project as he walked from the White House across Lafayette Park to the elegant brick home of the Chairman of the Senate Foreign Relations Committee, Charles Sumner. The flattery of senatorial egos sometimes brought fruitful results, and in this case Grant was reaching for a two-thirds vote. Politics was politics, after all. On the evening of January 2, 1870, in Washington, Sumner was offering good food and intense conversation to two politicos when Grant appeared at the door, uninvited and unexpected. Several awkward moments passed before the President revealed his mission to the powerful senator from Massachusetts. Would Sumner support a treaty of annexation for the Dominican Republic? Grant appeared impatient and only briefly sketched his case for this imperialist scheme. Sumner said simply that he would study the matter. Yet Grant, indulging in a bit of wishful thinking, departed persuaded that the senator would back the project. An American land grab seemed imminent—at least Grant thought so.

The Dominican Republic, or Santo Domingo, constantly strife-torn and invariably ruled by the unscrupulous, had long been within the United States' expansionist vision. The Navy coveted the harbor at Samaná Bay, a choice strategic site in the Caribbean. The island's raw materials, especially timber and minerals, and its undeveloped status invited the attention of foreign businessmen; others thought of the island as a potential sanitarium for isthmian canal workers struck by yellow fever. The Caribbean, in any case, was destined to become an American lake. Dominican President Buenaventura Baez, "an active intriguer of sinister talents," had been making the appropriate noises of subservience for months.[1] He seemed eager to part with his country. In July of 1869, Grant's personal secretary, General Orville Babcock, went to Santo Domingo to study the possibility of annexing this "Gibraltar of the New World."

Babcock was no saintly diplomat. Later exposed as a member of the Whiskey Ring, which defrauded the United

**Samaná Bay, Dominican Republic.** A central place in the Caribbean dreams of some American leaders. (*Harper's Weekly*, 1869)

States Treasury of millions of dollars, Babcock in this case also looked to personal profit. He befriended William Cazneau and Joseph Fabens, two American speculators and sometime diplomatic agents who owned key Dominican port facilities, mines, and banks. They also represented a steamship company that sought traffic between New York and the island. With Cazneau and Fabens in the wings, and American warships in Dominican waters, Babcock and Baez struck a deal in two treaties signed on November 29, 1869. In the first, the United States agreed to annex the Dominican Republic and assume the national debt of $1.5 million. The second treaty promised that if the United States Senate refused to take all of the country, Samaná Bay could be had for $2 million. After the signing, Babcock and Fabens prematurely hoisted the American flag at Samaná.

Babcock had done his work well, and Grant began to lobby for annexation. His visit to Sumner's house was a calculated step to build support. Yet the slow-moving and independent-minded Sumner remained noncommittal for months. The more Sumner and his colleagues heard, the more they recoiled from the untidy affair. Baez was a corrupt money-grabber about to be driven from office by rebels, who were being harassed in turn by the United States Navy. It appeared that Baez remained in power because the United States wanted him in power. Babcock was still a military officer, not a diplomatic official. After Babcock had negotiated the treaties, they were left to a lowly State Department functionary to sign. Fabens and Cazneau, furthermore, were notorious schemers who had obviously enthralled Grant and his advisers with their grand Dominican scenario. Finally, Haiti and Santo Domingo were nearly at war. Sumner grumbled against this set of unsavory facts.

Grant grew annoyed with Sumner's lethargy and worked vigorously for the treaty by personally buttonholing senators. He warned reluctant Cabinet members, who had not been consulted on annexation, to back the treaty or resign. The indignant but cautious Secretary of State, Hamilton Fish, whose department had been bypassed in the rush to grab Santo Domingo, threatened to quit, but a sense of loyalty and Grant's personal appeal kept him at his diminished post. Fish favored American hegemony over the island, but in the form of a "protectorate" rather than a formal territorial annexation. He could not persuade the stubborn President, who seemed bent on total victory or total defeat. On March 15, 1870, the Foreign Relations Committee, by a 5–2 vote, with Sumner in the lead, disapproved the treaty. Days later Sumner launched the debate on the Senate floor, disparaging annexation but favoring a "free confederacy" in the West Indies where the "black race should predominate" and be protected by the United States.[2]

Annexationists countered that absorption of the island would insure a steady flow of raw materials to the United States. They displayed pieces of Dominican hemp to prove their point and two senators performed a tug-of-war to demonstrate the fiber's power. Another predicted that the spindles of New England textile mills would "whirl" once the Dominicans began to buy American cotton goods. Anti-imperialists retorted that the island was infested with Spanish-speaking Catholics and nonwhites, two groups out of favor in white Anglo-Saxon Protestant America; that annexation would spur a larger navy, which would in turn involve the United States in foreign troubles; that Americans were acting too much like colonizing Europeans; that next they would be expected to annex adjacent black Haiti; and that Congress had a constitutional duty to check such presidential schemes. Sumner protested a "usurpation of power" by the executive branch, which was employing the Navy in the Caribbean in acts of hostility without congressional approval.[3]

To regain the offensive, Grant on May 31 sent a special message to Congress extolling the virtues of the tiny island. It read like an expansionist's shopping list: raw materials from mines and forests, excellent harbors, a naval base, national security, a market for American products, and a site from which to help settle the revolution raging in Cuba. America had to keep its word as recorded by the two treaties. Darkly, and without evidence, the President warned that if the United States did not take Santo Domingo, some other country would. The Monroe Doctrine would be endangered. He also had the audacity to report the result of a farcical rigged plebiscite in which the Dominicans registered their support for selling themselves to the United States by the rather remarkable vote of 15,169 in favor to only 11 against.

Sumner would not budge. Observers noticed a good deal of personal feuding in this issue. Grant had always considered Sumner an arrogant sort and a political challenger. Sumner had been cool to Grant's nomination in 1868, had opposed some of the President's appointees, and was linked to the radical wing of the Republican party—a faction to which Grant never warmed. Grant also felt betrayed, remembering that night in January when he believed Sumner had given his word of support. Sumner, for his part, had little respect for the error-prone and intellectually inferior Grant and probably felt pique at not being considered for the post of secretary of state. Sumner's explosive temper, exaggerated rhetoric, and attitude of intellectual certainty "excited obstinacy, anger and contempt" in Grant, noted Charles Francis Adams. The senator, commented one of his friends, treated "difference of opinion almost as moral delinquency."[4] Editor E. L. Godkin of *The Nation* remarked that Sumner "works his adjectives so hard that if they ever catch him alone, they will murder him."[5] The Dominican annexation treaty brought such personal antagonisms and different styles to the forefront.

On June 30, the Senate voted 28–28 on the treaty of annexation, well short of the two-thirds vote required for ratification. An agitated Grant reacted by abruptly firing the Ambassador to Britain, John L. Motley. That seemed a strange thing to do, but Motley was a close friend and confidant of Sumner's, who appeared to represent Sumner as much as the State Department. A strike against him meant a blow against the haughty Massachusetts senator. "I will not allow Mr. Sumner to ride over me," Grant declared.[6] Secretary Fish had opposed Grant's vengeful behavior, but he too grew annoyed with Sumner, who had stirred up trouble with the British over the *Alabama* claims issue and who seemed bent on making foreign policy in the Senate. Fish, Grant, and loyal party Republicans boldly set about to strip Sumner of his chairmanship of the Foreign Relations Committee.

Sumner began to lose support among his colleagues when he refused to accept Grant's proposal for a commission to study Dominican annexation. The senator saw it as a trick, a "dance of blood," and said so very dramatically in his famous "Naboth's Vineyard" speech (referring to the Biblical story of King Ahab, who coveted his neighbor's vineyard). Delivered to the Senate on December 21, 1870,

**Charles Sumner (1811–1874).** Harvard graduate, lawyer, abolitionist, critic of the Mexican War, Senator from Massachusetts, and Chairman of the Foreign Relations Committee (1861–1871), the strong-willed Sumner blocked attempts to annex the Dominican Republic and harassed England over the *Alabama* claims. (*Cosmopolitan,* 1887)

this intense oration reminded listeners of those pre-Civil War days when Sumner had blasted the defenders of slavery. Now Sumner chastised Cazneau and Fabens as "political jockeys" who had "seduced" Babcock. Santo Domingo, he insisted, belonged to the "colored" Dominicans and "our duty is as plain as the Ten Commandments. Kindness, beneficence, assistance, aid, help, protection, all that is implied in good neighborhood, these we must give freely, bountifully, but their independence is as sacred to them as is ours to us."[7] The Senate voted 32–9 to establish the commission (it issued a favorable report in early 1871), handing Sumner a severe defeat. Many senators voted "aye" not because they supported annexation, but because the commission was a face-saving device for Grant and a rebuke to the carping Sumner. In March, 1871, the Republican caucus voted 26–21 to remove Sumner altogether from the Foreign Relations Committee. Sumner, ill and irascible, had been duly punished for his opposition. Yet he still savored his victory over the Dominican land grab scheme. Grant could only walk through Lafayette Park, shake his fist at Sumner's house, and snap: "That man who lives up there has abused me in a way which I never suffered from any other man living."[8]

## Expansion and Imperialism

The foiled grab of Santo Domingo, coming so shortly after the Civil War, suggests that the sectional conflict was only a brief interlude in the continuity of American expansion. To be sure, most Americans in 1865 were not thinking about the Dominican Republic or foreign policy issues. But the United States government, even though it lacked well-defined, cohesive foreign "policies," very quickly set the nation once again on a course of empire. What changed after the Civil War was not the fact of imperial expansion, but the distant, often noncontiguous location of the peoples whom the United States chose to dominate, the increased use of "informal" means of control, and, for those areas formally annexed, a long-term colonial status rather than statehood.

The imperial path was not an easy or direct one, for, as the Dominican episode illustrates, domestic politics, the whims and antagonisms of personalities, and tension between the executive and legislative branches of government could intrude. There were many uncertainties and hesitancies in the 1865–1895 period, too, because anti-imperialist sentiment was strong and the United States sometimes lacked the power to work its will. American diplomacy was active on a global scale, but American power was confined largely to the western hemisphere and a few spots in the Pacific. A more concerted, less restrained, and less erratic foreign policy in the 1890s would consummate an imperial trend evident intermittently but persistently since the 1860s. During the last decade of the nineteenth century, the United States committed itself wholeheartedly to the exciting international race for commerce, land, and prestige.

To suggest that the United States was "expansionist" in the nineteenth century does not spark much controversy. To state that America has been "imperialist" for much of its history is something else, and historians have waged some heated verbal wars over the question. Popular political usage has clouded meaning. The key to the debate is definition. "Continental expansion" into Louisiana, the Floridas, Texas, California, and Oregon and the destruction or incarceration of Native Americans certainly had imperial characteristics. Yet some historians argue that America's only period of imperialism came briefly in the late 1890s, when it annexed noncontiguous colonies abroad. Their limited definition of imperialism, then, encompasses only the formal colonization of areas not part of the American continent.

Imperialism is the imposition of controlling authority by a stronger entity over a weaker one. If peoples or regions lose the freedom to make their own decisions, they stand in an imperial relationship with whoever is making those decisions. The crucial factor is controlling *power*, and formal means (annexation, for example) or informal means (economic manipulation) can be used to establish it. For example, the American economic domination of a country through trade and investment—an informal method of control—is imperialism, even though the United States does not formally annex the territory as a colony. Santo Domingo, to cite a case, was never formally taken as an American colony, but by the early twentieth century, after years of American expansion into the island, it had become subservient to the United States and hence part of the latter's empire. There is quite a difference, then, between imperialism and expansion. The latter refers only to an outward movement (of goods, people, ideas, etc.). Expansion sometimes leads to imperialism, to the domination of other peoples or regions. The United States was demonstrably "expansionist" in the period after the Civil War. In some instances, this expansion became imperialism.

The late nineteenth century witnessed an intense international rivalry for world influence, and the United States became an active participant. Americans had never been short on nationalism, and the events of the late nineteenth century released a torrent of nationalistic pride. Of course, history told Americans that they were a special people, even God-favored, who had enjoyed success through constant expansion. The generation of post-Civil War America lived in the wake of a national conflict which seemed to challenge that historical lesson. It had truly been a "civil" war, splintering the nation, exposing cross grains and opening gaping holes. The nation had to be rebuilt, and leaders set about to recreate a common national spirit and purpose, in part by reviving the rhetoric of Manifest Destiny. A considerable help was the impressive economic growth of the late nineteenth century, with its transcontinental railroads, population growth, technological improvements, and new industrial products. By the early 1890s the United States ranked first in the world in manufacturing, an accomplishment generating enormous pride, indeed. Then, too, American nationalists nurtured a vague sense of Anglo-Saxonism—a racial view that Anglo-Saxons, meaning the main stock of Americans, were a special breed equipped to lead others. The prevalence of Social Darwinist thought—that some peoples were in the natural order of things meant to survive and others to fail—encouraged similar notions of national superiority. A host of new patriotic associations organized in the early 1890s reflected the nationalism: Colonial Dames of America (1890), Daughters of the American Revolution (1890), and Society of Colonial Wars (1893).

Americans had traditionally thought themselves exceptional. Almost everybody who counted knew this exceptionalism to be so; they *felt* it, even measured it, and they were quick to correct any affronts to their assumption of national greatness. Furthermore, they expected to continue to expand even after historian Frederick Jackson Turner alarmed them by arguing that in 1890 the continental frontier was closing. Publicists like the Reverend Josiah Strong, whose widely read *Our Country* (1885) preached the extension of Anglo-Saxon superiority abroad, and Brooks Adams of the distinguished Adams family predicted the decay of civilized society

**"The Stride of a Century."** This Currier & Ives print captures the centennial spirit of 1876, which generated American nationalism and a celebration of the "progress" of the United States. (Library of Congress)

unless the United States enjoyed international commercial supremacy. Politicians like Ulysses S. Grant, William H. Seward, James G. Blaine, and Theodore Roosevelt, many farmers and businessmen, Protestant missionaries, and naval officers sought to perpetuate American greatness through expansion and imperialism. The imperialism of the European powers, who were carving up Africa and Asia, added fuel to American nationalism. The international rivalry for position and prestige was vigorous and seemed boundless. Vulnerable territories and populations were gobbled up. When the Europeans threatened to capture parts of the Pacific and Latin America, where Americans had already driven some stakes, the United States

## Makers of American Foreign Policy from 1865 to 1895

| Presidents | Secretaries of State |
| --- | --- |
| Andrew Johnson, 1865–1869 | William H. Seward, 1861–1869 |
| Ulysses S. Grant, 1869–1877 | Elihu B. Washburne, 1869 |
|  | Hamilton Fish, 1869–1877 |
| Rutherford B. Hayes, 1877–1881 | William M. Evarts, 1877–1881 |
| James A. Garfield, 1881 | James G. Blaine, 1881 |
| Chester A. Arthur, 1881–1885 | Frederick T. Freylinghuysen, 1881–1885 |
| Grover Cleveland, 1885–1889 | Thomas F. Bayard, 1885–1889 |
| Benjamin Harrison, 1889–1893 | James G. Blaine, 1889–1892 |
|  | John W. Foster, 1892–1893 |
| Grover Cleveland, 1893–1897 | Walter Q. Gresham, 1893–1895 |
|  | Richard Olney, 1895–1897 |

reacted with flexed muscles and warned off the intruders. Nationalism stimulated Americans to look outward, and when they did, they saw challengers. They forthrightly took up the challenge.

## The Expanding American Economy and Navy

An important component of this nationalism was the pride of the American people in their material achievements, their prosperity and economic growth. After the Civil War the United States entered a period of tremendous production. Urbanization, industrialization, capital formation—these phenomena were manifested in an unprecedented economic growth rate. Railroads knit the country together into a national market; oil wells tapped subterranean pools of black riches; adventuresome entrepreneurs like John D. Rockefeller and Andrew Carnegie created giant corporate structures and flaunted their affluence; sprawling, busy cities became the centers of national wealth. From the early 1870s to 1900 the gross national product more than doubled. In 1867 steel production equaled 20,000 long tons; in 1895 it passed the 6,000,000-ton figure. The United States had become an economic giant, and prominent Americans were proud of their accomplishments, despite considerable instability (major depressions in 1873–1878 and 1893–1897), business abuses necessitating antitrust and regulatory measures, the financial insolvency of the railroads, and the failure of consumption to keep pace with production.

Foreign trade constituted an important part of this economic growth. American exports expanded from $234 million in 1865 to $1.5 billion in 1900. Growing American productive efficiency, a decline in prices that made American goods less expensive in the world market, and improvements in transportation (steamships and the Suez Canal) and communications (a transatlantic cable in 1866) helped account for this impressive upturn in exports. Although about two-thirds of American products still went to Europe, a slight shift toward Latin America and Asia took place. The United States enjoyed a favorable balance of trade (exports exceeded imports) for the 1876–1894 period, and manufactured products claimed a larger share of total exports (from 19 percent in 1870 to 35 percent in 1900). Exports represented a very small percentage of the total gross national product

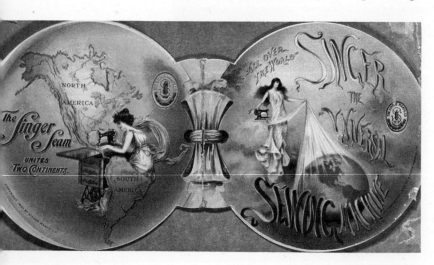

**Singer Sewing Machine Advertisement.** Selling "all over the world," the Singer Company enjoyed considerable foreign sales in the late nineteenth century, as did many other large American businesses. (Courtesy of The New-York Historical Society, New York City)

(between 6 and 7 percent), and the great majority of American businessmen concentrated on the domestic market. The opportunities for profits at home were more enticing.

Still, key segments of the economy needed foreign markets and earned a good proportion of their income from foreign sales. Farmers, especially producers of cotton, tobacco, and wheat, relied heavily upon the overseas markets. Over half of the annual American cotton crop was exported, and wheat growers in the period 1873–1882 received 30–40 percent of their gross annual income from exports. Two-thirds of American-refined oil was shipped abroad by the 1890s, with Standard Oil dominating this trade. By 1885 one-third of the New York Life Insurance Company's business was outside the United States and Canada. In the late nineteenth century, Singer exported about 40 percent of its sewing machines and penetrated South American and Chinese markets. Cyrus McCormick of International Harvester sent his famous reaper into Russian fields. Metal products firms like National Cash Register and Remington were active globally. Western Union participated in Canada's telegraph system, and Alexander Graham Bell and Thomas Edison first competed and then merged to initiate England's telephone network in 1880.

Historians disagree on the significance of foreign commerce and investment in the overall American economic growth of the late nineteenth century. Statistics tell only part of the story. The rest lies in attitude. Prominent Americans believed that foreign trade was important to the nation's well-being. They also thought that it must be expanded because United States factories and fields overproduced, creating a surplus that could not be absorbed by domestic consumers. Foreign trade, in this thinking, was one welcome source of relief for the domestic glut, especially in times of depression like those of the 1870s and 1890s: goods stacked up at home could be peddled abroad, thus stimulating the American economy and perhaps even heading off the social and political unrest that feeds on economic crises.

How did foreign trade and the belief in its necessity and significance affect American foreign policy? Some historians have dismissed the question altogether by arguing that foreign trade was simply not on the minds of most Americans, with overseas commerce usually representing less than 10 percent of the gross national product. That answer will not do. Even if only 1 percent of American products was exported, and that 1 percent involved the United States in foreign events or issues, foreign trade would be intertwined inescapably with American diplomacy—and hence a factor of importance. As the Navy's Policy Board concluded in 1890, anticipating conflicts and wars: "In the adjustment of our trade with a neighbor we are certain to reach out and obstruct the interests of foreign nations."[9] And even if all the efforts to expand trade produced minimal results, the quest itself would necessitate naval and diplomatic activity.

The question might be posed in another way: Why did American leaders think foreign trade was important? First, exports meant profits. That is the pocketbook issue. Second, exports might relieve social unrest at home caused by overproduction and unemployment. Third, foreign trade reflected a nation's economic power, itself one measurement of national greatness in international competition. Fourth, economic ties could lead to political influence (as in Hawaii and Mexico) without the formal necessity of military occupation and management. Fifth, foreign trade hand-in-hand with religious missionary work could be a force for "civilization" and human uplift. Missionaries, for example, joined Singer executives in proclaiming the sewing machine a "civilizing medium."[10] Josiah Strong urged merchants and missionaries to collaborate to shape the world in America's image. Sixth and last, to return to the theme of nationalism, foreign trade, if it conquered new markets abroad and helped bring prosperity to the United States, was an object of national pride. Foreign trade, then, held an importance beyond statistics. It was an intricate part of American "greatness"; leaders believed it important to the national interest.

The implications for foreign policy became evident. To expand and protect foreign commerce, a larger navy was needed. Commodore Robert W. Shufeldt explained to one congressman that "in the pursuit of new channels the trader seeks not only the unfrequented paths upon the ocean, but the unfrequented parts of the world. He needs the constant protection of the flag and the gun. He deals with barbarous tribes—men who appreciate only the argument of physical force. . . . The man-of-war precedes the merchantman and impresses rude people."[11] To fuel and disperse the Navy, naval stations were required. Leases and even colonies became necessary. Senator Albert Beveridge simplified the question: "Territorial extension is not desirable for itself alone. It is and will be merely an incident of commercial extension. And commercial extension is the absolutely necessary result of the overwhelming productive energy and capacity of the American people."[12] To make sure that competing countries did not deny Americans their economic stakes (investments, properties, or trade), interventions in the affairs of other nations became United States policy.

Official Washington also did what it could short of intervention to help expand foreign commerce, but its record was mixed. American products were displayed at international fairs, consular service officers prepared reports on commercial prospects, and the Navy scouted trade opportunities. The government negotiated commercial treaties and improved communications and transportation. Yet the diplomatic corps and consular service remained part of the domestic spoils system: political hacks instead of professionals filled their ranks. Although its impact on American foreign trade is not altogether clear, the tariff remained at high levels through the late nineteenth century, reaching a peak in the McKinley Tariff of 1890 (average duties of 49 percent). Certainly it aroused some retaliatory measures on the part of other countries, but American foreign trade expanded nonetheless. The American farmers and manufacturers could have their cake and eat it too. That is, they could keep out cheaper competitive foreign products on the one hand, and on the other, sell their goods in other countries. In the 1890s, when the theory that foreign trade could relieve overproduction became gospel, the United States gradually moved toward a tariff policy of reciprocity, wherein it would agree with other nations on mutual tariff reductions. Until the lower Underwood Tariff of 1913, America's high tariff policy probably proved only a mild detriment to the expansion of foreign trade.

The United States moved decisively, if slowly, in improving its Navy as an instrument of expansion. Captain Alfred T. Mahan especially popularized the relationship between a navy and expansion. An instructor at the Naval War College periodically after 1886, Mahan articulated in *The Influence of Seapower Upon History* (1890) what others had already been thinking. His thesis was simple: a nation's greatness depended upon its sea power. Victory in war and vigorous foreign trade, two measurements of greatness, depended upon an efficient navy.

That navy, in turn, would require colonies, and they, in turn, would further enhance foreign commerce and national power. The post-Civil War Navy that Mahan propagandized counted among its highest priorities the protection of American lives, property, and commerce overseas, and the expansion of American trade opportunities. "The Navy is, indeed," argued Commodore Robert Shufeldt, "the pioneer of commerce."[13] A group of spirited naval officers enthusiastically endorsed these purposes. Commodore Stephen B. Luce, father of the modern American Navy, was an effective naval politician instrumental in founding the Naval War College in 1884, instilling discipline and professional pride, and encouraging men like Mahan to publish their ideas.

Luce and Mahan had much to be unhappy about before the mid-1880s. Until that time, the Navy consisted of rotting hulks with worn-out boilers, resting in government-operated shipyards. Congress refused to appropriate funds for new ships. Shipyard officials and workers were political appointees little interested in naval improvement. As other nations moved to steel vessels, America nursed its barnacled, sail-driven, wooden craft and unseaworthy ironclad monitors. The naval officer corps was dominated by gentlemen of high social standing and by a dated naval strategy that emphasized coastal defense and commerce raiding in wartime. Less powerful nations had more impressive navies. To make matters worse, America's merchant fleet was also in decline.

Gradually in the 1880s the United States moved from sail to steel and from naval impotence to naval respectability, ranking seventh among the world's fleets by 1893. Listening more intently to thinking like Mahan's and Luce's, Congress appropriated funds for the construction of thirty new steel ships, including the *Boston*, which figured later in the American annexation of Hawaii, the *Maine*, which went to the bottom of Havana Harbor in 1898 and helped foment American intervention in Cuba, and the *Olympia*, Admiral George Dewey's flagship when he whipped the Spanish at Manila Bay. The Naval War College opened its doors, and professionalism came to characterize the younger officers. Consulting with Luce and Mahan, Secretary of the Navy Benjamin Tracy (1889–1893) launched the "new Navy" with emphasis on oceangoing battleships. Critical anti-imperialists protested that a larger navy would carry Americans to imperialism. Tracy was frank about it in 1891: "The sea will be the future seat of empire. And we shall rule it as certainly as the sun doth rise."[14]

**William H. Seward (1801–1872).** Once freed from the restraints of the Civil War, Secretary of State Seward vigorously pursued an enlargement of the American empire and purchased Alaska. (U.S. Signal Corps photo, Grady Collection, National Archives)

## Too Fast and Too Far: Secretary William H. Seward

Secretary of State William Henry Seward (1861–1869) provided a link between prewar and postwar imperialist thinking and behavior. During the Civil War he had to worry about keeping the European powers out of the internecine squabble. After the war, this vain, confident, and intelligent Republican leader, disheveled in appearance, enthusiastically redirected American foreign policy toward his vision of an imperial network. As historian Walter LaFeber has noted, "in the unfolding drama of the new empire William Henry Seward appears as the prince of the players."[15] The secretary foresaw a coordinated empire tied together by superior American institutions and commerce. Latin America, the Pacific islands, Asia, and Canada, Seward prophesied, would eventually gravitate toward the United States because of the contagion of American greatness and because of some immeasurable will of God. Wars of conquest were unnecessary; commerce would bind the distant areas together. Seward once speculated that Mexico would be an appropriate location for the new imperial capital. He indicated the means for acquiring this empire: improved foreign trade, immigration to provide cheap labor for productive American factories, high tariffs for the protection of American industry, liberal government land policies to open the American West for economic development, globe-circling telegraph systems, transcontinental railroads, a Central American canal, and, of course, annexation of territories.

In 1865 the ambitious secretary began negotiations with Denmark to purchase the Danish West Indies (Virgin Islands), whose excellent harbors were potential naval stations for the protection of American trade. The Danes balked; they sought more than the $5 million Seward offered, and urged a plebiscite of the islands' inhabitants. Two years later the islanders voted for American annexation. Seward

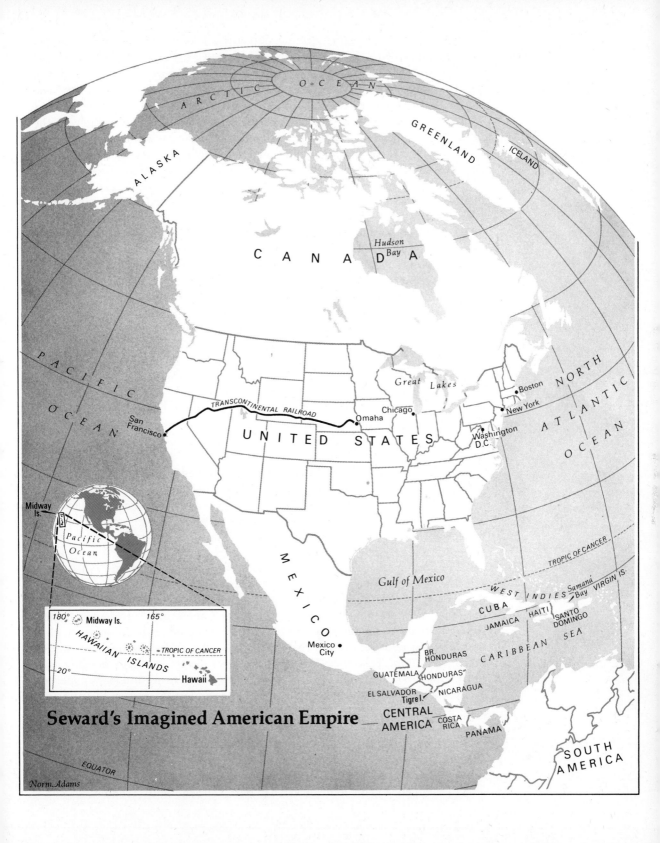

ARCTIC OCEAN

GREENLAND

ICELAND

ALASKA

CANADA

Hudson Bay

PACIFIC OCEAN

Great Lakes

Boston

Chicago

New York

NORTH ATLANTIC OCEAN

TRANSCONTINENTAL RAILROAD

San Francisco

Omaha

UNITED STATES

Washington D.C.

Midway Is.

Pacific Ocean

Gulf of Mexico

TROPIC OF CANCER

MEXICO

WEST INDIES

Samaná Bay

VIRGIN IS.

CUBA

HAITI

JAMAICA

SANTO DOMINGO

CARIBBEAN SEA

Mexico City

BR. HONDURAS

GUATEMALA

HONDURAS

EL SALVADOR

Tigre I.

NICARAGUA

CENTRAL AMERICA

COSTA RICA

PANAMA

SOUTH AMERICA

EQUATOR

180° Midway Is. 165°

HAWAIIAN ISLANDS

TROPIC OF CANCER

20°

Hawaii

Norm. Adams

## Seward's Imagined American Empire

raised his offer to $7.5 million for two of the islands, St. Thomas and St. John, but a combination of bad weather and heated politics undercut the treaty Seward signed with Copenhagen in October, 1867. When a devastating hurricane and tidal wave wracked St. Thomas, critics laughed at Seward's quest for "footholds." The treaty also had the misfortune of being introduced at the same time that President Andrew Johnson faced impeachment, and Seward himself lost credit with the Senate by supporting Johnson's unpopular Reconstruction policies. Incoming President Grant shelved the treaty, and the Virgin Islanders had to wait for American overlordship until 1917, when new factors prompted purchase.

Seward also wanted a piece of perpetually restive Santo Domingo. In 1866 he offered two million dollars for Samaná Bay, but the proposed deal remained open when he left office. Seward's vision encompassed Haiti, which he thought of annexing entirely, some small Spanish, French, and Swedish islands in the Caribbean, revolution-torn Cuba, Iceland and Greenland (both of which he hoped to buy), Honduras' Tiger Island, and Hawaii, fast becoming Americanized as more sugar was planted and more churches were built. Those imperialist ambitions went unfulfilled in Seward's day, but they foreshadowed later events.

Seward claimed some successes. The transcontinental railroad, high tariffs, the Atlantic cable in 1866, encouragements to immigration, and an expanded interest in foreign trade, although developments not wholly Seward's doing, moved the United States deeper into global affairs. The secretary did arrange two real estate transactions. The Midway Islands, some one thousand miles from Hawaii, were seized in August, 1867 by an American naval officer. Most Americans never heard again about these tiny imperial outposts until the great American-Japanese naval battle there in 1942. More attractive and more controversial was Seward's purchase of Alaska. Russia had put Alaska up for sale because it was proving unprofitable as colonial property, and because the Tsar feared that Britain would seize the undefended territory if the British and Russians tangled in a future war. Then, too, Russia seemed resigned to the inevitable. "The ultimate rule of the United States over the whole of America is so natural," the governor of Eastern Siberia told the Tsar, as early as 1853, "that we must ourselves sooner or later recede."[16] Edouard de Stoeckl, the Russian minister to the United States who negotiated the transfer, agreed over a decade later: "In American eyes this continent is their patrimony. Their destiny (manifest destiny as they call it) is to always expand."[17] Why not cultivate a "friend" and sell the 591,000 square miles (twice the size of Texas) to the United States? Seward alertly followed up well-placed Russian hints and quietly opened negotiations in Washington. The Cabinet and President remained largely ignorant of the talks, until they and the Congress were presented with a hastily drawn treaty and a bill for $7.2 million—not an inconsequential sum in March, 1867. One Treasury official estimated that the United States actually paid $43.4 million: $7.2 million in principal, $12.5 million in Army and Navy expenses for the transfer of the territory, and $23.7 million in lost interest on the principal had the money remained in the Treasury for twenty-five years. It was, nevertheless, a real bargain.

Contemporary critics howled anyway. Congress, which had to approve the treaty and appropriate the money, had been ignored by Seward. Some opponents balked because Seward was a member of the unpopular Johnson Administration. Others quipped about "Johnson's Polar Bear Garden" and "Frigidia" or com-

**"Our Irrepressible 'Bill'-Sticker."** "Tomorrow to fresh woods and pastures new" reads this cartoon. Already "posted" are Alaska and St. Thomas in the Virgin Islands. Cuba, Mexico, and Canada, it seems, are within reach. Anti-imperialists helped curb further postings. (*Harper's Weekly*, 1869)

plained that the cost was too high and that America could not populate the vast western lands it already owned. Seward beat back his opponents. He astutely won over Charles Sumner, who began to applaud Alaska's commercial potential and natural resources—minerals, fish, and seals among them. Sumner's influence, a vigorous educational program in which Seward compared Alaska to the Louisiana Purchase, the Russian minister's hiring of well-paid lobbyists and bribing of some congressmen, positive, if vague, feelings about Russian "friendship," and the immediate exhilaration over expanding American boundaries—all combined to carry the treaty through the Senate only ten days after it was signed. The House stalled, delaying fifteen months before voting the funds, but by then Seward had already ordered the Stars and Stripes raised over his imperial catch.

Seward acquired fewer territories than he desired, largely because of domestic obstacles. He was a Republican supporter of Democratic President Johnson and evinced little sympathy for the plight of freedmen in the South. Displaying their disapproval, angry Radical Republicans called for Seward's ouster from the Cabinet and helped block his imperialist schemes. Reconstruction, railroad growth, an inflated economy, landless freedmen, a recalcitrant South—such issues compelled many Americans to look inward and to skimp on foreign adventures that cost money. A nation that had just freed its slaves after a bloody civil war was not about to acquire Cuba, in which slavery flourished. Seward could only lament "how sadly domestic disturbances of ours demoralize the National ambition."[18]

The secretary's ambition was blocked, too, because committed and articulate anti-imperialists like Senator Carl Schurz, author Mark Twain, and editor E. L. Godkin spoke out. They called for the development of America's existing lands and for an American showcase of domestic social, political, and economic improvements as the best way to persuade other peoples to adopt American institutions. Whereas some imperialists were racists who wanted to subjugate "inferior" people, some anti-imperialists made racist arguments against adding more nonwhites to the American population. Godkin opposed the annexation of Santo Domingo because that country harbored 200,000 "ignorant Catholic Spanish negroes" who might seek United States citizenship.[19] Other anti-imperialists insisted that colonialism violated the principle of self-government and would increase the threat of foreign wars. Such men and such ideas, joined to the partisan struggle over Reconstruction, helped thwart Seward's efforts to create a larger empire. He was moving too fast for most Americans.

## Continued Rivalry with Great Britain

Anglo-American tensions, so evident before and during the Civil War, continued to claim a major part of the Department of State's attention in the 1865–1895 period. Union leaders were still irate over Britain's favoritism toward the South during the Civil War, especially the outfitting of Confederate vessels in British ports. At the end of the war, Seward filed damage claims against the British, even proposing at one point that Britain grant to the United States British Columbia or the Bahama Islands in lieu of a cash settlement. The secretary was further annoyed that British officials would not permit American soldiers to chase the destitute Sioux Indians into Canadian territory.

The British also had their grievances. It angered them that the United States sometimes sent anti-British Irish refugees back to Ireland as American consuls. Worse still, Washington seemed lax in controlling the United States–based Fenian Brotherhood. Organized in 1858 to promote Irish independence, the Fenians numbered about 10,000 in 1865. The following year they armed themselves and attacked Canada from Vermont. Seward actually tried to squelch them by sending troops to the border, but London complained that Washington moved too slowly. Then, too, some vociferous Americans still demanded that Canada be attached to the United States. They looked upon the creation of the unified Dominion of Canada in 1867 as a roadblock. Congress went so far as to pass a resolution proclaiming the new dominion a violation of the Monroe Doctrine.

The two powers continued to haggle over the question of the English-built Confederate ships (especially the *Alabama*) that had disrupted Union shipping. Irrepressible Charles Sumner added the naval damages to indirect damages that he derived by calculating that the war went on needlessly for two years because of British material help to and sympathy for the South; he totaled up a bill of $2.125 billion. One irate British diplomat explained that Sumner "was fool enough some year or so ago to marry a young and pretty widow. She found that he was not gifted with 'full powers' and has left him. . . . He therefore makes up by vigour of tongue for his want of capacity in other organs."[20] Some Americans felt the transfer of Canada to the United States would erase the debt. After months of informal talks, a Joint High Commission convened in Washington from February to May, 1871. Sumner's extravagant sum was set aside and the commissioners produced the Washington Treaty dated May 8. The British expressed regret for the actions of British-built Confederate raiders, and the signatories agreed to establish a tribunal to determine damages and claims. That commission, meeting in Geneva, struggled to reach a settlement after the Americans shocked the British by reviving Sumner's indirect claims. The United States again retreated from that extreme stance, and the tribunal finally issued its decision in September, 1872: Britain must pay the United States $15.5 million. "As the price of conciliating the United States, and protecting British naval interests," historian David P. Crook has written, "it was a bargain."[21]

The Washington Treaty attempted to settle two other Anglo-American disputes. Nestled between Vancouver Island (British Columbia) and territorial Washington in the Straits of Fuca were the San Juan Islands, claimed by both the United States and Britain on the basis of confusing geographical language in the Treaty of 1846. It was not much of an issue, except perhaps to the local inhabitants. The Treaty of Washington provided for arbitration by the German Emperor, who decreed in 1872 that the islands belonged to the United States. Another long-standing dispute was more rancorous and more serious—the rights of American fishermen in North Atlantic waters. The Washington Treaty gave permission to Yankee fishermen to cast their nets in British North American waters and to Canadians to fish the coastal regions of the United States above 39 degrees north latitude. In 1877 a fisheries commission ruled that the United States should pay Britain $5.5 million for the latter's having granted such generous fishing rights to Americans. The bill was paid, but in 1885 the United States canceled that part of the Washington Treaty dealing with fishing rights. The action opened tensions again and Canadians began seizing American vessels. An Anglo-American pact of 1888 never got by the Senate, but a modus vivendi cooled tempers. About the same time, British Minister Sir Lionel Sackville-West committed a sin of the first order for a diplomat—he privately recommended a particular candidate, Grover Cleveland, for re-election in 1888. His indiscreet advice became public and Irish-Americans demanded that he be handed his passports. Democrat Cleveland did just that before he was defeated by Benjamin Harrison in November. The angry Prime Minister, Lord Salisbury, refused to send a new minister until March of the next year.

Hardly quieted down after the Sackville-West incident and fisheries dispute, Anglo-American rivalry turned toward the issue of seals in the Bering Sea near Alaska. "Amphibious is the fur seal, ubiquitous and carnivorous, uniparous, gregarious and withal polygamous," historian Samuel Flagg Bemis has quipped.[22] By the late nineteenth century most of the seal herds lived in the Pribilof Islands near the Aleutians. American territorial law affecting Alaska forbade the killing of female or young seals and limited the slaughter of males. Yet foreign hunters slaughtered at will when the animals wandered on the high seas in search of food. In 1889 President Benjamin Harrison warned Canadians against "pelagic" sealing (killing animals in the ocean waters). When several Canadian sealing ships were seized in international waters, London and Ottawa protested. The United States had a better moral than legal case. American politicians, alert to their Irish constituencies, charged the British with trying to exterminate the seal herds in the North Pacific. A clash appeared to be in the offing. In mid-1890 the British sent four warships to the disputed region to watch as Canadian sealers shot seals to death. American cutters made no arrests this time. A temporary agreement halting pelagic sealing for a year was struck in 1891, and after another dispute the next year, London and Washington agreed to create an arbitral tribunal. Its members began to deliberate in early 1893 and their decree of August meant an American defeat, for it permitted pelagic sealing within prescribed limits. The herd further declined in number. Finally in 1911, Russia, Japan, Britain, and the United States set strict regulations to protect the furry creatures.

## Barbarians Versus Barbarians: China and the West

China beckoned as a commercial market and missionary field and hence drew the fascinated attention of foreigners, including the British and Americans. Although Americans seldom participated in the gunboat diplomacy that gained the British substantial rights in China, the Chinese did not consider Americans much different, for the latter soon demanded the rights granted other nations. Scholars have called this "hitchhiking diplomacy." The Chinese saw all westerners as barbarians. Americans at the same time depicted the Chinese as rat-eating, uncivilized, opium-drunk heathens. The 100,000 Chinese ("coolies") who lived in the United States by 1868 were unwelcome immigrants, believed to be too different in habits, dress, and religion to adapt to American institutions. White laborers saw them as competitors, for many Chinese entered the United States under labor contracts to American businessmen. Open insults and frequent violence—murders, lynchings, and beatings—haunted the Chinese in America, concentrated in their "Chinatowns." Writer Bret Harte protested such brutalities in an obituary to Wan Lee: "Dead, my revered friends, dead. Stoned to death in the streets of San Francisco, in the year of grace 1869 by a mob of half-grown boys and Christian school children."[23] While Westerners demanded treatment as equals in the Celestial Empire, they denied such status to the Chinese in the West.

Anson Burlingame, American minister to China (1861–1868), shared the pervasive American dream of a China market. Upon Burlingame's retirement in 1868, the Chinese hired him to lead a mission to the United States. He defined his task as opening China even further to missionaries and railroad developers. He had no such instructions from the Chinese, who actually hoped to use their "friend" Burlingame to deflect further Western intrusions. Accompanied by two Chinese diplomats, the envoy signed the Burlingame Treaty (1868) with Seward. It provided for the free immigration of each country's citizens and affirmed Sino-American friendship. Burlingame sailed next for Europe to negotiate other agreements, but died of pneumonia in St. Petersburg.

"**Pacific Chivalry.**" How Californians handled the Chinese. (*Harper's Weekly,* 1869)

The friendship between America and China, symbolized in the Burlingame Treaty, was superficial, for the Chinese under the Manchu dynasty were ardently antiforeign. One Chinese official wrote that foreign diplomats "think only of profit, and with the meretricious hope of profit they beguile the Chinese people."[24] In 1869–1870 Chinese nationalists demonstrated against Christians, missionaries and foreigners, killing many. The mutilation of nuns drew large headlines in American newspapers. Yet Chinese officials recognized their own weakness, rudely underscored in 1873 by the refusal of foreign diplomats to *kowtow* to the Empress Dowager in Peking. The Chinese foreign office, recognizing power realities, sought normal diplomatic relations. In 1878 the first Chinese diplomat, Ch'en Lap-pin, arrived in Washington with his associate Yung Wing, a graduate of Yale College. Both had been in Hartford, Connecticut earlier as superintendents of the Chinese Education Mission.

China was also powerless to protect its citizens in the United States or to challenge American immigration policy. In 1879, Congress legislated that only fifteen Chinese could arrive on any one ship in the United States. Although vetoed by President Rutherford B. Hayes as a violation of the Burlingame Treaty, this act illustrated the prevailing public reaction to the Chinese in America and the desire to stop the "Mongolian invasion." In 1880 a new immigration treaty negotiated with China permitted the United States to suspend, but not prohibit, Chinese immigration at will. Two years later Congress suspended Chinese immigration for ten years, initiating a practice that would be continued into the 1920s. The Chinese were also denied American citizenship. The violence persisted and everyone knew what "a Chinaman's chance" meant. In 1885, in one of the ugliest outbreaks of hatred, twenty-eight Chinese miners were murdered in Wyoming. The residents of Seattle, Washington, about the same time, sacked Chinese homes and deported several hundred Chinese immigrants to San Francisco. In California, members of provocateur Dennis Kearney's militantly anti-Oriental Workingmen's party committed numerous atrocities.

In China and much of Asia before the late 1890s the United States followed the British lead. Americans opposed any dismemberment of China, but seized opportunities created by the guns of other Westerners to expand commerce and missionary work. Fifty American companies operated in China by 1870, although trade with China remained a miniscule part of total American commerce abroad, amounting to $1 million in 1880, $4 million in 1895, and $15 million in 1900. By 1900 Americans had invested only $17.5 million in the Celestial Empire. Ex-President Grant's trip to Peking in 1879, wherein he urged China "to throw open her barriers and be one in commerce and trade with the outer world," was more a portent for the future than a significant event in its own day.[25] America's *interest* in China outstripped its *activity* there, yet Chinese nationalists resentfully included Americans among those imperial outsiders who had cost them control of their own sovereignty, lives, and properties.

## Pacific Prizes: Hawaii and Samoa

Hawaii, that commercial and naval jewel in the Pacific, was linked in the American mind to China. The Hawaiian (or Sandwich) Islands sat as convenient stations on the way to Asian markets. The port of Pearl Harbor was an admiral's dream, and sugar production had become big business. American missionaries acquired converts and property. The United States repeatedly emphasized that, although it was not itself ready to annex the islands, no other power would be permitted to do so. In 1875 the United States virtually bound Hawaii to the American economy through a Reciprocity Treaty. Under this arrangement, Hawaiian sugar could enter the United States duty-free, provided Hawaii did not grant territory to another country. Secretary of State James G. Blaine was explicit in 1881 when he warned the British to stay out of Hawaii, which was "essentially a part of the American system of states, and a key to the North Pacific trade."[26] In 1886 Hawaii granted the United States naval rights to Pearl Harbor, prompting an alarmed Britain, also ogling the islands, to call futilely for Hawaiian neutrality and equal commercial accessibility for all nations.

Reflecting the long-standing American interest in Hawaii, Secretary James G. Blaine informed President Harrison in 1891 that "Hawaii may come up for decision at any unexpected hour, and I hope we shall be prepared to decide it in the affirmative."[27] Like the expansionists of the 1840s, Americans hurried the hour. At the start of the decade Congress changed tariff laws, removing the duty-free provision for Hawaiian sugar, and sugar shipments to the United States declined. Hawaiian producers screamed in economic pain, and began to plot revolution against the anti-American, despotic native government of Queen Liliuokalani. The revolutionaries were influential wealthy white planters, who constituted a distinct minority of the population, but who owned a major part of the islands' land. Most of the 3,000 Americans in Hawaii's population of approximately 100,000 sought annexation to the United States to remove tariffs on sugar exports to mainland markets.

On January 16, 1893, the businessmen-revolutionaries bloodlessly toppled the Queen from her throne and proclaimed a provisional government. The revolution could not have succeeded without the assistance of American Minister John L. Stevens and the men of the U.S.S. *Boston.* An active partisan for annexation, Stevens sent 164 armed bluejackets from the American warship into Honolulu. They did not bivouac near American property to protect it, the announced pretext for landing, but quickly deployed to within a few hundred yards of the monarch's palace. Sipping lemonade while at the same time ostentatiously brandishing Gatling guns and cannon, the troops' very presence forced the Queen to give up. Minister Stevens recognized the provisional government, declared an American protectorate, and warned the State Department that the British might exploit this opportunity if the United States did not. The "Hawaiian pear is now fully ripe, and this is the golden hour for the United States to pluck it."[28] Native Hawaiians were never asked if they wished to be absorbed by the United States.

Although President Harrison had not authorized Stevens to intervene so directly, he was not displeased with the result and signed a treaty of annexation with a "Hawaiian" commission (four Americans and one Englishman) in February. Before it could be acted upon by the Senate, Harrison gave way to President Grover Cleveland. A few days after taking office, Cleveland withdrew the treaty for reflection and ordered an investigator, ex-Congressman James H. Blount, to the islands. Blount's report confirmed that the revolution was carried out with Stevens' collusion and that the majority of Hawaiians had never been consulted about annexation. Although an expansionist, Cleveland opposed taking colonies. He also worried about some tough questions. What would Southern Democrats think of incorporating a multiracial population in the Union? Could Hawaii, an "overseas" territory, ever become a state? What would happen if the native Hawaiians revolted against their white masters? Why stir up another heated issue when the United States was already beset by agrarian and labor protests? Secretary of State Walter Q. Gresham, himself an expansionist willing to annex territories if legal political processes were observed, said that he was "unalterably opposed to stealing territory, or of annexing a people against their consent, and the people of Hawaii do not favor annexation."[29] Cleveland thus killed the treaty. Meanwhile, the white leaders in Hawaii waited for a more friendly president in Washington and for propitious world events to persuade the United States to annex the islands.

Other nations had coveted Hawaii, and international rivalry throughout the Pacific was keen. Germany, Britain, and the United States collided in Samoa, a group of fourteen volcanic islands lying 4,000 miles from San Francisco along the trade route between the United States and Australia. American whalers had stopped there before the Civil War, and in 1839 Charles Wilkes of the United States Navy surveyed the islands as part of his exploring expedition in the Pacific. After the Civil War, nationals of the three great powers scrambled for privileges, urged their governments to annex Samoa, and exploited the chaotic and often violent tribal politics that had earned the Samoans some notoriety as the "Irishmen of the Pacific." At stake were coconut plantations, national pride stimulated by the three-cornered rivalry, and the excellent ports of Apia and Pago Pago. In 1872 a

**"Two Good Old Friends."** In this German cartoon, John Bull and Uncle Sam try to balance their Pacific interests in Samoa and Hawaii while the native inhabitants feel the weight of imperialism. (*Kladderadatsch* in *Review of Reviews,* 1893)

tribal chief granted the United States rights to a naval station at Pago Pago. Although this pact died because the Senate took no action on it and Grant, timid after the defeat of his Dominican scheme, did not push it, a new treaty was signed and ratified in 1878. Not only did the new treaty give Americans privileges at Pago Pago, but it also provided for American good offices in disputes between Samoa and outside nations, which were also collecting treaties of privilege.

In 1885–1886, after years of German intrigue, Secretary of State Thomas Bayard launched a more active American diplomacy. He protested to Berlin that "the United States had assumed the position of a benevolent protector, and the German intervention would mean the virtual displacement of the United States from that preferred status."[30] In 1887 Bayard convened a three-power Washington Conference, but it could not reach agreement and Germany landed marines on Samoa. Washington dispatched a warship and the English and Americans in Samoa refused to pay taxes to the German-dominated government. German Chancellor Otto van Bismarck remarked that "We must show sharp teeth."[31] Eager for a "bit of a spar with Germany," Theodore Roosevelt admitted that the Germans might burn New York City.[32] But, he reasoned, the calamity would persuade Americans to bolster coastal defenses. In early 1889 an aroused Congress authorized half a million dollars to protect Americans and their Samoan property and another $100,000 to build up a naval station at Pago Pago. Whether boldness or bluff, this American action helped persuade Bismarck to seek a peaceful solution. He was also encouraged by a typhoon which devastated Samoa and wrecked most of the American, British, and German warships. After that disaster, nobody had the weapons in Samoa with which to fight a war. At the Berlin Conference of 1889, the three powers carved Samoa into a tripartite protectorate (the United States got Pago Pago) and forced an unpopular king on the Samoans. Writer Robert Louis Stevenson, a prominent resident of the islands, futilely protested this violation of native sovereignty, this "Triple-Headed Ass."[33] Ten years later, in the aftermath of the Spanish-American War, the United States and Germany formally cut Samoa into colonies, with Britain compensated by other Pacific acquisitions.

## Peripheral Interests: Japan, Korea, and Africa

The Western nations also pushed for commercial advantages in Japan, which Commodore Matthew C. Perry had "opened" in the 1850s. In 1863–1864, despite the Civil War, the United States Navy deployed one delapidated warship alongside British, French, and Dutch vessels to punish the Japanese for their antiforeign riots and harassment of merchant ships. At Shimonoseki this firepower destroyed forts and boats, opening the strait to trade once again. Internally divided and militarily weak, the Japanese could not resist the $3,000,000 indemnity forced on them by the Western powers. (The United States received $785,000 of the amount, but returned it to Japan in 1883.) Then, in the Convention of 1866, Japan reluctantly bestowed commercial favors on the Western nations in the form of low tariffs. Soon the Japanese consciously adopted a policy of "westernization," persuading some Americans that the Japanese, unlike the Chinese, were "civilized." After Tokyo demonstrated its "progress" by thoroughly defeating the Chinese in the Sino-Japanese War of 1894–1895, the United States, following the British lead, ended extraterritoriality in Japan. Extraterritoriality, a symbol of foreign domination, was the practice of exempting foreigners from the legal jurisdiction of the

**Annihilation of a Korean Garrison, 1871.** The United States held negligible interests in Korea, but when Koreans resisted American intrusions, American gun power commanded the outcome: 350 Koreans and 3 Americans dead. (National Archives)

country in which they resided. The abolition of this Western privilege was a sure sign that Japan had to be reckoned with as an independent power, even a competitor, in Asia.

Korea was also dragged into contact with the West. This kingdom, called the "hermit nation" because of its isolation, was technically a dependency of China, but the latter's weakness invited outsiders to intervene in Korea. In the 1860s the French used gunboats against Korea to protest the maltreatment of Christian missionaries. In 1866, the United States was slower to act after an American trading ship, *General Sherman,* went aground. In a skirmish with Koreans, its crew was killed and the ship was burned. The United States sent an investigatory mission the following year, but not until 1871 did an American expedition sail to Korean waters to seek a treaty for the protection of shipwrecked Americans. Part of the flotilla, after heading for the capital in such a way as to convince Koreans that their nation was threatened, was fired upon. After leveling several Korean forts the American ships departed—without a treaty.

When the United States observed that Japan had received trading privileges from Korea in the 1870s, a new mission departed. In 1880, near the end of a government-sponsored two-year trading expedition to Asia and Africa, Commodore Robert Shufeldt of the United States Navy arrived in Korea aboard the U.S.S. *Ticonderoga.* He was rebuffed, but returned two years later and successfully signed a Korean-American treaty of peace, amity, commerce, and navigation. He had now, he declared, brought "the last of the exclusive countries within the pale of Western Civilization."[34] Throughout the 1880s American businessmen established trade links with Korea. Even Thomas Edison signed a contract for the installation of electric lights in the royal residence. For most Americans, however, Korea constituted a peripheral interest.

Africa also lay outside the mainstream of American expansion. From the 1870s on, American mining engineers followed prospectors to the gold and diamond regions of South Africa; American soldiers of fortune helped modernize the Egyptian army; missionaries labored in the Congo, and Salem traders exported

New England textiles to Zanzibar. Black nationalists like Bishop Henry Turner urged oppressed negroes to emigrate to Africa. Hundreds did so. Adventurer Henry M. Stanley, financed by the *New York Herald* in 1871, hiked through Africa in search of Dr. David Livingston, and thereby popularized the vast continent. In 1879 Commodore Shufeldt sailed the U.S.S. *Ticonderoga* to African waters to improve trade contacts. He pronounced South Africa an area of great trade possibilities, a prognostication that would make more sense in 1886 when gold was discovered there. In 1884 Shufeldt's son explored the interior of Madagascar. When Washington contemplated Africa, it thought largely of trade. In 1884 an American delegate participated in the Berlin Conference on the Congo and endorsed resolutions calling for freedom of trade and navigation in that Belgian-dominated region. President Cleveland, however, honoring the tradition of Amerian reluctance to join in binding *European* agreements, did not send the treaty to the Senate.

Washington could do little to interrupt the increasing European penetration of Africa. Even Liberia, recognized by the European powers as "American," was vulnerable. Settled and governed by American blacks with impetus from the American Colonization Society, Liberia was weakened in the 1870s by internal strife. The United States ordered warships there to squelch native rebellions against the "American"-Liberian government. When in the 1880s the British and French forced Liberia to cede some territory, Americans were unwilling to risk war through a forceful challenge. Nonetheless, the limited American patronage of Liberia may have forestalled full-scale European domination of that African nation. As it was, the United States was not an active competitor on the African continent. Lacking the power and the interest, it watched in the 1880s and 1890s as the British absorbed Egypt, the French took Tunisia, the Belgians grabbed the Congo, and the Germans seized East Africa and Southwest Africa. By 1895 most of Africa was partitioned. The United States stood as a bystander.

## Regional Power: The United States in Latin America

In the period 1865–1895 the United States became more active in Latin America than in any other part of the world. There it challenged the French and British, established economic links, invoked the Monroe Doctrine, intervened in inter-American disputes and revolutions (Haiti, Brazil, and Nicaragua, for example), tried to annex territories, lectured the Latin Americans about appropriate inter-American relations, and sought to unite them under the banner of Pan Americanism. Latin America was not yet a United States sphere of influence, but it was becoming so as Washington frequently instructed Europeans to stay out of hemispheric affairs. The foiled land grab of Santo Domingo was part of that relentless push. As the London *Times*, which knew something about imperialism, remarked in 1881: "The United States are indisputably the chief power in the New World. The time must arrive when the weaker States in their neighborhood will be absorbed by them."[35]

European competitors persisted in meddling in Latin American affairs, yet when the French in 1861 intervened militarily in Mexico and placed the young Archduke Ferdinand Maximilian of Austria on a Mexican throne, the Civil War-wracked United States could do little more than protest. Seward was angry, of course. The intervention seemed to pose a threat to American security and expansion, and the

United States read it as a blatant challenge to the Monroe Doctrine. Seward first arranged for some arms shipments to the forces of former Mexican President Benito Juárez. Once the Civil War subsided, the Grant Administration ordered 52,000 American soldiers to the Mexican border. Under the command of General Philip Sheridan, the troops showed all signs of readiness for battle as they conspicuously went through maneuvers. In early 1866 Seward firmly asked Napoleon III when French troops would be withdrawn. The Emperor, beset by opposition at home and Prussian competition in Europe, and faced by a noisy, well-armed, and victorious United States, had already decided to recall his troops. The abandoned and hapless "archdupe" Maximilian fell before a Mexican firing squad in 1867. Americans believed, much too simply, that they had forced France out and that the Monroe Doctrine, although not mentioned by name in this crisis, had been reinvigorated.

Another, but different, challenge sprang from Cuba, long within America's expansionist vision. From 1868 to 1878 the Spanish-owned island with its dreaded institution of slavery was bloodied by revolution. President Grant thought of recognizing the belligerency of the Cuban rebels, but Secretary Fish, wanting trade rather than war or territory in Latin America, dissuaded him. American hearts went out to the underdog Cubans as they and the Spanish mauled one another. The *Virginius* affair of 1873 ignited American protests. That Cuban-owned, gun-running vessel was captured by the Spanish, who shot as "pirates" fifty-three of the passengers and crewmen, some of whom were United States citizens. As Americans shouted for revenge, the levelheaded Fish demanded and got an apology and indemnity from Madrid for $80,000. Cuba continued to bleed until 1878, when the rebellion ended and slavery was abolished. From then until 1895, when a new revolution erupted, one which attracted a more militant American response, Cuba was like a carcass whose bones were being picked by the Spanish and other foreigners, including some Americans.

American economic interests were an important source of United States influence in Cuba and elsewhere in Latin America. American investments in and trade

**Hamilton Fish (1808–1893).** Graduate of Columbia University and lawyer, Fish served as a United States senator from New York (1851–1857) and opposed the expansion of slavery in the 1850s. More patient and tactful than President Grant, he recorded some achievements during his tenure as secretary of state (1869–1877): the Washington Treaty, nonintervention in the Cuban rebellion, and a reciprocity treaty with Hawaii. (*Harper's Weekly*, 1869)

with Latin American countries were conspicuous in Cuba (sugar and mines), Guatemala (the United States handled 64 percent of the country's trade by 1885), and Mexico (railroads and mines). In Mexico, according to historian Karl M. Schmitt, the United States "reduced its neighbor virtually to an economic satellite. . . . By the mid-1880s its economic stake in Mexico surpassed both the French and the British, which had been dominant in the country."[36] By the early 1890s, the United States was buying 75 percent of Mexico's exports and selling to Mexico about 50 percent of that nation's imports. The long, stable, and prosperous regime of dictator Porfirio Díaz (1876–1910) invited this foreign economic penetration. by 1890, American citizens had invested some $250 million in Latin America. Still, the region took only about 5 percent of total American exports that year. Most of the United States' trade (about 80 percent) remained with Europe. Although these economic ties with Latin America comprised a small part of the United States total world economic relationships, for countries like Cuba and Mexico they were vital and drew the United States into the internal affairs of each.

Central America attracted considerable American interest because of prospects for an isthmian canal linking the Pacific Ocean and Gulf of Mexico, thereby greatly reducing travel time between the eastern seaboard and Asian markets. The gala opening of the Suez Canal in 1869 spurred American canal enthusiasts. Panama and Nicaragua were identified as possible sites. The problem was the Clayton-Bulwer Treaty (1850), which held that a Central American canal had to be jointly controlled by Britain and the United States. Washington resented this limitation on American expansion, and when President Rutherford Hayes learned in 1880 that Ferdinand de Lesseps, builder of the Suez Canal, would attempt to construct a canal through Panama, he sent two warships to demonstrate United States concern. "A canal under American control, or no canal," exclaimed Hayes.[37] In 1881 Secretary Blaine forcefully but futilely asked the British to abrogate the Clayton-Bulwer Treaty, claiming that the United States "with respect to European states, will not consent to perpetuate any treaty that impeaches our right and long-established claim to priority on the American continent."[38] Three years later, in overt violation of the treaty, the United States signed a canal treaty with Nicaragua, although President Cleveland withdrew the offending pact from the Senate when he entered office. Nevertheless, the movement, led by naval officers, businessmen, and diplomats, for an exclusive United States canal was well under way. It was evident that some day it would be built; until that time no other nation would be permitted to undertake it. Meanwhile Central American conditions would have to be stabilized, as in Panama in 1885, when American sailors went ashore to protect American property threatened by civil war.

## Pan Americanism and the Humbling of Chile

The convocation of the first Pan American Conference in Washington in 1889 bore further witness to the growing United States influence in Latin America. "Jingo Jim" Blaine, hoping to expand American trade and boost his presidential aspirations, first recommended such a conference in 1881, but his departure in that year from the secretaryship of state left the question open until his return (1889–1892). The conference attracted representatives from seventeen countries. Six of the ten United States delegates were businessmen. After a grand tour of America's impressive industrial establishments in forty-one cities, the tired conferees assembled in Washington to hear Blaine's appeal for "enlightened and enlarged intercourse."[39] Unlike similar conferences in the twentieth century, the United States did not command all the results of this conclave. Blaine's ideas for a low-tariff zone and for compulsory arbitration of disputes were rejected, although the International Bureau of American Republics (later called the Pan American Union) was organized and reciprocity treaties to expand trade were encouraged. The conference also promoted inter-American steamship lines and railroads and established machinery to discuss commercial questions. The Pan American Union amounted to little in its early days. Its most significant impact was on the Washington landscape, where, with major financial help from steel baron Andrew Carnegie, the Pan Amercan Union put up one of the most impressive buildings in the nation's capital. Pan Americanism did not mean hemispheric unity; it really represented growing United States influence among neighbors to the south. For that reason European powers were disturbed by it.

Crises with Chile in 1891 and with Venezuela in 1895 (see next chapter) symbolized this growing United States hegemony. Chile attended the Pan American Conference as a rather fearless critic of the United States. The United States had clumsily attempted to end the War of the Pacific (1879–1883), in which Chile battled both Bolivia and Peru and won nitrate-rich territory. Civil war ripped through Chile in early 1891. The United States continued to recognize the existing government, which had tried to assume dictatorial powers. More than that, the United States minister indiscreetly favored it over the rebels, and the American Navy captured arms shipments purchased in the United States and destined for the revolutionaries. In the fall of 1891 the rebels won and openly expressed their anti-Yankee sentiments. Washington suspected growing British influence in Chile.

**Punishment for Chile, 1891.** An angry Uncle Sam is about to administer United States retribution to Chile after the exaggerated *Baltimore* affair. (*Harper's Weekly,* 1891)

A seemingly insignificant incident in October nearly exploded into a Chilean-American war. The American warship *Baltimore,* resting in Valparaiso Harbor, sent its men into town on leave. The exuberant sailors gave local taverns and brothels considerable business. At the True Blue Saloon, rum-drunk Americans and Chileans quarreled, fists flew, and knives slashed. Two Americans died and others were wounded; the Chilean police seemed oblivious to the tragedy.

President Benjamin Harrison, a former military man himself, reacted bitterly against this affront to the American uniform, especially because the Chilean government did not hurry to apologize. Captain Robley D. ("Fighting Bob") Evans of the *Yorktown,* also in Chilean waters, recorded, "I don't see how Mr. Harrison can help sending a fleet down here to teach these people manners."[40] The President fumed against "weaker powers" like Chile, but after American blustering and a change in the Chilean Cabinet, the now more cautious South Americans apologized in early 1892 and paid an indemnity of $75,000.[41] The Chileans had been humbled by the North American giant, and Latin Americans had to wonder what Pan-Americanism really meant. The United States "victory" over Chile boosted advocates of the expanding American Navy, but as one critic put it: "We do not need a steam hammer to crack nuts."[42] Senator George Shoup of Iowa drew another lesson: "The American Republic will stand no more nonsense from any power, big or little."[43]

## The Past as Prologue

In the late nineteenth century the United States moved toward global activism, but was restrained by self-imposed limitations on its own power. As an economic giant in competition with other nations it asserted its "rights." It added new territories to its domain and expanded its economy, foreign trade, and navy. More Americans than ever before, because of improved communications, were aware of and fascinated by foreign events. Consciousness was expanded. By 1895 the United States was self-confident, even cocky, steadied by a vibrant nationalism, yet rocked by a bad depression that convinced some leaders that domestic relief could best be found by expanding foreign markets. Latin America and Asia were prime targets, although only in the former could the United States work its will and meet European competition. Latin America, as a result of American interventions (political, naval, military, and economic), was being drawn closer to the United States. Not only did the United States intervene in Panama, Chile, and Venezuela, it also sent warships in 1894 to Brazil to thwart a rebellion against a government friendly with Washington. The process toward empire was by no means complete by the 1890s, but the trend was defined, and the United States considered the region off-limits to other powers.

There were impediments to expansion and to an enlargement of the American empire. Anti-imperialists, although weakened, continued their warnings. Congress still played politics with the diplomatic corps, consular service, Navy, and the tariff. In some areas of the world, the United States simply lacked the power to influence events. Some Americans argued that the answer to the domestic crisis of the 1890s was not to be found in foreign ventures, but in remedying ills at home.

Many skillful and articulate leaders, however, eyeing foreign grandeur, believed that they could arouse nationalist sentiment for the imperialist thrust that they thought necessary to the progress of the United States. In the early 1890s the

**Alfred Thayer Mahan (1840–1914).** Graduate of the United States Naval Academy, this bookish officer, historian, and respected naval politician articulated the necessity for overseas expansion and a large Navy. In 1890 he published *The Influence of Sea Power Upon History,* which influenced two key imperialists of the 1890s, Theodore Roosevelt and Henry Cabot Lodge. (*American Review of Reviews,* 1894)

future looked promising for extending the American frontier, and the need seemed urgent. As Senator Orville Platt of Connecticut put it: "A policy of isolation did well enough when we were an embryo nation, but today things are different. . . . We are sixty-five million of people, the most advanced and powerful on earth, and regard to our future welfare demands an abandonment of the doctrines of isolation."[44] In the late 1870s, renowned British scientist Thomas Huxley, after a trip to the United States, posed the problem somewhat cynically: "I cannot say I am in the slightest degree impressed by your bigness, or your material resources, as such. Size is not grandeur and territory does not make a nation. The great issue, about which hangs the terror of overhanging fate, is what are you going to do with all these things."[45] In their sense of change, of difference, of growth, and flush of power, Americans had a ready answer in the 1890s. At the close of the Civil War American leaders had considered the United States a world power; by 1895 they believed that it should act like one.

## Further Reading for the Period 1865–1895

General studies for this period include Robert L. Beisner, *From the Old Diplomacy to the New, 1865–1900* (1975), Charles S. Campbell, *The Transformation of American Foreign Relations, 1865–1900* (1976), Foster Rhea Dulles, *Prelude to World Power* (1968), John A. Garraty, *The New Commonwealth, 1877–1890* (1968), John A. S. Grenville and George B. Young, *Politics, Strategy, and American Diplomacy* (1967), Paul S. Holbo, "Economics, Emotion, and Expansion: An Emerging Foreign Policy," in H. Wayne Morgan, ed., *The Gilded Age* (1970), Walter LaFeber, *The New Empire* (1963), H. Wayne Morgan, *From Hayes to McKinley: National Party Politics, 1877–1896* (1969), Milton Plesur, *America's Outward Thrust* (1971), David M. Pletcher, *The Awkward Years: American Foreign Relations under Garfield and Arthur* (1962), Robert Wiebe, *The Search for Order* (1967), Richard Van Alstyne, *The Rising American Empire* (1960), and William A. Williams, *The Roots of the Modern American Empire* (1969).

For leading characters and their contributions to American foreign policy in the late nineteenth century, consult David Donald, *Charles Sumner and the Rights of Man* (1970), Allan Nevins, *Hamilton Fish* (1937), Ernest N. Paolino, *The Foundations of the American Empire* (1973) (on Seward), Charles C. Tansill, *The Foreign Policy of Thomas F. Bayard, 1885–1897* (1940), Alice Felt Tyler, *The Foreign Policy of James G. Blaine* (1927), Glyndon C. Van Deusen, *William Henry Seward* (1967), and essays by Gordon H. Warren, James B. Chapin, and Lester D. Langley on Seward, Fish, and Blaine in Frank Merli and Theodore A. Wilson, eds., *Makers of American Diplomacy* (1974). For short biographical sketches see John A. Garraty, ed., *Encyclopedia of American Biography* (1974).

The relationship between the American economy and foreign policy is treated in the works by Beisner, Campbell, Holbo, LaFeber, and Williams above and in William H. Becker, "American Manufacturers and Foreign Markets, 1870–1900," *Business History Review* (1973), Lloyd C. Gardner, ed., *A Different Frontier* (1966), David M. Pletcher, *Rails, Mines, and Progress: Seven American Promoters in Mexico, 1867–1911* (1958), Howard B. Schonberger, *Transportation to the Seaboard* (1971), Tom Terrill, *The Tariff, Politics, and American Foreign Policy, 1874–1901* (1973), and Mira Wilkins, *The Emergence of the Multinational Enterprise: American Business Abroad from the Colonial Era to 1914* (1970).

Improvements in the American Navy and its role in foreign relations are discussed in Kenneth J. Hagan, *American Gunboat Diplomacy and the Old Navy, 1877–1889* (1973) and "Alfred Thayer Mahan: Turning America Back to the Sea," in Frank Merli and Theodore A. Wilson, eds., *Makers of American Diplomacy* (1974), Walter R. Herrick, *The American Naval Revolution* (1966), Robert Seager II, *Alfred Thayer Mahan* (1977), and Harold and Margaret Sprout, *The Rise of American Naval Power, 1776–1918* (1944).

For relations with particular countries and regions see Charles S. Campbell, *From Revolution to Rapprochement: The United States and Great Britain, 1783–1900* (1974), Warren Cohen, *America's Response to China* (1971), Adrian Cook, *The Alabama Claims* (1975), Edward P. Crapol, *America for Americans: Economic Nationalism and Anglophobia in the Late Nineteenth Century* (1973), Fred Harvey Harrington, *God, Mammon, and the Japanese: Horace N. Allen and Korean-American Relations, 1884–1905* (1944), Ronald J. Jensen, *The Alaska Purchase and Russian-American Relations* (1975), Paul M. Kennedy, *The Samoan Tangle* (1974), Dexter Perkins, *The Monroe Doctrine, 1867–1907* (1973), Frederick B. Pike, *Chile and the United States, 1880–1962* (1963), Karl M. Schmitt, *Mexico and the United States, 1821–1973* (1974), Charles C. Tansill, *The United States and Santo Domingo, 1798–1873* (1938), Merze Tate, *The United States and the Hawaiian Kingdom* (1965), and Marilyn Blatt Young, "American Expansion 1870–1900: The Far East," in Barton J. Bernstein, ed., *Towards a New Past* (1968).

For an extensive bibliography use Campbell, *The Transformation,* and Norman A. Graebner, ed., *American Diplomatic History Before 1900* (1977). Also see the following notes.

# Notes to Chapter 5

1. Charles C. Tansill, *The United States and Santo Domingo, 1798–1873* (Baltimore: The Johns Hopkins Press, 1938), p. 134.

2. Quoted in David Donald, *Charles Sumner and the Rights of Man* (New York: Alfred A. Knopf, 1970), p. 443.

3. Quoted in Arthur M. Schlesinger, Jr., *The Imperial Presidency* (New York: Popular Library, 1973), p. 86.

4. Charles Francis Adams, *Before and After the Treaty of Washington* (New York: New York Historical Society, 1902), p. 76.

5. Rollo Ogden, ed., *Life and Letters of Edwin Lawrence Godkin* (New York: The Macmillan Company, 1907; 2 vols.), I, 304–305.

6. Quoted in Allan Nevins, *Hamilton Fish* (New York: Dodd, Mead, 1937), p. 372.

7. *The Works of Charles Sumner* (Boston: Lee and Shepard, 1870–1883; 15 vols.), XIV, 94–124.

8. Quoted in Adrian Cook, *The Alabama Claims: American Politics and Anglo-American Relations, 1865–1872* (Ithaca: Cornell University Press, 1975), p. 132.

9. Quoted in David Healy, *U.S. Expansionism: The Imperialist Urge in the 1890s* (Madison: University of Wisconsin Press, 1970), p. 44.

10. Quoted in Robert B. Davies, "'Peacefully Working to Conquer the World': The Singer Manufacturing Company in Foreign Markets, 1854–1889," *Business History Review*, XLIII (Autumn, 1969), 323.

11. Statement of 1878, quoted in Kenneth J. Hagan, *American Gunboat Diplomacy and the Old Navy, 1877–1889* (Westport, Conn.: Greenwood Press, 1973), p. 37.

12. Statement of 1898 quoted in John A. Thompson, "An Imperialist and the First World War: The Case of Albert J. Beveridge," *Journal of American Studies*, V (August, 1971), 135.

13. Quoted in Kenneth J. Hagan, "Alfred Thayer Mahan: Turning America Back to the Sea," in Frank Merli and Theodore Wilson, eds., *Makers of American Diplomacy* (New York: Charles Scribner's Sons, 1974), p. 288.

14. Quoted in Walter LaFeber, *The New Empire* (Ithaca, New York: Cornell University Press, 1963), p. 127.

15. *Ibid.*, p. 24.

16. Quoted in Oleh W. Gerus, "The Russian Withdrawal from Alaska: The Decision to Sell," *Revista de Historia de América*, LXXV–LXXVI (December, 1973), 162.

17. Quoted in Ronald J. Jensen, *The Alaska Purchase and Russian-American Relations* (Seattle: University of Washington Press, 1975), p. 55.

18. Quoted in Ernest N. Paolino, *The Foundations of the American Empire: William Henry Seward and U.S. Foreign Policy* (Ithaca, New York: Cornell University Press, 1973), p. 207.

19. Quoted in Robert L. Beisner, *Twelve Against Empire: The Anti-Imperialists, 1898–1900* (New York: McGraw-Hill, 1968), p. 72.

20. Quoted in Cook, *Alabama Claims*, p. 89.

21. Quoted in David P. Crook, *Diplomacy During the American Civil War* (New York: John Wiley & Sons, 1975), p. 131.

22. Samuel Flagg Bemis, *A Diplomatic History of the United States* (New York: Holt, Rinehart and Winston, 1965; 5th ed.), p. 413.

23. Quoted in Warren I. Cohen, *America's Response to China* (New York: John Wiley & Sons, 1971), p. 36.

24. Quoted in Foster Rhea Dulles, *Prelude to World Power* (New York: Macmillan, 1965), p. 80.

25. Quoted in Andrew H. Plaks, "Grant Takes Peking (1879)," *New York Times*, February 20, 1972.

26. Quoted in David M. Pletcher, *The Awkward Years: American Foreign Relations Under Garfield and Arthur* (Columbia: University of Missouri Press, 1962), p. 70.

27. Quoted in Julius W. Pratt, *Expansionists of 1898* (Chicago: Quadrangle Paperbacks [c. 1936], 1964), p. 25.

28. Quoted in Merze Tate, *The United States and the Hawaiian Kingdom: A Political History* (New Haven: Yale University Press, 1965), p. 210.

29. Quoted in Gerald G. Eggert, *Richard Olney: Evolution of a Statesman* (University Park, Pa.: Pennsylvania State University Press, 1974), p. 183.

30. Quoted in Paul M. Kennedy, *The Samoan Tangle: A Study in Anglo-American Relations, 1878–1900* (New York: Barnes & Noble, 1974), p. 53.

31. *Ibid.*, p. 76.

32. Quoted in Healy, *U.S. Expansionism*, p. 118.

33. Quoted in Jon D. Holstine, "Vermonter in Paradise: Henry Clay Ide in Samoa," *Vermont History*, XLIII (Spring, 1975), 140.

34. Quoted in M. Frederick Nelson, *Korea and the Old Orders in Eastern Asia* (Baton Rouge: Louisiana State University Press, 1946), p. 141.

35. Quoted in Pletcher, *Awkward Years*, p. 67.

36. Karl M. Schmitt, *Mexico and the United States, 1821–1973* (New York: John Wiley & Sons, 1974), p. 97.

37. T. Harry Williams, ed., *Hayes: The Diary of a President, 1875–1881* (New York: David McKay, 1964), p. 265.

38. Quoted in Richard W. Van Alstyne, *The Rising American Empire* (New York: W. W. Norton, [c. 1960], 1974), p. 163.

39. Quoted in Alice Felt Tyler, *The Foreign Policy of James G. Blaine* (Minneapolis: University of Minnesota Press, 1927), p. 178.

40. Robley D. Evans, *A Sailor's Log* (New York: D. Appleton, 1902), p. 265.

41. James D. Richardson, ed., *Messages of the Presidents* (Washington: Government Printing Office, 1898; 10 vols.), IX, 225.

42. Quoted in H. Wayne Morgan, *From Hayes to McKinley: National Party Politics, 1877–1896* (Syracuse: Syracuse University Press, 1969), p. 362.

43. Quoted in Ernest R. May, *Imperial Democracy: The Emergence of America as a Great Power* (New York: Harper and Row, [1961], 1973), p. 10.

44. Quoted in Robert L. Beisner, *From the Old Diplomacy to the New, 1865–1900* (New York: Thomas Y. Crowell, 1975), p. 72.

45. Quoted in J. William Fulbright, *The Crippled Giant* (New York: Random House, 1972), p. 275.

**Grover Cleveland (1837–1908).** This caricature of the two-term President, overweight from frequenting saloons as a young man, captured the gruff American attitude toward Britain during the Venezuelan crisis. (Courtesy of The New-York Historical Society, New York City)

# 6
# Imperialist Thrust, 1895–1900

## Diplomatic Crossroad: The Venezuelan Crisis, 1895

Grover Cleveland was pleased. On July 7, 1895, the same day his third daughter was born at the family summer home on Cape Cod, Massachusetts, he wrote an enthusiastic note to Secretary of State Richard Olney. Just a few days before, Olney, who also escaped from the sweltering summer temperatures of Washington to a residence on the cape, had personally delivered a 12,000-word draft document to the President. The secretary had been on the job only a few weeks and this draft of a major message to London on the Venezuelan boundary dispute was one of his first efforts. Energetic Olney, a successful corporate lawyer and former attorney general, was naturally anxious. He knew that Cleveland wanted the dispute cleared up, and Olney himself liked to keep his desk tidy. The President's note arrived bearing laudatory words: "It's the best thing of the kind I ever read." Cleveland suggested some minor changes, "a little more softened verbiage here and there," and directed Olney to send the document to London, which he did on July 20, 1895. Cleveland later christened it Olney's "twenty-inch gun." It was as much Cleveland's weapon as Olney's.[1]

The gun was aimed at Great Britain, which for decades had haggled with Venezuela over the boundary line separating that country and British Guiana. A Britisher, Robert Schomburgk, had drawn a line in the 1840s, but nobody liked it. Both sides made claims which went deep into the other's territory. In the 1880s, the discovery of gold in the disputed region—the largest nugget ever found, 509 ounces, was unearthed there—heightened competition. At stake, too, was control of the mouth of the Orinoco River, gateway to the potential trade of northern South America. In the 1870s Venezuela had begun to appeal to the United States for help, arguing that the poaching British were violating the Monroe Doctrine. Washington repeatedly asked the British to submit the issue to arbitration, but met constant rebuff. In his annual message to Congress in December, 1894, Cleveland renewed the call for arbitration. After another British refusal, the President grew impatient and ordered the State Department to prepare a report on the boundary question. The "twenty-inch gun" sounded Olney's memorable answer.

In retrospect it is easy to see why Cleveland and Olney were so agitated about the Venezuelan boundary question. First, the political dimension. William L. Scruggs, former American minister to Caracas, was hired in the early 1890s to propagandize Venezuela's case in the United States. He wrote a widely circulated pamphlet, *British Aggressions in Venezuela, or the Monroe Doctrine on Trial* (1895), which aroused considerable sympathy for the South American nation. Olney himself read it before preparing his blast of July 20. American sentiment soon congealed: the land-grabbing British were picking on a poor hemispheric friend of the United States. A unanimous congressional resolution of February, 1895, calling for arbitration, reflected the growing American concern. Cleveland listened attentively to such expressions, because his Democratic party had lost badly in the 1894 congressional elections and his Administration was being attacked, particularly by Republicans, as pusillanimous for not annexing Hawaii and for doing nothing when the British briefly landed troops in Nicaragua in April, 1895. Cleveland, it seemed, could deflect criticism and recoup Democratic losses by bold action. As one Democrat advised the President: "Turn this Venezuela question up or down, North, South, East or West, and it is a 'winner.'"[2]

The President did not need such political considerations to stimulate his interest. He was inclined toward action anyway because of momentous events in the 1890s. This was the golden age of European imperialism, when the powers were carving up territories in Asia, the Near East, and Africa. The British, already holding large stakes in Latin America, seemed intent upon enlarging them. Their intervention in Nicaragua was a fresh example. Nor was the French intervention in Mexico in the 1860s forgotten. Americans feared that new incursions could make Latin America another Africa. The boundary dispute in Venezuela seemed a symbol of the unwelcome European reach into the western hemisphere.

The American depression of the 1890s also helped fix attention on Venezuela. Many, including Cleveland, thought that overproduction was a major cause of the slump and that foreign trade expansion was a possible solution. Might the British close off the Orinoco River and hence the markets of the area? At that time, American economic involvement in Venezuela was ripening. For example, the National Association of Manufacturers, organized in 1895 to expand American exports, chose Caracas as the site for its first permanent overseas display of American products. In short, international competition and economic woes suggested that the national interest of the United States was tied to Venezuela's dispute with Britain.

Cleveland's own character and style colored his response. He did not like bullies pushing small fry around. He had already rejected Hawaiian annexation in part because he thought that Americans had bullied the Hawaiians against their will. It appeared to the President, exaggeration though it was, that America's perennial competitor Britain was arrogantly manhandling the Venezuelans. What he and the sometimes intemperate Olney needed was an intellectual peg upon which to hang the United States case. They found it in a refurbished Monroe Doctrine. Olney's "twenty-inch gun" of July 20, 1895, invoked that venerable principle in aggressive, bumptious, and exaggerated language that prejudged the issue against the British. The brash message noted that the British claim had grown larger and larger,

**"The Real British Lion."** A popular American depiction of the British global presence during the crisis over Venezuela. (*New York Evening World,* 1895)

cutting deeper and deeper into Venezuela. Further growth might lead to political control. It is conceivable, Olney stated, that the European struggle over the partition of Africa might be transferred to Latin America. The "safety," "honor," and "welfare" of the United States were at stake, and the Monroe Doctrine outlawed European intervention leading to control in the western hemisphere. Using history, Olney cited the successful application of the doctrine in the French-Mexican-American imbroglio of the 1860s. He quoted the doctrine at length and asserted that "any permanent political union between a European and an American state [was] unnatural and inexpedient."

Because its national interest was involved, the United States had to intervene in the dispute. "The states of America, South as well as North, by geographical proximity, by natural sympathy, by similarity of governmental constitutions, are friends and allies, commercially and politically, of the United States. To allow the subjugation of any one of them by a European power is, of course, to completely reverse that situation and signifies the loss of all the advantages incident to their natural relations with us." The forceful, overriding theme of Olney's proclamation was directed toward an international audience: "To-day the United States is practically sovereign on this continent, and its fiat is law upon the subjects to which it confines its interposition." And more: the United States' "infinite resources combined with its isolated position render it master of the situation and practically invulnerable as against any or all other powers."[3] Olney, finally, demanded arbitration, vaguely threatened United States intervention, and requested a British answer by the time of the President's annual message to Congress in December.

Ambassador to England Thomas Bayard delivered the document to the giant of European diplomats, Lord Salisbury, then doubling as the British prime minister and foreign secretary. The bearded sixty-five-year-old Salisbury struck an imposing figure—intelligent, aristocratic, cautious, and well read. He received the missive with some surprise and sent it to the Foreign Office for study. Through the summer months little was done, in part because vacations interrupted work. Salisbury saw no urgency, bothered as he was with crises elsewhere (especially in Africa). Anyway, in the late nineteenth century one expected American Anglophobic bombast. The issue, he thought, would probably fizzle out once American politics calmed down. Furthermore, he disliked arbitrating any question that might weaken the British Empire. Salisbury would never entrust British interests in the Orinoco area to the United States. Obviously, he did not appreciate how agitated the Cleveland Administration was. The British did not complete their reply until November 26, and it arrived in Washington after Cleveland's annual message (which was quite tame on the Venezuelan controversy). Salisbury's reply had a "ho-hum" quality. It discounted the applicability of the Monroe Doctrine and dismissed any United States interest in the dispute.

Cleveland, all 250 pounds of him, was duck-hunting in North Carolina when the British response reached Washington. Upon his return he read it and became "mad clean through."[4] Olney had already been working on a special congressional message. He had not counted on a flat British rejection. Now what? War? Retreat? Neither course would serve the national interest. Olney struggled for alternatives and finally selected one which left some maneuvering room, kept diplomacy in the hands of the executive branch, and avoided war or backstepping: an American study commission appointed by the President. Cleveland, although tired from his expedition among the ducks, stayed up all night to rewrite Olney's draft. He dispatched his special message to Congress on December 17 and it rang a bell of alarm. England must arbitrate; the United States would create an investigating

**"If There Must Be War."** Lord Salisbury and President Cleveland slug it out during the Venezuelan crisis as a substitute for full-scale war. (*Life,* 1896)

commission to set the true boundary line; and then American action would follow. Most observers labeled the message an ultimatum, with the possibility of war lurking throughout.

The nation buzzed over this verbal flexing of muscle. Congress appropriated funds for the investigating commission. Irish-Americans offered themselves as volunteers to fight the hated British; both Republicans and Democrats lined up behind the President, and Senator Henry Cabot Lodge noted with approval that "Jingoes are plenty enough now."[5] Theodore Roosevelt, always eager for a tussle, bubbled with enthusiasm: "Let the fight come if it must; I don't care whether our sea coast cities are bombarded or not; we would take Canada."[6] Many businessmen rallied behind the Administration, with Whitelaw Reid, editor of the *New York Tribune,* hyperbolically declaring that "This is the golden opportunity of our merchants to extend our trade to every quarter of Central and South America."[7] British Ambassador Sir Julian Pauncefote detected "in Congress and among the Public a condition of mind which can only be described as hysterical."[8]

This high wave of emotionalism subsided rapidly in early 1896. Many bankers and businessmen became alarmed when the stock market plummeted, in large part because British investors were pulling out. On second thought, some Americans calculated that a war was unconscionable with Britain, a country so close in race, language, and culture. Critics like E. L. Godkin, editor of *The Nation,* and respected international law specialist John Bassett Moore pointed out how haughtily Cleveland and Olney had acted. Ambassador Bayard was critical of the President's truculent stance: "I fear he has made a gross and great error of judgment and has been too *precipitate,* for I do not see why he should abandon suddenly his attitude of conservatism and go apparently into the camp of aggressiveness."[9] But Cleveland never wanted war. He wanted peace on American terms, even if it required aggressiveness.

## American Foreign Policy After Venezuela

What followed was anticlimactic. In a January 11, 1896 Cabinet meeting, Salisbury, still recommending delay, was overruled and instructed to begin negotiations with the United States. The British retreat was necessitated by a dispute with Germany over South Africa. England needed friends now, not enemies. Furthermore, Canada could not be defended and the Admiralty reported that the Royal Navy was inadequate in the North Atlantic and Caribbean. Formal talks ultimately began and dragged on until November, 1896, when Britain and the United States agreed to set up a five-person arbitral board to define the boundary, with each to name two members, who would in turn select the fifth. Finally, in October, 1899, the tribunal reached a decision that rejected the extreme claims of each party and generally followed the Schomburgk line. The pivotal Point Barima at the mouth of the Orinoco went to Venezuela, which came out of the dispute pretty well, considering the fact that neither the United States nor Great Britain cared much about what happened to *Venezuela's* national interest.

Indeed, a remarkable characteristic of this controversy was that the United States negotiated directly with Britain without consulting Venezuela. Venezuela had a duly accredited minister in Washington, but he was excluded from the talks. Olney never even gave the Venezuelans a copy of his "twenty-inch gun" (they eventually read it in the newspapers), and when they balked over the 1896

Anglo-American agreement he grew angry and simply told them what to do. He made one concession: Venezuela could name one of the five members of the arbitration board—so long as that person was not a Venezuelan. Scruggs complained that the United States was attempting to "over-awe and *bull-doze* Venezuela."[10] He was right, but Washington's vigorous diplomacy was directed at others besides that South American nation. The overweening theme of Olney's "twenty-inch gun" merits repeating: "To-day the United States is practically sovereign on this continent, and its fiat is law upon the subjects to which it confines its interposition."

The Venezuelan crisis, most scholars agree, was a significant event in American diplomatic history. Although Cleveland and Olney did not intend all the consequences which flowed from it, they did help move the United States toward world power status. As an example of forceful, even aggressive, American diplomacy, the Venezuelan controversy marked a time in history when the United States determined to demonstrate its weight in international affairs. Besides displaying a self-righteous disregard for the rights and sensibilities of small nations, it revealed a United States more sure of itself, more certain about the components of its "policy," and willing to flex its muscle. The episode stimulated American nationalism and pride, or what critics at the time called "jingoism." The Monroe Doctrine gained new stature as a warning to European nations to temper, if not abandon, their activities in the western hemisphere; the United States, nationalists were proud to relate, had humbled Great Britain and forced the olympian Salisbury to retreat. The executive branch kept the Venezuelan issue in *its* hands, thereby strengthening the foreign policy power of the President. Some congressmen and senators complained that Cleveland was committing the United States to possible war without appropriate consultation with the legislative branch.

Other ramifications became evident. Latin Americans learned once again that the United States intended to establish supremacy in the western hemisphere. They realized further that the United States would judge the national interests of other countries and intervene when it saw fit. The United States had always kept an eye on the Caribbean, but the Venezuelan crisis and the outbreak of revolution in Cuba in 1895 intensified American interest, a significant dimension of which was economic. The Venezuelan issue and the disposition of the Orinoco River also brought more attention to the theory of overproduction as a cause of depression, to be cured by exporting surplus goods. Commercial expansion, always a trend in American history, was given another boost.

The discord with Britain over Venezuela actually fostered Anglo-American rapprochement. Cooperation and mutual interest increasingly characterized relations between Washington and London. British diplomats sought United States friendship as a possible counterweight to growing German power, and one manifestation of the emerging détente was a self-conscious British decision to permit the United States to govern Caribbean affairs. One way, the chief way, the United States could manage events in that area was through naval power. The Venezuelan crisis, joined by crises in Asia and the belief that naval construction would employ those idled by depression, stimulated additional American naval expansion. The Navy Act of 1896, for example, provided for three new battleships and ten new torpedo boats. All told, the Venezuelan boundary dispute advanced the United States farther along the path of expansion.

That path, by the end of the decade, led to new United States colonies in the

Pacific, Far East, and the Caribbean, a decisive hold on Cuba, and Europe's recognition of the United States as the overlord of the Caribbean. By 1900, too, the United States had pledged itself to preserve the "Open Door" in China; it had built a navy that had just annihilated the Spanish fleet and ranked sixth in the world; and it had developed an export trade amounting to $1.5 billion. Its industrial might was symbolized by steel and iron production, which almost equaled that of Britain and Germany combined. American acquisition of new colonies after the Spanish-American War has led some observers to conclude that *only then*, about 1898, did the United States become an imperialist world power. But as we have seen, there was a continuity of expansionism and imperialism in nineteenth-century diplomacy. Seldom do major diplomatic squabbles or wars happen all of a sudden; they flow from cumulative events. Had William H. Seward lived in 1898, for example, he might have triumphantly emphasized the similarities between the 1890s and the 1860s. Had he been a good historian, he would have pointed out also that economic and political changes at home and increased competition with

European powers abroad had undermined anti-imperialist arguments and permitted his schemes for empire to be realized. Before the depression decade of the 1890s the United States had often taken halting steps toward a larger empire; in that decade it took the leap.

## The Making of American Foreign Policy in the 1890s

Theodore Roosevelt described the anti-imperialists in 1897 as "men of a by-gone age" and "provincials."[11] Indeed, anti-imperialism waned through the late nineteenth century. Increasing numbers of educated, economically comfortable Americans made the case for formal empire (colonies or protectorates) or informal empire (commercial domination). Naval officers, diplomats, politicians, farmers, skilled artisans, businessmen, and clergymen made up what might be called the "foreign policy public." Better read than most Americans and having access to lecterns to disperse their ideas, this "elite" helped move America to war and empire. Recent scholarly research has shown, contrary to a long-standing assumption, that it was not "public opinion," the jingoistic "yellow press," or the "people" in the 1890s that compelled the United States to war, but rather two key elements: a McKinley Administration very much in charge of its diplomacy through skillful maneuvering, and a majoritarian view within the articulate "foreign policy public" in favor of a vigorous outward thrust.

The "hows," rather than the "whys," of decisionmaking can be explained by noting problems with the phrase "public opinion." One often hears that "public opinion" or "the man in the street" influenced a leader to follow a certain course of action. But "public opinion" was not a unified, identifiable group speaking with one voice. Furthermore, political leaders and other articulate, knowledgeable people often shaped the "public opinion" they wanted to hear by their very handling of events and their control over information. That is, they *led* in the true sense of the word. In trying to determine who the "people" are and what "public opinion" is, social science studies demonstrate that the people who counted, the people who were listened to, the people who expressed their opinion publicly in order to influence policy—these people in the 1890s numbered no more than 1.5 million to 3 million, or between 10 and 20 percent of the voting public. This percentage—upper- and middle-income groups, educated, active politically—constituted the "foreign policy public." As Secretary of State Walter Q. Gresham put it in 1893: "After all, public opinion is made and controlled by the thoughtful men of the country."[12] The "public opinion" the President heard in the 1890s was not that of some collection we loosely call the "people," but rather that of a small, articulate segment of the American population alert to foreign policy issues. Although they

| Makers of American Foreign Policy from 1895 to 1900 | |
| --- | --- |
| *Presidents* | *Secretaries of State* |
| Grover Cleveland, 1893–1897 | Richard Olney, 1895–1897 |
| William McKinley, 1897–1901 | John Sherman, 1897–1898 |
| | William R. Day, 1898 |
| | John Hay, 1898–1905 |

counted anti-imperialists in their numbers, the "foreign policy public" was heavily weighted on the side of imperialism.

The President, as a consummate politician and good tactician, is often the master of policymaking, even thwarting the advice of the "foreign policy public" itself. President Cleveland, for example, successfully resisted pressure to annex Hawaii and withdrew the treaty from the Senate. He never let Congress or influential public opinion set the terms of his policy toward the Venezuelan crisis. Nor was President William McKinley stampeded into decisions; he tried *his* diplomacy before trying the war that many leaders, especially in Congress, had been advocating for months and years. An imperialist-oriented "foreign policy public," rather than some immeasurable "public opinion," helped move the United States along a path to war and larger empire, but the administrations determined the speed of the movement. Pressures from jingoes in Congress and a sensationalist press were evident, but the initiative in foreign affairs, unlike the 1860s and 1870s, was largely in the hands of the executive branch. In most historical periods, the public *reacts* to *immediate* events; the executive *acts, manages,* with *long-term* policy considerations.

## The Cuban Revolution and the United States, 1895–1897

Eighteen ninety-five was a year of momentous events. The Venezuelan crisis, Japan's defeat of China in the Sino-Japanese War, and the outbreak of revolution in Cuba—all carried profound meaning for American diplomacy. The sugar-rich island of Cuba, since the close of its unsuccessful war for independence (1868–1878), had stagnated in a state of political repression and massive poverty. After that war Cuban nationalists prepared for a new assault upon their Spanish overlords. From 1881 to 1895, Cuban national hero José Martí plotted from exile in the United States. In 1892 he organized the Cuban Revolutionary party, using American territory to recruit men and money for a return to his homeland. Martí's opportunity came when Cuba's economic development was hurt in 1894 by a new American tariff, which raised duties on imported sugar and hence reduced Cuban sugar shipments to the United States. On February 24, 1895, with cries of *"Cuba Libre,"* the rebels opened their drive for independence. They kept a cautious eye on the United States, for they knew its historical interest in Cuba and feared ultimate American control. As Martí remarked, "I have lived in the bowels of the monster and I know it."[13]

Cuban and Spanish military strategies were calculated to produce destruction and death. Led by General Máximo Gómez, a veteran of the 1868–1878 war, the *insurrectos* burned cane fields, blew up mills, and disrupted railroads, with the goal of rendering Cuba an economic liability to Spain. "The chains of Cuba have been forged by her own richness," Gómez proclaimed, "and it is precisely this which I propose to do away with soon."[14] Although outnumbered (about 30,000 Cuban troops against 200,000 Spanish) and lacking adequate supplies (often their weapons and ammunition did not match), the insurgents, with the sympathy of the populace, wore the Spanish down through guerrilla tactics. By late 1896 they controlled about two-thirds of the island, with the Spanish concentrated in coastal and urban regions. That year, to break the rebel stronghold in the rural areas, Governor-General Valeriano y Nicolau Weyler instituted the brutal reconcentration program. He divided the island into districts and herded Cubans into fortified camps. A half million Cubans were driven from homes and livelihoods into these centers, where frightful sanitation conditions, poor food, and disease contributed to the death of perhaps 200,000 people. Cubans outside the camps were assumed to be rebels and targets for death. In the countryside Weyler's soldiers destroyed crops, killed livestock, and polluted water sources. This effort to starve the insurgents and deprive them of physical and moral support, combined with the rebels' destructive behavior, made a shambles of Cuba's society and economy.

The Cleveland Administration, keeping control of its diplomacy against congressional pressures, faced several alternatives. It could recognize Cuban belligerency. That was ruled out because such an act, Olney noted, would relieve Spain of any responsibility for paying claims filed by Americans for properties destroyed in Cuba. Cleveland and Olney found recognition of Cuban independence even less appetizing, for they believed the Cubans incapable of self-government and feared anarchy and even racial war. That course might also arouse a Spanish declaration of war or force American belligerency because, logically, a Spanish attempt to conquer an "independent" Cuba would constitute a violation of the Monroe Doctrine. War seemed out of the question, as did outright annexation, although apparently Olney toyed with buying the island at one point. The Cleveland Administration settled on a dual policy of hostility to the revolution and pressure on Spain to grant some autonomy. Diplomacy and lecturing to a foreign government seemed to be working in the Venezuelan crisis; perhaps it would work in the case of Cuba.

Stirred by a Republican Congress (it passed a resolution in April, 1896, urging the President to recognize Cuban belligerency), by continued evidence of wholesale destruction, and by Spanish obstinacy in refusing reforms and adhering to force, Olney sent a note to Spain in April, 1896. He told Spain it could not win by force, but said the United States preferred continued Spanish control of the island. The United States took an active interest in Cuban affairs, he went on, because the American people always supported freer political institutions, the war was being conducted inhumanely, commerce was being disrupted, and American property was going the way of the torch. Spain should initiate reforms short of independence. Olney was principally concerned with the interests of Americans, not with those of the Cubans. American property was estimated at $50 million and the decline in sugar production wrought disaster to Cuban-American trade relations. In 1892 Cuba had shipped to the United States goods worth $79 million; by 1898 that figure had slumped to $15 million.

When Spain rejected Olney's advice, the Cleveland Administration seemed stymied. It did not desire war, but it meant to protect American interests. Congress kept asking for firm action. And in Havana, hotheaded American Consul-General Fitzhugh Lee was openly clamoring for American annexation. Cleveland did not feel he could fire Lee, nephew of General Robert E. Lee, because the noisy fellow had some political clout at home, and Cleveland needed political friends at a time when the Democratic party was dumping the incumbent President in favor of William Jennings Bryan. Olney kept Lee at bay by bombarding him with endless requests for information. Cleveland and Olney were further bothered by the news that Spain was approaching the courts of Europe for diplomatic support, with the argument that the Monroe Doctrine threatened all European powers. Spain's appeal went unheeded, but the apprehension lingered in the minds of American leaders that European nations might intrude in Cuba.

British Ambassador to Spain H. Drummond Wolff believed "what the United States required for Cuba was 'peace with commerce.'"[15] Cleveland proved this estimate accurate when he sent his annual message to Congress in December, 1896. With a slight echo of Olney's "twenty-inch gun" about the United States' "fiat" in the western hemisphere, the President reported that neither the Spanish nor the Cuban rebels had established their authority over the island. Americans felt a humanitarian concern, he said, but their trade and investments ("pecuniary interest") were also jeopardized. Furthermore, to maintain its neutrality, the United States had to police the coastline to intercept unlawful expeditions. Spain must grant autonomy or "home rule," but not independence, to "fertile and rich" Cuba to end the bloodshed and devastation. If Spain did not, he warned, the United States, having thus far acted with "restraint," might abandon its "expectant attitude."[16]

But Cleveland was more bark than bite. Through Olney he successfully buried a Senate resolution urging recognition of Cuban independence and contented himself with some limited Spanish reforms of February, 1897. Thereafter he let the Cuban issue fester, bequeathing it to the incoming McKinley Administration. His legacy to the new Republican President was nevertheless significant; he had declared that American interests were at stake in Cuba and that the United States would continue to lecture Spain about its Cuban problem.

## The Road to War: McKinley's Diplomacy, 1897–1898

William McKinley, inaugurated in March of 1897, was a veteran Republican politician, a deft manager of men. The election of 1896 had been rough, but McKinley, pegged as the "Advance Agent of Prosperity," had beaten back William Jennings Bryan with a quiet campaign based upon the theme of a bright future for America. The teetotaling Ohioan was a stable, dignified figure in a time of crisis. He represented deep religious conviction, personal warmth, sincerity, commitment to economic development and the revival of business, party loyalty, and support for expansion abroad. Yet McKinley often gave the appearance of being an infantile follower, a mindless flunky of the political bosses, a spineless leader. One joke went: "Why is McKinley's mind like a bed?" Answer: "Because it has to be made up for him every time he wants to use it." Plucky Theodore Roosevelt allegedly remarked that McKinley had no more backbone than a chocolate éclair. Such an image was created in large part by bellicose imperialists who believed that McKinley was not moving fast enough and critics of domestic policy like Bryan who saw McKinley as clay in the hands of big business and party machines. McKinley certainly was a party regular and friend of large corporations, but he was no lackey. A manager of diplomacy, who wanted expansion and empire without war and Spain out of Cuba without American military intervention, McKinley was his own man.

McKinley shared America's late nineteenth-century image of itself as an expanding nation of superior institutions and as a major power in Latin America. He agreed with Mahan and others that a large navy, overseas commerce, and foreign bases were essential to the well-being of the United States. He believed strongly, as he said time and time again, that America's surplus goods had to be exported. Although McKinley uttered almost nothing about foreign issues in the campaign of 1896, the Republican party platform overflowed with imperialist rhetoric and

**William McKinley (1843–1901).** An Ohioan who studied at Allegheny College, fought in the Civil War, and served several terms as a congressman, the twenty-fifth President was a supreme politician and successful imperialist. He was assassinated in Buffalo, New York in 1901. (Library of Congress)

conviction worthy of William H. Seward himself. Extolling a vigorous diplomacy, it urged American control of Hawaii, a Nicaraguan canal run by the United States, an enlarged navy, purchase of the Virgin Islands, and Cuban independence. Between election and inauguration, however, McKinley quietly joined Cleveland and Olney in successfully burying a Senate resolution for recognition of Cuba. He wanted a free hand. His appointment of the old and ailing Senator John Sherman as secretary of state suggested further that McKinley would take charge of his own diplomacy. His inaugural address vacuously urged peace, never mentioning the Cuban crisis.

McKinley's first tilt with Congress came in March, 1897, after he called a special session for revision of the tariff. Resolutions on Cuba sprang up repeatedly, but the President managed to bury them. He did satisfy imperialists by sending an Hawaiian annexation treaty to the Senate. The President was preparing for his own nonpublic diplomatic assault upon Spain. In June, Madrid received an American reprimand for Weyler's uncivilized warfare and for his disruption of the Cuban economy. "Capitalism and humanitarianism," historian Lester Langley has aptly noted, "had joined hands" in the American protest.[17] Spain, however, showed no signs of tempering its military response to the insurrection. American citizens suffered in Spanish jails; American property continued to be devastated. Fitzhugh Lee, who remained at his post in Havana, bellowed for American intervention. In July McKinley instructed the new American Minister to Spain, Stewart L. Woodford, to demand that the Spanish stop the fighting. Increasingly convinced that the Cuban insurrectos would not compromise, the President sought to persuade Spain to leave Cuba altogether. A new Spanish government assumed power in October and soon moderated policy by offering Cuba a substantial degree of self-government or autonomy. Even more, it removed the hated Weyler and promised to end reconcentration. Yet these reforms were not fully implemented and did not bring an end to the warfare.

McKinley's December 6, 1897 annual message to Congress (which had not been in session from July to December, thus giving the President little trouble) discussed the Cuban insurrection at great length. The crisis caused Americans the "gravest apprehension." What were the alternatives for the United States? McKinley rejected annexation as "criminal aggression." He argued against recognition of belligerency, because the rebels hardly constituted a government worthy of recognition. And he ruled out intervention because it was premature at a time when the Spanish were traveling the "honorable paths" of reform. He asked for patient waiting to see if Spanish changes would work, but hinted that the United States would continue to consider all policy options, including intervention "with force."[18]

By mid-January, however, evidence poured into Washington proving that the reforms had not moderated the crisis, that in fact insurgents, conservatives, and the Spanish army alike denounced them. Antireform, pro-army riots rocked Havana. The United States ordered the warship *Maine* to Havana on January 24, 1898 to demonstrate concern. On February 9, the State Department received a copy of a private letter written in late 1897 by Spanish Minister to the United States Enrique Dupuy de Lôme and sent to a Spanish editor touring Cuba. Intercepted in Cuba by a rebel sympathizer, the letter was forwarded to friends in the United States. Not only did it reach the State Department; William Randolph Hearst's flamboyant *New York Journal* published it that day with the banner headline: "Worst Insult to the United States in its History." De Lôme labeled McKinley "weak," a "bidder for the admiration of the crowd," and a "would-be politician."[19] McKinley, along with most Americans, was infuriated by de Lôme's remarks. The Administration particularly resented another statement that suggested that Spain did not take its reform proposals seriously and would persist in fighting to defeat the rebels. Spain, it appeared, had been tricking the United States. De Lôme's hasty recall hardly salved the hurt.

Trying to avoid war, a restless McKinley nevertheless recognized the trend. During the first four months of 1898 he had to take drugs to sleep. His demeanor was not improved by the rapidity of critical events. Less than a week after the de Lôme episode, on February 15, explosions ripped through the *Maine*, anchored audaciously in Havana Harbor. Over 250 American sailors died as the 6,700-ton vessel sank quickly. With no evidence, but considerable emotion, Americans jumped to the conclusion that Spain had committed the dastardly deed. Few asked why the *Maine* was there in the first place—in the dangerous waters of a Spanish colony in open rebellion. McKinley ordered an official investigation, but said little publicly. Some decried his caution, but he decided to try diplomacy and threat again. On March 3 Woodford protested in strong language to the Spanish government about

**The U.S.S. *Maine* Before and After.** Part of the battleship was raised in 1911, investigated, and sunk at sea with flag flying. The investigators concluded that the explosion that destroyed the vessel was external, but mystery still surrounds the causes of the catastrophe. (Before—*Harper's Weekly*, 1888; after—National Archives)

the de Lôme incident and the *Maine*. The Cuban crisis was "grave" and had to be resolved. On March 6 the President met with Joe Cannon, chairman of the House Committee on Appropriations, and asked him to present a bill providing $50 million for arms. "I must have the money to get ready for war."[20] Congress enthusiastically obliged three days later. Spain, Woodford reported, was stunned by the appropriation.

In mid-March Senator Redfield Proctor of Vermont, a friend of McKinley considered to be against going to war, stirringly told his colleagues about his recent trip to Cuba. He recounted ugly stories about the concentration camps. "Torn from their homes, with foul earth, foul air, foul water, and foul food or none, what wonder that one-half died and that one-quarter of the living are so diseased that they cannot be saved?"[21] Shortly after this moving speech, which convinced many congressmen and businessmen that Spain could not bring order to Cuba, the American court of inquiry on the *Maine* concluded that the vessel was destroyed by an external mine. The board could not determine who placed it there. A Spanish commission at about the same time correctly attributed the disaster to an internal explosion. We still do not know exactly what set off the forward powder magazine, but in 1898 vocal Americans pinned the crime squarely on Spain. "Remember the Maine, to hell with Spain" became the popular chant.

McKinley's options were certainly narrowed by these cumulative events and sentiments. He seriously thought of finding a way to buy Cuba, but it was evident Spain had no intention of selling. After consultation with advisers and congressional leaders, the President decided on an ultimatum. On March 27 Washington cabled the American demands: an armistice, McKinley's arbitration of the conflict if there was no peace by October, termination of the reconcentration policy, and relief aid to the Cubans. Implicit was the demand that Spain grant Cuba its independence. As a last-ditch effort to avoid American military intervention, the ultimatum had little chance of success. Spain's national pride and interest would block acceptance; it could not accept surrender. Madrid's answer was soon forthcoming: it had terminated reconcentration, would launch reforms, and would accept an armistice if the rebels did so first. By rejecting McKinley's offer of mediation and Cuban independence, the Spanish reply hardly satisfied the President. He did not think the Spanish were moving fast enough, so he began to write a war message in early April. On the ninth, Spain made a new concession, declaring a unilateral armistice "for such length of time" as the Spanish commander "may think prudent."[22] To McKinley, the declaration seemed too qualified and fell far short of independence. Could the Spaniards be trusted?

## Why War: Exploiting Opportunity

On April 11 McKinley sent a message to Congress, asking for authority to use armed force to end the Cuban war. Since neither the Cubans nor the Spaniards could stem the flow of blood, America would do the job. The United States would do so because of the "cause of humanity" and the "very serious injury to the commerce, trade, and business of our people, and the wanton destruction of property." And, recalling the sinking of the *Maine*, McKinley described the conflict as "a constant menace to our peace." At the very end of the message the President noted that Spain had recently accepted an armistice. He asked Congress to give this new information "your just and careful attention." This right after having aroused the legislators to war.[23]

Congress went to work. McKinley beat back an attempt to recognize the rebel Cuban government; he wanted no restraints on his freedom. He privately thought that Cuba would have to undergo American tutelage until the United States deemed the country ready for self-government. However, he failed to defeat the Teller Amendment, which disclaimed any American intention of annexing the island. It passed by voice vote and without much debate. Indeed, it was paid little attention in the emotional atmosphere of going to war. Some who voted for it feared that the United States might have to assume Cuba's large bond debt if it annexed the island. On April 19, Congress declared war, proclaiming Cuba independent, demanding Spain's withdrawal, and directing the President to use force to bring about these results.

Because of the Teller Amendment, the decision for war seemed selfless and humanitarian, and for many Americans it undoubtedly was. But the decision was not motivated so simply. Different people called for war for different reasons. McKinley himself stated several: humanitarian concern, property, commerce, and the removal of an annoyance. Republican leaders said that their party would lose the 1898 congressional elections if the President did not heed popular cries for war. Important businessmen, formerly hesitant, shifted in March and April to demand an end to the disruptive Cuban crisis. Farmers and businessmen interested in Asian and Latin American markets thought victory against Spain would open new trade doors by eliminating a colonial power. Many honest and sincere Americans simply felt compelled to end the bloodshed. Republican Senator George F. Hoar of Massachusetts, later an anti-imperialist, wrote that "we cannot look idly on while hundreds of thousands of innocent human beings . . . die of hunger close to our doors. If there is ever to be a war it should be to prevent such things as that."[24] Religious leaders, both Protestant and Catholic, marched in the war parade. Lyman Abbott, well-known pastor of Plymouth Church in Brooklyn, thought war the "answer to America to the question of its own conscience: Am I my brother's keeper?"[25] Church missionaries dreamed of new opportunities to convert the "uncivilized." Imperialists hoped war would add new territories to the American empire and encourage the growth of a larger navy. But the "warriors" were not synonymous with the "imperialists." Some people opposed empire and sincerely thought war would halt the long conflict in Cuba, whereas the imperialists seized upon war as an opportunity to expand the American empire.

Emotional nationalism also figured in the American thirst for war. The de Lôme and *Maine* incidents stmulated a national pride already infused with notions of American superiority, racial and otherwise. Imperialist Senator Albert Beveridge was ebullient: "At last, God's hour has struck. The American people go forth in a warfare holier than liberty—holy as humanity."[26] Journalist Finley Peter Dunne's popular Irish-American characters always seemed to have the fitting summary: "'We're a gr-reat people,' said Mr. Hennessy, earnestly. 'We ar-re,' said Mr. Dooley. 'We ar-re that. An' th best iv it is, we know we ar-re.'"[27] Excited statements by people like Roosevelt, who looked upon war as he looked upon horseback riding and cowboying in the Dakotas—it was sport, a game, fun—aroused martial fevers. Loud newspapers of the "yellow press" variety, like Hearst's *New York Journal* and Joseph Pulitzer's *New York World,* exaggerated stories

**"The Spanish Brute."** Grant Hamilton's angry cartoon captured the American attitude toward Spain in the 1890s, but especially after the sinking of the *Maine*, which added "mutilation to murder." (*Judge*, 1898)

of Spanish atrocities. Others proudly compared the Cuban and American revolutions. The American people, already steeped in a brash nationalism and prepared by earlier aggressive diplomatic triumphs, were receptive to this hyperbole. There was something exhilarating, furthermore, about competing with the imperialist "Joneses."

Both Washington and Madrid had tried diplomacy, but their diplomatic paths never crossed. McKinley wanted "peace" and independence for Cuba. The first, Spain could not deliver because the Cuban rebels were entrenched and bent on independence and Spanish forces were weak. The second, Spain could not grant immediately because it had its national pride too. Spain said it would fight the war more humanely and grant autonomy, but McKinley wanted much more, and he believed he had the right and duty to judge the affairs of Spain and Cuba.

Once McKinley insisted that Spain grant Cuba its independence, war seemed inevitable: here was one power, the United States, telling another power, Spain, how to manage its national interest. Critics said America might have been less haughty, letting the Cubans and Spaniards settle their own affairs. McKinley's actions in dispatching the *Maine* and asking Congress for $50 million probably encouraged the Cuban rebels to resist any compromise. He might have given Spain a bit more breathing space. Spain, after all, did fire Weyler, terminate reconcentration, and accept an armistice; most important, Madrid would have granted autonomy, which ultimately might have resulted in independence. Critics said the President should have recognized the Cuban insurgents and covertly aided them, and then American soldiers would not necessarily have had to fight in Cuba, the Philippines, and Puerto Rico. American materiel, not men, might have liberated Cuba. Or McKinley might have encouraged other European powers to press Spain jointly for a solution. Certainly the President never attempted to quiet the popular American emotion over Cuban affairs. Instead he chose war to end war. "The historical problem remains," historian Walter LaFeber has noted: "which power took the initiative in setting the conditions that resulted in armed conflict, and were those conditions justified?"[28]

## The Spanish-American-Cuban-Filipino War

Americans flocked to recruiting stations and enlisted in what they trumpeted as a glorious expedition to demonstrate United States right and might. They were cocky. Young author Sherwood Anderson joked that fighting Spain would be "like robbing an old gypsy woman in a vacant lot at night after a fair."[29] War almost seemed healthy. United States Ambassador to England John Hay called it a "splendid little war," and Theodore Roosevelt, who resigned as assistant secretary of the Navy to lead the flashy but overrated Rough Riders, remarked that "it wasn't much of a war, but it was the best war we had."[30] Yet the Spanish-American War, as a veteran recalled, was no "tin-foil" affair.[31] Much of the initial euphoria eroded in mosquito-infested camps, uncomfortable ships, and inadequate hospitals. It was a short war, ending August 12, but 5,462 Americans died in it—only 379 of them in combat. Most of the rest met death from malaria and yellow fever. The chief surgeon of the United States Volunteers witnessed the hundreds of disease-wracked men who came home to be quarantined on the tip of Long Island. "The pale faces, the sunken eyes, the staggering gait and the emaciated forms" marked some as "wrecks for life" and others as "candidates for a premature grave."[32]

That was not how it began. About 200,000 excited men entered army camps in April and May, 1898. Tampa, Florida became the busy base for the Cuban expedition. Camp life was tough. The amateur soldiers were plagued by poor food, including poisonous spoiled beef. They were issued heavy blue uniforms in a humid climate of rain and warm temperatures; most of the new brown tropical uniforms arrived at Tampa after the troops had left for Cuba. Sanitation earned low marks, diseases visited the camps early, and pungent body odors caused nausea. Black troops, in segregated units led by white officers, got no respite from the stings of racial insult and discrimination. Black resentment grew in the face of the epithet "nigger" and Jim Crow restrictions that barred them from "white only" public parks, bars, and cafes. A racial battle sparked by drunken whites rocked Tampa in early June; twenty-seven negroes and three whites had to be hospitalized. Although many blacks hoped to prove in war that they deserved white respect, others shared the views of a black chaplain: "Talk about fighting and freeing poor Cuba and of Spain's brutality; of Cuba's murdered thousands, and starving reconcentradoes. Is America any better than Spain?"[33]

Led by officers seasoned in the Civil War and campaigns against Native Americans, the new imperial fighters embarked from Florida in mid-June. The loading of ships was chaotic. Men rushed to the transports, fearful they would be left behind. Roosevelt's Rough Riders muscled out rivals competing for one vessel, but their horses were left behind for lack of space. Colonel Leonard Wood predicted that if the Americans did not fight the Spanish soon they would tear at one another. Seventeen thousand men, clutching their Krag-Jörgensen rifles, were stuffed into the flotilla for a week. They ate hardtack and tasteless canned beef, drank bitter coffee, waited anxiously, and got seasick. On the morning of June 22 they disembarked on Cuban soil, finding no Spanish resistance. Cuban insurgents met with American officers and agreed to help one another against Spanish forces.

Yet the big and surprising news had already arrived from the Philippine Islands, Spain's major colony in Asia. Only a few days after the American declaration of war, Commodore George Dewey sailed his Asiatic Squadron from Hong Kong to Manila Bay, where he smashed the Spanish fleet with the loss of one man. Every American ship in Manila Harbor, Senator Orville Platt of Connecticut proclaimed, was "a new *Mayflower* . . . the harbinger and agent of a new civilization."[34] Slipping by the strangely silent Spanish guns at Corregidor, Dewey had entered the bay at night. Early in the morning of May 1 his flagship *Olympia* began to demolish the ten incompetently handled Spanish ships. With his laconic order, "You may fire when ready, Gridley," Dewey quickly became a first-line hero. Some people, ignorant of American interests in the Pacific, the beckoning China market, and the feebleness of Spanish rule over the Philippines, wondered how a war to liberate Cuba saw its first action in Asia. Although probably few Americans knew the location of the Philippines, naval officials had pinpointed them in contingency plans as early as 1896 and were ready for the attack when war erupted. Often credited alone with ordering Dewey on February 25, 1898 to sail for Manila if war broke out, Assistant Secretary of the Navy Theodore Roosevelt was really a McKinley Administration functionary fulfilling policy that the President endorsed.

By late June, the American troops in Cuba were moving toward Santiago, where ill-equipped and disspirited Spanish soldiers manned antique guns. Joined by experienced Cuban rebels, the Americans approached the city, and on July 1 battled for San Juan Hill. Having given away their position by sending up an observation balloon, the American troops, spearheaded by the Rough Riders and the black soldiers of the Ninth Cavalry, finally captured the strategic promontory overlooking Santiago. It was a near defeat with heavy casualties, but an important victory. Two days later the Spanish fleet, which had been locked into Santiago Harbor for weeks by American warships, made a desperate, fatalistic daylight break for open sea. American officers were dumbfounded, having expected that the Spanish ships would attempt to sneak out at night. Some American vessels nearly collided as they hurried to sink the helpless Spanish craft, which went down with 323 dead. Its fleet destroyed, Spain entered its imperial death throes. Santiago soon fell, and the Americans easily occupied another Spanish colony, Puerto Rico. Manila collapsed in mid-August, after the Spanish put up token resistance in a deal with Dewey that salvaged Spanish pride and kept insurgent Emilio Aguinaldo from the walled city. Washington soon ordered Aguinaldo and the Filipino rebels, who had been fighting openly against the Spanish for independence since 1896 and had surrounded Manila for weeks, to remain outside the capital and to recognize the authority of the United States.

In July, to insure uninterrupted reinforcement of Dewey, the United States officially absorbed Hawaii, where ships touched en route to Manila. From 1893 to 1897, when Cleveland refused annexation, politics in Hawaii had changed little. The white revolutionaries would not give up power, especially after the Queen promised to behead them upon her return to the throne. McKinley's election removed the uncertainty. Committed to annexation, he negotiated a new agreement with the provisional Hawaiian government. But, fearful that the Senate would not give him the two-thirds vote needed for a treaty, the President decided to ask for a joint resolution. On July 7, 1898 Congress passed the resolution for annexation by a majority vote (290–91 in the House and 42–21 in the Senate), thereby formally attaching the strategically and commercially important islands to the United States.

## Peace and Empire: The Debate in the United States

Spain sued for peace, and on August 12 the belligerents proclaimed an armistice. To negotiate with the Spanish in Paris, McKinley appointed a "peace commission" loaded with imperialists and headed by Secretary of State William R. Day, friend and follower of the President's wishes. As the talks dragged on into the autumn, McKinley, who had made a political tour and recognized that the British would acquiesce in American imperialism, instructed the commissioners to demand all of the Philippines and Puerto Rico, as well as to make Cuba independent. Articulate Filipinos pleaded for their country's freedom but were rebuffed. Spanish diplomats were aghast at this American land grab, but they accepted it after the United States offered $20 million in salve. By early December the treaty was signed, and the American delegates walked out of the elegant French conference room with the Philippines, Puerto Rico, and Guam.

Anti-imperialists howled in protest against the treaty. They had organized the Anti-Imperialist League in Boston in November, 1898, but they were never truly united. They counted among their number such unlikely bedfellows as steel magnate Andrew Carnegie, labor leader Samuel Gompers, agrarian spokesman William Jennings Bryan, Senators Carl Schurz and George Hoar, President Charles W. Eliot of Harvard, and Mark Twain—people who had often been opponents

**"Hurrah for Imperialism."** This anti-imperialist cartoon suggested the fear that the United States was walking blindly along a disastrous path of empire. Anti-imperialists lost the debate in large part because Uncle Sam knew quite well where he was going in adding new territories to the American domain. (*Life,* 1898)

on domestic issues. Many of the anti-imperialists were inconsistent. Hoar, the most outspoken senator against the treaty, had voted for war and for the resolution to annex Hawaii. An expansionist, Carnegie apparently would accept colonies if they could be taken without force. "I am no little American," he asserted. "The day is coming when we shall own all these West Indian islands. They will gravitate to us of their own accord."[35] He even offered to write a personal check for $20 million to buy the independence of the Philippines. And the anti-imperialists were hampered by the *fait accompli,* possession and occupation of territory, handed them by McKinley. After all, argued the President, could America really let loose of this real estate so nobly taken in battle? The anti-imperialists, rejecting immediacy in favor of principle, denounced the thesis that greatness lay in colonies. They wanted trade too, but not at the cost of subjugating other peoples. Anti-imperialist David Starr Jordan, president of Stanford University, spoke of the "peaceful conquest" of Mexico by trade rather than by annexation.[36] Quoting the Declaration of Independence and Washington's Farewell Address as lessons from the past, these critics recalled America's tradition of self-government and *continental* expansion. Furthermore, the imposition of a government by force on another people was inhumane and immoral. Mark Twain wrote *The War Prayer* to mock statements that God was on America's side: "O Lord our God, help us to tear their soldiers to bloody shreds with our shells . . . , blast their hopes, blight their lives, protract their bitter pilgrimage."[37] Social reformer Jane Addams saw children playing war games in the streets of Chicago. The kids were *not freeing Cubans,* she protested, but rather *slaying Spaniards* in their not-so-innocent play. Some anti-imperialists insisted that the United States had serious domestic problems that demanded attention and resources first; others were racists who predicted that Filipinos and Puerto Ricans would ultimately corrupt Anglo-Saxon blood.

The imperialists, led by Senators Henry Cabot Lodge and Nelson Aldrich, Roosevelt, and McKinley, and backed strongly by articulate business leaders, engaged their opponents in vigorous debate in early 1899. They concentrated on pragmatic considerations, although they expressed common ideas of racial superiority and national destiny to civilize the savage world—to take up "the white man's burden." Social Darwinist philosophy was cited: that some were more fit than others to survive. The Philippines provided steppingstones to the rich China market and strategic ports for the expanding Navy that protected American commerce and demonstrated American prestige. International competition also dictated that the United States keep the fruits of victory, argued the imperialists; otherwise, a menacing Germany or expansionist Japan might pick up what America discarded. It was inconceivable to large numbers of Americans that the United States would relinquish territory it had acquired through blood. It became a question of national honor. Roosevelt, countering the protest that the Filipinos had never been asked if they wanted to be annexed to the United States, cited historical precedent. Jefferson, he delighted in telling Democratic anti-imperialists, took Louisiana without a vote by its inhabitants. Furthermore, said Richard Olney, Washington's Farewell Address had outlived its usefulness; there could be no more American isolation. Duty, destiny, defense, and dollars was the alliterative imperialist litany.

Battle-scarred Senator Lodge described the treaty fight as the "closest, most bitter, and most exciting struggle I have ever known, or ever expect to see in the Senate."[38] Shortly before the upper house took action, word reached Washington that Filipino insurrectionists and American soldiers had begun to fight. The news apparently stimulated support for the Treaty of Paris. Democrats tended to be anti-imperialists and Republicans imperialists, yet enough of the former endorsed the treaty on February 6, 1899 to pass it, just barely, by the necessary two-thirds vote, 57 to 27. William Jennings Bryan, believing that a rejection of the treaty would mean continued war, that a majority should rule in a democracy, and that the Philippines could be freed after terminating the hostilities with Spain, urged an "aye" vote upon his anti-imperialist friends. The Republicans probably had enough votes in reserve to pass the treaty even if Bryan had opposed it. The war was now over, the imperialist fruit was in the basket, and the United States undertook the task of controlling and extending the empire it had so easily wrested from the Spanish, Filipinos, Cubans, and Hawaiians.

## Asian Challenges: The Philippine Insurrection and the Open Door in China

Arranging the fruit in the basket became a larger chore than Americans expected. The Filipinos proved to be the most obstinate. By the end of the war, Aguinaldo and his insurgents held control over most of the islands, having routed the Spanish and driven them into Manila. Aguinaldo had been brought from exile in an American warship and believed that American leaders, including Dewey, had promised his country independence if he joined American forces in defeating the Spanish. After the Spanish-American armistice, he grew resentful of American

**Emilio Aguinaldo (1869–1964).** Of mixed Chinese and Tagalog ancestry, this Filipino nationalist was exiled by the Spanish from his country in 1897. He returned with American forces and later clashed with them when he declared independence for the Philippines. He was captured in 1901 and then declared allegiance to the United States. During World War II, however, he favored the Japanese, who occupied the islands, and he was briefly imprisoned by American authorities in 1945 when they re-established United States power over Manila. (U.S. Signal Corps, National Archives)

behavior. He and his men were ordered to stay out of the city, were gradually isolated from decisions, and were insulted by racial slurs, including "nigger" and "goo goo." American soldiers occupying the Manila area considered the Filipinos inferior, the equivalent of Indians and blacks at home. Imperialism had a way of exporting the worst in American life. In the fall and winter of 1898 American officers barred insurgent vessels from Manila Bay and showed no appreciation for the profound Filipino sentiment for independence. The Treaty of Paris angered the Filipinos, as did McKinley's dictate that the authority of the United States was supreme in the Philippines. In open defiance of Washington, Aguinaldo and other prominent Filipinos organized a government at Malolos, wrote a constitution, and proclaimed the Philippine Republic in late January, 1899.

Although anti-imperialist Senator Carl Schurz was probably correct when he said that the Filipino government was as virtuous as that of Chicago, McKinley believed his new colonials to be ill-fitted for self-government. In February, 1899 the Filipinos began fighting better-armed American troops. After bloody struggles, Aguinaldo was captured in March, 1901. Before the insurrection collapsed in 1902, over 5,000 Americans and 200,000 Filipinos died. One hundred and twenty-five thousand American troops had to be used to quell the insurrection, which cost the United States at least $160 million. Anti-imperialist William James, distinguished Harvard University philosopher, poignantly summarized the impact on the Philippines:[39]

> Here were the precious beginnings of an indigenous national life, with which, if we had any responsibility to these islands at all, it was our first duty to have squared ourselves. . . . We are destroying the lives of these islanders by the thousands, their villages and their cities. . . . We are destroying down to the root every germ of a healthy national life in these unfortunate people. . . . No life shall you have, we say, except as a gift from our philanthropy after your unconditional surrender to our will. . . . Could there be a more damning indictment of that whole bloated ideal termed "modern civilization" than this amounts to? Civilization is, then, the big, hollow, resounding, corrupting, sophisticating, confusing torrent of mere brutal momentum and irrationality that brings forth fruits like this!

Indeed, it was one of the ugliest wars in American history and both sides committed atrocities. Insurgents chopped off the ears of American prisoners. Americans burned *barrios* to the ground, placing villagers in reconcentration camps like those so detested in Cuba. To get information, Americans administered the "water cure" by forcing prisoners to swallow gallons of water and then stepping on or punching the swollen stomach to empty it quickly. American soldiers were tired, mosquito-bitten, and poorly fed, and their patience wore thin. Filipino guerrilla fighters harassed them. Racism and notions of white superiority surfaced. An American correspondent explained that "it is not civilized warfare, but we are not dealing with a civilized people. The only thing they know and fear is force, violence, and brutality; and we give it to them."[40] The civil governor of the Philippines from 1901 to 1904, William Howard Taft, put the question less crudely when he described the American mission as the creation of a Filipino government "which shall teach those people individual liberty, which shall lift them up to a point of civilization . . . , and which shall make them rise to call the name of the United States blessed."[41] Charles Francis Adams, Jr., a critic of the American

**"A Fair Field and No Favor."** Holding back the militant-minded imperialists of Europe, the United States permits China to inspect American wares. "I'm out for commerce, not conquest," asserts Uncle Sam. (*Harper's Weekly,* 1899)

**American Cigarettes in China.** An American soldier stationed in China at the turn of the century peddles some American-made cigarettes in a singular instance of private enterprise abroad. (Edward J. Parrish Papers, Duke University Library)

acquisition of the Philippines, ridiculed such thinking: "We are going to make them a self-governing community by forbidding them absolutely to discuss the principle of self-government. We are going to make them an independent people by putting them in jail if they mention the word 'independence.'"[42]

One of the prime attractions the Philippines held for the United States was their proximity to China, where American leaders predicted lucrative markets for American products. In early 1898 American businessmen organized the American Asiatic Association to stimulate public and governmental concern to protect and enlarge United States interests in China. Assistant Secretary of the Treasury Frank Vanderlip typically lauded the Philippines as the "pickets of the Pacific, standing guard at the entrances to trade with the millions of China and Korea, French Indo-China, the Malay Peninsula, and the islands of Indonesia."[43] American traders had long dreamed of an unbounded China market, and missionaries romanticized a Christian kingdom. These ambitions remained dreams more than reality. Yet dreams became a rationale for action, and during the 1890s the United States, despite limited power, began to speak in defense of its Asian interests, real and imagined. In that decade the European powers and Japan were dividing China, rendered helpless in 1895 after its disastrous defeat in the Sino-Japanese War, into spheres of influence and establishing discriminatory trading privileges in their zones. The McKinley Administration in early 1898 watched anxiously as Germany grabbed Kiaochow and Russia callously demanded and got a lease at Port Arthur on the Liaotung Peninsula. France, already ensconced in Indochina, leased

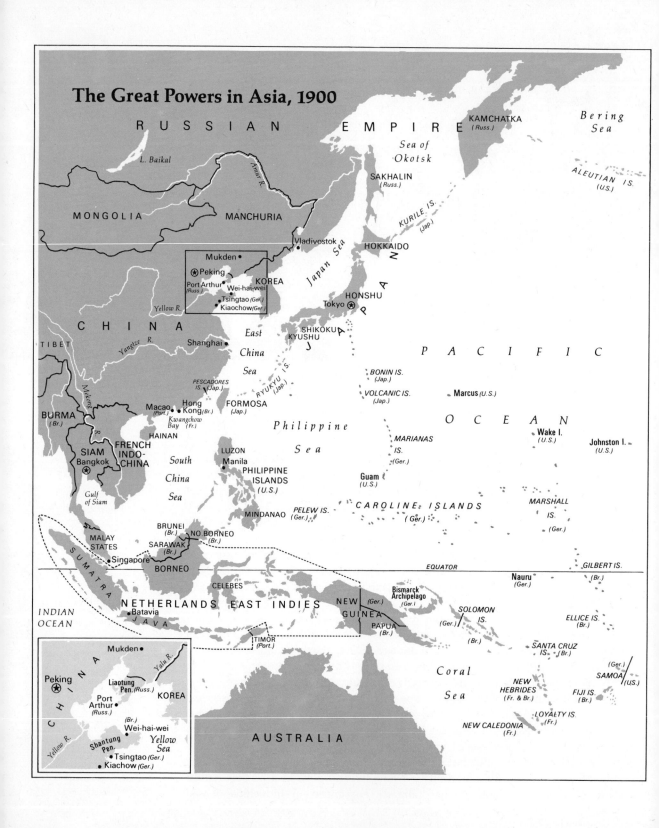

# The Great Powers in Asia, 1900

RUSSIAN EMPIRE

*Bering Sea*

KAMCHATKA
(*Russ.*)

*Sea of Okotsk*

MONGOLIA

MANCHURIA

SAKHALIN
(*Russ.*)

ALEUTIAN IS.
(*U.S.*)

L. Baikal

*Amur R.*

KURILE IS.
(*Jap.*)

Vladivostok

HOKKAIDO

Mukden

*Japan Sea*

Peking

Port Arthur
(*Russ.*)
Wei-hai-wei          KOREA

CHINA

Tsingtao (*Ger.*)
Kiaochow (*Ger.*)

HONSHU

Tokyo

Yellow R.

*East China Sea*

Shanghai

SHIKOKU
KYUSHU

PACIFIC

TIBET

*Yangtze R.*

*RYUKYU IS.
(Jap.)*

PESCADORES
IS. (*Jap.*)

BONIN IS.
(*Jap.*)

OCEAN

VOLCANIC IS.
(*Jap.*)

Marcus (*U.S.*)

BURMA
(*Br.*)

Macao
(*Port.*)
Hong Kong (*Br.*)
Kwangchow Bay (*Fr.*)

FORMOSA
(*Jap.*)

*Philippine Sea*

Wake I.
(*U.S.*)

Johnston I.
(*U.S.*)

HAINAN

MARIANAS
IS.
(*Ger.*)

FRENCH
INDO-
CHINA

*South China Sea*

LUZON
Manila

SIAM
Bangkok

PHILIPPINE
ISLANDS
(*U.S.*)

Guam
(*U.S.*)

*Gulf of Siam*

MINDANAO

PELEW IS.
(*Ger.*)

CAROLINE ISLANDS
(*Ger.*)

MARSHALL
IS.
(*Ger.*)

MALAY
STATES

BRUNEI
(*Br.*)
NO. BORNEO
(*Br.*)

SUMATRA

SARAWAK
(*Br.*)

Singapore

BORNEO

EQUATOR

GILBERT IS.
(*Br.*)

INDIAN
OCEAN

NETHERLANDS EAST INDIES

Batavia

CELEBES

JAVA

NEW
GUINEA
(*Ger.*)

Bismarck
Archipelago
(*Ger.*)

Nauru
(*Ger.*)

SOLOMON
IS.
(*Ger.*)

ELLICE IS.
(*Br.*)

TIMOR
(*Port.*)

PAPUA
(*Br.*)

(*Br.*)

SANTA CRUZ
IS. (*Br.*)

(*Ger.*)
SAMOA
(*U.S.*)

*Coral Sea*

NEW
HEBRIDES
(*Fr. & Br.*)

FIJI IS.
(*Br.*)

AUSTRALIA

NEW CALEDONIA
(*Fr.*)

LOYALTY IS.
(*Fr.*)

Mukden

CHINA

*Yalu R.*

Peking

Liaotung
Pen. (*Russ.*)

KOREA

Port Arthur
(*Russ.*)

(*Br.*)
Wei-hai-wei

Yellow R.

Shantung
Pen.

*Yellow Sea*

Tsingtao (*Ger.*)
Kiachow (*Ger.*)

Kwangchow Bay in southern China in April of that year. Japan already had footholds in Formosa and Korea. Britain approached Washington in March, 1898 and suggested a joint Anglo-American declaration on behalf of equal commercial opportunity in China. In the midst of the Cuban crisis, the United States gave little attention to the request. Britain then forced China to give up part of the Shantung Peninsula. China had become "the Sick Man of Asia."

With the annexation of the Philippines, and with trading and missionary interests in China, the United States became more than a bystander in Asian affairs. In September, 1899 Washington shot into action. Secretary of State John Hay sent an "Open Door" Note to Japan, Italy, Russia, Germany, Britain, and France asking them for assurances that equal trade opportunity for all nations would be observed in the various Chinese spheres. It was, of course, a traditional American principle, and given America's minimal naval or military power in Asia, it was the best the United States could do to curb the partition of China. Vague and noncommittal replies trickled back to Washington, but Hay read what he wanted into them and proclaimed the definitive acceptance of the "Open Door." Hereafter many Americans believed they could obtain what they wanted in Asia through simple declarations.

The Open Door policy was not empty of meaning, however. America knew it was weaker than the other imperialists in the Far East, but it also knew that a delicate balance of power existed there that the United States could unbalance. The European powers and Japan might be wary of excluding American commerce altogether from China, for fear that the United States would tip that balance by joining one of the powers against the others. They also feared that a world war might erupt from the competition in Asia. Americans hoped the Open Door policy would serve their goals in an area where American military power was feeble. The United States wanted the commercial advantages without having to employ military force, as it did in Latin America. The policy did not always work, but it fixed itself in the American mind as a guiding principle for Chinese affairs.

The Open Door Note notwithstanding, the Manchu dynasty (1644–1911) was near death and unable to cope with the foreign intruders. Resentful nationalistic Chinese, led by a secret society called *I-ho ch'üan* ("Righteous and Harmonious Fists," or the "Boxers"), undertook in 1900 to throw out the imperialist aggressors. The Boxers murdered hundreds of Christian missionaries and their Chinese converts, and laid siege to the foreign legations in Peking. To head off a complete gouging of China by vengeful Europeans and Japanese, Washington took two steps. It sent 2,500 American troops to Peking from the Philippines to join 15,500 soldiers from other nations to lift the siege. And Hay, without consulting the Chinese government, issued another Open Door Note on July 3, 1900. He defined United States policy as the protection of American life and property, the safeguarding of "equal and impartial trade," and the preservation of China's "territorial and administrative entity."[44] In short, keep the trade door open by keeping China intact. Certainly these actions did not save China from continued incursion (it was, for example, assessed over $300 million to pay for the Boxers' damages). The United States itself even asked for a territorial concession in late 1900 at Samsah Bay, Fukien Province. The Japanese, catching Hay redhanded, politely reminded him of his notes and he shelved the request. The United States continued to attempt to gain recognition for the Open Door and thereby immersed itself more and more in the boiling Asian cauldron. As historian Marilyn Blatt Young has concluded: "In the late nineteenth century Americans came to feel that having influence in Asia was a categorical imperative for a world power. America, after the Spanish-American War, was a world power, *ergo* it must take a key part in Far Eastern Affairs."[45]

## Toward World Power, 1895–1900

Venezuela, Cuba, Hawaii, the Philippines, Open Door Notes—together they meant an unprecedented set of commitments and responsibilities for the United States. Symbolic of this thrust to world power status was the ascendancy of the imperialist's imperialist, Theodore Roosevelt, to the office of the President in 1901. Peering into the twentieth century, Roosevelt warned Americans to avoid "slothful ease and ignoble peace." Never "shrink from the hard contests"; "let us therefore boldly face the life of strife."[46] Indeed, many diplomats looked back upon the triumphs of the 1890s as a testing time when the United States met the international challenge and rightfully asserted its place as a major world power. Europeans watched anxiously. Some, especially Germans, spoke of the "American peril" or "American menace." Italians worried that the United States would grab their poorly defended colonies. With its industrial and naval strength and its string of colonies, the United States, European leaders pointed out, was now a factor in the "balance of power." With whom, they asked in some trepidation, would the nation ally itself?

The odds seemed to favor Great Britain, although the Anglo-American courtship would be prolonged and marriage something for the future. Ever since the eye-opening Venezuelan crisis, London and Washington had been moving closer together in what has been called the "great rapprochement." Looking for support against an expansionist Germany, John Bull thought Uncle Sam a fit partner. During the Spanish-American War the British were noticeably friendly to the American side and to the subsequent absorption of Spanish colonies. Americans, in turn, sympathized with the British repression of the Boer Republics in South Africa, comparing that struggle to their own war with the Filipinos. Articulate Americans welcomed Britain's implicit acceptance of their imperialism. Germany seemed to replace Britain as the major power hostile to America. Vague Anglo-Saxonism and cultural ties joined British recognition of the power of the United States to forge more amicable relations. As the British Admiralty informed the Cabinet in December of 1899, "our squadron [West Indies], which in 1889 was superior to that of the United States, is now in 1899 completely outclassed by them."[47] Anglophobes continued to twist the lion's tail and Anglo-American commercial competition was intense, but the strands connecting the two powers grew tighter as they entered the twentieth century.

Britain still ranked first in naval power, but in the late 1890s the United States was growing, standing sixth by 1900. In 1898 alone, spurred by the war with Spain, the United States added 128 vessels to its Navy, at a cost of $18 million. At the 1898 American Historical Association meeting, Professor Edwin A. Grosvenor of Amherst College caught the new times in his address: "Barriers of national seclusion are everywhere tumbling like the great wall of China. Every nation elbows other nations to-day. . . . What was whispered at evening in the conclave of envoys and ambassadors is shouted the next morning by newsboys thousands of miles distant."[48] Many commentators reported that the United States, although

**Pears' Soap Advertisement.** This unusual mixture of commercial and diplomatic advertising salutes the Anglo-American rapprochement. (*Life,* 1898)

still divided North and South on many issues, was united as never before. Southern racists and Northern imperialists now had something in common: the need to
keep inferior peoples in their place. Senator Benjamin Tillman of South Carolina,
in noting the Filipino insurrection, put it this way: "No Republican leader . . . will
now dare to wave the bloody shirt and preach a crusade against the South's
treatment of the negro. The North has a bloody shirt of its own. Many thousands
of them have been made into shrouds for murdered Filipinos."[49]

The events of the 1895–1900 period meant further changes in the process of
decisionmaking. Both Cleveland and McKinley conducted their own foreign
policies, often thwarting or directing Congress. They helped establish the authority
of the President over foreign policy. In 1907, looking back upon the days of 1898
and citing the past, Woodrow Wilson, then president of Princeton University,
recorded the historical impact: "The war with Spain again changed the balance of
powers. Foreign questions became leading questions again, as they had been in the
first days of the government, and in them the President was of necessity leader.
Our new place in the affairs of the world has since that year of transformation kept
him at the front of our government, where his own thoughts and the attention of
men everywhere is centered on him. . . . The nation has risen to the first rank in
power and resources. . . . Our President must always, henceforth, be one of the
great powers of the world."[50] Wilson exaggerated America's power, for that
strength was still largely centered in the western hemisphere, but for the United
States, as the *Washington Post* editorialized in 1898, "the policy of isolation is
dead. . . . A new consciousness seems to have come upon us—the consciousness
of strength, and with it a new appetite, a yearning to show our strength. . . .
Ambition, interest, land-hunger, pride, the mere joy of fighting, whatever it may
be, we are animated by a new sensation. . . . The taste of empire is in the mouth of
the people, even as the taste of blood in the jungle."[51] After 1900 the task became
the translation of this consciousness into the actual management of the empire.

## Further Reading for the Period 1895–1900

For events and attitudes in the 1890s and America's path to empire, see some of
the works cited in Chapter 5 and the following: Robert L. Beisner, *From the Old
Diplomacy to the New* (1975), John A. S. Grenville and George B. Young, *Politics,
Strategy, and American Diplomacy* (1967), David Healy, *U.S. Expansionism: The Imperi-
alist Urge in the 1890s* (1970), Richard Hofstadter, *Social Darwinism in American
Thought* (1955) and "Manifest Destiny and the Philippines," in Daniel Aaron, ed.,
*America in Crisis* (1952), Walter LaFeber, *The New Empire* (1963), Ernest R. May,
*Imperial Democracy* (1961), H. Wayne Morgan, *America's Road to Empire* (1965),
William A. Williams, *The Roots of the Modern American Empire* (1969) and *The Tragedy
of American Diplomacy* (1962). Representative interpretations are collected in
Thomas G. Paterson, ed., *American Imperialism and Anti-Imperialism* (1973).

For the coming of the Spanish-American-Cuban-Filipino War, use the works
above and Philip S. Foner, *The Spanish-Cuban-American War and the Birth of American
Imperialism* (1972), Julius Pratt, *Expansionists of 1898* (1938), and Joseph E. Wisan,
*The Cuban Crisis as Reported in the New York Press, 1895–1898* (1934).

American leaders, imperialist and anti-imperialist, are treated in William N.
Armstrong, *E. L. Godkin and American Foreign Policy* (1957), H. K. Beale, *Theodore
Roosevelt and the Rise of America to World Power* (1956), Robert L. Beisner, *Twelve*

*Against Empire* (1968), John Braeman, *Albert J. Beveridge* (1971), Paolo E. Coletta, *William Jennings Bryan* (1964–1969), Gerald Eggert, *Richard Olney* (1973), John C. Farrell, *Beloved Lady: A History of Jane Addams' Ideas on Reform and Peace* (1967), Margaret Leech, *In the Days of McKinley* (1959), H. Wayne Morgan, *William McKinley and His America* (1963), Allan Nevins, *Grover Cleveland* (1932), Ronald Spector, *Admiral of the New Empire* (1974) (on Dewey), and E. Berkeley Tompkins, *Anti-Imperialism in the United States* (1970). For brief biographies consult John A. Garraty, ed., *Encyclopedia of American Biography* (1974).

For specialized studies consult Graham A. Cosmas, *An Army for Empire: The United States Army in the Spanish-American War* (1971), Willard B. Gatewood, Jr., *"Smoked Yankees" and the Struggle for Empire: Letters from Negro Soldiers, 1898–1902* (1971), and Gerald F. Linderman, *The Mirror of War: American Society and the Spanish-American War* (1974).

The Open Door policy and Asian events are discussed in Charles S. Campbell, *Special Business Interests and the Open Door Policy* (1951), Michael Hunt, *Frontier Defense and the Open Door: Manchuria in Chinese-American Relations, 1895–1911* (1973), Akira Iriye, *Across the Pacific* (1967), Thomas McCormick, *China Market* (1967), Paul A. Varg, *The Making of a Myth* (1968), and Marilyn Blatt Young, *The Rhetoric of Empire* (1968).

The Philippine rebellion receives scrutiny in Teodoro Agoncillo, *Malolos* (1960), Henry F. Graff, ed., *American Imperialism and the Philippine Insurrection* (1969), Daniel B. Schirmer, *Republic or Empire* (1972), and Leon Wolff, *Little Brown Brother* (1961).

For Anglo-American relations, including the Venezuelan crisis, see Alexander E. Campbell, *Great Britain and the United States, 1895–1903* (1960), Charles S. Campbell, *Anglo-American Understanding* (1957) and *From Revolution to Rapprochement* (1974), and Bradford Perkins, *The Great Rapprochement* (1968).

For lists of other relevant works, see Wilton B. Fowler, ed., *American Diplomatic History since 1890* (1975) and Paterson, *American Imperialism and Anti-Imperialism.* Also see the following notes.

## Notes to Chapter 6

1. Quoted in Gerald G. Eggert, *Richard Olney: Evolution of a Statesman* (University Park: Pennsylvania State University Press, 1974), p. 208.

2. Quoted in Ernest R. May, *Imperial Democracy: The Emergence of America as a Great Power* (New York: Harper & Row, [1961], 1973), p. 33.

3. *Papers Relating to the Foreign Relations of the United States, 1895,* Part I (Washington: Government Printing Office, 1896), pp. 545–562.

4. Quoted in Robert L. Beisner, *From the Old Diplomacy to the New, 1865–1900* (New York: Thomas Y. Crowell, 1975), p. 99.

5. Quoted in Howard K. Beale, *Theodore Roosevelt and the Rise of America to World Power* (New York: Collier Books, [1956], 1962), p. 60.

6. *Ibid.,* p. 61.

7. Quoted in Eggert, *Olney,* p. 223.

8. Quoted in Charles S. Campbell, *From Revolution to Rapprochement: The United States and Great Britain, 1783–1900* (New York: John Wiley & Sons, 1974), p. 182.

9. Memorandum of January 10, 1896, quoted in Allan Nevins, *Grover Cleveland: A Study in Courage* (New York: Dodd, Mead, 1932), p. 644.

10. Quoted in George B. Young, "Intervention Under the Monroe Doctrine: The Olney Corollary," *Political Science Quarterly,* LVII (June, 1942), p. 277.

11. Quoted in Richard E. Welch, Jr., *George Frisbie Hoar and the Half-Breed Republicans* (Cambridge, Mass.: Harvard University Press, 1971), p. 209.

12. Walter Q. Gresham to Carl Schurz, October 6, 1893, Walter Q. Gresham Papers, Library of Congress.

13. Quoted in Ramon Ruiz, *Cuba: The Making of a Revolution* (New York: W. W. Norton, [c. 1968], 1970), p. 73.

14. Quoted in Philip S. Foner, *The Spanish-Cuban-American War and the Birth of American Imperialism* (New York: Monthly Review Press, 1972; 2 vols.), I, 21.

15. Quoted in Eggert, *Olney*, p. 265 (August 14, 1896).

16. James D. Richardson, ed., *A Compilation of the Messages and Papers of the Presidents, 1789–1897* (Washington, D.C.: Government Printing Office, 1896–1899; 10 vols.), IX, 716–722.

17. Lester D. Langley, *The Cuban Policy of the United States: A Brief History* (New York: John Wiley and Sons, 1968), p. 97.

18. *Congressional Record,* 55th Cong., 2nd Sess., XXXI, 3–5.

19. *Papers Relating to the Foreign Relations of the United States, 1898* (Washington, D.C.: Government Printing Office, 1901), pp. 1007–08.

20. Quoted in Walter LaFeber, *The New Empire: An Interpretation of American Expansion, 1860–1898* (Ithaca, N.Y.: Cornell University Press, 1963), p. 349.

21. *Congressional Record,* 55th Cong., 2nd Sess., XXXI, 2916–19.

22. *Foreign Relations, 1898,* p. 746.

23. *Congressional Record,* 55th Cong., 2nd Sess., XXXI, 3699–3702.

24. Quoted in H. Wayne Morgan, *America's Road to Empire: The War with Spain and Overseas Expansion* (New York: John Wiley and Sons, 1965), p. 63.

25. May 7, 1898, quoted in Winthrop S. Hudson, "Protestant Clergy Debate the Nation's Vocation, 1898–1899" (unpublished manuscript, 1974).

26. Quoted in John Braeman, *Albert J. Beveridge: American Nationalist* (Chicago: University of Chicago Press, 1971), p. 23.

27. Finley Peter Dunne, *Mr. Dooley in Peace and War* (Boston: Small, Maynard, 1899), p. 9.

28. LaFeber, *New Empire,* p. 400.

29. Quoted in Gerald F. Linderman, *The Mirror of War: American Society and the Spanish-American War* (Ann Arbor: University of Michigan Press, 1974), p. 125.

30. Quoted in Ruiz, *Cuba,* p. 21.

31. Quoted in Frank Freidel, *The Splendid Little War* (Boston: Little, Brown, 1958), p. 306.

32. *Ibid.,* p. 295.

33. Quoted in Willard B. Gatewood, Jr., *"Smoked Yankees" and the Struggle for Empire: Letters from Negro Soldiers, 1898–1902* (Urbana, Ill.: University of Illinois Press, 1971), p. 28.

34. Quoted in Paul C. Nagel, *This Sacred Trust: American Nationality, 1798–1898* (New York: Oxford University Press, 1971), p. 252.

35. Quoted in David Healy, *U.S. Expansionism: The Imperialist Urge in the 1890s* (Madison: University of Wisconsin Press, 1970), p. 55.

36. Quoted in Robert L. Beisner, "1898 and 1968: The Anti-Imperialists and the Doves," *Political Science Quarterly, LXXV* (June, 1970), 200.

37. Mark Twain, *The War Prayer* (New York: Harper and Row, [1923], 1970).

38. Quoted in H. Wayne Morgan, *William McKinley and His America* (Syracuse: Syracuse University Press, 1963), p. 422.

39. From the *Boston Evening Transcript,* March 1, 1899, reprinted in Ray Ginger, ed., *The Nationalizing of American Life, 1877–1900* (New York: The Free Press, 1965), pp. 310–315.

40. Quoted in Stuart C. Miller, "Our Mylai of 1900: Americans in the Philippine Insurrection," *Transaction, VII* (September, 1970), 24.

41. Henry F. Graff, ed., *American Imperialism and the Philippine Insurrection* (Boston: Little, Brown, 1969), p. 36.

42. Charles Francis Adams to Moorfield Storey, February 24, 1902, Moorfield Storey Papers, Massachusetts Historical Society, Boston.

43. Quoted in Thomas J. McCormick, *China Market: America's Quest for Informal Empire, 1893–1901* (Chicago: Quadrangle Books, 1967), p. 119.

44. *Foreign Relations of the United States, 1901,* Appendix: "Affairs in China" (Washington: Government Printing Office, 1902), p. 12.

45. Marilyn Blatt Young, "American Expansion, 1870–1900: The Far East," in Barton J. Bernstein, ed., *Towards a New Past: Dissenting Essays in American History* (New York: Pantheon Books, 1968), p. 196.

46. Quoted in Beale, *Theodore Roosevelt,* p. 84.

47. Quoted in Alexander E. Campbell, *Great Britain and the United States, 1895–1903* (London: Longmans, 1960), p. 31.

48. American Historical Association, *Annual Report, 1898* (Washington: Government Printing Office, 1899), p. 288.

49. Quoted in C. Vann Woodward, *The Strange Career of Jim Crow* (New York: Oxford University Press, 1974; 3rd rev. ed.), p. 73.

50. Quoted in Arthur Link's essay in *Wilson's Diplomacy: An International Symposium* (Cambridge, Mass.: Schenkman, 1973), p. 6.

51. *Washington Post,* June 2, 1898.

**Teddy Roosevelt the Pirate.** In this swipe at Theodore Roosevelt, Frank Nankivell depicts him as a pirate—a depiction most Colombians certainly accepted after the strong-willed, tough-minded President "took" the Panama Canal area. (Swann Collection of Caricature and Cartoon)

# 7 Managing and Extending the American Empire, 1900–1914

## Diplomatic Crossroad: Taking Panama, 1903

"Revolution imminent," read the cable from the American consul at Colón, a normally sleepy Colombian seaport on the Atlantic side of the Isthmus of Panama. Acting Secretary of State Francis B. Loomis bridled his curiosity for an hour and five minutes. Then he fired off an inquiry to the United States consul at Panama City, on the Pacific slope: "Uprising on Isthmus reported. Keep Department promptly and fully informed." The response came back in four hours: "No uprising yet. Reported will be in the night. Situation is critical." Loomis' anxiety, already intense, increased sharply five minutes later when he learned that an "important message" intended for the U.S.S. *Nashville* anchored at Colón had miscarried, and troops of the Colombian government had landed in the city.

At the Department of State it was now 8:20 P.M., November 3, 1903. As far as Loomis knew, a revolution had not yet broken out on the isthmus. Nonetheless, he hurriedly drafted instructions for the consuls at Panama and Colón. "Act promptly," he directed in near desperation. Somehow convey to the commanding officer of the *Nashville* this order: "In the interests of peace make every effort to prevent [Colombian] Government troops at Colón from proceeding to Panama." Having ordered intervention against a friendly government during a revolution that to his knowledge had not yet begun, Loomis was left to agonize for another hour. Finally, a new cable arrived: "Uprising occurred to-night . . . no bloodshed. . . . Government will be organized to-night." Loomis no doubt sighed in relief. He had done his part to insure success in the reckless gamble for a canal controlled by the United States.

If November third was a busy day for Francis Loomis, it was far more hectic for José Augustín Arango and his fellow conspirators in Panama. The tiny mixed band of Panamanians and Americans living on the isthmus had been actively plotting revolution since August, when the Colombian Congress dashed their hopes for prosperity by defeating the treaty that would have permitted the United

States to construct an isthmian canal. By the end of October, they had become convinced that the North American colossus, frustrated in its overtures to Colombia, would lend them moral and physical support. Confident that American naval vessels would be at hand, they selected November fourth as the date of their coup d'état. To their dismay, however, the Colombian steamer *Cartagena* disembarked about 400 troops at Colón early in the morning of November 3. Because the "important message" directing him to prevent the "landing of any armed force . . . either Government or insurgent at Colón" had been delayed in transmission, Commander John Hubbard of the *Nashville* did not interfere with the landing.

Forced to rely on their own wits, the conspirators made good use of the transisthmian railroad. They deviously separated the Colombian commanding general from his troops, lured him aboard a train, and sped him ceremoniously across the isthmus to Panama City. At 6:00 P.M. on the third, the revolutionaries arrested their guest, formed a provisional government, and paraded before a cheering crowd at the Cathedral Plaza. But the revolution would remain perilously unfinished so long as armed Colombian soldiers occupied Colón. Too weak to expel the soldiers by force, the insurgents gave the colonel in charge $8000 in gold, whereupon he ordered his troops aboard a departing steamer. The American consul at Panama City cabled: "Quiet prevails." At noon the next day, Secretary of State John Hay recognized the sovereign Republic of Panama.

The frantic pace of American isthmian diplomacy continued. The new Panamanian government appointed as its minister plenipotentiary a Frenchman, Philippe Bunau-Varilla, who had long agitated for a Panama canal and who recently had conspired for Panamanian independence from Colombia. With Gallic flourish Bunau-Varilla descended upon Secretary Hay. He extolled the United States for rescuing Panama "from the barbarism of unnecessary and wasteful civil wars to consecrate it to the destiny assigned to it by Providence, the service of humanity, and the progress of civilization."[1] John Hay thoroughly understood the meaning of Bunau-Varilla's rhetoric and eagerly negotiated the treaty both men wanted. On November 18, 1903, less than two weeks after American recognition of Panama, they signed the Hay–Bunau-Varilla Treaty, by which the United States government would build, fortify, and operate a canal linking the Atlantic and Pacific oceans.

Hay had at last achieved a goal set by his chief, President Theodore Roosevelt, several years earlier. "I do not see why we should dig the canal if we are not to fortify it," Roosevelt had explained to navalist Alfred Thayer Mahan early in 1900. If an unfortified, neutral canal had existed in Central America during the recent war with Spain, Roosevelt argued in another letter, "we could have got the *Oregon* around in time," but the United States would have spent most of the war in "wild panic," fearful that the Spanish fleet would slip through the waterway and rush to the Philippines to attack Admiral Dewey. The lesson was manifest. Enemy fleets of the future must not be allowed to steam through an isthmian canal to strike the United States at exposed and vulnerable places. "Better to have no canal at all, than not give us the power to control it in time of war," Roosevelt expostulated.[2] What he really wanted, of course, was a canal run by Americans for the benefit of the United States.

The major barrier to that goal was the Clayton-Bulwer Treaty of 1850, stipulating joint Anglo-American construction and operation of any Central American canal. In December, 1898, flushed with victory over Spain, President William McKinley had directed Secretary Hay to discuss modification of that agreement

**Theodore Roosevelt (1858–1919).**
Graduate of Harvard, historian, Rough Rider, and New York governor, Republican Roosevelt became President in 1901 after William McKinley was assassinated. TR thought the presidency a "bully pulpit" and frequently used it as such. (Library of Congress)

with the British Ambassador, Sir Julian Pauncefote. The Hay-Pauncefote Treaty of February, 1900 permitted the United States to build a canal but forbade its fortification, much to the chagrin of Theodore Roosevelt, then governor of New York. He spearheaded an attack that defeated the treaty in the Senate, forcing renegotiation. On November 18, 1901, with Roosevelt now President, Hay and Pauncefote signed a pact satisfactory to the Rough Rider.

Then began the complex process of determining the route. In November, 1901, after an investigation lasting two years, the Walker Isthmian Canal Commission reported in favor of Nicaragua. The decisive criterion was cost, which in the case of Panama was made incalculable by the obduracy of the New Panama Canal Company, a French-chartered firm that held the Colombian concession for canal rights. The company estimated its assets on the isthmus at $109 million—

machinery, property, and excavated soil left by the defunct de Lesseps organization after its failure to cut through Panama in 1888. When coupled with the engineering costs, purchase of the New Panama Canal Company's rights and holdings would make construction through Panama prohibitively expensive, even though technologically easier. For these reasons, the House of Representatives on January 8, 1902 passed the Hepburn Bill authorizing a canal through Nicaragua.

The New Panama Canal Company's American lawyer, William Nelson Cromwell, described by one irritated congressman as "the most dangerous man this country has produced since the days of Aaron Burr—a professional revolutionist," swung into action.[3] Cromwell was a partner in the prestigious New York law firm of Sullivan and Cromwell, and his fixed purpose in 1902–1903 was to sell the assets of his French client for the highest possible price. The Walker Commission had estimated the company's worth at $40 million, a figure Cromwell reluctantly accepted in face of the passage of the Hepburn Bill. The attorney began an intense

lobbying campaign directed principally at President Roosevelt, Republican sena-tors Mark Hanna and John C. Spooner, and members of the Walker Commission. Cromwell was joined by Bunau-Varilla, formerly chief engineer for de Lesseps, in what has been described as one of the "masterpieces of the lobbyist's art."[4]

On January 18, 1902, the Walker Commission reversed itself and decided for the technologically preferable Panama passage, citing the company's willingness to sell out for the reduced sum of $40 million. Guided by Roosevelt, Spooner, and Cromwell, Congress five months later passed the Spooner Act, approving the Panama route. The State Department soon opened negotiations with Colombia. The price of the annual rental became a stumbling block, which Hay removed only by delivering an ultimatum to the Colombian chargé d'affaires, Tomás Herrán, in January, 1903. On January 22 he and Hay signed a treaty granting Colombia an initial payment of $10 million and $250,000 annually. The United States reaped control over the six-mile wide canal zone for 100 years, a privilege renewable at the "sole and absolute option" of the North American republic.[5]

The United States Senate approved the Hay-Herrán Treaty on March 17, 1903, but the Colombian government, although genuinely desiring American construc-tion of a canal, moved slowly. Faced with a treasury drained by a long and costly civil war, Bogotá attempted to extract a $10 million payment from the New Panama Canal Company for permitting the transfer of its assets to the American govern-ment. At this juncture Hay succumbed to the blandishments of William Nelson Cromwell. After meeting with the lawyer in April, the secretary bluntly announced that any discussion of a payment by the new Panama Canal Company to Colombia "would be in violation of the Spooner law and not permissible."[6]

As a second stratagem, the Colombian government attempted to raise the initial American cash payment from $10 to $15 million. Roosevelt waxed indignant, snapping to Hay that "those contemptible little creatures in Bogotá ought to understand how much they are jeopardizing things and imperilling their own future."[7] The President came to believe that "you could no more make an agree-ment with the Colombian rulers than you could nail currant jelly to the wall."[8] TR's intransigence and Hay's extraordinary intercession on behalf of a privately owned foreign corporation increased the anxiety felt by many Colombian con-gressmen about the Hay-Herrán Treaty's severe infringement upon Colombia's sovereignty over Panama. They unanimously defeated the treaty on August 12, 1903.

Bogotá's rejection did not catch Roosevelt altogether by surprise. Since April, Minister Arthur N. Beaupré had been warning that if the treaty were "submitted to the free opinion of the people it would not pass," and Roosevelt had begun to ponder undiplomatic alternatives.[9] On June 13 the ubiquitous Cromwell had met with Roosevelt and then planted a story in the *New York World* reporting that, if Colombia rejected the treaty, Panama would secede and grant to the United States "the equivalent of absolute sovereignty over the Canal Zone." Moreover, alleged the *World*, "President Roosevelt is said to strongly favor this plan."[10] As it became increasingly likely that Colombia would repudiate the Hay-Herrán pact, Roose-velt's contempt for the Colombian people mounted. In private letters to Hay and others he denounced them as "jack rabbits," "foolish and homicidal corruption-ists," and "cat-rabbits."[11] Hay, usually urbane and restrained, uttered a diatribe against "the government of folly and graft that now rules at Bogotá."[12]

Roosevelt and Hay now considered two options: seizure of Panama by force, or extension of instant recognition and support to any revolutionary regime in Panama. The President inclined sharply toward the latter course after a meeting with Bunau-Varilla on October 9, during which the Frenchman predicted an uprising. Although TR was guarded in his reply, he later admitted that Bunau-Varilla "would have been a very dull man" if unable to "guess" that the United States would respond favorably to a revolution.[13] One week later, on October 16, Secretary Hay informed Bunau-Varilla that American naval vessels were heading toward the isthmus. Bunau-Varilla shrewdly calculated the steaming time and cabled the revolutionaries waiting on the isthmus that American warships would arrive by November 2. Early that evening the U.S.S. *Nashville* dropped anchor at Colón as predicted.

In his annual message to Congress following the Panamanian revolution, Roosevelt urged swift ratification of the Hay–Bunau-Varilla Treaty so that the United States could "enter upon the execution of a project colossal in its size and of well-nigh incalculable possibilities for the good of this country and the nations of mankind."[14] When Democrats in the Senate questioned the President's role in the insurrection, Roosevelt averred: "No one connected with this Government had any part in preparing, inciting, or encouraging the late revolution."[15] With this determined if disingenuous presidential leadership, the Republicans overcame the opposition, and the Senate approved the treaty on February 23, 1904. Later, in 1911, TR boasted that "I took the Canal Zone and let Congress debate; and while the debate goes on the Canal does also."[16]

Construction began in mid-1904, and the fifty-mile-long canal opened to traffic on August 15, 1914. During the first year of operation alone, 1,058 merchant vessels slid through the locks, while the Atlantic and Pacific fleets of the United

**"Just Where the Paper Tore."** Roosevelt uses indelible ink to make his point across the Isthmus of Panama. Roosevelt defended himself at a Cabinet meeting and asked Secretary Elihu Root about his impressions of the spirited defense. Root replied: "You have shown that you were accused of seduction and you have conclusively proved that you were guilty of rape." (*Chicago Daily News,* 1903)

States Navy freely exchanged ships. In 1922 the United States paid "conscience money" or "canalimony" of $25 million to Colombia but did not formally apologize for having taken the canal zone. Although Roosevelt's handling of the Panama issue, according to historian William Harbaugh, constitutes "one of the ineradicable blots on his record," most Americans have applauded his bold meddling in the internal affairs of the sovereign nation of Colombia.[17] Roosevelt himself ranked his accomplishment alongside the Louisiana Purchase and the acquisition of Texas.

## The Conservative Shapers of the American Empire

The taking of Panama symbolized the new activism characteristic of American foreign policy after the Spanish-American War, and construction of the canal placed the United States in a physical position of undisputed domination over Latin America. Great Britain, the only Old World power that might have contested America's new pre-eminence, faced a stiff political and naval challenge from Germany. In a series of remarkable retreats beginning with the first Hay-Pauncefote Treaty, London diplomatically recognized the shifting balance of power in Europe and the Americas and acquiesced in United States hegemony over Latin America. President Roosevelt perceived more clearly than most Americans an opportunity to capitalize on this historic transformation. The Panama Canal marked one result.

In the late nineteenth century, Roosevelt had associated closely with the most vocal pressure group agitating for an American canal, the uniformed "professors of war" at the Naval War College.[18] He corresponded regularly with one of those officers, Alfred Thayer Mahan, the navalist who tirelessly explained the strategic advantages of a canal in the idiom of the 1890s. "Wherever situated, whether at Panama or Nicaragua," Mahan preached, "the fundamental meaning of the canal will be that it advances by thousands of miles the frontiers . . . of the United States."[19] In the course of expanding those frontiers during the "splendid little war" of 1898, the cruiser *Oregon* dashed at full speed from San Francisco to the tip of South America and through the Strait of Magellan to Cuba in time to help destroy the Spanish fleet off Santiago. The race of over 14,000 miles fired American imaginations, but it also consumed sixty-eight days and dramatically underscored the need for an interoceanic canal across Central America.

Roosevelt's sense of isthmian strategic necessity reflected a broad world view he shared with many "progressives" in the reform era of the early twentieth century. A conservative patrician reformer motivated by noblesse oblige, he "feared that unrest caused by social and economic inequities would impair the nation's strength and efficiency."[20] He saw a similar danger to American interests in unrest abroad, and he sought to exert United States influence to create order on a global scale. "More and more," Roosevelt told Congress in 1902, "the increasing interdependence and complexity of international political and economic relations render it incumbent on all civilized and orderly powers to insist on the proper policing of the world."[21] A quintessential chauvinist, Roosevelt talked about doing the "rough work of the world" and about the need to "speak softly and carry a big stick."[22] Like his contemporaries, TR had imbibed the Social Darwinist doctrines of "natural selection" and the "survival of the fittest," and he articulated racist notions about Anglo-Saxon superiority and the "white man's burden" to tutor "backward" peoples. For Roosevelt in particular, that superiority was best ex-

## Makers of American Foreign Policy from 1900 to 1914

| *Presidents* | *Secretaries of State* |
|---|---|
| Theodore Roosevelt, 1901–1909 | John Hay, 1898–1905 |
| | Elihu Root, 1905–1909 |
| | Robert Bacon, 1909 |
| William Howard Taft, 1909–1913 | Philander C. Knox, 1909–1913 |
| Woodrow Wilson, 1913–1921 | William Jennings Bryan, 1913–1915 |

pressed in war. "All the great masterful races have been fighting races," he lectured an audience at the Naval War College.[23] Progressive politicians, however, were decidedly split over foreign policy questions. Some joined Roosevelt in advocating a vigorous activism abroad. Others, like Wisconsin's Senator Robert M. LaFollette, were anti-imperialists and critics of war who believed that the corporate monopolies they were battling at home were dragging the United States into perpetual interventionism abroad.

Roosevelt always vigorously debated his critics and added his unique personal characteristics to American foreign policy. Often impatient and impetuous, having the instinct for the jugular, he centralized and personalized foreign policy decisionmaking, frequently bypassed Congress, and believed "the people" so ignorant about foreign affairs that they should not direct an informed president like himself. In the search for a stable world order and a balance of power, Roosevelt could assume the garb of the peacemaker trying to reconcile competing national interests. For example, he won the Nobel Peace Prize in 1906 for his mediating effort at the Portsmouth Conference (see below). The candid President disliked the pomp and ceremony of traditional diplomacy and on occasion disrupted protocol with a memorable incident: he once broke up a luncheon by demonstrating jujitsu holds on the Swiss minister. He could be seen running into the Potomac for a swim, a trail of exhausted, less active diplomats stumbling along behind him. But Roosevelt usually preserved his dignity. He dealt with foreign leaders "friend to friend, with the directness of a North Dakotan cowboy sheathed under the grace of aristocratic manners."[24]

Roosevelt and other shapers of American foreign policy between the Spanish-American War and the First World War were members of an American quasi-aristocracy and sure-footed devotees of "order." Most had graduated from prestigious eastern colleges and distinguished themselves in high political office or in the professions. They moved comfortably in the affluent, cosmopolitan, upper-class society of the Atlantic seaboard. Roosevelt, a graduate of Harvard College, had been assistant secretary of the Navy and governor of New York and was a prolific author. His successor, Ohioan William Howard Taft, a graduate of Yale, had served as a federal circuit court judge, governor of the Philippines (1901–1904), and secretary of war (1904–1908). Woodrow Wilson earned a Ph.D. from Johns Hopkins, wrote books on history, presided over Princeton, and governed New Jersey before entering the White House.

Their secretaries of state, with one exception, were members of the same caste. John Hay, secretary for 1898–1905, was born in Indiana and educated at Brown

University. Wealthy and recognized as a poet, novelist, biographer, and editor of the *New York Tribune,* he had served as Lincoln's personal secretary during the Civil War and later as McKinley's ambassador to Great Britain. He thought the "indispensable feature of our foreign policy should be a firm understanding with England," and he was one of the chief architects of the Anglo-American rapprochement of the early twentieth century.[25] His successor Elihu Root (1905–1909), a cautious conservative who praised Theodore Roosevelt as "the greatest conservative force for the protection of property and capital," was born in upstate New York, graduated from Hamilton College, took a law degree at New York University, and became one of America's most successful corporation lawyers.[26] As secretary of war from 1899 to 1904, he created mechanisms, such as the Platt Amendment for Cuba, for managing the American empire. Like TR, he believed that the "main object of diplomacy is to keep the country out of trouble" and maintain order abroad.[27] Philander C. Knox (1909–1913) followed Root. A corporation lawyer born in Pennsylvania, he had helped form the giant United States Steel Corporation. He served as attorney general and United States senator before entering the State Department. Habitually seeking leisure, Knox liked to play golf at Chevy Chase, spend summers with his trotters at his Valley Forge Farms estate, vacation in Florida in the winter, and delegate departmental work to subordinates. He advocated "dollar diplomacy" as a means of creating order in revolution-prone areas—that is, the use of private financiers and businessmen to promote foreign policy, and vice versa. The second man to serve under President Wilson was New Yorker Robert Lansing (1915–1920), a graduate of Amherst College, son-in-law of a former secretary of state, and practitioner of international law. Reserved and conservative, Lansing also would not tolerate disorder in the United States sphere of Latin America.

William Jennings Bryan, Wilson's first appointment (1913–1915), did not conform to the conservative elite status of most makers of foreign policy. The "boy orator" of Nebraska could mesmerize crowds by lamenting the "cross of gold" upon which eastern capitalists were crucifying western and southern farmers, but he could not win a presidential election (he ran in 1896, 1900, and 1908). The "Great Commoner" languished for years as the most prominent has-been of the Democratic party, until Wilson appointed him secretary of state out of deference to his long service to the partisan cause and as a reward for support at the convention of 1912. The President let Bryan appoint "deserving Democrats" to diplomatic posts and indulge his fascination with peace or "cooling off" treaties, but Wilson bypassed him in most important diplomatic decisions, even to the point of composing overseas cables on his own White House typewriter. In 1915 Bryan resigned in protest over Wilson's pro-British leanings during World War I.

These conservative managers of American foreign policy believed that a major component of national power was a prosperous, expanding economy invigorated by a healthy foreign trade. The principle of the "Open Door"—to keep open trade and investment opportunities—became a governing tenet voiced globally, although often tarnished in application. Mahan believed that commerce was the "energizer of material civilization," and Roosevelt declared to Congress in his annual message of 1901 that "America has only just begun to assume that commanding position in the international business world which we believe will more and more be hers."[28] In 1900 the United States exported goods valued at $1.5 billion. By 1914, at the start of World War I, that figure stood at $2.5 billion.

**Elihu Root (1845–1937).** Graduate of Hamilton College, corporate lawyer, Republican, Secretary of War (1899–1904), and Secretary of State (1905–1909), Root was a skilled administrator who helped devise methods for controlling the American empire. (*PBT*, Buenos Aires, 1906)

Exports to Latin America increased markedly from $132 million at the turn of the century to $309 million in 1914. Investments there in sugar, transportation, and banking shot up. By 1913 the United Fruit Company, the banana empire, had some 130,000 acres in cultivation in Central America, a fleet of freighters, and political influence as well. By 1914 the United States dominated nickel mining in Canada and sugar production in Cuba, and total American investments abroad equaled $3.5 billion.

But those statistics were not important solely as contributions to pocketbooks. Americans believed that economic expansion also meant that the best of "Americanism," the values of industriousness, honesty, morality, and private initiative, were carried abroad. Thus Yale University-in-China and the Young Men's Christian Association (YMCA) joined the Standard Oil Company and Singer Sewing in China as advance agents of civilization. And, as Secretary of War Taft said about the Chinese in 1908, "The more civilized they become the more active their industries, the wealthier they become, and the better market they will become for us."[29] President Wilson, who added a conspicuous tinge of missionary paternalism to the quest for order, said simply that he would "teach the South American Republics to elect good men."[30] As historian Jerry Israel has noted, "reforming cultures, making profits, and saving souls were not incompatible goals."[31] All were intertwined in the American compulsion to shape the lives of other people while denying any intention of dominating them.

## The Cuban Protectorate

President William McKinley faced a dilemma in 1898. The Teller Amendment, which he had unsuccessfully opposed, forbade the annexation of Cuba. Yet, in negotiating the preliminary protocol of peace he had insisted that Spain relinquish sovereignty over the island. Cuba lay athwart the approaches to the Gulf of Mexico and Caribbean Sea. Unless brought firmly within the American orbit, it could threaten the security of the Gulf states and United States hegemony over Central America. The President understandably equivocated. In his annual message of December, 1898, he promised to help the Cubans build a "free and independent" government, but he also warned that American military rule would continue until "complete tranquillity" and a "stable government" existed on the island.[32]

Two months later the Philippine insurrection erupted, sending shock waves through America's policy-makers. Secretary of War Elihu Root, charged with the formulation of Cuban occupation policy, feared that in Cuba the United States was "on the verge daily of the same sort of thing that happened to us in the Philippines."[33] To accelerate the evolution of Cuban democracy and stability, Root appointed General Leonard Wood the military governor of the island. A Harvard graduate with a degree in medicine, Wood had entered the Army for excitement. A spiritual relative and a friend of the adventurous Roosevelt, Wood favored outright annexation of Cuba, but he loyally subordinated his own preferences to the Administration's policy of patrician tutelage in the ways of progress and freedom. During his tenure as military governor (1899–1902), he worked to eradicate yellow fever, Americanize education, construct highways, and formulate an electoral law guaranteeing order. The general defined his objectives in a conservative manner: "When money can be borrowed at a reasonable rate of interest and when capital is willing to invest in the Island, a condition of stability will have been reached.''[34] Senator Joseph B. Foraker, an old Ohio rival of McKinley, viewed overseas investments in a less friendly light and sought to retard the annexationist tendencies that followed the flow of capital abroad. In February of 1899 he successfully attached an amendment to the Army Appropriation Bill that prohibited the American military government of Cuba from granting permanent economic concessions. However, Secretary of War Root outflanked the senator by granting revocable permits, beginning with a railroad franchise in 1901.

With the economic foundation of his policy safely laid, Root began construction of a Cuban-American political relationship designed to weather the storms of independence. Working closely with Senator Orville Platt, an Administration spokesman, Root fashioned the so-called Platt Amendment to the Army Appropriation Bill of 1901. By the Platt Amendment's terms, Cuba could not make a treaty with any nation that might impair its independence. Should Cuban independence ever be threatened, or should it fail to protect adequately "life, property, and individual liberty," the United States had the right to intervene. For these purposes, Cuba would cede to the United States "lands necessary for coaling or naval stations." The Platt Amendment also stipulated that "by way of further assurance" Cuba and the United States would "embody the foregoing provisions in a permanent treaty."[35]

Cubans howled. On Good Friday, 1901, the front page of Havana's *La Discusión* carried a cartoon of "The Cuban Calvary" depicting the Cuban people as Christ and Senator Platt as a Roman soldier. Many Americans agreed that the amendment

**"If General Wood Is Unpopular with Cuba, We Can Guess the Reason."** General Leonard Wood (1860–1927), before he served as military governor of Cuba (1899–1903), was a surgeon from Boston who entered the Army in 1886 and earned a promotion for his role in capturing Indian leader Geronimo. He also commanded the Rough Riders at San Juan Hill during the Spanish-American War. Later he helped govern the Philippines. (*Minneapolis Tribune* in *Literary Digest,* 1901)

relegated Cuba to the status of a protectorate. Theodore Roosevelt retorted that the critics were "unhung traitors . . . liars, slanderers and scandal mongers."[36] Root ingeniously informed Wood that intervention was not "synonymous with inter-meddling or interference with the affairs of a Cuban government," but the more straightforward general privately conceded that there was, "of course, little or no independence left Cuba under the Platt Amendment."[37] Wood himself forced a resistant Cuban convention to adopt the measure as an amendment to the new constitution on June 12, 1901, and the two governments signed a treaty embodying the provisions of the Platt Amendment on May 22, 1903. In 1903 the United States Navy constructed a naval base at Guantánamo Bay; "Gitmo," as the Marines christened it, was leased to the United States in perpetuity. A Reciprocity Treaty of 1902 permitted Cuban products to enter the United States at specially reduced tariff rates, thereby interlocking the economies of the two countries.

The first President of the Republic of Cuba, Tomás Estrada Palma, has been described as "more plattish than Platt himself."[38] Following his rigged re-election and second inauguration, discontented Cuban nationalists revolted. In a cable of September 8, 1906, the American consul-general in Havana reported Estrada Palma's inability to quell the rebellion or "protect life and property." He pleaded for warships.[39] President Roosevelt immediately ordered the cruiser *Denver* to Havana, but he failed in his instructions to leash the ship's commanding officer, who landed a battalion of sailors at Estrada Palma's request. Roosevelt summarily ordered the men back aboard ship, adding further to the political chaos. "Just at the moment I am so angry with that infernal little Cuban republic," exploded the Rough Rider, "that I would like to wipe its people off the face of the earth." All he wanted from the Cubans, he said, was that "they should behave them-selves."[40]

Into this turmoil stepped the portly Secretary of War, William Howard Taft, whom Roosevelt ordered to Cuba on a peace mission. Groping for a solution that would "put an end to anarchy without necessitating a reoccupation of the island by our troops," Roosevelt instructed Taft to mediate between the warring factions.[41] The Teller Amendment weighed upon the President's mind, as did memory of the bloody crushing of insurgent Emilio Aguinaldo in the Philippines. Army officers predicted that American suppression of the Cuban revolution would necessitate drastic reconcentration of the Cuban population, making political annexation inevitable. Estrada Palma resigned, permitting Taft to establish a new provisional government. Taft, the American secretary of war, thus became the provisional governor of Cuba on September 29, 1906. He soon lectured students of the National University of Havana that Cubans needed a "mercantile spirit," a "desire to make money, to found great enterprises."[42] Taft returned home in mid-October, leaving behind a government headed by an American civilian, administered by United States Army officers, and supported by over 5,000 American soldiers. For twenty-eight months Governor Charles E. Magoon attempted to reinstate Leonard Wood's electoral and humanitarian reforms, while Roosevelt publicly lectured the Cubans that if their "insurrectionary habit" persisted it was "absolutely out of the question that the Island should continue independent."[43] Privately he mused that "it is not our fault if things go badly there."[44]

Under his successor Taft, and under Taft's successor Woodrow Wilson, Ameri-can policy toward Cuba consisted of reflexive support for existing governments, by means of force if necessary. Taft and Wilson made no serious effort to reform

Cuba in the American image. In what has been called both "a preventive policy" and "Dollar Diplomacy," the United States sought order in Cuban politics and security for American investments and commerce, particularly in sugar.[45] The $50 million invested by Americans in 1896 jumped to $220 million in 1913. By 1920 American-owned mills produced about half of Cuba's sugar. Cuban exports to the United States in 1900 equaled $31 million, by 1914 $131 million, and by 1920 $722 million. When these interests were threatened by revolution, as in May of 1912 and February of 1917, the Marines went ashore. After Havana followed Washington's lead and declared war against Germany, in April, 1917, some 2,500 American troops were sent to Cuba for the protection of the sugar plantations that helped feed the Allied armies. Cuba, under the yoke of the Platt Amendment, the American military, and American economic interests, remained a protectorate of the United States. The island's "independence" was a myth, but its frustrated nationalism was a reality with which Americans always had to contend.

## Policing the Caribbean: Venezuela, the Dominican Republic, and the Roosevelt Corollary

President Theodore Roosevelt devoted a great deal of thought to Latin America in the winter of 1901–1902. He guided the second Hay-Pauncefote Treaty through the Senate, fretted over the route of his isthmian canal, and helped Elihu Root shape the terms of the occupation of Cuba. He also turned his mind toward the most hallowed of American doctrines, that propounded by James Monroe in 1823. In his first annual message, on December 3, 1901, Roosevelt emphasized the economic aspect of the doctrine: "It is really a guarantee of the commercial independence of the Americas." The United States, however, as protector of that independence, would "not guarantee any state against punishment if it misconducts itself, provided that punishment does not take the form of the acquisition of territory by any non-American power."[46] If a South American country misbehaved in its relations with a European nation, Roosevelt would "let the European country spank it."[47]

The President was thinking principally of Germany and Venezuela. Under the rule of Cipriano Castro, an unsavory dictator whom Roosevelt once characterized as an "unspeakable villainous monkey," Venezuela perpetually deferred payment on bonds worth more than $12.5 million and held by German investors.[48] Berlin became understandably impatient. Great Britain felt equally irritated by Venezuela's failure to meet its debts to British subjects. In December, 1902, after clearing the way with Washington, Germany and Britain delivered an ultimatum demanding immediate settlement of their claims, seized several Venezuelan vessels, bombarded two forts, and proclaimed a blockade closing Venezuela to commerce. To all of this Theodore Roosevelt acquiesced, but American congressional and editorial opinion reacted adversely. The *Literary Digest* of December 20 worried "that England and Germany will overstep the limits prescribed by the Monroe Doctrine" and concluded that many newspapers "think that the allies have already gone too far."[49]

In mid-January, 1903, the German Navy bombarded two more forts. Popular criticism of the intervention sharpened in the United States, while in Great Britain Rudyard Kipling denounced his government's cooperation with "the breed that have wronged us most."[50] Shaken by the American reaction, Kaiser Wilhelm II

**Roosevelt at Work.** TR was, according to biographer William Harbaugh, "a man of surpassing charm, extraordinary charisma, and broad intellectual interests . . . , a curious compound of realist and idealist, pragmatist and moral absolutist." A lover of power, he knew that one way to achieve it was through vigorous oratory. (*Kladderadatsch*, Berlin)

replaced his ill-informed ambassador with Hermann Speck von Sternburg, an old friend of Roosevelt. The President received Speck on the day of his arrival in Washington and urged a quick settlement to quell the clamor in Britain and the United States. Under this mounting criticism and pressure from Roosevelt, in early February Britain and Germany lifted the blockade and submitted the dispute to the Permanent Court at the Hague. Prime Minister Balfour poured oil on troubled Anglo-American waters by publicly denying any intention of acquiring additional territory in the western hemisphere and welcoming an "increase of the influence of the United States" in Latin America.[51] Even more, he accepted the Monroe Doctrine as international law. On February 22, 1904, the Hague Tribunal awarded preferential treatment to the claims of the two nations that had used force against Venezuela. A prominent State Department official complained that this decision put "a premium on violence" and made likely similar European interventions in the future.[52]

Theodore Roosevelt also worried increasingly about the chronic disorder and fiscal insolvency of the Dominican Republic, which had been torn continually by revolution since 1899. "I have about the same desire to annex it," Roosevelt said privately, "as a gorged boa constrictor might have to swallow a porcupine wrong-end to."[53] An American firm that formerly handled the country's tariff collections or customs claimed damages of several million dollars, and European creditors demanded action by their governments. The President had been "hoping and praying . . . that the Santo Dominigans would behave so that I would not have to act in any way." By the spring of 1904 he thought he might have "to do nothing but what a policeman has to do."[54] He preferred to do it after the presidential election of 1904.

After the electorate resoundingly endorsed his presidency, he described to Congress his conception of the United States as policeman of the western hemisphere. "Chronic wrongdoing, or an impotence which results in a general loosening of the ties of civilized society," he proclaimed, "may in America, as elsewhere, ultimately require intervention by some civilized nation, and in the Western Hemisphere the adherence of the United States to the Monroe Doctrine may force the United States, however reluctantly, in flagrant cases of such wrongdoing or impotence, to the exercise of an international police power."[55] With this statement of December 6, 1904, the twenty-sixth President of the United States added to the Monroe Doctrine his corollary, which fundamentally transformed that prohibition upon European meddling into a brash promise of United States regulation of the Americas.

The Rough Rider acted accordingly. In December the State Department initiated discussions with the Dominican Republic aimed at American collection and distribution of the Latin republic's customs revenues. A protocol to this effect was signed on February 7, 1905, but it ran into determined Democratic opposition in the Senate. Roosevelt, however, would not be deterred. He arranged a modus vivendi, assigning an American collector of the Dominican customs, an arrangement finally sanctified in a treaty negotiated by Secretary of State Root and approved by the Senate on February 25, 1907. While easing the new Dominican customs treaty through the Senate, Root explained the interrelationship between Latin American political stability and the security of the Panama Canal. The "inevitable effect of our building the Canal," he wrote, "must be to require us to police the surrounding premises."[56] The United States would reap "trade and control, and the obligation to keep order" and would simultaneously draw Latin America "up out of the discord and turmoil of continual revolution into a general public sense of justice and determination to maintain order."[57]

Taft's Secretary of State, Philander C. Knox, applauded Root's customs receivership in the Dominican Republic because it denied to rebels the funds they so eagerly "collected" through the capture of customs houses. Knox credited the receivership with curing "century-old evils."[58] The assassination of the Dominican President the following November, 1911, demonstrated that Knox spoke somewhat prematurely. And in 1912 revolutionaries operating from the contiguous country of Haiti marauded throughout the Dominican Republic. Their forays forced the closure of several customs houses that the United States had protected under the Treaty of 1907. To restore order, Taft in September, 1912 sent a commission backed by 750 Marines. The commissioners redefined the Haiti–Dominican Republic border, forced the corrupt Dominican president to resign by stopping his revenues from the customs service, avoided direct interference in a new election, and returned to Washington in December.

President Wilson and Secretary Bryan eloquently disparaged the evils of "dollar diplomacy" and promised that the United States would "never again seek one additional foot of territory by conquest."[59] That sounded new, but Roosevelt and Taft had already repudiated further American territorial acquisitions. Actually, Wilson's search for stability in Latin America retraced familiar steps. When, in September, 1913, revolution again threatened the Dominican government, Bryan warned "that this Government will employ every legitimate means to assist in the restoration of order and the prevention of further insurrections."[60] The Navy Department sent a cruiser to the island and Wilson urged political and economic reforms. Discouraged by a new revolutionary outburst in May of 1916, the Administration sent two warships, landed men, and permitted the admiral in command to threaten bombardment of the city of Santo Domingo if the leading revolutionary did not surrender. The Dominican and American governments thereupon debated terms of a treaty giving the United States full control over Dominican finances, while the United States Navy tightened its grip on the island. In November, as American involvement in the European war became increasingly probable, President Wilson proclaimed the formal military occupation of the Dominican Republic, ostensibly to curtail the activities of revolutionaries suspected of a pro-German bias. The American Navy governed the Dominican Republic until 1922.

## The Quest for Stability in Haiti and Nicaragua

The Dominican Republic shares the island of Hispaniola with Haiti, where revolution became an increasingly popular mode of changing governments after 1911. American investments in the country were limited to ownership of a small railroad and a one-third share in the Haitian National Bank. Nationals of France and Germany controlled the bank, and disorder thus could give either European nation a pretext for intervention. After the outbreak of World War I, the Wilson Administration worried about "the ever present danger of German control" of Haiti.[61] At stake was the security of the Panama Canal, along the approaches to which lay Haiti's deep water harbor of Môle Saint Nicolas. The Navy Department, content with bases in Cuba and Puerto Rico, no longer desired a station in Haiti, but

Wilson could not let Môle Saint Nicolas fall into the unfriendly hands of Germany. Moreover, the President realized that Haitian instability fueled the revolution in the Dominican Republic, which he was also combatting. He therefore pressed for an American customs receivership on the Dominican model.

The Haitians resisted successfully until July, 1915, when the regime of Guillaume Sam fell in an orgy of grisly political murders. Wilson could stomach no more, and he ordered the Navy to Haiti. While 2,000 Marines imposed martial law, Secretary of State Robert Lansing explained to the Haitians that his government expected "to be entrusted with the practical control of the customs, and such financial control over the affairs of the Republic of Haiti as the United States may deem necessary for an efficient administration."[62] Lansing drafted a treaty putting Americans in charge of all aspects of Haiti's finances, privately admitting to Wilson that "this method of negotiation, with our marines policing the Haytian Capital, is high handed."[63] The United States naval and diplomatic vise meant that Haiti would be ruled until 1934 by what historian David Healy has called "an American military regime which acted, when it pleased, through the [Haitian] president."[64]

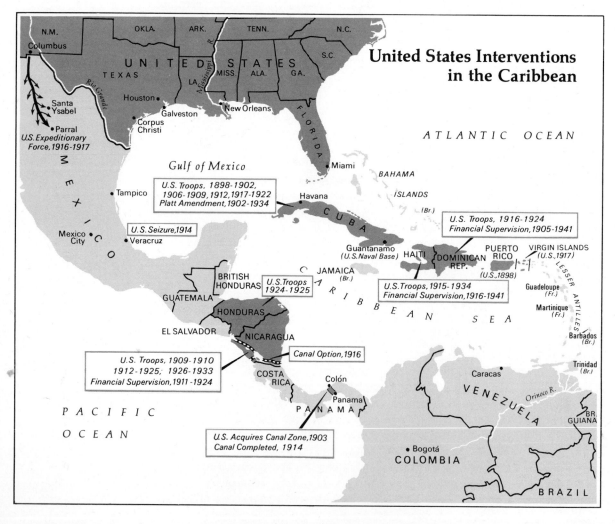

**United States Interventions in the Caribbean**

The United States also intervened, virtually at will, in hapless Nicaragua. For Theodore Roosevelt, Nicaragua had been important primarily as a potential canal route, a rivalry decided in Panama's favor in 1903. Subsequently, he manifested interest in Nicaragua only briefly, during 1907, when he and President Porfirio Díaz of Mexico proposed a peace conference to end the incessant warfare among Central American states. Secretary Root explained that the conduct of those countries was "important to us," because the Panama Canal put them "in the front yard of the United States."[65] Philander C. Knox continued the search for stability in Central America, but an abiding antipathy "to all Spanish-American modes of thought" made him more ready to countenance the use of force.[66] Thus, when José Santo Zelaya's Nicaraguan government executed two Americans for joining a revolutionary army in 1909, Knox broke diplomatic relations, gave "the revolution strong moral support," and tolerated an American naval interposition favoring the rebels in a decisive battle.[67] He then negotiated a treaty with the victorious revolutionaries led by Adolfo Díaz, providing for American control of the customs service and an American loan. The United States Senate refused ratification, but Knox and a group of bankers simply acted ad interim without the authorization of a treaty. In September, 1912, the Administration ordered the Marines into battle alongside Díaz's troops. After tipping the scales against the newest revolutionary army, the leathernecks returned home, leaving one hundred behind as a legation guard in Managua.

The Marines could prevent a coup d'état, but they could not easily put Díaz's house in fiscal order. Although critical of Taft's "dollar diplomacy," Bryan in the spring of 1913 dusted off a shelved draft treaty granting the United States a canal option in Nicaragua in exchange for three million dollars. Bryan hoped that this monetary prospect would "give sufficient encouragement" to American bankers to lend Díaz more money.[68] The secretary also added a clause similar to the Platt Amendment before sending the Bryan-Chamorro Treaty to the Senate. The upper house balked at this extension of American commitments and, to gain approval, the Wilson Administration had to delete the right of intervention. Ratification in February, 1916 did help to shore up Nicaragua's finances. The treaty also insured that European powers could not gain naval bases in the Gulf of Fonseca, and to make that point stick, Wilson ordered United States warships to cruise offshore during the 1916 Nicaraguan presidential campaign. Although nominally independent, Nicaragua remained a United States protectorate until 1933.

## Meddling in Mexico

Mexico changed governments with uncharacteristic frequency after the outbreak of revolution in 1910. In 1911 Francisco I. Madero toppled Porfirio Díaz, the aged dictator who had maintained order, personal power, and a healthy environment for American investments since the late 1870s. United States citizens owned over 40 percent of Mexico's property and thus the Mexican Revolution was tinged with an anti-American bias. President Taft grew angry with the chaos that threatened American lives and property, but he determined to "sit tight on the lid and it will take a good deal to pry me off."[69] In February, 1913, United States Ambassador Henry Lane Wilson encouraged one of Madero's trusted generals, Victoriano Huerta, to overthrow the revolutionary nationalist. Indeed, Huerta had Madero shot and then set about to consolidate his own power. The Taft Administration prepared to recognize Huerta's government in return for a settlement of claims against Mexico. But after Huerta requested formal oaths of allegiance from Mexican state governors, one of them, Venustiano Carranza, took up arms and led the "Constitutionalist" revolt on February 26. Americans and their property were caught in the crossfire. Just before leaving office, Taft recoiled from recognition of Huerta's government, insisting that it first punish the "murderers of American citizens" and "put an end to the discriminations against American interests."[70]

Woodrow Wilson seemed to worry less about the large private American investment of one billion dollars. He redefined American recognition policy, requiring governments to meet a test of morality. Referring to Mexico, he said he would not recognize a "government of butchers."[71] Despising Huerta's treachery, Wilson denounced the Mexican as a "diverting brute! . . . seldom sober and always impossible."[72] Unlike Ambassador Wilson, who advocated recognition of Huerta to protect American financial and commercial interests, the President remarked that he himself was "not the servant of those who wish to enhance the value of their Mexican investments."[73] In July, 1913 he had the ambassador recalled; a month later Henry Lane Wilson was dismissed from the diplomatic corps. Thereafter the President treated with Mexico through special emissaries, only one of whom spoke fluent Spanish. None was intimately familiar with Mexico and all were chosen because of earlier friendships with the President or Secretary Bryan.

On August 8, 1913, one of these representatives, John Lind, arrived in Mexico City, after landing on Mexican soil from an American warship. A rabid anti-Catholic and former governor of Minnesota, without diplomatic experience, Lind delivered Wilson's plan of "counsel and assistance." The American President wanted an armistice between Huerta's federalist troops and all revolutionary groups, "an early and free election," and Huerta's promise not to run for president. In exchange, the United States pledged recognition and aid to "the administration chosen and set up . . . in the way and on the conditions suggested." With sublime arrogance, Woodrow Wilson wondered, "can Mexico give the civilized world a satisfactory reason for rejecting our good offices?"[74] The Mexican minister of foreign relations thought he could. Already annoyed that Lind had arrived on a warship and held no formal diplomatic rank, Federico Gamboa issued a scathing reply on August 26, excoriating Wilson's "counsels and advice (let us call them thus)." Adherence to American dictates would mean that "all the future elections for president would be submitted to the veto of any President of the United States of America," and no government of Mexico would ever perpetrate "such an enormity" upon its people.[75] After this snub, Woodrow Wilson announced a restrained policy of "watchful waiting," clamped an embargo on arms to Mexico, and advised Americans to leave that country.[76]

Undeterred, Huerta in October dissolved an unruly legislature, arrested its members, and held a special election, which returned an entirely submissive congress ready to extend his presidency indefinitely. Wilson then turned to Carranza. He sent a personal representative to the revolutionary chief's headquarters in northern Mexico with the same proposal Huerta's foreign minister had rejected in August. Carranza proved an ardent nationalist as well as revolutionary. He contemptuously rejected Wilsonian mediation in the civil war and refused any solution short of his own triumph. Thoroughly isolated himself, Wilson on November 24 issued a circular note to the other powers informing them of his

**Woodrow Wilson (1856–1924).** The twenty-eighth President denounced "dollar diplomacy" and instead took up "missionary diplomacy." But the results were much the same for Latin Americans, who continued to feel pressure from the North. (U.S. Signal Corps, National Archives)

policy "to isolate General Huerta entirely; to cut him off from foreign sympathy . . . and so to force him out." But if political and economic pressure failed to induce Huerta's retirement, "it will become the duty of the United States to use less peaceful means to put him out."[77]

Most European powers had recognized Huerta and disapproved of Wilson's indignant opposition to him. The nation most deeply affected was Great Britain, whose capital investments in Mexico were second only to those of the United States. Also, the Royal Navy relied on Mexican oil as a backup to Middle Eastern sources. It took the British Foreign Office several months to realize that Wilson was serious about deposing Huerta. One senior official concluded darkly, "the United States cherish very sinister designs toward Mexico and desire that a condition of complete anarchy should supervene."[78] For London, however, the growing menace of Germany made American goodwill absolutely essential. In the event of conflict, England would need American war materiel. The Foreign Office therefore notified Huerta that it could not support him against the United States, advised him to retire as president, and recalled the British minister because of American antipathy toward him—all the while believing American views were "most impractical and unreasonable."[79]

With British compliance assured, Wilson acted. On February 1, 1914, he lifted the arms embargo, permitting large quantities of arms to flow to both factions. As Carranza's resupplied forces pushed south, the President sent American naval vessels to the busy port of Veracruz and the oil-producing town of Tampico, both on the Gulf of Mexico. On April 9, at Tampico, Huerta's inexperienced federal troops arrested several American sailors loading gasoline aboard a whaleboat docked provocatively near their forward outpost. The Mexican colonel in charge quickly disavowed the arrest, freed the sailors, and apologized orally. This redress failed to appease the hotheaded commander of the American squadron at Tampico, Rear Admiral Henry T. Mayo. He demanded a formal written apology and a twenty-one-gun salute to the American flag, because "taking men from a boat flying the American flag is a hostile act, not to be excused."[80] Wilson immediately warned the Mexican government "that unless the guilty persons are promptly punished consequences of [the] gravest sort might ensue." To reporters he bluntly said, "the salute will be fired."[81] He soon decided to use Herta's rejection of the Mayo ultimatum as justification for military intervention designed to humiliate the Mexican leader and drive him from power. In the early afternoon of April 20 Wilson requested congressional approval to use armed force "to obtain from General Huerta and his adherents the fullest recognition of the rights and dignity of the United States."[82] Meanwhile, Secretary of the Navy Josephus Daniels had learned of the imminent arrival at Veracruz of a German-owned steamer, the *Ypiranga,* carrying two hundred machine guns and over fifteen million cartridges. The United States could not allow these arms to reach Huerta on the eve of American military intervention. Thus Daniels ordered the Navy to interdict the shipment by seizing the customs house at Veracruz.

On April 21, 1914, eight hundred American sailors and Marines landed. Although most of Huerta's federal troops withdrew under orders from the Ministry of War, a local federalist commander freed and armed prisoners from city jails to resist the Americans. These desperadoes and other irregulars fought in the streets and sniped from hiding places so tenaciously that four Americans were killed and twenty were wounded on the first day alone. Nineteen Americans and several hundred Mexicans died before the fighting stopped. Wilson was stunned by the bloody turn of events. To one observer, the shaken President appeared "preternaturally pale, almost parchmenty," and to his personal physician Wilson moaned, "the thought haunts me that it was I who ordered those young men to their deaths."[83] Carranza added an angry rebuke, warning Wilson that the invasion could "drag us into an unequal war . . . which until today we have desired to avoid."[84] Newspaper editorials in the United States and abroad roundly denounced the aggression. Apparently chastened, Wilson accepted mediation when proposed by Argentina, Brazil, and Chile (the ABC powers) on April 25.

A month later, representatives of the United States, Huerta, and the ABC powers met on the Canadian side of Niagara Falls. From the outset, Wilson and Carranza doomed the mediation by their intransigence. The American President refused to allow his delegates to discuss the evacuation of Veracruz or Tampico, a major reason for convening the conference. He sought instead "the entire elimination of General Huerta" and creation of a provisional government under the Constitutionalists.[85] But Carranza indignantly refused to attend any foreign meeting dealing with Mexico's internal affairs. By early June the deadlock was complete, and one newspaper editor sarcastically proposed: "Why should not Abyssinia, Servia, and Senegabia—the A.S.S. powers—tender their good offices? Send out the SOS for the A.S.S."[86] On July 2 the hapless mediators adjourned; two weeks later Huerta fled to Europe, and on August 20 a triumphant Carranza paraded before enthusiastic throngs in Mexico City.

The Constitutionalist triumph was short-lived. One of Carranza's northern generals, Francisco (Pancho) Villa, soon broke from the ranks, marched south, and occupied Mexico City in December. Villa, an illiterate cattle rustler noted for his cunning and courage, beguiled Wilson by seeming to approve all aspects of the American President's Mexican policy, including the intervention at Veracruz. Wilson persuaded himself that "General Villa certainly seems capable of some good things and often shows susceptibility of the best influences," and encouraged him by refusing to recognize Carranza's government.[87] To avoid danger of a military clash with any Mexican faction, Wilson withdrew all American troops from Veracruz on November 23, 1914. Once again, Wilson watched and waited, thereby stimulating continued disorder in Mexico with his refusal to recognize the legitimacy of its government.

Mexican-American relations remained tense during the first months of 1915. Carranza's forces gradually drove Villa north, but in the process Mexico City became a no-man's-land, with bread riots and starvation threatening its inhabitants, including 2,500 Americans and 23,000 other foreign residents. Wilson gave some thought to relieving the city by force, perhaps with Pan American cooperation, but deteriorating German-American relations preoccupied him, especially after a German U-boat torpedoed the *Lusitania* in May. Resigned to failure in Mexico, Wilson seemed to repudiate all further interference in Mexican affairs: "Carranza will somehow have to be digested."[88] Two months later the United States extended partial, or de facto, recognition to the Constitutionalist government and permitted munitions exports, while embargoing arms to the Constitutionalists' enemies.

Forced north by Carranza's army, Villa plundered, looted, and killed Americans in his track. Infuriated by Wilson's grudging recognition of Carranza, the rebel

**Pancho Villa (1878–1923).** The colorful Mexican rebel bedeviled both Mexico and the United States. His daring and blood-stained raid on an American town prompted President Wilson to order General John J. Pershing to chase Villa, an experienced escape artist. (Library of Congress)

**Uncle Sam Shooting
Dice with Carranza.** The
Mexican leader tells a
grudging Uncle Sam in
1917 to put his dice
(army) back in the box.
(*Washington Evening Star,*
Library of Congress)

chieftain hoped to precipitate a Mexican-American war by attacking "the barbarians of the North."[89] In the predawn hours of March 9, 1916, he led a band of *Villistas* across the border into Columbus, New Mexico, initiating a bloody battle that left nineteen Americans and sixty-seven Mexicans dead. Within hours Wilson unleashed the United States Army against Villa. General John J. "Black Jack" Pershing commanded a Punitive Expedition, eventually totaling almost 7,000 men, which reached 350 miles into Mexico in a vain search for Pancho Villa. A clash with Carranza's forces in August occurred instead.

Carranza kept up drumfire pressure for American withdrawal, but Wilson hesitated for fear of appearing weak during a presidential election year. When United States participation in the European war finally became inescapable, Wilson disengaged from Mexico. On January 28, 1917, three days before Ambassador Johann von Bernstorff notified Secretary of State Lansing of Germany's resumption of unrestricted submarine warfare, Secretary of War Newton D. Baker announced that Pershing's troops were marching home. The last American soldier left Mexico on February 5. In late February, the secret Zimmermann telegram proposing an anti-American alliance between Germany, Japan, and Mexico came into the hands of the State Department, courtesy of British intelligence. This dire German ploy accelerated Wilson's movement toward full diplomatic relations with Carranza's government. The United States extended de jure recognition on August 31, 1917, in order to insure Mexican neutrality during the fight against

Germany. Thus, after four futile years, Wilson had given up on his haughty attempt to tell the Mexicans how to run their own affairs.

## The Open Door and Dollar Diplomacy in East Asia

Telling Asians how to run their affairs proved even more difficult. Secretary of State John Hay's endorsement of Chinese political and administrative integrity in the Open Door Notes of July, 1900 did not prevent the further emasculation of China. During the Boxer Rebellion Russia stationed 175,000 troops in Manchuria and demanded exclusive rights from China, including a commercial monopoly. President Roosevelt and Hay could do little to stop this infringement of China's sovereignty. The United States, they said, had "always recognized the exceptional position of Russia" in Manchuria and had merely sought the commercial freedom "guaranteed to us by . . . the whole civilized world."[90] Washington retreated from the Open Door Circular of 1900 because Roosevelt realized that the American people would not fight for nebulous principles of Chinese integrity in Manchuria, an area considered strategically remote and economically inconsequential. He understood the futility of trying, in historian Akira Iriye's words, "to play the role of an Asian power without military power."[91]

Japan viewed the question quite differently. Russia blocked Japanese economic expansion into Manchuria, posed a potential naval threat, and endangered the Japanese position in Korea. Tokyo covered its flanks with an Anglo-Japanese Alliance in 1902, opened negotiations aimed at explicit Russian recognition of nominal Chinese governance over Manchuria, and prepared for war. On February 8, 1904, the Japanese Navy suddenly captured headlines when it destroyed Russia's Far Eastern Fleet in a surprise attack at Port Arthur. At first Roosevelt cheered privately, "for Japan is playing our game," but as the enormity of Japanese victories became apparent he began to hope for peace "on terms which will not mean the creation of either a yellow peril or a Slav peril."[92] By the spring of 1905 Japanese soldiers had triumphed at Mukden, where Russia lost 97,000 men, and the navy had sunk the Russian Baltic Fleet in the straits of Tsushima. Still, the imperial treasury was drained and the army stretched thin. On May 31, Minister Kogoro Takahira requested Roosevelt, "on his own motion and initiative," to invite Russia and Japan to negotiate a peace treaty.[93]

Seizing the opportunity to balance the powers in order to protect America's territorial and commercial interests in the Pacific and Asia, the President invited Japanese and Russian representatives to meet at Portsmouth, New Hampshire on August 9, 1904. The Japanese delegates demanded Russia's leasehold on the Liaotung Peninsula and the railroad running from Harbin to Port Arthur, evacuation of Russian troops from Manchuria, and complete freedom of action for Japan in Korea. The Russians quickly conceded these points, but rejected additional Japanese requests for a monetary indemnity and cession of the island of Sakhalin. With negotiations deadlocked, Roosevelt telegraphed Tsar Nicholas II proposing division of Sakhalin between the belligerents and agreement "in principle" upon an indemnity. The Tsar agreed to partition the island but refused any payment. Needing peace more than money, Japan yielded on August 29.

The Roosevelt Administration's search for equipoise in East Asia neither began nor ended at Portsmouth. As early as March, 1904, TR had conceded to Japan a relationship with Korea "just like we have with Cuba."[94] Secretary of War Taft reaffirmed the concession during a discussion with Prime Minister Taro Katsura on July 27, 1905. In the Taft-Katsura "agreed memorandum of conversation," the Prime Minister also emphatically denied any Japanese designs on the Philippine Islands.[95] A year later southern Manchuria was reopened to foreign and American trade, although the Japanese systematically discouraged foreign capital investments.

This artful balancing of interests augured well for a continuation of traditional Japanese-American cordiality, until a local dispute in California abruptly undercut Rooseveltian diplomacy. On October 11, 1906, the San Francisco School Board created a special "Oriental Public School" for all Japanese, Chinese and Korean children. Japan immediately protested this racial discrimination against its citizens, and Theodore Roosevelt denounced the "infernal fools in California" whose exclusion of Japanese from all other public schools constituted "a confession of inferiority in our civilization."[96] At one point he wrote that the "feeling on the Pacific slope . . . is as foolish as if conceived by the mind of a Hottentot."[97] Yet there was little he constitutionally could do, other than rail against the recalcitrant school board, apply political pressure to the California legislature to prevent statewide discriminatory measures, and propose congressional legislation to naturalize Japanese residing permanently in the United States. The public outburst against naturalization finally convinced Roosevelt that he had seriously underestimated the depth of "genuine race feeling" throughout the United States, especially in California.[98] Always the political realist, Roosevelt accepted what he personally disliked and sought accommodation with Japan. By March, 1907, he had contrived a "Gentlemen's Agreement" with Tokyo sharply restricting Japanese immigration.

Two months later anti-Japanese riots and yellow journalistic agitation by what Secretary Root called the "leprous vampires" of San Francisco confirmed Roosevelt's apprehensions that local disturbances in California would create further crises with Japan.[99] The President shrewdly pressed for more battleships and fortification of Hawaii and the vulnerable Philippines, now America's "heel of Achilles," so that the United States would "be ready for anything that comes."[100] He also dramatized the importance of a strong navy to Congress and Japan by ordering the battle fleet on a cruise to the Pacific and around the world. The effect of this show of force by the "Great White Fleet" exceeded Roosevelt's expectations. In the spring of 1908 Congress endorsed a policy of building two battleships per year and Ambassador Takahira invited the cruising fleet to visit Tokyo, where it received a rousing popular reception. On the day the ships sailed from Tokyo Bay, Takahira received instructions to seek an agreement with the United States recognizing the Pacific Ocean as an open avenue of trade, pledging the integrity of Japanese and American insular possessions in the Pacific, supporting the status quo, and promising equal opportunity in China. After extensive refinement of rhetoric, these concepts were promulgated as the Root-Takahira declaration of policy on November 30, 1908. Japanese-American relations seemed to enter a period of mature harmony premised on mutual understanding of one another's national interests.

The new epoch did not materialize. William Howard Taft and Philander C. Knox chose to champion the "Open Door" and Chinese nationalism, thereby threatening Japan. The first explosion of twentieth-century Chinese nationalism had occurred in 1900, when the Boxers challenged both the Manchus and the Western powers exploiting the old dynasty. Angry Chinese patriots thereafter decried American participation in the suppression of the uprising, the concurrent bloody extirpation of Aguinaldo's Filipino partisans, and a racist 1904 act of Congress permanently barring Chinese immigration into the United States and its territories. Chinese nationalists inspired a popular boycott of American goods in 1904–1905 and official revocation of a railroad franchise held by financier J. P. Morgan. Roosevelt explained to the financial baron his "interest of seeing American commercial interests prosper in the Orient," but he restricted his diplomatic initiatives in East Asia to matters directly touching Japan.[101]

Not everyone shared Roosevelt's fixation on Japan. As early as 1905 Secretary of War Taft dreamed about the American share of "one of the greatest commercial prizes of the world," the China market.[102] During a trip to East Asia in 1905, Taft met the impressive, intensely anti-Japanese American Consul General in Mukden, Willard Straight. Two years later Straight proposed the creation of a Manchurian bank, to be financed by the American railroad magnate E. H. Harriman, only to have the economic panic of 1907 dash all hopes for subsidizing the Chinese administration of Manchuria. When Wall Street revived in 1908, Straight was

**"Jumping on Your Uncle Samuel."** Chinese nationalists, angered over American immigration restrictions, retaliated with a boycott of American products, trampling Uncle Sam. (*Philadelphia Inquirer,* in *Literary Digest,* 1906)

recalled to advise New York financiers on the exploitation of Manchuria. He arrived in time to condemn the Root-Takahira agreement as "a terrible diplomatic blunder," because it seemed to recognize Japan's exploitative position in Manchuria.[103] After Taft's inauguration he and the State Department inspired several New York banks to form a combination, headed by J. P. Morgan, to serve as the official agency of American railroad investment in China. As acting chief of the department's new Far Eastern Division, Straight instructed Minister William W. Rockhill in Peking to demand admission of the American bankers into a European banking consortium undertaking construction of the Hukuang Railway running southwest from Hankow. Having thus set up an American financial challenge in both Manchuria and China proper, Straight resigned from the State Department to become the Morgan group's roving representative.

Secretary of State Knox continued Straight's policy of injecting American capital into China and Manchuria. In November, 1909, Knox proposed to Britain the neutralization of Manchurian railroads through a large international loan to China for the purchase of the lines. Britain, however, joined both Japan and Russia to reject the neutralization proposal in January, 1910. "Instead of dividing Russia and Japan, and opening the door to American financial exploitation of Manchuria," historian A. Whitney Griswold has observed of Knox, "he had, as it were, nailed that door closed with himself on the outside."[104]

Although international resistance had shattered their Manchurian policy, Knox and Taft continued to seek American entrée to the British, French, and German consortium negotiating the Hukuang loan. They made persistent representations at the Court of St. James's, and Taft sent an extraordinary personal message to the Regent of China insisting upon "equal participation by American capital in the present railway loan."[105] At length, on November 10, 1910, a quadruple agreement expanded the consortium to include the American bankers, and the loan was floated the following June. But the Chinese Revolution of 1911, sparked in part by this new intrusion upon China's autonomy, delayed any actual railroad construction until 1913. "'Dollar' diplomacy," Willard Straight ruefully admitted, "made no friends in the Hukuang matter."[106]

This stringent assessment by one of dollar diplomacy's earliest advocates failed to dissuade Knox from coming to the financial aid of Yüan Shih-k'ai, the dominant leader of the 1911 revolution. Yüan asserted his power ruthlessly, but American missionaries overlooked his faults because he promised religious toleration. They saw in his new republic "the coming of the larger civilization of men which draws no national boundaries and which is controlled by good will. Jesus called it the Kingdom of God."[107] This "wishful thinking," as Akira Iriye describes it, reinforced the Taft Administration's pro-China orientation.[108] When Yüan sought dollars to bolster his nascent republic, Knox urged expansion of the four-power consortium to include Japan and Russia, whom he now thought might be restrained or co-opted by the others. Instead, Tokyo and St. Petersburg stipulated further erosion of Chinese sovereignty over Manchuria and Mongolia as the price for their participation. London and Paris backed them, but Peking resisted. Britain, France, Germany, and the United States then attempted to extort concessions from stubborn China by withholding diplomatic recognition throughout 1912.

Within days of Woodrow Wilson's inauguration, Straight and other representatives of the American banking group called the new President's attention to the convoluted result of dollar diplomacy in China. Wilson and Secretary Bryan at

**William Howard Taft (1857–1930).**
Ohioan, Yale graduate, lawyer, and judge, the good-natured and overweight Taft became civil governor of the Philippines in 1901, served as secretary of war (1904–1908), and succeeded Roosevelt to the presidency. (Library of Congress)

once perceived the infringement on Chinese sovereignty inherent in the proposed six-power loan, and the President repudiated American participation in the international consortium on March 18, 1913. Failure to cancel the loan, Wilson believed, would have cost the United States "the proud position . . . secured when Secretary Hay stood for the open door in China after the Boxer Uprising." Because he felt "so keenly the desire to help China," he extended diplomatic recognition to the struggling republic on May 2.[109] After less than two months in office Wilson had renewed America's commitment to the political integrity of China, a goal pragmatically abandoned by Roosevelt, unsuccessfully resuscitated by Taft, and consistently opposed by Japan.

Events in California shortly proved that, despite his moralistic disdain for dollar diplomacy, Wilson's disregard for Japan's sensibilities made his Far Eastern policy resemble Taft's more than Roosevelt's. In April, 1913, Democratic and Progressive politicians placed before the California legislature a bill denying residents "ineligible to citizenship" the right to own land. The measure struck directly at the 50,000 Japanese living in California, whose exceptional agricultural productivity had raised fears that they were, in the words of Governor Hiram Johnson, "driving the root of their civilization deep into California soil."[110] Racist passion erupted in California. One farmer pointed out that his neighbors were actually a Japanese man and a white woman with an interracial baby: "What is that baby? It isn't a Japanese. It isn't white. It is a germ of the mightiest problem that ever faced this state; a problem that will make the black problem of the South look white."[111] Basically sharing the Californians' anti-Japanese prejudices, and philosophically sensitive to states' rights, Wilson reacted cautiously. He urged restraint upon the California government, sent Bryan to Sacramento to beg for a euphemistic statute, and publicly discounted the "criminal possibility" of war when jingoes in Japan and the United States beat the drums.[112] But the California legislature passed the offensive bill on May 3, 1913, and when Japan protested strongly against the "unfair and intentionally racially discriminatory" measure, Wilson and Bryan took refuge in the legalistic defense that one state's legislation did not constitute a "national discriminatory policy."[113]

Wilson's antipathy toward Japan reappeared during the First World War. In the fall of 1914 Japan declared war on Germany, seized the German Pacific islands north of the equator, and swept across China's Shantung Peninsula to capture the German leasehold of Kiaochow. Tokyo immediately followed this grab with the Twenty-One Demands of January 18, 1915, by which it insisted upon a virtual protectorate over all of China. Stout resistance by Peking resulted in amelioration of the harshest exactions, but Japan emerged with extensive new political and economic rights in Shantung, southern Manchuria, and Mongolia. Preoccupied with Mexico, the British blockade, and the *Lusitania* crisis, the Wilson Administration limited its reaction to Secretary Bryan's caveat of May 11, 1915, refusing to recognize "any agreement . . . impairing the treaty rights of the United States and its citizens in China, the political or territorial integrity of the Republic of China, or . . . the open door policy."[114]

Wilson's nonrecognition policy was undermined, however, by secret treaties in which the European Allies promised to support Japan's conquests at the peace conference. Diplomatically isolated, the United States sought recourse in ambiguity. In an agreement with Viscount Kikujiro Ishii, signed November 2, 1917, Secretary Lansing admitted that "territorial propinquity creates special relationships between countries, and consequently . . . Japan has special interests in China," while Ishii pledged his nation's dedication to the Open Door and integrity of China.[115] Simultaneously, the Wilson Administration revived the international banking consortium as a means of checking further unilateral Japanese economic penetration of China proper. Once again, however, as in 1912, Britain, France, and the United States ultimately had to exclude the consortium from Manchuria as the price of Japanese participation. The wheel had turned full circle for Wilson. Like Taft before him, his attempt to succor Chinese independence had been thwarted by Japan.

## The Anglo-American Rapprochement

After the Venezuelan crisis of 1895, London and Washington sought closer relations, encouraging Theodore Roosevelt to conclude that "together . . . the two branches of the Anglo-Saxon race . . . can whip the world." Indeed, "I think the twentieth century will still be the century of the men who speak English."[116] But

TR's chauvinistic prediction first had to overcome serious strains in Anglo-American relations. Control of the isthmian canal ranked high as a point of contention. In December, 1898, President McKinley directed Secretary Hay to negotiate modification of the Clayton-Bulwer Treaty (1850), which forbade unilateral construction, operation, or fortification of a canal in Central America. For almost a year negotiations foundered on Ambassador Pauncefote's insistence that the United States make concessions along the ill-defined boundary of the Alaskan panhandle, in exchange for British compromises on the canal. At length, made painfully aware of their diplomatic isolation during the Boer War, and apprehensive of unilateral congressional abrogation of the Clayton-Bulwer Treaty, the British yielded and signed the first Hay-Pauncefote Treaty on February 5, 1900. The United States would now be permitted to construct and operate a canal, but one that was neutralized and not fortified.

Overcoming a self-proclaimed, if dubious, reluctance "to meddle in National Affairs," then New York Governor Theodore Roosevelt campaigned against the Hay-Pauncefote Treaty from the governor's mansion in Albany. Only a week after the agreement had been signed, Roosevelt argued publicly that complete American control of the canal was "vital, from the standpoint of our sea power, no less than from the standpoint of the Monroe Doctrine."[117] When the aggrieved Hay protested, Roosevelt praised him as "the greatest Secretary of State I have seen in my time," but advised him to "drop the treaty and push through a bill to build *and fortify* our own canal."[118] He then urged Senator Henry Cabot Lodge and other exponents of a "large policy" to amend the treaty so as to allow fortification and exclusive United States regulation of a canal.

Lodge and his allies succeeded in amending the Hay-Pauncefote Treaty as Roosevelt urged, but in March of 1901 Great Britain understandably rejected the butchered pact, forcing Pauncefote and Hay to reopen negotiations. This time the secretary of state worked closely with Lodge to forestall further embarrassing senatorial opposition, while Roosevelt, first as vice-president and then as president, lectured the British on the firm American resolve to build, fortify, and control the canal. Britain conceded every point in order to win American friendship, and a second Hay-Pauncefote Treaty was signed on November 18, 1901. President Roosevelt and his sympathizers in the Senate rushed it to ratification a month later. This British capitulation constituted the most important element of what one historian has called the "great rapprochement" marking Anglo-American relations between 1895 and 1914.[119]

Another obstacle to entente was overcome almost simultaneously and for the same reasons. After the discovery of gold along the Klondike in 1896, Canadian politicians revived an old boundary dispute with the Americans. The Anglo-Russian Treaty of 1825, which the United States inherited with Alaska in 1867, had left vague the territorial demarcation between the Alaskan panhandle and British North America. Advancing a maximum claim, Canada sought to run the line along the mouths of the numerous inlets reaching inland from the Pacific Ocean. The United States stood for a more easterly isogram at the water's high tide. Ottawa's interpretation would figuratively drive Americans into the sea, and Washington's claim would literally set the United States astride the avenues of approach to a suddenly valuable part of Canada. London initially supported the extreme Canadian claim by linking this issue to abrogation of the Clayton-Bulwer Treaty, hoping that the United States would sacrifice Alaskan territory in exchange for enlarged rights in Central America. Shrill European denunciations of Britain's painful suppression of the Boers in South Africa, coupled with benevolent official American silence on the same topic, persuaded Sir Julian Pauncefote to advocate separation of the two disputes in early 1900. "America seems to be our only friend just now," he commented to Foreign Secretary Lansdowne, "and it would be unfortunate to quarrel with her."[120] Disentanglement followed, but the Alaskan boundary dispute remained unresolved when Theodore Roosevelt entered the White House.

Declining arbitration by a third party on the grounds that the "manifestly clear and unanswerable" claim of the United States constituted a case where the "nation had no business to arbitrate," the President sent 800 soldiers to Alaska to impress England.[121] London hesitated, but the American criticism of British collaboration

**John Bull in Need of Friends.** Battered by criticism over its war against the Boers in South Africa and challenged by a rising Germany, Great Britain could have used some friends in the early twentieth century. London turned to the United States for one. (*Des Moines Leader* in *Literary Digest,* 1901)

with Germany in chastising Venezuela soon impelled the Foreign Office to eliminate all Anglo-American irritants. On January 24, 1903, Britain agreed to an
American proposal for a mixed boundary commission composed of six "impartial
jurists of repute," three from each side.[122] Roosevelt took no chances. He appointed Senator Lodge and Secretary Root, hardly disinterested judges, to the
commission. He informed them that the 1825 treaty "was undoubtedly intended to
cut off England, which owned the Hinterland, from access to the sea," and
informally warned London he would run the line himself if the commissioners
failed to agree.[123] After persuasion by Prime Minister Balfour, the British commissioner, Lord Chief Justice Alverstone, sided with the Americans, and on
October 20, 1903, by a vote of four to two, the commission officially decided for
the United States. Canada's claims had not been defeated because they lacked
historical foundation. They had been sacrificed as unworthy impediments to
improved Anglo-American relations.

Theodore Roosevelt later commented that the final definition "of the Alaskan
boundary settled the last serious trouble between the British Empire and ourselves," an observation especially pertinent to Anglo-American policies in the
western hemisphere.[124] In February, 1903, shortly after agreeing to the Alaskan
commission, British leaders silenced trans-Atlantic criticism of the intervention in
Venezuela by accepting international adjudication of the Anglo-German claims
and publicly praising the Monroe Doctrine. A month later the British Ambassador,
Sir Michael Herbert, half-jocularly admonished President Roosevelt to "be ready
to police the whole American Continent" since the United States no longer would
permit European nations to collect debts by force.[125] The Roosevelt Corollary
therefore neither surprised nor displeased Great Britain, and the same was true of
the denouement in Panama in 1903. London declined diplomatic assistance to
embattled Colombia prior to its rejection of the Hay-Herrán Treaty, and British
observers complacently watched the subsequent revolution lead to the Hay-
Bunau-Varilla Treaty.

English acquiescence also characterized another Anglo-American settlement of
Roosevelt's presidency, the North Atlantic fisheries dispute. Since 1782 American
fishermen, especially those from Massachusetts, had insisted on retaining their
pre-Revolutionary privileges along the coasts of Newfoundland. The modus
vivendi of 1888, by which they had fished for several years, collapsed in 1905 when
Newfoundland's Parliament placed restrictions on American fishing vessels.
Senator Lodge cried for warships to protect his constituents' livelihood. To avoid a
heated quarrel with Britain over a matter important largely to one state, Roosevelt
proposed, and London accepted, arbitration at the Hague Tribunal. In 1910 the
tribunal ruled that Britain could regulate fishing off Newfoundland if it established
reasonable regulations, that a fisheries commission would hear cases disputing the
definition of reasonableness, and that Americans could fish in large bays, outside a
limit of three miles from shore. This compromise defused the oldest dispute in
American foreign relations and symbolized London's political withdrawal from the
western hemisphere.

The naval retreat had occurred earlier, when the Admiralty abolished the North
Atlantic station based at Halifax. After 1902 the Royal Navy patrolled the Carib-
bean only with an annual visit by a token squadron of cruisers. Admiral Sir John
Fisher, who oversaw this historic retrenchment, wanted to concentrate his heavy

ships in the English Channel and North Sea as monitors of the growing German Navy, but he acted on the dual premise that the United States was "a kindred state with whom we shall never have a parricidal war."[126]

Even the aggressive hemispheric diplomacy of Taft and Wilson did not undermine the Anglo-American rapprochement. Although Britain criticized dollar diplomacy in Latin America, the complaints, in the words of historian Bradford Perkins, "were sporadic and carping rather than a rising crescendo of calls for positive action."[127] Wilson's quixotic efforts to dislodge Huerta from the presidency of Mexico met with little, if any, sympathy in England, but Foreign Secretary Sir Edward Grey tersely laid to rest all talk of a challenge: "His Majesty's Government cannot with any prospect of success embark upon an active counterpolicy to that of the United States, or constitute themselves the champions of Mexico or any of these republics against the United States."[128] In reciprocation, Wilson eliminated the one potentially dangerous British grievance inherited from his predecessor. Late in the Taft Administration, Congress had enacted a measure exempting American intercoastal shippers from payment of tolls at the Panama Canal. British opinion unanimously condemned this shifting of canal maintenance costs to other users. Wilson soon decided that the law unjustly discriminated against foreign shipping, and in June, 1914, Congress revoked the preferential treatment.

In the geographic area of secondary interest to the United States, the Far East, the Anglo-American rapprochement proved less fruitful. London negotiated the alliance with Tokyo in 1902 as a makeweight against Russian pressure upon China and as a means of concentrating more British battleships in home waters. Japan's defeat of Russia in 1904–1905 eliminated the alliance's principal theoretical opponent and removed any serious barriers to Japanese expansionism. The British faced a dilemma. They tried to maintain an alliance now valuable against the mounting German threat without sacrificing the equally vital harmony with the United States, the major power alternately accepting and resisting Japanese expansion. The Taft-Katsura and Root-Takahira exchanges, seemingly exhibiting Washington's acceptance, therefore elicited favorable comment from the British Foreign Office. Secretary of State Knox's neutralization and loan schemes, on the other hand, encountered a mixture of polite discouragement and firm disapproval.

The First World War simply accentuated Anglo-American differences over Japan and China. Britain welcomed Japanese expulsion of Germany from its insular positions in the Pacific and on the Shantung Peninsula of China, and British imperial forces seized all German islands south of the equator. On February 16, 1917, the two allies signed an additional, and secret, treaty pledging reciprocal support for their new territorial claims at the postwar peace conference. This rock lay beneath the deceptively tranquil surface of the Anglo-American wartime coalition, ready to surface when the tides of war receded.

## American Foreign Policy on the Eve of the "Great War"

Prior to the outbreak of the First World War, American policymakers largely adhered to the tradition of aloofness from continental European political and military affairs, as prescribed in Washington's Farewell Address and Jefferson's

**Naval Arms Race.** The vigorous international competition for large navies in the early twentieth century was foreboding. Disarmament talks at The Hague Conferences and arbitration treaties did not curb the arms buildup. Theodore Roosevelt's decision to send the "Great White Fleet" around the world in 1907–1908 may have encouraged both Japan and Germany to speed up their naval programs. (*Detroit News* in *Literary Digest,* 1904)

First Inaugural. Even Theodore Roosevelt, who appeared so impetuous, tampered only once with Europe's balance of power. In 1904 France acquiesced in British control of Egypt, in exchange for primacy in semi-independent Morocco. A year later, Germany decided to test the solidity of the new Anglo-French entente by challenging France's extension of power in Morocco. Speaking at Tangier, the Kaiser belligerently demanded a German political role in Morocco, which France at once refused. After a brief European war scare, in which Britain stood by her ally, Germany asked Roosevelt to induce France and England to convene a conference to settle Morocco's future. On the grounds that world peace was threatened, Roosevelt accepted the personal invitation only after assuring Paris that he was not acting on Berlin's behalf. During the conference, held in early 1906 at Algeciras, Spain, Roosevelt devised a compromise substantively favorable to Paris and persuaded the Kaiser to accept it. This political intervention isolated Germany and reinforced the Anglo-French entente, but it generated criticism at home. Roosevelt's successors made sure they did not violate the American policy of nonentanglement with Europe during the more ominous second Moroccan and Balkan crises preceding the "Great War."

Nonentanglement also doomed the sweeping arbitration treaties that Secretary of State Hay negotiated with several world powers. The Senate, always the jealous guardian of prerogative and aloofness, attached emasculating amendments, leading Roosevelt to withdraw the treaties because they now did "not in the smallest degree facilitate settlements by arbitration, [and] to make them would in no way further the cause of international peace."[129] After 1905 Secretary Root persuaded Roosevelt to accept watered-down bilateral arbitration treaties, and Secretary Bryan later negotiated a series of supplementary "cooling-off" treaties by which nations pledged to refrain from war during international investigations of serious disputes. None of these arrangements, however, effectively bound any of the signatories, and like the Permanent Court of Arbitration at The Hague, they represented a backwater in international diplomacy.

The mainstream of American foreign policy between 1900 and 1914 flowed through the Panama Canal. That momentous political, military, and technological achievement drew the United States physically into the Caribbean and Gulf of Mexico with unprecedented force. After ratification of the Hay–Bunau-Varilla Treaty, the United States became the unchallenged policeman of Central America. For Taft, the treaty "permits us to prevent revolutions" so that "we'll have no more."[130] In East Asia, American power was pale in comparison. The United States was in no position to challenge Japan or England, especially after the formation of the Anglo-Japanese Alliance in 1902 and the defeat of Russia in 1904–1905. As Roosevelt wrote Taft in 1910, the Open Door "completely disappears as soon as a powerful nation determines to disregard it."[131] Nor were American interests in Asia clearly discernible. The vulnerable Philippines needed protection, but diplomatic agreements were the only safeguards that even Theodore Roosevelt could devise, given the remoteness of the islands and congressional distaste for military spending. Beyond the Philippines, many Americans believed in what historian Paul Varg has called "the myth of the China market."[132] Straight, Taft, and Knox conceived of dollar diplomacy as a means of blocking Japanese expansion, sustaining Chinese independence, and stimulating American overseas investments and trade. Wilson's futile revival of the ill-fated consortium was largely a political act aimed at Japan. This persistent but ineffectual opposition to Japanese expansion constituted a most deleterious legacy. To the next generation it bequeathed war in the Pacific.

Another legacy of the 1900–1914 period was less measurable, but nevertheless a long-term consequence: American insensitivity to the nationalism of other peoples. The violent Filipino resistance to American domination, Cuban anger over the interventionist Platt Amendment, Colombian outrage over the "rape" of Panama, and Mexican rejection of Wilsonian meddling, bore witness to the depth of nationalistic sentiments. Like the European powers who were carving up Asia, Africa, and the Middle East, the United States was developing its empire and subjugating peoples, especially in Latin America. Driven by their own brands of nationalism, the imperialist powers trampled on the sovereign rights and national sympathies of others. Whether it was Roosevelt's "big stick," Taft's "dollar diplomacy," or Wilson's missionary zeal to remake flawed national characters, American foreign policy was imperialistic toward many Latin American countries because it prevented their citizens from freely making national choices. The American empire was not one of territorial aggrandizement, but rather of economic and political control, exercised through Marine contingents and financial advisers. (One exception was the purchase from Denmark of the Virgin Islands in 1917 for $25 million, because Washington feared Germany might seize the Danish West Indies.)

The much heralded rapprochement between Britain and the United States also meant mutual respect for each other's empires. Roosevelt, for example, encouraged London to resist firmly native aspirations for independence in India, while the British accepted the American suppression of the Filipinos and United States hegemony in Latin America. American leaders usually spoke favorably of independence for colonial peoples, but independence only after long-term education to make them "fit" and "civilized" enough to govern. In 1910 in Egypt, where Roosevelt applauded Britain's "great work for civilization," the ex-President even lectured restless Moslem nationalists about Christian respect for womanhood.[133]

This United States insensitivity to nationalism in the colonial world was evident especially in the new imperial possession of the Philippines. Although Aguinaldo was captured, Filipino resistance continued for years thereafter. From 1903 to 1914, for example, Artemio Ricarte harassed American military authorities with his hit-and-run tactics. Deported several times, he consistently refused to take an oath of allegiance to the United States. To silence less violent dissenters, the American colonial government imposed the Sedition Act of 1901, which made it unlawful to express any "scurrilous libels" against America.[134] Newspapers were censored and sometimes shut down. Recalcitrant dissidents were jailed. Some economic benefits, improvements in transportation and sanitation, and new educational facilities like the University of the Philippines (1906) accrued to the Filipinos, but American governors helped create an English-speaking, educated elite far removed from the mass of lower-class people. With American direction also came a misplaced pride in things "stateside"—a colonial mentality. Filipino history became "American" history. One Filipino critic wrote that "the history of our ancestors was taken up as if they were strange and foreign peoples who settled in these shores, with whom we had the most tenuous ties. We read about them as if we were tourists in a foreign land."[135]

In 1916, after years of Democratic party pledges, Congress passed and Wilson signed the Jones Act, promising Philippine independence, but setting no date. Thirty years later the United States would in fact relinquish the Philippines, gaining for itself the accolade from apologists of being a "good" imperialist, or—as historian Dexter Perkins has put it—an imperialist with an "uneasy conscience."[136] "Uneasy conscience" or not, Americans as imperialists behaved not unlike the European imperial warriors they so roundly condemned. Indeed, that phrase might better be applied to the American decision to intervene in the "Great War" that broke out in 1914, which permitted the United States to extend further the foreign interests it had cultivated in the previous two decades.

# Further Reading for the Period 1900–1914

For general studies of American foreign policy and the chief diplomats of this period, see Howard K. Beale, *Theodore Roosevelt and the Rise of America to World Power* (1956), Barton J. Bernstein and Franklin A. Leib, "Progressive Republican Senators and American Imperialism, 1898–1916: A Reappraisal," *Mid-America* (1968), John M. Blum, *The Republican Roosevelt* (1954), David H. Burton, *Theodore Roosevelt: Confident Imperialist* (1968), Paolo E. Coletta, *The Presidency of William Howard Taft* (1973) and *William Jennings Bryan* (1964–1969), John M. Cooper, Jr., "Progressivism and American Foreign Policy," *Mid America* (1969), Raymond A. Esthus, *Theodore Roosevelt and the International Rivalries* (1970), Norman A. Graebner, ed., *An Uncertain Tradition: American Secretaries of State in the Twentieth Century* (1961), William H. Harbaugh, *The Life and Times of Theodore Roosevelt* (1975), Philip C. Jessup, *Elihu Root* (1938), P. C. Kennedy, "LaFollette's Foreign Policy: From Imperialism to Anti-Imperialism," *Wisconsin Magazine of History* (1963), William Leuchtenberg, "Progressivism and Imperialism," *Mississippi Valley Historical Review* (1952), Ralph E. Minger, *William Howard Taft and United States Foreign Policy: The Apprenticeship Years, 1900–1908* (1975), Julius W. Pratt, *America's Colonial Experiment* (1950) and *Challenge and Reaction* (1967), Henry F. Pringle, *The Life and Times of William Howard Taft* (1939) and *Theodore Roosevelt* (1956), Walter V. and Marie V. Scholes, *The Foreign Policies of the Taft Administration* (1970), and E. Berkeley Tompkins, *Anti-Imperialism in the United States: The Great Debate, 1890–1920* (1970). For studies of Woodrow Wilson see the "further reading" section for Chapter 8.

United States relations with Latin America are examined in Peter Calvert, *The Mexican Revolution, 1910–1914* (1968), Clarence C. Clendenen, *The United States and Pancho Villa* (1961), Howard F. Cline, *The United States and Mexico* (1963), Kenneth J. Grieb, *The United States and Huerta* (1969), David Healy, *Gunboat Diplomacy in the Wilson Era: The U.S. Navy in Haiti, 1915–1916* (1976) and *The United States in Cuba, 1898–1902* (1963), James H. Hitchman, *Leonard Wood and Cuban Independence, 1898–1902* (1971), Warren G. Kneer, *Great Britain and the Caribbean, 1901–1913* (1975), Lester D. Langley, *Struggle for the American Mediterranean: United States-European Rivalry in the Gulf-Caribbean, 1776–1904* (1976), Allan R. Millett, *The Politics of Intervention: The Military Occupation of Cuba, 1906–1909* (1968), Dwight C. Miner, *The Fight for the Panama Route* (1940), Dana Munro, *Intervention and Dollar Diplomacy in the Caribbean, 1900–1921* (1946), Dexter Perkins, *The Monroe Doctrine, 1867–1907* (1937), Robert E. Quirk, *An Affair of Honor: Woodrow Wilson and the Occupation of Veracruz* (1962), Hans Schmidt, *The United States Occupation of Haiti, 1915–1934* (1971), and Karl M. Schmitt, *Mexico and the United States, 1821–1973* (1974).

America's interaction with Asia is the subject of Burton F. Beers, *Vain Endeavor: Robert Lansing's Attempt to End the American-Japanese Rivalry* (1962), Warren Cohen, *America's Response to China* (1971), Roy W. Curry, *Woodrow Wilson and Far Eastern Policy, 1913–1921* (1957), Raymond A. Esthus, *Theodore Roosevelt and Japan* (1966) and "The Changing Concept of the Open Door, 1899–1910," *Mississippi Valley Historical Review* (1959), A. Whitney Griswold, *The Far Eastern Policy of the United States* (1938), Akira Iriye, *Across the Pacific* (1967) and *Pacific Estrangement: Japanese and American Expansion, 1897–1911* (1972), Jerry Israel, *Progressivism and the Open Door: America and China, 1905–1921* (1971), Delber L. McKee, *Chinese Exclusion versus the Open Door Policy, 1900–1906* (1976), Charles E. Neu, *An Uncertain Friendship: Theodore Roosevelt and Japan, 1906–1909* (1967) and *The Troubled Encounter* (1975),

William J. Pomeroy, *American Neo-Colonialism: Its Emergence in the Philippines and Asia* (1970), Peter Stanley, *A Nation in the Making: The Philippines and the United States, 1899–1921* (1974), Eugene P. Trani, *The Treaty of Portsmouth* (1969), Paul A. Varg, *The Making of a Myth: The United States and China, 1897–1912* (1968), and Charles Vevier, *The United States and China, 1906–1913* (1955).

The history of United States relations with Europe is discussed in A. E. Campbell, *Great Britain and the United States, 1895–1903* (1960), Charles S. Campbell, *Anglo-American Understanding, 1898–1903* (1957), Calvin Davis, *The United States and the First Hague Peace Conference* (1962), Raymond A. Esthus, *Theodore Roosevelt and the International Rivalries* (1970), and Bradford Perkins, *The Great Rapprochement: England and the United States, 1895–1914* (1968).

Economic, racial, and military ingredients in American foreign policy are described in Richard D. Challener, *Admirals, Generals, and American Foreign Policy, 1898–1914* (1973), Roger Daniels, *The Politics of Prejudice: The Anti-Japanese Movement in California and the Struggle for Japanese Exclusion* (1962), Rubin F. Weston, *Racism in United States Imperialism* (1972), and Mira Wilkins, *The Emergence of Multinational Enterprise: American Business Abroad from the Colonial Era to 1914* (1970).

For brief biographies see John A. Garraty, ed., *Encyclopedia of American Biography* (1974).

For other readings, see Wilton B. Fowler, ed., *American Diplomatic History Since 1890* (1975) and the following notes.

## Notes to Chapter 7

1. This and previous quotations from U.S. Congress, *Diplomatic History of the Panama Canal*, Senate Document 474 (1914), pp. 345–363.
2. Elting E. Morison, ed., *The Letters of Theodore Roosevelt* (Cambridge: Harvard University Press, 1951–1954; 8 vols.), II, 1185–1187.
3. Quoted in Gerstle Mack, *The Land Divided* (New York: Alfred A. Knopf, 1944), p. 417.
4. Dwight C. Miner, *The Fight for the Panama Route* (New York: Columbia University Press, 1940), p. 75.
5. *Diplomatic History of the Canal*, p. 261.
6. Quoted in Miner, *Fight for the Panama Route*, p. 275.
7. Quoted in Henry F. Pringle, *Theodore Roosevelt* (New York: Harcourt, Brace, 1931), p. 311.
8. Quoted in Howard K. Beale, *Theodore Roosevelt and the Rise of America to World Power* (Baltimore: The Johns Hopkins Press, 1956), p. 33.
9. Quoted in Miner, *Fight for the Panama Route*, p. 251.
10. *New York World*, June 14, 1903.
11. Quoted in Pringle, *Roosevelt*, p. 311.
12. Quoted in Tyler Dennett, *John Hay* (New York: Dodd, Mead, 1933), p. 377.
13. Quoted in Mack, *Land Divided*, p. 459.
14. Quoted in Miner, *Fight for the Panama Route*, pp. 379–380.
15. James D. Richardson, ed., *A Compilation of the Messages and Papers of the Presidents, 1789–1897* (Washington, D.C.: Government Printing Office, 1896–1899; 10 vols.), IX, 6919–6923.
16. *New York Times*, March 25, 1911.
17. William H. Harbaugh, *The Life and Times of Theodore Roosevelt* (New York: Oxford University Press, 1975; rev. ed.), p. 197.
18. Ronald H. Spector, "'Professors of War': The Naval War College and the Modern American Navy" (Ph.D. dissertation, Yale University, 1967).
19. Quoted in Kenneth J. Hagan, "Alfred Thayer Mahan: Turning America Back to the Sea," in Frank Merli and Theodore Wilson, eds., *Makers of American Diplomacy* (New York: Charles Scribner's Sons, 1974), p. 298.
20. John M. Cooper, Jr., "Progressivism and American Foreign Policy: A Reconsideration," *Mid-America*, LI (October, 1969), 261.
21. Quoted in John Morton Blum, *The Republican Roosevelt* (New York: Atheneum, 1973 [1954]), p. 127.
22. Quoted in Beale, *Theodore Roosevelt*, p. 77 and G. Wallace Chessman, *Theodore Roosevelt and the Politics of Power* (Boston: Little, Brown, 1969), p. 70.
23. Quoted in Beale, *Theodore Roosevelt*, p. 140.
24. *Ibid.*, p. 13.
25. Quoted in Foster Rhea Dulles, "John Hay," in Norman A. Graebner, ed., *An Uncertain Tradition: American Secretaries of State in the Twentieth Century* (New York: McGraw-Hill, 1961), p. 24.
26. Quoted in Charles W. Toth, "Elihu Root," *ibid.*, p. 41.
27. Quoted in Richard W. Leopold, *Elihu Root and the Conservative Tradition* (Boston: Little, Brown, 1954), p. 50.

28. Quoted in David H. Burton, *Theodore Roosevelt: Confident Imperialist* (Philadelphia: University of Pennsylvania Press, 1968), p. 97, and *Congressional Record, XXXV* (December 3, 1901), 82–83.

29. Quoted in Ralph E. Minger, *William Howard Taft and United States Foreign Policy: The Apprenticeship Years, 1900–1908* (Urbana: University of Illinois Press, 1975), p. 179.

30. Quoted in Ray S. Baker, *Woodrow Wilson: Life and Letters* (Garden City, N.Y.: Doubleday, Doran, 1927–1939; 8 vols.), IV, 289.

31. Jerry Israel, "'For God, for China and for Yale'—The Open Door in Action," *American Historical Review, LXXV* (February, 1970), 807.

32. *Foreign Relations of the United States, 1898* (Washington, D.C.: Government Printing Office, 1901), pp. lxvi–lxvii.

33. Quoted in Philip C. Jessup, *Elihu Root* (New York: Dodd, Mead, 1938; 2 vols.), I, 286–287.

34. Quoted in David F. Healy, *The United States in Cuba, 1898–1902* (Madison: University of Wisconsin Press, 1963), p. 133.

35. *Congressional Record, XXXIV* (February 26, 1901), 3036.

36. Quoted in Healy, *United States in Cuba*, p. 177.

37. Quoted in Hermann Hagedorn, *Leonard Wood, A Biography* (New York: Harper and Brothers, 1931; 2 vols.), I, 362 and Healy, *United States in Cuba*, p. 178.

38. Quoted in Russell H. Fitzgibbon, *Cuba and the United States, 1900–1935* (New York: Russell & Russell, 1964 [1935]), p. 112.

39. Quoted in Allan R. Millett, *The Politics of Intervention* (Columbus: Ohio State University Press, 1968), p. 72.

40. Quoted in Burton, *Theodore Roosevelt*, p. 106.

41. Quoted in Millett, *Politics of Intervention*, p. 78.

42. Richardson, *Messages of the Presidents*, X, 7436–7437.

43. Quoted in Minger, *William Howard Taft*, p. 136.

44. Lawrence F. Abbott, ed., *The Letters of Archie Butt* (Garden City, N.Y.: Doubleday, Page, 1924), p. 325.

45. Fitzgibbon, *Cuba and the United States*, p. 145 and Millett, *Politics of Intervention*, p. 267.

46. Fred L. Israel, ed., *The State of the Union Messages of the Presidents, 1790–1966* (New York: Chelsea House, 1967; 3 vols.), II, 2038.

47. Morison, *Letters of Roosevelt*, III, 116.

48. *Ibid.*, IV, 1156.

49. *Literary Digest, XXV* (December 20, 1902), 823–824.

50. Quoted in Dexter Perkins, *The Monroe Doctrine, 1867–1907* (Baltimore: The Johns Hopkins Press, 1937), p. 358.

51. Quoted *ibid.*, p. 360.

52. Quoted *ibid.*, p. 420.

53. Quoted in Lloyd Gardner, "A Progressive Foreign Policy, 1900–1921," in William A. Williams, ed., *From Colony to Empire* (New York: John Wiley and Sons, 1972), p. 218.

54. Quoted in Perkins, *Monroe Doctrine*, p. 420.

55. Israel, *State of the Union Messages*, II, 2134.

56. Quoted in Jessup, *Root*, I, 471.

57. Elihu Root, *Latin America and the United States* (Cambridge: Harvard University Press, 1917), p. 275.

58. *Foreign Relations, 1912* (Washington, D.C.: Government Printing Office, 1919), p. 1091.

59. *Congressional Record, L* (November 3, 1913), 5845.

60. *Foreign Relations, 1913* (Washington, D.C.: Government Printing Office, 1920), p. 426.

61. Quoted in Dana G. Munro, *Intervention and Dollar Diplomacy in the Caribbean* (Princeton: Princeton University Press, 1964), p. 336.

62. Quoted in David F. Healy, *Gunboat Diplomacy in the Wilson Era* (Madison: University of Wisconsin Press, 1976), p. 109.

63. Quoted *ibid.*, p. 131.

64. *Ibid.*, p. 205.

65. Quoted in Munro, *Intervention and Dollar Diplomacy*, p. 155.

66. *Ibid.*, p. 160.

67. *Ibid.*, p. 181.

68. Quoted in Baker, *Wilson*, IV, 436.

69. Quoted in Paolo E. Coletta, *The Presidency of William Howard Taft* (Lawrence: University Press of Kansas, 1973), p. 176.

70. *Foreign Relations, 1912*, p. 846.

71. Quoted in Howard F. Cline, *The United States and Mexico* (New York: Atheneum, 1963; rev. ed.), p. 144.

72. Quoted in Arthur S. Link, *Wilson: The New Freedom* (Princeton: Princeton University Press, 1956), p. 360.

73. Quoted in Arthur S. Link, *Wilson: Confusions and Crises, 1915–1916* (Princeton: Princeton University Press, 1964), p. 317.

74. Quoted in Link, *Wilson: New Freedom*, p. 358.

75. Quoted *ibid.*, p. 360.

76. Quoted in Kenneth J. Grieb, *The United States and Huerta* (Lincoln: University of Nebraska Press, 1969), p. 137.

77. Quoted in Link, *Wilson: New Freedom*, pp. 386–387.

78. Quoted in Grieb, *United States and Huerta*, p. 137.

79. Quoted *ibid.*, p. 135.

80. Quoted in Robert E. Quirk, *An Affair of Honor* (Lexington: University of Kentucky Press, 1962), p. 26.

81. Quoted *ibid.*, pp. 32, 49.

82. Ray Stannard Baker and William E. Dodd, *Public Papers of Woodrow Wilson: The New Democracy* (New York: Harper and Brothers, 1926; 2 vols.), II, 102.

83. Quoted in Henry C. Lodge, *The Senate and the League of Nations* (New York: Charles Scribner's Sons, 1925), p. 18 and Cary T. Grayson, *Woodrow Wilson: An Intimate Memoir* (New York: Holt, Rinehart and Winston, 1960), p. 30.

84. Quoted in Link, *Wilson: New Freedom*, p. 402.

85. Quoted in Grieb, *United States and Huerta*, p. 160.

86. *Washington Post*, June 3, 1914.

87. Quoted in Arthur S. Link, *Wilson: The Struggle for Neutrality, 1914–1915* (Princeton: Princeton University Press, 1960), p. 239.

88. Quoted *ibid.*, p. 491.

89. Quoted in Herbert M. Mason, Jr., *The Great Pursuit* (New York: Random House, 1970), p. 227.

90. Morison, *Letters of Roosevelt*, III, 497–498.

91. Akira Iriye, *The Cold War in Asia* (Englewood Cliffs, N.J.: Prentice Hall, 1974), p. 35.

92. Morison, *Letters of Roosevelt*, IV, 724, 761.

93. *Ibid.*, p. 1222.

94. Quoted in Raymond A. Esthus, *Theodore Roosevelt and Japan* (Seattle: University of Washington Press, 1966), p. 101.

95. Quoted *ibid.*, p. 103.

96. Quoted in Charles E. Neu, *An Uncertain Friendship* (Cambridge: Harvard University Press, 1967), pp. 36, 47.

97. Quoted in Akira Iriye, *Across the Pacific* (New York: Harcourt, Brace & World, 1967), p. 107.

98. Quoted in Esthus, *Roosevelt and Japan*, p. 149.

99. Quoted *ibid.*, p. 173.

100. Morison, *Letters of Roosevelt*, V, 729–730, 761–762.

101. Quoted in Iriye, *Across the Pacific*, p. 109.

102. Quoted *ibid.*

103. Quoted in Herbert Croly, *Willard Straight* (New York: Macmillan, 1925), p. 276.

104. A. Whitney Griswold, *The Far Eastern Policy of the United States* (New Haven: Yale University Press, 1964 [c. 1938]), p. 157.

105. *Foreign Relations, 1909* (Washington, D.C.: Government Printing Office, 1914), p. 178.

106. Quoted in Croly, *Straight*, pp. 392–393.

107. Quoted in Iriye, *Across the Pacific*, p. 126.

108. *Ibid.*, p. 127.

109. Quoted in Link, *Wilson: New Freedom*, p. 286.

110. *New York Times*, May 5, 1913.

111. Quoted in Roger Daniels, *The Politics of Prejudice* (New York: Atheneum, 1968 [c. 1962]), p. 59.

112. Quoted in David F. Houston, *Eight Years with Wilson's Cabinet* (Garden City, N.Y.: Doubleday, 1926; 2 vols.), I, 66.

113. Quoted in Link, *Wilson: New Freedom*, pp. 300–301.

114. *Foreign Relations, 1915* (Washington, D.C.: Government Printing Office, 1924), p. 146.

115. *Foreign Relations, 1922* (Washington, D.C.: Government Printing Office, 1938; 2 vols.), II, 591.

116. Quoted in Beale, *Theodore Roosevelt*, pp. 81, 152.

117. Morison, *Letters of Roosevelt*, II, 1186–87.

118. Quoted in Beale, *Theodore Roosevelt*, p. 104.

119. Bradford Perkins, *The Great Rapprochement: England and the United States, 1895–1914* (New York: Atheneum, 1968).

120. Quoted in Charles S. Campbell, *Anglo-American Understanding, 1898–1903* (Baltimore: The Johns Hopkins Press, 1957), p. 190.

121. Quoted in Alexander E. Campbell, *Great Britain and the United States* (Westport, Conn.: Greenwood Press, 1974 [c. 1960]), pp. 105–106 and Morison, *Letters of Roosevelt*, III, 66.

122. Quoted in Perkins, *Great Rapprochement*, p. 168.

123. Quoted *ibid.*, p. 169.

124. Morison, *Letters of Roosevelt*, VII, 28.

125. Quoted in Perkins, *Monroe Doctrine*, p. 364.

126. Quoted in Arthur J. Marder, *From the Dreadnought to Scapa Flow: The Royal Navy in the Fisher Era, 1904–1919* (London: Oxford University Press, 1961–1970; 5 vols.), I, 125.

127. Perkins, *Great Rapprochement*, p. 195.

128. Quoted *ibid.*, p. 201.

129. Morison, *Letters of Roosevelt*, IV, 1119.

130. Quoted in Minger, *William Howard Taft*, p. 106.

131. Quoted in Jerry Israel, *Progressivism and the Open Door: America and China, 1905–1921* (Pittsburgh: University of Pittsburgh Press, 1971), p. 96.

132. Paul A. Varg, *The Making of a Myth* (East Lansing: Michigan State University Press, 1968), p. 36.

133. Quoted in Burton, *Theodore Roosevelt*, p. 190.

134. Quoted in Teodoro A. Agoncillo, *A Short History of the Philippines* (New York: New American Library, 1969), p. 156.

135. Quoted *ibid.*, p. 120.

136. Dexter Perkins, *The American Approach to Foreign Policy* (New York: Atheneum, 1968 [c. 1962], rev. ed.), p. 31.

**Mass Grave of *Lusitania* Victims.** In Queenstown, Ireland, a large burial ground holds more than a hundred victims of the *Lusitania* disaster of 1915, which rudely brought World War I to American consciousness. (U.S. War Department, National Archives)

# 8  World Reform
Through World War, 1914–1920

## Diplomatic Crossroad: The Sinking of the *Lusitania*, 1915

"Perfectly safe; safer than the trolley cars in New York City," claimed a Cunard Line official the morning of May 1, 1915.[1] Indeed, the majestic *Lusitania*, with her watertight compartments and swiftness, seemed invulnerable. The coal-burning steamer had already crossed the Atlantic one hundred times, and in 1907, the year of her maiden voyage, the *Lusitania* had set a speed record for transatlantic crossings. The British government, inspired by a German challenge to Britannia's supremacy of the seas, loaned Cunard the money to build this fast passenger liner, over twice as long as an American football field. The British Admiralty dictated many of the ship's specifications, so that the 30,396-ton vessel could be armed if necessary during war, and stipulated that half the *Lusitania*'s crew belong to the naval reserves.

"Lucy's" business was pleasure, not war. Resplendent with tapestries and carpets, the luxurious floating palace dazzled her passengers. One suitably impressed American politician found the ship "more beautiful than Solomon's Temple—and big enough to hold all his wives."[2] The 1,257 travelers were attended by a crew of 702 for the 101st transatlantic voyage, leaving from New York's Pier 54 on May 1; among them were renowned theatrical producer Charles Frohman and the multimillionaire playboy Alfred Vanderbilt. Deep in the *Lusitania*'s storage area rested a cargo of foodstuffs and contraband (4.2 million rounds of ammunition for Remington rifles, 1,250 cases of empty shrapnel shells, and eighteen cases of nonexplosive fuses). The Cunarder thus carried, said a State Department official, both "babies and bullets."[3]

In the morning newspapers of May 1 a rather unusual announcement, placed by the Imperial German Embassy, appeared beside the Cunard Line advertisement. The German "Notice" warned passengers that Germany and Britain were at war and that the waters around the British Isles constituted a war zone wherein British vessels were subject to destruction. One passenger called the warning

"tommy-rot" and only a handful canceled their bookings on the *Lusitania*. Few transferred to the *New York*, ready to sail under the American flag that same day. There was little time to shift vessels. Anyway, the unattractive *New York* was slow and for the American "smart set" socially unacceptable. Cunard officials at dockside reassured voyagers, and the State Department did not intercede to warn the one hundred and ninety-seven American passengers away from the *Lusitania*. Most Americans, in their "business-as-usual" attitude, accepted the statement of the Cunard Line agent: "The truth is that the *Lusitania* is the safest boat on the sea. She is too fast for any submarine. No German war vessel can get her or near her."[4] During this very time, Secretary of State William Jennings Bryan was trying to persuade President Woodrow Wilson that Americans should be prohibited from traveling on belligerent ships. He was making little headway.

Captained by an old sea dog, William T. Turner, the *Lusitania* steamed from New York into the Atlantic at half past noon on May 1. Manned by an ill-trained crew (the best had been called to war duty), "Lucy" enjoyed a smooth crossing in calm water. Perfunctory lifesaving drills were held, but complacency about the submarine danger characterized captain, crew, and passengers alike. Passengers joked about torpedoes, played cards, consumed gallons of liquor, and listened to concerts on deck. During the evening of May 6, as the *Lusitania* neared Ireland, Turner received a warning from the Naval Centre at Queenstown: "Submarines active off south coast of Ireland."[5] Earlier in the day two ships had been sunk in that vicinity. Captain Turner posted lookouts but took no other precautions, even after receiving follow-up warnings. He had standing orders from the Admiralty to take a zigzag path, to stay away from headlands, to steer a midchannel course, and to steam full speed—all to make it difficult for lurking German submarines to zero in on their targets. But Turner ignored these instructions.

May 7 was a beautiful day with unusually good visibility, recorded Lieutenant Walter Schwieger in his log. The young commander was piloting his U-20 submarine along the southern Irish coast. That morning it had submerged because

**The *Lusitania* and U-20.** The majestic passenger liner was sunk by German submarine U-20 off the coast of Ireland on May 7, 1915. (Peabody Museum of Salem; Bundesarchiv)

**Architects of Disaster.** Captain William T. Turner (1856–1933), left, of the *Lusitania* and Lieutenant Walter Schwieger (1885–1917) of U-20 never saw one another, but because their nations were at war, they were enemies nonetheless. (U.S. War Department, National Archives; Bundesarchiv)

British ships, capable of ramming the fragile, slender craft, were passing by. Schwieger surfaced at 1:45 P.M. and within a short time spotted a four-funneled ship in the distance. Carrying general orders to sink British vessels, Schwieger quickly submerged and set a track toward the *Lusitania,* eager to take advantage of this chance meeting (his specific orders, had he followed them, would have placed the U-20 near Liverpool). At 700 meters the U-20 released a torpedo. The deadly missile dashed through the water tailed by bubbles. A watchman on the starboard bow saw it and cried out. Captain Turner was unaccountably below deck, where he should not have been in those dangerous waters; and for some reason the bridge did not hear the lookout's warning called through a megaphone one minute before the torpedo struck. Had the message been received, the ship *might* have veered sharply and avoided danger. Thirty seconds before disaster a lookout in the crow's nest spied the torpedo and his frightened message sounded the alarm. Turner rushed to the bridge. He did not see the torpedo, but he heard the explosion as it ripped into the *Lusitania.* Schwieger watched through his periscope as the mighty vessel leaned on its starboard side and its bow dipped. The gold letters "LUSITANIA" became visible to the excited officer. "Great confusion ensues on board," he noted.[6] Panic swept the passengers as they stumbled about the listing decks or groped in the darkness below when the cut-off of electric power stranded elevators. Steam whistled from punctured boilers. Less than half the lifeboats were lowered; some capsized or were launched only partially loaded. Within eighteen minutes the "Queen of the Atlantic" sank, killing 1,198—128 of them Americans. A survivor remembered that when the *Lusitania* went down, "it sounded like a terrible moan."[7]

President Wilson had just completed a Cabinet meeting in the White House when he received the first sketchy news of the disaster. He was stunned, as was his special assistant Colonel Edward House, then dining in London with American Ambassador Walter Hines Page. "We shall be at war with Germany within a month," uttered the pro-British House, who, interestingly enough, had sailed on the *Lusitania* in February and had witnessed, much to his surprise, the hoisting of an American flag as the ship neared the Irish coast.[8] Secretary Bryan worried about war, and two days later he wrote the President that "ships carrying contraband should be prohibited from carrying passengers. . . . Germany has a right to prevent contraband going to the Allies and a ship carrying contraband should not rely upon passengers to protect her from attack—it would be like putting women and children in front of an army."[9] Bellicose ex-President Theodore Roosevelt was in Syracuse when he learned about the tragedy; he soon seared the air with his declaration that "this represents not merely piracy, but piracy on a vaster scale of murder than old-time pirates ever practiced."[10] American after American voiced horror and demanded that the President express the nation's collective moral indignation. But few wanted war. A troubled Wilson secluded himself to ponder an American response to this ghastly event. Just months before, he had warned Berlin that it would be held strictly accountable for the loss of any American ships or lives because of submarine warfare. "For the President of the United States," historian Arthur S. Link has noted, "this was by far the severest testing that he had ever known."[11]

After three days of reflection, which included reading memoranda from Bryan urging warnings to Americans not to travel on Allied ships carrying contraband, Wilson fulfilled a previous commitment and spoke in Philadelphia on May 10. His

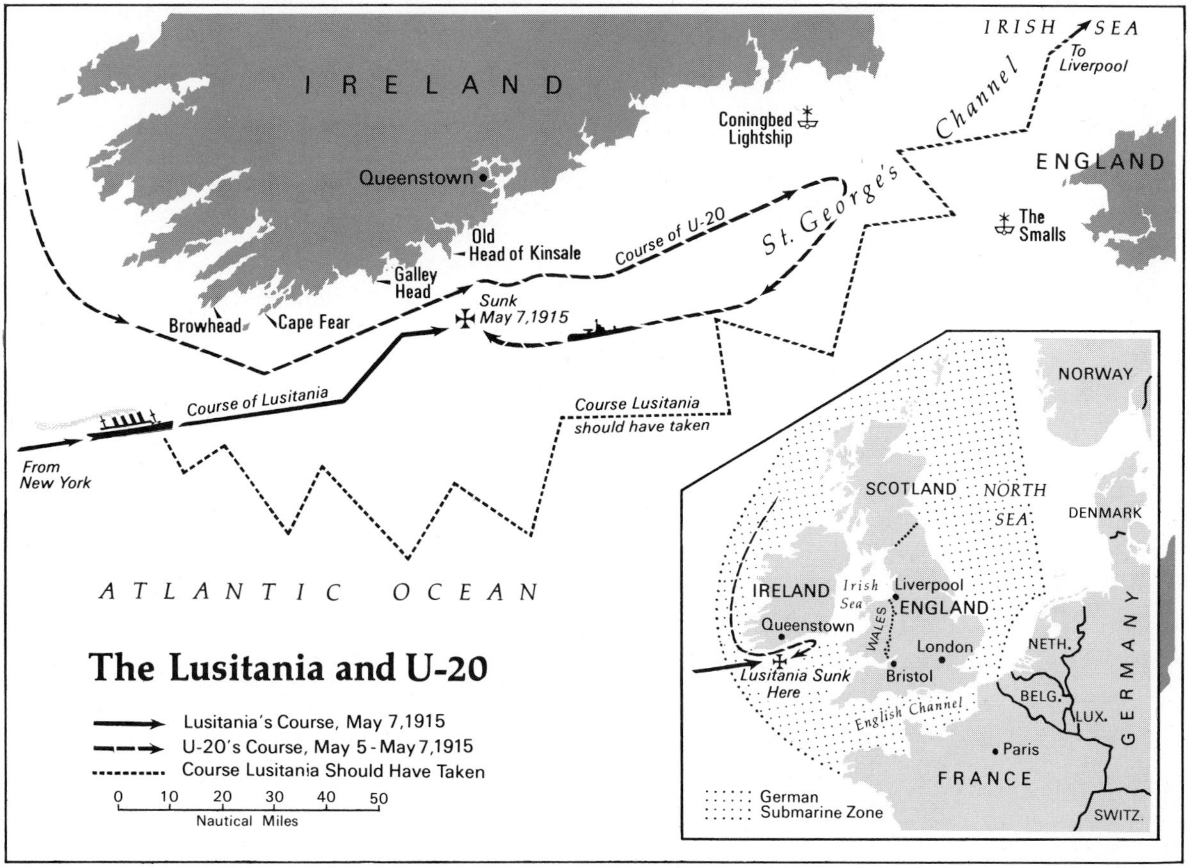
IRELAND
IRISH SEA
To Liverpool
Coningbed Lightship
St. George's Channel
ENGLAND
Queenstown
Old Head of Kinsale
Course of U-20
The Smalls
Galley Head
Browhead
Cape Fear
Sunk May 7,1915
Course of Lusitania
Course Lusitania should have taken
From New York
ATLANTIC OCEAN
Lusitania's Course, May 7,1915
U-20's Course, May 5 - May 7,1915
Course Lusitania Should Have Taken
0 10 20 30 40 50
Nautical Miles
NORWAY
SCOTLAND
NORTH SEA
DENMARK
IRELAND
Irish Sea
Liverpool
ENGLAND
WALES
Queenstown
London
NETH.
Lusitania Sunk Here
Bristol
BELG.
LUX.
GERMANY
English Channel
Paris
FRANCE
German Submarine Zone
SWITZ.

**The Lusitania and U-20**

words, much misunderstood, suggested he had no backbone: "There is such a thing as a man being too proud to fight. There is such a thing as a nation being so right that it does not need to convince others by force that it is right."[12] Both cheers and boos echoed across the nation, and Wilson regretted his impromptu choice of words. The next morning he told the Cabinet what he had decided. He would send a note to Berlin insisting that Americans had a right to travel upon the high seas and demanding a disavowal by the German government of the inhumane acts of its submarine commanders. Bryan approved this first "*Lusitania* note," but with a heavy heart, fearing war. Long upset about an apparent American double standard in protesting more against German than British violations of American neutral rights, the secretary pleaded with Wilson to send a simultaneous protest note to London. But only one note went out on May 13—to Berlin: "The Imperial Government will not expect the United States to omit any word or any act necessary to the performance of its sacred duty of maintaining the rights of the United States and its citizens and of safeguarding their free exercise and enjoyment."[13] In short, end submarine warfare, or else.

The German government was much less ecstatic than the German Navy about the destruction of the *Lusitania.* Chancellor Theobold von Bethmann-Hollweg had more than once chastised the Navy for inviting war with the United States through submarine attacks on neutral or Allied merchant vessels. On May 28 he sent an evasive reply to Wilson's note. The *Lusitania* case could not be settled, it read, until certain questions were clarified. The German note claimed that the ship was armed, that it carried munitions, and that it, like other merchantmen, had orders to ram submarines. Germany asked Washington to investigate. One angry American newspaper thought the reply "the answer of an outlaw who assumes no obligation toward society."[14] Nevertheless, the German reply raised serious issues.

Wilson convened the Cabinet on June 1 and asked for advice. When one member recommended a strong note demanding observance of American rights, another suggested as well a note to England to protest British interference with American commerce. Debate became heated. A majority denounced the idea of simultaneous notes. Bryan, obviously under strain, remarked that the Cabinet was pro-Ally. Wilson quickly rebuked him for "unfair and unjust" comments.[15] After this curt exchange, tension grew between Bryan and Wilson. Over the next days Wilson worked on a second "*Lusitania* note." This note, arguing the case for humanity, vigorously called for an end to warfare by submarine, which could not, given its method of attack, abide by the rules of reason and justice. Wilson rejected Bryan's plea for a warning to passengers and a protest note to England. A man of conscience, Bryan could no longer work for a President with whom he so profoundly differed. Realizing he was probably wrecking his own political career, he quietly resigned on June 8. Privately he complained to Wilson that "Colonel House has been Secretary of State, not I, and I have never had your full confidence."[16] Wilson, relieved that he no longer had to face Bryan, went to the golf links to relax and to free himself from the blinding headaches of the past several days. Bryan told a friend: "The President is wrong and history will not sustain him."[17]

Other notes on the *Lusitania* and the question of neutral rights on the seas would follow over the succeeding months. The *Lusitania* disaster was not forgotten, but diplomats in Washington and Berlin permitted it to drop from the front pages of newspapers. The crux of the issue was this: the United States insisted that Germany admit it had committed an illegal act; but Germany, unwilling to abandon one of its few effective weapons against British mastery of the ocean, refused to admit wrongdoing and asked for arbitration. Wilson grew impatient in early 1916, apparently ready to sever diplomatic relations with Berlin. Germany sought a compromise. On February 4 it expressed regret over the American deaths and offered to pay an indemnity (eventually paid in the early 1920s). Semanticists will debate whether this constituted a formal apology, but it surely did not equal an admission of guilt. Nevertheless, Wilson and his new Secretary of State Robert Lansing, eager to drop the *Lusitania* from their list of diplomatic squabbles, accepted what they recognized as a German concession.

Although a diplomatic settlement had been reached, the horrible deaths from the sinking of the *Lusitania* were etched on American memories. The torpedoing of the magnificent Cunarder represented a benchmark in German-American relations and the era of World War I. The Germans suffered a propaganda loss of significant proportions, as Englishmen and Americans alike depicted the "Huns" as depraved. The *Lusitania* disaster became a "naval victory worse than a defeat."[18] The sinking also hardened Wilson's opinion of Germany. The President refused henceforth to make diplomatic life easier for the Germans by simultaneously protesting British infractions. No, Germany could not count on equal treatment. The British were violating property rights, but the Germans were violating human rights. He also refused to warn Americans away from belligerent ships. In short, if a U-boat attacked a British ship with Americans aboard, Germany would have to take the consequences. Wilson did not reveal those consequences exactly, but the logical implication was war—just what Bryan feared. His resignation had placed pro-Ally Robert Lansing in the secretaryship of state. After the *Lusitania* crisis, Lansing recalled, he held the "conviction that we would ultimately become an ally of Great Britain."[19] The sinking of the *Lusitania* pointed up, for all to see, the complexities, contradictions, and uncertainties inherent in American neutrality during the European phase of the First World War, 1914–1917.

## The Unreality of Neutrality

Woodrow Wilson was virtually his own secretary of state during those troubled years. His secretary of the interior remarked that the President was "one of those men made by nature to tread the winepress alone."[20] British Prime Minister Lloyd George put it less kindly. Wilson, he said, "believed in mankind but . . . distrusted all men."[21] The President defined the overall character of American foreign policy—what historians call "Wilsonianism." Above all else, Wilson stood for an *open* world unencumbered by imperialism, war, or revolution. Barriers to trade and democracy had to be torn down, and secret diplomacy had to give way to public negotiations. The right of self-determination would force the collapse of empires. Constitutional procedures would replace revolution. A free-market, humanized capitalism would insure democracy. Disarmament programs would restrict the weapons of war. The economic competition that led to war would be harnessed by the Open Door of equal trade and investment opportunity. Wilson, like so many Americans, believed that the United States was exceptional among nations, that it was the redeemer nation. His reformist, inherently expansionist zeal, often called idealism, blended with realism. The President knew the nation's economic and strategic needs and devised a foreign policy that protected them. Yet many Americans questioned his definition of the national interest and feared that his world reforming efforts might invite war, dissipate American resources, and undermine reform at home. Hence Wilson led a divided nation, as his differences with Bryan suggested.

Few Americans, Wilson included, desired war, of course. Most watched in shock as the European nations savagely slashed at one another in 1914. Americans of the progressive reform era found it difficult to argue now that decent men had abolished immoral and barbaric war. The progressive faith in man's ability to right wrongs, the belief that war was part of the decadent past, the conviction that civilization had advanced too far for such blood-letting—all were ruthlessly challenged. It had seemed before 1914 that the new machine guns, howitzers, submarines, and dreadnoughts were simply too awesome to be unleashed by fair-minded human beings. The outbreak of World War I smashed illusions and tested innocence. "We were not used to smelling blood from vast human slaughterhouses," recalled reformer William Allen White.[22] The shock did not become despair, despite the horrible news of poison gas, U-boats, and civilian casualties. The "progressive" era was a time of optimism, and Americans, particularly the crusading Wilson, sought to retrieve the happier moments of the past by assuming the role of civilized instructors. America would help Europe come to its senses by teaching it the rules of human conduct. The carnage explained why the mission was necessary. In 1915 alone France suffered 1.3 million casualties, 330,000 of whom were deaths. For Germany the figure was 848,000, and 170,000 deaths. Britain followed with 313,000 casualties, and 73,000 deaths.

**Woodrow Wilson (1856–1924).** Scholar, professor, university president (Princeton), and governor (New Jersey), Woodrow Wilson was usually cocksure once he made a decision. He protested war and imperialism, but as America's chief diplomat he failed to avoid both. (*Cartoons,* 1912)

| Makers of American Foreign Policy from 1914 to 1920 | |
| --- | --- |
| *Presidents* | *Secretaries of State* |
| Woodrow Wilson, 1913–1921 | William Jennings Bryan, 1913–1915 |
| | Robert Lansing, 1915–1920 |
| | Bainbridge Colby, 1920–1921 |

There was good reason, then, for Americans to believe that Europe needed help in cleaning its own house. Furthermore, the outbreak of the war seemed so senseless. By June, 1914, the great powers had constructed two alliances, the Triple Alliance (Germany, Austria, and Italy) and the Triple Entente (France, Russia, and Great Britain). Some called this division of Europe a balance of power, but an assassin's bullet easily unbalanced it. Between Austria and Serbia (part of Yugoslavia today) lay Bosnia, a tiny province annexed by expansionistic Austria in 1909. The nationalistic Serbs had protested this absorption of fellow Slavs, and Bosnia became hotly disputed territory. Young Bosnian assassins, clutching bombs and pistols and apparently egged on by some Serbian officials, precipitated a world conflict. One of their number gunned down the heir to the Hapsburg Crown of Austria-Hungary, Archduke Franz Ferdinand, as his car moved through the streets of Sarajevo, the capital of Bosnia. Austria sent impossible demands to Serbia. The Serbs indignantly rejected them. Austria had already received encouragement from Germany, and Serbia had gotten a pledge of support from Russia, which in turn received backing from France. A chain reaction set in. On July 28 Austria declared war on Serbia; on August 1 Germany declared "preventive" war on Russia and two days later on France; on August 4 Germany invaded Belgium, and Great Britain declared war on Germany. In a few weeks Japan joined the Allies (Triple Entente) and Turkey the Central Powers (Triple Alliance). As Germany's Otto von Bismarck had once predicted, "some damned foolish thing in the Balkans" would start a world war.[23]

The Atlantic seemed at first a solid enough barrier to insulate the United States. In early August, Ambassador Walter Hines Page wrote the President: "Be ready; for you will be called on to compose their huge quarrel. I thank Heaven for many things—first the Atlantic Ocean."[24] Adhering to diplomatic tradition, Wilson on August 4 issued a Proclamation of Neutrality, followed days later by an appeal to Americans to be neutral in thought, speech, and action. It was a request laced with patriotic utterances ("Every man who really loves America . . ."), designed to cool the passions of immigrant groups who identified with the belligerents. Wilson warned that such alignments would be fatal to "our peace of mind." America, he implored, must demonstrate to a troubled world that it was "fit beyond others to exhibit the fine poise of undisturbed judgment, the dignity of self-control, the efficiency of dispassionate action."[25] A lofty call for restraint, an expression of America as the beacon of common sense in a world gone mad, a plea for unity at home—but difficult to achieve.

Few Americans, including officials of the Wilson Administration, were capable of neutral thoughts and deeds. Loyalties to fatherlands and motherlands were understandable. German-Americans naturally identified with the Central Powers.

Many Irish-Americans, nourishing their traditional Anglophobia at a time when Ireland was on the verge of rebellion against London, wished catastrophe upon Britain. But Anglo-American traditions and cultural ties, as well as slogans like "Remember LaFayette," pulled a majority of Americans toward a pro-Allied position. People with national origins in the British Isles and France outnumbered those from the Central Powers. Woodrow Wilson himself harbored some pro-British sentiment, believing as he did that a German victory would constitute a blow against government by law. Then, too, in his days as a scholar, Wilson had affirmed that the British parliamentary system of government was a preferable form of government and had once envisioned himself as a great prime minister. Wilson's advisers, Colonel Edward House and Robert Lansing, were ardently pro-British, as was the American Ambassador to London, Walter Hines Page. Page became so enthusiastic about British-American cooperation that once, after delivering to the British foreign minister an American protest note asserting the rights of neutral traders against British encroachments, he apologized for the American position and sat down to help draft a British reply to his own government.

German war actions, exaggerated by British propaganda, also undermined neutrality. The Germans, led by the boldly moustached, arrogant Kaiser Wilhelm II, were symbols to Americans of the dreaded militarism and conscription of the Old World. Even German Chancellor Theobold von Bethmann-Hollweg admitted that "we often got on the world's nerves."[26] Germany, too, was an upstart nation, an aggressive latecomer to the scramble for imperialist prizes, and appeared to be an intruder in the Caribbean, which even the British had acknowledged as an American lake. Eager to grasp world power and encouraging Austria to war, Berlin certainly had little claim on virtue. The rape of Belgium alone persuaded untold thousands of Americans to hate the "Hun." Belgium's neutrality in war was guaranteed by treaty, but Bethmann-Hollweg dismissed it as a "scrap of

**"Sport."** After Germany's tragic conquest of Belgium, Berlin drew critical commentary from cartoonists like A. B. Walker, who depicted the "Hun" in 1915 as the executioner of men, women, and children. (Historical Pictures Service, Inc., Chicago)

paper."[27] On August 4, 1914, hoping to get at France easily, the Germans attacked Belgium and, angered that the Belgians resisted, ruthlessly proceeded to raze villages, unleash firing squads against townspeople, and deport young workers to Germany. One current magazine was appalled by the brutality, declaring Belgium "a martyr to civilization, sister to all who love liberty, or law; assailed, polluted, trampled in the mire, heel-marked in her breast, tattered, homeless."[28] American hearts went out in the form of a major relief mission headed by a young, wealthy, and courageous mining engineer, Herbert Hoover. The British did not have to play up these atrocities for them to have an impact, but they undertook a hyperbolic propaganda campaign nevertheless, creating fictional stories of babies at the bloody ends of German bayonets and of Belgian women with breasts hacked off.

American economic links with the Allies also undermined Wilsonian appeals for neutrality. England had always been America's best customer and wartime conditions simply intensified the relationship. The Allies needed both war materiel and consumer goods. Americans, inspired by huge profits, a chance to pull out of a recession, and a "business-as-usual" attitude, obliged. In 1914 United States exports to England and France equaled $754 million; in 1915 the figure shot up to $1.28 billion, and in 1916 the amount more than doubled to $2.75 billion. Comparable statistics for Germany reveal why Berlin believed the United States was taking sides. In 1914 exports to Germany totaled $345 million; in 1915 they plummeted to $29 million, and in 1916 they fell to the negligible figure of $2 million. In 1914–1917 the prestigious banking house of J. P. Morgan Company of New York City served as an agent for England and France and arranged for the shipment of over $3 billion worth of goods. In April, 1915, Britain ordered shells from the American Locomotive Company costing $63.7 million, and that year Bethlehem Steel contracted for about $150 million in ammunition, to cite two examples. American copper, steel, cotton, wheat, oil, and munitions were part of this big business, which became a significant part of the Allied war chest.

Britain and France were hard pressed to pay for these huge shipments. First, they sold many of their American securities and liquidated investments. This netted them several billion dollars. Next, in cooperation with prominent American bankers and Secretary of State Robert Lansing, they appealed for loans. In 1914 Bryan discouraged private American loans to the belligerents, for, as he put it, "money is the worst of all contrabands because it commands everything else."[29] Yet in early 1915 the Wilson Administration did not object to a Morgan credit to France of $50 million. With Bryan's resignation and Lansing's ascent, the practice became common. As Lansing told Wilson in September, if Americans did not extend loans to the Allies, the United States would invite "restriction of output, industrial depression, idle capital, idle labor, numerous failures, financial demoralization, and general unrest and suffering among the laboring classes."[30] The Wilson Administration permitted loans to the Allies amounting to $2.3 billion during the period of American neutrality. Germany could garner only $27 million.

Berlin protested that such Allied-American economic ties were "unneutral." Yet to have curbed trade with Britain, which ruled the seas, would have been an unneutral act in favor of the Germans, for under international law a belligerent could buy, at its own risk, contraband and noncontraband goods from a neutral. Neutral or not, America's large trade with the Allies thoroughly alarmed the

Germans, who understood that the United States had become the arsenal of the Allied war effort. German-American propagandist George S. Viereck bitterly complained that Americans "prattle about humanity, while we manufacture poisoned shrapnel and picric acid for profit. Ten thousand German widows, ten thousand orphans, ten thousand graves bear the legend 'Made in America.'"[31] Berlin, in defining its national interest, felt compelled to interrupt this damaging trade with *unterseebooten*. "Without American assistance to the Allies," historian Ross Gregory has written, "Germany would have had no reason to adopt [a] policy injurious to the interests of the United States."[32]

## Murder on the High Seas: Submarines and Neutral Rights

The British planned to strangle Germany economically. They declared a loose and hence illegal economic blockade in 1914, mined the North Sea, defined contraband so broadly that it included foodstuffs and cotton by the end of the war, forced American ships into port for inspection, confiscated contraband from neutral vessels, interrupted American trade with Germany's neutral neighbors Denmark and Holland, armed British merchant vessels, used decoy ships to lure U-boats into traps, flew neutral (often American) flags, and rammed whenever possible any U-boats that complied with international law by surfacing to warn a British merchant vessel of its imminent destruction. The British "ruled the waves and waived the rules," as someone put it.[33] Defending America's traditional principles of neutral rights, the Wilson Administration issued protests, some mild, some tough, against these illegalities. London was not impressed. When it replied, the Foreign Office paid appropriate verbal deference to neutral rights and international law and went right on with its unorthodox behavior. It soothed America's hurt by compensating its businessmen for damages and purchasing large quantities of its goods at inflated prices. Americans thus came to accept the indignities of British economic warfare. Britain managed brilliantly to sever American economic lines to the Central Powers without producing a rupture in Anglo-American relations.

Germans protested vehemently against this seeming American acquiescence in British practice. They considered it a "hunger" or "starvation" blockade. If Germany expected to survive as a nation, to continue the battle against the Allies, it had to have imports. Furthermore, Germany had to curb the flourishing Anglo-American trade that fueled the Allied war machine. The German Navy, most of it bottled up in ports by British vessels, seemed inadequate for the task, so German leaders hesitantly turned to a relatively new experimental weapon of limited maneuverability, the U-boat or submarine. They possessed just 21 of them initially and at peak strength in October, 1917 they had only 127. Only a third of this fleet was at sea at any one time. On February 4, 1915 Berlin announced that it was retaliating against British strangulation by declaring a war zone around Britain. All *enemy* ships in the area would be destroyed. Neutral ships were warned to *stay out* of the zone because of the possibility of mistaken identity, a possibility given the British practice of hoisting neutral flags. Passengers from neutral countries like the United States were urged to *stay off* enemy passenger vessels. Six days later Wilson vigorously instructed Germany that it would be held to a "strict accountability" for the loss of American life and property.[34]

The English continued to arm their merchant vessels, which thereby became warships and theoretically ineligible to frequent neutral territory like the United States. But Washington invoked a fine point of law, made the distinction between offensive and defensive armaments and permitted such "defensively" weaponed British craft to visit American ports. The Germans detected some favoritism. They also thought that old international law, which Wilson piously invoked, did not fit the submarine. Traditional rules held that enemy merchant vessels about to be captured or sunk had to be adequately warned by the attacking cruiser so that the safety of passengers and crew could be insured. The submarine could not fulfill this requirement. If it surfaced in its sluggish fashion, the merchantman's crew might sink it with the blast from a deck gun or even a hand grenade, or ram the vulnerable and slow-moving craft. British vessels like the *Lusitania* had standing Admiralty orders to resist U-boats and to ram them. Before the sinking of the *Lusitania,* the Germans had lost eleven submarines—five by ramming. Imagine the problem for Schwieger of U-20 when he spotted the *Lusitania.* Had he surfaced to warn her, he would have imperiled his boat and crew. The *Lusitania* would probably have attempted to ram U-20 or flee and would have sent distress signals to British warships in the vicinity. Even if the *Lusitania* had submitted to the warning, it would have taken at least an hour for the passengers to be placed in lifeboats before the ship could be sunk, and by then, in all likelihood, British vessels would have closed in upon Schwieger. In short, from the German point of view, it was impossible to comply with an international law that did not include provision for the submarine. Wilson, said Berlin, was attempting to deny Germany the use of the one weapon that might break the British blockade. That weapon, Wilson and other Americans replied, brought horrible death to innocent people.

Secretary Bryan tried diplomacy in early 1915, asking Germany to give up use of unannounced submarine attacks in exchange for a British promise to disarm its merchant carriers and permit food to flow to Germany. The Germans seemed interested, but London, which would have to abandon its successful blockade, demurred. Some critics have stated that at this point Wilson should have been tough in pressuring the belligerents to alter their naval strategies or face the prospect of American warships convoying America's "neutral" ships. Or, he might have launched a vigorous diplomatic offensive to delay explosive events on the seas. Yet the war was still in infancy, its direction and length uncertain, and American armed convoys in the Atlantic could very well draw America into a war it did not want. A diplomatic offensive, given the intensity of nationalism and war fever in Europe, seemed doomed to an early and inglorious failure. Wilson had to ask if he could risk all this. In March, 1915, he did send Colonel House to Europe to sound out possibilities for mediation, but to no avail. Nonetheless, Wilson failed to adjust or shelve ancient international law, which had no provision for the submarine. He was willing to accept British alterations but not German ones, for reasons both of morality and economics.

Between February and early May, 1915, ninety ships were sunk in the war zone by marauding submarines. One American, on the British passenger ship *Falaba,* died in the sinking of that vessel on March 28. Washington did not protest, hoping that a crisis could be avoided and that the belligerents could yet be lured to the conference table. Then came the *Lusitania* in May. Something had to be done. Wilson tried his protest notes, and the American position became defined as uneasy tolerance of the violation of property rights by the British and as rejection of the violation of human rights by the Germans. The Germans, Wilson pointed out, were killing people, whereas the British were inconveniencing them. Secret German orders went out to U-boat commanders to cease sinking passenger liners, but on August 19 the *Arabic,* another British liner, was torpedoed with the loss of two American lives. A worried German ambassador pledged that never again would unarmed passenger ships be attacked without warning.

In early 1916, with the *Lusitania* issue still unresolved, the United States attempted to bring the warring parties to the conference table. In early January Colonel House arrived in London, talked with British officials for two weeks, but left with no promises for peace. He stopped next in Berlin, where the imperial German leaders gave no assurances. Both sides would fight on. "Hell will break loose in Europe this spring and summer as never before," House informed the President.[35] He traveled next to Paris for a round of talks with the French. Indiscreetly showing his pro-Allied colors, House assured them that *"in the event the Allies are successful during the next few months I promised that the President would not intervene. In the event that they were losing ground, I promised the President would intervene."*[36] The French were pleased at the prospect of American participation in the war against Germany. House apparently did not tell the President exactly what he had told the surprised French.

House then traveled to London again. Sir Edward Grey, British foreign secretary, did not want to send him back to Washington empty-handed: Grey deftly maneuvered House into the House-Grey Memorandum of February 22, 1916, a record of House's conversations with the French and British loaded with "ifs" and "probablys." The first paragraph read: "Colonel House told me that President Wilson was ready, on hearing from France and England that the moment was opportune, to propose that a Conference should be summoned to put an end to the war. Should the Allies accept this proposal, and should Germany refuse it, the United States would probably enter the war against Germany." The memorandum went on to report that House had said that the peace conference would secure terms "not unfavourable to the Allies."[37] Eager to mediate the world crisis at a peace conference, the President pronounced the memorandum a diplomatic triumph, although he amended it with two "probablys," one relating to the securing of favorable terms for the Allies and the other to leaving the conference on the side of the Allies if Germany was unreasonable. Wilson took the memorandum much more seriously than did the British Cabinet, which soundly rejected any idea of a peace conference in the near future.

Meanwhile, Lansing and Wilson were working on a particular problem: armed merchant vessels and submarines. As House moved about the European capitals, Lansing informed the Allied governments that the United States sought a modus vivendi to defuse naval crises: the Allies would disarm merchant vessels and the Germans would agree to follow international law by warning enemy merchant ships. This suggestion revealed that the Wilson Administration understood the German argument that armed merchantmen were in reality offensive craft, that is, warships. The British and Colonel House were aghast when they received this news, and were further set back when the Germans seemed to endorse the modus vivendi by declaring on February 10 that submarines would henceforth attack only *armed* merchant ships without warning. Suddenly Wilson reversed policy. He

**Edward M. House (1858–1938).** A Texan who loyally served President Woodrow Wilson, the colonel traveled widely as a special presidential emissary. Wilson called House "my second personality." (Sketch by Anthony Saris, American Heritage Collection)

abandoned the modus vivendi in order to restore his standing with the British and sustain House's efforts at mediation in London. Lansing announced, furthermore, that the United States would not prevent its citizens from traveling on "defensively" armed merchant ships.

## Passengers, Perils, and Pledges: Descent into World War I

These diplomatic confusions alarmed many Americans. Why let one American passenger and a trigger-happy U-boat captain bring Germany and the United States to war? asked public critics like Bryan. Why not, they inquired, keep Americans off belligerent ships and require them to sail on American vessels? From August, 1914 to mid-March, 1917 only three Americans (on the American oil tanker *Gulflight*, May 1, 1915) had lost their lives on an *American* ship torpedoed by a U-boat. In contrast, about 190 Americans, including the *Lusitania's* 128, died on belligerent ships. After the *Falaba* was sunk, Bryan, still secretary of state, recognized that Americans had a right to travel on belligerent vessels, but asked Wilson to ask them to forgo that right. "I cannot see," Bryan wrote the President, "that he [an American on a belligerent ship] is differently situated from those who by remaining in a belligerent country assume risk of injury."[38] Wilson had, after all, urged Americans to leave war-torn Mexico. The American Ambassador to Germany, James W. Gerard, wrote the President in July, 1915, that "when Americans have reasonable opportunity to cross the ocean [on American ships] why should we enter a great war because some American wants to cross on a ship where he can have a private bathroom?"[39] Senator William J. Stone, chairman of the Foreign Relations Committee, forcefully pointed out that the *Lusitania* passengers, duly warned about the risk, were in essence on "British soil." He continued: "Was not their position substantially equivalent to their being in the walls of a fortified city?"[40]

Wilson did not agree. Americans could not give up one right, or all rights would be jeopardized. In January, 1916, Congressman Jeff: McLemore of Texas introduced a resolution to prohibit Americans from traveling on armed belligerent vessels. In late February Senator Thomas P. Gore of Oklahoma followed with a similar resolution in his chamber. Joined as the Gore-McLemore resolution, these prohibitions very quickly gained support in both houses. Wilson, a firm believer in presidential supremacy in decisionmaking, was irate that his foreign policy leadership would be challenged by Congress. He attacked Gore-McLemore fiercely, unleashing Cabinet members with patronage muscle on timid congressmen, and suggesting that the resolution was a pro-German ploy. He issued a statement marked by lofty, almost embarrassing, phrases. To halt American passage on belligerent ships, Wilson intoned, would be to accept national humiliation and destruction of the "whole fine fabric of international law."[41] In short, he stuck with rigid, archaic concepts, refusing to adjust to the new factor of the submarine or to appreciate the impact on Germany of the obvious British violations of the same law. In early March, the Gore-McLemore resolution was beaten 68–14 in the Senate and 276–142 in the House. One congressman complained that the "President absolutely dominates Congress."[42] The Gore-McLemore resolution was one of the more sensible proposals for avoiding German-American conflict. It asked America to give up very little; despite Wilson's exaggerated rhetoric it did not besmudge national honor. Wilson's message to Berlin was unmistakable: do not use your submarines.

In March, 1916, another passenger ship, another U-boat, another torpedo, more American injuries: the French ship *Sussex*, moving across the channel, was badly mangled but not sunk. Aboard her was a young American scholar, Samuel Flagg Bemis, later to become a renowned diplomatic historian but then fresh from archival research on Jay's Treaty. Gazing over the calm sea, Bemis glimpsed the swirling wake of a torpedo moments before impact. "The entire bow was blown off and with it the people who were in the dining room," he recalled.[43] Although four Americans were injured, a wet Bemis escaped serious harm. Fortunately, he also saved his little bag of note cards. The *Sussex* attack violated the "*Arabic* pledge," even though the U-boat commander mistook the ship for a minelayer, and Lansing counseled the President to break diplomatic relations with Berlin. Wilson decided instead upon an ultimatum. He warned the Germans on April 18 that he would sever diplomatic relations if they did not pledge to halt their submarine warfare against passenger and merchant vessels; to emphasize the point he went to Congress the next day and repeated the warning. The German hierarchy was alarmed, fully expecting a rupture if the torpedo bays were not blocked. With the ground war going badly (a German offensive at Verdun was costing thousands of lives), Berlin was not willing to invite war with the United States. In early May Germany promised (the "*Sussex* pledge") that submarines would not attack passenger or merchant ships without proper warning. The Germans also reminded Washington that it should do something about British infractions of international law.

Meanwhile, the British, sensing favorable winds, clamped down even harder on trade with the Central Powers. In July they issued a "blacklist" of firms; over eighty American companies that had traded with the Central Powers were on it, and even Woodrow Wilson now fumed that he was "about at the end of my patience with Great Britain and the Allies."[44] He contemplated a prohibition on loans and exports to them, but he did little. Many Americans also condemned the brutal British success in smashing the Irish Easter rebellion in April of 1916.

Shortly after the presidential election of 1916, punctuated with the Democrats' slogan "He Kept Us Out of War," the President launched another diplomatic offensive. In December Wilson boldly asked the belligerents to state their war aims. Actually, neither Berlin nor London, still seeking elusive military victory, welcomed Wilson's mediation, which would deny them the spoils of war. Germany intended to obtain Poland, Lithuania, Belgium, and the Belgian Congo; Britain sought German colonies; France wanted the return of Alsace-Lorraine. To these ardent war aims, Wilson seemed oblivious, especially when, on January 22, 1917, he called for a "peace without victory" because only through a peace founded on the "equality of nations" could a lasting world order be achieved. He proposed that "nations should with one accord adopt the doctrine of President Monroe as the doctrine of the world."[45] French Premier Georges Clemenceau's newspaper was cynical about Wilson's new appeal: "Never before has any political assembly heard so fine a sermon on what human beings might be capable of accomplishing if only they weren't human." And the radical *L'Oeuvre* contemptuously asked: "What about Cuba?"[46] The grand old man of French letters, Anatole France, revealing the French quest for revenge, put it this way: "Peace without victory is bread without yeast . . . , love without quarrels, a camel without humps, night without moon, roof without smoke, town without brothel."[47]

## Woodrow Wilson and the Decision for War, 1917

In early 1917 crises mounted quickly. On January 31 Berlin announced that, starting the next day, German submarines would attack without warning and sink all vessels, enemy and neutral, found near British waters. This declaration of unrestricted submarine warfare expressed Germany's calculated risk that England would be defeated before the United States could mobilize and send its soldiers overseas. The cocky German naval minister was emphatic: "From a military standpoint, America's entrance is as nothing."[48] German naval officers convinced the Kaiser that the U-boats, now numbering about 100, could shrink United States munitions shipments and hence knock Britain out of the war in six months. Army officers, bogged down in trench warfare, were eager to end their costly immobility through a bold stroke. Field Marshal Paul von Hindenburg overcame the arguments of a more cautious Chancellor Bethmann-Hollweg by insisting persuasively that "we are counting on the possibility of war with the United States, and have made all preparations to meet it. Things cannot be worse than they are now."[49] But an adviser to Bethmann-Hollweg fatalistically recorded in his diary that "despite all promises of the navy it remains a leap into the dark."[50]

Wilson still did not want war with Germany, though he was incensed by Berlin's most recent decision. He had become, according to Lansing, "more and more impressed with the idea that 'white civilization' and its domination over the world rested largely on our ability to keep this country intact, as we would have to build up the nations ravaged by the war."[51] Yet Wilson had also committed himself in notes and impassioned rhetoric to a forceful response to unrestricted submarine warfare. So on February 3 Washington severed diplomatic relations with Berlin. Allied and neutral vessels soon succumbed to U-boat torpedoes, and fearful American owners kept their merchant ships in port. Goods stacked up on wharves and many leaders predicted economic doom for the United States.

Added to this threat to America's economic interests and the intense Wilsonian defense of human rights was an implied threat to United States security. In late February the British passed to Ambassador Page an intercepted and decoded telegram sent to Mexico by German Foreign Minister Arthur Zimmermann. The remarkable message proposed a military alliance with the Latin American country. And should war with the United States break out, Germany would help Mexico "gain back by conquest" the territory lost in 1848: Arizona, California, and New Mexico.[52] Wilson read the telegram as a direct slap at American honor and a challenge to American security. Although the threat was potential rather than real, it deeply angered Washington, in large part because the United States was plagued at the time by stormy relations with a revolution-torn Mexico. Germany, it appeared, would stop at nothing. Theodore Roosevelt said he would "skin him alive" if the President did not declare war on Germany.[53]

One day after Wilson learned of Zimmermann's cable, he asked Congress for authority to arm American merchant vessels. On March 1, to create a favorable public opinion for the request, he released the offensive Zimmermann telegram to the press. But antiwar senators Robert LaFollette and George Norris led a filibuster—a "little group of willful men," said Wilson—that killed the armed ship legislation.[54] Stubbornly ignoring the Senate, Wilson ordered the arming anyway. Nevertheless, ship after ship was sunk by the U-boats: in March 16–18 alone the American ships *City of Memphis, Illinois,* and *Vigilancia* went down. Buttressed by the unanimous support of his Cabinet, the President decided for war.

On April 2 Wilson solemnly addressed a special joint session of Congress and appealed for a declaration of war against Germany—a war that Berlin had "thrust" upon the United States. His words were inspired, moving his audience to nationalistic enthusiasm. The President depicted the "unmanly business" of using submarines as "warfare against mankind." Freedom of the seas, commerce, American lives, human rights—all were challenged by the "outlaw" U-boats. A combination of economic self-interest, morality, and national honor compelled Americans to fight. He characterized the German government as a menacing monster striking at the "very roots of human life." The "Prussian autocracy" was also stirring up trouble through spies and the Zimmermann note. He acknowledged, too, that the Russian Revolution of March made fighting on the Allied side easier because now all the Allies would be democracies. Then came the memorable words: "The world must be made safe for democracy."[55] The address simplified issues and claimed too much for American participation in World War I. But the moment required patriotic fervor, not sophisticated analysis. "It had been a moving oration," Ross Gregory has written, "and when the President had finished, most of his listeners—there remained a few diehard dissenters—were ready to grasp the Hun by the collar, feeling that surely God was on their side, and if He was not, God this one time must be wrong."[56] By votes of 82–6 (Senate, April 4) and 373–50 (House, April 6), Congress endorsed Wilson's appeal for a war for peace.

Most historians agree that submarine warfare precipitated the American decision to enter the war. Such a conclusion is not inaccurate, but it is incomplete. Certainly had there been no submarine to menace American lives, property, and the United States definition of international law, there would have been no American soliders sent to France. From the German perspective, however, use of the submarine was justified by the long list of unfriendly American acts: American acquiescence in the British blockade, part of a general American pro-British bias; large-scale American munitions shipments to, and other commerce with, the Allies; large American loans; an interpretation of neutral rights, which insisted that American passengers could sail anywhere, even into a war zone, and which thereby rendered the submarine an impotent weapon. Take away those acts, which the Germans considered unneutral, and they might not have launched the U-boats. It seems questionable that American ideals and interest could depend so perilously on a ship loaded with contraband, heading for Britian, and steaming through a war zone. Yet that is how Wilson and his advisers defined the problem; dissenters like Gore and McLemore disagreed, but they were in the minority.

Evident in Wilson's policies was the traditional American belief that others must conform to American prescriptions, self-professed as they were, and that America's ideals were a beacon for mankind. "We created this Nation," the President once proclaimed, "not to serve ourselves, but to serve mankind."[57] When the Germans defied America's rules, ideals, and property, and threatened its security through a proposed alliance with Mexico, they had to be punished. Here was an opportunity to protect both humane principles and commercial interests. When Wilson spoke passionately of the right of a neutral to freedom of the seas, he demonstrated how intertwined were American moral, economic, and strategic concerns. Wilson sought the role of peacemaker and he promised to remake the world in the American image: that is, to create a world order in which barriers to political democracy and the "Open Door" were eliminated, in which revolution and aggression were abolished. This missionary zeal served, at least in Wilson's mind, the national interest (trade and the Open Door) and high principles (respect for human rights, self-determination, and democracy). War came to the United States not simply because of German submarines, but because expansionist American leaders were finally willing to fight in order to implant in the Old World the best principles and goods America had to offer.

## Preparing for War

Berlin had risked war with the United States because it assumed that American soldiers could not reach France fast enough to reverse an expected German victory. That proved to be a gross misjudgment, for American military muscle and economic power decisively tipped the balance against Germany. Given the information available in early 1917, however, the German assumption does not seem so unrealistic. In April the United States was hardly prepared to send a major expedition to the Western Front. At that date the Regular Army counted only 130,000 officers and men, backed by 180,000 National Guardsmen. Although some American officers had been seasoned by military interventions in Cuba, the Philippines, and recently in Mexico, many soldiers were poorly trained. Weapons such as the machine gun were in short supply. The "Air Service," then part of the Army, did not have a plane of modern design with a machine gun, and some ships in the Navy had never fired a gun. German calculations based upon these facts seemed at the time sensible; what the Germans underestimated badly was American capacity for organization and the intense nationalism and remarkable productive power of the United States.

An American "preparedness movement" had been under way for months, encouraged by prominent Americans like the tough-minded Rough Rider and military evangelist, General Leonard Wood, who overstated the case when he argued that America's military weakness invited attack, but rang true when he noted that the United States was not recognized as an important military power. After 1914, Wood, Theodore Roosevelt, the National Security League, the Army League, and the Navy League lobbied actively for bigger military appropriations. The belief that "preparedness" was an insurance against war grew more popular. One propaganda film, *The Fall of a Nation*, depicted a helpless United States invaded by spike-helmeted attackers. In mid-1915 one hundred of America's wealthiest men pledged thousands of dollars to help the Navy League plead its case before Congress, and by September of that year twenty-eight governors had joined the National Security League.

Wilson himself decided to prepare the nation for possible war. After consulting senior Army and Navy officers, he presented his plan to Congress in December, 1915. He dramatically asked for a half-billion-dollar naval expansion program, including ten battleships and one hundred submarines, to bring the United States to first rank with Britain in five years. Land forces would also be enlarged and reorganized. Perpetuating the antimilitarist tradition of great numbers of Americans, Senator Robert LaFollette, House Majority Leader Claude Kitchin, and such prominent citizens as Jane Addams, William Jennings Bryan, Lillian Wald, and Oswald Garrison Villard spurred a movement against these measures. Those peace advocates, the Women's Peace Party, and the League to Limit Armaments argued that war would interrupt reform at home, benefit big business, and curtail civil liberties. Their arguments were formidable and their numerical strength impressive. The President faced a serious test.

In January, 1916, Wilson set out on a two-month speaking tour, often having to criticize members of his own party for their opposition to a military buildup. U-boat sinkings aided the President's message. Finally, in May, 1916, Congress passed the National Defense Act, increasing the Regular Army to over 200,000 men and 11,000 officers, and the National Guard to 440,000 men and 17,000 officers. Provision was made, too, for summer training camps, modeled after one held in 1915 for the social and economic elite in Plattsburg, New York. In June, 1916, Wilson asserted that "mankind is going to know that when America speaks she means what she says."[58] The Navy bill passed in August, 1916 and was followed by the shipping bill providing $50 million to enlarge the merchant marine. With these successes, Wilson entered the presidential campaign under the banner of "reasonable" preparedness and "He Kept Us Out of War." Peace groups thought the measures went too far; Teddy Roosevelt, of course, believed they fell short.

**"In the Front Line at Early Morning."** A soldier stares across "no-man's-land" from a World War I trench in this painting by Harvey Dunn. American generals vowed to end the stalemate of costly trench warfare. (Smithsonian Institution)

When the United States voted for belligerency in April, 1917, it was preparing for war, but was not yet ready. Wilson requested 500,000 more soldiers in his war message. The Selective Service Act of May, 1917 began a registration process that included all males between the ages of eighteen and forty-five. By the end of the conflict, 4,800,000 soldiers, sailors, and marines had been mobilized. Officer training camps turned out "ninety-day wonders," thousands of commissioned officers drawn largely from people of elite background. One camper remarked about the spirit of his group: "There are so many Roosevelts that you can't turn around without stumbling over one."[59] Actually, Theodore Roosevelt was not there. The old Rough Rider had asked Wilson for permission to recruit and lead a volunteer unit into battle; no doubt taking some revengeful pleasure in denying the request, Wilson argued that special volunteer divisions would raise havoc with military organization. As historian Edward M. Coffman has concluded: "A dilettante at war with a political reputation and political ambitions was out of place in the American army of 1917–18."[60] Roosevelt was to die peacefully in January, 1919, after tragically losing his youngest son in the war.

Right after the American declaration of war, Allied military missions flocked to the White House to beg for soldiers. General John J. "Black Jack" Pershing, veteran fighter against Apaches, Filipinos, and Mexicans, and now head of the American Expeditionary Force to Europe, soon sent a "show the flag" contingent to France to stimulate Allied morale. Neither Wilson nor Pershing would accept, however, the European recommendation that American troops be inserted in Allied units where needed. American units would cooperate in joint maneuvers with other forces, but the United States Army would remain separate and independent. National pride dictated this decision, but so did the realization that Allied commanders had for years wasted the lives of hundreds of thousands in vicious trench warfare. The United States would not supply more bodies for such an unsuccessful strategy. It wanted freedom of choice and no identification with exploitative Allied war aims. Thus the United States insisted on calling itself an "associated" rather than an "allied" power in the war.

## Over There: Winning the War

On July 4, 1917, General Pershing reviewed the first unit of American troops to arrive in France. A battalion of the 16th Infantry marched proudly through the streets of Paris, as nearly a million Parisians madly tossed flowers, hugged the doughboys, and cheered wildly. The American soldiers were enthusiastic but ill-trained recruits. One company commander recalled that "these men couldn't even slope arms. They were even more dangerous with a loaded rifle."[61] But to the war-weary French, accustomed to viewing haggard men exhausted by the agony of the trenches, these fresh American troops were inspirational. Speeches were delivered with accustomed Independence Day rhetoric. One colonel proclaimed, "Lafayette, we are here!" and back home the *New York Times* echoed, "the old debt is being paid."[62]

Preparations continued in the United States. To the tune "Johnny Get Your Gun," innocent but eager recruits—draftees and volunteers—were sent from their hometowns with fanfare and full stomachs from church dinners. Many got drunk on the mobilization trains. "Hurry up and wait," a military tradition, greeted the young soldiers in camp. The six-month training program demanded a seven-

**Recruiting Poster.** James Montgomery Flagg's famous poster urged young people to join the American crusade in World War I. (Library of Congress)

teen-hour day, including "policing the area" (i.e., picking up cigarette butts), a military custom considered instructive for "discipline." The soldiers ate well, slept on straw mattresses and cots, and drilled, often without the benefit of weapons. Some never fired a rifle until stationed in France. War hero Private Alvin C. York, of Tennessee's mountain country, remarked that many of his fellow warriors "missed everything but the sky" during marksmanship training. "Of course, it weren't no trouble nohow for me to hit them big army targets. They were so much bigger than turkey's heads."[63]

To the chagrin of American leaders, taverns and brothels quickly surrounded army camps. Alcohol and prostitution were, of course, taboos during the progressive era. "Fit to Fight" became the government's slogan, as it moved to close down "red-light districts"; "sin-free zones" around camps were declared, and the sale of liquor to men in uniform was prohibited. Secretary of the Navy Josephus Daniels preached that "Men must live straight if they would shoot straight."[64] The military conquered the venereal disease problem in the United States. As historian Allen F. Davis has concluded, "it was a typical progressive effort—a large amount of moral indignation combined with the use of the most scientific prophylaxis."[65] Groups like the YMCA and the Jewish Welfare Board helped work against sin by sending song leaders to camps. Movies, athletic programs, and well-stocked stores were also designed to keep the soldier on the base by making him feel "at home." These activities could not deal with a major flu epidemic, which struck several camps in

1918. The death rate was awesome. At Camp Sherman, Ohio, one of the bases hit hardest, 1,101 men died between September 27 and October 13. According to army records for the war as a whole, 62,000 men died of diseases of many kinds. Battle deaths numbered less—about 51,000.

Approximately 400,000 black troops suffered the intolerance of American racism and discrimination during this war "to make the world safe for democracy." Camps were segregated and "white only" signs posted. In 1917 in Houston, Texas, whites provoked negroes into a riot that left seventeen whites and two blacks dead. Over a hundred black soldiers were courtmartialed; thirteen were executed by hanging. In the army, three out of every four black soldiers were assigned to labor units, where they wielded a shovel, not a gun, or where they cooked or unloaded supplies. They received poor training and became dispirited under the leadership of white officers. Even black officers were assigned second-class quarters during the transatlantic trip. Black troops in France won high praise from French leaders, but Americans insensitively poked fun by quipping that it would be difficult to get a load of watermelons across the Atlantic to reward them. Many black soldiers earned the coveted medal "Croix de Guerre," but Americans preferred to emphasize an uneven performance by two black units in the Meuse-Argonne offensive near the end of the war. To be black in World War I was to be reminded of the

**Black "Kitchen Engineers."** In Marseilles, France these black members of the United States Army peel potatoes, one of the "service" functions performed by segregated blacks, who ironically participated in a war to "make the world safe for democracy." (U.S. Signal Corps, National Archives)

blotted lives of slave ancestors and the utter contradiction between America's wartime rhetoric and reality. In the nation as a whole in 1917 there were seventy lynchings.

After training in the Unites States, troops went to France for two more months of preparation. There they endured frequent rain and mud, slept in barns and stables, fought off "cooties" (lice), and ate "monkey-meat" (canned corned beef from Madagascar). One soldier, battling the lice, remarked that he knew full well why Napoleon was always pictured with his hand in his shirt. They made friends, some lasting, with French villagers, although some resented Americans who flaunted their wealth among people who knew only wartime sacrifice. Wine and women occupied spare hours. American reformers in the camps back home had said that they hoped to give the soldiers enough social armor before they reached France so that they would not be tempted by sin overseas. But they either overestimated the self-control of American men or underestimated the power of French women, because the venereal disease rate spiraled up alarmingly. Every morning General Pershing had a venereal disease chart laid on his desk. What to do? French Prime Minister Georges Clemenceau generously offered to supply the American Army with licensed—health-inspected—prostitutes. A cautious Pershing commented that the offer was "too hot to handle," and forwarded it to Raymond Fosdick, Chairman of the Commission on Training Camp Activities. Fosdick carried it to Secretary of War Newton Baker, who in shock expostulated: "For God's sake, Raymond, don't show this to the President or he'll stop the war."[66] Clemenceau's offer was never taken up, but disease prevention programs and the threat of court-martial confronting any infected soldier helped reduce the problem. We shall always remember the problem existed, however, because one of the French ladies of ill repute was immortalized in some of the unprintable words of the popular song "Mademoiselle from Armentières."

Pershing established headquarters outside Paris and tried to acquaint his soldiers with the hardships of trench and gas warfare. The first American deaths came from limited combat in October, 1917. Despite the impatience of the French and British, Pershing was reluctant to commit his green soldiers to full-scale battle. As it was, great numbers of troops were shipped over in British vessels and had to borrow French weapons. And by early 1918 the Allies were mired in a murderous strategy of throwing ground forces directly at other ground forces. German troops were mauling Italian forces, and the French army was still suffering from the mutinies of the year before. In March Germany forced an exhausted and revolution-wracked Russia out of the war in the draconian Brest-Litovsk Treaty, which stripped the victim of valuable land and people. President Wilson, trying to avoid vindictiveness, nevertheless waxed militant. He told a Baltimore audience in April that Americans must employ "Force, Force to the utmost, Force without stint or limit, the righteous and triumphant Force which shall make Right the law of the world, and cast every selfish dominion down in the dust."[67] American soldiers soon trooped into battle.

In March the German armies, swollen by forty divisions from the Russian front, launched a great offensive. Allied forces were hurled back, and by late May the Kaiser's soldiers encamped near the Marne River less than fifty miles from Paris. Saint-Mihiel, Belleau Wood, Cantigny, Château-Thierry—sites where American soldiers shed their blood against Germany—soon became household words at home. In June at Château-Thierry the doughboys dramatically stopped a German advance. From May through September of 1918 over a million American troops went to France; two million would be there by the armistice in November. In mid-July the Allies launched a counteroffensive and nine American divisions fought fiercely near Château-Thierry, helping to lift the German threat from Paris. In the Meuse-Argonne offensive (begun on September 26), over a million American soldiers joined French and British units in penetrating the crumbling German lines.

## Preparing for Peace: The Fourteen Points, Armistice, and Allied Competition

In the fall of 1918, German leaders began to think peace, as the Allied offensive steadily struggled forward. On October 4, as American soldiers fought in the thick Argonne Forest, the German chancellor asked Wilson for an armistice. German troops were mutinous; revolution and riots plagued German cities; Bulgaria had left the war in September. Turkey would drop out in late October, and Austria-Hungary would surrender on November 3. Germany had no choice but to surrender. The Kaiser fled to Holland. On November 11, in a railroad car in the Compiègne Forest, German representatives capitulated. At the time, American troops controlled 21 percent of the Western Front: the United States, through its men and supply, had made the difference in defeating Germany. In the sports vernacular of the day, the *Rochester Post-Express* concluded that the "trouble with this war game was that it ran into extra innings and Germany had no relief pitcher or pinchhitters."[68] The Allies had the Americans, and the latter would not let the former forget it.

During the combat, President Wilson had begun to explain in very general terms his plans for the peace. His message of a "peace without victory" was trumpeted most dramatically in his "Fourteen Points" speech before Congress on January 8, 1918. The first five points promised an "open" world after the war, a world distinguished by "open covenants, openly arrived at," freedom of navigation upon the seas, equal trade opportunity and the removal of tariffs, reduction of armaments, and an end to colonialism. Points six through thirteen called for self-determination for national minorities in Europe. Point fourteen was paramount: a "general association of nations" to insure "political independence and territorial integrity to great and small states alike."[69] His Fourteen Points, joined by later elaborations, signaled from the American perspective a generous, nonpunitive postwar settlement. They served as effective American propaganda against revenge-fed Allied aims and Russian Bolshevik appeals for European revolution.

Leaders in France, Britain, and Italy grew angry at Wilson, fearing he would deny them the spoils of war. In 1915 the Allies had signed secret treaties carving up German territories, including colonies in Africa and Asia. Nursing deep war wounds and dreaming of imperial expansion at the expense of a defeated Germany, the Allies sneered at Wilson's prescriptions. They did not appreciate the "modern St. George," as publicist Herbert Croly depicted Wilson, or his attempts to slay the "dragons of reaction" in Europe.[70] Furthermore, Europeans, surveying the comparative wartime suffering and human loss, believed that Wilson "had bought his seat at the peace table at a discount."[71] When, in September and October of 1918, Wilson exchanged notes with Germany and Austria-Hungary about an armistice, the Allied powers grew restless. They expressed strong reservations about the Fourteen Points. General Tasker Howard Bliss, the Ameri-

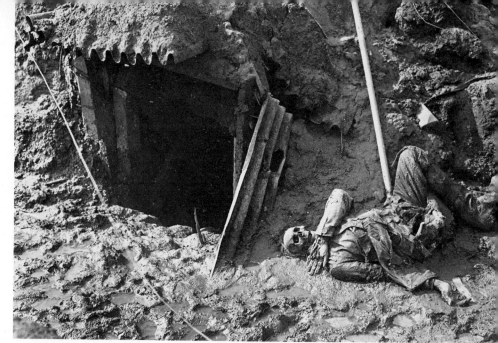

**A German Soldier.** This disturbing picture of an unburied German soldier of the First World War, and others like it, convinced many Americans to abstain in the future from European squabbles that might lead to United States military action. (Imperial War Museum, London)

can representative on the Supreme War Council (established in the fall of 1917 to coordinate the Allied war effort), recognized the Allied thirst for revenge. "Judging from the spirit which seems more and more to actuate our European allies," he informed Washington in October, "I am beginning to despair that the war will accomplish more than the abolition of *German* militarism while leaving *European* militarism as rampant as ever."[72] To counter the Allied assault upon the Fourteen Points, presidential aide Colonel Edward House and Wilson hinted that the United States might negotiate a separate peace with the Central Powers. House further warned that the President might go before Congress and publicize the exploitative Allied war aims. The colonel also contemplated economic coercion in the form of a reduction in American shipments to Europe. London, Paris, and Rome reluctantly agreed, in the armistice of November, to begin peace negotiations on the basis of the Fourteen Points.

Wilson, at the peak of his diplomatic career, relished the opportunity to shape the postwar world. The war had been won by the infusion of American arms, and the United States was about to claim a major role in deciding world events. The pictures of dying men dangling from barbed wire fences, and the reality of battle shock victims who staggered home convinced many Americans of the frightful costs of war and the need to prevent another conflagration. Wilson's call for a just peace commanded the backing of countless foreigners as well. The President thus headed for the Paris Peace Conference at Versailles with a reputation as an apostle of peace.

He also went as a person with human weaknesses and olympian ambitions. It became a personal tragedy that the sacred garb of peace, so carefully tailored by Wilson himself, would be stripped from the President by recalcitrant European leaders, critical senators, and his own disaffected advisers. But, as most historians point out, Wilson invited calamity by compromising too much in Europe and too little at home. A personal tragedy the peacemaking was; whether it was a national tragedy remains an open question.

In telling fashion, the President weakened his position even before he reached the peace conference. Against the advice of many friends he had decided to go personally to Paris to conduct the meetings. Congressional leaders wanted him to stay home to handle domestic problems. Advisers like Lansing feared that in the day-to-day bickering of a conference he would lose his exalted image. He would have only one vote, whereas from Washington he could symbolically marshall the votes of mankind. Wilson retorted that distance contributes to confusion, that he had already pledged the United States to a direct hand in the peacemaking, and that his presence would prevent an Allied retreat from the Fourteen Points. The President rejected the apparently sounder advice that he open the conference, engage in preliminary discussions, and then exit, leaving the daily quarreling to American diplomats. No, this would be Wilson's show: "I must go."[73]

In late October, 1918, Wilson appealed to Americans to return a Democratic Congress loyal to him. Anything less, he said, would be read abroad as a repudiation of his leadership and ideas. Republicans, partisans themselves, were angry that he attempted to identify himself and the Democratic party with the well-being of the nation. The Republicans proceeded to capture the November election and a majority in both houses of Congress; now they would sit in ultimate judgment of Wilson's peacemaking. Not only did Wilson undercut himself at home by arousing partisanship; he also weakened his position at the conference table. European leaders, some of them fresh from political victories, may have agreed with Wilson-baiter Theodore Roosevelt that "Mr. Wilson has no authority whatever to speak for the American people at this time. His leadership has just been emphatically repudiated by them."[74] The President also made the political mistake of not appointing either an important Republican or a senator to the American Peace Commission. Wilson, House, and Lansing sat on it; they were joined by General Bliss and Henry White, seasoned diplomat and nominal Republican. One critical editor listed the members this way:[75]

| Name | Occupation | Representing |
|------|-----------|-------------|
| Woodrow Wilson | President | Himself |
| Robert Lansing | Sec. of State | The Executive |
| Henry White | None | Nobody |
| Edward M. House | Scout | The Executive |
| Tasker H. Bliss | Soldier | The Commander-in-Chief |

It was a handpicked group tied to the President. Wilson also failed to consult with the Senate Foreign Relations Committee before he departed for Paris. Some concessions to his political opposition, and to senatorial prerogatives in foreign affairs, might have smoothed the path later for his peace treaty.

## Making the Peace: The Paris Conference at Versailles

On December 4, with great fanfare, Wilson departed from New York harbor aboard the *George Washington*. He settled into a quiet voyage, surrounded by advisers and nearly 2,000 reports produced by "The Inquiry," a group of scholars who for over a year had studied international problems likely to arise at the peace conference. There were many reports, but few plans. In fact, Wilson's friends were alarmed that the President continued to speak in vague terms and still had not produced a blueprint for the League of Nations. Wilson landed in France on

**David Lloyd George (1863–1945).**
One of Wilson's antagonists at Versailles, the British Prime Minister (left) grew annoyed with Wilson's pontificating lectures. (Sketch by Anthony Saris, American Heritage Publishing Company)

**Georges Clemenceau (1841–1929).**
Auguste Rodin's bronze (right) aptly conveys the formidable stature of "The Tiger" from France, eager for revenge against Germany. (The Rodin Museum, Philadelphia Museum of Art)

**Wilson in Dover, England, 1919.** Demonstrations of adulation like this one buoyed Wilson's faith that he represented mankind in the quest for peace. (U.S. Signal Corps, National Archives)

December 13, and soon began a tiring round of receptions and speeches. Enthusiastic Paris crowds cheered him, and thousands in England and Italy greeted him with admiration verging on the religious. Wilson assumed that this generous outpouring meant that *his* version was universally popular and that *he* had a missionary duty to carry it forward. He would soon discover that such ambiguous "man-in-the-street" opinion was not shared by the more sober David Lloyd George, Prime Minister of Britain, by French Premier Georges Clemenceau, or by Italian leader Vittorio Orlando, his antagonists at the Paris Conference.

Germany and Bolshevik Russia were excluded from the conference of January–May, 1919, but thirty-two nations sent delegations, which essentially followed the lead of the "Big Four." Most of the sessions were conducted in secrecy, hardly befitting Wilson's first "point." Clemenceau, dubbed "The Tiger," was imposing—his face masked by a bushy moustache and his mind dominated by French revenge against Germany. He did not like Wilson, snorting that "God gave us the Ten Commandments, and we broke them. Wilson gives us the Fourteen Points. We shall see."[76] Lloyd George, the "Welsh Witch," was more conciliatory, eager to build a strong France and to head off a reduction in German purchases of British exports. Orlando was a fervent Italian nationalist, concerned primarily with those issues that would enlarge Italian interests. All of them distrusted American power, harbored dreams of bigger empires, sought security and postwar reconstruction, and resented Wilson's "sermonettes." Lloyd George, who complained that the United States was bullying Europe, concluded that Wilson "was the most extraordinary compound I have ever encountered of the noble visionary, the implacable and unscrupulous partisan, the exalted idealist and the man of rather petty personal rancour."[77]

One of the thorniest issues at the conference was the disposition of colonies and the establishment of new countries. Wilson had appealed for self-determination, but the belligerents had already signed secret treaties of conquest. After hard negotiating, the conferees mandated former German and Turkish colonies to the countries which had conquered them, to be loosely supervised under League of Nations auspices. Under the mandate system—a compromise between outright annexation and complete independence—France and Britain obtained parts of the Middle East, and Japan acquired China's Shantung Province and Germany's Pacific islands. After Wilson's reluctant acceptance of the Shantung arrangement, the President lamented to a friend that "the settlement was the best that could be had out of a dirty past."[78] The victimized Chinese were naturally irate. France was granted occupation of the German Rhineland and a stake in the coal-rich Saar Basin. Italy annexed South Tyrol and Trieste from the collapsed Austro-Hungarian Empire. A total of 1,132,000 square miles changed hands. Newly formed or independent countries also emerged: Austria, Czechoslovakia, Hungary, Poland, and Yugoslavia. The Allies further exploited nationalism to establish a ring of hostile states around Bolshevik Russia: Finland, Estonia, Latvia, and Lithuania, all formerly part of the Russian Empire. The map of Europe was redrawn. The mandate system smacked of imperialism, in violation of the Fourteen Points. But the new states in Europe were examples of Wilson's self-determination pledge—although some critics argued that the new countries were very weak and vulnerable to outside pressures, thereby inviting international conflict. France itself felt insecure. To assuage French fears of a revived Germany, Britain and the United States signed a security pact with France guaranteeing its border, but the pact was never ratified by the Senate.

Reparations proved a knotty issue. The peace conference, recalled American adviser Bernard Baruch, "was dealing with blood-raw passions still pulsing through people's veins."[79] The United States wanted a limited indemnity for Germany, to avoid a harsh peace that might arouse long-term German resentment or debilitate the German economy and politics. "If we humiliate the German people and drive them too far," Wilson remarked before Versailles, "we shall destroy all form of government, and Bolshevism will take its place."[80] France, hoping to cripple Germany, pushed for a large bill of reparations. Britain, suffering a milder case of revenge, sided with France. The conferees wrote a "war guilt clause," which held Germany responsible for all of the war's damages. Although the reparations settlement was shortsighted, Wilson felt compelled to give in to heavy pressure, always confident that his League of Nations would ameliorate any severity. With little regard for Germany's ability to pay, the Reparations Commission in 1921 presented a hobbled Germany with the outrageous indemnity of thirty-three billion dollars. The Paris reparations agreement plagued international relations for the next decade.

Wilson's primary concern, unlike that of the other participants, was the League of Nations. He directly supervised the drafting of the League's covenant. This charter provided for an influential council of five big powers (permanent) and representatives from smaller nations (by election). An assembly of all nations for discussion was also created. Wilson argued that the heart of the covenant was Article 10, a provision designed to curb aggression and war: "The Members of the League undertake to respect and preserve as against external aggression the territorial integrity and existing political independence of all Members of the League. In case any such aggression or in case of any threat or danger of such aggression the Council shall advise upon the means by which this obligation shall be fulfilled."[81] Wilson succeeded in persuading the conferees to merge the League covenant and the peace terms in a package. The League charter, then, constituted the first 26 articles of a 440-article Treaty of Paris. The League covenant was the noblest part of all—"It is practical, and yet it is intended to purify, to rectify, to elevate."[82]

The Germans, when first handed the long document, refused to sign, pleading that some of its provisions violated the Fourteen Points. The Allies were not in a forgiving mood, so the losers bowed to the inevitable humiliation on June 28 in Versailles' elegant Hall of Mirrors. Germany was stripped of 13 percent of its territory, 10 percent of its population, and all its colonies. Lansing, believing the harsh peace terms would make the League unworkable, complained: "The League might as well attempt to prevent the growth of plant life in a tropical jungle."[83] A German nationalist bitterly wrote a year later: "Among all those who shoveled at the grave of our people, none was more clever or more successful than Woodrow Wilson."[84]

## Principle and Partisanship: The League Fight at Home

Wilson spent almost six months in Europe drawing up his plans for the postwar peace. From February 24 to March 14, he returned to the United States for executive business; during that brief respite from the Paris Conference, Wilson's handiwork came under attack. Upon landing in Boston in late February, he castigated critics. "America is the hope of the world," he lectured. Wilson would not let "minds that have no sweep beyond the nearest horizon" reject the American purpose of making men free. "I have fighting blood in me," he asserted.[85]

Within days he met with the House Foreign Affairs Committee and Senate Foreign Relations Committee. Republicans peppered him with questions about the degree to which the covenant limited American sovereignty. Senator Frank Brandegee of Connecticut was not impressed with Wilson's performance: "I feel as if I had been wandering with Alice in Wonderland and had tea with the Mad Hatter."[86] In early March, Republican Senator Henry Cabot Lodge of Massachusetts engineered a "Round Robin," a statement by thirty-nine senators (enough to deny the treaty a two-thirds vote) that questioned the League covenant and requested that the peace treaty and the covenant be acted upon separately. Many of the signers feared that the League would limit United States freedom to act independently in international affairs.

A defiant Wilson sailed again for France, cocksure that the "pygmy" minds in America would not destroy his precious League. Still, he was politician enough, and stung enough, to seek slight changes in Paris. He did not think his senatorial opponents had much sense, but he knew they had votes. So he amended the covenant, to the effect that League members could refuse mandates, that the League had no jurisdiction over purely domestic issues, and that the Monroe Doctrine was safeguarded against League action. He would not alter Article 10. When he returned to the United States in July, criticism had not subsided; indeed, it was more insistent. Wilson submitted the 264-page Treaty of Paris to the Senate on July 10, with an address that resembled an evangelical sermon: "The stage is set, the destiny disclosed. It has come about by no plan of our conceiving, but by the hand of God, who led us into this way. . . . The light streams upon the path ahead, and nowhere else."[87] There was no doubt about the outcome in Wilson's mind, for as he told a reporter, *"The Senate is going to ratify the treaty."*[88] Asked by the French ambassador if he would accept senatorial "reservations" to the treaty, Wilson snapped: "I shall consent to nothing. The Senate must take its medicine."[89]

Both friends and foes were asking if Wilson could have avoided the compromises, the land-grabbing, the harsh reparations bill, and the less than open diplomacy at the conference. Most historians agree that Wilson, against strong odds, gained a good percentage of his goals as outlined in the Fourteen Points. Self-determination for nationalities was established as never before in Europe, and the League, despite later failings, was a notable achievement. Wilson did compromise, however, especially when faced by formidable opposition like that thrown up by Clemenceau, who spoke for the many Europeans unable easily to forget the war's death count. During the conference, too, both Italy and Japan had threatened to walk out unless they realized some territorial goals. Wilson's problem with his domestic critics was that he had so built up a case for his ability to deliver an unselfish peace that when the conquerors' hard bargaining, rather than charity, characterized the conference, observers could only conclude that the President had failed badly to live up to his own ideals. In short, Wilson, through his pompous and vague rhetoric, had misled. The millenium he promised was obviously unattainable. Some of his critics said that he should have left Paris in protest, refusing to sign, or that he should have threatened the European powers with American economic power by curbing postwar loans and trade. Believing ardently that the League, with Article 10, would rectify all, Wilson instead had accepted embarrassing compromises.

Wilson would not compromise at home, however. Nor would he give systematic technical analysis to the many clauses of the treaty or admit that it might be flawed. He simply expected the Senate dutifully to ratify his masterwork. Yet his earlier bypassing of that body and his own partisan speeches and self-righteousness insured debate with influential critics. Progressives among them, like Senator George Norris, tended to think that the League did not go far enough in reducing the possibility of war, that it was an ill-disguised device to continue great power domination. Conservative critics, like Senator Henry Cabot Lodge, argued on the other hand that the League deprived the United States of too much sovereignty. Senator James Reed of Missouri added a racist touch: "Think of submitting questions involving the very life of the United States to a tribunal on which a nigger from Liberia, a nigger from Honduras, a nigger from India . . . each have votes equal to that of the great United States."[90] Article 10 seemed to bother everybody. Two questions were uppermost: Would League members be obligated to use force? Did the article mean that the status quo would always be upheld? The article did not require members to use force, but it implied they should. Senator William Borah complained that "I may be willing to help my neighbor . . . , but I do not want him placed in a position where he may decide for me when and how I shall act or to what extent I shall make sacrifice."[91] Article 10 also implied that territorial adjustments or rebellions, such as those in Ireland, India, and Egypt, would not be permitted. Senator Robert LaFollette called the League an imperialist club, which would keep colonies in bondage against their will by invoking Article 10. The article was simply too open-ended. Yet Wilson argued that without such a commitment to halt warmakers in the future the League would be feeble. "In effect," historian Roland N. Stromberg has noted, "Wilson and the Democrats wanted to accept an obligation that we might thereafter refuse, while Lodge and the Republicans wanted to refuse an obligation we might thereafter accept."[92]

Wilson's chief legislative obstacle was Henry Cabot Lodge. Chairman of the Senate Foreign Relations Committee, nationalist-imperialist, author, Ph.D., Republican partisan, like Wilson a scholar in politics, Lodge packed his committee with anti-League senators, dragged out hearings for weeks, kept most Republicans together on treaty votes, and nurtured a personal animosity toward Wilson matched only by Wilson's detestation for Lodge. It is frankly unclear whether or not Lodge sought to kill the League in infancy: in any case, his method of attack was indirect. He proposed a series of "reservations" to the League covenant. Although in retrospect these reservations, intended to guard American sovereignty, do not appear to have been death blows to the League, at the time they were hotly debated. They addressed the question of American national interest—the degree to which the United States would limit its freedom of action, the degree to which the United States should engage in collective security. Many of the fourteen reservations stated the obvious—such as, that Congress would retain its constitutional role in foreign policy. Others excluded the Monroe Doctrine from League oversight more explicitly than the covenant's version, and denied the League jurisdiction over American domestic legislation such as immigration laws. The reservation that struck at Article 10 was important: The United States assumed no obligation to preserve the territorial integrity or political independence of another country unless authorized by Congress.

The Senate divided into four groups. Loyal to Wilson were about forty Democrats called the Non-Reservationists. Another group, the Mild-Reservationists, led by Frank B. Kellogg, numbered about thirteen Republicans. The third faction, managed by Lodge, were known as the Strong-Reservationists. They counted in

**Henry Cabot Lodge (1850–1924).** Aristocratic, wealthy, haughty, partisan, and conservative, "the scholar in politics" held a Ph.D. in history from Harvard and chaired the Senate Foreign Relations Committee. From that position he called for a declaration of war after the *Lusitania* sinking and blocked American membership in Wilson's League of Nations. (Library of Congress)

**Woodrow Wilson after His Stroke.** On September 25, 1919, the President collapsed in Pueblo, Colorado during a speaking tour on behalf of the League of Nations. Thereafter he succumbed to a paralytic stroke and stubbornly resisted senatorial attempts to revise the Treaty of Paris. He died in 1924. (Library of Congress)

their number some twenty Republicans and a handful of Democrats. The fourth group, consisting of sixteen Irreconcilables, ardently opposed the treaty with or without reservations. Most of them were Republicans, including LaFollette, Norris, and Borah.

Wilson refused to accept any reservations whatsoever. He also argued that a treaty ratified with reservations would have to go back to another international conference for acceptance; he was unwilling to invite that possibility, because every nation would then rush in with its pet reservations. Later this argument was weakened when the British announced that they would accept American reservations just so that the League could be launched and the treaty passed. In September, 1919, noting that Lodge was hoping delay would sour the American people on the treaty, Wilson decided to dig his spade into the grass roots. He set off on an 8,000-mile trip across the United States. It was a tragic journey. Weak, tired, irritable, and plagued by severe headaches, he pounded the podium for forty speeches before he collapsed in Pueblo, Colorado. He took the offensive, blasting his traducers as "absolute, contemptible quitters."[93] He also appealed to patriotism by denouncing hyphenated Americans (a response to Irish- and German-American opposition to the treaty) and by comparing his critics to Bolsheviks (both destructive, he said). He confused his audiences when he stated that Article 10 meant that the United States had a moral but not legal obligation to use armed force. He insisted that America could still decide which wars it wanted to enter. Wilson's erratic practice of mixing impassioned rhetoric with occasional sober analysis undercut his effectiveness.

After his collapse, he returned to Washington, where he fell victim to a stroke that paralyzed his left side. Wilson's poor health probably did not affect the outcome; sick or healthy, he was adamant against compromise. After his stroke, however, he isolated himself, apparently ashamed of his physical weakness. The brain damage and impaired vision resulting from the stroke hindered concentration and promoted stubbornness. His wife, Edith Bolling Wilson, helped run his political affairs, screening messages and visitors, and such advocates of conciliation as Colonel House and Secretary Lansing fell from presidential grace. House was unable even to get an appointment with the ailing President, and in February, 1920, Lansing was abruptly dismissed, replaced by the more pliable Bainbridge Colby, a Wilson admirer. "Better a thousand times to go down fighting," Wilson told his wife, "than to dip your colors to dishonorable compromise."[94] Wilson held firm, but so did the critics.

In November, 1919, the Senate balloted on the complete treaty *with* reservations and rejected it, 39–55 (Irreconcilables and Non-Reservationists in the negative). Then it voted on the treaty *without* reservations and also rejected it, 38–52 (Irreconcilables and Reservationists in the negative). The President kept loyal Democrats in line, forbidding them to accept any "reserved" treaty, yet realistically such was the only kind that would have fulfilled his dream of American membership in the League. In March, 1920, another tally saw many Democrats break ranks to vote in favor of reservations. Still not enough, the treaty was rejected 49–35, short of the two-thirds majority required for ratification. "It is dead," Wilson lamented to his Cabinet, "and lies over there. Every morning I put flowers on its grave."[95] Still a fighter, he avowed that the election of 1920 would be a "solemn referendum" on the treaty. It was not. A multitude of other questions blurred the League issue in that campaign, and Warren G. Harding, who as a senator had supported reservations, was elected President. In July, 1921, Congress officially terminated the war, and in August by treaty with Germany the United States claimed as valid for itself the terms of the Treaty of Paris—exclusive of the League articles.

The memorable League fight was over. The negative outcome can be blamed on political partisanship, personal animosities, senatorial resentment at having been slighted in the peacemaking, and disinterest and confusion in the public, which increasingly diverted its attention to the problem of readjusting to a peacetime economy. Then, of course, there was Wilson himself—stubborn, pontificating, and combative. He might have conceded that the peace was imperfect. He might have provided more careful analysis of a complicated document of 264 pages. He might, further, have admitted that his opponents held a respectable intellectual position. Instead he chose an often shrill rhetoric and a rigid self-righteousness, excessively defensive of his authorship of a parchment that he considered almost sacred. Most important, he refused compromise because the difference between himself and his critics was fundamental: whether it was in America's national interest to participate in collective security or seek safety unilaterally. In essence, then, traditional American nationalism and nonalignment, or unilateralism, decided the debate against Wilson.

America's absence from the League was not catastrophic. None of the great powers wished to bestow significant authority on the League. Even if the United States had joined, it too probably would have continued to act outside the League's auspices, especially regarding its own imperialism in Latin America. No international organization at that time could have outlawed war, dismantled empires, or scuttled navies. Wilson overshot reality in thinking that he could reform world politics through a new international organization: certainly the League was a commendable cry for restraint, but it was no panacea for world peace.

## Containing the Bolshevik Specter: Intervention in Russia

"Paris cannot be understood without Moscow," wrote Wilson's press secretary in France, Ray Stannard Baker. "Without ever being represented at Paris at all, the Bolsheviki and Bolshevism were powerful elements at every turn."[96] Indeed, throughout the conference "there rose the specter of chaos, like a black cloud out of the east, threatening to overwhelm and swallow up the world."[97] As he traveled to France aboard the *George Washington,* President Wilson complained about the "poison of Bolshevism."[98] Revolutionary and anticapitalist, the Bolsheviks, or Communists, threw fright into the established leaders of Europe and America. David Lloyd George worried that Western statesmen would be unable to dam the "waters of Revolution."[99] At home and abroad the peacemakers battled the radical left. In the United States the Wilson Administration trampled on civil liberties during an exaggerated "Red Scare," which sent innocent people to jail or deported them. Abroad Wilson first hoped to tame the Bolsheviks, to reform them, to contain them; finally he hesitantly aligned with other powers in a futile attempt to destroy them.

Most Americans applauded the Russian Revolution of March, 1917, which toppled Tsar Nicholas II. Wilson himself viewed it as a thrust against autocracy, war, and imperialism. But when the moderate Provisional government under Alexander Kerensky fell to the radical Bolsheviks in October, shocked Americans responded with hostility. American anger was further aroused in March, 1918,

**Vladimir Ilyich Lenin (1870–1924).** A Bolshevik revolutionary who had been exiled by the Tsar, Lenin returned to Russia in early 1917 proclaiming that the "people needs peace; the people needs bread; the people needs land." Wilson and the European leaders vowed to thwart the Lenin-sponsored "social revolution" that threatened to spread across Europe. (Library of Congress)

when the Bolsheviks signed the Brest-Litovsk Treaty with Germany. It was a harsh peace for the Russians, for they had to relinquish the territories of the Ukraine and Finland, among others—a total of 1,267,000 square miles, 62,000,000 people, and one-third of Russia's best agricultural land. From the Bolshevik perspective, it was a necessary peace for a nation incapable of continued fighting. From the Allied point of view, the treaty was a stab in the back, an end to the war's eastern front, and a victory for Germany. Some irate American officials began to think that the Bolsheviks were pro-German. V. I. Lenin's travel through Germany in early 1917, with the apparent permission of German authorities, fed this mistaken notion.

A number of methods were open to Wilson and the Allies to smash Bolshevism: military intervention, economic blockade, exclusion from the peacemaking, non-recognition, encirclement with hostile countries (*cordon sanitaire*), food relief, and aid to anti-Bolshevik forces within Russia. They tried all, but Wilson was never sure about the viability of the methods. "I have been sweating blood over the question what it is right and feasible to do in Russia," Wilson wrote Colonel House. "It goes to pieces like quicksilver under my touch."[100] In June, 1918, Wilson decided to send American troops to northern Russia. They were ordered to avoid military action in the Russian civil war, but inevitably they supported French and British units in military efforts to roll back Bolshevik influence. Wilson announced that the expedition was authorized only to prevent German seizure of military supplies and a railroad, but he did not reveal his hope that the venture would help cripple the Red Army. Eventually 5,000 American soldiers, many constituting the "Polar Bears," or 339th Infantry Regiment from Michigan, were stationed there. One hundred and thirty-nine died on Russian soil. They suffered through a bitter winter of fifty below zero temperatures and few daylight hours. Their morale sagged and mutiny threatened. As George F. Kennan has noted: "They alone had to endure this purgatory, and this for reasons never adequately explained to them."[101] Remaining even beyond the armistice of World War I, they departed in June, 1919.

Wilson had hoped to avoid military action, to draw the Bolsheviks peacefully somehow into a nebulous world order. But the pressure from the deeply anticommunist French and British and expansionist Japanese persuaded him to send another expedition, this time to Siberia, where he envisioned the growth of a non-Bolshevik Russian bastion. In July he approved the expedition, later officially explaining to the American people that the troops (eventually numbering 10,000) were being dispatched to rescue a group of Czechs stranded in Russia. The Czech legion had been organized during the war as part of the Russian army to fight for a Czech homeland in Austria-Hungary, but in 1918 it was fighting the Bolsheviks along the Trans-Siberian Railroad. Wilson said he hoped they could get out and back to central Europe to fight Germans.

Wilson's official explanation masked his more general strategy of opposing Bolshevism. Historians disagree on Wilson's motives. Some argue that the official reason (saving the Czechs) is the only one; others say that he wanted to preserve the "Open Door" against the Japanese, who sent some 72,000 troops to Siberia; still others point to the President's anti-Bolshevik intentions. Whether his inten-

**American Troops in Vladivostok, Siberia.** A contingent of the 10,000 United States troops sent by President Wilson to Siberia in 1918 during the Russian civil war. (U.S. Signal Corps, National Archives)

tions were anti-Bolshevik or not, his actions certainly became so. The very presence of American troops in Russia during a civil war, and American support for non-Bolshevik groups, constituted hostility to the Communist regime. Then, too, there is no question that the Czechs were anti-Bolshevik and that the other powers intended their military expeditions to crush the radicals. Wilson and the Allies for a time hoped that anti-Bolshevik White Russian leader Admiral A. V. Kolchak would marshal enough strength to form a pro-Western constitutional government. They funneled money and supplies to him, but he proved an immoderate and ineffective leader, and Kolchak's movement collapsed in late 1919. American troops were finally withdrawn in early 1920 after thirty-six deaths.

At the Paris Peace Conference, the victors tried to isolate what they considered a revolutionary contagion. The Bolsheviks were, of course, excluded from the meeting, certainly a serious mistake: a strike against Wilson's own desire for world unity, and a denial of his pledge of self-determination. "Bolshevism is gaining ground everywhere," Colonel House noted in his diary. "We are sitting on an open powder magazine and some day a spark may ignite it."[102] The organization of the Third International in Moscow in early 1919 alarmed postwar leaders, as did Communist Bela Kun's successful revolution in Hungary in March, 1919, which only lasted until August. At Versailles, the conferees granted territory to Russia's neighbors (Poland, Rumania, and Czechoslovakia) and created the nations of Finland, Estonia, Latvia, and Lithuania as a ring of unfriendly states around Russia. During the conference, besides the military interventions, the Allies imposed a strict economic blockade on Russia, continued aid to the White forces, and sent relief assistance to other countries, like Austria and Hungary, to stem political unrest.

Critics protested against these counterrevolutionary efforts and suggested that alternatives were possible. Raymond Robins (a Red Cross official) and Senator Robert LaFollette, among others, called for recognition of Lenin's government and opposed the policy of isolating Russia from the peace conference. Robins, who met frequently with Lenin, urged the Wilson Administration in early 1918 to send aid to the Bolsheviks so that they could resist the German peace terms eventually written into the Brest-Litovsk Treaty. Other critics, like Walter Lippmann, urged a policy of noninterference—let the Russians settle their own affairs. But Wilson could not tolerate the Bolsheviks; they had betrayed the Allies, expropriated commercial and church property, established a dictatorship, denounced capitalism, and planted seeds of revolution elsewhere. Wilson wanted to reform capitalism; Lenin sought to eliminate it. Wilson believed imperialism and war could be contained through an international organization; Lenin was adamant that war and imperialism were an inevitable outgrowth of expansionist capitalist institutions.

Certainly no ideological compromise was possible. But recognition of the Moscow regime and a diplomatic accommodation appear to have been options. Wilson attempted to end the civil war in Russia in January, 1919, when he invited the warring groups to meet on Prinkipo Island in the Sea of Marmara. The Bolsheviks cautiously accepted the invitation, but the anti-Bolsheviks flatly rejected it and the meeting never took place. Next, in February, Colonel House arranged to send William C. Bullitt, a member of the American delegation at Versailles, and Lincoln Steffens, radical muckraking journalist, to Russia to talk with the Soviets. Wilson envisioned a factfinding mission. The ambitious Bullitt, however, dreamed of an agreement whereby Allied troops would be withdrawn from Russia and Lenin would make territorial concessions to his adversaries to end the civil war. Believing that the Moscow government was well established, Bullitt and Steffens returned to Paris convinced they had struck such an agreement. Lloyd George squelched it; Wilson ignored it. Bullitt, already disgusted by Wilson's compromises with the Allies at Paris, resigned in protest.

The Allied counterrevolution was costly to the future of international relations. The scar ran deep. "Few in the West recall the war of East and West of 1918–20," Frederick L. Schuman has written. "Every city, town, and village in Russia preserves momentoes of these tragic years."[103] In 1959, for example, Premier Nikita Khrushchev reminded Americans of their oft-forgotten intervention. At a time when Soviet leaders were locked in a life-or-death struggle against internal enemies, they had to resist a foreign invasion that prolonged the agony of civil war. The blatant Allied tactics ultimately backfired, as the Bolsheviks capitalized on the nationalistic feelings aroused by foreign troops on Russian soil. Wilson's dream of a cooperative and harmonious world was dealt another blow. William Bullitt resolved to lie on the beaches of the Mediterranean and "watch the world go to hell."[104] "He went. And it did."[105]

## American Expansion and World War I

About 130,000 Americans died in the First World War and the conflict cost the United States government over thirty billion dollars. A third of the figure was paid through taxes; the other two-thirds represented borrowed money, which would have to be paid off by postwar generations. If one counts the long-term expense of veterans' benefits, the cost to the United States probably equaled three times the immediate direct costs. But the price and consequences of World War I can be reckoned in other ways. What President Dwight D. Eisenhower would later call the "military-industrial complex" had its origins in the government-business cooperation during that war; economic decisionmaking for the nation was centralized as never before, and efficient methods in manufacturing were applied comprehensively, contributing to American economic power. In foreign affairs, the White House, under Wilson's heady leadership, assumed more authority in initiating policy and controlling execution. The State Department read diplomatic messages after Wilson had typed them on his own machine. Wilson bypassed Congress on a number of occasions, failing even to consult that body, for example, about the Fourteen Points, the goals at Versailles, and the intervention in the Russian civil war. He acted, according to his biographer Arthur S. Link, "like a divine-right monarch in the conduct of foreign relations."[106] The Senate finally rebelled by rejecting the League of Nations, but that negative decision did not undercut the trend of growing presidential power in the making of foreign policy.

The era of World War I also witnessed domestic events that in turn affected foreign affairs: racial conflict, evidenced by twenty-five race riots in 1919; suppression of civil liberties under the Espionage and Sedition Acts, by which innocent people who dissented from the war were silenced; the crippling of radical commentary (Socialist party leader Eugene Debs was jailed for opposing the war) and hence the growth of an uncritical consensus; the emasculation of the reform impulse. Wars tend to demand conformity at home because leaders insist on

**"We Are Making a New World."** British painter Paul Nash rendered this gloomy landscape as a commentary on the ugly devastation wrought by the guns of World War I. (Imperial War Museum, London)

patriotism and commitment to the "crusade." Those who question the foreign venture can face ostracism and harassment.

Over 10 million lives were annihilated in World War I. Russia lost 1.7 million, Germany gave up 1.8 million, and Britain lost 1 million. One out of every two French males between the ages of twenty and thirty-two (in 1914) died during the war. It had been a total war, involving whole societies, not merely their marching armies. Europe's landscape was trampled. Never before had a war left the belligerents so exhausted, so battered. New destructive weapons had been introduced—tanks, airplanes, poison gas, the Big Bertha gun, and submarines. Journalist Hanson Baldwin has commented that World War I "provided a preview of the Pandora's box of evils that the linkage of science with industry in the service of war was to mean."[107] Many Americans turned away in disgust from the slaughter and the new weapons of destruction. The sight of men singing as they marched to their deaths seemed incongruous. The desire to avoid a major war was strong after the European conflict, and Americans would henceforth be cautious about entering a conflagration in Europe. The *New Republic* editorialized: "THIS IS NOT PEACE. Americans would be fools if they permitted themselves to be embroiled in a system of European alliances. . . . America should withdraw from all commitments which would impair her freedom of action."[108] Disillusioned intellectuals like Ernest Hemingway and John Dos Passos mocked the carthaginian peace. E. M. Remarque's *All Quiet on the Western Front* (1929) captured the antiwar mood: "A hospital alone shows what war is." [109]

World War I, as someone remarked, stacked the cards for the future. Empires were broken up—the Turkish, Austro-Hungarian, German, and Russian—creating new and weak nations. Nationalists in Asia, such as Mahatma Gandhi in British-dominated India and Ho Chi Minh in French-controlled Indochina, set goals of national liberation based in part upon Wilson's ideal of self-determination. Sun Yat-sen's Chinese revolution jarred Asian relationships. The rather closed, Europe-oriented diplomatic system of the turn of the century had fragmented and expanded to include the several new states in central and eastern Europe, Japan, and the United States, as well as the new League of Nations. In Latin America, prewar European economic stakes were loosened, inviting the United States to expand its interests there. The international system was quite fluid, made more so by the rise of Bolshevism in Russia. The world had to be put back together again: the adjustments to new relationships would not come easily. Because of fear of communism, leaders tried to isolate Soviet Russia. Because of fear of a revived Germany, leaders tried to strip it of power, creating bitter resentments in the German people. Because the victors faced reconstruction problems at home, they tagged Germany with a huge reparations bill that would disorient European and world economics. Nobody seemed happy with the postwar settlement; many would attempt to recapture lost opportunities or to redefine the terms. Wilsonianism enjoyed but a brief prominence; the lessons Wilson sought to impress upon an offending mankind were taught, but unlearned. World War I had, surely, created as many problems as it solved. "Politically, economically, socially," Wilson informed Congress in 1919, "the World is on the operating table, and it has not been possible to administer any anesthetic." [110] Wilson had his prescription for the cure, but so did others, including the Russians with their competing ideology of communism.

To Americans, World War I bequeathed an unassailable legacy: the United States became the world's leading economic power. As Wilson confidently put it in August, 1919: "The financial leadership will be ours. The industrial primacy will be ours. The commercial advantage will be ours. The other countries of the world are looking to us for leadership and direction." [111] During the war years, to meet the need for raw materials, American companies expanded operations in developing nations. Goodyear went into the Dutch East Indies for rubber, Swift and Armour expanded in South America, tin interests tapped Bolivia, copper companies penetrated Chile, and oil firms sank new wells in Latin America. The government took considerable interest in and gave encouragement to this economic expansion. By 1920, America produced about 40 percent of the world's coal, 70 percent of its oil, and about half of its pig iron.

Because the United States government and American citizens loaned heavily to the Allies during the war, the nation shifted abruptly from a debtor to a creditor status, with Wall Street replacing London as the world's financial center. By early 1919 the Allied governments owed the United States government $10 billion. Whereas before the war Americans owed foreigners $3 billion, after the conflict foreigners owed Americans $13 billion. A gradual shift had begun before the war, but the wartime experience accelerated it tremendously. Americans had devised plans to seize the apparent economic opportunities given them by the war—the Edge Act to permit foreign branch banks, and the Webb-Pomerone Act to allow trade associations to continue to combine for export trading without fear of antitrust action, for example—but a key question remained: how could Europeans pay back their debt to the United States? The answer lay somewhere in a complicated tangle of loans, reparations, tariffs, and world trade. "We are on the eve of a commercial war of the severest sort," predicted Wilson in early 1920.[112]

Economic disorder, then, coupled with political instability, was a legacy of the war. Wilson, who tried to plan against it, warned Congress in August, 1919: "We must face the fact that unless we help Europe to get back to her normal life and production a chaos will ensue there which will inevitably be communicated to this country. . . . In saving Europe, she [United States] will save herself. . . . Europe is our best customer. We must keep her going or thousands of our shops and scores of our mines must close. There is no such thing as letting her go to ruin without ourselves sharing in the disaster."[113] Whether this awareness of the interdependence of the world economy would be matched by policies to stabilize economic conditions was the supreme question for postwar leaders. In 1920, as they contemplated the future, it appeared that World War I had made the world safe neither for American democracy nor for American commerce and capital. American diplomats, with a sense of America's new power, would next try nonmilitary methods.

## Further Reading for the Period 1914–1920

For the foreign policy of Woodrow Wilson and the era of World War I, see Paul Birdsall, "Neutrality and Economic Pressure, 1914–1917," *Science and Society* (1939), Edward H. Buehrig, ed., *Wilson's Foreign Policy in Perspective* (1957), John M. Cooper, *The Vanity of Power: American Isolationism and the First World War* (1969), Patrick Devlin, *Too Proud to Fight: Woodrow Wilson's Neutrality* (1975), Ross Gregory, *The Origins of American Intervention in the First World War* (1971), Sondra Herman, *Eleven Against War* (1969), Arthur S. Link, *Wilson* (1960–1965) and *Wilson the Diplomatist* (1963), Ernest R. May, *The World War and American Isolation, 1914–1917* (1959), Daniel M. Smith, *The Great Departure* (1965), and Charles C. Tansill, *America Goes to War* (1938).

For American participation in and diplomacy during the First World War, consult Edward M. Coffman, *The War to End All Wars* (1968), Harvey A. DeWeerd, *President Wilson Fights His War* (1968), and David Trask, *The United States in the Supreme War Council* (1961).

The peacemaking at Versailles and the fate of the League of Nations in the Senate are discussed in Thomas A. Bailey, *Woodrow Wilson and the Lost Peace* (1944) and *Woodrow Wilson and the Great Betrayal* (1945), Lawrence E. Gelfand, *The Inquiry: American Preparations for Peace* (1963), Herbert Hoover, *The Ordeal of Woodrow Wilson* (1958), Warren F. Kuehl, *Seeking World Order: The United States and International Organization to 1920* (1969), Keith Nelson, *Victors Divided: America and the Allies in Germany, 1918–1923* (1973), Robert E. Osgood, *Ideals and Self-Interest in American Foreign Relations* (1953), Ralph A. Stone, *The Irreconcilables* (1970), and Seth P. Tillman, *Anglo-American Relations at the Paris Peace Conference, 1919* (1961).

America's response to the Bolshevik Revolution in Russia is treated in Lloyd C. Gardner, ed., *Wilson and Revolutions, 1913–1921* (1976), George F. Kennan, *Russia Leaves the War* (1956) and *The Decision to Intervene* (1958), N. Gordon Levin, *Woodrow Wilson and World Politics* (1968), Arno Mayer, *Peacemaking: Containment and Counter-*

*revolution at Versailles* (1967), and John Thompson, *Russia, Bolshevism, and the Versailles Peace* (1966). See Betty Unterberger, ed., *American Intervention in the Russian Civil War* (1969) for representative essays.

The following works study prominent participants: Allen F. Davis, *American Heroine: The Life and Legend of Jane Addams* (1974), John A. Garraty, *Henry Cabot Lodge* (1953), Ross Gregory, *Walter Hines Page* (1970), and Daniel M. Smith, *Robert Lansing and American Neutrality* (1958). For brief biographies, see John A. Garraty, ed., *Encyclopedia of American Biography* (1974).

For other studies, see Wilton B. Fowler, ed., *American Diplomatic History Since 1890* (1975), a bibliographical list, Daniel M. Smith, "National Interest and American Intervention, 1917: An Historiographical Appraisal," *Journal of American History* (1965), Samuel F. Wells, Jr., "New Perspectives on Wilsonian Diplomacy," *Perspectives in American History* (1972), and the following notes.

## Notes to Chapter 8

1. Quoted in Thomas A. Bailey and Paul B. Ryan, *The Lusitania Disaster* (New York: The Free Press, 1975), p. 81.
2. Quoted in Edward Robb Ellis, *Echoes of Distant Thunder: Life in the United States, 1914–1918* (New York: Coward, McCann & Geoghegan, 1975), p. 195.
3. Quoted in Bailey and Ryan, *Lusitania Disaster*, p. 94.
4. *Ibid.*, p. 82.
5. *Ibid.*, p. 133.
6. *Ibid.*, p. 150.
7. Quoted in C. L. Droste and W. H. Tantum, eds., *The Lusitania Case* (Riverside, Conn.: 7 C's Press, 1972), p. 172.
8. Quoted in Burton J. Hendrick, *Life and Letters of Walter Hines Page* (Garden City, N.Y.: Doubleday, Page, 1922–1925; 3 vols.), II, 2.
9. William Jennings Bryan and Mary B. Bryan, *Memoirs* (Chicago: John C. Winston, 1925), pp. 398–399.
10. Quoted in William H. Harbaugh, *The Life and Times of Theodore Roosevelt* (New York: Oxford University Press, 1975; rev. ed.), p. 448.
11. Arthur S. Link, *Wilson: The Struggle for Neutrality, 1914–1915* (Princeton: Princeton University Press, 1960), p. 379.
12. Ray Stannard Baker and William E. Dodd, eds., *Public Papers of Woodrow Wilson: The New Democracy* (New York: Harper and Brothers, 1926; 2 vols.), I, 321.
13. U.S. Department of State, *Foreign Relations of the United States, 1915, Supplement* (Washington: Government Printing Office, 1928), p. 396.
14. *New York World*, quoted in Link, *Wilson: Struggle for Neutrality*, p. 410.
15. David F. Houston, *Eight Years with Wilson's Cabinet, 1913 to 1920* (Garden City, N.Y.: Doubleday, Page, 1926; 2 vols.), I, 137.
16. Quoted in Ernest R. May, *The World War and American Isolation, 1914–1917* (Chicago: Quadrangle Books, [1959], 1966), p. 155.
17. Quoted in Paolo E. Coletta, *William Jennings Bryan* (Lincoln: University of Nebraska Press, 1964–1969; 3 vols.), II, 343.
18. Bailey and Ryan, *Lusitania Disaster*, p. 340.
19. Robert Lansing, *War Memoirs* (Indianapolis: Bobbs-Merrill, 1935), p. 128.

20. Franklin K. Lane, quoted in Robert E. Osgood, *Ideals and Self-Interest in American Foreign Relations* (Chicago: University of Chicago Press, 1953), p. 173.
21. Quoted in Rohan Butler, "The Peace Settlement of Versailles, 1918–1933," in C. L. Mowat, ed., *The New Cambridge Modern History*, vol. XII: *The Shifting Balance of World Forces, 1898–1945* (Cambridge: Cambridge University Press, 1968), p. 214.
22. Quoted in George H. Knoles, "American Intellectuals and World War I," *Pacific Northwest Quarterly*, LIX (October, 1968), 203.
23. Quoted in Barbara Tuchman, *The Guns of August* (New York: Dell, [1962], 1963), p. 91.
24. Quoted in Hendrick, *Life and Letters of Walter Hines Page*, I, 310.
25. Baker and Dodd, *Public Papers: The New Democracy*, I, 157–159.
26. Quoted in Tuchman, *Guns of August*, p. 349.
27. *Ibid.*, p. 153.
28. Quoted from *Life* magazine, in Mark Sullivan, *Our Times* (New York: Charles Scribner's Sons, 1926–1937; 6 vols.), V, 59.
29. Quoted in Ray Stannard Baker, *Woodrow Wilson: Life and Letters* (New York: Doubleday, Doran, 1927–39; 8 vols.), V, 175.
30. Quoted in Paul Birdsall, "Neutrality and Economic Pressures, 1914–1917," *Science and Society*, III (Spring, 1939), 221.
31. Quoted in Bailey and Ryan, *Lusitania Disaster*, p. 99.
32. Ross Gregory, *The Origins of American Intervention in the First World War* (New York: W. W. Norton, 1971), p. 131.
33. Quoted in Bailey and Ryan, *Lusitania Disaster*, p. 29.
34. *Foreign Relations, 1915, Supplement*, p. 99.
35. Quoted in Arthur S. Link, *Woodrow Wilson and the Progressive Era, 1910–1917* (New York: Harper & Row, 1954), p. 203.
36. Quoted in Arthur S. Link, *Wilson: Confusions and Crisis, 1915–1916* (Princeton: Princeton University Press, 1964), p. 125n. Italics in original.
37. *Ibid.*, pp. 134–135.
38. Bryan and Bryan, *Memoirs*, p. 397.
39. *Foreign Relations, 1915, Supplement*, p. 461.

40. Quoted in Bailey and Ryan, *Lusitania Disaster*, p. 128.

41. Baker and Dodd, *Public Papers: The New Democracy*, II, 122–124.

42. Claude Kitchin, quoted in May, *World War and American Isolation*, p. 189.

43. Samuel Flagg Bemis, "A Worcester County Student in Wartime London and Paris (via Harvard): 1915–1916," *New England Galaxy*, XI (Spring, 1970), 20.

44. Quoted in Patrick Devlin, *Too Proud to Fight: Woodrow Wilson's Neutrality* (New York: Oxford University Press, 1975), p. 517.

45. Baker and Dodd, *Public Papers: The New Democracy*, II, 407–414.

46. Quoted in Jean-Baptiste Duroselle's essay in *Wilson's Diplomacy: An International Symposium* (Cambridge, Mass.: Schenkman, 1973), p. 21.

47. Quoted in Arthur S. Link, *Wilson: Campaigns for Progressivism and Peace, 1916–1917* (Princeton: Princeton University Press, 1965), p. 274.

48. *Ibid.*, p. 289.

49. Quoted in May, *World War and American Isolation*, p. 414.

50. Quoted in Konrad H. Jaransch, *The Enigmatic Chancellor: Bethmann Hollweg and the Hubris of Imperial Germany* (New Haven: Yale University Press, 1973), p. 301.

51. Lansing, *War Memoirs*, p. 212.

52. Quoted in Link, *Wilson: Campaigns*, p. 343.

53. Quoted in Harbaugh, *Life and Times of Theodore Roosevelt*, p. 467.

54. Quoted in Baker, *Woodrow Wilson: Life and Letters*, VI, 481.

55. Ray Stannard Baker and William E. Dodd, eds., *Public Papers of Woodrow Wilson: War and Peace* (New York: Harper & Brothers, 1927; 2 vols.), I, 6–16.

56. Gregory, *Origins of American Intervention*, p. 128.

57. Quoted in Osgood, *Ideals and Self-Interest*, p. 177.

58. Quoted in May, *World War and American Isolation*, p. 337.

59. Quoted in J. Garry Clifford, *The Citizen Soldiers: The Plattsburg Training Camp Movement, 1913–1920* (Lexington, Ky.: University Press of Kentucky, 1972), p. 234.

60. Edward M. Coffman, *The War To End All Wars: The American Military Experience in World War I* (New York: Oxford University Press, 1968), p. 27.

61. Quoted *ibid.*, p. 4.

62. *Ibid.*

63. *Ibid.*, p. 67.

64. Quoted in Allen F. Davis, "Welfare, Reform, and World War I," *American Quarterly*, XIX (Fall, 1967), 530.

65. *Ibid.*

66. *Ibid.*, p. 531.

67. Baker and Dodd, *Public Papers: War and Peace*, I, 202.

68. Quoted in *Literary Digest*, LIX (November 30, 1918), 15.

69. Baker and Dodd, *Public Papers: War and Peace*, I, 159–161.

70. Quoted in Selig Adler, *The Isolationist Impulse* (New York: Collier Books [c. 1957], 1961), pp. 60–61.

71. H. G. Nicholas' essay in *Wilson's Diplomacy*, p. 81.

72. Quoted in David F. Trask, *The United States in the Supreme War Council: American War Aims and Inter-Allied Strategy, 1917–1918* (Middletown, Conn.: Wesleyan University Press, 1961), p. 155.

73. Quoted in Daniel M. Smith, *The Great Departure* (New York: John Wiley and Sons, 1965), p. 115.

74. Quoted in Julius W. Pratt, *America and World Leadership, 1900–1921* (New York: Collier Books [c. 1967], 1970), p. 175.

75. George Harvey, quoted in Ralph Stone, *The Irreconcilables* (Lexington, Ky.: University Press of Kentucky, 1970), p. 35.

76. Quoted in Smith, *Great Departure*, p. 109.

77. Quoted in Herbert Hoover, *The Ordeal of Woodrow Wilson* (New York: McGraw-Hill, 1958), p. 254.

78. Quoted in Ross Gregory, "To Do Good in the World: Woodrow Wilson," in Frank Merli and Theodore Wilson, eds., *Makers of American Diplomacy* (New York: Scribner's, 1974), p. 380.

79. Bernard M. Baruch, *The Making of the Reparation and Economic Sections of The Treaty* (New York: Harper & Brothers, 1920), p. 7.

80. Quoted in N. Gordon Levin, Jr., *Woodrow Wilson and World Politics: America's Response to War and Revolution* (New York: Oxford University Press, 1968), p. 134.

81. Article 10 of the League covenant.

82. Baker and Dodd, *Public Papers: War and Peace*, I, 428.

83. Quoted in Hoover, *Ordeal of Woodrow Wilson*, p. 239.

84. Quoted in Ernst Fraenkel's essay in *Wilson's Diplomacy*, p. 65.

85. Baker and Dodd, *Public Papers: War and Peace*, I, 432–440.

86. Quoted in D. F. Fleming, *The United States and the League of Nations, 1918–1920* (New York: Russell & Russell, 1968), p. 134.

87. Baker and Dodd, *Public Papers: War and Peace*, I, 551–552.

88. Quoted in Thomas A. Bailey, *Woodrow Wilson and the Great Betrayal* (Chicago: Quadrangle Books [1945], 1963), p. 9.

89. Quoted in Arthur S. Link, *Wilson the Diplomatist* (Chicago: Quadrangle Books [1957], 1963), p. 131.

90. Quoted in Stone, *Irreconcilables*, p. 88.

91. Quoted in Osgood, *Ideals and Self-Interest*, p. 286.

92. Roland N. Stromberg, *Collective Security and American Foreign Policy* (New York: Frederick A. Praeger, 1963), p. 37.

93. Baker and Dodd, *Public Papers: War and Peace*, I, 624.

94. Quoted in Hoover, *Ordeal of Woodrow Wilson*, p. 281.

95. Quoted in E. David Cronon, ed., *The Cabinet Diaries of Josephus Daniels, 1913–1921* (Lincoln: University of Nebraska Press, 1963), p. 520.

96. Quoted in John M. Thompson, *Russia, Bolshevism, and the Versailles Peace* (Princeton: Princeton University Press, 1966), pp. 3–4.

97. Quoted in Arno J. Mayer, *Politics and Diplomacy of Peacemaking* (New York: Vintage Books [c. 1967], 1969), p. 10.

98. *Ibid.*, p. 21.

99. Quoted in Hoover, *Ordeal of Woodrow Wilson*, p. 168.

100. Quoted in Charles Seymour, *The Intimate Papers of Colonel House* (Boston: Houghton Mifflin, 1926–1928; 4 vols.), III, 415.

101. George F. Kennan, *Russia and the West under Lenin and Stalin* (Boston: Little, Brown, 1960), pp. 88.

102. Quoted in Thompson, *Russia, Bolshevism, and the Versailles Peace*, p. 389.

103. Frederick L. Schuman, *Russia Since 1917* (New York: Alfred A. Knopf, 1957), p. 109.

104. Quoted in Beatrice Farnsworth, *William C. Bullitt and the Soviet Union* (Bloomington: Indiana University Press, 1967), p. 70.

105. Walter LaFeber and Richard Polenberg, *The American Century* (New York: John Wiley & Sons, 1975), p. 127.

106. Arthur S. Link, *The Higher Realism of Woodrow Wilson* (Nashville: Vanderbilt University Press, 1971), p. 83.

107. Quoted in Gordon A. Craig, "The Revolution in War and Diplomacy," in Jack J. Roth, ed., *World War I: A Turning Point in Modern History* (New York: Alfred A. Knopf, 1967), p. 12.

108. Quoted in Arthur A. Ekirch, Jr., *Ideas, Ideals, and American Diplomacy* (New York: Appleton-Century-Crofts, 1966), p. 121.

109. E. M. Remarque, *All Quiet on the Western Front* (London: Putnam, 1929), p. 224.

110. Baker and Dodd, *Public Papers: War and Peace*, I, 560.

111. *Ibid.*, p. 640.

112. Quoted in John A. DeNovo, "The Movement for an Aggressive American Oil Policy Abroad, 1918–1920," *American Historical Review, LXI* (July, 1956), 858.

113. Baker and Dodd, *Public Papers: War and Peace*, I, 568–569.

**Franklin D. Roosevelt (1882–1945).** "Happy Days Are Here Again" was his campaign song. Although crippled by polio, this energetic man from Hyde Park, New York was elected four times to the White House. He launched major changes in domestic and foreign policy, including the recognition of Soviet Russia in 1933. (United Press International)

# 9 Power Without Punch: Relations with Europe, 1920–1939

## Diplomatic Crossroad: Franklin D. Roosevelt and the Recognition of Russia, 1933

"Gosh, if I could only, myself, talk to some one man representing the Russians," remarked the President to his close friend and soon-to-be Secretary of the Treasury Henry Morgenthau, Jr., "I could straighten out this whole question."[1] The problem was the sixteen-year-old American policy of nonrecognition of Soviet Russia. Franklin D. Roosevelt decided in early 1933 to bring "this whole Russian question into our front parlor instead of back in the kitchen."[2] The tall, balding, inarticulate, but forceful Morgenthau wanted to sell surplus American cotton to the Russians, and in union with such advocates as Senator William Borah and Colonel Edward House, he encouraged the shift toward recognition. Rather than use the services of the Department of State, which Roosevelt considered still in the "horse and buggy age,"[3] the President preferred personal emissaries like Morgenthau and William C. Bullitt. Bullitt, who had undertaken the abortive mission to Lenin in 1919, was considered a friend of Russia. Ambitious, headstrong, and irascible, Bullitt in 1933 served as special assistant to the secretary of state. In reality, he represented Roosevelt—a "Colonel House in disguise," as one senator put it.[4]

In early October, 1933, at Roosevelt's request, Bullitt began meeting with Boris Skvirsky, director of the Soviet Information Bureau in Washington. He handed Skvirsky a presidential invitation to open discussions "to end the present abnormal relations." But, Bullitt hastened to add, the President's note was only a draft, not a formal document. He instructed the somewhat surprised Russian official to send the invitation to Moscow "by your most confidential code, and learn if it is acceptable to your people." If Russian leaders found it acceptable, they should forward a draft response and, when approved in Washington, both the invitation and Soviet answer would be made public. However, if the Soviet reply should be negative, "Will you give me your word of honor that there will never be any publicity in regard to this proposed exchange of letters and that

301

the whole matter will be kept a secret?"[5] Secrecy being nothing new to Soviet diplomacy, Skvirsky gave his word.

Moscow responded favorably and on October 20 Roosevelt, who liked surprises, published his letter to Russian titular head Mikhail Kalinin, as well as Kalinin's missive to the President. The letters were purposely vague, although the often hyperbolic FDR managed to say at his press conference that "they describe the situation 100 per cent."[6] The President's cordial letter invited the Russians to engage in "frank, friendly conversations" with him "personally." Kalinin responded that he too sought to end the abnormality of nonrecognition, which had an "unfavorable effect not only on the interests of the two states concerned, but also on the general international situation, increasing the element of disquiet, complicating the process of consolidating world peace and encouraging forces tending to disturb that peace."[7]

The last, oblique reference to Japanese aggression in China suggested that the Russians, as well as the Americans, placed the upcoming negotiations in a global context. Since 1917 the Soviets had unsuccessfully sought recognition from the United States, but had been told repeatedly that they must first assume their "international obligations." A world depression and Japanese aggression along Russia's Far Eastern border—trade and security questions—changed attitudes. In early 1933, American officials like Bullitt met informally with Russian diplomats in Europe, and both sides intimated interest in opening diplomatic relations. Bullitt assured Commissar for Foreign Affairs Maxim Litvinov in London that Americans were talking with him "as if he were a human being and not a wild man," and Bullitt advised the President to recognize the Soviet Union because "the two

**"So You're the Big Bad Bear!"** Roosevelt and Soviet Commissar for Foreign Affairs Maxim Litvinov met in Washington in 1933. The atmosphere was friendly. (*Washington Evening Star,* Library of Congress)

countries will henceforth be intimately related in their policy towards Japan and if we should have first-rate men in both countries we might to a large extent control their common actions or at least prevent their acting in a way of which we disapprove."[8] Litvinov likewise hoped American recognition would stand as a warning to Tokyo, which might wonder whether the United States would join forces with Russia if war broke out. Litvinov may even have wanted something approximating an alliance. The fact that Moscow later named its foremost expert on Japan, Alexander Troyanovsky, as the first ambassador to the United States further suggests the Russian preoccupation.

Russia's chief diplomat, Litvinov himself, came to Washington for the negotiations in November, 1933. The chubby round-faced commissar was "regarded as the sharpest trader in Europe," according to Under Secretary of State William Phillips.[9] Morgenthau found him a "warm, friendly man, sparkling in conversation, abundant in hospitality," and Louis Fischer, considered one of the most knowledgeable journalists on Soviet affairs, commented that the intelligent, English-speaking Litvinov "talks quickly on the platform and swallows at least one syllable in each word."[10] On his arrival in the United States on November 7, Litvinov amused reporters when he said that the negotiations would take less than half an hour. In Washington Secretary of State Cordell Hull greeted the visiting envoy and grumbled privately that the President should have used State Department machinery to contact Russia. Actually this was one of the few functions Hull would undertake during the Litvinov visit, because Roosevelt had deliberately scheduled the negotiations knowing full well that his silver-haired secretary would soon be departing for a Pan American Conference in Montevideo, Uruguay. The show would belong to the charming and self-confident Roosevelt, an example of his "personal diplomacy." When the President first met Litvinov in the Blue Room of the White House, he tried to humor the Russian by cracking that the Red Room would be a more appropriate site.

Humor aside, the United States had serious reasons for a turnaround on the question of recognition. Nonrecognition of a major country simply made no diplomatic sense. It had not altered the Soviet system or foreign policy. Fischer summarized widespread opinion when he said it was wrong "not to be in touch with a power which was half of Europe and which occupied a most important strategic position in relation to Japan and China."[11] Phillips concluded that, "since most of the other great powers had already taken the step, to continue to be not on speaking terms had become an absurdity."[12] Although they were divided on the issue, with the American Federation of Labor and the American Legion, among other groups, opposed, more Americans favored recognition in 1933 than ever before. Opening relations, then, might even prove a political success at home. Also, increased trade with Russia beckoned in the hard days of the depression. Many businessmen sought Russian markets, and humorist Will Rogers quipped that "we would recognize the Devil with a false face if he would contract for some pitchforks."[13] Furthermore, of prime strategic importance in American calculations was Japan, recent conqueror of Manchuria: as an Asian power itself, the Soviet Union was a potential bulwark against further Japanese expansion. "The world is moving into a dangerous period both in Europe and Asia," Hull once told the President. "Russia could be a great help in stabilizing this situation as time goes on and peace becomes more and more threatened."[14] No American official ever precisely explained how Russia and the United States might cooperate to tame

Japan, but the common assumption prevailed that somehow Japan would think recognition implied something formal, hence dictating caution in Asia.

A number of Russian-American issues from the past also claimed attention in 1933. This "rich food for debate," as Hull put it, included the debts-claims question.[15] By American accounts Russia owed Americans and the United States government about $636 million for loans extended during World War I and compensation for property confiscated during the Bolshevik Revolution. Moreover, Russia was to many Americans the epitome of anti-God; to gain support from American religious leaders, most notably Father Edmund Walsh of Georgetown University, Roosevelt promised to seek Soviet pledges guaranteeing religious freedom for Americans in Russia. Anticapitalist propaganda directed at the United States also aroused antagonism to communism, as did the uncertainty of legal rights for Americans charged with crimes in Russia. The State Department, which for years had been collecting data and formulating arguments against recognition, was now directed to shift its position, much against its will. It prepared documents on these outstanding questions, making the case that solutions should precede the extension of recognition. Secretary Hull himself seemed lukewarm toward recognition, not simply because Roosevelt was bypassing him, but because he thought Moscow-directed Communists were fomenting revolution in Cuba. His attitudes did not command presidential notice. Anyway, Hull was packing his bags for Montevideo.

The first serious talks, dealing with what Roosevelt called the "mechanical procedure" of sifting through hundreds of "details and figures," went badly.[16] Litvinov insisted on recognition before negotiations. Roosevelt broke the impasse on November 10 when he again humored the commissar by suggesting they meet alone so that "they could, if need be, insult each other with impunity."[17] In subsequent tête-à-tête meetings on the 12th, 15th, and 16th, the two amiable negotiators moved like two bookworms eating toward one another from opposite ends of the shelf, as Bullitt put it. The knottiest question was debts-claims. Much of the amount, Litvinov insisted, was owed by the defunct Tsarist and Provisional governments, not by the Bolsheviks. That amount would never be paid. Unable to resolve their differences, the parties initialed a "gentleman's agreement" acknowledging that they would discuss debts and claims in the future.

Late in the evening of November 16, Litvinov and Roosevelt signed and exchanged a series of letters outlining their agreements: establishment of diplomatic relations, cessation of Soviet subversive activities and propaganda against the United States, protection of religious freedom and legal rights for Americans in Russia, and settlement of debts and claims through future negotiations. There was no mention of Japan or trade in the documents, although the questions were on everybody's mind. Nor was provision made for an American loan to finance Soviet-American trade—a loan the Russians had apparently set as a goal in the negotiations. The imprecise agreements did not satisfy the legalists in the State Department, who complained further that FDR kept no memoranda of his meetings.

When Josef Stalin heard about recognition he uttered *"Ne Razkhlebasta"* or "Keep your shirt on. Don't display our excessive glee."[18] Russian and American expectations for healthy relations *at the time* ran high, despite the Department of State's lack of optimism. Soviet expert George F. Kennan complained later that the popular "idea of trying to enlist Soviet strength in a cause [against Japan] for which we were unwilling to develop and mobilize our own seemed to me particularly dangerous."[19] Kennan's harsh criticism suggests an important consideration: America and Russia were using one another against a third power because alone each was too weak. For the rest of the decade each would attempt to increase its own strength, but in 1933 both looked upon recognition as a stopgap solution to the Asian crisis and depression-plagued trade. "I hope it lasts," Hull remarked when he heard about the Litvinov-Roosevelt accord.[20] It did not, for both Moscow and Washington pursued independent foreign policies that obstructed cooperation against what Morgenthau called the "roughnecks" of international relations.[21]

## Independent Internationalism: Diplomats and Diplomacy Between the Wars

The history of the 1933 recognition of Russia illustrates well some of the key themes of interwar diplomacy. It demonstrates that the United States was seeking nonmilitary methods to implement its foreign policy of thwarting hostile powers in traditionally significant areas. It reveals the importance of trade questions and the impact of the Great Depression on diplomacy. It suggests that at times ideological differences, or emotional dislike for a dreaded and alien social-political system, could be subordinated to the national interest. It demonstrates how a President, if an activist, can master the foreign affairs process, even using such devices as isolating his own State Department and signing vague agreements. The recognition of Soviet Russia, finally, proves that the United States in the interwar years was not following a course of simple "isolationism."

The United States had emerged from World War I a recognized world power. Postwar American diplomats, closer to a global perspective than ever before, knew that the American frontier had been extended, that even if they wanted to, Americans could not be bystanders in world affairs. True, between the First and Second World Wars Americans hoped to avoid foreign entanglements and concentrate on domestic matters. But, within the limits of United States power, American leaders largely pursued an active foreign policy befitting their nation's high international status. On the whole, they did not put themselves helplessly at the mercy of events, but worked to create a world of peaceful nations characterized by legal and orderly processes, the Open Door, and economic and political stability. Washington emphasized nonmilitary means—treaties, conferences, disarmament, economic and financial arrangements—in its pursuit of that elusive order. One President pointed to this attempted retreat from military methods when he observed that "we can never herd the world into the paths of righteousness with the dogs of war," and a secretary of state remarked that the United States championed a "commercial and non-military stabilization of the world."[22]

America was "isolationist" between the wars only in the sense that it wanted to isolate itself from war, to scale down foreign military involvements, and to preserve the freedom to make independent decisions in international affairs in order to serve the national interest of prosperity and security. Historian Joan Hoff Wilson's apt phrase, "independent internationalism," rather than "isolationism," characterized American practice and attitude—active on an international scale, but independent in action.[23] There was some recognition in the United States that its influence abroad had limits: where the United States lacked viable power, such as in Asia, it moved haltingly. Where it possessed power, as in Latin America, it moved vigorously. As for Europe, where United States influence was extensive, Americans ultimately concluded they could not solve Europe's problems if Europeans themselves would not do so, and Congress adopted "neutrality" legislation.

**Charles Evans Hughes (1862–1948) and Warren G. Harding (1865–1923).** The secretary of state and President were quite different in background and intelligence, but as conservatives both sought a stable nonrevolutionary world order. (Ohio Historical Society)

Unwilling to become entangled once again in European military squabbles and balance-of-power machinations, the United States did try, however ineffectually, to heal the wounds of World War I through economic diplomacy, disarmament, and the outlawry of war. Yet, by 1939, Washington had decided again that risking war was necessary to achieve world order.

After Woodrow Wilson's Administration and until that of Franklin D. Roosevelt, the American foreign policy process was characterized by weak presidential leadership, congressional-executive competition, and increased professionalism in the Foreign Service. Presidents Warren G. Harding and Calvin Coolidge gave minimal attention to foreign affairs, leaving that field to their secretaries of state. Harding's world was his hometown of Marion, Ohio. He was "most comfortable in the realm of clichés and maxims, and left it to others to supply the necessary intellectual content."[24] Furthermore, Wilson's League of Nations fiasco at home persuaded Harding to eschew a conspicuous role in foreign policy. On one occasion, when a European correspondent for the *New York Times* talked with Harding, the President cut him short: "I don't know anything about this European stuff."[25]

Calvin Coolidge managed in his autobiography to avoid mentioning foreign policy, although as a politician he had often waxed noisy on the issue of Bolshevism. Congressman Lewis Douglas described the taciturn Coolidge as "much like a wooden Indian except more tired looking."[26] Coolidge could deflate anybody's interest in most topics. His relaxed approach to problems, exemplified by the long afternoon naps he took in the White House and by his fawning worship of American business, created a deceptively passive image. Compared to Franklin D. Roosevelt, he certainly was passive—but Coolidge was not withdrawn from foreign policymaking as much as Harding was. The simple man from Vermont, preaching the virtues of self-reliance, did grow impatient with Europeans—who, he believed, always looked to the United States to bail them out. "I think I have stated in some of my addresses," he noted in 1926, "that we couldn't help people very much until they showed a disposition to help themselves."[27]

Herbert Hoover held much the same philosophy, but he was knowledgeable about foreign affairs and committed to an active presidential role. He was a practitioner of independent internationalism. His distinguished career included experience in international business (mining), food relief (Belgium and Russia), and diplomacy (reparations adviser at Versailles). As secretary of commerce under Harding and Coolidge, he used his office energetically to expand American economic interests abroad. Coolidge had considered his millionaire deputy the "smartest 'gink' I know."[28] Known as the "Great Engineer," Hoover had a telephone installed at his elbow in the White House, further contributing to his reputation as a specialist in administrative efficiency. A plodding speaker with a shy personality, Hoover had the misfortune to enter the presidency as the Great Depression struck, thereby wrecking his political career. True to his Quaker background, he sought nonmilitary, noncoercive solutions to international crises. He believed that world order could be maintained largely through stable economic relations.

The secretaries of state in the 1920s often compensated for some of the presidential shortcomings. Majestical Charles Evans Hughes, facetiously called by Louis Brandeis the "most enlightened mind of the eighteenth century," was a distinguished jurist (Supreme Court), an experienced politician (governor of New York and unsuccessful candidate for President in 1916), and a confirmed nationalist and expansionist.[29] Under Harding and Coolidge, the patient and pragmatic Hughes enjoyed considerable freedom in diplomacy, receiving little presidential instruction. The observance of international law and the sanctity of treaties were his primary guides to the attainment of world order. Still, "foreign policies are not built upon abstractions," he said. "They are the result of practical conceptions of national interest arising from some immediate exigency or standing out vividly in historical perspective."[30] Hughes's successor was Frank B. Kellogg, ingloriously called "Nervous Nellie" because of his shaky appearance (one blind eye and a trembling hand). A former senator and ambassador to Britain, Kellogg was cautious, often consulting a major critic of interventionism, the irrepressible "Lion"

**Herbert Hoover
(1874–1964).** Graduate of Stanford University, mining engineer, millionaire, and secretary of commerce before he became the thirty-first President, the cautious and stubborn Hoover advocated healthy trade relations as a route to peace. (*The Reporter*, 1953, Copyright 1953 by Fortnightly Publishing Co., Inc.)

## Makers of American Foreign Policy from 1920 to 1939

| Presidents | Secretaries of State |
| --- | --- |
| Woodrow Wilson, 1913–1921 | Bainbridge Colby, 1920–1921 |
| Warren G. Harding, 1921–1923 | Charles E. Hughes, 1921–1925 |
| Calvin Coolidge, 1923–1929 | Frank B. Kellogg, 1925–1929 |
| Herbert C. Hoover, 1929–1933 | Henry L. Stimson, 1929–1933 |
| Franklin D. Roosevelt, 1933–1945 | Cordell Hull, 1933–1944 |

from Idaho, Senator William Borah. Kellogg broke no new ground in diplomacy, leaving only the much derided Kellogg-Briand peace pact as a legacy. Both he and Hughes had to contend with jurisdictional disputes as Hoover expanded the international offices and functions of the Department of Commerce.

President Hoover's secretary of state was the trim, moustachioed Henry L. Stimson, one of America's distinguished public servants. The strong-willed, wealthy lawyer lived on his Long Island estate like an English squire. His social pedigree included Phillips Andover Academy, Yale University, Harvard Law School, and tutelage under the eminent Elihu Root. Tenacious, cold, confident, aloof, reserved, punctual, mannered, stern—his characteristics befitted an American aristocrat. Before becoming secretary of state, Stimson had served as secretary of war under Taft, as a diplomatic troubleshooter in Nicaragua in 1927, and during 1927–1929 as governor-general of the Philippines. He had been Colonel Stimson in World War—and let few forget it. Indeed, his athletic and strenuous life style reminded many of Theodore Roosevelt. Hoover apparently did not like the man, finding his personality too combative and disapproving of his eagerness to use force in foreign affairs.

That kind of strong personality was just what Franklin D. Roosevelt did not want for his secretary of state. Roosevelt, like Theodore Roosevelt and Woodrow Wilson before him, wanted foreign policymaking in his own hands. FDR came to office with some foreign affairs experience, having served in the Navy Department under Wilson, and unlike the Republican Presidents of the 1920s, he was an activist diplomat. He admired both the big-sticking of his cousin Theodore and the liberal internationalism of Wilson. As a vice-presidential candidate in 1920, Roosevelt had defended the League and the Treaty of Versailles, but in the 1932 campaign he abandoned support for the League in order to garner the endorsement of influential newspaper magnate William Randolph Hearst. Considerable debate has centered on whether Roosevelt was an "isolationist." Without contradiction, the historian can conclude that he was both a Wilsonian and an "isolationist." That is, he was Wilsonian because he believed that collective security through an international organization directed by the large powers would help stabilize world politics, and that the world should be "democratized." He was an isolationist because he shared, although in differing degrees, the basic components of isolationist thought: (1) abhorrence of war; (2) limited *military* intervention abroad; (3) freedom of action in international relations. He was very much part of the age of independent internationalism.

Roosevelt conducted personal diplomacy, often taking command of negotiations and appointments and more than once failing to tell the Department of State what he was doing. He centralized decisionmaking in the White House, but, because too often he possessed only a superficial understanding of other national cultures and histories, dangers lurked in his methods. Sometimes he misled diplomats with his easy smile and tendency to be agreeable at the moment; sometimes his agreements were imprecise, depending for their authority on the honor of gentlemen's words; sometimes the "spirit" of a meeting was not properly captured in the formal diplomatic document; sometimes American diplomacy moved forward with the dizziness of a confused bureaucracy. Then, too, as a consummate politician always conscious of hostile opinion, he compromised frequently, leaving his ideals a bit tattered. Roosevelt was not above deception when he believed it would serve his goals. He has been likened to a physician who lies to the patient for his own good. Historian Willard Range has noted that FDR was "something of an intellectual jumping-jack and was often guilty of hopping helter-skelter in several directions at once."[31]

Roosevelt's secretary of state was Tennesseean Cordell Hull. A powerful senator whose primary interest was the improvement of international trade, the sixty-one-year-old Hull accepted the assignment reluctantly. FDR picked him not for his foreign views (Roosevelt knew little about them), but because the appointment would be popular with old Democratic party members, southern conservatives, and unreconstructed Wilsonians. Once Hull was appointed, Roosevelt often ignored him, although he and the State Department did influence Asian and Latin American policy. Rexford Tugwell, a presidential assistant, noted in 1933 that "I'm sure Hull doesn't know half of what goes on."[32] For example, Roosevelt sent Hull to the World Economic Conference in London that year without consulting him on the makeup of the delegation, and then embarrassed him by suddenly withdrawing the United States from the meeting. Once dubbed "Miss Cordelia Dull" for being so distant from the center of American foreign policymaking, Hull had contemplated resigning even before the conference broke up, because the President had decided to delay sending Hull's pet project, the reciprocal trade bill, to Congress. Hull possessed a deliberate style that annoyed the President, who preferred quickness of thought and decision. The secretary resented the President's practice of sending personal envoys like Harry Hopkins overseas, of conspicuously excluding Hull from important conferences, and of consulting with friends like Sumner Welles (after 1937 under-secretary of state), Morgenthau, and Bullitt, instead of Hull himself. Hull nevertheless stayed on until 1944, the longest tenure of any secretary of state, forever disliking the pomp of official dinners and receptions, always charming his listeners with his hill-country drawl and lisp, and impressing all with his personal dignity, hard work, and deep commitment to the premise that wars grew out of international economic competition. The loyal Hull recalled later that he suffered "humiliations" but "just kept right on."[33]

The Foreign Service over which Hull presided made important strides toward professionalism in the interwar period, reflecting the increased involvement of the United States in world affairs. It had certainly needed reform. Frequenting the dark corridors, black leather rocking chairs, and Victorian furnishings of the old State, War, and Navy Building on Pennsylvania Avenue were American diplomats noted for their elite backgrounds (urban, wealthy, eastern, and Ivy League-educated) and their loyalty to the diplomatic club. Roosevelt thought them snobbish and too preoccupied by social amenities. Often derided as "cookie pushers" and "striped pants," as purveyors of "pink peppermint and protocol," they were paid insufficient salaries, thereby insuring that only people of independent means would seek diplomatic posts. President Coolidge, who knew little about the Foreign Service and its responsibilities, met in 1925 with his new Ambassador to Argentina, Peter Jay. The exchange is illustrative, if exaggerated: *Jay:* "You know Mr. President that my salary as Ambassador is $17,500, and I will have to spend $15,000 on my rent." *Coolidge:* "What are you going to do with the other $2,500?"[34] Many appointees were unqualified, unable to speak the language of the country to which they were assigned. Under the spoils system, faithful politicians were given diplomatic posts.

The heavy work load imposed on Foreign Service personnel during World War I had exposed the shortcomings. Congressman John J. Rogers concluded after the war that, "as adequate as [the Foreign Service] may have been when the old order prevailed and the affairs of the world were free from the present perplexities, it has ceased to be responsive to present needs."[35] The immigration laws of 1921 and

**Cordell Hull (1871–1955).** A career politician from Tennessee, the long-tenured secretary of state (1933–1944) was often left out of important diplomatic decisions by President Roosevelt. In trade and tariff questions, however, Hull charted his own course. (Franklin D. Roosevelt Library)

1924, establishing quotas for nationals from abroad, demanded a more efficient consular staff; the revolution in China required observers who could intelligently report on that major event; and economic expansion depended upon efficient reporting abroad. The Rogers Act of 1924 brought some improvements. It merged the previously unequal consular and diplomatic corps into the Foreign Service of the United States and provided for examinations, increased salaries, promotion by merit, and living expense allowances abroad. It also created the Foreign Service School. At about the same time, the State Department began training specialists in Soviet affairs, with George F. Kennan and Charles E. Bohlen (both later to serve as ambassadors to Russia) as initiates who mastered the language and culture of Russia. President Roosevelt, however, desiring to keep the instruments of foreign policymaking in the White House, weakened the influence of the Foreign Service by simply not utilizing it in key policy formulation. The depression forced salaries down and the service became badly understaffed. Politics still intruded, and aristocratic pretensions still characterized the Foreign Service, but overall it was becoming more efficient and professional in handling the global questions facing the United States.

## American Expansion and the Shaky World Economy

The Foreign Service helped facilitate the conspicuous American economic expansion abroad in the 1920s, since the developing economic ties frequently required American diplomats to protect "American lives and property." After World War I, measured by statistics, the United States was the most powerful nation in the world, accounting for 70 percent of the world's petroleum and 40 percent of its coal production. Most impressive, the United States produced 46 percent of total world industrial goods (1925–1929 figures). It also ranked first as an exporter, shipping over 15 percent of total world exports in 1929, and it replaced Great Britain as the largest foreign investor and financier of world trade. Throughout the decade the United States enjoyed a favorable balance of trade, exporting more than it imported. In the period 1914–1929, the value of exports more than doubled, to $5.4 billion, and American private investments abroad grew fivefold—from $3.5 billion in 1914 to $17.2 billion by 1930.

"The growth of U.S. stakes abroad during the 1920s represented not simply an increase in scale," historian Mira Wilkins has noted. "Rather, U.S. companies were (1) going to *more countries,* (2) building *more plants* in a particular foreign country, (3) manufacturing or mining *more end products* in a particular foreign land, (4) investing in a single alien nation in a *greater degree* of integration, and (5) diversifying on a *worldwide* basis."[36] U.S. Rubber bought its first Malayan plantation; Anaconda moved into Chilean copper mining; General Electric joined international cartels and invested heavily in Germany; oil companies began to penetrate the Middle East; Radio Corporation of America built high-power radio stations in Poland; General Motors purchased Opel, by 1929 the best-selling automobile in Germany; Henry Ford helped build an automobile plant in Russia; Borden and International Telephone and Telegraph expanded in England; and American firms handled about one-third of oil sales in France. Direct American investments in Europe more than doubled during the 1920s.

This economic surge on a worldwide scale had to overcome adversities at the beginning of that decade. Mexican nationalism, confiscation of property in Russia, European resentment over American prosperity, a wrecked German economy,

**The Weight of the United States in the World Economy:**
Relative Value of Industrial Production, 1925–1929*

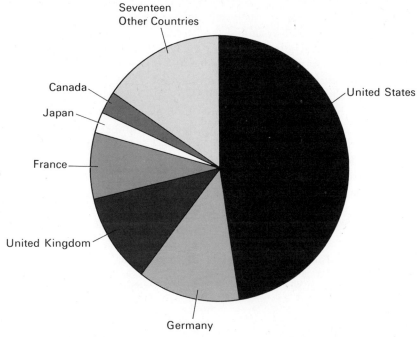

*Source: U.S. Department of Commerce, *The United States in the World Economy* (Washington, D.C.: Government Printing Office, 1943), p. 28.

wartime destruction in Europe, growing tariff walls, and the nightmarish dislocation of international finance caused by World War I debts and reparations—all placed hurdles before enterprising American businessmen and American diplomats. The recession of 1920–1921 further disrupted commerce and investments. Some of these obstacles soon disappeared; expansion was spurred by need for capital, by the availability of rich raw materials and growing markets in Latin America (where competing Europeans were nudged out), by aggressive American entrepreneurs, and by the active encouragement of the United States government. New tools, which proved to be of welcome but limited help, were provided by the Webb-Pomerene Act (1918), which permitted American companies to combine for purposes of foreign trade without prosecution under the antitrust laws; the Edge Act of 1919, which legalized branch banks abroad; and the Merchant Marine Act of 1920, which authorized the federal government to sell vessels to private companies and to make loans for the construction of new ships. Useful also were American tax laws that permitted foreign tax credits for American investors abroad. Secretary Hoover put the Department of Commerce behind trade expansion by providing businessmen with research data and advice. To help financiers avoid unproductive foreign lending and the purchase of risky foreign bonds, official Washington tried to oversee loans and bond sales, but the practice was never consistent or thorough. Businessmen were granted considerable freedom to make their own lending choices. For example, the government discouraged the sale in the United States of the bonds of a Czech brewery because it would violate the "spirit" of prohibition laws, but tolerated an unproductive loan for a sports palace in Germany. Overall, American leaders considered foreign economic expansion essential for prosperity at home.

The United States continued to proclaim the Open Door policy, but applied it selectively and imperfectly. It was usually invoked where the United States faced vigorous competition, as in Asia and the Middle East. In Latin America and the Philippines, however, where American capital and trade dominated, something approximating a "closed door" was in effect. Europeans complained bitterly that the United States was following a double standard. They also resented American tariff policy, which made it more difficult for other nations to sell to the United States—as they had to do in order to get the dollars necessary to buy from the United States. The tariff acts of 1922 (Fordney-McCumber) and 1930 (Hawley-Smoot) raised duties to protect domestic producers and invited retaliation against American products. A group of over a thousand economists protested the Hawley-Smoot Tariff: "There are few more ironical spectacles than the American Government as it seeks, on the one hand, to promote exports . . . , while, on the other hand, by increasing tariffs it makes exportation ever more difficult." More generally, they concluded, "a tariff war does not furnish good soil for the growth of

**The Contracting Spiral of World Trade:**
January, 1929 to March, 1933*
(Total imports of 75 countries in millions of dollars)

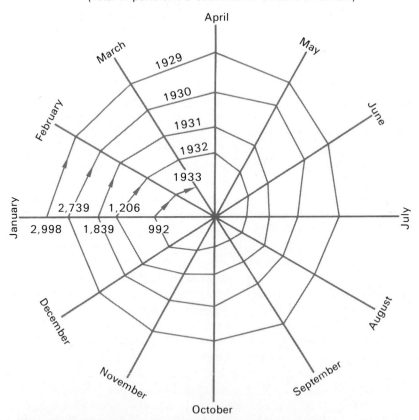

*Source: Charles P. Kindleberger, *The World in Depression, 1929–1939* (Berkeley and Los Angeles: University of California Press, 1973), p. 172. Copyright © 1973 by The Regents of the University of California; reprinted by permission of the University of California Press.

world peace."[37] Some twenty-five nations by 1932 had indeed retaliated against American imports; even some Latin American countries imposed trade controls. Hoover and others in authority held that high tariffs and overseas economic expansion could proceed hand in hand, and until the Great Depression struck in 1929 the seeming contradiction appeared to work.

The depression raised havoc with the international economy. Economic nationalism guided most countries as they tried to protect themselves from the cataclysm with higher tariffs, import quotas, and preferential and discriminatory trade agreements. World trade declined 40 percent in value and 25 percent in volume from 1929 to mid-1933. In 1934 the United States exported goods worth $2.2 billion, down from the 1929 figure of $5.4 billion. American capital stayed at home and foreign holders of American loans defaulted. American private investments abroad slumped to $13.5 billion, down from the $17.2 billion figure of 1930. Hoover simply blamed the economic trouble on the rest of the world. His successor, Franklin D. Roosevelt, facing the problem of 15 million unemployed Americans when he took office in 1933, also succumbed to economic nationalism as he created his New Deal recovery program at home. He abruptly withdrew the United States from the London Economic Conference. But gradually Hull persuaded him that lowered tariffs would spur American foreign trade and hence spark recovery at home. Furthermore, argued Hull, healthy world trade would contribute to stable politics and peace at a time when Japan, Germany, and Italy were turning to political extremes and aggressive foreign policies. It was feared, furthermore, that Bolshevism might exploit Europe's economic and social disequilibrium. "International commerce conducted on a fair and mutually profitable basis," the inspired secretary told a congressional committee, "is not only calculated to aid materially in the restoration of prosperity everywhere, but it is the greatest civilizer and peacemaker in the experience of the human race."[38]

In 1934 Hull piloted through Congress the Reciprocal Trade Agreements Act, which empowered the President to reduce tariffs by as much as 50 percent after making agreements with other nations under the doctrine of the most-favored nation. This principle, which had traditionally guided American trade, did not mean that one nation was more favored than another. Rather, it meant that the United States was entitled to the lowest tariffs imposed by a country (in short, the best favor that country granted any other nation) with which the United States had a reciprocal agreement, and vice versa. The reciprocal trade program did not bring immediate results, but it did slow the deterioration of world trade and placed it on a path toward freer commercial intercourse. Hull also created in 1934 the Export-Import Bank, a governmental agency designed to provide loans to expand foreign trade. It not only assisted in commercial expansion; it also became an important diplomatic weapon, as Washington gave or withdrew credits to satisfy foreign policy goals.

The reciprocal trade program and the bank, however, came too late to help solve one of the major troubling legacies of World War I and Versailles—the debts-reparations tangle. Whereas before the war United States citizens owed some $3 billion to Europeans, after the war European citizens owed private Americans $3 billion and their governments owed another $10 billion, largely because of wartime loans. America had gone dramatically from a debtor to a creditor nation. But how would the European countries pay such a huge sum? Besides American dollar investments and the sale of goods to the United States to raise dollars, there was the income from German reparations payments. But the Germans were incapable of meeting the indemnity of $33 billion, so in the early 1920s the British began asking for a cancellation of the debts, arguing that they should be considered an American contribution to the Allied victory. Europeans, then, looked upon the war loans as essentially political in character, rather than as normal business transactions. Anyway, they pointed out, they had given lives and had endured destruction and damage of property. The United States, on the other hand, had not suffered military trampling and had enjoyed unprecedented profits from the sale of goods to the Allies. America indignantly rejected this argument and soon earned the label "Uncle Shylock." Coolidge complained that "this money has to be paid by our taxpayers unless it is paid by the taxpayers" of the debtor nations.[39] He also reportedly snapped, "They hired the money, didn't they?"[40] Will Rogers captured the American mood in a joke: "There is only one way we could be worse with the Europeans, and that is to have helped them out in two wars instead of one."[41] Congress created the War Debt Commission in 1922 to negotiate for full payment. The commission ultimately forgave or canceled about half of the Allied debts, while Washington continued to demand repayment to ward off popular criticism in the United States. Europeans remained piqued.

Germany held a key place in the debts-reparations tangle. Wild inflation, a crippled economy, inadequate exports, and anti-Versailles hostility prompted the Germans to default on reparations payments in 1922–1923. France and Belgium thereupon aggravated Germany's plight by seizing the rich Ruhr Valley. Britain called again for cancellation of debts. To alleviate the German economic crisis, Americans had been for years pumping millions in capital into the struggling nation. In 1924 the State Department sponsored the Dawes Plan, whereby American investors like the J. P. Morgan Company loaned millions to Germany. A systematic reparations payment schedule was also devised. It proved to be a superficial solution, for the European economy simply could not bear the heavy debts (Europeans also owed money to other Europeans) and the reparations. Nor could American capital continue to keep Europe afloat. Under the Young Plan of 1929, another salvaging effort was made: German reparations were reduced to nine billion dollars. In 1931 Hoover initiated a one-year moratorium on debts payments. Neither worked; thereafter the debtors defaulted and the Germans stopped paying reparations. Only Finland continued to meet its debt obligations, forever winning a place in American hearts. American financial diplomacy had failed, although the United States remained the giant and manager of the world economy. There was no easy solution to the tangle so long as the Allies insisted on burdening Germany with reparations and the United States kept its tariff walls up, believing that, through the collection of debts and extension of capital, its economic power could provide answers.

## Peace, the League, and Disarmament: The Failed Alternatives

If Europeans and Americans failed to resolve the mammoth problems plaguing the international economy, they also failed to curb a growing arms race. Peace sentiment ran high in the 1920s, but it was seldom translated into concrete programs or treaties. In 1922 publisher Edward Bok sponsored an essay contest for the best peace plan and offered $100,000 to the winner. There were 22,165 entrees, including one from Franklin D. Roosevelt. Some peace advocates, such as the World

**William E. Borah (1865–1940).** As a Republican senator (1907–1940), the leather-lunged orator from Idaho helped generate support for the Kellogg-Briand Pact. As an "irreconcilable," he fought American membership in the League of Nations. As an anti-imperialist, he opposed interventions in Latin America, and as an isolationist, he favored neutrality in European squabbles. People were surprised, a Washington joke went, that when Borah took his daily horseback ride he consented to face in the same direction as the horse. (Franklin D. Roosevelt Library)

Peace Foundation and the Carnegie Endowment for Peace, placed their faith in collective security through the League of Nations or in law through the World Court, with American membership. Pacifists, members of such groups as the Fellowship of Reconciliation and the War Resisters League, renounced individual participation in war. Religious groups emphasized the un-Christian characteristics of war and tried to generate a spiritual and moral revulsion against it. Salmon Levinson, a Chicago lawyer who organized the American Committee for the Outlawry of War, argued that "war is an institution in the same sense as the church, the school or the home. It will never cease to be an institution until it becomes illegal."[42] Some businessmen, like Thomas J. Watson of International Business Machines (IBM), endorsed the theme of "world peace through world trade."[43] Still others, who believed that stockpiles of weapons contributed to war rather than deterred it, pressed for disarmament. Radical pacifists and antiwar advocates agitated for fundamental social and economic change in order to remove social injustice, which they saw as the capitalist wellsprings of imperialism and war. The National Council for the Prevention of War, founded in 1921, served as an organizational umbrella for the divergent peace groups.

Most peace activists or peace-conscious citizens were strong nationalists who believed that the United States, because of its basically democratic and pacific intents, could regenerate habitually war-prone Europe. At the time, such reformist ideas did not seem farfetched: arms seemed controllable (technology had not yet produced global bombers or atomic weapons); domestic economies did not yet rely heavily for their prosperity on defense production; the revulsion against World War I was intense; and few warmongers were in immediate sight. Still, most Americans were more interested in sports, movies, and the radio in the "roaring twenties" than in questions of peace. The peace advocates were, as historian Merle Curti has noted, "mere chips and foam on the surface of the stream of American life."[44]

One of the few achievements of the peace people was the Kellogg-Briand Pact of 1928. The French, prodded by James T. Shotwell, a Columbia University professor and trustee of the Carnegie Endowment for Peace, publicly invited the United States to sign a bilateral treaty outlawing war. The security-conscious French, ever worried about a revived Germany, were hoping that an alliance with the United States would prevent any rebirth of German militarism. The invitation met with a cool reception in Washington. But a publicity campaign for a multilateral treaty launched by Shotwell, Levinson, and Senator William Borah put the State Department on the spot. Something had to be done. At first reluctant, Kellogg soon took the lead. In February of 1928 he sent a draft treaty to France and other powers. Foreign Minister Aristide Briand felt betrayed; he had wanted a Franco-American treaty for security, much like the abortive one Wilson devised at Versailles. Kellogg and the peace advocates had converted his idea into a universal declaration against war. That August in Paris, the signatories, eventually numbering sixty-two, agreed to "condemn recourse to war for the solution of international controversies, and renounce it as an instrument of national policy."[45] Occasional poet Robert Underwood Johnson struck the euphoric moment for some Americans:[46]

> Lift up your heads, ye peoples,
> The miracle has come
> No longer are ye helpless,
> No longer are ye dumb.

The Kellogg-Briand Treaty was a harmless, feeble document, a statement of principle, requiring no real sacrifices and establishing no precise responsibilities. In January, 1929, the Senate approved it 85–1, the lone dissenter being John J. Baline of Wisconsin, a confirmed Anglophobe. Senator Hiram Johnson of California who voted "aye," parodied the treaty's lack of enforcement authority by quoting François Villon:[47]

> To Messur Noel, named the neat
> By those who love him, I bequeath
> A helmless ship, a houseless street
> A wordless book, a swordless sheath
> An hourless clock, a leafless wreath
> A bell sans tongue, a saw sans teeth,
> A bed sans sheet, a board sans meat,
> To make his nothingness complete.

Senator Carter Glass of Virginia also voted for the treaty, after belittling it as worth no more than a postage stamp. American statesmen were not lulled into a sense of security by the treaty; indeed, on the same day the Senate approved funds for fifteen new cruisers. They saw Kellogg-Briand as a wishful hope for peace. Peace advocates were not so naive as to think it guaranteed a peaceful world. The much maligned, ineffectual pact should not be dismissed too lightly; for in alerting the American conscience to think again of the costs of war, it held important educational value. And the pact was revived after World War II by the Allies to punish German leaders at the Nuremburg Trials.

The League of Nations, itself designed to check wars, opened in Geneva without the United States, and Washington at first impolitely ignored communications from the League. But by 1925 American diplomats were quietly attending and discreetly participating in League functions. By 1930, unofficial American "observers" had participated in over forty League conferences on such questions as health, prostitution, suppression of obscene materials, codification of international law, and opium. In 1931–1932 American representatives sat formally in League discussions of Japanese thrusts into China, but Washington would not push the League to do any more than timidly invoke the Kellogg-Briand pact and condemn

Japan for aggression. The United States almost joined the League-sponsored Permanent Court of International Justice. This Geneva-based World Court sought to arbitrate international disputes when requested to do so. In 1926 the Senate approved American membership, but so qualified it that the court could not accept the American proposal. Finally, in 1935, a treaty of membership was defeated in the Senate and hopes for a World Court–United States linkage were daunted. Nevertheless, outstanding jurists like Charles Evans Hughes sat as judges in the international body.

American participation in disarmament conferences in 1922 (Washington), 1927 (Geneva), 1930 (London), 1932–33 (Geneva), and 1935–36 (London) also demonstrated America's international but independent diplomatic course. At those conferences, the United States sought limitations especially on navies, in part because it hoped to restrain others at a time when Congress restrained American growth. Except for some naval restrictions imposed by the Washington Treaty of 1922 (discussed in the next chapter) and the London Conference of 1930, little was accomplished. The reasons are clear. The United States, a leading naval power, was seeking to check the quantitative growth of others; France would not endorse disarmament until its security was guaranteed; the British had a huge empire to protect and police by sea; Italy and Germany under dictators Benito Mussolini and Adolf Hitler were bent on military expansion; Japan eyed naval expansion in the Pacific. German rearmament under Hitler in the early 1930s and Japanese renunciation of the Washington Treaty restrictions in 1934 provided stark evidence not only that arms limitation efforts had failed, but also that the Versailles Treaty and the League of Nations had proven impotent.

## The Uncertainty of Soviet-American Relations

The Russians were the first to sign the Kellogg-Briand Treaty and were permitted to join the League of Nations in 1934. Yet these acts did not nullify the fact that between the wars most European nations and the United States treated Bolshevik Russia as an outsider, a revolutionary disease to be isolated. Only when Europe tottered on the brink of war in 1939 did Germany on the one hand and France and Britain on the other seriously woo the Soviet Union. Nevertheless, most powers grudgingly established diplomatic and commercial contact with the Soviet Union in the interwar years, unable any longer to nurse their fantasies that somehow Bolshevism would be tossed out of Moscow, or to ignore a country that figured in both European and Asian politics. The roller-coaster characteristic of ups and downs in Soviet-American relations was typical of Western relations with the Soviets.

Despite Russian interest in gaining official diplomatic recognition from Washington in the 1920s, the Republican administrations adhered to the nonrecognition policy set by Woodrow Wilson. The Bolsheviks, they pointed out, had confiscated American-owned property valued at $336 million and had rejected compensation. Russia owed another $192 million to the United States government and still another $107 million to American nationals (Tsarist and Provisional government debts). Until the roughly $636 million was paid, until Moscow met its obligations, recognition would be denied. Behind this official position lay an antiradical sentiment, harshly expressed in the Red Scare of 1919–1920, and an attitude among many prominent Americans in the 1920s that the threatening Bolsheviks were godless, uncivilized, anticapitalist, violent, destructive revolutionaries who chained their workers like slaves to an authoritarian system. The *New York Times* and the American Federation of Labor, among others, bitterly castigated the Soviet experiment. President Samuel Gompers of the AFL thought Soviet Russia a "villainous despotism."[48] Secretary Stimson, like other Americans annoyed by the rantings of the American Communist party, declared in 1930 there would be no recognition until Russia "ceased to agitate for the overthrow of American institutions by revolution."[49] Only a few Americans, like Senator Borah and the International Ladies Garment Workers Union, urged tolerance and recognition, although even they did not admire the Soviet system.

If most Americans kept at arm's length from the dreaded Bolsheviks, others, for a variety of reasons, got closer. In 1921 Russia suffered a devastating famine. When writer Maxim Gorky appealed for help, Secretary of Commerce Herbert Hoover began to mobilize support for assistance. In 1919 Hoover had told President Wilson that relief aid to Russia would be more humane than military intervention, and that it would bring about Russian political stability by weakening the authority of the Bolsheviks. For both humanitarian and anti-Soviet purposes, Hoover signed an agreement with Moscow in 1921 and organized the shipments of valuable food and medicine to needy areas of Russia. Hoover believed that food would help implant American influence in Russia and serve as a counterrevolutionary force. From 1921 to 1924 the American Relief Administration collected $50 million from the federal government and private citizens for assistance to approximately 10 million Russians. Colonel William Haskell, who headed the effort in Russia, reported his accomplishment in 1923: the relief mission, he concluded rather incorrectly, had left communism "dead and abandoned."[50]

Businessmen, for profit and adventure, sought commercial contacts. The State Department divorced its distaste for Bolshevism from its desire for economic expansion and permitted important commercial relations to develop. Companies like International Harvester, General Electric, and DuPont signed trade and technical assistance contracts with the Soviet government, often through its purchasing agency in New York, the Soviet-owned Amtorg Trading Corporation. By 1924 Soviet purchases of American products had jumped seven times over the 1923 figure. In 1925 W. Averell Harriman, two decades later an ambassador to Russia, received monopolistic rights to rich manganese deposits valued at a billion dollars, although the project never got under way. By 1927, 85 percent of Russia's tractors were American-built "Fordsons." Russia's plans for industrialization and collectivization could not have moved forward without the influx of American machinery, technology, and engineers (1000 by 1931). Improvements in steel and agriculture in particular depended upon American businessmen and technicians, although German trade and investments also figured heavily in Soviet economic growth.

To people who believed that capitalism and communism could never meld, these economic ties were startling. It surprised many in 1929 that a business hero of the 1920s, Henry Ford, signed a Soviet contract. He agreed to supply technical information needed to build the large Nizhni-Novgorod automobile factory near the Volga River, which would buy Ford parts and produce a car like the Model A and a truck like the Model AA. It was a multimillion-dollar venture, and Ford eventually lost $578,000 (the arrangement terminated in 1934). Nevertheless, conclude two Ford biographers, "to give his ideas a practical illustration on the world stage, Henry Ford would gladly have sacrificed twice that sum."[51] Ford was attracted to the Soviets because they were enthusiastic about his mass production methods (*Fordizatsia*). The Russians saw him as a radical individual, an efficiency expert who could speed up industrial production and reduce drudgery in the fields. Ford tractors were popular throughout the country. One American observer returned from a tour of Russian villages to report that "next to Lenin, Trotsky, and Kalinin, Ford is possibly the most widely known personage in Russia."[52] To Ford, Russia looked like an engineer's dream: central planning, regulated materials and work force, and a zeal for efficiency. So in their respect for the wonders of machine and man in harmony, capitalists and Bolsheviks embraced.

American-Russian economic ties began to loosen in the early 1930s. The Great Depression had sent capitalism to its knees, and government and business officials were not amused by Soviet announcements in the United States that jobs were available in Russia. Most important, Russia began selling goods in the world market below American prices, and the United States charged Moscow with "dumping." In mid-1930 Soviet paper pulp was denied entry into the United States because the material was allegedly produced by convict labor. In retaliation and because of inadequate American capital to fund purchases, the Soviets reduced drastically their buying of American goods. In 1932 American exports to Russia declined 90 percent from the 1931 trade. Businessmen eager for markets began to argue that official diplomatic recognition might restart stalled commercial relations. The Reconstruction Finance Corporation, a government agency set up to battle the depression, helped some by extending Russia a $4 million credit for the purchase of American cotton.

**Ford in Russia.** Under a banner of Josef Stalin, a 1929 Model A Ford automobile rolls from a Russian assembly line. Henry Ford's contract with the Soviets proved a losing investment, but the venerable auto king nevertheless relished the experiment. (*Tass* from Sovfoto)

The Roosevelt Administration, because it wanted to improve trade and stop Japan, and simply because nonrecognition served no useful purpose, recognized the Soviet Union in November, 1933. But the exchange of embassies did not smooth relations or halt Japan. American trade with Russia did not improve very much, despite the signing of a trade treaty in 1935, its renewal in 1937, and the establishment of the Export-Import Bank. The debts question went unsolved. When some American Communists spoke critically of the United States at Moscow's Seventh International Communist (Comintern) Congress in 1935, Cordell Hull sent a protest against the violation of the no-propaganda pledge. During the 1933 negotiations, Roosevelt and Litvinov had apparently discussed the possibility of an American loan, and Litvinov departed with the notion that one would be forthcoming. The loan never materialized and its absence further exacerbated friction over the recognition agreement. To many American observers, the dashed hopes meant that the United States could not trust the Russians.

After recognition other issues disrupted Soviet-American relations. William Bullitt was named the first ambassador to Moscow; he left America in 1933 as a friend of Russia. Two years later an embittered Bullitt preached the "hard line" and resigned his post. Difficult living conditions in Moscow, spies among his servants, daily indignities at the hands of rude Soviet bureaucrats, and the conspicuous Soviet tyranny—all helped change his mind. The Comintern Congress of 1935 angered him, because it seemed to violate Russia's promise not to permit propaganda activities to originate from its soil. "Honor" and "fair dealing" were at stake; "friendly" relations with Russia could not be expected. With pride the often hotheaded Bullitt in later years recalled that "I deviled the Russians. I did all I could to make things unpleasant."[53] American correspondent Louis Fischer, who frequented the embassy rooms in Moscow, remembered that the ambassador urged reporters every day to "fan the flames of anti-Sovietism in America."[54] Bullitt did just that himself in the years ahead. In 1946 he had this exchange with Congressman John Rankin:[55]

RANKIN: Is it true that they eat human bodies in Russia?
BULLITT: I did see a picture of a skeleton of a child eaten by its parents.
RANKIN: Then they're just human slaves in Russia?
BULLITT: There are more human slaves in Russia than ever existed anywhere in the world.

Bullitt was also moved toward the "hard line" by the ghastly purges, which began in earnest in 1935. George F. Kennan, a member of the embassy staff and later ambassador to Russia, found those days "a sort of liberal education in the horrors of Stalinism."[56] For Kennan, who attended many of the purge trials in person, Russia had become a nightmarish scene of political murders, secretiveness, conspiratorial thinking, cruelty, and opportunism. Like most diplomats who have been stationed in the suspicious, isolated environment forced on foreigners in Moscow, Bullitt and Kennan became intense in their rejection of things Soviet. So did some liberal and leftist Americans who had previously urged tolerance for the Soviet experiment. Journalist Eugene Lyons, for example, a United Press correspondent in Russia from 1928 to 1934, became sickened by the callousness of the Soviet regime. When he returned to the United States he wrote a controversial article for *Harper's* magazine (1935) titled "To Tell or Not to Tell," an anguished autobiography which did the former. "The great tragic themes of peasant liquidation, persecution of intellectuals, tightening food shortage were bodied forth in hundreds of individual tragedies," he sadly wrote.[57]

If the ugly purges stunned many Americans, the Nazi-Soviet pact of August, 1939 outraged them. Premier Stalin believed he had no choice but to sign this agreement in order to protect his country from a menacing Germany. From the Russian point of view the Western European powers and the United States had let Hitler expand uninhibited, because he harbored conquerer's designs toward Russia. Moscow believed itself abandoned by others to face alone the German military onslaught. And Stalin had so depleted the officer ranks of his army through the purges that he was in no position to stave off an expected German attack. In the United States, the nonaggression pact, which secretly divided Poland, proved charges that Hitler and Stalin were one and the same, even that fascism and communism were similar ideologies. When World War II erupted in September, 1939, many Americans blamed Russia.

There were some light moments during the deterioration of Soviet-American relations. Shortly after Bullitt's arrival in Russia, the ambassador threw a party for Red Army generals. Amidst the tables covered with plates of caviar, duck, pheasant, and the usual bottles of vodka sat Bullitt and the Soviet commissar of war. With the help of Charles Thayer, a prank-prone interpreter bored with his job, the conversation turned to polo. The Russians enthusiastically requested American polo instruction, having learned that the sport was good for the cavalry, and in due course the American embassy imported the necessary balls and mallets. The Russians selected their best horsemen and sent them to an open field near the Moscow River, where Bullitt tried desperately to explain the game. Once the match started, the refereeing ambassador lost control over the fierce competitors, who paid little attention to fouls as madly galloping men and horses collided. Then, of course, Thayer had forgotten to translate Bullitt's words regarding the relationship between the whistle and the end of the game. Finding no other way to halt the thundering mob of players, Thayer dashed on the field and sent the ball into the Moscow River. It was an unsuccessful effort, for an exuberant Russian rider retrieved it and the melee went on. Thayer then lunged at the ball, tucked it under his arm, and begged the horsemen to stop. Weeks later, after Moscow ordered the best ponies shipped to its polo teams, the first formal match was staged before the elite of the Soviet government. As Europe moved toward war, however, the Russian cavalrymen went off on maneuvers, abandoning their "polo for the proletariat."[58]

## Hitler's Germany, Appeasement, and the Coming of War

By exploiting the depression-afflicted economy and the vehement attitudes against the Versailles Treaty in Germany, Nazi leader Adolf Hitler came to power in January, 1933. Racist toward Jews, emphatically anti-Bolshevik, and fanatical in his quest for personal power, Hitler created a regime that set out to recapture past glory through the expansionist concept of Pan Germanism. In October, 1933, Hitler withdrew Germany from the faltering League of Nations and denounced disarmament talks. Defiantly, he told an associate that the European powers would "never act! They'll just protest. And they will always be too late."[59] Indeed, France and Britain settled upon a timid policy, ultimately called "appeasement," hoping thereby to satisfy what they thought were Hitler's limited goals and to

**Adolf Hitler (1889–1945).** The anti-Communist, anti-Semitic Nazi leader, here reviewing German youth, catapulted Europe into war after securing control of Germany through nationalistic appeals. (Library of Congress)

avert another European war. By 1935 Hitler was rearming Germany, building an air force and a huge army. Britain, France, Italy, and the League of Nations censured Germany in April, 1935. Yet at the same time, Britain agreed that Germany should be permitted to rebuild its navy to 35 percent of the size of the British Navy. It proved a costly concession to German militarism.

Hardly adjusted to the rise of Nazi Germany, the world was shocked by another example of military extremism when Italy invaded the African state of Ethiopia in October, 1935. Fascist Benito Mussolini had governed Italy since 1922, and had long dreamed of creating an Italian empire. Already holding Somaliland and Eritrea as African colonies, Mussolini gradually built up pressure on Ethiopian leader Haile Selassie until military skirmishes broke out. Then he struck in a bold invasion and annexation of Ethiopia that encouraged new European appeasement. The League did impose an embargo on the shipment of war-related goods (except oil) to Italy. But the French, with their own empire in Africa, and the British, worried that Italy might impede their imperial lifeline in the Mediterranean, seemed willing to sacrifice Ethiopia, a mere "corridor for camels."[60] Also, they hoped that Italy might stand with them against German expansion.

Apparently encouraged by Anglo-French docility over Ethiopia, Hitler in March, 1936 ordered his goose-stepping troops into the Rhineland, the area bordering Belgium and France that the Versailles Treaty had declared permanently demilitarized. Gambling that the French would not resist this audacious act, Hitler envisioned a potential military avenue through Belgium into France. After World War I, the French had erected the Maginot Line, a series of large gun emplacements and defensive bunkers along the German-French border. By seizing the Rhineland, Germany was now in a position to skirt the supposedly impregnable Maginot. The French, fearful of igniting another war, did not resist the German advance into the Rhineland. Meanwhile, in June, the League of Nations lifted the economic sanctions against Italy. In October, 1936, Germany and Italy arranged a tenuous alignment, the Rome-Berlin Axis; and a month later Germany and Japan, then deep into China, joined in the Anti-Comintern Pact aimed at Russia. The aggressors had joined hands.

Spain provided another battleground. "Nationalist" soldiers under General Francisco Franco started the Spanish Civil War in July of 1936 by attacking the "Loyalist" Republican government in Madrid. Eager to mold in Spain a Franco government hostile to France, Hitler and Mussolini poured military equipment and troops into the Nationalist effort. The Anglo-French response was the tepid International Non-Intervention Committee of twenty-seven nations, remarkably including Germany and Italy. Although the signatories pledged to stay out of the Spanish conflict, Hitler and Mussolini continued covert aid, and France and Britain lived with the fiction that the Spanish Civil War had been isolated. Russia and Mexico sent help to the Republicans, and some Americans volunteered and fought alongside them in the Lincoln Brigade, but Franco battled his way to bloody victory in early 1939.

The mid-1937 election of Neville Chamberlain as British Prime Minister enshrined the "appeasement" policy. Chamberlain believed that Germany had good reason to want to throw off the humiliating Versailles Treaty (Hitler called it a "dictated treaty"[61]) and to claim status as a major power. He was resigned to German dominance of Central Europe and tolerant of Hitler's demand for mastery over people of German descent living in Austria, Czechoslovakia, and Poland. Historian Raymond J. Sontag has described Chamberlain's view: "As Germany became economically prosperous, as Germany attained equality as a colonial power, and as Germans lost the feeling their fellow Germans in other countries were treated unjustly, the neurotic excitability which made Germany a difficult neighbor would subside."[62] Furthermore, an appeased Germany could serve as a useful restraint on communist Russia.

**Benito Mussolini (1883–1945).** The Fascist dictator who apparently made the trains run on time in Italy, ''El Duce'' excited a revival of Italian imperial grandeur by attacking Ethiopia in 1935. (U.S. Information Agency, National Archives)

**Neville Chamberlain
(1869–1940).** The British
Prime Minister (1937–
1940), a Conservative
party member from a
wealthy, elite family,
became the architect of
the ill-fated appeasement
policy. He resigned from
office in May of 1940.
(U.S. Information Agency,
National Archives)

Chamberlain's ideas were tested in 1938. In March, German troops crossed into Austria and annexed it to the German Reich. Months of terrorism against Jews and opponents of Nazism in Austria followed. In September, Hitler grabbed the Sudeten region of Czechoslovakia, where three million ethnic Germans lived. Britain and France (which had a defense treaty with Prague) decided to let Hitler have this additional prize. Abandoned, Czechoslovakia capitulated. Hitler assured Chamberlain that this was Germany's last territorial demand. The end of Czech independence was confirmed at the Munich Conference of September 29–30, 1938, where Italy, Germany, France, and Britain agreed never to make war against one another and to sever the Sudetenland from Czechoslovakia. The Munich agreement was negotiated without consulting the Czechs themselves. They were not invited to the conference. Nor were the Russians or Americans. Chamberlain proclaimed "peace with honour" and "peace for our time," but as a precaution Britain launched a rearmament program.[63] Hitler soon initiated a brutal program against German Jews and in March of 1939 swallowed the rest of Czechoslovakia. The following month Italy absorbed Albania.

Poland came next. Refusing Hitler's demands for the city of Danzig, the Poles soon suffered German pressure. But London and Paris, questioning Hitler's professions about limited goals, announced in March, 1939, that they would stand behind an independent Poland. "Hitler is highly intelligent," mused Chamberlain, "and therefore would not be prepared to wage a world war."[64] Hitler commented privately that "while England may talk big . . . she is sure not to resort to armed intervention in the conflict."[65] Russia then emerged as a central actor in the European tumult. Germany, Britain, and France opened negotiations with Moscow in attempts to gain Russia's allegiance. Germany won. On August 23, Nazi Germany and Soviet Russia signed the nonaggression pact, essentially assuring Berlin that Russia would remain neutral and not align with an Anglo-French coalition. Poland, the immediate victim, was to be divided between the two powers. Hitler had accomplished another stunning feat—in this case cavorting with the Bolshevik devil itself. So much for Stalin's denunciations of Nazism and Hitler's shrill harangues against Bolshevism. Yet Western outcries against the Nazi-Soviet pact seemed hypocritical, for Russia had done much the same thing that Britain and France had done at Munich. Hypocrisy or not, Germany was ready for another conquest. On September 1, German soldiers invaded Poland. Two days later, Britain and France buried appeasement and declared war against Germany. "Everything that I have worked for," lamented Chamberlain, "has crashed into ruins."[66]

Throughout these years of descent into World War II, Hitler apparently did not consider the United States a nation of much consequence. In his warped view, shaped by limited knowledge, the United States could not and would not be a vital factor in international affairs. Although his diplomatic advisers, including German Ambassador to the United States Hans Dieckhoff, warned the Fuehrer that American "isolationism" was not permanent and could not be counted upon, Hitler believed that America could be nothing else than a weak, noninterventionist nation. Even in the period 1939–1941, when the United States took measures to aid the Allies, he did not alter his view. The United States, he said, "was incapable of conducting war." It was a "Jewish rubbish heap," incapacitated by economic and racial crisis, crime, and inept political leadership. "The inferiority and decadence of this allegedly new world is evident in its military inefficiency," he claimed. For

**Joachim von Ribbentrop (1893–1946) and Josef Stalin (1879–1953).** The German foreign minister and Soviet Premier smile their approval of the Nazi-Soviet nonaggression pact signed in August, 1939. (World War II Collection of Seized Enemy Records, National Archives)

Hitler a nation was powerful, and thus to be taken seriously, if its racial composition was pure and if it was a land power. Because the United States was a so-called "melting pot" of ethnic diversity, "half Judaized, half negrified," and because it was largely a sea power, Hitler underestimated it.[67] This gross misperception, this subjective view, would ultimately mean his undoing, as the United States after 1938 increasingly tied its fortunes to Britain and France in the European squabbles.

## American ''Isolationism'' and the Neutrality Acts

"This nation will remain a neutral nation," the President announced on September 3, 1939, "but I cannot ask that every American remain neutral in thought as well."[68] Actually, at the start of the war, the United States was not quite neutral in thought or deed. But this nascent unneutrality was a recent phenomenon. During the early 1930s the United States attempted to shield itself from conflict in Europe, to let Europeans settle their own political differences, and to remain neutral.

Although most Americans responded to the rise of Nazism with hostility, and strongly disapproved of Hitler's machinations at home and abroad, they tried to isolate themselves politically from what they considered European decadence, from a continent prone to self-destruction. If Britain and France could not handle German aggression in their own backyards, America could not do the job for them.

Americans also drew lessons from the bloody experiences and inconclusive peace of World War I. Disillusioned writers and "revisionist" historians argued that Germany was not alone to blame for the outbreak of war in 1914, that Wilson was pro-British and influenced by businessmen and propagandists, and that the costs and results of war—the national interest—would not justify American involvement. In 1934 a best-selling book titled *Merchants of Death* (by Helmuth Englebrecht and Frank Hanighen) was offered by the Book-of-the-Month Club. Its message, that profiteering manufacturers of armaments were active members of the American economic and political system and had helped compromise American neutrality during the First World War, reflected popular opinion. A Senate committee under the leadership of Gerald P. Nye held hearings during 1934–1936 to determine if munitions makers and bankers had lobbied Wilson into war. The committee never proved the allegation, but did uncover substantial evidence that these entrepreneurs were hardly agents of peace. As John Wiltz, historian of the investigation, has concluded, the Nye Committee "exhibited documents which shocked Americans into the realization that there was a difference between selling instruments of human destruction and selling sewing machines or automobiles."[69] Nye wailed against "rotten commercialism."[70] Such revelations fed popular sentiment that World War I had been a tragic blunder—Americans would stay out of the next one. Historian and isolationist Carl Becker complained that, in regard to the First World War, the United States, rather than defending its property or making the world safe for democracy, had actually lost millions of dollars in bad debts and helped make the world safe for dictators.

Peace groups, scientist Albert Einstein, celebrated pilot Charles Lindbergh, Herbert Hoover, anti-Semite Father Charles E. Coughlin, historian Charles Beard, President Robert Hutchins of the University of Chicago, and senators like William Borah and George Norris shared some of these ideas. The antiwar movement was particularly strong on college campuses and among women. Princeton University students organized the Veterans of Future Wars in 1936 and demanded $1000 each as a bonus *before* going into battle, because few, they predicted, would live through the next war. "Hello Sucker" posters picturing maimed soldiers aroused antiwar consciences. In 1938, Congressman Louis Ludlow introduced a constitutional amendment calling for a national referendum on decisions for war. A motion to discharge his resolution from the Rules Committee failed by only twenty-one votes, 209–188. Warned Ludlow: "The art of killing people en masse and maiming and wrecking human bodies has been perfected until it is impossible to imagine the next large-scale war being anything less than a vast carnival of death."[71] Roosevelt had worked against the referendum, claiming that it "would cripple any President in his conduct of our foreign relations," and isolationist Senator Arthur Vandenberg protested that it "would be as sensible to require a town meeting before permitting the fire department to put out the blaze."[72]

Many of the so-called "isolationists" were liberal reformers who believed that American involvement in a European war would undercut the New Deal's attempts to recover from the depression. They remembered how Wilson had turned against critics in World War I, suppressing civil liberties. They remembered, too, that he cooperated with big business to win the war. Some reformers were convinced that businessmen were harbingers of war; hence they sought to curb business adventures abroad that entangled the United States and compromised what they believed to be the national interest. The statistics were not as readily available to them as they are now to historians. In 1937, for example, 20 of the top 100 American corporations were involved in important agreements with Nazi Germany, some of them with the backbone of the German military machine, the I. G. Farben Company. Companies like DuPont, Union Carbide, and Standard Oil were closely tied to Germany through contracts. Standard Oil helped Germany develop both synthetic rubber and hundred-octane aviation fuel, and, true to its arrangement with Farben, refused to develop the fuel for the United States Army. As historian Arnold A. Offner has concluded: "American businessmen publicly opposed war as much as anyone else. But it would seem that the one price they would not pay for peace was private profit."[73] A notable exception was the Wall Street law firm of Sullivan and Cromwell, which severed profitable ties with Germany in protest against the persecution of Jews.

The abhorrence of war and its potential for harm in the United States, the desire to avoid intervention in another European squabble, and the nationalist conviction that the United States should find a way to protect its freedom of action, all contributed to the passage of the Neutrality Acts of 1935–1937. Roosevelt, sharing much of the isolationist thought, wanted a neutrality act, but he sought the discretionary power to decide to which belligerent in a war an embargo on arms shipments should be applied. Suspicious of presidential power in foreign policy-making, Congress refused and passed the Neutrality Act of 1935, which prohibited American ships from transporting war goods to all sides, after the President had officially declared the existence of war. The President could not, in short, designate and punish the aggressor. Subsequent acts added that loans were forbidden to the belligerents (Act of 1936), that the United States was neutral in the Spanish Civil War (Amendment of 1937), and that belligerents wishing to trade with the United States would have to come to this country and carry away the goods in their own ships ("cash and carry"), after payment upon delivery (Act of 1937). The last legislation also forbade American citizens to travel on belligerent vessels.

The Neutrality Acts were a mistake; they provided for no discrimination among the belligerents, no punishment of the aggressor. They denied the United States any forceful word in the cascading events in Europe. They amounted to an abdication of power. Yet, at the same time, much of what the isolationists said about the fruits of war was true. Their criticisms of imperialism and business expansion were honest and telling. They scored the British Empire and American intervention in Latin America. They compared Italy's subjugation of Ethiopia to Britain's supremacy in India. Many of them warned about increasing the power of the President in foreign affairs beyond congressional reach. Their commitment to peace, and their rejection of war as a solution to human problems, were compelling and ennobling. They cannot simply be dismissed as obstructionist crackpots who left the nation unprepared for war, for many were nationalists who did vote defense funds. "Isolationism was," historian Manfred Jonas has written, "the considered response to foreign and domestic developments of a large, responsible, and respectable segment of the American people."[74] In condemning all imperialism—American, British, or German—the isolationists often refused to make the choice of the lesser of two or three evils, as human necessity requires. However praiseworthy some components of their thought (and later generations have learned to heed many of their criticisms about intervention abroad), their formulas for the 1930s were mistaken—as mistaken, certainly, as Britain's appeasement policy.

## Roosevelt and the United States on the Eve of War

President Franklin D. Roosevelt, sensitive to the political weight of the prevailing American sentiment against involvement in European bickering and territorial rearrangements and sharing much of the isolationist loathing of war, responded haltingly to the events of the 1930s. His foreign policy fed appeasement. When Germany began to rearm and when Italy attacked Ethiopia, Roosevelt stated that the United States sought above all to avoid war. America would set a peaceful example for other nations to follow. The idea of the United States as a "showcase" of righteousness drew upon American tradition. He and Hull invoked the Neutrality Act in the Italo-Ethiopian conflict, warned Americans not to travel on belligerent ships, and suggested a moral embargo against trade with the warring parties. Actually American businessmen ignored the moral embargo and increased commerce with Italy, especially in oil. In August of 1936 the President gave a stirring speech at Chautauqua, New York, recalling memories of World War I: "I have seen war. . . . I have seen blood running from the wounded. I have seen men coughing out their gassed lungs. I have seen the dead in the mud. . . . I have seen the agony of mothers and wives. I hate war. I have passed unnumbered hours, I shall pass unnumbered hours, thinking and planning how war may be kept from this nation."[75]

In January, 1937, the Roosevelt Administration asked Congress for an arms embargo against Spain, then wracked by civil war. Congress obliged, but the

**Franklin D. Roosevelt Stood the Heat.** In the 1930s the President moved steadily away from the Neutrality Act and isolationism as he reacted to alarming European events. Here he is seen in 1938 mopping his brow after a cruise in the hot sun aboard the U.S.S. *Houston*. (United Press International)

decision sparked considerable debate, because the embargo clearly worked against the "Loyalist" Republican government and in favor of Franco, who received arms from Germany and Italy. Many isolationists protested neutrality—the sacrifice of Spanish democracy—in this case. The issue was agonizing: How can one be committed to both peace and liberty? Roosevelt and Hull chose strict neutrality, in essence following the lead of Britain and France in trying to contain the civil war and bowing to pro-Franco Catholic sentiment at home. Throughout 1937 Roosevelt wondered how the United States might stem the tide of aggression. In the summer of that year he thought vaguely about calling an international conference, but he took no action, uncertain that the United States could perform any magic. "I haven't got a hat and I haven't got a rabbit in it," he sighed.[76] In July, when Japan plunged into undeclared war against China, Roosevelt favored China by not invoking the Neutrality Act, thereby permitting the Chinese government to buy and import American war goods. Then in October he delivered his famous "quarantine" speech, calling for the isolation of international lawbreakers, the disease carriers. But he offered no plan on how Germany, Italy, and Japan might be curbed. That fall, also, Roosevelt's friend and State Department officer Sumner Welles revived the idea for a world peace conference to set laws of international conduct. Roosevelt encouraged him, but Hull stepped in to dissuade the uncertain President from the venture. Again in January, 1938, Welles and Roosevelt contemplated such a conference. This time the Americans approached the British with the idea. Chamberlain complained about this "bolt from the blue" and lectured Washington that London preferred to handle Germany in its own way[77]—a "douche of cold water" that Welles resented.[78] Nothing ever came of the idea.

During the Czech crisis of 1938 the United States kept at a safe distance. The President appealed for negotiations to head off war, but he informed Hitler that the United States had "no political involvements in Europe and will assume no obligations in the conduct of the present negotiations."[79] He refrained from criticizing Germany for fear that Czechoslovakia would be encouraged to resist. "Good man," Roosevelt cabled Chamberlain when he heard that the Prime Minister would go to Munich.[80] When the Munich accord was announced, Roosevelt accepted it as a measure for peace and Hull remarked that Munich provided "a universal sense of relief."[81] Yet the dismemberment of Czechoslovakia, combined with the Japanese terror in China, profoundly troubled the President. To stop the lawlessness he began to shed his isolationist proclivities; within months after Munich, he admitted privately that he was ashamed of his earlier response. He got encouragement for this shift in attitude from former ambassador to Germany William Dodd and Assistant Secretary of State George Messersmith, both of whom roundly condemned appeasement.

In October of 1938 Roosevelt asked Congress for $300 million for national defense. He encouraged the State Department and Senator Key Pittman, that hard-drinking, gun-packing, incompetent chairman of the Foreign Relations Committee, to lobby for the repeal of the arms embargo law. In November, in protest against Hitler's vicious persecution of the Jews, he recalled Ambassador Hugh Wilson from Berlin and never let him return. Wilson had endorsed the appeasement policy, applauding Munich as opening the way "to a better Europe."[82] He, like many other Americans, hoped that a strong Germany would stand as a bulwark against Bolshevik Russia. That same month, Roosevelt initiated a major airplane building program, in order to "have something to back up my words."[83] He invited the French to discuss the purchase of American aircraft, and in January the Roosevelt Administration agreed to sell bombers to France. In December of 1938 the United States rallied behind a declaration of joint defense against aggression in the western hemisphere and loaned $25 million to China.

In his annual message to Congress in January, 1939, the President lashed out against the aggressors and suggested that the neutrality legislation be revised. Because it applied to both sides in a conflict, he thought it might "actually give aid to an aggressor and deny it to the victim. The instinct of self-preservation should warn us that we ought not to let that happen any more."[84] After much delay, in March, he proposed to Congress that it repeal the arms embargo altogether to permit sales of weapons to belligerents on a cash-and-carry basis. Yet through the spring he was content to let Pittman direct the effort. Never one to risk battle against sizable political odds, Roosevelt failed to provide leadership at a crucial time. In April he asked Hitler and Mussolini to refrain from attacking the countries named specifically on a list, but the suggestion met open derision, Mussolini indicating that Italy would not be influenced by "convivial vociferations, or Messiah-like messages."[85] The Senate Foreign Relations Committee, by a vote of 12–11, refused in July to report out a bill for repeal of the arms embargo. "I've fired my last shot," Roosevelt intoned. "I think I ought to have another round in my belt."[86] Hull told Congress that the arms embargo was "directly prejudicial to the highest interests and to the peace and security of the United States."[87] Not until three weeks after Germany's blitz against Poland did Congress repeal the arms embargo, thereby placing the United States squarely on the side of Britain and France in the Second World War.

Even in the fall of 1939, however, Americans joined their President in wanting to avoid participation in the war. Antiwar sentiment ran high, as did sympathy for the Allies. The inherited lessons of World War I still tugged at Americans. They would not be duped again by a European war. They would stand above the melee as an example of a civilized, pacific nation. They would let Europe clean its own house. The 1940 Democratic party platform was emphatic: "We will not participate in foreign wars, and we will not send our army, naval or air forces to fight in foreign lands outside of the Americas except in case of attack." But it also said: "Weakness and unpreparedness invite aggression. . . . We propose to provide America with an invincible air force, a navy strong enough to protect all our seacoasts and our national interests, and a fully equipped and mechanized army."[88] As in World War I, because most of them were internationalists, because American power became intricately involved in the war, and because they gradually abandoned neutrality to aid the Allies, Americans once again faced the dilemma of risking war to serve peace. The interwar quest for order had failed; the Neutrality Acts had failed; independent internationalism had failed. The time was ripe for diplomatic change.

## Further Reading for the Period 1920–1939, Relations with Europe

For general studies of this period, see Selig Adler, *The Isolationist Impulse* (1957) and *The Uncertain Giant* (1965), Robert A. Divine, *The Reluctant Belligerent* (1965), Jean-Baptiste Duroselle, *From Wilson to Roosevelt* (1963), L. Ethan Ellis, *Republican Foreign Policy, 1921–1933* (1968), William E. Leuchtenburg, *Franklin D. Roosevelt and the New Deal* (1963), Sally Marks, *The Illusion of Peace* (1976), Arnold Offner, *The Origins of the Second World War* (1975), Robert Freeman Smith, "American Foreign Relations, 1920–1942," in Barton J. Bernstein, ed., *Towards a New Past* (1968), Raymond Sontag, *A Broken World, 1919–1939* (1971), William A. Williams, *Tragedy of American Diplomacy* (1962), and John Wiltz, *From Isolation to War, 1931–1941* (1968).

Leading participants and their diplomacy are treated in McGeorge Bundy, *On Active Service in Peace and War* (1948) (on Stimson), James M. Burns, *The Lion and the Fox* (1956) (on Roosevelt), Wayne S. Cole, *Senator Gerald P. Nye and American Foreign Relations* (1962), Richard Current, *Secretary Stimson* (1954), Robert Dallek, *Democrat and Diplomat: The Life of William E. Dodd* (1968), Robert A. Divine, *Roosevelt and World War II* (1969), Robert Ferrell, *American Diplomacy in the Great Depression* (1957), Betty Glad, *Charles Evans Hughes and the Illusions of Innocence* (1967), Waldo Heinrichs, *American Ambassador* (1966) (on Joseph C. Grew), Robert James Maddox, *William E. Borah and American Foreign Policy* (1969), Elting E. Morison, *Turmoil and Tradition: A Study of the Life and Times of Henry L. Stimson* (1960), Julius Pratt, *Cordell Hull* (1964), Merlo J. Pusey, *Charles Evans Hughes* (1951), Willard Range, *Franklin D. Roosevelt's World Order* (1959), Arthur M. Schlesinger, *The Age of Roosevelt* (1957–1960), essays on Hughes, Kellogg, and Stimson by John C. Vinson, L. Ethan Ellis, and Richard Current in Norman A. Graebner, ed., *An Uncertain Tradition* (1961), and Joan Hoff Wilson, *Herbert Hoover* (1975). For short biographies of the leading figures in this period see John A. Garraty, ed., *Encyclopedia of American Biography* (1974). See also Robert Schulzinger, *The Making of the Diplomatic Mind: The Training, Outlook, and Style of United States Foreign Service Officers, 1908–1931* (1975).

Problems of economic diplomacy receive attention in Frederick Adams, *Economic Diplomacy: The Export-Import Bank and American Foreign Policy, 1934–1939* (1976), Joseph Brandes, *Herbert Hoover and Economic Diplomacy* (1962), Herbert Feis, *The Diplomacy of the Dollar* (1950), Lloyd C. Gardner, *Economic Aspects of New Deal Diplomacy* (1964), Michael J. Hogan, *Informal Entente: The Private Structure of Cooperation in Anglo-American Economic Diplomacy* (1977), Burton I. Kaufman, *Efficiency and Expansion: Foreign Trade Organization in the Wilson Administration, 1913–1921* (1974), Cleona Lewis, *America's Stake in International Investments* (1938), Carl Parrini, *Heir to Empire: United States Economic Diplomacy, 1916–1923* (1969), George Soule, *Prosperity Decade* (1947), Harris G. Warren, *Herbert Hoover and the Great Depression* (1959), Mira Wilkins, *The Maturing of Multinational Enterprise: American Business Abroad from 1914 to 1970* (1974), and Joan Hoff Wilson, *American Business and Foreign Policy, 1920–1933* (1971).

For questions of peace, the League of Nations, and disarmament, see Thomas Buckley, *The United States and the Washington Conference, 1921–1922* (1970), Merle Curti, *Peace or War* (1936), Roger Dingman, *Power in the Pacific: The Origins of Naval Arms Limitation, 1914–1922* (1976), Robert Ferrell, *Peace in Their Time* (1952), D. F. Fleming, *The United States and World Organization, 1920–1933* (1938), Harold Josephson, *James T. Shotwell and the Rise of Internationalism in America* (1976), and Stephen Pelz, *Race to Pearl Harbor: The Failure of the Second London Naval Conference and the Onset of World War II* (1974).

Soviet-American relations and recognition are discussed in Edward Bennett, *Recognition of Russia* (1970), Donald G. Bishop, *The Roosevelt-Litvinov Agreements* (1965), Robert Browder, *The Origins of Soviet-American Diplomacy* (1953), Beatrice Farnsworth, *William C. Bullitt and the Soviet Union* (1967), Peter Filene, *Americans and the Soviet Experiment, 1917–1933* (1967), George F. Kennan, *Russia and the West under Lenin and Stalin* (1960), Anthony Sutton, *Western Technology and Soviet Economic*

*Development, 1917 to 1930* (1968), William A. Williams, *American-Russian Relations, 1781–1947* (1952), and John Hoff Wilson, *Ideology and Economics: U.S. Relations with the Soviet Union, 1918–1933* (1974).

American "isolationism," neutrality, the rise of European fascism, and the coming of World War II are treated in many of the works cited above and in Warren Cohen, *The American Revisionists* (1967), James V. Compton, *The Swastika and the Eagle: Hitler, the United States and the Origins of World War II* (1967), Robert A. Divine, *The Illusion of Neutrality* (1962), Manfred Jonas, *Isolationism in America* (1966), Lawrence Lafore, *The End of Glory* (1971), Arnold Offner, *American Appeasement* (1969), Thomas G. Paterson, "Isolationism Revisited," *The Nation* (1969), Richard Traina, *American Diplomacy and the Spanish Civil War* (1968), and John Wiltz, *In Search of Peace: The Senate Munitions Inquiry* (1963).

Also see Wilton B. Fowler, ed., *American Diplomatic History Since 1890* (1975), the "Further Reading" sections for chapters 10 and 11, and the following notes.

## Notes to Chapter 9

1. Quoted in John M. Blum, *From the Morgenthau Diaries: Years of Crisis, 1928–1938* (Boston: Houghton Mifflin, 1959–1967; 3 vols.), I, 55.
2. *Ibid.*
3. Quoted in Dean Acheson, *This Vast Eternal Realm* (New York: W. W. Norton Company, 1973), p. 288.
4. Quoted in Beatrice Farnsworth, *William C. Bullitt and the Soviet Union* (Bloomington: Indiana University Press, 1967), p. 86.
5. Quoted in Edward M. Bennett, *Recognition of Russia* (Waltham, Mass.: Blaisdell, 1970), pp. 111–112.
6. Edgar B. Nixon, ed., *Franklin D. Roosevelt and Foreign Affairs* (Cambridge: Harvard University Press, 1969; 3 vols.), I, 434n.
7. U.S. Department of State, *Foreign Relations of the United States, 1933,* II (Washington: Government Printing Office, 1949), 794–795.
8. Nixon, *Roosevelt and Foreign Affairs,* I, 293–294.
9. William Phillips, *Ventures in Diplomacy* (Boston: Beacon Press, 1952), pp. 156–157.
10. Blum, *From the Morgenthau Diaries,* I, 57 and Louis Fischer, *Men and Politics: An Autobiography* (New York: Duell, Sloan and Pearce, 1941), p. 130.
11. Fischer, *Men and Politics,* p. 211.
12. Phillips, *Ventures in Diplomacy,* p. 156.
13. Will Rogers, *How We Elect Our President* (Boston: Little, Brown, 1952), p. 148.
14. Cordell Hull, *Memoirs* (New York: Macmillan, 1948; 2 vols.), I, 297.
15. *Ibid.,* p. 292.
16. Nixon, *Roosevelt and Foreign Affairs,* I, 468.
17. Robert P. Browder, *The Origins of Soviet-American Diplomacy* (Princeton: Princeton University Press, 1953), p. 133.
18. Quoted in Fischer, *Men and Politics,* p. 299.
19. George F. Kennan, *Memoirs, 1925–1950* (Boston: Little, Brown, 1967), p. 57.
20. Hull, *Memoirs,* I, 302.
21. Blum, *From the Morgenthau Diaries,* I, 57.
22. Herbert Hoover, quoted in Robert F. Smith, "Republican Policy and the Pax Americana, 1921–1932," in William A. Williams, ed., *From Colony to Empire* (New York: John Wiley

and Sons, 1972), p. 292; and Henry L. Stimson, quoted in Melvyn P. Leffler, "Political Isolationism: Economic Expansionism or Diplomatic Realism? American Policy toward Western Europe, 1921–1933," *Perspectives in American History,* VIII (1974), 419.
23. Joan Hoff Wilson, *American Business and Foreign Policy, 1920–1933* (Boston: Beacon Press, 1973 [c. 1971], p. x.
24. Robert K. Murray, *The Politics of Normalcy* (New York: W. W. Norton, 1973), p. 21.
25. Quoted in L. Ethan Ellis, *Republican Foreign Policy, 1921–1933* (New Brunswick, N.J.: Rutgers University Press, 1968), p. 40.
26. Diary, December 9, 1927, Box 87, Lewis W. Douglas Papers, University of Arizona Library (from the notes of Professor Thomas G. Smith).
27. Howard H. Quint and Robert H. Ferrell, eds., *The Talkative President: The Off-the-Record Press Conferences of Calvin Coolidge* (Amherst: University of Massachusetts Press, 1964), p. 298.
28. Quoted in Joan Hoff Wilson, *Herbert Hoover: Forgotten Progressive* (Boston: Little, Brown, 1975), p. 122.
29. Quoted in John Chalmers Vinson, "Charles Evans Hughes," in Norman A. Graebner, ed., *An Uncertain Tradition: American Secretaries of State in the Twentieth Century* (New York: McGraw-Hill, 1961), p. 133.
30. *Ibid.,* p. 132.
31. Willard Range, *Franklin D. Roosevelt's World Order* (Athens: University of Georgia Press, 1959), p. xii.
32. Quoted in Frank Freidel, *Franklin D. Roosevelt: Launching the New Deal* (Boston: Little, Brown, 1973), p. 459.
33. Quoted in Louis B. Wehle, *Hidden Threads of History* (New York: Macmillan, 1953), p. 131.
34. Quoted in Lewis Einstein, *A Diplomat Looks Back* (New Haven: Yale University Press, 1968; ed. by Lawrence E. Gelfand), p. 29.
35. Quoted in William Barnes and John H. Morgan, *The Foreign Service of the United States* (Washington: Department of State, 1961), p. 203.
36. Mira Wilkins, *The Maturing of Multinational Enterprise: American Business Abroad from 1914 to 1970* (Cambridge: Harvard University Press, 1974), p. 138.
37. *New York Times,* May 5, 1930.

38. Quoted in Julius W. Pratt, *Cordell Hull* (New York: Cooper Square, 1964; 2 vols.), I, 112.

39. Quint and Ferrell, *Talkative President*, p. 196.

40. Quoted in John D. Hicks, *Republican Ascendancy, 1921–1933* (New York: Harper and Row, 1960), p. 136.

41. Will Rogers, *Letters of a Self-Made Diplomat to His President* (New York: A. & C. Boni, 1926), p. xii.

42. Quoted in Harold Josephson, *James T. Shotwell and the Rise of Internationalism in America* (Rutherford, N.J.: Fairleigh Dickinson University Press, 1975), p. 140.

43. Quoted in Charles DeBenedetti, "Peace Was His Profession: James T. Shotwell and American Internationalism," in Frank Merli and Theodore A. Wilson, eds., *Makers of American Diplomacy* (New York: Charles Scribner's Sons, 1974), p. 390.

44. Merle Curti, *Peace or War: The American Struggle, 1636–1936* (New York: W. W. Norton, 1936), p. 262.

45. *The General Pact for the Renunciation of War* (Washington: Government Printing Office, 1928).

46. Quoted in Robert H. Ferrell, *Peace in Their Time* (New York: W. W. Norton, [c. 1952], 1969), p. 201.

47. Quoted in L. Ethan Ellis, "Frank B. Kellogg," in Graebner, *Uncertain Tradition*, p. 166.

48. *Foreign Relations, 1923, II* (Washington: Government Printing Office, 1938), 760.

49. Quoted in David J. Danelski and Joseph S. Tulchin, eds., *The Autobiographical Notes of Charles Evans Hughes* (Cambridge: Harvard University Press, 1973), p. 262.

50. Quoted in Peter G. Filene, *Americans and the Soviet Experiment, 1917–1933* (Cambridge: Harvard University Press, 1967), p. 82.

51. Allen Nevins and Frank E. Hill, *Ford: Expansion and Challenge, 1915–1933* (New York: Charles Scribner's Sons, 1952), p. 683.

52. Maurice Hindus (*The Outlook*) quoted *ibid.*, p. 603.

53. Quoted in Farnsworth, *Bullitt and the Soviet Union*, p. 153.

54. Fischer, *Men and Politics*, p. 308.

55. Quoted in James Aronson, *The Press and the Cold War* (Indianapolis: Bobbs-Merrill, 1970), p. 32.

56. Kennan, *Memoirs, 1925–1950*, p. 67.

57. Eugene Lyons, "To Tell or Not to Tell," *Harper's*, CLXXI (June, 1935), 102.

58. Charles W. Thayer, *Bears in the Caviar* (Philadelphia: Lippincott, 1951), p. 115.

59. Quoted in Arnold A. Offner, *American Appeasement: United States Foreign Policy and Germany, 1933–1938* (New York: W. W. Norton, 1976 [c. 1969]), p. 50.

60. Quoted in Raymond J. Sontag, *A Broken World, 1919–1939* (New York: Harper and Row, 1971), p. 290.

61. Quoted in Lawrence Lafore, *The End of Glory: An Interpretation of the Origins of World War II* (Philadelphia: J. B. Lippincott, 1970), p. 158.

62. Sontag, *A Broken World*, p. 316.

63. Quoted in A. J. P. Taylor, *The Origins of the Second World War* (New York: Fawcett Publications, 1966 [c. 1961]), p. 181.

64. *Foreign Relations, 1939, I* (Washington: Government Printing Office, 1956), 288.

65. Quoted in Sontag, *A Broken World*, p. 374.

66. *Ibid.*, p. 381.

67. Quoted in James V. Compton, *The Swastika and the Eagle: Hitler, the United States, and the Origins of World War II* (Boston: Houghton Mifflin, 1967), pp. 17, 25, 33.

68. Samuel I. Rosenman, ed., *Public Papers and Addresses of Franklin D. Roosevelt, 1939* (New York: Macmillan, 1938–50; 13 vols.), VIII, 463.

69. John E. Wiltz, "The Nye Committee Revisited," *The Historian*, XXIII (February, 1961), 232.

70. Quoted in Wayne S. Cole, *Senator Gerald P. Nye and American Foreign Relations* (Minneapolis: University of Minnesota Press, 1962), pp. 126–127.

71. Quoted in Thomas G. Paterson, "Isolationism Revisited," *The Nation*, CCIX (September 1, 1969), 167.

72. Quoted in Robert A. Divine, *The Reluctant Belligerent* (New York: John Wiley and Sons, 1965), p. 49; and in John E. Wiltz, *From Isolation to War, 1931–1941* (New York: Thomas Y. Crowell, 1968), p. 16.

73. Offner, *American Appeasement*, p. 103.

74. Manfred Jonas, *Isolationism in America, 1935–1941* (Ithaca, New York: Cornell University Press, 1966), p. viii.

75. Rosenman, *Public Papers, 1936*, V, 289.

76. Quoted in Dorothy Borg, *The United States and the Far Eastern Crisis of 1933–1938* (Cambridge: Harvard University Press, 1964), p. 374.

77. Quoted in Offner, *American Appeasement*, p. 219.

78. Sumner Welles, *The Time for Decision* (New York: Harper & Brothers, 1944), p. 66.

79. *Foreign Relations, 1938, I* (Washington: Government Printing Office, 1955), 685.

80. *Ibid.*, p. 688.

81. *Ibid.*, p. 703.

82. Quoted in Offner, *American Appeasement*, p. 215.

83. Quoted in Blum, *From the Morgenthau Diaries: Years of Urgency, 1938–1941*, II, 49.

84. Rosenman, *Public Papers, 1939*, VIII, 4.

85. Quoted in William L. Langer and S. Everett Gleason, *The Challenge to Isolation, 1937–1940* (New York: Harper and Brothers, 1952), p. 87.

86. *Ibid.*, p. 143.

87. Quoted in Robert A. Divine, *The Illusion of Neutrality* (Chicago: Quadrangle Books, 1968 [1962]), p. 280.

88. Kirk H. Porter and Donald B. Johnson, eds., *National Party Platforms, 1840–1972* (Urbana: University of Illinois Press, 1973), p. 382.

**"The Open Door."** The Japanese thrust into Manchuria in 1931 called into question the peace and disarmament agreements of the previous decade. (*The Outlook,* 1931)

# 10 A Question of Power: Relations with Asia and Latin America, 1920–1939

## Diplomatic Crossroad: The Manchurian Crisis, 1931–1932

It apparently started with thirty-one inches of steel. At 10:30 P.M., a few miles outside the Manchurian capital of Mukden during the night of September 18, 1931, an explosion apparently blasted a short section from the South Manchurian Railway. Apparently Japanese soldiers shot and killed some Chinese attempting to escape from the area. Apparently? Yes, because Japanese army officers had a most difficult time explaining the events of that dark night. The Mukden Express had somehow managed to cross over that very section of track *after* the alleged explosion. The train must have jumped the gap, the Japanese lamely answered. American officials who inspected the steel fragments noted that they did not carry the imprint of the Carnegie Steel Works as did the track still in place. Indeed, it appears compelling that the "Mukden Incident" of September 18 was fabricated by young Japanese officers of the Kwantung (Manchurian) Army. They had plotted for months to seize Manchuria and sever it permanently from China. Feverish in their quest for Japanese grandeur and Asian power, they or their followers had already, in 1930, assassinated the Japanese premier. So when the news from Mukden reached Tokyo, one civilian official remarked with resignation, "They've done it at last."[1]

Manchuria was to Tokyo, civilian and military alike, a vital Japanese interest. It served as a defensive buffer against the hated Russians and their communism. More important, it teemed with the raw materials (coal, iron, timber, soybeans) so desperately needed by the import-hungry Japanese islands. More than half of Japan's foreign investments were in Manchuria. The Japanese-run South Manchurian Railway served as the nerve center of these large economic holdings. Ever since their victory in the Russo-Japanese War, the Japanese had been driving in their imperial stakes. By treaty they had acquired the right to station troops along the railroad. The United States had recognized Japan's primacy in Manchuria through the Root-Takahira and Lansing-Ishii agreements.

Chinese nationalists throughout the 1920s had harassed their Asian brethren. Nationalist leader Chiang Kai-shek encouraged thousands of Chinese to emigrate to Manchuria and sought to build a railroad to compete with the South Manchurian. The Chinese boycotted Japanese products, a particularly alarming practice during the Great Depression, when Japan's foreign trade faced a serious slump. Both Chinese and Japanese blood was spilled in isolated incidents. Such cumulative provocations amounted to "a case where a thousand pinpricks equalled a slash of the saber,"[2] and the haughty Japanese response came in the darkness of September 18, 1931.

The Mukden news reached an irritable Secretary of State Henry L. Stimson, worn low by Washington's exceedingly hot, humid temperatures before the age of the air conditioner. The weather accentuated a Stimsonian personality trait. President Herbert Hoover thought the moustachioed Stimson "more of a warrior than a diplomat," and Stimson himself pointed to his "combat psychology."[3] The forthright secretary shared prevalent American attitudes toward "inferior" races and believed that he understood the "Oriental mind."[4] He also embraced the Open Door policy and the sanctity of law. "Respect for treaties was the very foundation of peace," he said.[5] Japanese aggression in Manchuria violated treaties signed at the Washington Conference (1922), which endorsed the Open Door, and the Kellogg-Briand Pact (1928), which outlawed war. Thus, Stimson concluded that the Manchurian crisis was "an issue between the two great theories of civilization and economic methods."[6]

Stimson hoped at first that the "Mukden Incident" was a localized mutiny of the Japanese army. No American wanted the United States to become ensnarled "'all

**Henry L. Stimson (1867–1950) and Herbert Hoover (1874–1964).** The secretary of state (left) and President differed on how the United States should protest Japanese machinations in Manchuria. Stimson's "combat psychology" clashed with Hoover's caution. (Herbert Hoover Presidential Library)

by itself' in the jungle of this Chinese-Japanese-Manchurian mixup—which is full of hidden explosives, dense underbrush, [and] quicksand," noted Chief of the State Department's Division of Far Eastern Affairs Stanley K. Hornbeck.[7] One of Stimson's aides depicted the secretary as "a small boy at the edge of a pool which is cold, just not quite willing to get in there in one plunge and swim."[8] Caution was quite in order. The United States possessed little power in Asia. The British, interested in preserving their own Asian empire and hobbled by economic crisis at home, preferred to appease their former ally Japan. The French were caught in their usual domestic political confusion. Soviet Russia, still not recognized by the United States, could hardly be called upon for help. The League of Nations was notably feeble, its big power members openly contemptuous of Wilson's creation. Neither the United States nor Russia belonged to it.

Stimson decided on a meek policy of letting "the Japanese know we are watching them."[9] On September 24, 1931, he gently urged the Chinese and Japanese to cease hostilities. A few days later the League began to discuss the Manchurian crisis, and the United States permitted an American representative to sit at the League table only as an "observer." Stimson and Hoover feared that the international organization would "dump" the "Manchurian baby" in Washington's lap,[10] but the League passed meaningless resolutions for peace and set up the Lytton Commission to investigate. Japanese soldiers kept marching, meeting little resistance from ineptly led Chinese forces, and within months they had seized all of Manchuria. Humorist Will Rogers quipped that nations would run out of stationery for their many protest notes before the Japanese ran out of soldiers.

The secretary of state did not have many diplomatic tools with which to work. He could not intervene militarily. He could not call on Britain, France, Russia, or the tepid League. And when he suggested to Hoover, in December, 1931, that the United States and others impose economic sanctions on Japan, the President strongly rejected the idea. Stimson knew that Japan depended upon imports of American oil, that it was the third largest buyer of American exports, and that the United States took about 40 percent of Japan's exports. Maybe economic pressure would force Tokyo to reverse its military thrust through Manchuria. Hoover, however, responded that the United States should not venture forth alone "sticking pins in tigers."[11] The risk of war was too great, the President cautioned.

Thus, nonrecognition. Drawing upon Secretary of State William Jennings Bryan's protest in 1915 against the Japanese Twenty-One Demands on China, Stimson on January 7, 1932 issued what became known as the "Stimson Doctrine." (Hoover, his political fortunes flagging at home, thought it should be called the "Hoover Doctrine.") Stimson threw tradition and law against Japan: the United States would not recognize any arrangements in China that might impair American treaty rights, violate the Open Door policy, or subvert the Kellogg-Briand Pact. Defiantly, on January 28, the Japanese marched into Shanghai. Stimson grew belligerent and convinced Hoover to reinforce the American military garrison in that city. Reminded of the German attack on Belgium in 1914, the secretary drew an historical lesson and set his jaw against this new aggressive outrage.

There was nothing left to try but bluff. He wanted to frighten Japan without its knowing that it had no reason to be afraid. On February 23, 1932, Stimson sent a public letter to Senator William Borah, chairman of the Senate Foreign Relations Committee. Privately the secretary hoped it would "encourage China, enlighten the American public, exhort the League, stir up the British, and warn Japan."[12] A rather ambitious set of goals, for sure. Employing the Open Door policy as an instrument, Stimson chastised Japan for violating the administrative and territorial integrity of China and the Kellogg-Briand agreement. He repeated his earlier denial of recognition and threatened to fortify Guam and build up the American Navy in the Pacific if Japan did not halt its aggression. The protest letter made little impact, although Japan soon signed an armistice in Shanghai and the League endorsed nonrecognition. In February, Japan actually reconstituted Manchuria as the puppet state of Manchukuo, and in September recognized it. The next month the Lytton Commission squarely blamed Japan for the Manchurian crisis. Perturbed but unchecked, Japan resigned from the League of Nations in early 1933, claiming it was being crucified like Christ on the cross. Stimson's bluff had failed. The secretary, biographer Elting E. Morison concludes, "wound up like a man before a breaking dam with a shovel in his hands." Stimson himself remarked that he was armed only with "spears of straw and swords of ice."[13]

## The Quest for a Nonmilitary Foreign Policy

Stimson's diplomacy raises questions that help us comprehend the 1920–1939 period. Was it wise for Stimson to rail so vigorously against Japanese machinations in Manchuria? Did it do any good? Did it help the Japanese military faction gain support from other nationalists who also considered Manchuria of supreme importance? Did the policy of nonrecognition reveal how weak the United States was in Asia? Was it read as bluff? Did it not also expose China's vulnerability, its abandonment by other nations? Should Stimson have ignored the violations of the treaties? Would it have been wiser to let the Asians settle their own differences—especially since the United States lacked sufficient naval and military power to intervene in the area? Was America's national interest affected by the Manchurian crisis?

Years after 1931, Stimson admitted that nonrecognition had not worked. It did not alter the balance of power in Asia. Japan was not cowed. Moral exhortation and lecturing may only have soothed the American conscience and stirred up the aggressor, to nobody's benefit. Diplomat Hugh Wilson reflected on Stimson's tactics: "If the nations of the world feel strongly enough to condemn, they should feel strongly enough to use force. . . . To condemn only merely intensifies the heat." He went on: "Condemnation creates a community of the damned who are forced outside the pale, who have nothing to lose by the violation of all laws of order and international good faith."[14]

Stimson tried lecture and bluff because he had no other viable options. As an aristocrat committed to law and order, it seemed to him natural and gentlemanly to isolate the disorderly and to identify the damned. Further, although American economic interests in Manchuria were small, the cherished principle of the Open Door, both as diplomatic tool and as ideology, was at stake. The Japanese were shutting the door. If the Open Door could be violated so callously in Manchuria, it could be jeopardized elsewhere. Stimson spoke out for the principle that bolstered American economic interest overseas—hence his reference to the struggle in Manchuria as one between different economic methods.

America's timid response to the Manchurian crisis demonstrated that the United States, because it lacked power, could not manage affairs in Asia. United States gunboats still chugged along the Yangtze, American troops were garrisoned on

| Makers of American Foreign Policy from 1920 to 1939 | |
|---|---|
| *Presidents* | *Secretaries of State* |
| Woodrow Wilson, 1913–1921 | Bainbridge Colby, 1920–1921 |
| Warren G. Harding, 1921–1923 | Charles E. Hughes, 1921–1925 |
| Calvin Coolidge, 1923–1929 | Frank B. Kellogg, 1925–1929 |
| Herbert C. Hoover, 1929–1933 | Henry L. Stimson, 1929–1933 |
| Franklin D. Roosevelt, 1933–1945 | Cordell Hull, 1933–1944 |

Chinese soil, and the Philippines remained a colony, but in the Pacific the Japanese were far superior. America could lecture, but not enforce. By contrast, the United States held considerable power—economic, naval, military, political—in Latin America. It was to the United States what China, especially Manchuria, was to Japan. The Japanese, in fact, often commented that what they were doing in China was what the United States had been doing for decades in Latin America. In Latin America the United States practiced the "closed door"; in Asia it appealed for the "Open Door." In both areas, the viability of American foreign policy depended upon power.

The Manchurian crisis also revealed the feebleness of the treaties of the 1920s and the reluctance of the European powers to check aggression in the 1930s, when appeasement was the policy of the day. Britain and France would not act; the League of Nations was weak and devoid of commitment from its chief members. Under these circumstances, and under the debilitating effects of the Great Depression, Americans understandably nurtured their independent internationalism. Given the timid policies of the Europeans and the League, Americans seemed to recognize the limits of their own power and the difficulty of taking unilateral action. They may have overextended themselves in words, but not in deeds. Their power did not reach as far as their desires. Still they did not withdraw from international events. Rather, the United States sought to create with nonmilitary means a world characterized by legal, orderly processes, the Open Door, and economic and political stability. The Hoover-Stimson response to the Manchurian episode typified these goals and methods. To quote Hoover again: "we can never herd the world into the paths of righteousness with the dogs of war."[15] Practicing "independent internationalism," America hoped to muzzle the dogs of war, not solely in the abstract, but to stimulate domestic prosperity, expand foreign trade, and insure national security.

## The Washington Conference: Navies and Asia

The American pursuit of independent internationalism and a nonmilitary foreign policy was evident at the Washington Naval Conference of November 12, 1921 through February 6, 1922. After World War I a naval arms race loomed between the United States, Britain, and Japan. None of the parties really welcomed the spiraling financial costs of such a contest. Japan was pumping as much as one-third of its national budget into naval construction. The United States, possessing the second largest navy in the world, alarmed third-ranked Japan by shifting the main part of its battle fleet to the Pacific, by developing the base at Pearl Harbor, and by talking about fortifying the Philippines and Guam. First-ranked Britain already had Singapore, but lacked funds to engage in a naval arms race. The United States Congress might not appropriate funds either. Thus all three powers embraced arms control in order to check one another. With some prodding from Senator William Borah, the Harding Administration invited eight nations (Britain, France, Italy, Japan, China, Belgium, Netherlands, and Portugal) to Washington to discuss with the United States naval arms limitations and competition in Asia.

The Washington Conference opened with dramatic words from bewhiskered Secretary of State Charles Evans Hughes. Disdaining the usual generalities of welcoming statements, Hughes cut quickly to the problem. Calmly but deliberately he announced that the United States would scrap thirty ships. Then he turned to the British delegation and sank twenty-three of its ships. British Admiral Lord David Beatty, noted a reporter, leaned forward like a "bulldog, sleeping on a sunny doorstep, who has been poked in the stomach by the impudent foot of an itinerant soap canvasser." Spellbound now, the delegates heard Hughes scuttle twenty-five Japanese vessels. One commentator wrote that "Hughes sank in thirty-five minutes more ships than all the admirals of the world have sunk in a cycle of centuries."[16]

Despite grumblings of doom from naval advisers, the diplomats hammered out a naval limitations pact—the Five Power Treaty. It set a ten-year moratorium on the construction of capital vessels, defined as warships of more than 10,000 tons displacement or carrying guns larger than eight inches in bore diameter. The treaty also limited the tonnage for aircraft carriers, and established a tonnage ratio for capital ships of 5:5:3:1.75:1.75 (United States:Britain:Japan:France:Italy; 1 = approximately 100,000 tons displacement). The top three naval powers agreed to dismantle a total of seventy ships. They also pledged not to build new fortifications in their Pacific possessions, such as the Philippines and Hong Kong, thus giving protection to the Japanese, who had sarcastically accepted naval inferiority by translating 5:5:3 as Rolls Royce:Rolls Royce:Ford. Another treaty—the Four Power—abolished the Anglo-Japanese Alliance and stated simply that the signatories would respect each other's Pacific territories. All delegations also signed the Nine Power Treaty, a polite endorsement of the Open Door for the preservation of China's sovereignty and equal trade opportunity there. Other agreements were struck. Japan consented to evacuate troops from the Shantung Peninsula; the United States was given cable rights to the Pacific island of Yap; and Japan agreed to end its occupation of parts of Russian Siberia and the northern half of Sakhalin Island. President Harding, who had little to do with the conference, claimed these results as a political achievement, demonstrating, he said, that he was "not so much of a duffer as a good many people expected me to be."[17]

The treaties signed in Washington essentially recognized the status quo in Asia. Japan had the upper hand, and the other powers were in no position to challenge it without undertaking massive naval construction and prohibitively expensive fortifications. Hughes knew he could not drive the Japanese out of Manchuria, so he skirted that issue. Geography clearly worked in Japan's favor in Asia, as it did for the United States in Latin America. The United States gave up little in the treaties, except the *potential* of naval superiority. It secured temporary protection of the vulnerable Philippines and abolition of the Anglo-Japanese Alliance, a threatening vestige of the old imperialism against which the Open Door was aimed. Each power accepted some naval disarmament in its national interest, as a way of checking a costly arms race and protecting its Asian interests. But as the Japanese prime minister noted: "While armed conflict has cooled off, economic competition is becoming more and more intense."[18]

There were shortcomings. The Five Power Treaty did not limit submarines, destroyers, or cruisers, thus permitting an arms race in those categories, which was only partially checked by agreements at the London Conference of 1930. Russia, which had stakes in Asia, was not invited to the Washington Conference, since the major powers were still attempting to isolate the Bolsheviks. There was no enforcement provision in the Nine Power Treaty. China, torn by factionalism and civil war, was a loser at the conference. It was represented by the feeble Peking regime, rather than Sun Yat-sen's Kuomintang government in Canton, although the latter sent a watchdog. Most Chinese groups resented the Western powers' maintenance of imperial privileges, the very symbols of China's inferiority. As historian Warren Cohen has written: "In answer to China's demand to be allowed to set its own tariff rates, the powers offered a 5 percent increase on imports and a promise of subsequent discussion. In answer to the Chinese demand for an end to extraterritoriality, the powers offered only a commission to study the problem. In answer to the Chinese demand for the withdrawal of foreign troops from Chinese soil, nothing was done."[19] The great powers had protected their own rights, not China's; they had intended to stabilize China for their own sake, not China's. There were no compromises with Chinese nationalism. The Washington Conference constituted a worthy step toward disarmament, but it still left China at the mercy of foreigners. Hence Japan in 1931, without any countervailing power from foreign nations or China itself, could easily emasculate the generalities of the Nine Power Treaty.

## The Rise of Chinese Nationalism

United States policy toward Asia had to contend not only with expansionist Japan, but also with anti-imperialist, nationalist Chinese. In 1898 the Philippines had been seized in large part because they were perceived as steppingstones to China; three decades later, in an historical flipflop, a strong China friendly to the United States seemed necessary to protect those defenseless islands. China thus took on some strategic importance for Americans in the 1920s and 1930s. Also, many Americans were still mesmerized by the mirage of the China market and the ostensible inviolability of the Open Door principle. Stanley K. Hornbeck affirmed that "our people and our Government have, from the beginning of our national life, asserted that in the commercial relationships of sovereign states there should *not* be a 'closed door' *anywhere*."[20] Sentimental considerations partially accounted for the American attachment to China, especially in the 1930s. Pearl Buck's best-selling *The Good Earth* (1931), made into a powerful movie six years later, captured for Americans the romance of the hard-working, persevering Chinese peasants. This Sinophile's book humanized the people then being victimized by the Japanese. John Paton Davies, a young Foreign Service officer in China during the depression decade, has commented that Americans held a "righteous infatuation" with China, stemming from years of missionary activity and a misguided and self-congratulatory belief that America was China's special friend by virtue of the Open Door Notes. In Asia, Davies has concluded, "Washington preached to everyone, including the Chinese."[21]

Washington directed its preaching at the principal activists in Asia between the world wars: Japan, Russia, and the Chinese Nationalists. Each defined a new "order" that excluded the United States and the other Western imperialists. For the United States, "order" meant peaceful change or "orderly processes," in the words of Cordell Hull.[22] It meant the Open Door, protection of American property and citizens, and the treaty rights of trade and judicial extraterritoriality (criminal trials for its nationals in American rather than Chinese courts). To protect its interests and to preserve order, the United States maintained troops on Chinese soil and gunboats on Chinese rivers. What would Americans think, someone asked, if China sent armed junks up the Mississippi River to "protect" Chinese laundrymen in Memphis? Sun Yat-sen, the leader of the Chinese Revolution from its outbreak in 1911 until his death in 1925, bristled when American gunboats from the South China Patrol visited Canton in 1923 to halt a potential Chinese takeover of foreign-dominated customs houses. After declaring that the Chinese Revolution took its inspiration from America, Sun lamented that "we might well have expected that an American Lafayette would fight on our side in this good cause. In the twelfth year of our struggle towards liberty there comes not a Lafayette but an American Admiral with more ships of war than any other nation in our waters."[23]

There were two roadblocks to Japanese expansion—Russia and the Chinese Nationalists—but the United States did not cooperate with or strengthen either. Few American leaders paid heed to the 1921 prophecy of Minister to China Jacob G. Schurman that "only the Chinese can solve China's problems and they will do it in a Chinese way."[24] Americans applauded the Chinese nationalistic spirit, preached the Open Door, but then asked that American treaty privileges be perpetuated. Finding minimal sympathy in Washington, the Chinese turned to another possible means of support, Bolshevik Russia; and Moscow, seeking to restrain Japan, spank imperialist capitalists, and implant communism, sent advisers to China. Under the guidance of agent Michael Borodin, the Soviets helped the Nationalists centralize the structure of the Kuomintang party. Americans understood neither the depth of Chinese nationalism nor Sun Yat-sen's use of Russians for Chinese purposes; Americans at first compared Sun with the unruly Chinese warlords he was fighting, and when that analogy collapsed, they attributed China's intense antiforeign sentiment to Bolshevik agitation. A lucid understanding of Chinese nationalism was made extremely difficult by the tumult and factionalism of the Chinese Revolution. Although Sun was the recognized Nationalist leader, he by no means had firm control of China. Events were confusing and moved quickly. Few Americans could foresee who would win.

In 1925, Sun died and the Nationalist outpouring in the May 30th Movement of that year led to attacks on American and other foreign property and citizens. The 10,000 Christian missionaries who lived in China were subjected to threats and violence. Anti-imperialist opinion at home, and Chinese determination to gain control of their own country, combined to prompt a reconsideration of American treaty privileges by Washington. The outbreak of civil war within the Nationalist ranks also dictated a re-evaluation. The clever and ambitious Kuomintang leader, Chiang Kai-shek, turned fiercely on his Communist allies in 1926–1927. Borodin was booted ingloriously from China. Chinese Communists were murdered by the thousands or chased into the hills; their leader, Mao Tse-tung, fled south to Kiangsi Province, where he set up a rebel government. Although the United States used gunboats in 1927 to protect its nationals and property in Nanking, it did respond to

**Chiang Kai-shek (1887–1975).** Ambitious and often ruthless, Chiang took command of the Nationalist movement in China, drove the Communists into the hills, and cultivated cordial relations with the United States in the 1920s. (Library of Congress)

Chiang's assertion of power by signing in 1928 a new treaty restoring tariff autonomy to China and providing for most-favored-nation treatment. Still, Sino-American trade and investment remained in a category labeled "potential." By 1930 over 500 American companies were operating in China, with investments amounting to $155 million, yet they represented only 1 percent of total American foreign investments. From 1923 to 1931 the United States sent only 3 percent of its total exports to China. American trade with Japan totaled twice as much.

Despite minimal trade and the continued elusiveness of the mythical China market, Americans warmed toward Chiang. He had joined their crusade against communism, and in 1930 he announced that he had been converted to Christianity. Furthermore, and quite important, he gave up a previous wife and two concubines and married Meiling Soong, the ambitious daughter of American-educated Chinese businessman Charles Soong. A Wellesley College honors graduate, she spoke flawless English and soon established ties with prominent Americans in the United States, later called the "China Lobby." Madame Chiang was beautiful, intelligent, poised, and "westernized." Americans were captivated by her. She was the right Chinese woman in America's dream of a stable, God-fearing, and Open Door China.

## The "New Order" and Japanese-American Conflict

The Japanese were motivated by an intense nationalism of their own. They were driven by a fear of inferiority spawned by a shortage of land for a growing population (in 1931, 65 million lived in an area smaller than Texas), by a dependence upon outside sources for raw materials, and by an awareness that Western nations had for years intruded into their sphere of influence and come to control products like oil vital to their economy. Japan sought self-sufficiency. One Japanese leader argued that a "tree must have its roots," and cited the United States "roots" in Latin America as an example.[25] Without an empire, it was believed, Japan could not survive as a nation. A Monroe Doctrine for Asia, or "Greater East Asia Co-Prosperity Sphere," would insure the Japanese full stomachs and satiated egos. They were compulsive about seeking "equality" with the Occidental powers, and they often explained their expansion and rationalization of the Asian sphere in the broadest terms: all major powers were doing it. With a high degree of fatalism, the Japanese recognized that an imperialist thrust into Manchuria and China could very well bring them into war with the United States or Russia.

Despite past efforts to defuse their rivalry, in the 1920s and 1930s Tokyo and Washington took actions that intensified their differences. Indeed, in 1923 Japan ranked the United States first in its list of potential enemies. A Japanese Navy War College study of 1936 stated that "in case the enemy's [America's] main fleet is berthed at Pearl Harbor the idea should be to open hostilities by surprise attacks from the air."[26] Naval competition, despite the Washington Conference, continued. Historian Waldo Heinrichs has noted that American naval leaders of the interwar years "regarded war with Japan as practically inevitable some day," and used Japan as the enemy on the war game board at the Naval War College.[27] The limits were taken off that rivalry in 1935–36 when the London Conference broke up without agreement and Japan announced its abrogation of the Washington and London treaties. The American Immigration Act of 1924, blatantly discriminatory in excluding Japanese citizens from entering the United States, rankled the sensitive Japanese. Secretary of State Hughes, less alarmed than West Coast racists about the threat of a domestic "Yellow Peril" to American institutions, lamented that the legislation had "undone the work of the Washington Conference and implanted the seeds of an antagonism sure to bear fruit in the future."[28] Angry Japanese, as if to emphasize their power in Asia, contemptuously remarked that, although they could not enter America, they could still go to China. Commercial rivalry also increased. Inexpensive Japanese goods, especially textiles, entered the American market to bring havoc to some domestic producers. "Buy America" campaigns and public boycotts of Japanese goods followed. Japan began to close the trade and investment door in China and that angered Washington. The Japanese considered Western lecturing against expansion a double standard. One diplomat complained that the Western powers taught Japan the game of poker, but after acquiring most of the chips they pronounced the game immoral and took up contract bridge. Japan and the United States did have two common interests: their mutual trade continued at high levels, and both feared communism and Soviet Russia (Japan joined the Anti-Comintern Pact with Germany in 1936).

When Roosevelt took office in early 1933, his Administration continued Stimson's nonrecognition policy. The British ambassador, after a conversation with the President, reported to London that FDR's "view is that there is nothing to be done at present to stop [the] Japanese government and that the question can only be solved by the ultimate inability of Japan to stand the strain any longer. His policy would be to avoid anything that would tend to relieve that strain."[29] This nonintervention attitude was necessitated by American weakness in Asia and was made possible, at least until 1937, by the long lull in fighting between China and Japan. Little American action seemed required.

Through the 1930s, the Roosevelt Administration did improve the Navy and take other steps to increase the "strain" on Japan. Shortly after taking office, Roosevelt moved to bring the Navy up to the strength permitted by the Washington and London conference treaties. Under New Deal relief programs in 1933, the President allocated funds for thirty-two new vessels, including two aircraft carriers, and by 1937 naval appropriations had doubled. Two years earlier large-scale naval maneuvers near Midway Island in the Pacific alarmed the Japanese. American leaders believed that a large and conspicuous navy would help deter Japanese expansion, because, some argued, the Japanese were a military people who respected military might. Actually, the American naval buildup convinced the Japanese in 1936 to terminate the treaty limitations, thus setting off a vigorous naval arms race. Roosevelt's diplomatic recognition of Soviet Russia in 1933 was in part an effort to frighten Japan with the suspicion that Russia and America were teaming up in Asia. Four years later, Captain Claire Chennault, retired from the United States Army Air Corps, joined the Chinese air force as chief adviser. His "Flying Tigers" unit was staffed by mercenary American pilots and tolerated by American officials. These efforts, official and unofficial, to strengthen both the United States and China did not risk war for the former. Washington sought to *alert* the Japanese to American disapproval, but not to *threaten* them.

A more interventionist American policy developed after the eruption of new Sino-Japanese warfare in 1937. During the evening of July 7, Japanese and Chinese units clashed at the Marco Polo Bridge near Peking. This skirmish grew quickly into the "China Incident" (it was not called a "war" because the Kellogg-Briand Pact outlawed wars), with fighting throughout China. Shanghai fell to Japan in November after a costly battle and the cruel bombing of helpless civilians. A

**Shanghai, China, 1937.** This moving UPI photograph of a baby amidst the ruins of North Station after Japanese bombing galvanized American opinion. (United Press International)

stirring United Press International photograph of a crying baby in the midst of the bombed ruins of Shanghai aroused American emotions and, as Barbara Tuchman has written, the picture "humanized the war for Americans. . . . Journalists flocking to the drama . . . reported tales of heroism, blood and suffering. China was seen as fighting democracy's battle and personified by the steadfast Generalissimo and his marvelously attractive, American-educated, unafraid wife."[30] President Roosevelt responded at first by refusing to invoke American neutrality, thereby permitting valuable trade to continue with the beleaguered Chinese. It was hardly enough to save China. To make matters worse, the civil war between Chiang's Kuomintang forces and Mao Tse-tung's Communists further sapped China. The Communists had declared war on Japan in 1932 and had charged Chiang with appeasing Tokyo. And until 1937 Chiang fought the Communists more than the Japanese. From 1935 to 1937, the Communists took the dramatic "Long March" from their southern haven to Yenan in the north—an expedition of 6,000 miles. In late 1936 Chiang was actually kidnapped by dissident army forces in Manchuria. They wanted to end the civil war by creating a coalition government. Russia and the Chinese Communists persuaded them to release Chiang, for they saw him as a bulwark against Japan. The outcome was a tenuous and largely ineffective united front against Japan in 1937.

Roosevelt addressed a Chicago audience on October 5, 1937 and used a medical metaphor to describe American "policy" after the China Incident. He called vaguely for a "quarantine" on aggressors to check the "epidemic of world lawlessness." Americans, he declared, could not be safe in a "world of disorder."[31] After the speech the President admitted he had no plan; indeed, it was an attitude more than a "policy." Privately he toyed with economic warfare—a naval blockade or embargo—but American isolationists responded to the speech by warning him against any bold action. Senator Gerald P. Nye, citing historical lessons, complained that "we are once again being caused to feel that the call is upon the United States to police a world that chooses to follow insane leaders. Once again we are baited to thrill to a call to save the world. We reach a condition on all fours with that prevailing just before our plunge into the European war in 1917."[32] In November Roosevelt sent American representatives to a conference in Brussels, but it disbanded without taking a stand—only the Soviet Union pushed for reprisals against Japan. The following month the war came closer to America. The American gunboat *Panay*, escorting on the Yangtze River three small Standard Oil Company tankers flying American flags and well-marked with the symbol "S," was sunk by zealous Japanese pilots. Under pressure from Ambassador Joseph Grew, Tokyo quickly apologized and offered reparations. Many Americans were relieved, some remembering the war fevers aroused by the sinking of the *Maine* in 1898 and others suggesting that the vessel should not have been there in the first place.

As Japan tightened its grip on China in 1938, the Roosevelt Administration cautiously initiated new measures designed to strengthen both China and American defenses in Asia. First, through the purchase of Chinese silver, the United States gave China dollars with which to buy American military equipment. Second, Secretary Hull imposed a "moral embargo" on the sale of aircraft to Japan. Third, the United States extended technical assistance to improve the Chinese transportation system. Fourth, a naval bill authorized the construction of two new carriers and the doubling of naval airplanes. Fifth, the United States occupied

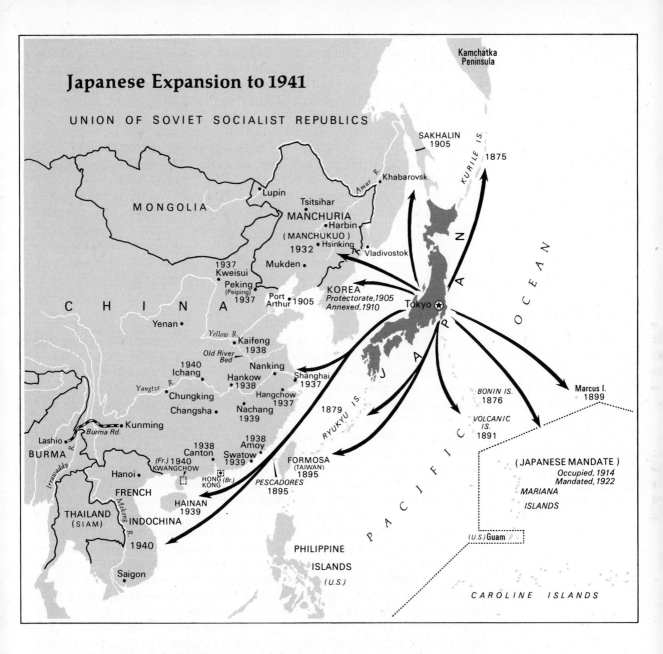

## Japanese Expansion to 1941

UNION OF SOVIET SOCIALIST REPUBLICS

Kamchatka
Peninsula

SAKHALIN
1905

KURILE IS. 1875

MONGOLIA

Lupin

Tsitsihar

MANCHURIA
(MANCHUKUO)
1932

Harbin

Hsinking

Vladivostok

Khabarovsk

Mukden

Port
Arthur 1905

KOREA
Protectorate, 1905
Annexed, 1910

Tokyo

J A P A N

C H I N A

1937
Kweisui

Peking
(Peiping)
1937

Yenan

Yellow R.

Kaifeng
1938

Old River
Bed

Nanking

1940
Ichang

Hankow
1938

Shanghai
1937

Chungking

Hangchow
1937

Changsha

Nachang
1939

1938
Amoy

RYUKYU IS.

1879

BONIN IS.
1876

Marcus I.
1899

VOLCANIC
IS.
1891

Yangtze R.

Kunming

Burma Rd.

Lashio

BURMA

Irrawaddy R.

Hanoi

FRENCH

THAILAND
(SIAM)

INDOCHINA

Mekong R.

Saigon

1938
Canton

(Fr.) 1940
KWANGCHOW

HONG
KONG (Br.)

HAINAN
1939

Swatow
1939

FORMOSA
(TAIWAN)
1895

PESCADORES
1895

1940

PHILIPPINE

ISLANDS

(U.S.)

(JAPANESE MANDATE)
Occupied, 1914
Mandated, 1922
MARIANA
ISLANDS

(U.S.) Guam

P A C I F I C   O C E A N

CAROLINE   ISLANDS

several Pacific islands (Enderbury, for example) as potential naval bases. These actions of 1938 did not deter the brazen Japanese, who by the end of that year had gained authority in almost all major Chinese seaports, declared a "New Order" for Asia, and established exploitative development companies. An American trade commissioner in Shanghai charged quite correctly that the "Open Door" was being "banged, barred, and bolted."[33] The "New Order" meant the ouster of Western imperialism and the creation of a self-sufficient Asian bloc united economically and racially.

In 1939 Roosevelt and Hull remained cautious, unwilling to take steps that might risk war in Asia. Events in Europe were more significant for the American national interest. In mid-1939 the United States abrogated the 1911 Japanese-American Treaty of Commerce and Navigation, hoping this application of economic leverage would shock the Japanese into tempering their onslaught in China. In 1938 the United States had supplied Japan with 44 percent of its imports, a sizable portion of which consisted of automobiles, machinery, copper, oil, iron, and steel. The abrogation, effective January, 1940, by no means ended trade, for the Roosevelt Administration remained reluctant to impose a rigid trade embargo. Grew's talks with the Japanese foreign minister in the fall of 1939 failed to secure American trading rights in China, but did elicit a Japanese pledge to curtail brutalities against foreigners. In November of 1939 another American naval bill authorized two more battleships. By then the Second World War had begun to bloody Europe, and Japanese-American relations were stalemated, with every new Japanese jab into the "sick man of Asia" convincing American diplomats that a showdown was in the offing. By late 1939, with Pearl Harbor two years ahead, the United States had moved in Asia a considerable distance from its weakness of 1931–1932, but its methods remained timid and its power limited.

## Good Neighbors in Latin America

In contrast with Asia, American power in the western hemisphere remained unmatched and American methods bold. Indeed, shortly after World War I, American armed forces used the Caribbean for maneuvers and planning—as preparation for a possible war with Japan in the Pacific. And when Germany and Japan marched aggressively in the 1930s, the United States brought most of the Latin American states into a virtual alliance to resist any foreign intrusions in the United States sphere of influence. Earlier, Japanese leaders observed that their "New Order" in Asia was simply a copying of United States hegemony in Latin America. The United States imperial net in Latin America had been stitched before and during the First World War, especially in Central America and the Caribbean, through military occupations, naval demonstrations, the Panama Canal, the management of national finances, the threat of intervention, nonrecognition, and economic ties. The Roosevelt Corollary to the Monroe Doctrine provided the overriding justification. In the 1920 presidential campaign, after some Republicans insisted that the United States reject League membership because the British controlled six votes, Democratic vice-presidential candidate Franklin D. Roosevelt rebutted happily that the United States would control twelve votes—eleven from Latin America. The chief of the State Department's Division of Latin American Affairs expressed a typical attitude in a 1925 speech to the Foreign Service School. He mentioned the "low racial quality" of Latin Americans, but concluded that they were "very easy people to deal with if properly managed."[34] The sight of swaggering American Marines in the streets of Havana, Managua, or Port-au-Prince represented only the most conspicuous evidence of the United States' imperial management.

The use of Marines as instruments of policy, however, was becoming unpopular and counterproductive, and some limitations were placed on United States power by nationalist sentiment, especially in Mexico and Argentina. Anti-imperialists like Senators George Norris and William Borah, citing the Wilsonian ideal of self-determination, demanded it for Latin Americans. Congressmen increasingly resented the costs of military interventions, as well as the President's usurpation of

**Uncle Sam as Seen by Latin America.** This angry cartoon from *Critica* (Buenos Aires) represented one view of the United States in the western hemisphere. (*Current History and Forum,* 1927)

their power to declare war when as Commander-in-Chief he unilaterally dispatched soldiers to the Caribbean. Businessmen came to believe that military expeditions, because they aroused anti-United States sentiment and violence, endangered rather than protected their properties. The United States was also caught in its own imperialist posture in Latin America when Japan seized Manchuria in 1931. The double standard was embarrassing. Henry L. Stimson, who had supported American occupation before, commented in 1932: "If we landed a single soldier among those South Americans now . . . it would put me absolutely in the wrong in China, where Japan has done all this monstrous work under the guise of protecting her nationals with a landing force."[35] Pragmatic American diplomats recognized that armed interventions generated hostile nationalism and violence, and thereby undermined the basic American goal of tranquil order.

Between the world wars, therefore, the United States attempted to find means other than direct military intervention to continue its influence over Latin America. Increasingly Washington foreswore armed interference and employed the methods of economic penetration, political subversion, nonrecognition, support for stable dictators, arbitration treaties, Pan Americanism, Export-Import Bank loans, and the training of national guards. These tactics were summarized in a catchy phrase popularized, but not invented, by Franklin D. Roosevelt—the Good Neighbor policy. The President declared in early 1933 that "I would dedicate this Nation to the policy of the good neighbor—the neighbor who resolutely respects himself and, because he does so, respects the rights of others—the neighbor who respects his obligations and respects the sanctity of his agreements in and with a world of neighbors."[36] Some observers quickly declared a new era in inter-American relations, and Latin Americans welcomed the seemingly new spirit. What had changed was not the goal of United States hegemony over Latin America, but the methods for insuring it. After the Good Neighbor policy, however, Washington was more hesitant to defend exploitative American companies and more willing to entertain mutual decisionmaking. Roosevelt defined the "new approach" toward Latin America: "Give them a share. They think they are just as good as we are, and many of them are."[37] And as an Axis threat was perceived in the late 1930s, the Good Neighbor policy came to mean close cooperation against the European totalitarians.

The history of the famous 1928 memorandum by Under Secretary of State J. Reuben Clark illustrates that the Good Neighbor policy meant new tactics, not new goals. This report repudiated the Roosevelt Corollary by stating that the Monroe Doctrine could not be cited as a rationale for American intervention in Latin America, for that doctrine referred specifically to European intrusions, not to the right of the United States to intervene. Many contemporaries and historians have applauded the Clark Memorandum as a forerunner of the Good Neighbor policy. Yet the report did not denounce the right of intervention, only its sanction by the Monroe Doctrine. Furthermore, neither the Hoover nor Roosevelt administrations paid much attention to the memorandum. For many Latin Americans it simply meant that Washington would find other explanations for intervention. The imperialist elements of coercion, imposition, and external authority largely remained.

## The Annexation of Wealth: Economic Ties with Latin America

Economic decisions made by American leaders, private and governmental, held immense importance for the life of Latin American nations, especially in the Caribbean, Mexico, and Central America. In the Dominican Republic, Cuba, and Haiti, for example, officials had to obtain United States consent before borrowing foreign capital. The Chilean ambassador to Washington in the early 1930s spent much of his time trying to anticipate American decisions on copper purchases and Chilean bonds, both essential to his nation's livelihood. In that decade "never had Chile felt so totally controlled by the unpredictable attitudes of a foreign power."[38] In Cuba, where American interests accounted for about two-thirds of sugar production, American investments helped lock the country into a risky one-crop economy subject to fluctuating world sugar prices. Sumner Welles reported in 1924 that in Honduras, where the United Fruit Company and Standard Fruit Company accounted for most of the country's revenue, American interests provided essential cannon and machine guns to one political group that conducted a successful coup. In Venezuela, one-half of the nation's tax revenues came from oil taxes—hence from foreign-owned oil companies. In 1929 American firms produced more than one-half of Venezuela's oil. Their bribery of Venezuelan government officials, including the President, was not uncommon. Over 1,000 American-controlled businesses exercised significant influence in at least three-fourths of the Latin American countries by 1920. As historian J. Fred Rippy has noted: "The operation of these numerous business enterprises requires many intimate associations and a multitude of contacts. . . . Thousands of businessmen and technicians from the United States were brought into close touch with millions of Latin Americans almost every day in the year."[39]

Argentine writer Manuel Ugarte was blunt in the mid-1920s when he tagged the United States a "new Rome." The United States, he complained, annexed wealth rather than territory, and thereby enjoyed the "essentials of domination" without the "dead-weight of areas to administrate and multitudes to govern." He deplored the consequences of America's economic penetration: "Its subtle intrusion into the private affairs of each people has always in consecrated phrase invoked peace, progress, civilization, and culture; but its motives, procedure, and results have frequently been a complete negation of these premises."[40] Latin American leaders, when making economic, political, and diplomatic decisions, had to consider what

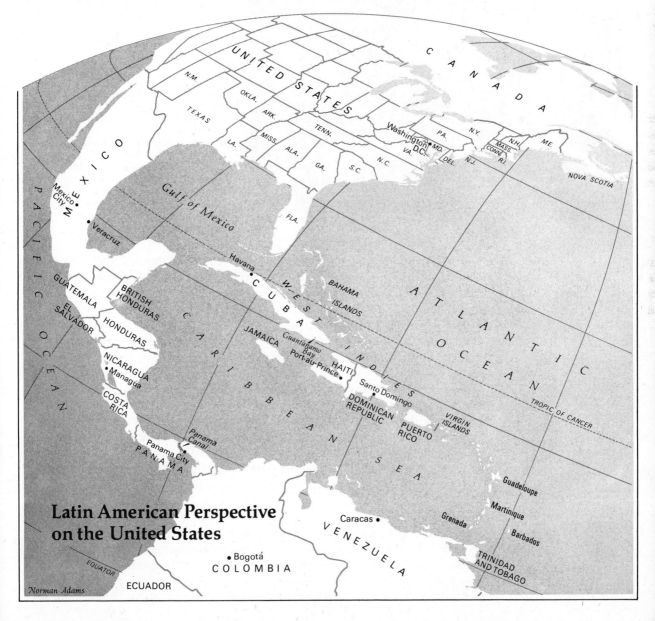

**Latin American Perspective on the United States**

*Norman Adams*

**Herbert Hoover, Good Neighbor.** As secretary of commerce and President, Hoover improved trade relations with Latin America and spawned the Good Neighbor policy before Roosevelt popularized the phrase. Shortly after his election as President, Hoover traveled for several weeks on a "good will" tour of Latin American states. (*La Nacion,* Santiago, Chile in *American Review of Reviews,* 1929)

North Americans thought and what they owned. Ambassador to Chile William D. Culbertson made no apologies in 1930: "American capital will be the controlling factor in public and private finance in these [South American] countries. . . . Opposition and criticism may divert or slow down these tendencies but they cannot defeat the final result, namely, that American civilization, material and cultural, is bound to impress itself upon, and I believe, benefit these peoples. If anti-American critics wish to describe this as our 'imperialism' let them make the most of it."[41]

Economic expansion characterized United States foreign relations after World War I, and investments in and trade with Latin America reached a "boom" stage. Although European, especially British, interests remained important there, United States businessmen gradually nudged them out of first rank. The direct investments of ̕United States citizens (excluding bonds and securities) jumped from $1.26 billion in 1914 to $3.52 billion in 1929, mostly in electric power, railroads, bananas, sugar, oil, and minerals. By 1936, because of the devastating impact of the worldwide depression on economic relations, the amount dropped to $2.77 billion. These figures represented about one-third of total United States investments abroad. One of the nation's largest corporations, Standard Oil of New Jersey, was active in eight countries, and the United Fruit Company held a large stake in the "banana republics" of Central America. International Telephone and Telegraph controlled communications in Cuba, where, between 1919 and 1933, overall American investments increased 536 percent. Worried about diminishing oil reserves in the United States after World War I, the Harding Administration, particularly under the leadership of Secretary of State Charles E. Hughes and Secretary of Commerce Herbert Hoover, decided to "urge our oil companies to acquire oil territory in South America and elsewhere before the European companies preempted all of it." As Hoover further recounted, "a conference of the leading oil producers was called and such action taken that most of the available oil lands in South America were acquired by Americans."[42] Then, too, fourteen Latin American nations floated bonds in the United States in the 1920s, many of them for unproductive public works, such as a marble palace for the Peruvian President. This "easy money" returned a respectable profit for North Americans, but generally had a damaging effect upon Latin American economies. Latin American nationalists also complained that large profits went back to the United States. In the period 1925–1929, the average annual income outflow from United States investments was $100 million more than the United States capital inflow.

"Trade follows investments" was a popular slogan of the time. From 1914 to 1929 United States exports to Latin America tripled in value, reaching the billion dollar figure, representing about 20 percent of total United States exports. Although trade declined in the 1930s and most United States commerce continued to be with Europe, for many Latin American countries commercial relationships with the United States were vital. Nicaragua, for example, shipped 96 percent of its exports to the United States by 1941. In 1920 the United States supplied Cuba with 73 percent of its imports; that trade shrank to 59 percent in 1929 because of the depressed state of the Cuban sugar economy. Cuba's exports to the United States also dropped off, although they remained at the high level of 68 percent of all the island's exports. If trade with Cuba was declining, it improved with other nations farther south. Large American investments in and trade with Venezuela moved the British out and helped that country to become the world's leading exporter of oil and the second-ranked oil producer, behind only the United States. Trade with Chile in nitrates and copper jumped after American investments there doubled from $200 million in 1920 to $400 million in 1928. United States capital represented 92 percent of the total amount invested in Chilean copper mining by the mid-1920s. Worried by declining world trade during the crippling depression of the 1930s, Secretary of State Cordell Hull was alive to the possibilities of increasing markets in Latin America when he launched the Export-Import Bank (and directed some of its loans to inter-American commerce) and the Reciprocal Trade Agreements Program. His efforts helped increase the value of exports to Latin America from $244 million in 1933 to $642 million in 1938.

## Santo Domingo and Nicaragua: Learning New Methods

After Spain left the Dominican Republic in 1865 and until the American military occupation began in 1916, that impoverished Caribbean country knew little peace. Corrupt politics and the mismanagement of the national revenues produced economic stagnation, political factionalism, and foreign indebtedness. Americans had long been interested in the Dominican Republic. Since the nineteenth century businessmen were active in sugar and finance there, and the Navy had its eye on the harbor of Samaná Bay. President Theodore Roosevelt seized control of Dominican finances in 1905, but for years insurrections fractured Dominican order. In May of 1916, when a contest between the Dominican Congress and President threatened to postpone American demands for expanded United States authority, American Marines went ashore. Within months they had subdued embittered Dominicans, occupied major cities, and established martial law. Sumner Welles, American commissioner to the Dominican Republic (1922–1924), later observed that a new government began to function, "headed by an officer of the American Navy, with a cabinet composed of officers of the United States Navy or Marine Corps, none of whom had any knowledge or experience of Dominican affairs or problems, and the great majority of whom could not even speak the language of the country."[43]

The military intervention in the Dominican Republic, more so than other American interventions, became a hot political issue in the United States and abroad. The Republicans went on record in 1920 as favoring withdrawal. *The Nation* (1920), in denying the imperialist argument that occupation was justified because the United States had improved educational facilities and health, wrote that the "Germans improved sanitation during their occupation of some of the villages of northern France, but no officer of the Marine Corps ever suggested that these reforms justified German presence in France."[44] Washington decided to make a virtue out of adversity and to withdraw in 1924. The United States soon cited the Dominican occupation, and withdrawal, as an example of its good intentions toward Latin America. As Hughes ingeniously argued in 1928, the departure proved that the United States was "anti-imperialistic."[45] Franklin D. Roosevelt agreed, in a 1928 article in *Foreign Affairs:* "We accomplished an excellent piece of constructive work, and the world ought to thank us."[46] Happy with its newfound showcase, the United States continued to manage fiscal matters until 1941, aligning itself with a dictator who served American interests.

Rafael Leonidas Trujillo was an offspring of the American occupation. In early 1919 he was commissioned a second lieutenant in the United States–created national constabulary; he earned high marks from American military officers and became chief of staff of the reorganized National Army in 1928. Through the election of 1930, characterized by violence, fraud, and a boycott by political opponents, Trujillo became President. The vote, roughly 224,000 to 1,900, demonstrated that he held a firm grip on the country. Washington was wary, fearing that his authoritarian methods would spawn new insurrections, but gradually warmed to him when it became clear that his strong-arm tactics would create internal order and thereby eliminate the need for American military intervention. Thanks to beneficent American control of the customs, Trujillo was able to divert considerable funds to his army for the suppression of internal dissent. Political corruption, military muscle, torture, murder, nepotism, commercial monopolies, and raids on the national treasury permitted Trujillo to quiet all opposition and increase his fortune to $800 million.

From 1930 until his assassination in 1961, sometimes as President, sometimes through puppets, "Benefactor of the Nation" Trujillo ruled the Dominican Republic. American military arms filled Dominican arsenals. American businessmen, who dominated the sugar production of the country, endorsed him. Most imports came from the United States, and the economic links were profitable. The National City Bank was designated the official depository for Dominican revenues. In July of 1939, Trujillo traveled to the United States, not as President, but as commander of the armed forces. FDR greeted him in good neighborly fashion. By World War II the Dominican Republic stood as a success story for the new Good Neighbor policy. But, asked many critics, pointing to the brutalities and poverty of Dominican life, good neighbors with whom? Roosevelt gave an answer in reference to Trujillo: "He may be an S.O.B., but he is our S.O.B."[47]

Nicaragua, like the Dominican Republic, developed in the twentieth century under the weight of American military occupation and the Good Neighbor policy. From 1912 to 1925 the United States ruled Nicaragua and kept in power its favorite group, the Conservative party. Nicaragua by 1925 appeared to be solvent, secure, and stable. The Marines departed, but in late 1926 they returned. Even ardent imperialists found it hard to swallow the explanation for this intervention given by the Coolidge Administration. It charged, in an exaggerated report titled "Bolshevik Aims and Policies in Mexico and Latin America," that Communists were fomenting trouble in Nicaragua. It had no evidence of such activity and historians can find none, but such rhetorical rationalization was typical in that era of prevailing anti-Bolshevism. Actually the Nicaraguan Liberals had used Mexico as a sanctuary to organize a countermovement against the Conservatives. "We are not making war on Nicaragua," Coolidge opined, with tones of the Roosevelt Corollary, "any more than a policeman on the street is making war on passersby."[48]

The Nicaraguan intervention generated heated debate in the United States. The assertion of a Communist plot convinced few. Congress again resented a military action taken by the executive, which bypassed its power to declare war. Senator George Norris suggested critically that, if the Coolidge Administration thought Marines could insure honest elections, they should be sent first to Philadelphia and Pittsburgh, cities notorious for their political corruption. Bloodshed and destruction in Nicaragua raised further outcries after Secretary of the Navy Curtis D. Wilbur matter-of-factly reported in 1928: "Several houses were destroyed in the village of Quilali in order to prepare a landing field for airplanes so that 19

**Rafael Trujillo (1891–1961).** The strong man of the Dominican Republic graduated from an American military training school and went on to rule his nation from 1930 to 1961, when he was assassinated. (*The Reporter,* 1961. Copyright 1961 by The Reporter Magazine Co.)

**"The Congressional Castigator."** The intervention in Nicaragua sparked considerable debate in the United States. Uncle Sam is beleaguered by the terrain, a sniping congressman, and the bite of the rebel Sandino. (*The Outlook*, 1928)

wounded Marines could be evacuated to a hospital."[49] Despite extensive American military operations, Liberal leader César Augusto Sandino escaped subjugation; his flight to the hills and his daring struggles against some 5,000 American troops gained him an international reputation as a battler against "Yankee imperialism."

Sensitive to the large-scale criticism of and resistance to the American presence in Nicaragua, special emissary Henry L. Stimson engineered withdrawal (1933). He brought Liberals and Conservatives together in the "Peace of Tipitapa" (1927) and provided for United States supervision of the election of 1928. Most important, he helped create an American-trained national guard to insure the domestic order which American Marines had imposed. Shortly after withdrawal, Sandino signed a truce with the Nicaraguan government. But he was assassinated by the new American-instructed constabulary; the United States, historian Neill Macaulay has written, supplied the "murder weapon."[50] The Guardia Nacional came under the control of a former Liberal rebel, General Anastasio Somoza, who seized power in 1936 and established a brutal dictatorship, which lasted until 1956. Somoza and the United States struck an uneasy alliance. An American collector-general remained to handle customs collections until 1944, and the United States retained canal rights and a naval base. In the late 1930s Somoza complained that the United States was undermining the economic development of his country by

**César Augusto Sandino (1895–1934).**
The Nicaraguan rebel and Latin American hero battled American Marines for years before his death. (Marine Corps, National Archives)

not building a canal. To assuage the dictator's discontent, the Roosevelt Administration in 1939 offered to build an interoceanic highway (Rama Road) for several million dollars. Somoza actually used the road as much for moving his guardsmen as for transporting goods.

Few benefits accrued to the United States from its years of interference in Nicaragua. Trade and investments never reached important levels. From 1914 to 1930 American investments grew from $4.5 million to $13 million, the latter a miniscule part of overall investments in Latin America. Although the occupation of Nicaragua sparked strong resentment and helped foster the Good Neighbor policy, for Nicaragua that policy meant continued foreign financial management and replacement of the United States Marine Corps by a home-grown dictator and a constabulary traveling the Rama Road.

**Comic Strips in Nicaragua.** In this 1927 photograph of the tranquil side of American intervention, American soldiers read comic strips to appreciative Nicaraguan children. (Marine Corps, National Archives)

## When the Marines Ran Haiti

A Marine officer depicted the Haitians as "real nigger and no mistake—there are some very fine looking, well educated polished men here but they are real nigs beneath the surface."[51] When American soldiers went abroad, of course, they carried American prejudices as well as canteens. For nineteen years, from 1915 to 1934, United States Marines governed the tiny black French-speaking nation of Haiti in the Caribbean. The occupation hardly stood as an example of benevolent imperialism, and even the most charitable historian is taxed to salvage much good from the venture. The Wilson Administration ordered the Marines into Haiti on July 28, 1915, after a civil war had erupted there. The United States was interested in the fine harbor at Môle Saint Nicolas, fearful of suspected German intrigue during World War I, protective of American financial interests (largely those of the National City Bank of New York), and insistent, in general, on establishing order in the Caribbean. Franklin D. Roosevelt figured prominently in the story: as assistant secretary of the Navy, he helped write the 1918 Haitian Constitution, and in 1934, as President, he oversaw the evacuation.

The United States occupation touched every aspect of Haitian life. Americans built roads, technical schools, lighthouses, a telephone network, hospitals, and railroads. They improved public health and sanitation. Contemporary critics complained that Haitians could have undertaken most of these projects on their own with some American assistance and without American military subjugation. The improvements never eradicated Haiti's profound human squalor. By the mid-1960s Haiti had the lowest life expectancy (35 years) and the lowest literacy rate (10 percent) in Latin America. Even the new highways soon fell into disrepair, for Americans failed to impart maintenance skills to the Haitians. Many of the roads had been built in 1916–1918 by forced labor—the *corvée* system under which Admiral William Caperton ordered workers into labor gangs and treated them like prisoners. NAACP official James Weldon Johnson, who toured Haiti in 1920, protested: "They were maltreated, beaten and terrorized. In fact, they were in the same category with the convicts in the Negro chain gangs that are used to build roads in many of our southern states."[52] Haitians rebelled against the *corvée*; in 1919 alone the Marines had to kill some 2,000 to quell the insurrection.

American racism and Jim Crow reached into Haiti. American personnel introduced to Haitians the words "nigger," "gook," and "coon" and enforced segregation between blacks and whites. Americans favored mulattoes (the "elite") over the *authentique* (black), but treated all with utter disregard for human dignity. For many Haitians the Marine initials U.S.M.C. meant *Un Salaud Mal Costume*, a sloppy bum. Racism was not the property solely of American soldiers stationed in the field: officials in Washington shared the prevalent view of blacks as inferiors. Secretary of State Robert Lansing, three years after sending the Marines to Haiti, wrote that the "African race" had an "inherent tendency to revert to savagery and to cast aside the shackles of civilization which are irksome to their physical nature. Of course there are many exceptions to this racial weakness but it is true of the mass, as we know from experience in this country."[53] To Americans, if the Haitians were not savage, they were indolent or capable of mastering only menial tasks.

The United States also meddled in the economic affairs of Haiti, sometimes beneficially. New highways, railroads, and bridges expanded commercial contacts between cities and rural farmers. Pan American Airways began flights between Miami and Port-au-Prince. Irrigation systems and a telephone network contributed to economic growth. Sugar and cotton exports increased, although the heavy dependence on one crop, coffee, left Haiti susceptible to fluctuations in world coffee prices. The United States became Haiti's largest trading partner. American capital investments grew from $11.5 million in 1914 to $28.5 million in 1930. The Banque Nationale was owned by the National City Bank of New York. Under American financial supervision, Haiti actually paid its foreign debts (largely

French) ahead of schedule, causing some to complain that the money might have been better spent on economic improvements at home. Haiti's economic life was determined in the United States—although the economic rewards for Americans (or Haitians) hardly justified the occupation.

United States military authorities trained a national guard, the *Garde d'Haiti*, to keep domestic order—to quell revolutions. A majority of the officers of this gendarmerie were actually Americans and no Haitian had reached captain's rank by 1930. The first commandant was Marine Major Smedley D. Butler, a brash veteran previously experienced in putting down "natives" in China, Honduras, Nicaragua, Panama, and Mexico. Mothers in Nicaragua used to discipline their children by warning, "Hush! Major Butler will get you."[54] The national guardsmen enforced the rules of American occupation, served as judges, tax collectors, and paymasters for teachers, and enforced the frequent declarations of martial law. For over two decades after the American military withdrawal in 1934, the *Garde d'Haiti* was the deciding political force.

The United States failed in its years of occupation to establish respect for honest government by law and neglected to train efficient civil servants. The 1918 constitution was drafted in Washington and forced on the Haitians; local elections were rigged, and the press censored. When President Philippe Sudre Dartiguenave's term ended in 1922, he was jilted in favor of wily Louis Borno, a lawyer and perfect stage villain more favorable to the American presence. Borno teamed up with the American High Commissioner, General John H. Russell of Georgia, to rule Haiti from 1922 to 1930. Borno "has never taken a step without

**"The Rights of Small Nations: Haiti."** A harshly critical view of the American military occupation of Haiti, 1915–1934. (*Good Morning,* 1921)

consulting me," Russell boasted.[55] The American general wrote Haitian legislation, took personal command of public projects, and when Borno seemed unduly obstinate, ordered the American financial adviser to withhold the President's salary. The Department of State in Washington criticized Russell's authoritarian rule, but accepted it as necessary for maintaining order.

Haitians resented their colonial status. The peaking of resentment in 1929 coincided with a slump in coffee prices and exports during the Great Depression and with exposure of Borno's political machinations. Protests and strikes spread across the country. President Hoover rejected a full-scale military response and appointed instead an investigating commission. Chaired by W. Cameron Forbes, former governor-general of the Philippines, the commission's report of 1930 combined a delicate mixture of praise and criticism: "The failure of the Occupation to understand the social problems of Haiti, its brusque attempt to implant democracy by drill and harrow, its determination to set up a middle class—however wise and necessary it may seem to Americans—all these explain why, in part, the high hopes of our good works in this land have not been realized."[56] The Forbes Commission promoted a "Haitianization" process to ease Haitians into positions of responsibility. Hoover started the withdrawal; Roosevelt completed it in 1934.

After American Marines left Haiti, Haitians celebrated a "Festival of the Second Independence." Thereafter, however, Haiti was ruled by strong-arm presidents with the help of Export-Import Bank loans and ties with Washington. During World War II the United States used Haitian bases, and until 1947 American officials supervised Haitian national finances. A revolution in 1946 placed the government in the hands of the *Garde,* and the revolution of 1956–1957 produced one of the most callous dictatorships in hemispheric history, that of Dr. François ("Papa Doc") Duvalier. He ruled until his death in 1971, when his rotund son "Baby Doc" assumed power. The Duvaliers were not American creations or creatures. As historian Rayford Logan has noted, however, the "American occupation contributed little to the amelioration of Haiti's plight, rooted in poverty, illiteracy, overpopulation, excessive reliance upon a single crop, and a lack of sturdy democratic political and social traditions and institutions."[57] A Haitian nationalist in 1927 summarized the impact of the American occupation: "They have made themselves the allies of the evil past of oppression and tyranny; they have abolished liberty, justice, independence; they are bad administrators of the public funds. . . . They push forward like the rising tide; they attack our traditions, our soul. . . . They are exploiters." He concluded bitterly: "How can they teach us when they have so much to learn themselves?"[58]

## The Subversion of Cuban Nationalism

Many Cubans thought similarly, as they bristled under the Platt Amendment and American military interventions. Through the 1920s and into the 1930s the United States helped conduct strife-torn elections, enlarged the national army, managed the national budget, and maintained economic control over Cuba. American investments, particularly in sugar, equaled $50 million in 1895; they jumped to $220 million in 1913, and to $1.5 billion in 1929. With the help of a commercial treaty with the United States, Cuba shipped most of its valuable sugar there.

Gerardo Machado, an admirer of Italy's Benito Mussolini, became President in 1924 and conducted national affairs through corruption and brutality. During his rule from 1924 to 1933, he suppressed free speech, jailed or murdered political leftists, journalists, labor leaders, and students, and used the army as a political weapon. He received loans from American bankers and gained the approval of American businessmen by prohibiting strikes.

Cuban resentment against Machado intensified in the late 1920s when sugar prices began to drop. Dependent upon sugar and exports to the United States, Cuba sank further into economic crisis when the United States imposed the restrictive Smoot-Hawley Tariff of 1931. Unemployment rates shot up. Protests and violence spread. Machado sent his soldiers to club the dissenters, closed Havana University, and generally defied his growing opposition. American officials grew disenchanted—he had become an obvious source of disorder. Shortly after entering office, Roosevelt and his advisers decided that an armed American intervention would be blatantly contrary to the newly stated Good Neighbor policy, so Machado had to be eased out.

Suave Sumner Welles, a Groton school friend of Roosevelt and already experienced in the Dominican Republic, was sent as ambassador to Havana in 1933. While American warships patrolled Cuban waters, Welles began to subvert the Machado regime. Fearful that students and leftists might gain authority once Machado stepped down, the ambassador organized a group of old-style politicians. Welles's pressure, a general strike, and more violence convinced Machado to flee. But Welles lost control of the revolution; "his" government, led by Carlos Manuel de Céspedes, lasted less than a month. Céspedes was, said Welles, a "most sincere friend of the United States,"[59] but he was also a lackluster, relatively unknown leader. On September 4, 1933, army men, commanded by Sergeant Fulgencio Batista, staged the "Sergeants' Revolution," deposed the hapless Céspedes, and installed Professor Ramón Grau San Martín as President.

An exile under Machado, a strong critic of the Platt Amendment, and a friend of the left, Grau, according to scholar Luis Aguilar, stood as "the hope and the symbol of the forces of nationalism, patriotism, and reform."[60] But the American ambassador would not suffer him, and "no government here can survive for a protracted period without recognition by the U.S.," Welles bragged.[61] He contemplated landing troops, but Secretary Hull vetoed that unneighborly suggestion in preference for visits by a few warships. In September, Grau abrogated the Platt Amendment and promulgated a host of economic and social reforms to "liquidate the colonial structure that has survived in Cuba since independence."[62] His government suspended payment on Chase National Bank loans, seized some American-owned sugar mills, and threatened a Cuban takeover of all land. The timid in Grau's revolutionary following began to drop off, as it seemed that his economic nationalism might invite American intervention. Army leaders especially were critical of the revolutionary measures. The Communists, on the other hand, considered Grau's government too moderate. Welles began to talk with Batista, the one man who seemed to represent authority in Cuba. To Washington Welles reported that Communists were taking over the Grau government, a patently erroneous depiction. Although Welles left Cuba in December, 1933 (he later became under secretary of state for Latin American affairs), United States pressure continued. In January, 1934, Batista moved against Grau, who fled to Mexico. A

**Fulgencio Batista (1901–1973).** Cuban dictator and American friend, Batista (second from right) was driven from power in early 1959 by Fidel Castro. He died in exile in Portugal. Here he and his family and friends arrive in Miami, 1938. (U.S. Information Agency, National Archives)

Batista-backed President took over, and the United States quickly granted recognition.

Batista ruled Cuba, sometimes as President, sometimes from the shadows, from 1934 to 1959. At the start of the "Era of Batista," the United States abrogated the unpopular Platt Amendment (1934), lowered the sugar tariff, granted a favorable quota to Cuban sugar imports (1934), and issued Export-Import Bank loans ($8 million in 1934). In 1940, Cuba granted American armed forces the use of ports and airfields (besides Guantánamo) in exchange for military aid. An angry Cuban revolutionary, Julio Cesar Fernández, wrote in reflection on the lost opportunity of 1933: "American diplomacy has many resources; when the steel of her warships is not convenient, she uses the docile backbone of her native lackeys."[63] Indeed, the American subversion of the Cuban government and United States economic domination provided an example of the nonmilitary tactics of the Good Neighbor policy.

## A Different Case: Compromise with Mexican Nationalism

The ongoing Mexican Revolution, which began in 1910, presented the United States with one of its few serious obstacles in Latin America and in the 1930s a test of the nonmilitary emphasis of the Good Neighbor policy. Before the 1920s it had appeared that Mexico would be treated like some of America's other neighbors—invaded, occupied, and owned by Americans, who by 1910 controlled 43 percent of Mexican property and produced more than half of Mexico's oil. In 1914,

American sailors bombarded Veracruz, and two years later General John Pershing crossed into Mexico to chase that colorful bandit Pancho Villa. Pershing ran into the Mexican army instead. Mexican nationalists resented *el peligro yanqui*, the Yankee peril.

The Mexican Constitution was proclaimed the same day the last American soldier withdrew from Mexico—February 5, 1917. The radical document alarmed capitalist Americans, because its Article 27 held that all "land and waters" and all subsoil raw materials belonged to the Mexican nation. Three hundred million dollars in American investments in oil and mines were jeopardized. Mexico also began to tax American oil producers heavily. As historian Karl M. Schmitt has written, "for the first time in the modern industrial age a weak, underdeveloped, and economically penetrated state insisted on modifying if not abolishing its dependence on a highly industrialized, militarily powerful overlord."[64]

The United States continued to claim economic rights for its nationals in Mexico and refused to recognize the Mexican government. In 1923, however, Mexico and the United States signed the Bucareli Agreements. In exchange for American recognition, Mexico agreed that Americans who held subsoil rights before the 1917 Constitution could continue those concessions and that Americans who had their agricultural lands expropriated would receive Mexican bonds in compensation. At the time Americans owned just over 50 percent of Mexico's oil industry. But a new law passed by the Mexican Congress in 1925 stated that oil lands secured before 1917 could only be held for a maximum of fifty years. Despite vigorous appeals from American special interest groups to intervene, Washington demonstrated its movement toward nonmilitary methods.

In early 1927, Calvin Coolidge selected an old college chum, a partner in the elite Wall Street firm of J. P. Morgan and Company, as the new ambassador to Mexico City. "After Morrow come the Marines," chanted some Mexicans, but Dwight W. Morrow personified the nonmilitary solutions typical of American foreign policy of that period.[65] Learning a little Spanish, having "Lone Eagle" Charles Lindbergh fly nonstop from Washington, D.C., and even bringing humorist Will Rogers to the Mexican capital, Morrow ingratiated himself with officials. He then negotiated an agreement which confirmed *pre-1917* ownership of petroleum lands. Thus in 1927–1928, the oil controversy seemed defused through compromise: the United States protected the oil investments of its citizens, and Mexico received a tacit American concession that Mexico legally controlled its own raw materials. This arrangement lasted until 1938, when Mexican President Lázaro Cárdenas defiantly expropriated the property of all foreign oil companies, which had grown haughtily obstinate during an oil workers' strike for higher wages. United States economic expansion and Mexican nationalism clashed again, posing a major question for the twentieth century: What were the rights of American businessmen in foreign countries?

The American ambassador in Mexico City in 1938 was Josephus Daniels, who as secretary of the Navy in 1914 had ordered the Marines to occupy Veracruz. Committed to temperance (the embassy served mineral water) and the Golden Rule in diplomacy, the mild-mannered Daniels had dispelled early suspicions and won the admiration of leading Mexicans since his appointment in 1933. "The oil and other big interests here have no sympathy with the Good Neighbor policy," Daniels informed Hull in early 1938. "They go to bed every night wishing that

Díaz were back in power and we carried the Big Stick and had Marines ready to land at their beck and call."[66] Daniels would not tolerate such behavior. Nor would he accept Hull's "get tough" policies, although he disapproved of expropriation. Daniels softened an intemperate State Department blast when he delivered it to the Mexican foreign minister. He ignored Hull's instructions to return to Washington. Hull grew furious with this insubordination. Meanwhile, Washington tried economic coercion by reducing American purchases of Mexican silver, a step Daniels characterized as Big Stick. He urged a reconsideration, and wrote the President that "We are strong. Mexico is weak. It is always noble in the strong to be generous and generous and generous."[67] For their part the American oil companies refused to sell petroleum equipment to Mexico, and they persuaded shipping companies not to carry Mexican oil. Standard Oil of New Jersey financed utterly false propaganda in the United States with the message that Cárdenas was a Communist bent on creating a Soviet Mexico. *Atlantic Monthly* magazine ran a pro-Standard Oil article in its July, 1938, number, and soon admitted with some embarrassment that the issue had been financed by the oil companies. "Rotten oil propaganda," Daniels snarled.[68]

FDR ruled out United States intervention and decided on negotiations to gain compensation for lost properties. That choice was prompted in part by fears that Mexico was moving toward fascist Germany and Italy, which had increased their purchases of Mexican oil during the controversy. Japan too increased trade with Mexico. If the Americans would not sell them equipment or ship their oil, the Mexicans argued, their only chance of economic survival rested in such sales. Long and difficult Mexican-American talks resulted in an agreement in 1941. The United States conceded the principle that Mexico owned its own raw materials, and Mexico promised to pay the oil companies and other Americans for expropriated properties. The Export-Import Bank prepared to extend a $30 million loan. Although Washington's ultimate compromise with Mexican nationalism was an exceptional case, the nonmilitary methods used were typical of the Good Neighbor policy. Mexico remained one of the United States' leading trading partners and loyally joined the United States' fight against the Axis powers in World War II.

## Pan Americanism and the Approach of War

In 1889, under Secretary of State James G. Blaine's initiative, the International Bureau of American Republics was created. In 1910 it was renamed the Pan American Union, and the United States secretary of state became its permanent chairman. "Pan Americanism" was at first concerned with the improvement of trade in the western hemisphere and symbolized a mythical inter-American unity. The union's elegant quarters, financed by steel baron Andrew Carnegie, stood, significantly, a short distance from the Department of State Building. One Argentine diplomat sneered that "there is no Pan Americanism in South America; it exists only in Washington."[69] The declarations of neutrality during World War I by seven Latin American governments annoyed Washington and exposed the shallowness of Pan American solidarity.

In 1923 the Fifth Pan American Conference met in Santiago, Chile. The United States controlled the agenda, and the delegates endorsed a Treaty to Avoid or Prevent Conflicts Between the American States (Gondra Treaty). The Havana

Conference of 1928, however, was quite a different matter. Arriving at Havana shortly after American troops were landed in Nicaragua, the conferees assembled in a rebellious mood. American officials had anticipated trouble and had thus appointed former Secretary of State Hughes to head the American delegation. Even President Coolidge traveled to Cuba to address the conference with commonplaces. The cooperative Machado dictatorship ordered newspapers to abstain from critical comment about the United States.

At the conference, the delegate from tiny El Salvador rose and moved that "no state has the right to intervene in the internal affairs of another."[70] Mexico and Argentina backed this challenge to the United States. Hughes had the resolution sent to a study committee chaired by himself. The committee recommended that the question of intervention be considered at the *next* conference. Yet El Salvador's courageous Dr. Gustavo Guerrero reintroduced his nonintervention resolution at the plenary meeting, forcing Hughes to defend the right to intervene with language not altogether dissimilar from that of the Roosevelt Corollary: "We do not wish to intervene in the affairs of any American Republic. We simply wish peace and order and stability and recognition of honest rights properly acquired so that this hemisphere may not only be the hemisphere of peace but the hemisphere of international justice."[71] His words did not persuade many, but the power of the United States did, and the issue of intervention was tabled until the next conference. Professor Samuel Guy Inman of the American delegation critically assessed the meaning of the conference: "We still hold to the old pre-war diplomacy. And the United States still calls for more volunteers to hunt Sandino in Nicaragua and to be ready to act in any country near the Panama Canal where we have a 'moral mandate' to see that they conduct elections as we do in Pennsylvania, Illinois, or Oklahoma. And Latin America still holds her protest meetings . . . , while her officials float new loans in New York to pay their way to the numerous new Pan American conferences."[72]

The Seventh Pan American Conference, in Montevideo, Uruguay (1933), convened with considerable optimism, for it followed Roosevelt's inauguration and met amidst the aura of the Good Neighbor policy. The expected resolution was introduced ("No state has the right to intervene in the internal or external affairs of another"), and Cordell Hull cast an affirmative vote. The jubilation was not uniform, however, for Hull announced that the United States would reserve its right to intervene "by the law of nations as generally recognized and accepted."[73] In other words, the United States still held to intervention as a right. Further confusion about the meaning of the nonintervention pledge was added at the 1936 Buenos Aires Conference, where the United States seemingly endorsed an unequivocal statement of nonintervention. The American definition, however, was that *military* intervention was outlawed, whereas many Latin American countries (especially Mexico) interpreted it to mean that the United States could not interfere through economic or political pressure when countries nationalized American-owned property.

Pan Americanism took a decided turn toward continental solidarity and hemispheric security in the late 1930s, as Germany, Italy, and Japan attempted to improve their economic and political standing in Latin America. "To me the danger to the Western Hemisphere was real and imminent," Cordell Hull recalled. "It was not limited to the possibility of a military invasion. It was more acute in its indirect form of propaganda, penetration, organizing political parties, buying some adherents, and blackmailing others. We had seen the method employed with great success in Austria and in the Sudetenland."[74] Nazi activists were evident in Argentina, Uruguay, Brazil, and Guatemala. Although the United States clearly exaggerated the Nazi threat to the western hemisphere, the fears were nevertheless real, and Washington moved to squash the perceived danger at the Lima Conference of 1938. Argentina, Uruguay, and Chile provided opposition at Lima to United States efforts to knit the Latin American countries together in a quasi-alliance. They argued that they should not break their ties with Europe and become more dependent upon the United States. Hull, through extensive lobbying, beat back attempts to undermine his plan for solidarity. The evident anti-German sentiment of most of the delegates, aroused by the recent Munich crisis, made his task easier. Hence the conference strongly endorsed the Declaration of Lima, wherein the "American Republics" pledged to cooperate in resisting any "foreign intervention or activity that may threaten them."[75] A year later, in the Declaration of Panama, they established a security belt around the western hemisphere to rebuff potential Axis intrusions. At the same time, the United States persuaded Latin American nations to reduce or cease trade with the Axis powers and to ship valuable raw materials to the United States. So, through the late 1930s and into World War II, a perceived threat encouraged methods that continued United States hegemony in Latin America.

## On the Eve of War

Japan was still marching in Asia, violating the Open Door and audaciously denying the United States a place in China's destiny. Unintimidated Mexican nationalism had just dealt the United States a rude setback through the expropriation of large American oil properties. Argentina was flirting with Nazi Germany. The post-World War I search for order in international relations had indeed broken down by 1939. In both Asia and Latin America, nationalists challenged the United States. In both areas the success and viability of American diplomacy was determined by the power the United States possessed and exercised. In Asia, after the Manchurian crisis of 1931–1932, the United States sought, without success, to build a counterforce to Japan; but even the Philippines, as Theodore Roosevelt had noted years before, was a virtual hostage that the military said it could not defend. Asia became a Japanese sphere of influence, and the Japanese told Americans that Tokyo was only doing in Asia what the United States was doing in Latin America. Indeed, in Latin America the United States suffered few competitors. As Washington perceived a Nazi threat in the late 1930s, it drew its neighbors even more snugly under its paternalistic wing.

In both Asia and Latin America the United States looked down on "inferiors" from the grand heights of paternalism. America thought it was China's best friend, even though little could be done to save that friend. In Latin America the long-standing paternalistic attitude was enhanced by the lofty language of the Good Neighbor. Historian Paul A. Varg has noted that the "phrase 'Good Neighbor Policy,' carrying with it the same kind of philanthropic ring as the earlier 'Open Door Policy,' appealed to the public's illusory wish to believe that foreign policy could be altruistic."[76] The self-determination principle was much abused in practice, for the United States acted on the premise that it knew what was best for its southern neighbors. Despite Pan Americanism, Washington still treated Latin Americans as protégés rather than as associates.

American paternalism, however, was being challenged by militant nationalism, a force of considerable power, defining new "orders" that excluded American influence. Cuban nationalism, Mexican nationalism, Chinese nationalism, Japanese nationalism—all demanded the exclusion of imperialists, including (and in some cases especially) the United States. Nationalism might become contagious, and hence more dangerous, thought American leaders. Secretary Cordell Hull mused during the oil crisis of 1938: "What if Mexican nationalism spilled over into Venezuela?"[77] Intolerant of nationalism, yet not altogether able to check it, the United States made compromises. The Big Stick was shelved during the Mexican oil controversy, and the result was not lost on other Latin Americans: Mexico gained an American concession that it controlled its own natural resources—it stood up boldly to the "Colossus of the North" and essentially won. The United States still dominated Latin America by World War II, but its hold was certainly less firm, and Latin Americans enjoyed a new measure of self-determination.

The Great Depression had helped undermine American authority in world affairs. That economic catastrophe worked gouging damage on international relations. World trade and investment collapsed; tariffs went up. The island-bound and trade-conscious Japanese were encouraged to seek a "co-prosperity" sphere in Asia. In Latin America, many of whose states depended upon the exportation of one crop for economic survival, revolutions and coups erupted, feeding on incipient nationalism. Social unrest and political instability rocked the area from which the United States was withdrawing its Marines. Santo Domingo, Argentina, Brazil, and Chile in 1930, Peru in 1931, Cuba in 1933 . . . The political upheavals in the United States' sphere of influence were met with the new nonmilitary tactics of the Good Neighbor. Hegemony was maintained, yet compromises with nationalism jeopardized Washington's authority. Latin Americans, devastated by the depression, gained a new awareness of the extent to which their national choices were made by foreigners, and the degree to which foreign companies drained profits from them. By World War II, Latin Americans held a more favorable image of the United States, because the latter had seemingly abandoned military intervention. But they harbored fresh suspicions that inter-American economic relations would continue United States hegemony. Yankeephobia simmered, while the United States continued largely to take Latin American subservience for granted.

On the eve of World War II many Americans were less certain about the wisdom of continuing nonmilitary methods in diplomacy. Of course Americans wanted no part of war in Europe or Asia, but increasing numbers came to believe that more forceful diplomacy and military preparedness would prevent American involvement in the conflagration. Should those tougher methods fail to deter adversaries bent on aggression that endangered American interests, war was the next step. The lessons of the 1930s, then, became clear to reflective American leaders. Interests and commitments, like the Philippines or American commerce, must be defended with power; principles like the Open Door must be buttressed by muscle; power and order go hand in hand; treaties must have enforcement clauses; an international organization, like the League of Nations, unless its members desire to utilize it, is a weak instrument of peace; the United States cannot count on other nations to maintain the peace; nonmilitary tactics must be joined by the willingness to use force. Never again, reasoned American diplomats, would they permit American principles to be so callously trampled or American interests to be jeopardized. Never again would the United States be caught short on power, for persuasive diplomacy hinged on it. One day after Pearl Harbor, the President asserted that Americans "will make it very certain that this form of treachery shall never again endanger us."[78]

Noting the integral relationship between economics and politics, American leaders also vowed to create a healthy world economy and hence a stable political order. Near the end of World War II, Hull identified one of the chief lessons of the 1930s and a core idea of the American outlook: "A world in economic chaos would be forever a breeding ground for trouble and war."[79] Vice-President Henry A. Wallace reflected a few months after Pearl Harbor that "We failed our job after World War I. . . . But by our very errors we learned much, and after this war we

**FDR Reviews the Fleet.** Aboard the U.S.S. *Houston* with Admiral Claude Bloch, the President, always a "big Navy" man, plays Commander-in-Chief for a day, July 14, 1938, at a time when the United States began to beef up its military status. (Franklin D. Roosevelt Library)

shall be in position to utilize our knowledge in building a world which is economically, politically, and, I hope, spiritually sound."[80] Two days after Pearl Harbor, FDR expressed a similar attitude when he said in a fireside chat that the future would be different, indeed: "We are going to win the war, and we are going to win the peace that follows."[81]

## Further Reading for the Period 1920–1939, Relations with Asia and Latin America

For general studies of this period and biographies, see some of the works listed in the "Further Reading" section of Chapter 9.

Tumultuous events in Asia leading to conflict with Japan are studied in Irvine H. Anderson, *The Standard-Vacuum Oil Company and United States East Asia Policy, 1933–1941* (1975), Dorothy Borg, *The United States and the Far Eastern Crisis of 1933–1938* (1964), Dorothy Borg and Shumpei Okamoto, eds., *Pearl Harbor as History: Japanese-American Relations, 1931–1941* (1973), Russell D. Buhite, *Nelson T. Johnson and American Policy Toward China, 1925–1941* (1968), Richard Dean Burns and Edward M. Bennett, eds., *Diplomats in Crisis* (1974), Warren I. Cohen, *America's Response to China* (1971), Roger Dingman, *Power in the Pacific: The Origins of Naval Arms Limitations, 1914–1922* (1976), Herbert Feis, *The Road to Pearl Harbor* (1950), Akira Iriye, *Across the Pacific* (1967) and *After Imperialism* (1969), James W. Morley, ed., *Deterrent Diplomacy: Japan, Germany and the U.S.S.R., 1935–1940* (1977), Charles E. Neu, *The Troubled Encounter* (1975), William L. Neumann, *America Encounters Japan* (1963), Armin Rappaport, *Henry L. Stimson and Japan, 1931–1933* (1963), Barbara Tuchman, *Stilwell and the American Experience in China, 1911–45* (1971), and Gerald Wheeler, *Prelude to Pearl Harbor: The United States Navy and the Far East, 1921–1931* (1963).

United States relations with Latin America are treated in Richard Abrams, "United States Intervention Abroad: The First Quarter Century," *American Historical Review* (1974), E. David Cronon, *Josephus Daniels in Mexico* (1960), Alexander DeConde, *Herbert Hoover's Latin American Policy* (1951), Donald Dozer, *Are We Good Neighbors?* (1959), Alton Frye, *Nazi Germany and the American Hemisphere, 1933–1941* (1967), Irwin F. Gellman, *Roosevelt and Batista* (1973), David Green, *The Containment of Latin America* (1971), Stanley Hilton, *Brazil and the Great Powers, 1930–1939* (1975), William Kamman, *A Search for Stability: United States Diplomacy Toward Nicaragua, 1925–1933* (1968), Lester D. Langley, *The Cuban Policy of the United States* (1968), Neil Macaulay, *The Sandino Affair* (1967), Frank McCann, *The Brazilian-American Alliance, 1937–1945* (1973), Dana Munro, *United States and the Caribbean Republics, 1921–1933* (1974), Robert I. Rotberg, *Haiti* (1971), Ramon Ruiz, *Cuba: The Making of a Revolution* (1968), Hans Schmidt, *The United States Occupation of Haiti* (1971), Karl M. Schmitt, *Mexico and the United States* (1974), Robert F. Smith, *The United States and Cuba* (1960) and *The United States and Revolutionary Nationalism in Mexico, 1916–1932* (1972), Dick Steward, *Trade and Hemisphere* (1975), Joseph Tulchin, *The Aftermath of War: World War I and U.S. Policy Toward Latin America* (1971), and Bryce Wood, *The Making of the Good Neighbor Policy* (1961).

For an extensive list of studies, see David F. Trask, Michael C. Meyer, and Roger Trask, *A Bibliography of United States–Latin American Relations Since 1810* (1968).

Also see the following notes.

1. Quoted in Elting E. Morison, *Turmoil and Tradition: A Study of the Life and Times of Henry L. Stimson* (New York: Atheneum, 1964), p. 312.

2. Robert H. Ferrell, "The Mukden Incident: September 18–19, 1931," *Journal of Modern History*, XXVII (March, 1955), 67.

3. Quoted in Morison, *Turmoil and Tradition*, p. 308.

4. Quoted in Richard N. Current, "Henry L. Stimson," in Norman A. Graebner, ed., *An Uncertain Tradition* (New York: McGraw-Hill, 1961), pp. 171, 169.

5. Quoted in John E. Wiltz, *From Isolation to War, 1931–1941* (New York: Thomas Y. Crowell, 1968), p. 39.

6. Quoted in Frank Freidel, *Franklin D. Roosevelt: Launching the New Deal* (Boston: Little, Brown, 1973), p. 120.

7. Quoted in Richard Dean Burns, "Stanley K. Hornbeck: The Diplomacy of the Open Door," in Richard Dean Burns and Edward M. Bennett, eds., *Diplomats in Crisis* (Santa Barbara, Cal.: ABC-CLIO Press, 1974), p. 103.

8. Quoted in Morison, *Turmoil and Tradition*, p. 306.

9. Quoted in Christopher Thorne, *The Limits of Foreign Policy: The West, the League and the Far Eastern Crisis of 1931–1933* (New York: Capricorn Books edition, 1973), p. 158.

10. Quoted in Morison, *Turmoil and Tradition*, p. 310.

11. *Ibid.*, p. 315.

12. Quoted in Norman A. Graebner, "Hoover, Roosevelt, and the Japanese," in Dorothy Borg and Shumpei Okamoto, eds., *Pearl Harbor as History* (New York: Columbia University Press, 1973), p. 30.

13. Morison, *Turmoil and Tradition*, p. 332.

14. Hugh R. Wilson, *Diplomat Between the Wars* (New York: Longmans, Green, 1941), p. 280.

15. Quoted in Robert F. Smith, "Republican Policy and the Pax Americana, 1921–1932," in William A. Williams, ed., *From Colony to Empire* (New York: John Wiley & Sons, 1972), p. 292.

16. Quoted in Thomas H. Buckley, *The United States and the Washington Conference, 1921–1922* (Knoxville: University of Tennessee Press, 1970), pp. 72–73.

17. Quoted in Roger Dingman, *Power in the Pacific: The Origins of Naval Arms Limitations, 1914–1922* (Chicago: University of Chicago Press, 1976), p. 212.

18. Quoted in Akira Iriye, *The Cold War in Asia* (Englewood Cliffs, N.J.: Prentice-Hall, 1974), p. 18.

19. Warren Cohen, *America's Response to China* (New York: John Wiley & Sons, 1971), p. 106.

20. Stanley K. Hornbeck, *The United States and the Far East* (Boston: World Peace Foundation, 1942), p. 10.

21. John Paton Davies, *Dragon by the Tail* (New York: W. W. Norton, 1972), p. 95.

22. Quoted in Hornbeck, *United States and Far East*, pp. 3–4.

23. Quoted in Akira Iriye, *Across the Pacific* (New York: Harcourt Brace & World, 1967), p. 148.

24. Quoted in Cohen, *America's Response to China*, p. 104.

25. Quoted in Wiltz, *From Isolation to War*, p. 25.

26. Quoted in Asado Sadao, "The Japanese Navy and the United States," in Borg and Okamoto, *Pearl Harbor as History*, p. 238.

27. Waldo Heinrichs, Jr., "The Role of the U.S. Navy," *ibid.*, pp. 202–203.

28. Quoted in William L. Neumann, *America Encounters Japan* (Baltimore: The Johns Hopkins Press, 1963), p. 176.

29. Quoted in Freidel, *Franklin D. Roosevelt: Launching*, p. 104.

30. Barbara W. Tuchman, *Stilwell and the American Experience in China, 1911–45* (New York: Bantam Books, 1972 [c. 1971]), p. 214.

31. Samuel I. Rosenman, ed., *Public Papers and Addresses of Franklin D. Roosevelt* (New York: Macmillan, 1938–1943; 13 vols.), VI, 406–411.

32. Quoted in Wayne S. Cole, "The Role of the United States Congress and Political Parties," in Borg and Okamoto, *Pearl Harbor as History*, p. 314.

33. Quoted in Frederick C. Adams, *Economic Diplomacy: The Export-Import Bank and American Foreign Policy, 1934–1939* (Columbia: University of Missouri Press, 1976), p. 233.

34. Quoted in Robert D. Schulzinger, *The Making of the Diplomatic Mind: The Training, Outlook & Style of United States Foreign Service Officers, 1908–31* (Middletown, Conn.: Wesleyan University Press, 1975), p. 95.

35. Quoted in Arthur P. Whitaker, "From Dollar Diplomacy to the Good Neighbor Policy," *Inter-American Economic Affairs*, IV (Spring, 1951), 18.

36. Rosenman, *Public Papers*, II, 14.

37. Quoted in David Green, *The Containment of Latin America* (Chicago: Quadrangle Books, 1971), p. 38.

38. Frederick B. Pike, *Chile and the United States, 1880–1962* (South Bend, Ind.: University of Notre Dame Press, 1963), p. 236.

39. J. Fred Rippy, *Globe and Hemisphere* (Chicago: Henry Regnery Company, 1958), pp. 46–47.

40. Quoted in C. Neale Ronning, ed., *Intervention in Latin America* (New York: Alfred A. Knopf, 1970), pp. 42–49.

41. Quoted in Joan Hoff Wilson, *American Business & Foreign Policy, 1920–1933* (Boston: Beacon Press, 1973 [c. 1971]), p. 160.

42. Herbert Hoover, *Memoirs: The Cabinet and the Presidency, 1920–1933* (New York: Macmillan, 1952), p. 69.

43. Sumner Welles, *Naboth's Vineyard* (New York: Payson and Clark, 1928; 2 vols.), II, 797–798.

44. Quoted in Joseph R. Juarez, "United States Withdrawal from Santo Domingo," *Hispanic American Historical Review*, XLII (May, 1962), 180.

45. *Ibid.*

46. Franklin D. Roosevelt, "Our Foreign Policy: A Democratic View," *Foreign Affairs*, VI (July, 1928), 583.

47. Quoted in Robert F. Smith, *The United States and Cuba: Business and Diplomacy, 1917–1960* (New York: Bookman Associates, 1960), p. 184.

48. Quoted in Albert K. Weinberg, *Manifest Destiny* (Chicago: Quadrangle Books, 1963 [c. 1935]), p. 441.

49. United States Department of the Navy, *Operation of Naval Service in Nicaragua* (Senate Doc. No. 86, 70th Cong., 1st Sess., 1928), pp. 5–6.

50. Neill Macaulay, *The Sandino Affair* (Chicago: Quadrangle Books, 1967), p. 257.

51. Colonel Littleton Waller, quoted in Robert I. Rotberg, *Haiti: The Politics of Squalor* (Boston: Houghton Mifflin, 1971), pp. 137–138.

52. James Welton Johnson, "The Truth About Haiti," *The Crisis*, XX (September, 1920), 223.

53. Quoted in Rayford W. Logan, *Haiti and the Dominican Republic* (New York: Oxford University Press, 1968), p. 126.

54. Quoted in Hans Schmidt, *The United States Occupation of Haiti, 1915–1934* (New Brunswick: Rutgers University Press, 1971), p. 81n.

55. Quoted in Donald B. Cooper, "The Withdrawal of the United States from Haiti, 1928–1934," *Journal of Inter-American Studies*, V (January, 1963), 83.

56. Quoted in Dana G. Munro, *The United States and the Caribbean Republics, 1921–1933* (Princeton: Princeton University Press, 1974), pp. 314–315.

57. Logan, *Haiti and Dominican Republic*, pp. 141–142.

58. Quoted in Emily Greene Balch, ed., *Occupied Haiti* (New York: Winters, 1927), pp. 179–180.

59. Quoted in Luis E. Aguilar, *Cuba 1933: Prologue to Revolution* (New York: W. W. Norton, 1974 [1972]), p. 150.

60. *Ibid.*, p. 167.

61. Quoted in Hugh Thomas, *Cuba: The Pursuit of Freedom, 1762–1969* (New York: Harper and Row, 1971), p. 655.

62. Quoted in Aguilar, *Cuba 1933*, p. 175.

63. *Ibid.*, pp. 228–229.

64. Karl M. Schmitt, *Mexico and the United States, 1821–1973* (New York: John Wiley & Sons, 1974), p. 158.

65. Quoted in John W. F. Dulles, *Yesterday in Mexico* (Austin: University of Texas Press, 1961), pp. 324–325.

66. Quoted in E. David Cronon, *Josephus Daniels in Mexico* (Madison: University of Wisconsin Press, 1960), p. 185.

67. *Ibid.*, p. 198.

68. *Ibid.*, p. 210.

69. Quoted in J. Lloyd Mecham, *A Survey of United States–Latin American Relations* (Boston: Houghton Mifflin, 1965), p. 100.

70. Quoted in Samuel Guy Inman, *Inter-American Conferences, 1826–1954* (Washington, D.C.: University Press, 1965; ed. by Harold E. Davis), p. 117.

71. Quoted in Mecham, *Survey of United States–Latin American Relations*, p. 107.

72. Inman, *Inter-American Conferences*, pp. 118–119.

73. Quoted in Bryce Wood, *The Making of the Good Neighbor Policy* (New York: Columbia University Press, 1961), p. 119.

74. Cordell Hull, *Memoirs* (New York: Macmillan, 1948; 2 vols.), I, 602.

75. *Ibid.*, I, 608.

76. Paul A. Varg, "The Economic Side of the Good Neighbor Policy: The Reciprocal Trade Program and South America," *Pacific Historical Review*, XLV (February, 1976), 49.

77. Quoted in Lloyd C. Gardner, *Economic Aspects of New Deal Diplomacy* (Madison: University of Wisconsin Press, 1964), pp. 117–118.

78. Rosenman, *Public Papers*, X, 515.

79. Hull, *Memoirs*, II, 1681.

80. Quoted in John L. Gaddis, *The United States and the Origins of the Cold War* (New York: Columbia University Press, 1972), p. 2.

81. Rosenman, *Public Papers*, X, 530.

**Church Service, *Prince of Wales.*** On August 10, 1941, President Franklin D. Roosevelt and Prime Minister Winston S. Churchill, with their staffs, attended a memorable church service aboard the British vessel during the Atlantic Charter Conference. (Franklin D. Roosevelt Library)

# 11 World War II: The Ordeal of Allied Diplomacy, 1939–1945

## Diplomatic Crossroad: The "Atlantic Charter" Conference, 1941

It was the longest walk that the tall, greying man had attempted since being stricken by polio twenty years earlier. Holding a cane in his right hand and helped by his son Elliott, President Franklin D. Roosevelt slowly limped the entire length of the battleship H.M.S. *Prince of Wales* to take his place of honor on the quarterdeck. More than fifteen hundred men, including British Prime Minister Winston S. Churchill, stood at rigid attention as the President took his tortured steps. "He was making a tremendous effort," observed a Britisher, and "he was determined to walk along that deck even if it killed him."[1] Finally, Roosevelt reached his seat near the bow, side-by-side with Churchill. British and American chiefs of staff stood behind them, with impressive ranks of sailors and marines on each side. Facing them was the *Prince of Wales'* forward turret, its fourteen-inch guns protruding "like rigid pythons."[2] Roosevelt and Churchill were attending church services together in the quiet waters of Placentia Bay near the harbor of Argentia, Newfoundland that Sunday of August 10, 1941.

Sunday services aboard the *Prince of Wales* marked the high point of the four-day summit meeting between the two leaders (August 9–13, 1941), some four months before Pearl Harbor catapulted the United States into World War II as a formal belligerent. The text of the sermon, from Joshua 1:1–9, seemed directed at the President: "There shall not any man be able to stand before thee all the days of thy life; as I was with Moses, so I will be with thee: I will not fail thee, nor forsake thee." Also suggesting the need for the United States to aid its sister democracy in the war against Hitler was the stirring hymn, "Onward Christian Soldiers," with its call for volunteers "marching as to war." For Roosevelt, who had already assisted the British with destroyers, Lend-Lease, and other aid short of war, the moment evoked a rush of emotion. His handkerchief dabbed at his eyes. "If nothing else had happened," he later told his son, "that would have cemented us. 'Onward Christian Soldiers.' We *are*, and we *will*, go on, with God's help."[3] Churchill later wrote of the symbolism of that Sunday morning—"the Union Jack and the Stars and Stripes draped side by side on the pulpit; . . . the highest naval, military, and air officers of Britain and the United States grouped together behind the President and me; the close-packed ranks of British and American sailors, completely intermingled, sharing the same books and joining fervently in the prayers and hymns familiar to both."[4] None of those praying on the *Prince of Wales* could know, of course, that the majestic battleship would be destroyed by Japanese bombs off the coast of Malaya on December 10, 1941.

The four-day meeting in Placentia Bay was the first of many conferences between Roosevelt and Churchill during World War II; altogether, the two leaders would spend some 120 days in each other's company. Notwithstanding the fears of presidential assistant Harry Hopkins that the meeting foreordained a clash of "prima donnas," the personalities blended nicely.[5] "I am sure I have established warm and deep personal relations with our great friend," Churchill cabled London.[6] The tactful British leader's willingness to pay deference to a man he regarded "almost with religious awe" and his own pride in being half-American (his mother) made Churchill an ardent advocate of Anglo-American solidarity.[7] Roosevelt, although he sometimes saw the Prime Minister as the last of the Victorians, reciprocated Churchill's friendship, and the two heads of government built over the next four years a degree of cooperation unmatched in modern times. "It is fun to be in the same decade with you," FDR wrote his British partner in early 1942.[8]

Aside from the personal equation, the other results of Argentia were less clear-cut. The British asked for men, ships, planes, and tanks. Churchill urged that the American Navy extend its convoying of British vessels farther into the German submarine–infested North Atlantic. The British military chiefs, remembering the frightful casualties of World War I, and perhaps hoping to make military intervention more palatable to the Americans, argued that bombing, blockades, and propaganda might so weaken the Germans that they would surrender without a cross-channel operation. Even with landings, said the British, the burden of fighting would be carried by armored units rather than the large infantry forces of 1914–1918. The Americans, particularly Army Chief of Staff General George C. Marshall, favored a more direct strategy, insisting on large ground armies. Marshall declared further that an American military buildup had to take priority over British demands for weapons and equipment; "the hungry table," as Churchill once described American defense production, simply did not have enough for all who wanted to eat.[9] The one tangible military commitment at Argentia was Roosevelt's promise to order his Navy to convoy British merchant ships as far as Iceland. The President delayed any public declaration until September, when a German submarine torpedoed the American destroyer *Greer* off the coast of Iceland. Neglecting to mention that the *Greer* had been shadowing the U-boat for three hours prior to the attack, Roosevelt announced over worldwide radio on September 11 that henceforth American naval vessels would shoot at German submarines, "the rattlesnakes of the Atlantic."[10] An undeclared naval war was as far as Roosevelt would go in the months before Pearl Harbor.

Discussions about Japan exposed British and American differences at Argentia. Sir Alexander Cadogan of the Foreign Office argued that Japan, which had recently occupied the southern half of French Indochina, should receive an explicit American warning against further encroachments, and that the United States should commit itself to war if the Japanese attacked British or Dutch territory in Southeast

**Winston S. Churchill (1874–1965) at Placentia Bay, 1941.** Familiar cigar in place, the British Prime Minister moves his bulldog posture across the deck at the seaborne conference near Newfoundland where he and President Roosevelt devised the Atlantic Charter. (Franklin D. Roosevelt Library)

Asia. Under Secretary of State Sumner Welles avoided any definite commitment. The best that the British could get was a Rooseveltian promise to deliver a "mighty swat" to Japan. When the President returned to Washington, however, Secretary of State Cordell Hull watered down the proposed statement. Whereas the original draft had stated that further Japanese aggression would cause the United States to take measures that "might result in war," the actual postconference warning to the Japanese ambassador merely read that Washington would take steps necessary "toward insuring the safety and security of the United States."[11] Despite British pressures for a hard line and despite the American embargo of oil to Japan the previous month, Roosevelt preferred to delay a confrontation in the Pacific until his Army and Navy were stronger, public opinion more favorable, and two-front war more advantageous. Roosevelt's policy was to beat Hitler first.

The most famous product of the Churchill-Roosevelt summit conference was the eight-point statement of war aims—the Atlantic Charter. Reminiscent of Woodrow Wilson's Fourteen Points, the Atlantic Charter, in deliberately vaguer terms, reaffirmed the old Wilsonian principles of collective security, national self-determination, freedom of the seas, and liberal trading practices. The signatories also denied themselves any territorial aggrandizement and pledged economic collaboration leading to "social security." Behind the vision of a postwar world in which "all the men in all the lands may live out their lives in freedom from fear and want," however, lay Anglo-American differences. The Americans, particularly Sumner Welles, whom Cadogan said had "swallowed a ramrod in his youth," pressed for a statement explicitly endorsing freer trade.[12] The British wanted to protect their discriminatory system of imperial preferences. The compromise called for "access, on equal terms, to the trade and to the raw materials of the world which are needed for their economic prosperity," leaving the British an escape clause that promised "due respect for their existing obligations." Hull, when he read this vague language later, was "keenly disappointed."[13] Churchill failed to gain Roosevelt's backing for a new League of Nations. The President said that he did not favor a new League Assembly, at least not until England and the United States, acting as policemen, had time to pacify and disarm international troublemakers. Not wishing to arouse either isolationists or fervent internationalists, Roosevelt accepted only "the establishment of a wider and permanent system of general security."[14] As "both realist and idealist, both fixer and preacher, both a prince and a soldier," the President wanted to be as cautious as he was eloquent about postwar goals.[15] "I have not the slightest objection toward your trying your hand at an outline of the post-war picture," he had told an assistant secretary of state in June, 1941. "But for Heaven's sake don't ever let the columnists hear of it."[16]

The Atlantic Charter became a moral and ideological propaganda tool for the war against the Axis. "Every one of the eight points . . . was a challenge to the practice of the Axis Powers, and a challenge to which they could give no effective answer."[17] In September, 1941, at an Inter-Allied meeting in London, representatives of the nations battling Hitler formally adhered to the "common principles" set forth in the Atlantic Charter.[18] The Soviet Union also gave qualified approval. Twenty-six nations, on January 1, 1942, signed the Declaration of the United Nations, which pledged cooperation in achieving the aims of the Atlantic Charter. Churchill and Roosevelt, however, provided no procedures for enforcement or implementation of the principles. Indeed on September 9, in the House of Commons, the Prime Minister insisted that the charter applied only to "nations of Europe now under the Nazi yoke," not to "the regions and peoples which owe allegiance to the British Crown."[19] As early as December, 1941, Josef Stalin, when rebuffed in his call for Polish territory, remarked: "I thought that the Atlantic Charter was directed against those people who were trying to establish world dominion. It now looks as if the Charter was directed against the USSR."[20] As for Roosevelt, he came to view the principles as guides or inclinations rather than set rules. However much the President believed in the ideals set forth at Argentia, he was always willing to postpone their application or compromise them to accommodate pressing military and diplomatic priorities. "I dream dreams but am, at the same time, an intensely practical person," he once said.[21]

By meeting secretly with Winston Churchill on board a British battleship, President Roosevelt demonstrated America's commitment to the defense of Britain by all means short of war. Notwithstanding outcries from American isolationists, and whatever hopes he might have held that the theatrics of Argentia would galvanize American opinion for a firmer policy, Roosevelt could not commit the United States to war prematurely. "There isn't the slightest chance of the U.S. entering the war until compelled to do so by a direct attack on its own territory," reported one British participant shortly after the conference.[22] Yet the Atlantic Charter, the Churchill-Roosevelt friendship, the Anglo-American strategic conversations, even the divergent views with respect to international organization and postwar economic policy—all struck chords that would echo through the next four years of war. The fact that the Soviet Union, which had been invaded by Germany some six weeks earlier, was not represented at Argentia did not mean that the question of Russian cooperation against the Axis was absent from discussions. Harry Hopkins, Roosevelt's good friend and Churchill's "Lord Root of the Matter," had visited Moscow some two weeks before the Argentia conference, and his assurances that the USSR would withstand the Nazi onslaught were a constant topic of conversation for the two leaders. In a joint communication to Stalin from Argentia, Churchill and Roosevelt hailed "the splendid defense that you are making against the Nazi attack" and promised the "very maximum" of supplies.[23] This Anglo-American commitment to cooperation with the Soviet Union against Hitler also carried large implications for the future.

## Step by Step Toward War with Germany, 1939–1941

The conversations at Placentia Bay exemplified Roosevelt's distinctly personal approach to diplomacy during World War II. The President delighted in face-to-face confrontations, always confident of his ability to charm and understand foreign leaders. The meeting with Churchill whetted his appetite for more. It mattered little to Roosevelt that Secretary of State Cordell Hull learned of the conference when he read about it in the newspapers. The President did not mind that his military and naval advisers were often given short notice to prepare for meetings. Roosevelt kept close aides like Harry Hopkins and Sumner Welles nearby and watched the spotlight focus on himself. His cigarette holder omnipresent, the buoyant Roosevelt reveled in the power and drama that were his to command. If not the evil Machiavelli of isolationist fantasy, the President, with his confident style and strong personality, could be unsettling. As British Foreign Secretary Anthony Eden later put it: "[Roosevelt] seemed to see himself disposing of the fate of so many lands, allied no less than enemy. He did all this with so much grace that it was not easy to dissect. Yet it was too like a conjurer, skillfully juggling with balls of dynamite, whose nature he failed to understand."[24]

The juggling act had begun some two years before the "Atlantic Charter" Conference, when Germany started World War II by attacking Poland. On September 3, 1939, two days after the German invasion, FDR spoke to the American people in a fireside chat. "This nation will remain a neutral nation," he declared, "but I cannot ask that every American remain neutral in thought as well."[25] Thus, in words pointedly different from Woodrow Wilson's in 1914, did Roosevelt project for the next twenty-six months American policy toward the war in Europe. Historian Robert A. Divine has compared the evolution of that policy to a game of giant steps, where the President always "moved two steps forward and one back before he took the giant step ahead."[26] Roosevelt proceeded from neutrality to nonbelligerency to undeclared war in the Atlantic and finally, after Pearl Harbor, to full-scale war against the Axis powers. Hoping to avoid war, while at the same time giving as much aid as possible to Hitler's opponents, the President was not always candid with the public about the possible and ultimate contradiction between these two goals.

## Makers of American Foreign Policy from 1939 to 1945

| Presidents | Secretaries of State |
|---|---|
| Franklin D. Roosevelt, 1933–1945 | Cordell Hull, 1933–1944 |
| | Edward R. Stettinius, Jr., 1944–1945 |
| Harry S Truman, 1945–1953 | James F. Byrnes, 1945–1947 |

On September 21, 1939 Roosevelt requested that Congress repeal the arms embargo in the Neutrality Act as the best way to keep the United States from entering the war. He stressed this deceptive argument, knowing that the real purpose of the repeal was to permit England and France, with their superior sea power, to purchase arms and munitions on a cash-and-carry basis. He persuaded William Allen White, the Republican sage from Emporia, Kansas, to form a Non-Partisan Committee for Peace through Revision of the Neutrality Act. Although isolationists like Republican Senator Arthur H. Vandenberg of Michigan fumed that the United States could not be "an arsenal for one belligerent without becoming a target for the other," the President's tactics worked.[27] By a vote of 63–30 in the Senate and 243–181 in the House, the revised Neutrality Act became law on November 4.

The Pan American Conference at Panama City (September 23–October 3, 1939) also signaled the pro-Allied emphasis of United States policy. The conferees proclaimed neutrality, established a hemispheric committee for economic coordination, and created a neutral zone three hundred miles wide along the entire coast of the western hemisphere (except Canada), in which belligerent naval operations were prohibited. Roosevelt had told his Cabinet as early as April, 1939, that the United States Atlantic fleet would patrol such areas and "if we fire and sink an Italian or German [submarine] . . . we will say it the way the Japs do, 'so sorry.' 'Never happen again.' Tomorrow we sink two."[28] These "neutrality patrols" actually became the first step toward Anglo-American naval cooperation. By the late summer of 1940 conversations between staff officers began in London, soon to be followed by exchanges of personnel, actual coordination against German naval operations (such as the sighting and sinking of the battleship *Bismarck* in May, 1941), and, in the autumn of 1941, the convoying of merchant ships across the Atlantic. Justified in terms of contingency planning and aid short of war, such naval measures nonetheless led the Chief of Naval Operations, Admiral Harold R. Stark, to conclude early in 1941: "The question as to our entry into the war seems to be *when* and not *whether*."[29]

Germany's *blitzkrieg* humbled Poland in two weeks, and then came, in the winter of 1939–1940, a period of some quiet called the "phony war" or *sitzkrieg*. Most battle news, from November to March, flowed from Northern Europe, where Russia defeated Finland in the "Winter war." Roosevelt sent his sympathies but little else to Finland. The fall of France in June, 1940, stung FDR into bold measures. In a speech of June 10 Roosevelt condemned Italy for holding the dagger that "struck . . . the back of its neighbor," and pledged to England "the material resources of this nation."[30] A week later he named prominent Republicans Henry L. Stimson and Frank Knox, both ardent advocates of aid to Britain, as secretary of war and secretary of the navy, respectively. Then, after careful preparations and intricate negotiations, the President announced on September 3, 1940, that he was, by executive agreement, transferring to England some fifty old destroyers in exchange for leases to eight British bases stretching from Newfoundland to British Guiana. Two weeks later, he signed into law the Selective Training and Service Act of 1940, the first peacetime military draft in American history.

That Roosevelt could accomplish so much in the summer of 1940, at a time when isolationist sentiment still prevailed and he was seeking a controversial third term as President, testifies to his political astuteness. As to both selective service

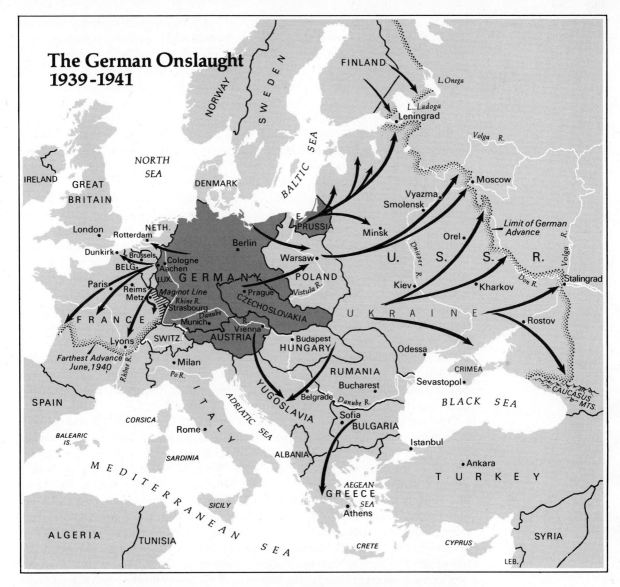

## The German Onslaught 1939-1941

and the destroyers-for-bases agreement, FDR ascertained through intermediaries that his Republican presidential opponent, Wendell L. Willkie, would not make a campaign issue of either measure. Also, in both cases Roosevelt encouraged influential private citizens (the Century Group for the destroyer deal and the Military Training Camps Association for selective service) to lobby for his objectives. That summer the larger Committee to Defend America by Aiding the Allies, headed by William Allen White, rallied behind the President and served as a counter to the isolationist America First Committee set up in September, 1940. FDR avoided congressional scrutiny of the destroyer deal by negotiating it as an executive agreement rather than a treaty, and he deflected political opposition to conscription by having men of integrity, such as Secretary Stimson and Army Chief of Staff General George C. Marshall, attest to the military need for a draft. Public sympathy for beleaguered Britain also helped. "Every time Hitler bombed

London we got another couple of votes," noted future Selective Service Director Lewis W. Hershey.[31] Furthermore, Roosevelt continued to promise that his policies would keep America out of war. Although the destroyers-for-bases agreement could be considered a *casus belli* by Germany, FDR called it instead "the most important action in the reinforcement of our national defense . . . since the Louisiana Purchase."[32] Churchill privately considered it a "decidedly unneutral act" vital to British survival.[33] The President defended his pro-Allied foreign policy in the fall campaign. When Willkie made last-minute charges that Roosevelt secretly sought war, the White House unequivocally struck back: "Your boys are not going to be sent into any foreign wars." Willkie exploded: "That hypocritical son of a bitch! This is going to beat me!"[34] He was right.

While Roosevelt was celebrating victory on a postelection cruise in the Caribbean, Churchill spelled out Britain's desperate need for arms and munitions and concluded that "the moment approaches when we shall no longer be able to pay cash for shipping and other supplies."[35] On returning to Washington Roosevelt held one of his breezy, jaunty press conferences, telling reporters that he favored a policy of lending or leasing to Britain whatever supplies it needed. Saying that "I am trying to . . . eliminate the dollar sign," he likened his policy to lending a garden hose to a neighbor whose house was burning. Once the fire is out, "he gives it back to me and thanks me very much for the use of it," or, if damaged, he replaces it with a new product.[36] In a fireside chat on December 29, FDR admitted that sending armaments to Britain risked involvement in the war, but "our national policy is not directed toward war. Its sole purpose is to keep war away from our country and our people." Then, in a ringing phrase, Roosevelt called upon the United States to "become the great arsenal of democracy."[37]

Over the next two months, as FDR later put it, the Lend-Lease Bill was debated in Congress, "in every newspaper, on every wave length—over every cracker barrel in all the land."[38] Although the final victory of 60–31 in the Senate and 317–71 in the House was substantial, the White House did not win without a struggle. Isolationist Senator Burton K. Wheeler, a Democrat from Montana, immediately labeled the bill "the New Deal's triple A foreign policy; it will plow under every fourth American boy." Roosevelt shot back at a press conference, calling Wheeler's statement "the rottenest thing that has been said in public life in my generation."[39] A bit of benevolent deception occurred in the numbering of the bill in the House. The Administration's floor manager, Representative John W. McCormack, worried because the Irishmen of his South Boston constituency were sure to protest any "McCormack Bill" designed to aid the British Empire, induced the House parliamentarian to tag the Lend-Lease Bill H.R. 1776. McCormack was relieved. Nonetheless, one irate constituent berated him on the street later that winter. The future Speaker of the House thought quickly: "Madam, do you realize that the Vatican is surrounded on all sides by totalitarianism? Madam, this is not a bill to save the English, this is a bill to save Catholicism."[40]

Formally titled "An Act to Promote the Defense of the United States," the bill was signed into law on March 11, 1941. Under its terms the President was permitted "to sell, transfer title to, exchange, lease, lend, or otherwise dispose of" defense articles to "any country whose defense the President deems vital to the defense of the United States."[41] Although the initial appropriation totaled $7 billion, by the war's end the United States had expended more than $50 billion on Lend-Lease. Fittingly enough, the United States included 900,000 feet of fire-hose in the first shipment of goods to England, which was to receive $31.6 billion in Lend-Lease assistance during the war. "We have torn up 150 years of traditional American foreign policy," cried Senator Vandenberg. "We have tossed Washington's Farewell Address in the discard."[42]

With German U-boats operating in wolf packs and sinking more than 500,000 tons of shipping a month, it seemed likely that the United States would use its Navy to see that Lend-Lease supplies reached England safely. But Roosevelt hesitated, because "public opinion was not yet ready."[43] The President compromised in April by extending naval "patrols" halfway across the Atlantic, announcing publicly that American vessels would watch for German warships and monitor their movements. American troops also occupied Greenland the same month. Stimson, Knox, Treasury Secretary Henry Morgenthau, Jr., and Interior Secretary Harold Ickes all urged the President to speak out candidly for convoys of British ships. The impatient Stimson thought his chief was "tangled up in the coils of his former hasty speeches on possible war and convoying as was Laocoon in the coils of the boa constrictors."[44]

When Hitler occupied the Balkans and launched his attack on the USSR in June, 1941 Roosevelt acted decisively. The President announced the next month that some 4,000 American Marines would occupy Iceland for hemispheric defense— surely the first time anyone had placed Iceland within the western hemisphere. He also began military Lend-Lease aid to Russia in November, notwithstanding opinions from the State Department and his military advisers that the Soviet Union would quickly fall. (By the end of the war Russia received $11 billion in

**Lend-Lease to Russia.** An American Lend-Lease official checks a shipment of American food destined for Russia's hard-pressed people. The Russians eventually lost 15–20 million dead and received over $11 billion in Lend-Lease aid, which the President defended as necessary to an Allied victory. (U.S. Information Agency, National Archives)

Lend-Lease.) Roosevelt also ignored the suggestion of Democratic Senator Harry S Truman of Missouri: "If we see that Germany is winning the war we ought to help Russia and if Russia is winning we ought to help Germany, and . . . let them kill as many as possible."[45] As for Churchill's remarks on his new ally Russia: "If Hitler invaded Hell I would make at least a favorable reference to the Devil in the House of Commons."[46] When bureaucratic tangles and military lethargy inhibited the flow of goods to Russia, a short-tempered Roosevelt lectured his Cabinet that "the only answer I want to hear is that it is under way."[47] Then the President held his dramatic meeting with Churchill at Placentia Bay, and in early September, after a German submarine fired torpedoes at the *Greer,* he publicly ordered naval convoys as far as Iceland and issued a "shoot-on-sight" command to the Navy.

By the autumn of 1941, Roosevelt, even though he wanted to limit American military efforts to naval and air support, probably sought an "incident" to induce American entry into the war against Hitler. After the Placentia Bay conference, Churchill told the British War Cabinet that the President "had said that he would wage war, but not declare it, and that he would become more and more provocative. If the Germans did not like it, they could attack American forces."[48] When a U-boat torpedoed the destroyer *Kearny* off Iceland, killing eleven men on October 17, the President seized the moment. "The shooting has started. And history has recorded who fired the first shot," he intoned on October 27. "The U.S.S. *Kearny* is not just a Navy ship. She belongs to every man, woman, and child in this Nation. Hitler's torpedo was directed at every American, whether he lives on our sea coasts or in the innermost part of the country."[49] Roosevelt then flourished a  map which purportedly showed how Nazi henchmen planned to reorganize Central and South America as vassal states. Through these histrionics the President hoped to persuade Congress to repeal the sections of the 1939 Neutrality Act that prohibited the arming of merchant ships and banned such vessels from war zones. After the destroyer *Reuben James* was sunk, with the loss of over 100 men, on October 31, the isolationist America First Committee charged that the White House was "asking Congress to issue an engraved drowning license to American seamen."[50] Following a very bitter debate, repeal passed in November by narrow margins, 50–37 in the Senate and 212-194 in the House. For the first time since the outbreak of war in 1939, American merchant vessels were permitted to carry arms and munitions to England. Roosevelt must have suspected that Hitler, unless he courted defeat, could not allow American cargo ships to cross the Atlantic unmolested. American naval escorts were provocative enough. Hitler himself had said on October 3: "When I see the enemy leveling his rifle at me, I am not going to wait till he presses the trigger. I would rather be the first to press the trigger."[51]

Roosevelt charted an oblique path toward war because he believed he had no other choice. The President "devoted considerable time and energy to assessing public opinion"[52] and was particularly impressed by the scientific polling of Gallup, Roper, and others, a new technique based on representative samples of the population. Every poll showed a manifest desire to stay out of the war. In September, 1941, nearly 80 percent of the American people opposed participation in the war. At the same time they strongly wished to defeat Hitler. Thus, so long as Roosevelt defined American policy as building the arsenal of democracy, saying that this would be the best way to avoid war, the American people could have both of their wishes fulfilled. The narrow vote over repeal of the Neutrality Act in November dramatized the power of isolationist sentiment and reinforced the

President's reluctance to ask for outright intervention. As Robert E. Sherwood put it, "he had no more tricks left. The hat from which he had pulled so many rabbits was empty."[53] This inability to go to Congress for a declaration of war was to some extent self-inflicted: that is, FDR had said for months that the United States would not enter the war, that aiding the Allies would prevent the need for American military intervention; now he could not easily reverse his opinions without appearing a hypocrite. The only recourse was to wait for the Germans to fire the first shot. Hitler was slow to oblige, restraining his admirals from all-out war in the shipping lanes while he tried on land to knock Russia out. News of the Japanese attack at Pearl Harbor reached Berlin at a time when German armies had bogged down short of Moscow. In the mistaken belief that Japanese intervention would keep Americans occupied in the Pacific, the Fuehrer jubilantly announced war against the United States on December 11, 1941, saving Roosevelt himself from the difficult task of first having to pilot through Congress a declaration of war against Berlin.

### Toward Pearl Harbor: Japanese-American Relations, 1939–1941

Events in Asia, not Europe, plunged the United States into World War II. Ambassador Joseph C. Grew, the grizzled diplomat with the fierce, bushy eyebrows, was surprised at the increased signs of anti-Japanese sentiment during a trip home in the summer of 1939. The ambassador listened to his old Groton and Harvard friend Franklin Roosevelt talk truculently of intercepting the Japanese fleet if it moved against the Dutch East Indies. When the State Department gave formal notice in July that the 1911 commercial treaty with Japan would be terminated in six months, Grew feared that economic sanctions would follow, and perhaps war as well. "[It] is going to be up to me," he noted, "to let this American temper discreetly penetrate into Japanese consciousness. Sparks will fly before long."[54]

Grew, with his Far Eastern preoccupation, had failed to grasp the Europe-first emphasis of Roosevelt's foreign policy. After 1937, when Japan marched deep into the "stubble" of China, Washington angrily reacted with protests, but limited its intervention on behalf of China.[55] As in the 1920s and early 1930s, American power was insufficient to challenge Japanese predominance in East Asia. Even Roosevelt's much-heralded tactic of refusing to apply the Neutrality Act to the "incident" in China, thus making it legal to sell arms and munitions to Chiang Kai-shek's government, could not obscure the preponderance of American trade with Japan. As late as 1940, $78 million in American exports went to China, whereas $227 million were shipped to Japan. Abrogation of the 1911 commercial treaty permitted economic sanctions against Japan, but oil, the most vital ingredient in Japan's war machine, was not withheld until July, 1941. In keeping with Roosevelt's policy of all-out aid to England short of war, the Navy revised its strategic thinking in November, 1940. "Plan Dog" called for a defensive posture in the Pacific, depicted Germany as the country's number one enemy, and made preservation of England its principal goal. Opposed to any appeasement of Japan, Roosevelt still hoped to avoid a confrontation, because "I simply have not got enough Navy to go around—and every little episode in the Pacific means fewer ships in the Atlantic."[56]

Japanese movement into Southeast Asia, in apparent coordination with Hitler's *blitzkrieg* in Europe, placed Washington and Tokyo on a collision course. With the

Asian colonies of France and the Netherlands lying unprotected, Japanese expansionists demanded a thrust southward, thus completing the strangulation of China and transforming the whole region into the Greater East Asia Co-Prosperity Sphere. Japan pressed England and France to close supply routes to the Kuomintang through Burma and Indochina. Tokyo also demanded economic concessions from the petroleum-rich Dutch East Indies. Then came the shocking news of late September, 1940. Just four days after Vichy French representatives allowed Japanese troops to occupy northern Indochina, Japanese Foreign Minister Yosuke Matsuoka, on September 27, signed the Tripartite Pact with Germany and Italy. Each signatory pledged to aid one another if attacked by a nation not currently involved in the war. Since the Soviet Union was explicitly exempted by the pact, Washington had no doubt about being its target. "This is not the Japan I have known and loved," wrote a disgruntled Ambassador Grew.[57] The aggressors of Europe and Asia had apparently banded together.

A new more militant Japanese government, with Prince Fumimaro Konoye as prime minister and General Hideki Tojo as war minister, took the fateful steps. Matsuoka, who had spent nine years in America as a youth and thought he understood Americans, articulated the advantages of boldness—"one cannot obtain a tiger's cub unless he braves the tiger's den."[58] The intent of the Tripartite Pact, as Matsuoka saw it, was to deter the United States from intervening in either the Atlantic or Pacific, and to facilitate a rapprochement between Japan and the Soviet Union, which was still aligned with Germany in the Nazi-Soviet Pact. Chiang Kai-shek might then be induced to accept a reasonable settlement, after which Japanese troops could be gradually withdrawn and Tokyo's civilian control over the army finally reasserted. Japan, moreover, could peacefully carve out its East Asian Co-Prosperity Sphere. "Held together by a long chain of 'ifs,'" as historian Barbara Teters has written, Matsuoka's scenario could also lead to war.[59] The Japanese Navy, which would bear the brunt of any war with England and the United States, fought against the Tripartite Pact. "Our opposition," wrote one admiral, "was like paddling against the rapids only a few hundred yards upstream from Niagara Falls."[60]

Washington flashed warning signals. In July, 1940, Roosevelt clamped an embargo on aviation fuel and top-grade scrap iron sought by Japan. In September, at the time of the Tripartite Pact, he extended the embargo to all scrap metals. Even Grew urged firmness. His famous "green light" telegram of September 12, 1940 labeled Japan "one of the predatory powers," lacking "all moral and ethical sense . . . frankly and unashamedly opportunist, seeking at every turn to profit by the weakness of others."[61] Administration "hawks" like Stimson, Knox, Ickes, Morgenthau, and even Eleanor Roosevelt, pressed the President to shut off oil exports as well. Backed by Secretary Hull and the joint chiefs, however, Roosevelt, in historian Charles Neu's phrase, "swallowed hard and remained in touch with reality."[62] As FDR wrote Grew in January, 1941: "We must recognize that hostilities in Europe, in Africa, and in Asia are all parts of a single world conflict. . . . Our policy of self-defense must be a global strategy."[63] Within this global strategy, however, the President still hoped to aid England, while avoiding a showdown in the Pacific.

The first six months of 1941 saw vigorous private and official transpacific efforts to avoid war. In February, Admiral Kichisaburo Nomura became ambassador to Washington. Well-known for his pro-Western opinions and a personal friend of

Franklin Roosevelt, Nomura accepted the appointment only when assured by Konoye and Matsuoka that peace with the United States took precedence over Japan's commitment to the Axis. Otherwise, he said, his task would be "like chasing two rabbits in different directions."[64] A group of private citizens known as the "John Doe Associates" and led by two Catholic missionaries, Father James M. Drought and Bishop James E. Walsh, also tried to effect conciliation. They held interviews with Prince Konoye, Hull, and Roosevelt. Having a vague understanding of the issues and a strong desire for peace, the John Doe intermediaries told each government what it wanted to hear. Father Drought enthusiastically forwarded a "Draft Understanding" to Secretary Hull on April 9, which, among other points, called for a Konoye-Roosevelt meeting in Hawaii and American pressure on China to recognize the Japanese domination of Manchuria, in exchange for a virtual Japanese disavowal of the Tripartite Pact. Hull, who thought the "Understanding" was a Japanese proposal, accepted it as a basis of discussion, but told Nomura that any Japanese-American agreement had to satisfy four basic principles: respect for the territorial integrity and sovereignty of all nations; noninterference in the internal affairs of other nations; respect for the equality of commercial opportunity, or Open Door; and support for only peaceful change of the status quo in the Pacific. Japan, on the other hand, thought the "Draft Understanding" an American proposal, and Nomura failed to attach appropriate importance to Hull's four points when he reported to Tokyo. Not until September did Tokyo learn that Hull's four principles were crucial and a major obstacle to any settlement of the China war. The amateur diplomatic activities of the Doe Associates had confused Japanese-American relations. The question of a Pacific meeting between Konoye and Roosevelt was a case in point. The "Draft Understanding" of April recommended such a conference; Japan initially indicated that an agreement in principle on key issues was required before a Konoye-Roosevelt meeting could be held. But in August the Japanese reversed themselves and asked for the meeting they thought the Americans had proposed in April. The Doe Associates, of course, not the Americans, had originally urged the conference. By August, however, Washington first wanted assurances from Tokyo on outstanding problems and hence rejected a high-level meeting. Japan then grew annoyed, sure that the United States was retreating from an original position. "The fundamental misconception that had been planted in April," Professor Robert J. C. Butow has written, "had become a tangled, impenetrable growth by August."[65]

The efforts of diplomats, including the Doe Associates, were ultimately doomed by Japan's determination to hold China and to expand farther. "The Japs are having a real drag-down," Roosevelt told Ickes in early July, 1941, "trying to decide which way they are going to jump—attack Russia, attack the South Seas . . . or whether they will sit on the fence and be more friendly with us."[66] When word reached Washington on July 24 that troop transports bearing the Rising Sun were steaming toward Camranh Bay and southern Indochina, FDR signed an executive order freezing all Japanese funds in the United States. In practice, this meant stopping all trade with Japan—including oil. "From now on," Herbert Feis has noted, "the oil gauge and the clock stood side by side. Each fall in the level brought the hour of decision closer."[67]

The diplomacy of proposals and counterproposals in the remaining months of 1941 proved ineffective. Unless the flow of American oil resumed, Japan determined to seize Dutch and British oil fields. But the United States would not turn on the oil spigot until Tokyo agreed to Hull's four principles, especially the pledge to respect China's sovereignty and territorial integrity. Key American officials also knew from cracking the Japanese code ("Operation Magic") that the forces of Nippon were massing to strike southward after mid-November. But many in the Roosevelt Administration did not think Japan would battle the United States. Hard-liners like Henry L. Stimson had advocated embargoes for more than a year, arguing that the Japanese were "notorious bluffers" who backed down when confronted firmly.[68] As late as November 27, when "Magic" was reporting a Japanese strike somewhere very soon, State Department Asian expert Stanley K. Hornbeck, who probably did not know about the intercepts, offered odds of five to one that war with Japan would not occur by December 15. "Tell me of one case in history," he challenged his colleagues, "when a nation went to war out of desperation."[69] Amid such an atmosphere, the urging of Army and Navy leaders to string out negotiations until the Philippines could be reinforced went unheeded. An eleventh-hour modus vivendi proposed a small trickle of oil to Japan and negotiations between Chungking and Tokyo, while maintaining American aid to China; Japan would have to abrogate the Tripartite Pact and accept basic principles of international conduct. Not trusting the Japanese, Hull and Roosevelt decided to shelve the proposal. "I have washed my hands of it," muttered Hull on November 27, "and it is now in the hands of . . . the Army and Navy."[70]

The Japanese attack on Pearl Harbor, as political scientist Bruce M. Russett has written, cannot "be explained simply as an act of 'irrationality,' an impulsive act by an unstable leader."[71] After months of discussion among civilian and military leaders, a commitment was made at the Imperial Conference of September to fight Americans if the life-strangling embargo on strategic materials was not lifted by October 15. The date was later extended to November 25, then November 30. With 12,000 tons of oil used each day by Japan, moderates and militants alike saw American pressure as provocative. The choices were fighting the United States or pulling out of China, and no Japanese leader counseled the latter. American power and industrial potential were well known, but, as General Tojo put it, "sometimes a man has to jump with his eyes closed, from the veranda of Kiyomizu Temple."[72] The man ordered to plan the Pearl Harbor attack, Admiral Isoroku Yamamoto, had no illusions about ultimate victory. "If told to fight regardless of consequence," he said, "I shall run wild considerably for the first six months or a year, but I have utterly no confidence for the second and third years."[73] At dawn on November 25, 1941, a task force that included six carriers and two battleships headed across three thousand miles of open sea. The planes struck on Sunday, December 7, 1941 a few minutes before eight o'clock, Hawaiian time. Within two hours eight American battleships sank to the bottom of Pearl Harbor and more than 2,400 Americans died.

"Millions of words," Robert E. Sherwood has written, "have been recorded by at least eight official investigating bodies and one may read through all of them without arriving at an adequate explanation of why, with war so obviously ready to break out *somewhere* in the Pacific, our principal Pacific base was in a condition of peacetime Sunday morning somnolence instead of in Condition Red."[74] After World War II, critics argued that Roosevelt, aided by his top advisers, had deliberately sacrificed the Pacific fleet to get into the war against Hitler via the "back door."[75] Most scholars reject the conspiracy theory and explain the Pearl

Harbor disaster as the consequence of mistakes, missed clues, overconfidence, and plain bad luck. American leaders, partly due to the "Magic" intercepts, thought that the Japanese would strike in Southeast Asia, for troop transports were sighted heading for Thailand, and underestimated Japan's capacity to undertake two major operations at once. As to the many hints of major Japanese interest in Pearl Harbor, including Ambassador Grew's warning in February, 1941, of a possible sudden attack, historian Roberta Wohlstetter has written: "After the event a signal is always crystal clear; we can now see what disaster it was signalling, since the disaster has occurred. But before the event it is obscure and pregnant with conflicting meanings. . . . In short, we failed to anticipate Pearl Harbor not for want of the relevant materials, but because of a plethora of irrelevant ones."[76] Many "ifs" cloud the question. If the radar operator had been able to convince his superiors on Oahu that the blips were really planes, if General Marshall's last-minute warning had been sent by Navy cable instead of Western Union telegraph, if a "Magic" decoding machine had been at Honolulu, if . . . .

The attack on Pearl Harbor gave Japan a smashing tactical victory. Yet it was a strategic disaster. In Samuel Eliot Morison's words, "one can search military history in vain for an operation more fatal to the aggressor."[77] When Roosevelt, referring to the "date which will live in infamy," asked for a declaration of war,

**Pearl Harbor.** A Japanese pilot's perspective on Ford Island, Pearl Harbor, Hawaii. On December 7, 1941, a "date which will live in infamy," the Japanese attackers sank much of the United States Pacific fleet. (Navy Department, National Archives)

Congress responded with a unanimous vote in the Senate and only one dissent in the House on December 8, 1941.[78] For Senator Arthur H. Vandenberg, Pearl Harbor "ended isolationism for any realist."[79]

## The Character of Wartime Diplomacy

The "Atlantic Charter" Conference and the events of 1939–1941 illustrate well some of the themes of wartime diplomacy. The emphasis on giving material aid to Hitler's opponents through the "arsenal of democracy" foreshadowed the main American contribution to victory over the Axis. Washington's commitment to a "Europe First" strategy derived from Anglo-American staff discussions prior to Pearl Harbor, as did the different American and British conceptions of that strategy. Americans favored a "massive thrust at the enemy's heart" and the British preferred "successive stabs around the periphery . . . like jackals worrying a lion before springing at his throat."[80] During the war Americans also revived Wilsonianism, but combined it with a pragmatic determination to avoid Wilson's

"**Jap . . . You're Next!**" James Montgomery Flagg, who had become famous with his "I Want You" Uncle Sam poster of World War I, returned in the Second World War to render this 1942 interpretation of the "Europe First" strategy. (National Archives)

mistakes. This time the United States would join an international organization to maintain peace, even if it meant adding balance-of-power features to the institution and paying court to sensitive Republican senators. There would be no debts-reparations tangle because Lend-Lease would eliminate the dollar sign. This time, too, the enemy would have to surrender unconditionally. Particularly evident during the war years was the State Department's desire to reduce tariffs abroad and to create an open world, reflecting Secretary Hull's Wilsonian belief that trade discrimination was one of the prime causes of war.

If total war inspired visions of total peace, victory over the Axis also required compromises and short-term decisions that were not always Wilsonian. The marriage of convenience with the Soviet Union involved perhaps the most serious departure from Wilsonian ideals, if only because Russian security needs and drives in Eastern Europe clashed with the principle of national self-determination. But Franklin Roosevelt had learned as much about statecraft from his cousin Theodore as from Woodrow Wilson. His vision of the "Four Policemen" (Russia, China, Britain, and the United States) maintaining world peace implied spheres of influence more than true collective security. Roosevelt was committed, with some precautions, to continuing Soviet-American cooperation into the postwar world. Because the Red Army bore the brunt of the fighting until mid-1944, and because the Kremlin ostentatiously played down its commitment to world revolution after June 22, 1941, it thus became prudent, even necessary, to postpone difficulties with Moscow until the end of the war. Despite wartime propaganda about the similar revolutionary and anti-imperialist pasts, Soviet-American differences remained profound. Fears on both sides that the other would make a separate peace with Germany provided sufficient evidence of the continued tension between the two nations.

The growing influence of the military was another wartime characteristic. That Roosevelt took his joint chiefs, not Secretary Hull, to Argentia and other wartime conferences symbolized the extent to which military decisions determined foreign policy. As a former Assistant Secretary of the Navy, FDR delighted in the duties of Commander-in-Chief. He liked to concentrate on grand strategy, enjoyed the company of admirals and generals, made the joint chiefs principal advisers during the war, and generally left postwar planning and congressional liaison to the State Department. Cordell Hull, although influential in formulating Japanese policy before Pearl Harbor, grudgingly acquiesced because he had never been Roosevelt's "complete agent."[81] The former Tennessee judge pouted: "If the President wishes to speak to me all he has to do is pick up that telephone, and I'll come running. It is not for me to bother the President."[82] Frequently Hull did not learn of Roosevelt's decisions until Secretary of War Stimson told him. So confusing did procedures become that at one point in 1944 the State Department was formulating plans for the occupation of Germany that contradicted decisions the President had made at the Teheran Conference a few months earlier. Roosevelt did not tell Hull what happened at Teheran and Hull apparently never asked.

The ordeal of global war brought new power and confidence to American diplomacy. The Atlantic Charter reflected a commitment to shaping the postwar world in an American image. As Henry Luce's best-selling *American Century* phrased it in 1941, the United States must "exert upon the world the full impact of our influence, for such purposes as we see fit and by such means as we see fit."[83] By rearming, acquiring new bases, raising an army of sixteen million, welding hemispheric unity, and revving up its industries, the United States possessed the sinews of global power even before Pearl Harbor. "The United States was now pursuing an imperialist policy," complained Adolf Hitler in November, 1940. "It was not fighting for England, but only trying to get the British Empire into its grasp, helping England at best to further its own rearmament and to reinforce its military power by acquiring bases. . . . The United States have no business in Europe, Africa, or Asia."[84] Winston Churchill himself told Roosevelt in 1944: "You have the greatest navy in the world. You will have, I hope, the greatest air force. You will have the greatest trade. You have all the gold." But Churchill hoped that the Americans "will not give themselves over to vainglorious ambitions, and that justice and fair-play will be the lights that guide them."[85] The United States used its power for both political and military purposes, but, as Roosevelt told Churchill, political settlements "must be definitely secondary to the primary operations of striking at the heart of Germany."[86]

## The Grand Alliance: Strategy and Fissures, 1941–1943

The diplomacy of the "Grand Alliance" of the United States, Britain, and the Soviet Union centered on two issues: boundaries in Eastern Europe, and the timing of an Anglo-American "second front" in Western Europe. When Anthony Eden went to Moscow just after Pearl Harbor, Premier Stalin said he had no objections to declarations like the Atlantic Charter, which he regarded as "algebra," but he preferred "practical arithmetic"—that is, an agreement guaranteeing Soviet boundaries with Eastern Europe as they stood prior to Hitler's attack in 1941.[87] The British, after an initial refusal, were inclined to grant what Stalin wanted. The Americans, particularly Cordell Hull and most officers of the State Department, worked to postpone such issues until postwar conferences and plebiscites. The second front was another matter. The Russians, fighting some two hundred German divisions and dying by the hundreds of thousands, urged a cross-channel attack as quickly as possible, and the American military, despite British reluctance, wished to comply. "We've got to go to Europe and fight," an American staff officer noted as early as January, 1942. "If we're to keep Russia in, save the Middle East, India and Burma; we've got to begin slugging with air at West Europe; to be followed by a land attack as soon *as possible*."[88] When the Soviet foreign minister visited Washington that May, Roosevelt, partly to defer the question of Russian frontiers, "authorized Mr. Molotov to inform Mr. Stalin that [the President] expected the formation of a second front this year."[89] But the Anglo-American invasion of France did not take place until June 6, 1944, and during the interim, as FDR said, "the Russian armies are killing more Axis personnel and destroying more Axis material than all other twenty-five United Nations put together."[90] The delay, to say the least, produced fissures in the Grand Alliance.

American military leaders urged a cross-channel attack by the spring of 1943 at the latest, but the British, with Roosevelt's compliance, decided otherwise. A new plan, Operation TORCH, called for the invasion of French North Africa in November, 1942, a decision that led logically to operations against Sicily and Italy in the summer of 1943 and effectively postponed a cross-channel attack (later dubbed Operation OVERLORD) until 1944. American generals were bitter. When General Dwight D. Eisenhower learned that the second front had been postponed, he muttered that it might be the "blackest day in history" if Russia were not kept in the war.[91] At numerous military conferences in 1942–1943, from Quebec to Cairo, the Americans argued with their British counterparts, always suspicious that fixation on the Mediterranean reflected a British desire to shore up imperial lifelines, and not, as the British said, a coherent strategy to bloody Germany on the periphery before launching a full-scale invasion of France. Sometimes there was real acrimony, as described by one American general at the Cairo Conference of November, 1943, when British Chief of Staff Alan Brooke exchanged heated words with American Admiral Ernest J. King: "Brooke got nasty and King got good and sore. King almost climbed over the table at Brooke. God, he was mad. I wished he had socked him."[92] Apart from Roosevelt's desire to have Americans fighting Germans somewhere in 1942, the main reason that British strategy predominated in the two years after Pearl Harbor was that England was fully mobilized, while America was not, and any combined operation had to depend largely on British troops, British shipping, and British casualties. "The possibility of extensive losses is very great," Churchill told Soviet Ambassador Ivan Maisky. "We are a small country" and Britain must "cut her coat according to her cloth."[93] Once American production and manpower began to assert their weight by mid-1943, combined strategy gradually shifted to Operation OVERLORD. A confrontation between Churchill and General Marshall in January, 1944, was symbolic. Churchill insisted on an invasion of the island of Rhodes off the Turkish coast. "No American is going to land on that god-damn island," barked Marshall.[94] No American did.

Roosevelt and Churchill knew how intensely Marshal Stalin wanted a full-scale second front in France, not in North Africa or Italy. The Red Army had stopped the Germans short of Moscow in 1941, but in the summer of 1942 German *panzers* drove into the Caucasus oil fields and laid siege to Stalingrad on the Volga River. Churchill told Stalin in August, 1942 that a cross-channel attack was planned for the spring of 1943. Yet a few months later Stalin was informed that the attack was postponed until August, 1943. Not until June, 1943, did the Russians learn officially that there would be no cross-channel assault at all that year. "Need I speak of the dishearteningly negative expression that this fresh postponement of the second front . . . will produce in the Soviet Union?" Stalin wrote Roosevelt on June 11.[95] Tensions increased that summer, when the Soviet Union broke off diplomatic relations with the Polish exile government in London after the Poles had asked the International Red Cross to investigate charges that the Russians had murdered some 15,000 Polish prisoners in the Katyn Forest in 1941. The Russians also complained when Allied convoys carrying valuable Lend-Lease supplies to Murmansk had to be suspended because of shipping needs in the Mediterranean and Pacific. In August, 1943 Stalin sent a sharp message to Roosevelt, complaining about the separate peace negotiations that the American and British were conducting with Italy. (The Italians formally surrendered in early September, then declared war against Germany, only to have German forces occupy most of the peninsula before Anglo-American troops could be reinforced.) "To date it has been like this," accused the Soviet leader, "the U.S.A. and Britain reached agreement between themselves while the U.S.S.R. is informed . . . as a third party looking passively on. I must say that this situation cannot be tolerated any longer."[96]

Roosevelt and Churchill did what they could to conciliate their testy ally. The Prime Minister urged the Poles not to protest the Katyn massacre because "nothing you can do will bring them [the dead officers] back."[97] The President expedited

Lend-Lease supplies to Russia without the usual quid pro quo arrangements. Probably the most controversial attempt to reassure the Russians came at the Casablanca Conference in January, 1943, when Roosevelt announced that "the elimination of German, Japanese, and Italian war power means the unconditional surrender by Germany, Italy, and Japan." He added, "it does not mean the destruction of the population [of these countries], but it does mean the destruction of the philosophies in those countries."[98] Coming shortly after the so-called Darlan Deal, wherein the Anglo-Americans made an agreement with the Vichy French collaborator Admiral Jean-François Darlan to gain French cooperation in North Africa, Roosevelt's "unconditional surrender" announcement was meant as a signal to a suspicious Stalin that England and the United States would not make a separate peace with one of Hitler's subordinates. Although the doctrine may have encouraged German soldiers to fight harder, as Eisenhower later claimed, its enunciation brought a modicum of Allied unity by concentrating on a total military victory over Hitler, deferring troublesome peace terms until afterward. As long as the United States had to rely on Soviet troops in Europe, however, FDR was in no position to confront the Soviets over political issues like the Polish border.

The Russians became less contentious in late August, 1943, and called for a Big Three foreign ministers' conference in Moscow. Stalin apparently feared that the Italian surrender might bring the Anglo-Americans quickly into Central Europe at a time when, with postwar boundaries unsettled, the advancing Russian armies were still six hundred miles from the 1941 frontiers. The foreign ministers' meeting in Moscow (October 19–30) established an Advisory Council for Italy to coordinate Allied policy and a European Advisory Commission to make recommendations for a final peace settlement. The conferees also called for "a free and independent Austria." The Russians told Secretary of State Cordell Hull that the 200,000 American battle casualties were insignificant—"we lose that many each day before lunch. You haven't got your teeth in the war yet."[99] Hull in turn lectured Commissar for Foreign Affairs V. M. Molotov against gobbling up neighbors: "When I was young I knew a bully in Tennessee. He used to get a few things his way by being a bully and bluffing other fellows. But he ended up by not having a friend in the world."[100] The high point for the ill, seventy-two-year-old Hull, who was "almost mystical in his approach," was a Declaration of Four Nations on General Security (China was included).[101] This was the first definite statement about a postwar replacement for the defunct League of Nations. Hull thereafter exulted to Congress rather naively that "there will no longer be need for spheres of influence, for alliances, for balance of power, or any other of the special arrangements through which, in the unhappy past, the nations strove to safeguard their security and promote their interests."[102]

Moscow seemed a mere appetizer for the first Big Three summit meeting at Teheran, Iran, November 28–December 1, 1943. "The eternal triangle is perhaps as much a threat to politicians as it is to lovers," historian Warren F. Kimball has written, and Teheran proved it as far as the Churchill-Roosevelt relationship was concerned.[103] Meeting the moustachioed Russian leader for the first time, FDR came away from an early conversation thinking Stalin "very confident, very sure of himself, moves slowly—altogether quite impressive, I'd say."[104] At the first plenary session, as an American Army Air Force general recalled, "Uncle Joe had talked straight from the shoulder about how to carry on the war against Germany," telling Churchill and Roosevelt that he favored a firm commitment to OVERLORD as

## Major Wartime Conferences, 1941–1945

| Conference | Date | Participants | Results |
|---|---|---|---|
| Argentia, Newfoundland | August 9–12, 1941 | Roosevelt, Churchill | Atlantic Charter |
| Washington, D.C. | December 22, 1941– Jan. 14, 1942 | Roosevelt, Churchill | Combined Chiefs of Staff; priority in war effort against Germany; United Nations Declaration |
| Washington, D.C. | June 19–25, 1942 | Roosevelt, Churchill | North African campaign strategy |
| Moscow, USSR | August 12–15, 1942 | Churchill, Stalin, Harriman | Postponement of Second Front |
| Casablanca, Morocco | January 14–24, 1943 | Roosevelt, Churchill | Unconditional surrender announcement; campaign against Sicily and Italy |
| Washington, D.C. | May 12–25, 1943 | Roosevelt, Churchill | Schedule for cross-channel landing set as May 1, 1944 |
| Quebec, Canada | August 14–24, 1943 | Roosevelt, Churchill | Confirmation of cross-channel landing (OVERLORD); Southeast Asia Command established |
| Moscow, USSR | October 19–30, 1943 | Hull, Eden, Molotov | Postwar international organization to be formed; Russian promise to enter the war against Japan after Germany's defeat; establishment of European Advisory Commission |
| UNRRA, Washington, D.C. | November 9, 1943 | 44 nations | Creation of UNRRA |
| Cairo, Egypt | November 22–26, 1943 | Roosevelt, Churchill, Chiang Kai-shek | Postwar Asia: China to recover lost lands; Korea to be independent; Japan to be stripped of Pacific Islands |
| Teheran, Iran | November 27–December 1, 1943 | Roosevelt, Churchill, Stalin | Agreement on cross-channel landing and international organization; Soviet reaffirmation of entry into war against Japan |
| Bretton Woods, New Hampshire | July 1–22, 1944 | 44 nations | Creation of World Bank and International Monetary Fund |
| Dumbarton Oaks, Washington, D.C. | August 21–Oct. 7, 1944 | U.S., Britain, USSR, China | United Nations Organization |
| Quebec, Canada | Sept. 11–16, 1944 | Roosevelt, Churchill | "Morgenthau Plan" for Germany |
| Moscow, USSR | October 9–18, 1944 | Churchill, Stalin | Spheres of influence in Balkans (percentage scheme) |
| Yalta, USSR | February 4–11, 1945 | Roosevelt, Churchill, Stalin | Polish governmental structure, elections, and boundaries; United Nations; German reparations; USSR pledge to declare war against Japan and to recognize Chiang's government; Asian territories to USSR |
| San Francisco, California | April 25–June 26, 1945 | 50 nations | United Nations Organization Charter |
| Potsdam (Berlin), Germany | July 16–August 2, 1945 | Truman, Churchill/Attlee, Stalin | German reconstruction and reparations; Potsdam Declaration to Japan; Council of Foreign Ministers established |

opposed to any Anglo-American operations in the Balkans.[105] When Churchill persisted in cataloguing the advantages of an Adriatic landing, Stalin broke in with a blunt question: "Do the British really believe in OVERLORD or are they only saying so to reassure the Russians?" Churchill lamely retorted that "it was the duty of the British Government to hurl every scrap of strength across the channel."[106] At a dinner party two nights later Stalin playfully baited Churchill further by calling for the summary execution of 50,000 German officers. The Prime Minister protested that the British would "never tolerate mass executions."[107] Roosevelt interceded by joking that only 49,000 should be shot. Churchill walked out in a huff. As General Marshall recalled, Stalin "was turning the hose on Churchill all the time, and Mr. Roosevelt, in a sense, was helping him."[108]

At Teheran, Roosevelt refused to meet with Churchill alone lest the Russians suspect an Anglo-American deal. Yet the President had three conferences *à deux* with Stalin. FDR called for an international organization to be dominated by the "Four Policemen," who would deal immediately with any threat to the peace. Stalin commented that Europe might not like domination by the "Four Policemen," and that China was too weak to be of much use as a policeman. He suggested two regional committees—in Europe, the Big Three and one other power, and in Asia, the Big Three and China. The President also told Stalin that the United States would supply only air and naval support in the event of a crisis in postwar Europe; troops would have to come from Britain and Russia. The Russian agreed with Roosevelt that the future United Nations Organization "should be world-wide and not regional" and that France should be treated as an inconsequential power in the postwar world.[109]

The subjects of Eastern Europe and Germany also came up. Earlier in the conference Churchill, pushing three matchsticks, had proposed moving Poland's boundaries a considerable distance to the west, incorporating German lands. Polish territory in the east would be transferred to the Soviets for the security of their western frontier. Roosevelt told Stalin that he acquiesced in these plans for Poland, but he could not "publicly take part in any such arrangement at the present time." The election of 1944 loomed ahead, and FDR, "as a practial man," did not want to risk losing the votes of six to seven million Polish-Americans. Roosevelt mentioned that there were also many Americans of Lithuanian, Latvian, and Estonian origin who wanted the right of self-determination in the Baltic states. Stalin bristled. Those states, he insisted, were part of the Soviet Union. Roosevelt replied that the American people "neither knew nor understood." Stalin shot back that they "should be informed and some propaganda work should be done."[110] But in the remaining months of the war the President never tried to explain publicly the differences between the Atlantic Charter and Russian desires for security in Eastern Europe. On the subject of Germany, Stalin said he favored dismemberment. Roosevelt suggested the division of Germany into five autonomous regions and international control of the Ruhr and Kiel Canal. "To use an American expression, the President has said a mouthful," observed a disconcerted Churchill, who then proposed a solution that reduced Prussia to impotence and linked the rest of Germany to Austria and Hungary in a Danubian confederation.[111] Stalin objected to Churchill's plan, saying that all Germans, not just the Prussians, fought like devils. Specific postwar plans for Germany were recommended for future consideration.

Even though many of the discussions were inconclusive, the Americans were pleased with Teheran, especially because Stalin had confirmed a previous promise to Secretary Hull that, once Hitler was defeated, Russia would help the United States defeat Japan. In response to this good news, Roosevelt suggested that the Russians might be rewarded with a Chinese "free port" at Dairen. Stalin's preference for OVERLORD instead of a Balkans operation also gratified the American joint chiefs and seemed to clinch their position in the interminable debate with the British. General sentiment in favor of a peace dictated by the big powers, an international organization, and a weakened postwar Germany represented important Allied cohesion. Roosevelt was also impressed when Stalin paid tribute to Lend-Lease and the United States manufacture of 10,000 aircraft a month: "Without these planes from America the war would have been lost."[112] At a Teheran dinner in celebration of Churchill's sixty-ninth birthday, Roosevelt toasted the Big Three: "We can see in the sky, for the first time, that traditional symbol of hope, the rainbow." Churchill drank to "Stalin the Great." Stalin hailed his "fighting friend Churchill," adding one last jibe, "if it is possible for me to consider Churchill my friend."[113] On his return to Washington the President optimistically told a national radio audience: "I 'got along fine' with Marshal Stalin. . . . I believe that we are going to get along very well with him and the Russian people—very well indeed."[114] The Grand Alliance had temporarily closed some of its fissures.

## Problem Client: China and the War in Asia

When Winston Churchill journeyed to Washington in December, 1941 to discuss grand strategy, he was astonished at "a standard of values which . . . rated the Chinese armies as a factor to be mentioned in the same breath as the armies of Russia."[115] America's romanticized infatuation with China, its support for the Open Door, the false image of Chiang Kai-shek as a democatic leader—all had persisted in American policy during the months before Pearl Harbor. Some Americans, President Roosevelt included, even envisioned a strong, united China as a postwar client of the United States. China's military importance soon diminished, however, as Japanese victories in early 1942 sent the British and Americans reeling. The fall of Burma in May closed the last remaining land route to Generalissimo Chiang Kai-shek's capital at Chungking. Thereafter the only way to send supplies was by flying them over the "hump" of the Himalayas. And given available resources and military priorities, "hump" transport was pitifully small—less than one hundred tons a month during the summer of 1942. The Americans wanted to keep China in the war, yet Roosevelt could not send troops because they were needed elsewhere. He sent General Stilwell instead.

Joseph W. Stilwell was fifty-eight years old when he arrived in Chungking with the impressive titles of Chief of Staff to Generalissimo Chiang Kai-shek and Commanding General of the United States Forces in India, Burma, and China. An aggressive soldier, "diplomacy was not his long suit."[116] As a junior officer he had served two tours of duty in China, had become fluent in Chinese, and had developed great admiration for the Chinese people. But he thought Chiang an untrustworthy scoundrel. Blunt to reporters, Stilwell was even blunter in his diary, where he referred to Chiang as "the Peanut," the British as "pigfuckers," and President Roosevelt as "just a lot of wind."[117] "Vinegar Joe's" principal task in Chungking was to train and equip Chinese divisions. With these modernized forces, plus British help from India, Stilwell planned to reopen Burma, increase supplies to China, and thus make the mainland the staging point for the final invasion of Japan.

Stilwell's plans for military reform cut at the core of Chiang Kai-shek's power structure. The general sputtered in his diary: "Why doesn't the little dummy [Chiang] realize that his only hope is the 30-division plan, and the creation of a separate, efficient, well-equipped, and well-trained force?"[118] In actuality, most of Chiang's armies were controlled by twelve commanders, virtually autonomous warlords whose loyalties were manipulated by the Generalissimo in masterful Byzantine fashion. Chiang wanted Stilwell's equipment, but not his advice. Nor did the Chinese leader want to commit his own forces to battle. Perhaps 500,000 of the Kuomintang's best troops were blockading the Communists in Yenan. Chiang wanted to wait out the war, play one barbarian off against the other, and then muster his strength for the final showdown with Mao Tse-tung. He would not fight in Burma unless the British and Americans gave more support. Much to Stilwell's chagrin, the "hump" tonnage that Washington promised came in trickles, and the British continually balked at a Burma campaign. "That China is one of the world's four great powers is an absolute farce," said Churchill privately, as he pushed for higher Anglo-American priorities in the Mediterranean.[119] Shortly after the landings in North Africa, Stilwell described his strategic dilemma bitterly: "Peanut and I are on a raft, with one sandwich between us, and the rescue ship is heading away from the scene."[120]

President Roosevelt urged a more conciliatory diplomacy toward China. He warned that Chiang was "the Chief Executive as well as the Commander-in-Chief, and one cannot speak sternly to a man like that or exact commitments from him the way we might do from the Sultan of Morocco."[121] To Chungking the President sent a stream of personal emissaries to buoy up Chinese morale and listen to complaints about Stilwell. Chiang was given a half-billion dollar loan in 1942, and in January, 1943, the State Department negotiated a treaty abolishing the American right of extraterritoriality in China. The following month Roosevelt hosted Madame Chiang Kai-shek at the White House; the immaculately attired Wellesley College alumna also addressed Congress, where she was received as enthusiastically as Churchill. At the Cairo Conference in November, 1943, Churchill and Roosevelt met with Chiang and formally pledged the return of all Japanese-held territories after the war. In December Congress repealed the exclusion laws, which had prohibited Chinese immigration. Roosevelt talked confidently of postwar China, one of his "Four Policemen" to keep the peace. Such sentiment derived partly from sincerity, partly from a felt need to compensate China for wartime neglect, and partly from the assumption that the Chinese would be grateful to the United States. As historian Warren Cohen has written, "Roosevelt was almost Oriental in his attempts to give Chiang 'face' when he could not or would not give anything more substantial."[122]

Roosevelt also endorsed a plan of General Claire Lee Chennault. The organizer of the famed "Flying Tiger" volunteers boasted that with 105 fighters and 42 bombers he could "destroy the effectiveness of the Japanese Air Force" and thereby achieve "the downfall of Japan."[123] Building up air forces in China did not require large numbers, nor did it disturb Chiang's juggling act, so Roosevelt gave the older flyer the wares. The result was near disaster. As Stilwell and Marshall had predicted, when Chennault's bombers began to draw blood in the spring of 1944, Japanese armies launched a massive counterattack and nearly overran all the

**The Cairo Conference.** Chiang Kai-shek, FDR, Churchill, and Madame Chiang pose for photographers at the Cairo Conference of November, 1943, where they agreed that China would be restored territorially after the war. (Franklin D. Roosevelt Library)

American air bases. Chiang then balked at fighting. This time Roosevelt made the extraordinary proposal that Chiang give Stilwell unrestricted command of all forces, Chinese and foreign, in China. The Generalissimo stalled for two months; then Roosevelt sent an ultimatum that Stilwell gleefully delivered in person. "Mark this day in red on the calendar of life," he wrote in his diary on September 19, 1944. "A hot firecracker. I handed this bundle of paprika to the Peanut and then sank back with a sigh. The harpoon hit the little bugger right in the solar plexus, and went right through him."[124] Chiang was never to forgive Stilwell for such a personal humiliation. The vain Chinese leader's reply to Roosevelt hinted that he might accept some other American in command of Chinese forces, but not Stilwell. The President, after some hesitation, decided to replace his unpopular commander. By the autumn of 1944, following the Navy's capture of the Marianas and MacArthur's landings in the Philippines, the likelihood that China would play a major role in the defeat of Japan seemed minimal. The Russians had promised at Teheran that they would enter the Pacific war after the defeat of Hitler, and Roosevelt was counting on Soviet armies, not Chinese, to neutralize Japanese forces on the mainland. It was better not to antagonize an ally by insisting on Stilwell.

Enter General Patrick J. Hurley, a sixty-one-year-old Oklahoma Republican sent by Roosevelt to facilitate Stilwell's appointment as full commander. Actually the Generalissimo persuaded Hurley to support Stilwell's recall. Hurley then became the American ambassador, in November, 1944, replacing Clarence Gauss, a career diplomat known for his disdain toward the corruption in Chiang's government. In his own way every bit as much a bull in the china shop as Stilwell had been, Hurley concentrated his energies on forming a coalition between Chiang's government and the Communists. The Americans had sent an "Observer Mission" to Yenan in July, 1944, and its members liked what they saw. Using guerrilla tactics, the People's Liberation Army had achieved successes against the Japanese, in marked contrast to the inaction of Chiang's forces. Morale seemed excellent, and Mao's followers possessed a remarkable intelligence network extending behind Japanese lines. One downed American pilot was able to hike more than a thousand miles from eastern Hopei to Yenan with the aide of "Red" guides. Mao Tse-tung, Chou En-lai, and other Communist leaders welcomed the American observers and requested direct military aid. The Communist revolutionary leadership, according

# The United States Pushes Japan Back
# 1942-1945

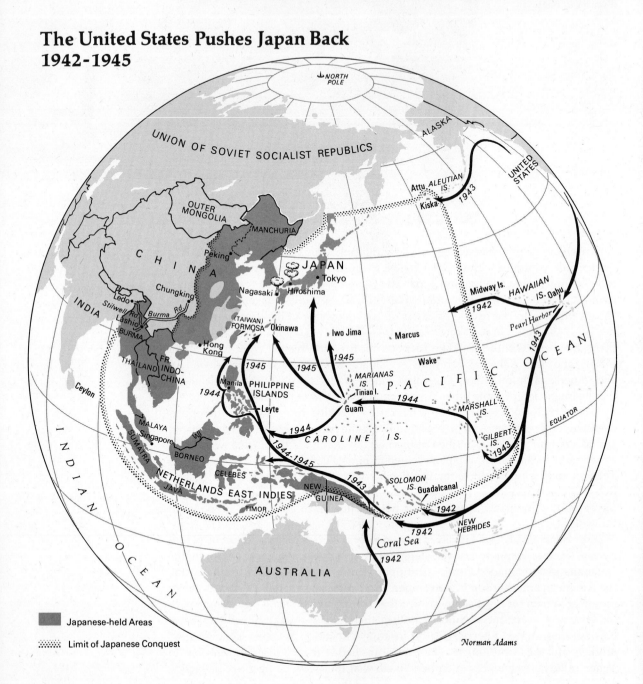

Japanese-held Areas

Limit of Japanese Conquest

*Norman Adams*

**General Patrick J. Hurley (1883–1963) in Yenan, China.** At Communist headquarters, the rambunctious anti-Communist ambassador to China met with Mao Tse-tung, Lin Tze-haw, Chu Teh, and Chou En-lai (left to right) in his vain effort to create a coalition government. The time was November, 1944. (Western History Collections, University of Oklahoma Library)

to Foreign Service Officer John S. Service in October, 1944, "has improved the political, economic and social status of the peasant. . . . As the Japanese cannot defeat these forces of the people, neither can the Kuomintang. . . . The Communists are certain to play a large, if not dominant, part in China's future."[125] This belief—that the Communists might win in a postwar struggle for power—was widespread among Americans in China, and so Hurley had unified support for his initial attempts at coalition.

The "Genbassador's" first visit to Communist Yenan, in November, 1944, was a grand spectacle. Hurley alighted from his plane "with enough ribbons on his chest to represent every war . . . in which the United States had ever engaged except possibly Shays' Rebellion."[126] Then he completely discombobulated Chou En-lai by letting out Choctaw war whoops. Later, after the Communists rejected Chiang's offer of a virtually worthless seat on the National Military Council in return for merging the Yenan army under Nationalist control, Hurley accepted Mao's counterproposal for full coalition and a Communist sharing in Lend-Lease supplies. Back in Chungking, however, Chiang continued to insist on merger of the two armies without real coalition, and Hurley seemed to acquiesce. Mao exploded, calling Chiang and Hurley "turtle eggs," whereupon Hurley snapped, Mao "tricked meh!"[127]

At this point Hurley began to diverge markedly from his subordinates, including the young Foreign Service Officers. Without ever having been so instructed by either Roosevelt or the State Department, the ambassador decided that his mission was not to mediate, but rather to "sustain Chiang Kai-shek" and "to prevent the collapse of the Nationalist government."[128] The Communists would undoubtedly come to terms eventually. Hurley was encouraged in these beliefs by an earlier visit to Moscow in August, 1944, when Molotov had told him that the Chinese Communists "had no relation whatever to Communism" and the Russians would support Chiang Kai-shek.[129] The other Americans in China (representatives of the Army, Office of Strategic Services, and Treasury, as well as Foreign Service Officers) knew that Mao's followers were agrarian-based Communists, and they feared that if the United States denied him aid, Mao would obtain assistance from Moscow and thus create a postwar squabble between the United States and Russia over China. Contrary to Hurley, these "China hands" believed that the rifts between the Communist and Kuomintang were deep and long-standing, and that the only way to obtain unity was to pressure Chiang Kai-shek by dealing with Yenan separately. Preliminary talks had already begun in Yenan, and on January 9, 1945, the head of the American Military Observers Mission cabled that "Mao and Chou will be immediately available either singly or together for exploratory conference at Washington should President Roosevelt express desire to receive them at White House as leaders of a primary Chinese party."[130] Hurley ignored his staff, and when Kuomintang-Communist negotiations stalled, he became convinced that disloyal subordinates were undermining his position by encouraging the Communists. He quickly blocked any meeting between Mao and Roosevelt. "You want me to pull the plug on Chiang Kai-shek," he bellowed to his startled embassy assistant, John Paton Davies.[131]

The predictable explosion occurred when Hurley returned to Washington in February, 1945 for consultations following the Yalta Conference, where Roosevelt had made concessions to Stalin regarding China without consultation with the Kuomintang government. In Hurley's absence, the embassy officers at Chungking sent a long telegram to Washington urging the President to "inform Chiang Kai-shek in definite terms that we are required by military necessity to cooperate with and supply the Communists and other suitable groups who can aid in this war against the Japanese."[132] These young "China hands" did not know that Stalin had reaffirmed Russian entry into the Japanese war at Yalta and, accordingly, that the military rationale for a Kuomintang-Communist coalition now became less urgent. Hurley roared like a wounded lion when he read the telegram. He stormed about Washington telling all who would listen that his subordinates were treasonous and that he would get an agreement between Mao and Chiang by April. He called on Roosevelt, then about to take what would be his final journey to Warm Springs, and the weary President gave him what he wanted—unqualified backing for Chiang's regime. The disputatious diplomats, including Service and Davies, were transferred out of China as a frightened State Department kowtowed to the rambunctious ambassador.

Roosevelt's wartime policy toward China exposed the disparity between his military strategy and postwar political goals. When it became obvious in 1944 that China would not play a major role in the Japanese war and hardly deserved rank as one of the "Four Policemen," Roosevelt faced a choice. He could accelerate American military activities in China and press Chiang to undertake the reforms necessary to maintain him in power. Or the President could scale down his political expectations for China and limit his military operations there. In fact, as James MacGregor Burns has pointed out, Roosevelt "tried to do both and ran the risk of succeeding in neither. He kept talking to and about China as a great power even while he was giving higher and higher military priorities to other military theaters."[133] Similarly, when the feud between Hurley and the China hands ignited, Roosevelt chose to drift with existing policy rather than take a hard look at Chinese politics. As happened often, when the smiling squire of New York could not easily resolve dichotomies, he left them to the future. In this case delay raised the ominous prospect of a full-fledged civil war between the Kuomintang and the Communists.

### Witness to the Holocaust: Americans and the Plight of the European Jews

Another problem left to the future was that of the refugees, hundreds of thousands of them Jews from Nazi-occupied territories. Many sought asylum in the United States. Although most Americans denounced Hitler's drive to preserve the purity of the "Aryan race" through the persecution and extermination of European Jews, translating moral revulsion into policy proved difficult. United States immigration laws, traditional anti-Semitism, the depression, bureaucratic procedures, wartime fear of spies, and domestic politics shaped the timid American response.

The dark story began in 1933 when Hitler initiated his attacks upon "non-Aryans." Throughout the 1930s, they were systematically eliminated from the professions and denied their businesses. In 1935, under the Nuremberg Laws, Jews were stripped of their civil and political rights, in essence becoming stateless beings. Signs reading "whoever buys from a Jew is a traitor" were plastered on buildings.[134] In November, 1938, a young, distraught Jewish boy living in Paris entered the German embassy and shot and killed a German official. He had learned that his parents had been placed in a boxcar for shipment to a concentration camp. Germany erupted in anti-Semitic violence. Several hundred synagogues were sacked and burned; Jews were beaten in the streets; Jewish shops were destroyed. After this *Kristallnacht* or "Night of the Breaking Glass," the German government fined its Jewish subjects $400 million. Fifty thousand Jews were sent to concentration camps at Dachau and Buchenwald, then detention centers later fitted with equipment for extermination. President Roosevelt called the American ambassador home in protest against the blatant persecutions, remarking, "I myself could scarcely believe that such things could occur in a twentieth century civilization."[135]

The brutal events were repeated in Austria, Czechoslovakia, Poland, Hungary, and elsewhere as the Third Reich overran Europe. Americans read about the cruelties in their newspapers. Unprecedented numbers of urgent requests for transit to the United States flooded American embassies and consulates. American immigration law, however, prescribed a quota for each country. Openly discriminatory, the National Origins Act of 1924 was designed to limit immigration from eastern and southern Europe, home, as Congressman J. M. Tincher of Kansas crudely put it, of "Bolshevik Wops, Dagoes, Kikes and Hunkies."[136] The annual quota for Great Britain and Ireland was 83,575, for Germany and Austria 27,370, for Poland 6,000, for Italy 5,500, and for Rumania 300. American consular officers also inhibited easy immigration to the United States from areas overrun by Nazism by strictly enforcing procedures. Potential immigrants had to present as many as fifty pages of documents attesting to their crime-free background, birth, health, and financial status. Many of these papers had to be obtained from Nazi officials. Furthermore, Americans rigidly denied entry to people "likely to become a public charge." This clause meant that persons could gain a place on the quota list only if they proved that they could support themselves once in the United States. Yet under Nazi law Jews could not take their property or savings from Germany. These restrictions, combined with the evaporation of American jobs during the depression, created a revealing statistic for the period 1933–1938: 174,067 people entered the United States and 221,239 departed, or a net *loss* of 47,172. To have opened America's doors to the persecuted abroad, in short, would not have inundated the United States. For a nation of 130 million the admission of several hundred thousand refugees should have been inconsequential.

Not so, said the restrictionists in the interwar years. The American Federation of Labor and patriotic groups lobbied against any revision in the quotas or relaxation of the visa requirements. Foreigners, they argued, should not be permitted to enter the United States to compete with American citizens for scarce jobs—a telling argument during the depression. Long-standing anti-Semitism fed such nativist thought. Father Charles E. Coughlin, the fiery Catholic priest from Michigan, led the anti-Semitic forces. He equated Judaism and communism in his radio broadcasts, which reached 3.5 million listeners a week. Even distinguished diplomat George Messersmith, who was outraged over Hitler and Nazism, opposed the establishment of a University of Exile at the New School for Social Research in New York because he feared that Jews hired there would undermine the basic Anglo-Saxon Protestant nature of American society. Opinion polls in the 1930s revealed that over 80 percent of Americans opposed revision of the quotas to admit European refugees. Although the *New Republic* magazine appealed for "common decency," Congress stood firmly behind the quota system.[137] Roosevelt was sensitive to political realities. Already blistered by charges that his domestic reform program was a "Jew Deal," a label attached because Jews like Henry Morgenthau, Jr. and Felix Frankfurter were prominent in his Administration, the President played it safe. Thwarted in his ill-fated "court-packing" attempt in 1937 and his futile effort to purge conservatives from the Democratic party in 1938, Roosevelt did not wish to risk another political setback. "For God's sake," insisted a congressional spokesman, "don't send us any more controversial legislation!"[138]

Roosevelt left the refugee problem to the Department of State, which "clung to a policy that was timid, rigidly legal, and without innovation."[139] In 1934 the department lobbied successfully against a Senate resolution condemning Germany's treatment of the Jews, fearful that the resolution would spark German comment about the segregation of black Americans. Secretary Hull also opposed boycotts organized by American Jews against German products because such behavior interrupted normal trade channels. Although he did relax enforcement of the "likely to become a public charge" clause, many Jews, caught in circumstances of fear and chaos, still could not obtain the necessary documents. The result: the German-Austrian quota went unfilled in 1933–1938 and 1940–1945; only in 1939 was it filled. For the entire period 1933–1945, only 35.8 percent of the German-Austrian quota was used. Congressman Emanuel Celler of New York thought the State Department a "heartbeat muffled in protocol."[140]

In 1938 Roosevelt called for an international meeting on refugees, which met in Evian, France and established an Intergovernmental Committee on Refugees. No real plans emerged and the committee proved ineffective. Hitler sneered: "It is a shameful example to observe today how the entire democratic world dissolves in tears of pity, but then, in spite of its obvious duty to help, closes its heart to the poor, tortured people."[141] In early 1939 Senator Robert Wagner of New York introduced a bill to allow 20,000 German refugee children to enter above the quota as a "symbol of our faith in the ideals of human brotherhood."[142] The Roosevelt

Administration remained silent. The bill died in committee. In mid-1939 the ship *St. Louis* steamed toward Cuba from Hamburg carrying 930 Jewish refugees. Havana officials, however, would not permit them to land because their visas had not been obtained properly. The ship headed for Miami, tailed by Coast Guard cutters. American immigration officials would not let the passengers disembark. Despite appeals to Washington from concerned American liberals, the *St. Louis* was forced to return to Europe, its passengers ultimately scattered to Britain, the Netherlands, Belgium, and France after refugee societies pressured their governments. "The cruise of the *St. Louis,*" editorialized the *New York Times,* "cries to high heaven of man's inhumanity to man."[143]

The plight of Jewish refugees did not improve after the outbreak of war. The State Department actually tightened visa requirements because it feared refugees might include Nazi or Communist spies. American consuls increasingly rejected applications for visas, and ships headed to American shores half empty. Washington tried futilely to persuade Latin American countries to take refugees. When the State Department asked the British to approach Portugal about opening its African colony of Angola, Lord Halifax snapped: "Let the Americans do it."[144] Schemes to provide havens in British Guiana and French Madagascar fell through. Britain also restricted the movement of Jews to Palestine. The record of other countries, in other words, was as bad as that of the United States. In the State Department, refugee questions fell under the authority of Breckinridge Long, a Southern aristocrat, old Wilsonian, former ambassador to Italy, and large financial contributor to the Democratic party. Believing that refugees might become a fifth column of spies in the United States, he and other officials blocked numerous private efforts to save them and actually suppressed information about Hitler's plan to exterminate European Jewry.

In early 1942 reliable evidence reached the State Department that Germany planned to exterminate the entire Jewish population of Europe. The information seemed beyond imagination, too cruel to be true. The thought of Jews being sent by cattle car to extermination camps, gassed, and then burned in crematoria seemed too farfetched. Yet the evidence mounted. After invading Russia in 1941, special German squads rounded up Jews and massacred them. In two days in September, 33,000 were murdered in Kiev. One of the first extermination camps was built at Auschwitz, Poland, where one million people died. At its peak, Auschwitz executed 12,000 people a day. Using Zyklon B gas and large crematoria, German officials competed for efficiency ratings in human destruction. The Jewish ghetto in Warsaw became a target of German barbarity; by the fall of 1942 only 70,000 of its 380,000 residents remained, and they desperately rebelled in the spring of the next year. Italian and Greek Jews were shipped by rail to Auschwitz. Of the ten million Jews who lived in 1939 in areas overrun by the Nazis, an estimated six million had died by the end of the war. Appeals throughout the war years for American planes to bomb the rail lines leading to the death camps and the crematoria went unheeded by the War Department, on the grounds that such diversions would delay victory, itself the best hope for the Jews. Ultimately, two scholars have concluded, "Hitler was able to exult that nobody wanted the Jews and so, since there was nowhere for them to go, he had no option but to destroy them."[145]

In early 1943 representatives of Britain and the United States met in Bermuda to discuss the refugee problem; in essence they reported that they had done all they could to help. After the conference, Hull informed the President: "The unknown cost of moving an undetermined number of persons from an undisclosed place to an unknown destination, a scheme advocated by certain pressure groups, is, of course, out of the question."[146] Hull never sought to solve the unknowns. Secretary of the Treasury Henry Morgenthau, Jr. did. He asked his general counsel, Randolph Paul, to prepare a study of the State Department's handling of the refugee crisis. Paul turned in a *Report to the Secretary on the Acquiescence of This Government in the Murder of the Jews*, a startlingly frank critique of Breckinridge Long and the State Department. "It takes months and months to grant the visa and then it usually applies to a corpse." Morgenthau reported directly to Roosevelt that the rescue of Jews "is a trust too great to remain in the hands of men indifferent, callous and perhaps hostile."[147] In January, 1944, the President created the War Refugee Board, outside the auspices of the State Department. Using private and public funds, board operatives established refugee camps in Italy, Morocco, Hungary, Italy, Sweden, Palestine, and Switzerland. Thousands were saved from the gas chambers. Still, the War Refugee Board had come too late, eleven years after Hitler's first efforts to persecute the Jews. Cordell Hull, after leaving office, could accurately say that "President Roosevelt at no time complained to me that the Department had not done enough."[148] The quota system lasted until 1965. In

**Freeing Prisoners at the Wobbelin Concentration Camp.** This prisoner near Berlin escaped the ghastly mass murder perpetrated by the Third Reich. (U.S. Office of War Information)

large measure the Jewish refugees themselves took command of their survival after the war by leading the "exodus" to Palestine and creating the new nation of Israel in 1948.

## Planning for the Postwar Peace, 1943–1945

American leaders began thinking about the contours of the postwar world early in the war. Interdepartmental committees identified potential problems and suggested courses of action. Determined that never again would isolationism, economic depression, and war threaten American interests, the United States cooperated with other nations to devise a number of international organizations to secure peace and prosperity. The oft-repeated principles of the Atlantic Charter provided useful guides, but, as always, principles were modified in practice and after compromise. During 1943–1945 the United Nations Relief and Rehabilitation Administration (UNRRA), World Bank, International Monetary Fund, and United Nations Organization took form. Unlike World War I, this time the establishment of postwar institutions would not await the grand deliberations of one conference. Nor would plans to reform Germany.

On November 9, 1943, at the White House, forty-four nations signed the UNRRA Agreement to plan and administer "measures for the relief of victims of war . . . through the provision of food, fuel, clothing, shelter and other basic necessities, medical and other essential services."[149] The humanitarian relief program would, said a State Department official, help create "a more stable world order."[150] Some leaders feared that the millions of hungry displaced people might, in desperation, turn to political extremes like communism. Food and medicine would help stem postwar political chaos. The Department of State successfully insisted throughout the negotiations that an American be named head of UNRRA. In existence until mid-1947, UNRRA enjoyed a budget of $4 billion, $2.7 billion of which was donated by the United States. UNRRA dispensed nine million tons of food, built hundreds of hospitals, administered medicine to prevent epidemics of diphtheria, typhoid, cholera, and venereal disease, revived transportation systems, and cared for over one million displaced persons. China, Italy, Greece, and Austria absorbed about half of UNRRA's assistance. The other half was spent in Poland, other Eastern European nations, and the Soviet Union. Therein lay American criticism after the war that American money was being spent through an international organization to shore up Communist governments. In fact, UNRRA tried to avoid politics and to help anybody who was destitute, whether that person lived in a Communist country or not. As part of American foreign aid, however, food was expected to bring political returns. When it did not, Washington killed UNRRA in 1947 by cutting off funds.

Two other organizations proved more permanent. From July 1 to 22, 1944, the delegates of forty-four nations negotiated at Bretton Woods in the scenic White Mountains of New Hampshire. Working from an Anglo-American proposal, the conferees created the International Bank for Reconstruction and Development or World Bank and the International Monetary Fund. The World Bank was designed to extend loans to "assist in the reconstruction and development" of members, to "promote private investment," and to "promote the long-range balanced growth of international trade."[151] The fund was designed to grease world trade by stabilizing the international system of payments through currency loans. "The question," Senator Robert Wagner of New York declared in support of the Bretton Woods agreements, "is whether by default we allow the world to repeat the tragic blunders of the 1920s and 1930s."[152] After much debate, with critics worried about America's possible loss of sovereignty to international organizations, Congress passed the Bretton Woods Agreements Act in July of 1945.

From the start the two organizations were dominated by the economic power of the United States. They were located in Washington, D.C., top posts went to Americans (an American has been president of the World Bank since its formation), and the United States possessed one-third of the votes in the bank by subscribing $3.175 billion of the total of $9.100 billion. The United States also held one-third of the votes in the fund. As payer of the "piper," complained the *Manchester Guardian*, the United States would "call the tune."[153] Britain begrudged American control but joined. Although Russia attended the Bretton Woods Conference, it did not join the bank or fund, because the Soviets practiced state-controlled trade and finance, feared having to divulge economic data, and could not accept the emphasis on "private" enterprise or the American domination. Russia's absence did not prove disruptive, but it augured poorly for postwar Allied cooperation.

From August to October, 1944, representatives of the United States, Britain, Russia, and China met in the handsome Georgetown mansion at Dumbarton Oaks in Washington, D.C. Cordell Hull had been tooling up for this conference since early in the war. Public opinion polls indicated that Americans strongly endorsed a new world organization, and Congress had passed favorable resolutions. Roosevelt had spoken of the "Four Policemen" as guardians of the peace, and at the conference the American delegation helped shape the United Nations Organization (UN) under this concept. The Big Four, with considerable unanimity, hammered out the UN's preliminary charter, providing for a powerful Security Council dominated by the great powers and a weak General Assembly. The Security Council, empowered to use force to settle crises, had five permanent members. When the United States pushed China as a permanent member, Britain proposed France. Churchill had protested that China was not a world power, but a "faggot vote on the side of the United States."[154] Russia, after some grumbling, accepted both China and France, feeling secure in the veto power that each permanent member of the Security Council possessed.

Two issues dogged the conferees: the voting procedure in the Security Council and membership in the Assembly. Russia advocated an absolute veto for permanent members, whereas the United States argued that parties to a conflict should not be in a position to veto discussion or action. The issue was left unsettled. (At the Yalta Conference in early 1945 the Allies agreed to a compromise whereby the veto could not be used for procedural questions but could be applied to substantive questions like economic or military sanctions.) As for membership in the Assembly, Russia at Dumbarton Oaks boldly requested seats for all sixteen Soviet republics. That outlandish request derived from Moscow's fear of being badly outnumbered in the Assembly by the British Commonwealth "bloc" and the United States–Latin American "bloc." The Soviet Union, like Britain and the United States, was playing the great power game. The participants decided to defer the question. (At Yalta a compromise of three Soviet votes in the Assembly was struck.) The President declared that 90 percent of the issues at Dumbarton Oaks had been resolved: "Well, that is what we used to call in the old days a darn good batting average."[155]

During the Dumbarton Oaks Conference, Republican presidential candidate Thomas Dewey scored the meeting for subjecting "the nations of the world, great and small, permanently to the coercive power" of the Big Four.[156] Secretary Hull angrily disagreed and managed to dissuade Dewey from further political attacks on the fledgling United Nations Organization. That nonpartisanship, and the inclusion of senators in the Dumbarton Oaks delegation, helped the Roosevelt Administration build its case for the UN with the American people. There would be no Wilsonian League of Nations fiasco this time. Still, some critics wondered how cohesive the new institution would be. One compared the members to marbles in a dish: "put your toe on the dish and the marbles will scatter, each to its own corner."[157] A sign that the advocates, not the critics, would dominate the subsequent debate over American membership in the United Nations came on January 10, 1945, in the Senate. Influential Arthur H. Vandenberg of Michigan, an arch prewar isolationist who was expected to insist on reservations much as Lodge had a generation earlier, delivered a stunning speech urging resuscitation of the Atlantic Charter and American participation in collective security as a curb on aggression—presumably he meant the Soviet variety. Furthermore, he advised the major Allies to sign a security treaty to keep the Axis nations permanently demilitarized; he hoped thereby to allay Soviet fears of a revived Germany and hence render Soviet expansion unnecessary. Vandenberg could accept American membership in the United Nations Organization, because "this is anything but a wild-eyed internationalist dream of a world State. . . . I am deeply impressed (and surprised) to find Hull so carefully guarding our American veto in his scheme of things."[158]

Roosevelt rewarded the vain Vandenberg for his support by naming him a delegate to the San Francisco Conference of April 25–June 26, 1945. Before that meeting, Russia had soured on the new international organization—in part because the provisional pro-Communist government of Poland had not been invited. Just before Roosevelt died on April 12, he appealed to Stalin to send Commissar Molotov to the San Francisco conference as a sign of Soviet seriousness. When Stalin expressed his sadness over the President's death, he also indicated that Molotov would travel to San Francisco. However, the new President, short-tempered Harry S Truman, who had become angry over Soviet manipulation in Poland, exploded that "if the Russians did not wish to join us they could go to hell."[159]

The new secretary of state after Hull's retirement on November 27, 1944, Edward R. Stettinius, Jr., managed the conference in the elegant setting of the San Francisco Opera House. "The Conference opens today—with Russian clouds in every sky," Vandenberg noted in his diary. "I don't know whether this is Frisco or Munich."[160] The 282 delegates did not make decisions without prior approval of the representatives of the big powers, who met each evening in Stettinius' penthouse at the Fairmont Hotel. Still, controversy marred the lofty mood of the conference. The United States again refused to admit Poland, because its government had not been reorganized as required by Yalta. But then the American delegation shocked the conferees by asking for participation by Argentina, which had only declared war against Germany in March. Molotov considered the government in Buenos Aires fascist and thought it "incomprehensible" that Poland

**United Nations Symbol.** A sign for a postwar peace yet unrealized. (United Nations)

would be refused entry and Argentina admitted.[161] The United States, believing that the Latin American republics would not vote for three Soviet seats in the Assembly unless Argentina were included, would not relent. By the lopsided vote of 32 to 4, with 10 abstentions, Argentina was seated.

Journalist Walter Lippmann detected an American "steamroller" at San Francisco.[162] So did Russia, which objected in blunt language. And so did smaller states, which protested their isolation from key decisions and their impotence in the new United Nations Organization. Fifteen nations abstained, for example, in the vote on the veto formula. The UN Charter, as finally adopted, included the Economic and Social Council and the Trusteeship Council. The latter looked to the eventual independence of colonial areas, but left the British and French empires intact and permitted the United States to absorb former Japanese-dominated islands in the Pacific (Marianas, Carolines, and Marshalls). *Time* magazine aptly termed the United Nations "a charter for a world of power."[163] Indeed, that characterization was evident not only in the veto provision, but in Article 51, which permitted regional alliances such as that the United States and Latin America outlined in the Act of Chapultepec in March. The United States, as War Department official John J. McCloy observed, would "have our cake and eat it too"— freedom of action in the western hemisphere and an international organization to curb aggression in Europe.[164] Amidst memories of 1919, the Senate debated the UN Charter. Senator Tom Connally of Texas, a delegate at San Francisco, thundered: "They know that the League of Nations was slaughtered here in this chamber. Can't you see the blood?—there it is on the wall."[165] The Senate approved the charter on July 28, 1945, by a vote of 89 to 2.

While these plans for the victors unfolded, American officials debated plans for the defeated. The debate over Germany centered on a "constructive" policy (rehabilitation, economic unity, and integration into the European economy) or a "corrective" policy (strict reduction in industry, large reparations, and a decentralized economy).[166] At the center of the controversy stood Secretary of the

**"Uncle Sam Pulls the Lever at the UN."** Many foreign commentators believed that the United States dominated the new United Nations Organization. (*Ta Kung Pao* of Shanghai–Hong Kong in *United Nations World,* 1951)

Treasury Henry Morgenthau, Jr. As in the case of the refugee problem, Morgenthau stepped outside normal jurisdictional boundaries and proposed a "corrective" plan designed to despoil Germany of industries having potential military value. In early September, 1944 he had informed Roosevelt that the coal- and iron-rich Ruhr area, "the heart of German industrial power," should be stripped of industry.[167] The President introduced this idea at the Quebec Conference of September 12–16, 1944, where he gained Churchill's reluctant signature to a memorandum: "This programme for eliminating the war-making industries in the Ruhr and in the Saar is looking forward to converting Germany into a country primarily agricultural and pastoral in its character."[168] Apparently a bargain was struck at Quebec, wherein Churchill approved the Morgenthau scheme in exchange for the promise of a postwar American loan.

Back in Washington, however, critics lambasted the "Morgenthau Plan." Secretaries Hull and Stimson opposed a harsh economic peace because Germany was the vital center to a revived Western European economy. "Sound thinking teaches that prosperity in one part of the world helps to create prosperity in other parts of the world," Stimson advised Roosevelt. "It also teaches that poverty in one part of the world induces poverty in other parts."[169] Germany had to be revived to encourage postwar prosperity. Using his special access to the President, Morgenthau persuaded Roosevelt in late September to approve an interim Joint Chiefs of Staff directive (JSC/1067), the final version of which came in April, 1945. JCS/1067 ordered programs of denazification and demilitarization, the dismantling of iron, steel, and chemical industries, a controlled economy, and limited rehabilitation. The new President, Harry S Truman, however, thought "Morgenthau didn't know sh— from apple butter" and began a gradual retreat from the Morgenthau Plan and JCS/1067, especially after easing Morgenthau out of office in July of 1945.[170] By the end of the war, then, American plans for postwar Germany remained unsettled.

## The Yalta Conference

Near the end of the European war Churchill, Roosevelt, and Stalin met once again, this time at the Livadia Palace near Yalta in the Crimea. The Prime Minister penned a ditty: "No more let us falter! From Malta to Yalta! Let nobody alter!"[171] Meeting from February 4 to 11, 1945, the Big Three, after considerable compromise, made important decisions for the war against the Axis and for the postwar configuration of international affairs, the Yalta "system." After the conclave, Yalta aroused heated controversy akin to the Munich Conference. To later critics, Yalta symbolized a "sell-out" to—or appeasement of—the Soviets, an example of Roosevelt's coddling of the Communist menace. Roosevelt was tired, worn low by the illness that would take his life two months later. His physical weakness and his propensity for personal diplomacy, argued detractors, subjected him to the temptations of a guileful Stalin. But Roosevelt's poor health did not decide the outcome at Yalta. Nor did the presence of Alger Hiss. Later convicted of perjury and denounced by right-wing anti-Communists as a spy for Moscow, Hiss seemed to them an insidious agent of the Communist conspiracy, who undermined American interests. Although at Yalta Hiss was an adviser on questions of international organization, no evidence exists that he influenced Roosevelt or the results of the conference. Other critics have complained that Roosevelt ignored the rights of weak nations like China and Poland, went into sessions unprepared, and failed to use superior American economic and military might to force Soviet concessions. Many of the agreements, furthermore, were secret at the time. Above all else, Yalta became a topic of acrimony because the agreements, cast in vague language, ultimately broke down.

The Big Three entered the conference with different goals. Britain sought a zone in Germany for France, a curb on Soviet expansion into Poland, and protection of the British Empire. Russia wanted reparations to rebuild the devastated Soviet economy, possessions in Asia, a Soviet-influenced Poland, and a Germany so weakened that it could never again march eastward. The United States wanted the United Nations as an institution for postwar world order and American influence, a Russian declaration of war against Japan, a reduction of the Communist presence in Poland, and elevation of China to big power status. Each participant suspected the others' intentions. But, "although the Great Powers differed in their initial viewpoints," historian Diane Shaver Clemens has noted, "a high incidence of consensus was reached at the Conference."[172]

The "consensus" at Yalta was determined not only by a willingness to reconcile differences, but also by the military and diplomatic realities of the moment. Anglo-American troops were bogged down in the Battle of the Bulge in Belgium from mid-December to mid-January, 1945. Churchill had appealed to Stalin to take pressure off the Western Front by stepping up the Russian winter offensive in the east. Russia obliged on January 12. "I am most grateful to you for your thrilling message," a relieved Churchill wrote Stalin.[173] Throughout 1944 the Red Army had cut deeply into German lines on the Eastern Front. Indeed, by the time of the Yalta Conference, Russian soldiers were sweeping westward along a wide front through Poland, Czechoslovakia, and Hungary, with Rumania already freed from German clutches. Thus, the Russians held a formidable bargaining position at Yalta because of their military exploits.

In the Far East also, military realities shaped diplomatic decisions. Japan was fiercely battling American forces in Luzon and the Marianas, and still had a million soldiers in China, two million in the home islands, and another one million in Manchuria and Korea. Americans were taking heavy losses in planes, ships, and men. Iwo Jima, Okinawa, and the atomic bomb still lay in the future. As historian Forrest C. Pogue has concluded, "all in all, the military backdrop for the Yalta negotiations . . . did not yet afford Roosevelt and Churchill the luxury of renouncing or forgoing Soviet military cooperation in Europe and Asia."[174] The point was conspicuous: as close as victory was, Britain and the United States still needed the Russians to win the war.

The setting itself impressed the conferees with the costs of the war. Gutted buildings, abandoned vehicles, and gnarled railways blotted the snow-blanketed countryside around the resort town on the Black Sea. The villas of bygone dukes and tsars still stood grandly, although Nicholas II's Livadia Palace had been badly looted by the retreating Germans. As hosts for the first tripartite conference held on Russian soil, the Soviets strained to make their guests comfortable, with servants and lavish meals. The only complaints were registered against a paucity of toilets and bathtubs and a plethora of bedbugs. The meetings were generally amicable, although Stalin once became ruffled when he misunderstood that Roosevelt's name for him—"Uncle Joe"—was a term of endearment, not ridicule. Molotov wore his customary stone face, but Stalin, Churchill, and Roosevelt

**The Yalta Conference.** A physically distraught President confers with the Prime Minister in uniform at the Yalta Conference, February, 1945. Although FDR was ill (he died two months later), he helped write agreements considered at the time a high point of the wartime alliance and a real hope for a peaceful future. (Franklin D. Roosevelt Library)

debated in good humor and frankness, sharing a desire to maintain the Grand Alliance. Stalin especially beamed over Churchill's spirited and belabored defense of the British Empire.

For Churchill, Poland was "the most urgent reason for the Yalta Conference."[175] Seven of the eight plenary sessions grappled with the Polish issue. "We ought to do something," Roosevelt said, "that will come like a breath of fresh air in the murk that exists at the moment on the Polish question."[176] There were actually two Polish governments. The British and Americans recognized the conservative exiled government in London, led by Stanislas Mikolajczyk. Moscow recognized the Communist-led provisional government in Lublin. Stalin was emphatic that any Polish government must be eastward leaning. He reminded his counterparts at the conference that Soviet security was at stake, that the Polish corridor had been the route of deadly German attacks on Russia twice in this century. He insisted not only on Allied support for the Lublin government, but also on Polish boundaries that gave Poland part of Germany (Oder-Neisse line in the west) and Russia part of Poland (Curzon line in the east). Churchill and Roosevelt opposed a Communist Poland but were in no position to bargain effectively, since Soviet troops occupied much of the country. Churchill fumed: "Poland [must] be mistress in her own house and captain of her soul."[177] What he sought was a pro-British Polish regime. Roosevelt said he had several million Polish voters back home who demanded a more representative Polish government. Stalin, castigating the anti-Sovietism of the conservative London Poles, remained adamant.

Compromises were reached. The Curzon line was temporarily set as the eastern boundary. The Yalta agreement read also that a "more broadly based" government would be created in Poland, that the "Provisional Government which is now functioning in Poland should be therefore reorganized on a broader democratic basis with the inclusion of democratic leaders from Poland itself and from Poles abroad," and that "free and unfettered elections" would be held soon.[178] The Communist Lublin group, then, would serve as the nucleus of the postwar Polish state. Much controversy would surround this language later, for the Americans interpreted it to mean that an altogether new government would develop from the reorganization. "Mr. President," said Chief of Staff William D. Leahy, "this is so elastic that the Russians can stretch it all the way from Yalta to Washington without technically breaking it." "I know, Bill—I know it," responded Roosevelt. "But it's the best I can do for Poland at this time."[179] Churchill swallowed the bitter pill, in part because Stalin assured him that the Soviet Union would not intrude in British-dominated Greece, then suffering from civil war. Compromises on other issues also made the Polish settlement tolerable.

Britain, although not keen about dividing Germany, accepted "dismemberment" so long as its ally France received a zone of occupation. Noting that Roosevelt had said that American troops would not long remain in Europe, Churchill cited France as a bulwark against Germany. Stalin protested: France had hardly fought during the war; indeed, the Vichy government had collaborated with the Germans. But Stalin finally accepted a French zone. On reparations, which the Soviets vigorously demanded, Britain and America hedged. They agreed on German reparations "in kind," but refused to set a figure until Germany's ability to pay was determined. The Big Three stated only that they would *discuss* in the future the amount of $20 billion, half of which would go to Russia. Stalin probably assumed that the United States and Britain would henceforth support the $10 billion figure.

Further compromises were struck over the Far East. The American military and the President wanted Soviet participation in the war against Japan. Anticolonialist that he was, Roosevelt also told Stalin privately that he wanted to break up the British Empire, even giving Hong Kong to China, and prevent a French return to Indochina. Although the Yalta accords did not treat these imperial questions, they did include trade-offs between Russia and the United States. Stalin promised to declare war against Japan two or three months after Hitler's defeat, enough time to permit the transfer of his troops to Asia. He agreed to sign a pact of friendship and alliance with Chiang Kai-shek's regime, rather than with Mao Tse-tung's rival Communist group. In return, Russia regained territories and privileges it had lost in 1905: the southern part of Sakhalin, Darien as a free port, Port Arthur as a Soviet naval base, and joint operation of the Chinese Eastern and South Manchurian Railroads. The Kurile Islands were also awarded to the Soviet Union. These agreements, it should be emphasized, were forged without consultation with China, a clear loser at Yalta.

The Allies also compromised on the United Nations Organization. France and China had been added at Dumbarton Oaks as "permanent" members of the Security Council, possessing the veto. Although Churchill had complained earlier that China would vote with the United States, Roosevelt and Stalin knew as well that France was inclined toward British positions. Feeling outnumbered in the Council, Stalin thus asked at Yalta for membership of all sixteen Soviet republics in the General Assembly. He also insisted upon an absolute veto in the Council on all issues, procedural and substantive. Roosevelt agreed to grant the Soviets three seats in the General Assembly and Stalin agreed that the veto could not be cast on procedural questions, such as whether the Council should take up an issue to which the permanent member is a party. The conferees also set April 25 as the date for the organizing meeting of the United Nations in San Francisco.

Besides a restatement of the Atlantic Charter in the "Declaration of Liberated Europe," the establishment of a Reparations Commission, and inconclusive statements on Iran, Yugoslavia, and the Dardanelles, these were the sum of the agreements. Yalta marked a high point of the alliance, the "dawn of the new day," said Harry Hopkins. "We were absolutely certain that we had won the first great victory of the peace—and, by 'we,' I mean *all* of us, the whole civilized human race."[180] But Yalta was not as free of self-interest as Hopkins suggested. The sovereignty of weak nations had been violated. As Churchill told his colleagues: "The eagle should permit the small birds to sing and care not wherefore they sang."[181] France and China had been excluded from the negotiations. Spheres of influence had, in essence, been recognized. Although tough questions had been postponed, each power went home with something from this conference of traditional diplomatic give-and-take that reflected diplomatic and military needs and realities. Roosevelt had played the great power game as deftly as Stalin and Churchill.

Later, when the Yalta agreements collapsed, critics ignored the advantages the United States carried away from the conference—broadening of the Polish government, Russian promise to fight Japan, Russian recognition of Chiang's government, a voting formula in the United Nations, postponement of the reparations question—and charged that Roosevelt had given away too much. But he had little to give away. The United States might have used its economic power in the form of reconstruction aid as a diplomatic weapon, but that would have spoiled the spirit of compromise at Yalta, which served American interests. Nor did Stalin play one of his trump cards: the capture of Berlin during the conference. From Yalta Stalin ordered Marshall G. K. Zhukov to halt the Berlin offensive. His generals were not sure why, but contemporaries and historians have suggested that Stalin wanted to avoid a dramatic conquest, which might have created suspicions and destroyed cooperation at Yalta. Sir Alexander Cadogan thought, for example, that Stalin showed "no bluster: [military] success, instead of going to his head, seemed to have given him the added assurance enabling him to take broad views and to be unafraid of making concessions."[182] Churchill recognized the necessity of compromise: "What would have happened if we had quarrelled with Russia while the Germans still had three or four hundred divisions on the fighting front?"[183] Averell Harriman, although angry that the Yalta accords did not hold up, later offered a sobering perspective on the significance of the conference: "If we hadn't had the Yalta agreement *we* would have been blamed for all the postwar tensions."[184]

## To Each His Own: Allied Divergence and Spheres of Influence

At Yalta and throughout the diplomacy of World War II, the Allies attempted to protect and, if possible, extend their spheres of influence. Churchill's spirited defense of the British Empire, from Argentia through Yalta, was an ever present characteristic of wartime diplomacy. "If the Americans want to take Japanese islands which they have conquered," he informed his Foreign Secretary Anthony Eden, "let them do so with our blessing and any form of words that may be agreeable to them. But 'Hands Off the British Empire' is our maxim."[185] With vital interests in the Mediterranean and Persian Gulf, as well as the Far East, Britain resisted any machinery for postwar United Nations-mandated trusteeships. "I will not have one scrap of British Territory flung into that area," Churchill boomed.[186] Some Americans suspected that Churchill's constant postponement of the second front and his strategies for North Africa and Italy aimed at protecting imperial lifelines from either Germany or Russia. His advice to American military leaders, near the war's end, that they drive quickly to Berlin, and if possible even farther into Eastern Europe, to beat the Russians, provided further evidence for this suspicion.

The Churchill-Stalin percentage agreement of October, 1944 illustrated well the movement toward spheres of influence. In early 1944 Churchill concluded that "we are approaching a showdown with the Russians" in the Balkans. It was time for a frank settlement. Roosevelt warned against "any post-war spheres of influence," but agreed to a trial division of authority.[187] The "showdown" could be measured

**Pacific Fleet Carriers.** A major reason for United States victories in the Pacific theater and for a substantial American role in postwar Asian affairs was the air superiority provided by these *Essex*-class ships (27,000 tons each). The U.S.S. *Essex* leads this flotilla in 1943. (Navy Department, National Archives)

in Rumania, where Soviet troops dominated, Yugoslavia, where independent Communist Josip Tito and his Partisans were emerging, Bulgaria, where an indigenous Communist movement grew with Soviet influence, and Greece, a British-dominated area in the throes of a burgeoning civil war. At a conference with Stalin in Moscow in October, Churchill scribbled some percentages on a piece of paper. In Rumania, Russia would get 90 percent of the power and Britain 10 percent, in Greece Britain would enjoy 90 percent and Russia 10 percent, in Yugoslavia and Hungary a 50–50 split, and in Bulgaria 75 percent would go to Russia and 25 percent to "others." As Churchill recalled, he "pushed this across to Stalin," who "took his blue pencil and made a large tick upon it." Churchill, fearful that posterity would think such important issues had been disposed of in an "offhand manner," suggested that the paper be burned. "No, you keep it," said Stalin.[188] Roosevelt did not remonstrate over the bargain. Always following the path of least resistance, Roosevelt probably "had come to agree with Churchill that some such arrangement as the one reported was advisable, if not essential."[189] The percentage bargain did not last, in large part because local conditions denied the maintenance of artificial percentages of influence. But the agreement probably reinforced Stalin's view that his developing sphere had tacit Western approval.

If Britain was trying to save its sphere of influence, especially in Greece, Russia was attempting to expand its in Eastern Europe. Soviet support for the Lublin Polish government, demands for Polish and Rumanian territory, efforts to exclude the United States and Britain from the joint control commissions in Eastern Europe, and seizure of German-operated property (including Standard Oil equipment in Rumania) alerted American officials to the growing power of Russia vis-à-vis its neighbors. The Soviet handling of the Warsaw uprising of July 31, 1944 alarmed Western observers, convincing many that Soviet callousness had few limits. With Soviet armies some twelve miles from Warsaw, the Polish underground gambled and attacked German forces, believing that the Soviet troops would dash to their aid. But the Soviet Army stopped. For two months the Germans pummeled the Polish fighters, who owed their allegiance to the exiled government in London. The Germans killed 166,000 Poles and leveled half the city. Churchill persuaded Stalin in September to drop supplies to the besieged city, but the Russian leader called the Warsaw uprising a reckless, futile undertaking. He begged off from further support, pointing out that his troops were meeting heavy German resistance. To requests that American planes be permitted to land at Russian airfields after carrying supplies to Warsaw, Stalin first said *"nyet,"* and then permitted landings in mid-September. Whatever the military realities, many charged that Stalin abetted the slaughter of the Warsaw Poles. Churchill spoke of the Soviet "tale of villainy and horror," and British Air Marshall John Slessor later wrote: "How, after the fall of Warsaw, any responsible statesman could trust any Russian Communist further than he could kick him, passes the comprehension of ordinary men."[190] The liberation of Poland by Soviet forces in 1944 ultimately fixed a Communist regime in Warsaw—one that Roosevelt's compromises at Yalta essentially recognized.

The United States itself was expanding and building spheres of influence during the war, although it disapproved of spheres for others. Having already drawn most of the Latin American states into a defense community at the Lima Conference (1938) and in the Declaration of Panama (1939), the United States moved to drive

**"Gone with the Wind . . ."** In this critical Argentine cartoon of 1940, Uncle Sam, his pledges of neutrality and isolationism discarded, tends the armaments he uses to seduce Latin America. (Antonio Arias Bernal, The Swann Collection of Caricature and Cartoon)

German investments and influence from the western hemisphere. The Export-Import Bank loaned $130 million to twelve Latin American nations in 1939–1941 to help them oust German businesses, cut trade with the Axis, stabilize their economies, and bring them into alignment with American foreign policy. During the war, the United States increased its stake in Bolivian tin, helped build Brazilian warships, expanded holdings in Venezuelan oil, acquired bases in Panama and Guatemala, and nourished the dictatorship of Rafael Trujillo in the Dominican Republic. The American military also began to coordinate armaments and military training with Latin American forces. During the war Latin America shipped 50 percent of its exports, largely much needed raw materials, to the United States. At the Rio de Janeiro Conference (January 15–28, 1942), all but Chile and Argentina voted to break diplomatic relations with the Axis nations. In March of 1945, in the Act of Chapultepec, the United States and Latin America took another step toward a regional defense alliance. Furthermore, American officials recognized that Latin Americans would vote with the United States at the new United Nations. An unwitting and embarrassing statement of February, 1945 by Secretary Stettinius in Mexico City, reminded many that the United States still considered its southern neighbors subservient: "The United States looks upon Mexico as a good neighbor, a strong upholder of democratic traditions in this hemisphere, and *a country we are proud to call our own.*"[191]

American leaders also sought to direct events in postwar Italy and Asia. They essentially excluded the Soviets from the Italian surrender agreement in 1943 and denied them a role in the control commission. Some American officials recognized that Italy, where predominant power rested in American hands, set a precedent for later Soviet predominance in Rumania and Hungary. American officials also insisted on holding the conquered Japanese islands in the Pacific and in unilaterally governing Japan itself. "You're dead right in believing that after this war's over the sentiment of the people will be in favor of having what the government thinks will be enough to maintain our power in the Pacific," Secretary of War Henry L. Stimson told a congressman.[192] Washington also anticipated Chiang's China as an ally in this area of enlarged American influence.

In the Middle East the United States also expanded. In 1939 the Arabian-American Oil Company (Aramco) began to tap their 440,000-square mile concession in Saudi Arabia's rich oil fields. By 1944 American corporations controlled 42 percent of the proved oil reserves of the Middle East, a nineteenfold increase since 1936. In 1944, American companies, with Washington's encouragement, applied for an oil concession in Iran, then occupied by British and Soviet troops and used as a corridor for Lend-Lease shipments to Russia. This request touched off a three-cornered competition for influence in the heretofore British-dominated country. When Roosevelt informed Churchill in 1944 that the United States did not intend to deprive the British of their traditional stakes in the Middle East, the Prime Minister tartly replied: "Thank you very much for your assurances about no sheeps' eyes at our oil fields in Iran and Iraq. Let me reciprocate by giving you fullest assurance that we have no thought of trying to horn in upon your interests or property in Saudi Arabia."[193]

On a global scale, then, the Big Three jockeyed for power and influence. "Spheres of influence do in fact exist," concluded the State Department in early 1945, "and will probably continue to do so for some time to come. . . . In view of the actual Eastern European sphere and the Western Hemispheric bloc (Act of Chapultepec), we are hardly in a position to frown upon the establishment of measures designed to strengthen the security of nations in other areas of the world." Unfortunately, "such measures represent power politics pure and simple."[194] The Atlantic Charter had not restrained the Allies from reaching for postwar spheres of influence in their wartime diplomacy. Therein lay growing fissures in Big Three relations.

With Germany's surrender on May 8, 1945 the Third Reich collapsed in the rubble of bombed-out Berlin. President Truman quickly ended Lend-Lease aid to Russia (he soon partially restarted it), thereby stirring up a "hornets nest" in Moscow, which interpreted the abrupt cutback as diplomatic pressure.[195] With this issue and the Polish question troubling Soviet-American relations, the President sent Harry Hopkins to see Stalin in May, to "use diplomatic language or a baseball bat," as Truman later recalled.[196] The Russians, said the President, "were like people from across the tracks whose manners were very bad."[197] Hopkins chose diplomatic language when he met an irate Stalin. The Marshal told the special envoy that the sudden Lend-Lease cessation had been "brutal": "If the refusal to continue Lend-Lease was designed as pressure on the Russians in order to soften them up," lectured Stalin, "then it was a fundamental mistake."[198] Hopkins denied that the United States practiced economic coercion, and warned that Americans were growing restive about Russia's failure to carry out the Yalta agreement on Poland—a symbol of Soviet-American trust. Stalin frankly explained why he could not permit the anti-Soviet London group, who would probably have won free elections, to govern postwar Poland:[199]

> In the course of twenty-five years the Germans had twice invaded Russia via Poland. Neither the British nor American people had experienced such German invasions which were a horrible thing to endure and the results of which were not easily forgotten. . . . Poland has served as a corridor for the German attacks on Russia. . . . It is therefore in Russia's vital interest that Poland should be both strong and friendly.

Ambassador Harriman reported to Truman that Stalin could not "understand why we should want to interfere with Soviet policy in a country like Poland, which he considers so important to Russia's security, unless we have some ulterior motive."[200] Hopkins got the Marshal to budge a little. Stalin agreed that a handful of ministries should rest in the hands of non-Lublin Poles. He also promised Hopkins, as at Yalta, that Russia would enter the war against Japan and respect Chiang's government in China. Overall, Truman was pleased that Russia had attempted to conciliate American wishes, but he desired to break up the developing Soviet sphere of influence and to consolidate American interests.

## Triumph and Tragedy: Potsdam and the Legacy of World War II

When the Big Three gathered in Berlin for the Potsdam Conference (July 16–August 2, 1945), the war in Asia was nearing an end, and the reconstruction of Germany was an immediate reality. Sir Alexander Cadogan described the Berlin environs as a "staggering sight. . . . I don't think it could ever be rebuilt."[201] During the conference, Truman wrote his family that "you never saw such pig-headed people as are the Russians."[202] As for Stalin, "I thought he was an S.O.B.," Truman said after the meeting. "But, of course, I guess he thinks I'm one, too."[203] Gone indeed was the special personal relationship between Roosevelt and Stalin. Truman had come to make final decisions, and, like his advisers, he grew impatient with the Russians. Admiral Leahy thought Stalin "a liar and a crook," and Harriman called the Russians "those barbarians."[204] Churchill, who would leave the conference after the defeat of his Conservative party in British elections (Clement Attlee replaced him), fiddled with his cigars and grunted throughout the sessions. But he took a liking to the new President, whom he described as a "man of exceptional character and ability with . . . simple and direct methods of speech, and a great deal of self-confidence and resolution."[205] Some of that resolution at Potsdam derived from the news Truman learned on the second day of the conference: the successful explosion of an atomic device on July 16 in New Mexico.

By the time of Potsdam, American policy toward postwar Germany had moved a good distance from the Morgenthau Plan and JSC/1067, toward a policy of reconstruction. Germany was now seen by many American officials as a vital link in the economic recovery of Western Europe. Thus, when Germany came up for discussion, Truman resisted dismemberment and large reparations. The final Potsdam accord stated that Germany was to be managed by military governors in each of the four zones, treated as "a single economic unit," and permitted a standard of living higher than its low level of 1945.[206] Transportation, coal, agriculture, housing, and utilities industries were to be rehabilitated. As for reparations, desired by Russia for both revenge and the recovery of its hobbled economy, the United States refused to set a firm figure until Germany's ability to pay was determined. In defense of the American position, Truman recalled the post-World War I reparations tangle. Stalin protested, but all he could get was an agreement that each nation should take reparations from its own zone and that Russia would get some reparations in industrial equipment from the Western zones. In return for the latter Russia would send food to the other three zones. The reparations issue, postponed once at Yalta, was essentially postponed again. The result was, as diplomat George F. Kennan put it, "catch as catch can."[207]

The conferees tangled over Poland. Every time Churchill complained about the absence of free elections in Poland, Stalin mentioned the British domination of Greece. They did agree, however, to set the Oder-Neisse line as Poland's temporary western boundary, thereby granting Poland large chunks of German territory. The Soviet Union agreed to accept Italy as a member of the United Nations. The big powers also established the Council of Foreign Ministers to continue discussion on issues not resolved at Potsdam: peace treaties for the former German satellites; the withdrawal of Allied troops from Iran; postwar control of the Dardanelles; internationalization of inland waterways; and the disposition of Italian colonies. Stalin promised again to enter the war against Japan, although American leaders were less eager about that with the atomic bomb looming as a major weapon. Finally Britain and the United States issued the "Potsdam Declaration" to Japan, demanding unconditional surrender and threatening it with destruction.

The seemingly minor issue of waterways illustrated the tension at Potsdam and became for Truman a test of Soviet intentions. At the conference he pushed for an international authority to govern the eighteen-hundred-mile long Danube River, which wound its way through several countries, including Russia, to the Black Sea. Essentially a combination of two traditional American principles—free navigation and the Open Door—the proposal antagonized the Russians. They countered with a commission limited to riparian states. For Russia the Danube was analogous to America's Panama Canal and Britain's Suez Canal. When Churchill backed Truman on the question, Molotov pressed: "If it was such a good rule why not apply it to the Suez?"[208] Churchill evaded the comparison, and Truman fumed when his personal appeal to Stalin for acceptance of an internationalized Danube was rebuffed. In his *Memoirs* the President drew an exaggerated conclusion. Stalin's attitude on waterways "showed how his mind worked and what he was after. . . . The Russians were planning world conquest."[209] Former State Department official and historian Herbert Feis has written: "History hints that what is done during the first few months after a great war ends is likely to determine the fate of the next generation."[210] The Potsdam Conference demonstrated that.

Potsdam, aptly code-named TERMINAL, left the world much as it had found it—divided and devastated. World War II officially ended on August 14, 1945. Japanese officials surrendered aboard the battleship *Missouri* on September 2. But peace remained elusive, in large part because of the troubling legacy of the war: the vast social, economic, and political dislocations in Europe and Asia. Thirty-five million Europeans had died during the conflict, between fifteen and twenty million of them Russians. The Soviet government's bold machinations in Poland, and call for heavy German reparations, could be partly explained by that tragedy. A generation of young European people in their twenties and thirties had been virtually eliminated. Millions of displaced persons were sadly separated from their homelands. Transportation systems and communications networks were destroyed. Factories were bombed out. Cities were reduced to ashes, including the German city of Dresden, which Allied planes had punished in February, 1945, in a merciless attack of questionable necessity. Parts of Asia also lay in ruins. Tokyo had been fire-bombed, leaving 100,000 dead. China was badly mauled, and faced a civil war. These wrenching effects of the war confronted postwar diplomats with incomparable reconstruction problems, and leftist politicians challenged discredited, but still entrenched, elites.

With the imperial powers in disarray, their colonies, long yearning for the moment and in Asia encouraged by Japan during the waning days of the war, became rebellious. Unable to apply the necessary resources and manpower to curb the nationalist revolutions, the European empires began to crumble. The Dutch battled their Indonesian subjects; France fought the Vietnamese in French Indochina; Britain reluctantly began its exit from Burma, India, and Ceylon.

The rise of Soviet Russia as a major international player was another result of World War II. The "greatest crime of Hitler," said Ambassador Harriman, was that his defeat opened parts of Europe to Russian influence.[211] Russia insisted on being treated as an equal and resented any intimation that it should not have an

**Bombed-out French Town, 1944.** Europe lay in ruins at the end of the war and American help seemed essential to the reconstruction effort. (U.S. Office of War Information, National Archives)

influential voice in postwar questions. Reeling from its heavy wartime losses and facing massive reconstruction tasks, Russia asked for much and grabbed what it could before the war ended. "You know we have never been accepted in European councils on a basis of equality," Maxim Litvinov complained. "We were always outsiders."[212] Never again.

Russia rose, Britain fell, China floundered, and the United States galloped. Its economy, the "arsenal of democracy," untouched by enemy bombers or marauding armies, was in high gear at war's end. The American gross national product jumped from $88.6 billion in 1939 to $198.7 billion five years later. Observers spoke of an American "production miracle."[213] One Englishman resentfully penned a poem:[214]

> In Washington Lord Halifax
> Once whispered to Lord Keynes:
> "It's true *they* have the money bags
> But *we* have all the brains."

A British Foreign Office diplomat complained that "we shall have to suffer from American arrogance."[215] As the unsurpassed economic leader of the world, alone in a position to provide the capital and goods for recovery abroad, Washington was flushed with power. Imbibing lessons from the 1930s about the need to avoid Munichs, Americans looked forward to shaping a world of peace and prosperity. With greatly increased power, the United States seemed capable of creating the stable world order that had eluded it between the two world wars. State Department official Dean Acheson observed that the "great difference in our second attempt to establish a peaceful world is the wide recognition that peace is possible only if countries work together and prosper together. That is why the economic aspects are no less important than the political aspects of the peace."[216] Through the war years the United States had constructed institutions—UNRRA, World Bank, International Monetary Fund, United Nations—to insure that peace. Despite this attraction to international organizations, the United States pursued its traditional unilateralism as well, especially in Latin America.

The war also wrought changes in the foreign affairs decisionmaking process in the United States. As Richard Barnet has put it, the United States underwent a "bureaucratic revolution."[217] Agencies in the government handling national security matters ballooned in size. The defense establishment became more active in making diplomatic choices. In comparison, the State Department, so frequently bypassed by President Roosevelt, slipped in power. The war spawned a large espionage establishment, beginning with the Office of Strategic Services (OSS) in 1941 and culminating in the Central Intelligence Agency (CIA) six years later. The President as Commander-in-Chief centralized decisionmaking in the White House, while Congress gave up its foreign affairs prerogatives in the constitutional system and applauded bipartisanship. "War had accustomed those in charge of foreign policy to a complacent faith in the superior intelligence and disinterestedness of the executive branch," historian Arthur M. Schlesinger, Jr. has noted.[218] Another consequence of the war was the enlargement of what came to be called the "military-industrial complex," a partnership between businessmen eager for lucrative defense contracts and military men eager for increased budgets. A bureaucratic momentum of defense spending grew from this relationship. Universities, which had been recruited during the war, were not left untouched by it.

Professors of the sciences had developed the atomic bomb at the universities of Chicago and California, Berkeley. "The universities transformed themselves into vast weapons development laboratories," the editor of *Scientific American* concluded.[219] Postwar federal subsidies flowed to colleges not only for arms development, but also for research on Russian studies and intelligence gathering. These lasting changes wrought by the experiences of World War II were not easily identifiable in 1945; their impact would be measured in the immediate future as the Allies struggled to transform their military victory into a stable peace.

## Further Reading for the Period 1939–1945

For general accounts of American foreign policy and Allied relations during World War II, see James M. Burns, *Roosevelt: The Soldier of Freedom* (1970), Winston S. Churchill, *Second World War* (1948–1953), Robert A. Divine, *Roosevelt and World War II* (1969), Herbert Feis, *Churchill, Roosevelt, Stalin* (1957), Victor Israelian, *The Anti-Hitler Coalition* (1971), Gabriel Kolko, *The Politics of War* (1968), Ralph B. Levering, *American Opinion and the Russian Alliance* (1976), William H. McNeill, *America, Britain, and Russia* (1953), William L. Neumann, *After Victory* (1967), Robert E. Sherwood, *Roosevelt and Hopkins* (1948), Gaddis Smith, *American Diplomacy During the Second World War* (1965), and John L. Snell, *Illusion and Necessity* (1963).

American diplomacy toward Europe, 1939–1941, is recounted in Patrick Abbazia, *Mr. Roosevelt's Navy: The Private War of the Atlantic Fleet, 1939–1942* (1975), Mark Chadwin, *The Hawks of World War II* (1968), Wayne S. Cole, *America First: The Battle Against Intervention* (1953), James V. Compton, *The Swastika and the Eagle* (1967), R. H. Dawson, *The Decision to Aid Russia, 1941* (1959), Robert A. Divine, *The Reluctant Belligerent* (1965), Saul Friedlander, *Prelude to Downfall: Hitler and the United States, 1939–1941* (1967), Warren F. Kimball, *The Most Unsordid Act: Lend-Lease, 1939–1941* (1969), William L. Langer and S. Everett Gleason, *The Challenge to Isolation, 1937–1940* (1952), Arnold A. Offner, *The Origins of the Second World War* (1975), and Theodore A. Wilson, *The First Summit: Roosevelt and Churchill at Placentia Bay, 1941* (1969).

For the advent of war with Japan, see Dorothy Borg and Shumpei Okomoto, eds., *Pearl Harbor as History: Japanese-American Relations, 1931–1941* (1973), Richard Dean Burns and Edward M. Bennett, eds., *Diplomats in Crisis* (1974), Robert J. C. Butow, *Tojo and the Coming of the War* (1961) and *The John Doe Associates: Backdoor Diplomacy for Peace, 1941* (1974), Herbert Feis, *The Road to Pearl Harbor* (1950), Samuel Eliot Morison, *The Rising Sun in the Pacific* (1973), Charles Neu, *The Troubled Encounter* (1975), Bruce M. Russett, *No Clear and Present Danger: A Skeptical View of the U.S. Entry into World War II* (1972), Paul W. Schroeder, *The Axis Alliance and Japanese-American Relations, 1941* (1958), Charles C. Tansill, *Back Door to War* (1952), and Roberta Wohlstetter, *Pearl Harbor: Warning and Decision* (1962).

Wartime diplomacy and strategy are discussed in Stephen Ambrose, *The Supreme Commander* (1970), Robert Beitzell, *The Uneasy Alliance: America, Britain, and Russia, 1941–1943* (1972), A. Russell Buchanan, *The United States and World War II* (1964), Thomas M. Campbell, *Masquerade Peace: America's UN Policy, 1944–1945* (1973), Diane Shaver Clemens, *Yalta* (1970), Robert A. Divine, *Second Chance: The Triumph of Internationalism in America During World War II* (1967), Herbert Feis, *Between War and Peace: The Potsdam Conference* (1960), Kent R. Greenfield, *American Strategy in World War II* (1963), George C. Herring, Jr., *Aid to Russia, 1941–1946* (1973),

William Langer, *Our Vichy Gamble* (1947), Samuel Eliot Morison, *Strategy and Compromise* (1958), Raymond G. O'Connor, *Diplomacy for Victory: FDR and Unconditional Surrender* (1971), Elmer Potter, *Nimitz* (1976), John L. Snell, ed., *The Meaning of Yalta* (1956), Richard W. Steele, *The First Offensive, 1942* (1973), and Llewellyn Woodward, *British Foreign Policy in the Second World War* (1970–1971).

Sino-American relations during the Second World War are treated in David D. Barrett, *Dixie Mission* (1970), Russell D. Buhite, *Patrick J. Hurley and American Foreign Policy* (1973), Warren I. Cohen, *America's Response to China* (1971), John Paton Davies, *Dragon By the Tail* (1972), Herbert Feis, *The China Tangle* (1953), E. J. Kahn, Jr., *The China Hands* (1975), Tang Tsou, *America's Failure in China, 1941–1950* (1963), and Barbara Tuchman, *Stillwell and the American Experience in China, 1911–1945* (1971).

For wartime politics, see Robert A. Divine, *Foreign Policy and U.S. Presidential Elections, 1940–1948* (1974) and for wartime planning for postwar defense, see Michael S. Sherry, *Preparing for the Next War* (1977).

Among the numerous biographical studies are John M. Blum, ed., *From the Morgenthau Diaries* (1959–1972) and *The Price of Vision: The Diary of Henry A. Wallace, 1942–1946* (1973), Waldo H. Heinrichs, *American Ambassador: Joseph C. Grew and the Development of the United States Diplomatic Tradition* (1966), Warren Kimball, "Churchill and Roosevelt: The Personal Equation," *Prologue* (1974), Joseph P. Lash, *Roosevelt and Churchill, 1939–1941* (1976), Elting E. Morison, *Turmoil and Tradition: The Life and Times of Henry L. Stimson* (1960), Forrest C. Pogue, *George C. Marshall* (1963–1973), and Edward R. Stettinius, Jr., *Roosevelt and the Russians* (1949). For short biographies see John A. Garraty, ed., *Encyclopedia of American Biography* (1974).

The sad chronicle of American diplomacy and the refugee problem is recounted in Henry L. Feingold, *Politics of Rescue* (1970), Saul S. Friedman, *No Haven for the Oppressed* (1973), Arthur D. Morse, *While Six Million Died* (1968), Arnold Offner, *American Appeasement* (1964), and David Wyman, *Paper Walls* (1968).

For representative essays and a bibliography, see Warren Kimball, ed., *Franklin Roosevelt and the World Crisis, 1937–1945* (1973). Other works are listed in Wilton B. Fowler, ed., *American Diplomatic History since 1890* (1975) and E. David Cronon and Theodore D. Rosenof, eds., *The Second World War and the Atomic Age, 1940–1973* (1975).

Also see the following notes.

## Notes to Chapter 11

1. Quoted in Theodore A. Wilson, *The First Summit: Roosevelt and Churchill at Placentia Bay, 1941* (Boston: Houghton Mifflin, 1969), p. 109.

2. H. V. Morton quoted *ibid.*, p. 84.

3. Elliott Roosevelt, *As He Saw It* (New York: Duell, Sloan, and Pearce, 1946), p. 33.

4. Winston S. Churchill, *The Grand Alliance* (Boston: Houghton Mifflin, 1950), p. 431.

5. Quoted in Robert E. Sherwood, *Roosevelt and Hopkins* (New York: Harper and Brothers, 1948), p. 236.

6. Francis L. Loewenheim, Harold D. Langley, and Manfred Jonas, eds., *Roosevelt and Churchill: Their Secret Wartime Correspondence* (New York: Saturday Review Press/E. P. Dutton, 1975), p. 155.

7. Harold Nicolson, *Diaries and Letters: The War Years, 1939–1945* (New York: Atheneum, 1966–1968; 3 vols.), II, 385.

8. Quoted in Warren F. Kimball, "Churchill and Roosevelt: The Personal Equation," *Prologue*, VI (Fall, 1974), 179.

9. Quoted in Forrest C. Pogue, *George C. Marshall: Ordeal and Hope, 1939–1942* (New York: Viking Press, 1963–1973; 3 vols.), II, 46.

10. Quoted in Robert A. Divine, *Roosevelt and World War II* (Baltimore: The Johns Hopkins University Press, 1969), p. 44.

11. Quoted in Raymond Esthus, "President Roosevelt's Commitment to Britain to Intervene in a Pacific War," *Mississippi Valley Historical Review, L* (June, 1963), 31.

12. David Dilks, ed., *The Diaries of Sir Alexander Cadogan, 1938–1945* (New York: G. P. Putnam's Sons, 1971), p. 399.

13. Cordell Hull, *Memoirs* (New York: Macmillan, 1948; 2 vols.), II, 975–976.

14. For the Atlantic Charter text, see *Foreign Relations, 1941* (Washington, D.C.: Government Printing Office, 1958), I, 368–369.

15. James MacGregor Burns, *Roosevelt: The Soldier of Freedom* (New York: Harcourt Brace Jovanovich, 1970), p. 550.

16. Quoted *ibid.*, p. 129.

17. Llewellyn Woodward, *British Foreign Policy in the Second World War* (London: Her Majesty's Stationary Office, 1970–1971; 3 vols.), II, 204.

18. *Foreign Relations, 1941, I*, 378.

19. Quoted in William H. McNeill, *America, Britain, & Russia: Their Co-operation and Conflict, 1941–1946* (London: Oxford University Press, 1953), p. 41.

20. Quoted in Anthony Eden, *The Reckoning: Memoirs* (Boston: Houghton Mifflin, 1965), p. 343.

21. Quoted in Burns, *Soldier of Freedom*, p. 609.

22. Quoted in Wilson, *First Summit*, p. 260.

23. Quoted *ibid.*, p. 210.

24. Eden, *The Reckoning*, p. 433.

25. Samuel I. Rosenman, ed., *Public Papers and Addresses of Franklin D. Roosevelt, 1939* (New York: Macmillan, 1938–1950; 13 vols.), VIII, 463.

26. Divine, *Roosevelt and World War II*, p. 37.

27. *Congressional Record, LXXIV* (October 4, 1939), 98.

28. Quoted in John M. Blum, *From the Morgenthau Diaries: Years of Urgency, 1938–1941* (Boston: Houghton Mifflin, 1965), p. 91.

29. Quoted in Patrick Abbazia, *Mr. Roosevelt's Navy: The Private War of the U.S. Atlantic Fleet, 1939–1942* (Annapolis: Naval Institute Press, 1975), p. 142.

30. Rosenman, *Public Papers, 1940, IX*, 263.

31. Quoted in John G. Clifford, "Grenville Clark and the Origins of Selective Service," *Review of Politics, XXXV* (January, 1973), 31–32.

32. Rosenman, *Public Papers, 1940, IX*, 391.

33. Winston S. Churchill, *Their Finest Hour* (Boston: Houghton Mifflin, 1949), p. 404.

34. Quoted in Robert A. Divine, *Foreign Policy and U.S. Presidential Elections, 1940–1948* (New York: New Viewpoints, 1974), pp. 82–83.

35. Loewenheim *et al.*, *Roosevelt and Churchill*, p. 125.

36. Rosenman, *Public Papers, 1940, IX*, 607.

37. *Ibid.*, pp. 640–643.

38. Quoted in George C. Herring, Jr., *Aid to Russia, 1941–1946: Strategy, Diplomacy, and the Origins of the Cold War* (New York: Columbia University Press, 1973), p. 4.

39. Quoted in Warren F. Kimball, *The Most Unsordid Act: Lend-Lease, 1939–1941* (Baltimore: Johns Hopkins Press, 1969), p. 154 and Rosenman, *Public Papers, 1940, IX*, 711–712.

40. Quoted in Kimball, *Most Unsordid Act*, p. 153.

41. *Congressional Record, LXXVII* (March 8, 1941), 2097.

42. Quoted in Herring, *Aid to Russia*, p. 5.

43. Quoted in Blum, *From the Morgenthau Diaries: Years of Urgency*, p. 251.

44. Quoted in Elting E. Morison, *Turmoil and Tradition: A Study of the Life and Times of Henry L. Stimson* (Boston: Houghton Mifflin, 1960), p. 429.

45. *New York Times*, July 24, 1941.

46. Churchill, *Grand Alliance*, p. 370.

47. Quoted in Blum, *From the Morgenthau Diaries: Years of Urgency*, p. 264.

48. August 19, 1941, CAB 65/19, War Cabinet Records 84, Public Record Office, London, England (from the notes of Walter LaFeber).

49. Rosenman, *Public Papers, 1941, X*, 438, 439.

50. Quoted in Wayne S. Cole, *America First: The Battle against Intervention, 1940–1941* (Madison: University of Wisconsin Press, 1953), p. 163.

51. Quoted in William L. Langer and S. Everett Gleason, *The Undeclared War, 1940–1941* (New York: Harper and Brothers, 1953), p. 760.

52. Richard W. Steele, *The First Offensive, 1942: Roosevelt, Marshall, and the Making of American Strategy* (Bloomington: Indiana University Press, 1973), p. 47.

53. Sherwood, *Roosevelt and Hopkins*, p. 383.

54. Quoted in Edward M. Bennett, "Joseph C. Grew: The Diplomacy of Pacification," in Richard Dean Burns and Edward M. Bennett, eds., *Diplomats in Crisis: United States-Chinese-Japanese Relations, 1919–1941* (Santa Barbara, Cal.: ABC-CLIO, 1974), p. 78.

55. Herbert Feis, *The Road to Pearl Harbor* (New York: Atheneum, 1967), p. 17.

56. Harold L. Ickes, *The Secret Diary of Harold L. Ickes: The Lowering Clouds* (New York: Simon and Schuster, 1953; 3 vols.), III, 567.

57. Quoted in Waldo H. Heinrichs, *American Ambassador: Joseph C. Grew and the Development of the United States Diplomatic Tradition* (Boston: Little, Brown, 1966), p. 320.

58. Quoted in Charles E. Neu, *The Troubled Encounter: The United States and Japan* (New York: John Wiley and Sons, 1975), p. 168.

59. Barbara Teters, "Yosuke Matsuoka: The Diplomacy of Bluff and Gesture," in Burns and Bennett, eds., *Diplomats in Crisis*, p. 288.

60. Quoted in Asada Sadao, "The Japanese Navy and the United States," in Dorothy Borg and Shumpei Okamoto, eds., *Pearl Harbor as History: Japanese-American Relations, 1931–1941* (New York: Columbia University Press, 1973), p. 248.

61. *Foreign Relations of the United States, 1940* (Washington: Government Printing Office, 1955), IV, 602.

62. Neu, *Troubled Encounter*, p. 175.

63. Quoted in Arnold A. Offner, *The Origins of the Second World War* (New York: Praeger, 1975), p. 193.

64. Quoted in Hilary Conroy, "Nomura Kichisaburo: The Diplomacy of Drama and Desperation," in Burns and Bennett, eds., *Diplomats in Crisis*, pp. 300–301.

65. Robert J. C. Butow, "Backdoor Diplomacy in the Pacific: The Proposal for a Konoye-Roosevelt Meeting in 1941," *Journal of American History, XXXIX* (June, 1972), 59.

66. Quoted in Feis, *Road to Pearl Harbor*, p. 206.

67. *Ibid.*, p. 244.

68. Ickes, *Secret Diary*, III, 346.

69. Quoted in James C. Thomson, Jr., "The Role of the Department of State," in Borg and Okamoto, eds., *Pearl Harbor as History*, p. 101.

70. Quoted in Feis, *Road to Pearl Harbor*, p. 321.

71. Bruce M. Russett, *No Clear and Present Danger: A Skeptical View of the U.S. Entry into World War II* (New York: Harper and Row, 1972), p. 55.

72. Quoted in Neu, *Troubled Encounter*, p. 187.

73. Quoted in Samuel Eliot Morison, *The Rising Sun in the Pacific: 1931–April 1942* (Boston: Little, Brown, 1948), p. 46.

74. Sherwood, *Roosevelt and Hopkins*, p. 434.

75. For example, Charles C. Tansill, *Back Door to War* (Chicago: Henry Regnery, 1952).

76. Roberta Wohlstetter, *Pearl Harbor: Warning and Decision* (Stanford: Stanford University Press, 1962), p. 387.

77. Morison, *Rising Sun*, p. 132.

78. Rosenman, *Public Papers, 1941*, X, 514.

79. Arthur H. Vandenberg, Jr., ed., *The Private Papers of Senator Vandenberg* (Boston: Houghton Mifflin, 1952), p. 1.

80. Samuel E. Morison, *Strategy and Compromise* (Boston: Little, Brown, 1958), p. 25.

81. Memorandum of Conversation with Cordell Hull, September 29, 1944, "Black Notebooks," Box 1, Arthur Krock Papers, Princeton University Library.

82. Charles E. Bohlen, *Witness to History, 1929–1969* (New York: W. W. Norton, 1973), p. 129.

83. Quoted in Geoffrey Perrett, *Days of Sadness, Years of Triumph: The American People, 1939–1945* (Baltimore: Penguin, 1973), p. 197.

84. Saul Friedlander, *Prelude to Downfall: Hitler and the United States, 1939–1941* (New York: Alfred A. Knopf, 1967), p. 161.

85. Quoted in Kimball, "Churchill and Roosevelt," p. 181.

86. Winston S. Churchill, *Triumph and Tragedy* (Boston: Houghton Mifflin, 1953), p. 338.

87. Eden, *The Reckoning*, pp. 336–337.

88. Alfred D. Chandler, *et al.*, eds., *The Papers of Dwight David Eisenhower: The War Years* (Baltimore: The Johns Hopkins Press, 1970; 5 vols.), I, 66.

89. Quoted in Sherwood, *Roosevelt and Hopkins*, p. 563.

90. Quoted in Herbert Feis, *Churchill, Roosevelt, Stalin* (Princeton: Princeton University Press, 1957), p. 42.

91. Quoted in Harry C. Butcher, *My Three Years with Eisenhower* (New York: Simon and Schuster, 1946), p. 29.

92. Quoted in Arthur Bryant, *Triumph in the West, 1943–1946* (London: Collins, 1959), p. 78.

93. Quoted in Ivan Maisky, *Memoirs of a Soviet Ambassador: The War, 1939–1943* (New York: Charles Scribner's Sons, 1968), p. 276.

94. Quoted in Morison, *Strategy and Compromise*, p. 51.

95. *Correspondence between the Chairman of the Council of Ministers of the U.S.S.R. and the Presidents of the U.S.A. and the Prime Ministers of Great Britain during the Great Patriotic War of 1941–1945* (Moscow: Foreign Languages Publishing House, 1957; 2 vols.), II, 70–71.

96. Quoted in Robert Beitzell, *The Uneasy Alliance: America, Britain, and Russia, 1941–1943* (New York: Alfred A. Knopf, 1972), p. 159.

97. Winston S. Churchill, *The Hinge of Fate* (Boston: Houghton Mifflin, 1950), p. 759.

98. Quoted in Raymond G. O'Connor, *Diplomacy for Victory: FDR and Unconditional Surrender* (New York: W. W. Norton, 1971), p. 52.

99. "Memorandum of Conversation with Cordell Hull," November 30, 1943, "Black Notebooks," Box 1, Arthur Krock Papers, Princeton University Library, Princeton, New Jersey.

100. Hull, *Memoirs*, II, 1297.

101. Robert Murphy, *Diplomat Among Warriors* (Garden City: Doubleday, 1964), p. 208.

102. Hull, *Memoirs*, II, 1314–1315.

103. Kimball, "Churchill and Roosevelt," p. 179.

104. Quoted in Roosevelt, *As He Saw It*, p. 176.

105. Henry H. Arnold, *Global Mission* (New York: Harper and Brothers, 1949), p. 465.

106. *Foreign Relations of the United States: The Conferences at Cairo and Teheran, 1943* (Washington, D.C.: Government Printing Office, 1961), p. 539.

107. Churchill, *Hinge of Fate*, p. 374.

108. Quoted in Pogue, *Marshall: Organizer of Victory, 1943–1945*, III, 313.

109. Quoted in Beitzell, *Uneasy Alliance*, p. 348.

110. *Foreign Relations, Cairo and Teheran*, pp. 594–595.

111. Churchill, *Hinge of Fate*, p. 401.

112. Quoted in Burns, *Roosevelt: Soldier of Freedom*, p. 411.

113. *Foreign Relations, Cairo and Teheran*, pp. 583, 585 and Bohlen, *Witness to History*, p. 149.

114. Rosenman, *Public Papers, 1943*, XII, 558.

115. Churchill, *Hinge of Fate*, p. 133.

116. Warren I. Cohen, *America's Response to China: An Interpretive History of Sino-American Relations* (New York: John Wiley and Sons, 1971), p. 157.

117. Quoted in Jonathan Spence, *To Change China: Western Advisers in China, 1620–1960* (Boston: Little, Brown, 1969), p. 236 and in Christopher Thorne, "Indochina and Anglo-American Relations, 1942–1945," *Pacific Historical Review*, XLIV (February, 1976), 76.

118. Theodore H. White, ed., *The Stilwell Papers* (New York: William Sloane Associates, 1948), p. 157.

119. Quoted in Akira Iriye, "The United States as an Asian-Pacific Power," in Gene T. Hsiao, ed., *Sino-American Détente and Its Policy Implications* (New York: Praeger, 1974), p. 12.

120. Quoted in Herbert Feis, *The China Tangle: The American Effort in China from Pearl Harbor to the Marshall Mission* (Princeton: Princeton University Press, 1953), p. 51.

121. Quoted in Burns, *Roosevelt: Soldier of Freedom*, p. 377.

122. Cohen, *America's Response to China*, p. 162.

123. Quoted in Charles F. Romanus and Riley Sunderland, *Stilwell's Mission to China* (Washington, D.C.: Department of the Army, 1953), p. 253.

124. White, ed., *Stilwell Papers*, p. 333.

125. *Foreign Relations of the United States, 1944* (Washington, D.C.: Government Printing Office, 1967), VI, 631–632.

126. David D. Barrett, *Dixie Mission: The United States Army Observer Group in Yenan, 1944* (Berkeley: University of California China Research Monographs, 1970), p. 56.

127. Quoted in John Paton Davies, Jr., *Dragon by the Tail* (New York: W. W. Norton, 1972), p. 381.

128. Quoted in Feis, *China Tangle*, p. 213.

129. Quoted in Russell D. Buhite, *Patrick J. Hurley and American Foreign Policy* (Ithaca: Cornell University Press, 1973), p. 152.

130. Quoted in Barbara W. Tuchman, "If Mao Had Come to Washington: An Essay in Alternatives," *Foreign Affairs*, L (October, 1972), 44.

131. Quoted in Davies, *Dragon by the Tail*, p. 386.

132. Quoted in Feis, *China Tangle*, p. 269.

133. Burns, *Roosevelt: Soldier of Freedom*, p. 545.

134. Quoted in Moshe Gottlieb, "The Berlin Riots and Their Repercussions in America," *American Jewish Historical Quarterly*, LIX (March, 1970), 306.

135. Quoted in Cyrus Adler and Aaron M. Margalith, *With Firmness in the Right: American Diplomatic Action Affecting Jews, 1840–1945* (New York: American Jewish Committee, 1946), p. 381.

136. Quoted in Saul S. Friedman, *No Haven for the Oppressed: United States Policy Toward Jewish Refugees, 1938–1945* (Detroit: Wayne State University Press, 1973), p. 21.

137. Quoted in Robert A. Divine, *American Immigration Policy, 1924–1952* (New Haven: Yale University Press, 1957), p. 98.

138. Quoted in James MacGregor Burns, *Roosevelt: The Lion and the Fox* (New York: Harcourt, Brace and World, 1956), p. 339.

139. Arnold A. Offner, *American Appeasement: United States Foreign Policy and Germany, 1933–1938* (New York: W. W. Norton, 1976 [c. 1969]), p. 92.

140. Quoted in Henry L. Feingold, *Politics of Rescue: The Roosevelt Administration and the Holocaust, 1938–1945* (New Brunswick, N.J.: Rutgers University Press, 1970), p. 19.

141. Quoted in Friedman, *No Haven*, p. 83.

142. Quoted *ibid.*, p. 103.

143. Quoted in Irwin F. Gellman, "The *St. Louis* Tragedy," *American Jewish Historical Quarterly*, LXI (December, 1971), 156.

144. Quoted in A. J. Sherman, *Island Refuge: Britain and Refugees from the Third Reich, 1933–1939* (Berkeley: University of California Press, 1973), p. 207.

145. Peter Calvocoressi and Guy Wint, *Total War: The Story of World War II* (New York: Pantheon Books, 1972), p. 238.

146. Quoted in Arthur D. Morse, *While Six Million Died: A Chronicle of American Apathy* (New York: Random House, 1968), p. 63.

147. Quoted *ibid.*, pp. 93, 95.

148. Cordell Hull, *Memoirs* (New York: Macmillan, 1948; 2 vols.), II, 1540.

149. Quoted in George Woodbridge *et al.*, *The History of the United Nations Relief and Rehabilitation Administration* (New York: Columbia University Press, 1950; 3 vols.), I, 4.

150. Francis B. Sayre in *Department of State Bulletin*, IX (October 23, 1943), 275.

151. U.S. Department of State, *Treaties and Other International Acts* (Washington, D.C.: Government Printing Office, 1946), series 1501–1502.

152. Quoted in Thomas G. Paterson, *Soviet-American Confrontation: Postwar Reconstruction and the Origins of the Cold War* (Baltimore: The Johns Hopkins University Press, 1973), p. 147.

153. Quoted in Richard N. Gardner, *Sterling-Dollar Diplomacy: The Origins and the Prospects of Our International Economic Order* (New York: McGraw-Hill, 1969; rev. ed.), p. 267.

154. Quoted in Diane Shaver Clemens, *Yalta* (New York: Oxford University Press, 1970), p. 48.

155. Quoted in Robert A. Divine, *Second Chance: The Triumph of Internationalism in America During World War II* (New York: Atheneum, 1967), p. 226.

156. Quoted in Thomas M. Campbell, *Masquerade Peace: America's UN Policy, 1944–1945* (Tallahassee: Florida State University Press, 1973), p. 22.

157. Quoted in Divine, *Second Chance*, p. 229.

158. Diary entry of May 11, 1944 in Gabriel Kolko, *The Politics of War* (New York: Random House, 1968), pp. 270–271.

159. *Foreign Relations of the United States, 1945* (Washington, D.C.: Government Printing Office, 1967), V, 253.

160. Vandenberg, *Private Papers*, p. 176.

161. Quoted in Divine, *Second Chance*, p. 290.

162. Quoted *ibid.*, p. 291.

163. Quoted *ibid.*, p. 297.

164. Quoted in Kolko, *Politics of War*, p. 470.

165. Tom Connally, *My Name Is Tom Connally* (New York: Thomas Y. Crowell, 1954), p. 286.

166. Arnold Wolfers, *United States Policy toward Germany* (New Haven: Yale Institute of International Studies, 1947), p. 3.

167. Quoted in Paterson, *Soviet-American Confrontation*, p. 237.

168. *Foreign Relations, Conference at Quebec, 1944* (Washington, D.C.: Government Printing Office, 1972), p. 467.

169. Henry L. Stimson to the President, September 15, 1944, Box 100, James Forrestal Papers, Princeton University Library.

170. Notebooks, Interview with Harry S. Truman, November 12, 1949, Box 85, Jonathan Daniels Papers, University of North Carolina Library, Chapel Hill, North Carolina.

171. Churchill, *Triumph and Tragedy*, p. 338.

172. Clemens, *Yalta*, p. 287.

173. *Correspondence Between the Chairman . . .*, I, 295.

174. Forrest C. Pogue, "The Struggle for a New Order," in John L. Snell, ed., *The Meaning of Yalta* (Baton Rouge: Louisiana State University Press, 1956), pp. 33–34.

175. Churchill, *Triumph and Tragedy*, p. 366.

176. Quoted *ibid.*, p. 372.

177. Quoted in Department of State, *Foreign Relations of the United States: The Conferences at Malta and Yalta, 1945* (Washington, D.C.: Government Printing Office, 1955), p. 668.

178. This and subsequent quotations from the accords are from *ibid.*

179. William D. Leahy, *I Was There* (New York: Whittlesey House, 1950), pp. 315–316.

180. Quoted in Sherwood, *Roosevelt and Hopkins*, p. 870.

181. Quoted in Charles E. Bohlen, *Witness to History, 1929–1969* (New York: W. W. Norton, 1973), p. 181.

182. Dilks, *Diaries of Sir Alexander Cadogan*, p. 717.

183. Churchill, *Triumph and Tragedy*, p. 402.

184. Quoted in *New York Times*, February 8, 1970.

185. Quoted in Kolko, *Politics of War*, p. 465.

186. Quoted in Clemens, *Yalta*, p. 241.

187. Quoted in Woodward, *British Foreign Policy in the Second World War*, III, 116–118.

188. Feis, *Churchill, Roosevelt, Stalin*, p. 451.

189. Churchill, *Triumph and Tragedy*, pp. 227–228.

190. Churchill quoted in Louis Fischer, *The Road to Yalta: Soviet Foreign Relations, 1941–1945* (New York: Harper and Row, 1972), p. 179; and Slessor in John Wheeler-Bennett and Anthony Nicholls, *The Semblance of Peace* (New York: W. W. Norton, 1974 [c. 1972]), p. 191.

191. Quoted in Richard L. Walker, *E. R. Stettinius, Jr.* (New York: Cooper Square Publishers, 1965), p. 333. Emphasis added.

192. Quoted in Kolko, *Politics of War*, p. 465.

193. *Foreign Relations, 1944* (Washington: Government Printing Office, 1965), III, 103.

194. Quoted in Kolko, *Politics of War*, p. 482.

195. Harry S. Truman, *Memoirs* (Garden City, N.Y.: Doubleday, 1955–1956; 2 vols.), I, 228.

196. *Ibid.*, p. 258.

197. Quoted in John Morton Blum, *The Price of Vision: The Diary of Henry A. Wallace, 1942–1946* (Boston: Houghton Mifflin, 1973), p. 451.

198. *Foreign Relations, Berlin, I*, 33.

199. *Ibid., I*, 39.

200. *Ibid., I*, 61.

201. Dilks, *Diaries of Sir Alexander Cagodan*, p. 762.

202. Truman, *Memoirs, I*, 402.

203. Quoted in Lisle A. Rose, *After Yalta: America and the Origins of the Cold War* (New York: Charles Scribner's Sons, 1973), p. 51.

204. Journal, August 1, 1945, Box 19, and Memorandum of Conversation with Harriman, July 17, 1945, Box 18, Joseph Davies Papers, Library of Congress.

205. Winston Churchill, "Note of the Prime Minister's Conversation with President Truman at Luncheon, July 18, 1945," Premier 3, 430/8, Prime Minister's Office Records, Public Record Office, London, England.

206. *The Tehran, Yalta & Potsdam Conferences: Documents* (Moscow: Progress Publishers, 1969), p. 323.

207. George F. Kennan, *Memoirs, 1925–1950* (Boston: Little, Brown, 1967), p. 260.

208. *Foreign Relations, Berlin, II*, 365.

209. Truman, *Memoirs, I*, 412.

210. Herbert Feis, *Between War and Peace: The Potsdam Conference* (Princeton: Princeton University Press, 1960), p. 25.

211. Quoted in Walter Millis, ed., *The Forrestal Diaries* (New York: The Viking Press, 1951), p. 79.

212. "Notes on Conversation in Moscow with Maxim Litvinov," by Edgar Snow, December 6, 1944, Box 68, President's Secretary's File, Franklin D. Roosevelt Papers, Franklin D. Roosevelt Library, Hyde Park, New York.

213. Peter F. Drucker, *The Concept of the Corporation* (New York: New American Library, 1964; 2nd ed.), p. xi.

214. Quoted in Gardner, *Sterling-Dollar Diplomacy*, p. xvii.

215. H. D. Clarke in Foreign Office Minutes on the Political Situation in the United States, August 20, 1945, AN2505/4145, Foreign Office Correspondence, Public Record Office.

216. *Department of State Bulletin, XXII* (April 22, 1945), 738.

217. Richard J. Barnet, *Roots of War* (Baltimore: Penguin Books, 1973 [c. 1972]), p. 23.

218. Arthur M. Schlesinger, Jr., *The Imperial Presidency* (New York: Popular Library, 1974), p. 128.

219. Quoted in Barnet, *Roots of War*, p. 42.

**Atomic Blast.** The second atomic bomb fell on Nagasaki, August 9, 1945, killing at least 35,000. (U.S. Air Force)

# 12 The Origins of the Cold War, 1945–1950

### Diplomatic Crossroad: "The Greatest Thing in History" at Hiroshima, 1945

The crewmen of the B-29 group scrawled rude and poignant anti-Japanese graffiti on the "Little Boy." A major, thinking about his son in the states and a quick end to the war, scratched "No white cross for Stevie" on the 10,000-pound orange and black bomb.[1] The 509th Bombardment Group had been training on the Mariana Island of Tinian since May. At last, it seemed that the United States secret atomic development program ("the Manhattan Project") was nearing fruition. In the evening of August 5, 1945 Colonel Paul "Old Bull" Tibbets informed his men for the first time that their rare cargo was "atomic." He did not explain the scientific process in which two pieces of uranium (U-235), placed at opposite ends of a cylinder, smashed into one another to create tremendous energy. They knew what the equivalent of 20,000 tons of TNT meant, however. At midnight they settled down to a preflight meal, played poker, and waited.

At 1:37 A.M. on August 6 three weather planes took off in the darkness for the urban targets of Hiroshima, Kokura, and Niigata. At 2:45, after photo snapping and well wishing, Tibbets' heavily laden ship, the *Enola Gay*, named after his mother, lifted ponderously off the Tinian runway. The six-hour flight was uneventful, marked by the dodging of cumulus clouds and the nerve-wracking final assembly of the bomb's inner components. Followed by two observation planes stocked with cameras and scientists, the *Enola Gay* spotted the Japanese coast at 7:30 A.M. The weather plane assigned to Hiroshima, the primary target, reported clear skies. Tibbets headed for that city.

"This is history," he intoned over the intercom, "so watch your language."[2] But in those anxious moments someone actually forgot to switch on the tape recorder. At 31,600 feet and 328 miles per hour the *Enola Gay* began its run on Hiroshima. Crew members fastened on welder's goggles. Bombardier Thomas Ferebee prepared to cross the hairs in his bombsight. At 8:15 A.M. he shouted "bombs away." The *Enola Gay* swerved quickly to escape. The hefty "Little Boy"

**Enola Gay.** On August 6, 1945, just before takeoff, Colonel Paul Tibbets waved from the cockpit of his aircraft *Enola Gay*. Tibbets hailed from Miami and was a veteran of the European theater. For commanding the atomic mission, Tibbets was awarded the Distinguished Service Cross. (U.S. Air Force)

**"Little Boy."** The nuclear weapon detonated over Hiroshima was 120 inches long and 28 inches in diameter, and weighed about 10,000 pounds. (Los Alamos Scientific Laboratory, courtesy of the Harry S Truman Library)

fell for fifty seconds and then exploded about 2,000 feet above ground, a near perfect hit at hypo-center. A brilliant flash of light temporarily blinded the fliers. The ship trembled, hit by a wave of sound like a baseball bat hitting an ash can. Crew members looked back. "My God," sighed co-pilot Captain Robert Lewis, as he watched the huge, purplish cloud of smoke, dust, and debris rise 40,000 feet into the atmosphere. "Even though we had expected something terrific," he remembered, "what we saw made us feel that we were Buck Rogers twenty-fifth century warriors."[3]

Hiroshima was Japan's eighth largest city, with 250,000 people. Manhattan Project director Lieutenant General Leslie Groves, with the President's approval, had ranked it first on the target list because it housed regional military headquarters, but it was largely a residential and commercial city. On the cloudless, warm morning of August 6, 1945, Hiroshima's inhabitants heard the bombing alert siren. An "all clear" sounded when it was discovered that only a weather plane had passed over. Everything seemed routine, for Hiroshima had largely been spared from American bombs during the war. Forty-five minutes later, at 8:15 A.M., people labored at their jobs or moved fearlessly in the streets. Few heard the *Enola Gay* overhead. Suddenly a streak of light raced through the sky. A blast of lacerating heat traveling at the speed of light rocked the city. The temperature soared to suffocating levels. Trees were stripped of their leaves. Buildings blew apart like firecrackers. Debris shot through the air like bullets. Permanent shadows were etched into concrete. The sky grew dark, lighted only by the choking fires that erupted everywhere. Winds swirled violently and raindrops intermittently struck the cluttered ground. Some victims thought the Americans were now unleashing gasoline drops to feed the spreading fires. It seemed as though a huge scythe had leveled Hiroshima.

As the giant mushroom cloud churned above, dazed survivors stumbled about like scarecrows, their arms raised to avoid the painful rubbing of burned flesh. The victims' condition was gruesome: skin peeling off like ribbons; gaping wounds; vomiting and diarrhea; intense thirst. A badly wounded Dr. Michihiko Machiya noted that "no one talked, and the ominous silence was relieved only by a subdued rustle among so many people, restless, in pain, anxious, and afraid, waiting for something else to happen."[4] The nightmare was later recorded in statistics: 70,000–80,000 dead, as many wounded, and 81 percent of the city's buildings destroyed.

President Harry S Truman, upon hearing the news about the successful mission of August 6, remarked that "this is the greatest thing in history."[5] A second atomic bomb destroyed Nagasaki on August 9, killing at least 35,000. The Japanese surrendered on August 14. At home Americans went on a two-day victory binge. Presidential adviser Admiral William D. Leahy did not share the euphoria, for he thought that "in being the first to use it, we had adopted the ethical standard common to the barbarians of the Dark Ages. I was not taught to make war in that fashion, and wars cannot be won by destroying women and children."[6] The atomic age had begun with a ghastly record, indeed.

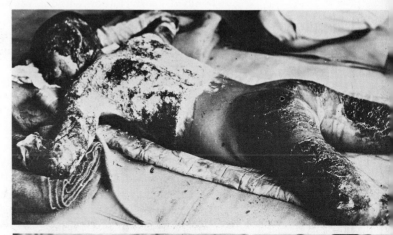

**Victims at Hiroshima.** Flash-burned victims shortly after the destruction of Hiroshima. Some of them died later. (Photographs courtesy of Dr. A. A. Liebow, Army Institute of Pathology)

As Leahy's comment attests, the decision to use the atomic bomb against an urban center met criticism within the small circle of government officials and scientists who were privy to the Manhattan Project. Although Truman always claimed that he never lost a night's sleep over his momentous decision, several advisers and physicists were restless. They presented what they thought were viable alternatives to dropping the bomb on a civilian population: (1) follow up Japanese peace feelers; (2) blockade and bomb Japan conventionally; (3) have Russia declare war on Japan; (4) warn Tokyo about the bomb and threaten its use; (5) demonstrate the bomb on an unpopulated island or area with international observers, including Japanese; (6) conduct a military landing on the outlying Japanese island of Kyushu. The overriding themes were that use of the bomb would constitute a moral blot on the American record, that it would jeopardize the chances of postwar international control of the awesome weapon, and that it was unnecessary because Japan was near military defeat anyway.

The general thrust of those who, like Truman himself, chose to drop the atomic bomb on a populated target was that the war should be ended as quickly as possible to save American lives. That simple reason helps to explain the decision, but decisions seldom derive from single factors and this one is no exception. Three primary and intertwined motives induced policymakers to inflict atomic horror upon the citizens of Japan. Together, the three suggest the central point: Truman found no compelling reasons against dropping atom bombs on Hiroshima and Nagasaki and important advantages in doing so.

The first motive—emotion—dated from December 7, 1941, when the Japanese bombed Pearl Harbor without warning. Vengeful Americans never forgot or forgave that disaster. The Japanese, as Truman said time and time again, could not be trusted. Revenge was the order of the day; they had to be repaid in kind. This popular attitude was strengthened by the racist American image of the Japanese, which drew upon a long tradition of anti-Oriental prejudice. The Japanese were stereotyped as crafty and sadistic. Hollywood movies portrayed suicidal, mad, grinning Nipponese pilots bearing down upon American aircraft with bloodthirsty delight. The *kamikaze* attacks fed such images in 1945. Americans hated the Japanese—the "slant-eyes"—more than the Germans, and 13 percent in a Gallup poll of December, 1944 recommended the extermination of all Japanese. Others advised sterilization. "We are drowning and burning the bestial apes all over the Pacific," Admiral William Halsey boasted on a newsreel, "and it is just as much pleasure to burn them as to drown them."[7] This irrational emotion was influential. Truman himself said on August 11, 1945: "When you have to deal with a beast you have to treat him as a beast."[8]

The second motive—military momentum—merged with the first and dated from the establishment of the Manhattan Project in August, 1942. This program began after European scientists, through a letter from Albert Einstein to President Franklin D. Roosevelt, warned that Germany might develop a nuclear device for military purposes. From the start, the assumption underlying the two-billion-dollar secret American project was that once a bomb was developed it would be used to end the war. Truman inherited this assumption from the Roosevelt Administration. His decision was not so much a decision to drop the bomb, but rather a decision *not* to reject that assumption, not to break the momentum. Furthermore, the large-scale bombing of civilian populations, such as those of Dresden and Tokyo, was an accepted practice by 1945. By August, 1945, however, this compel-

**Hiroshima.** The ruins of Japan's eighth largest city carry the meaning of the new atomic age. (U.S. Air Force)

ling momentum had taken on an irrational quality, for the Germans had been knocked out of the war and Japan faced certain defeat.

The third factor that helped persuade Truman to unleash the atomic bomb was the diplomatic advantage that might accrue to the United States. The diplomatic bonus materialized when American leaders, while at the Potsdam Conference, learned about the successful test explosion at Alamogordo, New Mexico on July 16, 1945. Throughout the war, Churchill and Roosevelt had kept the secret of the bomb from Russia, in part to use it for diplomatic leverage in the postwar period. Some scientists and advisers protested that excluding Russia, an ally, from any knowledge, would jeopardize or kill opportunities for successful postwar negotiations. At the Potsdam meeting, Truman did casually and cryptically inform Stalin that the United States had "a new weapon of unusual destructive force."[9] Stalin muttered that he hoped America would use it against the Japanese. It is likely that the Soviet dictator already knew from his intelligence network about the existence of the joint Anglo-American atomic development program, although he probably did not know the magnitude of the bomb and certainly did not know how soon or whether it would be used.

Churchill learned about the test in New Mexico directly from the American delegation at Potsdam. "Now I know what happened to Truman yesterday," the Prime Minister noted. "When he got to the meeting after having read this report [on the New Mexico success] he was a changed man. He told the Russians just where they got on and off and generally bossed the whole meeting."[10] Two diplomatic advantages suggested themselves. First, the bomb might gain diplomatic concessions by strengthening the United States' negotiating position vis-à-vis the Soviets. Russia might be intimidated to make concessions on Eastern European questions if the bomb revealed its destructive power on a Japanese city. Second, the use of the bomb might end the war in the Pacific before the Russians could declare war against Japan; such a circumstance would deny Russia any part in the postwar control of Japan and perhaps forestall Russian military entry into Manchuria. Until the explosion at Alamogordo the United States had desired Soviet military action against Japan; the bomb's triumph in the sands of New Mexico expunged that desire.

All three factors—emotion, military momentum, and diplomatic advantage—explain the tragedies at Hiroshima and Nagasaki. The diplomatic aspect was added as a late bonus; the bomb would have been dropped whether such a consideration existed or not. To have decided against dropping the atomic bomb, Truman would have had to deny the passion and momentum which had built up by midsummer, 1945. Pearl Harbor could be avenged, the war ended quickly, American lives

**James F. Byrnes (1879–1972) and Harry S Truman (1884–1972).** Both the secretary of state and the President, here on their way back from the Potsdam Conference, anticipated that the atomic bomb would serve as a diplomatic bargaining weapon in the postwar period. South Carolinian Byrnes served as secretary of state for 1945–1947. (U.S. Navy, courtesy of the Harry S Truman Library)

saved, and the American diplomatic position shored up—the advantages far outweighed the disadvantages in the American mind. Still, the costs were not inconsequential. Some of the alternatives, or a combination of them, might have terminated the war without the heavy death toll and the grotesque suffering of the survivors. The failure to discuss atomic development and control with the Russians during the war bequeathed to the postwar generation both division and fear. The United States never directly threatened to use the weapon in the early Cold War to gain Soviet concessions; the threat was *implied* only. Yet "the bomb" fixed itself as a corrosive feature of the Soviet-American confrontation.

## Soviet-American Confrontation

If Hiroshima symbolized the destructive power possessed by the United States in 1945, a war-wracked Europe, resembling a rubble heap, constituted one of the United States' major postwar problems. It is awesome indeed to realize that 35 million people died in Europe during the Second World War. Those Europeans who survived were homeless and hungry, and the contrast with prosperous Americans, untouched by enemy bombers or soldiers, was stark. Then, too, the French, British, and Dutch, weakened by the war, were no longer able to manage their rebellious colonial domains, particularly in Asia, and began to pull back. Britain, for example, granted independence to India in 1947 and Burma in 1948, and the Dutch left Indonesia a year later. Throughout the postwar period, the decolonization process begun by World War II continued, presenting challenges to the United States.

The United States also faced a major new power bent upon asserting its authority in international relations. Soviet Russia assumed a demanding postwar position and its pushy behavior, its suspicion, and its blunt language antagonized Americans. Diplomat Dean Acheson said the Soviets were not housebroken, and Truman complained that they negotiated "with a boorishness worthy of stable boys."[11] At the end of the war, the Soviet Union had troops in most of the Eastern European countries and Germany. It lacked an effective navy or air force and did not possess the atomic bomb, but it had become a strong regional power by virtue of its military exploits. Motivated by traditional Russian nationalism, a fervent Communist ideology, a craving for security against a revived Germany, and the huge task of reconstruction, the leaders of the Kremlin determined to make the most of the limited power they held. Often rude and abusive, yet cautious and realistic, Josef Stalin determined never again to see his country invaded through Eastern Europe. The image of "Uncle Joe" soon dissipated. Nevertheless, compared to the United States, as chargé d'affaires George F. Kennan reported from Moscow, Russia was still the "weaker force."[12]

The United States emerged from World War II a global power for the first time in its history. American diplomats were self-conscious about their supreme power and attempted to use it to shape an American-oriented postwar world. With troops in Asia and Europe, the world's largest navy and air force, a monopoly of the atomic bomb, and a high-gear economy, the United States demanded first rank in world affairs. As one scholar has put it, the United States held the "prime weapon of *de*struction—the atomic bomb—and the prime weapon of *recon*struction—such wealth as no nation hitherto had possessed."[13] President Truman heralded America as the "giant of the economic world," and British Ambassador Lord Halifax

**Josef Stalin.** As the ruthless leader of Russia since the 1920s, Stalin created an authoritarian state within his country and conducted external affairs with a suspiciousness that irritated. Lenin had complained that Stalin was "too rude," and most international leaders agreed. (*The Reporter*, 1952. Copyright 1952 by Fortnightly Publishing Co. Inc.)

reported that "by contrast with the exhausted and devastated countries of western Europe, the United States sees itself, as a result of the war, endowed with colossal productive and fighting capacity."[14] While public pressure compelled Truman to demobilize the armed forces faster than he wished, the Soviet Union itself demobilized, although it still retained a large standing army.

Washington was encouraged to exercise its power by the fundamental factors of ideology and the economic requirements of the nation. American ideology integrated political and economic tenets in a "peace and prosperity" philosophy. Simply stated, this ideology held that world peace and order depended upon the existence of prosperity and political democracy. Poverty and economic depression, on the other hand, bred totalitarianism, revolution, communism, the disruption of world trade through economic competition, and war. Prosperity became the handmaiden of stability, political freedom, unrestricted trade, and peaceful international relations. This thinking was not new to the postwar era, for Americans had long believed that they were prosperous because they were democratic and democratic because they were prosperous.

American leaders determined that *this time*, unlike after World War I, the United States would seize the opportunity to fulfill its ideological premises. As historian Gaddis Smith has described diplomat Dean Acheson's historical understanding, "only the United States had the power to grab hold of history and make it conform."[15] The lessons of the 1920s and 1930s tugged at the leaders of the 1940s, and there was a good deal of arrogance in both American ideology and behavior nurtured by this desire to throw off the mistakes of the past. The British complained about America's "irritating cockahoop moods."[16] On the simplest level

## Makers of American Foreign Policy from 1945 to 1950

| Presidents | Secretaries of State |
|---|---|
| Harry S Truman, 1945–1953 | Edward R. Stettinius, Jr., 1944–1945 |
| | James F. Byrnes, 1945–1947 |
| | George C. Marshall, 1947–1949 |
| | Dean G. Acheson, 1949–1953 |

Americans believed themselves a successful people, with admirable institutions and ideals worthy of universal adoption. The postwar period seemed an opportune time to install America's concept of "peace and prosperity" as the world's way—a time to express traditional American expansionism.

Postwar expansionism was also stimulated by another factor of a fundamental character: the vital needs or requirements of the American economy. Truman and other leaders frankly stated the facts: the United States *had* to export American goods and *had* to import strategic raw materials. By 1947 United States exports accounted for one-third of total world exports and were valued at $14 billion a year. Pivotal industries, such as automobiles, trucks, machine tools, steel, and farm machinery relied heavily upon foreign trade for their well-being. Farmers exported about half of their wheat. Many Americans, remembering the Great Depression, predicted economic catastrophe unless American foreign trade continued and

"**What Next?**" Jack Lambert's 1946 cartoon of Truman captured the feeling of many Americans that the President, new at his job, was overwhelmed by postwar problems. (Jack Lambert, *Chicago Sun Times*)

expanded. Although less than 10 percent of the GNP, exports exceeded in volume such elements of the GNP as consumers' expenditures on durable goods, total expenditures by state and local governments, and private construction. Furthermore, imports of manganese, tungsten, and chromite, to name a few, were essential to America's industrial system. Foreign trade, however, was threatened by the sickness of America's best customer, Europe, which lacked the resources to purchase American products, and by nationalists in former colonial areas, who controlled raw materials sources for both Europe and America. To protect its interests and to fulfill its ideology the United States undertook foreign aid programs that eventually became global in scale.

President Harry S Truman felt the flush of American power, shared the ideology, and knew well the economic needs of the country. A self-confident party regular from the Pendergast machine in Kansas City, Truman had long experienced the rough-and-tumble of politics. Whereas Roosevelt had been charming and often evasive, Missouri-bred Truman was blunt and straightforward. "The buck stops here" read a sign on his desk. He prided himself on simple, direct language and quick decisions. Critics said he frequently shot before he thought. "Give 'em hell Harry," the crowds shouted. Truman had the "steady energy of a commission salesman, the aplomb and brashness of a riverboat gambler," and the "sass" of a bantam rooster, wrote one biographer.[17] With his intense eyes peering through thick lenses, Truman relished the verbal brawl. His hurried simplification of issues, his amateurish application of lessons from the past, and his quick-tempered style spawned jokes that often fit the truth. Why did the President arrive late for a press conference? "He got up this morning a little stiff in the joints and had trouble putting his foot in his mouth." Somebody rewrote a proverb: "To err is Truman."

A statesman's style may reveal his nation's bargaining position. In April, 1945, Soviet Foreign Minister V. M. Molotov visited the White House and President Truman gave him a vigorous tongue-lashing. Stubborn Molotov stormed out of the office, stung by language more suitable for a ward politician in Missouri who had not delivered enough votes to the machine. After the encounter, the first meeting between the new President and a high-ranking Soviet official, Truman gloated to a friend: "I gave it to him straight 'one-two to the jaw.' I let him have it straight."[18] Truman's confident style drew strength from actual American power. He could "get tough," as the saying went at the time, because the United States was in fact powerful. Truman told Ambassador to Russia W. Averell Harriman that he was not afraid of the Soviets, because they "needed us more than we needed them." He did not expect to win 100 percent of the American case, but "we should be able to get 85 percent."[19] Overall, United States foreign policy after World War II was neither accidental nor aimless, but rather self-conscious and forceful.

The confrontation between the United States and Russia, the "Cold War," had its origins in the different postwar needs, ideology, style, and power of the two rivals and drew upon an historical legacy of distrust. Each saw the other, in mirror image, as the world's bully. Each charged the other with assuming Hitler's aggressive mantle. Americans compared Nazism and Communism, Hitler and Stalin, and coined the phrase "Red Fascism." The international structure or balance was in a shambles. Putting it back into some kind of order would automatically generate tension. Conflict was inevitable, but perhaps the Cold War was not. Here is where American style and tactics counted. The heated American rhetoric,

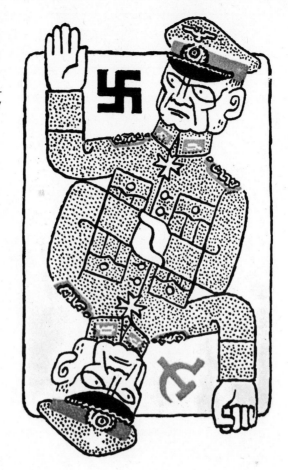

**"Red Fascism."** This popular notion among Americans suggested that German nazism and Russian communism were really one and the same and that the 1940s would see totalitarian aggression like that of the 1930s. Such thinking aroused fears of another "Munich" and "appeasement" and thereby hindered negotiations. (*The Reporter,* 1950. Copyright 1950 by Fortnightly Publishing Co. Inc.)

constant alarms, "get tough" style, unilateral decisions, manipulation of international agencies, rejection of reasonable alternative policies, uncompromising stances, use of foreign aid as a diplomatic weapon—all helped bring on the Cold War.

## Diplomatic Battleground in Eastern Europe

By the end of the war Eastern Europe had become a Soviet sphere of influence. It was the one area of the world largely closed off to American influence, where the Soviet Union stood most powerful. Although some observers considered Eastern Europe an impenetrable and solid Soviet bloc, the region looked more like a patchwork quilt. The Soviet presence in Eastern Europe before 1947–1948 was neither uniform nor consistent. Russia had no imperial blueprint for its neighbors. Poland, with its Communist Lublin government in control, was firmly within the Soviet grasp. Rumania, an anti-Soviet German satellite during the war, suffered under a Soviet-imposed government. The Soviet Union gained territory at the expense of Poland, Finland, and Rumania after postwar boundary settlements. Bulgaria had a large indigenous Communist movement, which gained control through elections without much help from Moscow.

NORTH
SEA

NORWAY

SWEDEN

BALTIC
SEA

FINLAND

*Leased to Russia
until 1955*

*Gulf of Finland*

L. Ladoga

*To
Russia*

• Leningrad

ESTONIA
*To Russia*

L. Pskov

LATVIA
*To Russia*

SOVIET RUSSIA

LITHUANIA
*To Russia*

*Niemen R.*

*To Russia*

DENMARK

NETH.

U.S.

BRITISH
ZONE

*Elbe R.*

Berlin
•

GERMANY
E.

BELG.

W.

*Rhine R.*

FRENCH
ZONE

Danzig

EAST
PRUSSIA
*To Poland*

*Vistula R.*

*To
Poland*

RUSSIAN
ZONE

*Oder R.*

*Neisse R.*

POLAND

*To Russia*

*Don R.*

UNITED
STATES
ZONE

CZECHOSLOVAKIA

NORTHERN
BUKOVINA

FRANCE

SWITZ.

FRENCH

U.S.
AUSTRIA
BRITISH

Vienna

RUSSIAN

BRATISLAVIA
BRIDGEHEAD
*To Czech.*

SUBCARPATHIAN
RUTHENIA

*Dniester R.*

BESSARABIA
*To Russia*

*Pruth R.*

VENEZIA–GIULIA
*To Yugoslavia*

HUNGARY

*To France*

*Po R.*

Trieste
•

*Drava R.*

RUMANIA

BLACK
SEA

CORSICA

Rome •

ITALY

ADRIATIC
SEA

YUGOSLAVIA

*Danube R.*

DOBRUJA
*To
Bulgaria*

SARDINIA

ALBANIA

BULGARIA

SICILY

GREECE

TURKEY

*AEGEAN

SEA*

## Changes in Europe After World War II

DODECONESE IS.
*To Greece
from Italy*

*CRETE*

Territorial Changes After World War II

*MEDITERRANEAN   SEA*

Hungary and other nations developed differently. The conservative Hungarian Smallholders' party of Ferenc Nagy won national elections in November, 1945 by routing the Communists, who managed to get only 17 percent of the vote. The Nagy government remained in office until a Communist coup in the spring of 1947. In Finland, to demonstrate the political complexity in Eastern Europe further, non-Communist leaders recognized their precarious position with respect to neighboring Russia and adopted a neutral position vis-à-vis the Soviet-American confrontation. Finland thus retained its independence and in 1948 even ousted from its Cabinet the lone Communist member. Yugoslavia, although a Communist state, established its independence from Moscow under the leadership of Josip Broz Tito. The growing schism became public in 1948 when Belgrade and Moscow bitterly split. Finally, there was the tragic case of Czechoslovakia, an independent socialist country with a democratic political process and ties with the West. Czech officials recognized the advisability of a middle course. A coalition government under non-Communist President Eduard Beneš and Foreign Minister Jan Masaryk assumed office after free elections in May, 1946. Communists held membership in the government, with 9 of 26 top-level positions and 114 of 300 National Assembly seats, but the Soviet Union for a time refrained from meddling directly in Czech affairs. Not until February, 1948, after the Cold War was well advanced, did the Communists seize control of Czechoslovakia during a domestic crisis.

The Soviet presence in Eastern Europe before 1948, then, was conspicuous and often repressive, but not absolute. Communists were active, sometimes gaining control of repressive ministries of interior (police). Stalin seemed hesitant and uncertain, having a different policy for each Eastern European country. The Russian leader said he wanted "friendly governments," not satellites. In early 1945, in stating his case regarding Poland, Stalin emphasized security: "Throughout history Poland has been the corridor for attack on Russia. We have to mention that during the last thirty years Germany twice has passed through this corridor. The reason for this was that Poland was weak. Russia wants a strong, independent, and democratic Poland. . . . It is not only a question of honor for Russia, but one of life and death."[20] Still bitter over the *cordon sanitaire* the Western powers constructed around Russia after World War I, staggering from the loss of 15–20 million Russian dead during the recent war, and fearing that some day Germany might march again, Soviet leaders demanded security through influence among their neighbors. They also believed that the 1944 Moscow percentage bargain, armistice agreements, and Yalta accords acknowledged their primary position in Eastern Europe. Thus the Soviets began building their own *cordon sanitaire*.

United States goals for the area clashed with those of the Soviet Union. Washington sought "free elections" and the "Open Door" for trade, both traditional principles calculated in part to reduce Soviet influence. The Soviets signed bilateral trade treaties with many of the Eastern European states, which established favors anathema to America's Open Door policy and multilateral approach to trade. Although Americans had minimal commercial ties with Eastern Europe, American diplomats preached the Open Door as a way of driving a wedge into the area. The application of the principle of "free elections" also proved difficult in Eastern Europe. There was little tradition of democracy, except in Czechoslovakia, and free elections in most of those nations would have meant strongly anti-Soviet governments threatening Soviet security (such as the London Poles). The question of elections in Hungary demonstrates the complexity of the question. During late

1946 it was the *non-Communist* Nagy who delayed elections, because he knew the Communists would lose badly and that result might trigger an intrusive Soviet response. What both the United States and the Soviet Union wanted in Eastern Europe was not democratic, but friendly governments. After all, critics asked, if "free elections" were the ultimate and universal goal of American diplomacy, why was the principle not applied to the United States sphere of influence in Latin America, where Washington recognized a host of military dictators?

The Soviets hence charged the United States with a double standard. When American leaders consciously excluded Russia from participation in the postwar reconstruction of Italy and Japan, the Soviets cited the Italian example as a precedent for their machinations in Eastern Europe. Secretary of War Henry L. Stimson was alive to the problem in 1945: "Some Americans are anxious to hang on to exaggerated views of the Monroe Doctrine and at the same time butt into every question that comes up in Central Europe."[21] Furthermore, V. M. Molotov dipped into the 1946 edition of the *World Almanac* to illustrate how economically strong the United States was compared to the war-weakened states. He contended that an Open Door in Eastern Europe would actually mean ultimate American economic domination, because the United States had no real economic competitors. In short, the Soviet Union looked upon American goals in Eastern Europe as guises for United States expansion in an area of vital importance to its own security. The Americans, in rebuttal, pointed out that the Russians had emasculated the Declaration of Liberated Europe agreed to at Yalta.

At the Yalta and Potsdam conferences, at the Foreign Ministers conferences in London (September–October, 1945) and Moscow (December 1945), at the Paris Peace Conference (April–October, 1946), and in numerous diplomatic notes, the United States sought influence in Eastern Europe to counter the Soviets. It tried nonrecognition of the pro-Soviet governments, but abandoned that after slight Soviet concessions, such as the addition of a handful of non-Communists to the Polish government. Some American leaders thought the continued United States monopoly of the atomic bomb would force Soviet concessions. Stimson recorded in his diary that Byrnes "looks to having the presence of the bomb in his pocket" at the London Conference.[22] A telling incident occurred at that conference. Molotov, as if he had been reading Stimson's diary, asked Byrnes if "he had an atomic bomb in his side pocket. 'You don't know Southerners,' Byrnes replied. 'We carry our artillery in our hip pocket. If you don't cut out all this stalling and let us get down to work, I am going to pull an atomic bomb out of my hip pocket and let you have it.'"[23] Molotov apparently laughed, but his suspicious mind must have fixed on the implications of the answer to his light question. Still, the implied threat of the bomb did not budge the Soviets from Eastern Europe, and the United States never practiced a conscious "atomic diplomacy" of direct threat.

Stimson opposed the use of the bomb as a diplomatic weapon in September, 1945. He had earlier embraced the thought of forcing Soviet concessions, but reversed himself when he told the President that the United States should share the secret of the bomb to spur postwar cooperative relations. "For if we fail to approach them now and merely continue to negotiate with them, having this weapon rather ostentatiously on our hip, their suspicions and their distrust of our purposes and motives will increase." Stimson, then seventy-eight, and a former Cabinet officer under William Howard Taft, Herbert Hoover, and Franklin Roosevelt, offered Truman some sage advice: "The chief lesson I have learned in a long life is the only way you can make a man trustworthy is to trust him; and the surest way you can make a man untrustworthy is to distrust him and show your distrust."[24] Stimson gained the support of Secretary of Commerce Henry Wallace, but Secretary of the Navy James V. Forrestal rejected any effort to "buy [Russian] understanding and sympathy. We tried that once with Hitler."[25] Truman sided with Forrestal.

The United States also used foreign aid as a diplomatic weapon in Eastern Europe. Byrnes stated the policy in 1946: "We must help our friends in every way and refrain from assisting those who either through helplessness or for other reasons are opposing the principles for which we stand."[26] In short, no loans or aid for Eastern Europe. This policy backfired, for it left those countries dependent upon Soviet aid and drove them deeper into the Soviet orbit. In Czechoslovakia, for example, the United States in 1946 abruptly severed an Export-Import bank loan to press Beneš to remove the Communists from his government. As non-Communist Foreign Trade Minister Hubert Ripka complained bitterly in late 1947 about American behavior, "these idiots started the usual blackmail: 'Okay, you can have 200,000 or 300,000 or even 500,000 tons of wheat, but on one condition only—that you throw the Communists out of the Czechoslovak Government.'" The result: "And now these idiots in Washington have driven us straight into the Stalinist camp."[27]

The United States, through such pressure tactics on the Soviet sphere of influence, helped intensify the Cold War. That is, during 1947–1948 the Russians read American policies, including American encouragement to dissident anti-Soviet political groups, as threats to their security and so tightened their grip. George F. Kennan has suggested, for example, that the Czech coup was the Soviet

"I Can't Give You All Up For One Angel Of Peace." The burly Russian savors the attention of the Eastern Europeans in this critical Turkish cartoon. (*ULUS,* Ankara, in *United Nations World,* 1947)

response to the Marshall Plan, a major American aid program that the Soviets considered a challenge to their tenuous position in Eastern Europe. Overall, Washington exaggerated the extent of Soviet control in Eastern Europe and pressed the peoples of that region to align with the West. Yet the Eastern Europeans, so close to Russian power, could not and would not affront the Soviet Union. Washington treated only Finland and Yugoslavia as exceptions, forwarding some aid to them. American policymakers showed little understanding of the difference between an independent country (like Czechoslovakia) influenced by the Soviet Union and a subjugated country (like Poland). To Americans all were Soviet satellites, and because the Soviets were uncompromising in their heavy-handedness in manipulating governments, they deserved utter condemnation. Yet, as contemporary critics asked, would the Eastern Europeans have retained some of their independence and been better off had Washington cooled its rhetoric, meddled less, recognized what it ultimately could not change, and maintained economic and political ties through foreign aid? Perhaps. What we do know is that Russian behavior did not happen in a vacuum. American pressure aroused Soviet fears and hence countermeasures damaging to the Eastern Europeans.

## Getting Tough with the Russians, 1946

The question of Eastern Europe broke up the London Conference of Foreign Ministers (September–October, 1945). Byrnes demanded representative governments in Bulgaria and Rumania before he would sign any peace treaties with the former German satellites. Molotov countered with questions about British-dominated Greece and American-dominated Japan. The conferees left London unable to agree even on a public communiqué. Byrnes became convinced that the Soviets had welshed on the Yalta Declaration on Liberated Europe and that they could not be trusted. At the Moscow Conference in December, 1945, the secretary of state tempered his tough stand somewhat and got Stalin to accept a token broadening of the Rumanian and Bulgarian regimes. The Russians also accepted Byrnes's ideas for a general peace conference to be held in Paris in 1946 and a United Nations Atomic Energy Commission to prepare plans for international control.

Yet Truman grew impatient. Byrnes had not kept the President informed about the Moscow proceedings. More important, Truman had decided upon a firmer line against the Soviet Union. As he put it in January of 1946, "I'm tired of babying the Russians."[28] The new "get tough" policy developed through the early months of 1946. Republican leaders like Senator Arthur Vandenberg of Michigan helped shape it with their denunciations of "appeasement," recalling the horrors of the 1930s and warning against new Munichs. The news of a Canadian spy ring that had sent atomic secrets to Russia broke in February, about the same time that Stalin gave a cocky pre-election speech that convinced some Americans that Russia was arming for war. From Moscow, on February 22, chargé d'affaires George F. Kennan wrote an alarmist and influential cable which declared that "we have here a political force committed fanatically to the belief that with [the] US there can be no permanent modus vivendi."[29] The "long telegram" was widely circulated in Washington and devoured with relish by those who believed there could be no compromise with Russia. Kennan later apologized that the cable read like a primer published by "the Daughters of the American Revolution, designed to arouse the citizenry to the dangers of the Communist conspiracy."[30]

On March 5, Winston Churchill, no longer prime minister, spoke in Fulton, Missouri. President Truman sat prominently on the platform and heard the eloquent orator declare that the United States "stands at this time at the pinnacle of world power." Churchill then lashed out at the Soviets: "From Stettin in the Baltic to Trieste in the Adriatic, an iron curtain has descended across the continent."[31] Most Americans applauded his stiff anti-Russian tone, but they warmed much less to his call for an Anglo-American alliance outside the fledgling United Nations Organization. "Don't be a ninny for imperialist Winnie," pickets later chanted in New York City.[32] Truman was pleased with Churchill's forceful language. Secretary Wallace, however, a dissenter from the "get tough" approach, feared that the Anglo-Americans were trying to "strut around the world and tell people where to get off."[33] An angry Stalin asserted that nations were not willing to exchange the "lordship of Hitler for the lordship of Churchill."[34] The war of words escalated.

The Iranian crisis peaked in early 1946 just as the Truman Administration was deciding to throw its power into making the Soviet Union more cooperative. The crisis began quietly in 1944 when British and American oil companies applied for Iranian concessions, and it became a classic example of competition for spheres of influence. Unwilling to be excluded from a bordering country, Russia soon applied for an oil concession too. The British, who had long dominated Iran, were no longer powerful enough to sustain their position. Reluctantly London looked to Washington for backing, and was pleased to find that the wartime and postwar American quest for petroleum in the Middle East served as a counterweight against the Soviets. By 1944 American corporations controlled 42 percent of the "proved" oil reserves of the Middle East, a nineteen-fold increase in American holdings there since 1936.

**V. M. Molotov (1890—).** Popularly known as "stone ass," the Soviet foreign minister was a tough-minded negotiator who cleared most decisions with Stalin. When he became angry, a bump appeared on his forehead, a sure signal to American diplomats that something dramatic was about to break out. He organized a "Molotov Plan" to counter the "Marshall Plan." (*The Reporter,* 1956. Copyright 1956 by The Reporter Magazine Co.)

A 1942 treaty with Iran allowed the British and Soviets to occupy the country and required them to leave six months after the end of the war. American supply units and soldiers were also there, largely shipping Lend-Lease goods to Russia. In mid-1945 an indigenous rebellion in northern Iran (Azerbaijan) was encouraged by the Soviets. In January, 1946, working with American officials, Iran took the question of Soviet meddling to the United Nations Organization. The Soviets were irate, pointing out that British troops remained. Iran and Russia entered direct negotiations, but they did not reach an accord by March 2 when all foreign troops, by treaty, had to depart. American soldiers had withdrawn in January, but, very important, left military advisers behind; British troops departed in early March. The Russians thus stood alone in defiance of the treaty and aroused considerable international protest. In April, however, Moscow and Teheran concluded an agreement and Soviet forces left. In exchange for this withdrawal, Iran agreed to establish a joint Iranian-Soviet oil company, subject to approval by its parliament. After this agreement, the Iranian Prime Minister took a strong stand against Russia and the rebels in Azerbaijan, often following the advice of American Ambassador George V. Allen. In late 1946, Iranian armed forces, advised by Major General Robert W. Grow of the United States Army, squelched the insurrection in northern Iran. Russia took no steps to defend its Azerbaijani friends. Not until October, 1947, did the legislature consider the joint oil company; it rejected the agreement by a convincing vote of 102 to 2.

The Soviets exploded in anger. They had been eased from Iran while Britain and the United States had driven in stakes. Arthur C. Millspaugh, former United States financial adviser to the Iranian government, pinpointed the issue when he commented that "Iran's geographic relation to the Soviet Union is roughly comparable to the relation of Mexico or Canada to the United States."[35] It was as if Mexico City or Ottawa had become allied with Moscow—a spheres-of-influence and security question. The Russians wanted what the British and Americans already had: oil and influence. Moscow feared the foreign penetration of a neighboring state. Years later, Truman embellished the Iranian story by claiming that he had sent the Russians an ultimatum to get out of Iran or face American troops. He may have contemplated sending one, but the State Department has denied the existence of such a message. Yet this myth is indicative of the simple lesson Americans drew from the conflict: "Get tough" and the Russians will give way. Secretary Henry A. Wallace saw it differently and told a Madison Square Garden audience in September, 1946: " 'Getting tough' never brought anything real and lasting—whether for schoolyard bullies or businessmen or world powers. The tougher we get, the tougher the Russians will get."[36] For this speech and Wallace's criticism of American foreign policy, Truman fired him from the Cabinet. "The Reds, phonies and 'parlor pinks' seem to be banded together and are becoming a national danger. I am afraid they are a sabotage front for Uncle Joe Stalin," concluded the President with tortured exaggeration.[37]

## A Multitude of Disputes: Loans, Atomic Bombs, and Germany

Three other issues, which flared in 1946 and continued beyond, illustrated Truman's new "get tough" policy: an abortive loan to Russia, the Baruch Plan for atomic control, and Germany. The loan issue began during the war when the Soviet Union requested a reconstruction loan of one billion dollars, later raised to six billion. Some American leaders, like Wallace and Secretary of the Treasury Henry Morgenthau, Jr., thought such a loan would stimulate trade with Russia as well as contribute to amicable relations. Ambassador Harriman and Truman reasoned, on the other hand, that the Russian need for economic help should be exploited for diplomatic leverage. Economic assistance was "one of the most

**W. Averell Harriman (1891—).** Graduate of Yale, heir to the Harriman railroad empire, investment banker of Brown Brothers, and diplomat, Harriman has been one of America's busiest public servants in the twentieth century. As an architect of the "get tough" policy toward Russia, he advocated using foreign aid in diplomatic bargaining. He served as ambassador to Russia (1943–1946), ambassador to Great Britain (1946), secretary of commerce (1946–1948), and U.S. representative in Europe for the Marshall Plan. Later he became a foreign affairs adviser and negotiator for Presidents John F. Kennedy and Lyndon B. Johnson. (*The Reporter*, 1950. Copyright 1950 by Fortnightly Publishing Co. Inc.)

effective weapons at our disposal" to influence events in Europe, Harriman informed Washington in 1944.[38] Truman "felt we held all the cards and that the Russians had to come to us," and he intended to "play them as American cards."[39]

The "cards" were foreign aid. In early 1946, after months of silence on the issue, the United States reopened the loan question by requesting concurrent discussion on Eastern Europe and Soviet participation in the World Bank. The Soviets hesitated in various diplomatic notes, hardly interested in opening talks designed to weaken their position in Eastern Europe. Nor did they wish to join the American-dominated World Bank. In May, however, they vaguely agreed to discuss Eastern Europe in a *preliminary* fashion. Washington was actually baffled, for it no longer expected Soviet concessions and it did not have enough money left in the Export-Import Bank to grant a large loan. So the State Department responded that it could not accept merely a preliminary exchange of views. The loan issue died with that message, although the general question of foreign aid for Russia would arise again when the Marshall Plan began. Would a loan have eased the increasingly bitter Soviet-American relations? We cannot be sure, but we know that the Soviets faced a major reconstruction problem, that the assistance was badly needed, and that Moscow had made a concession, however vague. Some observers concluded that the Soviet demand for German reparations hardened because of the loan failure, and Harriman suggested that American loan policy "may have contributed to their avaricious policies" in Eastern Europe.[40] The diplomatic use of economic power, by any nation possessing it, is to be expected and may be helpful in achieving mutually beneficial negotiations. Yet the Truman Administration chose to brandish the loan as a diplomatic weapon before negotiations, rather than to utilize it as a bargaining tool at the conference table, thereby producing further schism. In contrast, the United States negotiated with the British and granted a $3.75 billion loan in mid-1946, using aid as a tool to convince London to alter the preferential trading behavior of its Sterling Bloc.

The Baruch Plan was presented to the United Nations Atomic Energy Commission on July 14, 1946 and it also divided the two powers. Although the result of months of discussion within the Administration, the final touches were those of Bernard Baruch, the ubiquitous adviser to Presidents. He outlined the American proposal for control of atomic weapons: (1) the creation of an international authority; (2) the international control of fissionable raw materials by this authority; (3) inspections to prevent violations; (4) no Security Council vetoes of control or inspections; (5) global distribution of atomic plants for peaceful purposes; (6) cessation of the manufacture of atomic bombs; (7) destruction of existing bombs; (8) these procedures to be taken in stages, with the last stage being the abandonment of the American atomic bomb monopoly.

Not until the last stage, after the Russians had given up atomic bomb development and fissionable materials within their country, and submitted to inspections, would the United States relinquish its monopoly. Furthermore, the United States would control a majority of the members of an international authority, and most of the plants would be in areas friendly to the United States. The Soviets thought they would have to jeopardize their security during these various stages. "In other words," Wallace wrote the President, "we are telling the Russians that if they are 'good boys' we may eventually turn over our knowledge of atomic energy to them."[41] Moscow rejected the Baruch Plan, and the stalemate persisted until 1949, when the Russians successfully exploded their first atomic device. The issue

**Berlin Airlift.** Citizens of Berlin watch an American cargo plane fly in supplies as part of "Operation Vittles" to circumvent the Soviet blockade of the beleaguered city. (Official U.S. Air Force photo)

seemed insoluble. The Russians obviously could not accept the American plan, and the United States could not be expected to surrender its atomic advantage in such a turbulent world seemingly threatened by a large Red Army. Truman, Byrnes, and Baruch, however, drew the exaggerated conclusion that the Soviet rejection of their plan was further evidence that Moscow intended to obstruct peaceful international relations.

The issue of Germany—zones, reparations, central administration, demilitarization, and the dismantling of war-oriented factories—deepened the schism between the former Allies. France, Britain, the USSR, and the United States each had a zone in defeated Germany and in Berlin, and each did what it liked. The vengeful French proved to be the most obstructionist, refusing to permit any centralized German agencies and arguing for permanent dismemberment. The Soviets tried with mixed success to grab reparations, thereby weakening the entire German economy. The British tried to bestow socialism on their district, but generally wanted a strong Germany to which they could sell goods and from which they could receive coal. The United States sought, according to the Potsdam accords, to treat Germany as one economic unit to speed reconstruction. Americans were not about to pour dollars into Germany for its recovery only to see those dollars flow out as reparations. By 1946 the Morgenthau Plan was near death. Steel- and coal-rich Germany was the vital center of the European economy and had to be reconstructed.

The dismantling of industrial plants slowed down, and in May of 1946, American Military Governor Lucius Clay halted all reparations shipments from the

American zone. No more reparations, he told the Russians, until they contributed to German economic unity. As Secretary Forrestal rhetorically asked, "Are we going to try to keep Germany a running boil with the pus exuding over the rest of Europe, or are you going to try to bring it back into inner society?"[42] In December, 1946, the British and Americans combined their zones into "Bizonia." The Federal Republic of Germany (West Germany), a consolidation of "Bizonia" with the French zone, was created in May, 1949. The Soviets, on the other hand, economically exhausted their zone and retaliated in October, 1949 with the establishment of their puppet German Democratic Republic (East Germany).

The Berlin blockade (June, 1948–May, 1949) was calculated by the Soviets to stop the unilateral Western issuance of a new German currency. To them, the currency was another sign of a resurgent, unified Germany. For months, after the Soviets sealed off land access to the city of Berlin, American aircraft swept into West Berlin with cargoes of food and supplies. The outstretched hands of alarmed West Berliners captivated a world audience moved to disgust by this Soviet travesty. Some Americans recommended that United States troops march through East Germany to free Berlin, and incidentally start a war with Russia, or that Truman threaten to use the atomic bomb. Truman chose the less provocative airlift, although he said frankly that he would not hesitate to use "the bomb" if it became necessary. For their part, the Soviets never shot down an American plane. Russia eventually lifted the blockade, suffering a serious defeat. The Russians actually hastened in the crisis what they most wanted to avoid: a unified, rearmed West Germany. Berlin became another oversimplified lesson, like Iran: the United States had not flinched in the face of Communist aggression, and had won.

## The Truman Doctrine and Containment

On March 12, 1947 President Harry S Truman spoke dramatically to a special joint session of Congress. Greece and Turkey, he said, were gravely threatened. Unless the United States offered help, "we may endanger the peace of the world—and we shall surely endanger the welfare of this Nation." History seemed to be repeating itself. The Greek-Turkish crisis, the President suggested, was Hitler and World War II all over again. Truman invoked the peace and prosperity idiom when he declared that the "seeds of totalitarian regimes are nurtured by misery and want." The most famous words became known as the Truman Doctrine, the commanding guide to American foreign policy in the Cold War: "I believe that it must be the policy of the United States to support free peoples who are resisting attempted subjugation by armed minorities or by outside pressures."[43] Truman asked for $400 million to insure this policy's success. The President's moving address was short on analysis of the civil war in Greece and the Soviet-Turkish controversy over the strategic Dardanelles, but long on clichés, alarmist language, and panacea. He played on the words "free" and "democratic," leaving the mistaken impression that they fit the Greek and Turkish governments. Truman, however, was not interested in educating people, but in persuading them. The drafters of the speech thought it was the "most important thing that had happened since Pearl Harbor."[44] Unlike Roosevelt's "quarantine" speech, Truman's warning would be followed by action.

The immediate catalysts for the Truman Doctrine were a British request for help in Greece and a lingering squabble over who governed the Dardanelles. When the

Germans withdrew from hobbled Greece in 1944, much of the countryside was controlled by Communist and other leftist Greek nationalist resistance fighters, the ELAS, or National Popular Liberation Army and their political arm the EAM, or National Liberation Front. To re-establish Greek subservience to London, the British soon installed a government in Athens. Violence between the competing factions erupted in December, 1944. British troops, transported to Greece on American ships, joined by rightest sympathizers, and spurred by Churchill's pledge of "no peace without victory," engaged the leftists in vicious warfare.[45] The rebels, in control of most of the nation and thinking themselves within reach of political power through elections, signed a peace treaty in February, 1945 and laid down their arms.

From then until March, 1946, when the civil war flared again, the British-sponsored Athens regime, corrupt, inefficient, and ruthless, set about to eliminate its political foes. The United States sent warships to Greek ports and offered aid through the Export-Import Bank. In September, 1946, Secretary Forrestal announced that the United States would maintain a permanent fleet in the Mediterranean. Although Washington was uneasy about the harsh methods of the Athens government and its close alliance with Britain, still, a friendly regime was better than a leftist or Communist one. Greece limped along, staggered by war-wrought devastation, poor leadership, and civil turmoil. Britain, suffering its imperial death throes, could no longer pay the Greek bill. On February 21, 1947, the British informed Washington that they were pulling out. American officials responded to the British appeal with uncommon alacrity with Truman's special message.

Many congressmen resented Truman's having handed them a fait accompli on March 12, 1947. Critics argued that Truman was bypassing the United Nations in giving direct aid to Greece and Turkey, that the Greek regime was venal, that the program would cost too much, that economic—not military—aid was preferred, that Russia would be antagonized, and that the United States was entering an ill-defined global crusade. To win its case the Truman Administration enlisted the support of Republican Senator Vandenberg in a prime example of bipartisan foreign policy. Truman had scared people with his speech. "Washington," editorialized the *New Republic*, "was smothered under gusts of apprehension."[46] Vandenberg, who often warned against another Munich, predicted a "Communist chain reaction from the Dardanelles to the China Sea and westward to the rim of the Atlantic."[47] Most leaders accepted what would later be called the "domino theory." On April 22 the Senate passed the bill for aid to Greece and Turkey by a 67 to 23 vote; the House followed on May 15 with a positive voice vote. Truman signed the act on May 22.

Critics had pressed the Administration on its contention that Greece and Turkey were threatened by Soviet aggression, but received lame answers. It became clear why. The EAM, although Communist-led, had minimal ties with Russia. Churchill more than once said that Stalin had kept the bargain he made at their 1944 Moscow conference to stay out of the Greek imbroglio. In fact, Stalin disliked the Greek Communists because they were nationalists and they admired the independent-minded Yugoslav leader Tito, who gave them aid. Yet Truman simplified the question, enamored as he and many other Americans were with the notion that all Communists took their orders from Moscow.

The issue over the Dardanelles was also more complex than Truman portrayed it. The United States urged international control over the straits. The Soviets saw the issue quite differently, for they had witnessed Turkish behavior during World War II that permitted German warships to drive through the straits into the Black Sea. Soviet security was at stake. Stalin insisted at Yalta that Russia could no longer "accept a situation in which Turkey had a hand on Russia's throat."[48] For its part, Turkey refused any form of joint control with the Soviets. The Soviets grew angry, verbally blasting the Turks and threatening to take action. Turkey, stated one State Department report, "constitutes the stopper in the neck of the bottle through which Soviet political and military influence could most effectively flow into the eastern Mediterranean and Middle East."[49] Stalin, on the other hand, asked: "What would Great Britain do if Spain or Egypt were given this [Turkish] right to close the Suez Canal, or what would the United States Government say if some South American Republic had the right to close the Panama Canal?"[50] The Truman Administration presented the delicate, and perhaps insoluble, issue in the simplest way: the Soviets wanted to subjugate Turkey. The Soviets probably would have liked to, but there was little evidence that they were trying to.

The Dardanelles issue became a perennial Cold War subject, whereas the Greek civil war came to a conclusion when the rebels capitulated in October, 1949. American aid and advisers had flowed to Greece after 1947. American diplomats intervened in Greek politics. Over 350 American officers accompanied the Greek army in its campaign against the EAM in 1947–1949. Lieutenant General James A. Van Fleet advised the Greek general staff. By 1952 the United States had spent $500 million to build up Greek forces. Understandably Greece became dependent upon American assistance. Truman claimed another Cold War victory, but it was not that simple: the Greek insurgents lost not only because of American intervention, but because the Soviet Union refused to help them and Tito decided to seal off the Yugoslav border to deny Greek leftists a sanctuary. Americans nevertheless drew another lesson from this experience: Moscow-inspired communism could be stopped. Soothing and distorting simplicity had overcome complexity in American thinking. As one student of America's response to revolutions has concluded: "The fifth-column analogy from World War II dominated official thinking. The possibility that men had taken to the hills for reasons of their own and not as agents of a foreign power was never seriously considered."[51]

Another statement of what came to be called "containment" flowed gracefully from the gifted pen of George F. Kennan, director of the State Department's Policy

**George F. Kennan (1904– ).** Graduate of Princeton, Pulitzer Prize–winning historian, career diplomat, and recognized "expert" on Soviet affairs, Kennan was Mr. "X" in 1947 when he articulated the containment doctrine. This brilliant man served W. Averell Harriman in Moscow and then returned home to head the State Department's Policy Planning Staff (1947–1949). Later he became ambassador to Russia (1952) and Yugoslavia (1961–1963). In his memoirs he argued that he had not meant that containment should be implemented militarily or universally. (Princeton University Library)

Planning Staff. The July, 1947 issue of the prestigious journal *Foreign Affairs* carried an article titled "The Sources of Soviet Conduct," written by a mysterious Mr. "X", soon revealed as Kennan. The United States must adopt a "policy of firm containment," he wrote, "designed to confront the Russians with unalterable counterforce at every point where they show signs of encroaching upon the interests of a peaceful and stable world." Such pressure might force the "mellowing" of Soviet power. Kennan sketched a picture of an aggressive, uncompromising Russia driven by ideology. Mechanistic Soviet power, he wrote, "moves inexorably along a prescribed path, like a persistent toy automobile wound up and headed in a given direction, stopping only when it meets some unanswerable force."[52] Kennan was vague on whether economic or military means should be used to implement containment—a key question thereafter.

One of the most vocal critics of containment, journalist Walter Lippmann, predicted trouble. In a series of articles published as *The Cold War* (1947), Lippmann called containment a "strategic monstrosity," because it did not discriminate geographically—did not distinguish vital from peripheral areas. Containment would test American resources and patience without limit. What if Congress should decide, as was its constitutional prerogative, not to fund some presidential ventures in "counter-force?" Lippmann also prophetically observed that the "policy can be implemented only by recruiting, subsidizing and supporting a heterogeneous array of satellites, clients, dependents and puppets." He argued that the answer to world tension was not a seemingly limitless global crusade, but a primary effort to remove foreign troops from all of Europe. He denied the popular notion that the Soviet Union's military force was poised for an attack on Western Europe, a point on which he and Kennan agreed. Finally, Lippmann sadly concluded that Truman and Mr. "X" in their major statements had abandoned their essential responsibility—diplomacy. "For a diplomat to think that rival and unfriendly powers cannot be brought to a settlement is to forget what diplomacy is about."[53]

## The Marshall Plan

By 1947 the United States had granted or loaned about nine billion dollars to Europe to help reconstruct its broken economy, to relieve hunger, to encourage trade with America, to avert contagious depression, and to stem radicalism. Despite assistance through the United Nations Relief and Rehabilitation Administration, the World Bank, and the International Monetary Fund, plus the loan to Britain and expenditures for the military occupation of Germany, Washington had failed to secure peace and prosperity. Europe remained prostrate, and Americans predicted that Communists, especially in France and Italy, would exploit the economic chaos. Furthermore, Europe's multibillion dollar deficit posed a real danger to the American economy—Europeans could not buy American products unless they received dollars from the United States. A comprehensive, coordinated program was required, and Secretary of State George C. Marshall called for one when he addressed a Harvard University commencement audience on June 5, 1947. Marshall was a halting, quiet orator, but his message of only 1500 words was lucid. A distraught Europe had to have help to face "economic, social and political deterioration of a very grave character."[54] He vaguely called upon the European nations to initiate a collective plan. British Foreign Minister Ernest Bevin contacted

**The Marshall Plan Team.** Truman, Secretary of State George C. Marshall (1947–1949), Paul Hoffman, and W. Averell Harriman discuss the European Recovery Program in 1948. Hoffman, president of Studebaker Corporation, served as administrator. (U.S. Information Agency, National Archives)

French Foreign Minister Georges Bidault. They met in Paris in mid-June and reluctantly invited Molotov to join them.

The seemingly open Marshall invitation and the Bevin-Bidault request must have stimulated intense discussion among Kremlin leaders. They sniffed a capitalist trap. The Soviets had hardly completed their diatribes against the Truman Doctrine. *Pravda* first commented that Marshall's plan was designed "for political pressure with the help of dollars, a plan for interference in the domestic affairs of other countries."[55] Yet the Soviets convened in Paris with England and France in late June and early July. Molotov thought Bevin and Bidault had plotted something behind his back. Bidault suspected that Molotov's economic advisers were really spies working with the French Communist party. Bevin did not want Russia in a European recovery program at all—a point the scowling Molotov got quickly. The Paris conferees reached a stalemate. Russia could not accept a program dominated by the United States; it sought instead a loosely structured system to protect individual national sovereignties. That was unacceptable to the United States, and hence to Britain and France. Molotov abruptly left town. "East" and "West," as in Germany, were going their own ways.

The United States had never wanted Soviet participation in the Marshall Plan or European Recovery Program (ERP). Throughout the 1947 discussions, diplomats stated that the United States had to run the plan very tightly. The American strategy was to invite all European nations to join, without mentioning any by name, and to keep firm control over the program. If Russia did not accept American terms, the propaganda value would be immense, for it would appear that Russia had rejected a generous American offer and so further divided the world. Yet it is understandable why the Soviets snubbed the Marshall Plan. The open invitation came at a time when the anti-Soviet Truman Doctrine was only a few months old, and furthermore, Eastern Europe was expected to ship raw materials to industrial Western Europe. Thus the postwar effort of the Eastern Europeans and Russians to industrialize, to become less dependent on Western Europe for manufactured goods, was being challenged. And anyway Russia wanted those raw materials. Also, since Soviet influence in Eastern Europe in 1947 was not comprehensive, from Moscow's perspective, a massive influx of American dollars into the region would have represented a real threat to Russia.

The invitation was probably disingenuous in the first place. It would have been illogical and contradictory for Congress to approve funds for Russia so shortly after it had been persuaded to fund the anti-Soviet Truman Doctrine. The invitation amounted to a diplomatic gesture. It worked, because Americans—participants and historians—could say that Russia made the negative decision, or in more general language, that Russia caused the Cold War. Russia formed a feeble Molotov Plan to counter the Marshall Plan's Organization of European Economic Cooperation and revitalized the old Comintern into a new propaganda agency called Cominform. Moscow forced some Eastern European nations to reject the Marshall Plan; others remained outside, not willing to antagonize the Soviet Union by taking the American side in the Cold War. The already existing but weak Economic Commission for Europe was bypassed, and economically vital West Germany was integrated into the ERP.

After months of discussion about how much to spend and after a huge administration advertising campaign, Congress in March, 1948 passed the Economic Cooperation Act. The coup in Czechoslovakia, scheduled elections in Italy (would they go Communist?), and the growing crisis over Germany, together with a March 17 Truman war scare speech to a joint session of Congress (which revived memories of 1939), garnered the Marshall Plan a vote of 69 to 17 in the Senate and 329

**Essen, Germany.** In the rubble of this German city rests a new citizen, who, because of American reconstruction aid, enjoys a full stomach. (Harry S Truman Library)

to 74 in the House. Four billion dollars were approved for its first year. Before it ended in 1952, the Marshall Plan, under the Economic Cooperation Administration, sent over thirteen billion dollars into the needy European economy. People went back to work as factories and mines reopened. Although agricultural production recovered slowly, industrial production improved. The European Recovery Program, said Bevin, was "like a lifeline to sinking men."[56]

The generous Marshall Plan stimulated recovery for people in dire need. Americans believed that peace depended upon prosperity, and they knew that the American economy required exports to European markets. Many of the Marshall Plan billions came home to purchase American products. The Marshall Plan, then, was a matter of serious national interest for the United States as well as a humanitarian effort. It had shortcomings too. Europe became dependent upon American aid, less able to make its own choices. Some American funds were used to continue European domination over colonial areas. The program bypassed the United Nations and the Economic Commission for Europe, where, some critics suggested, it might have been carried out with less divisiveness. The Marshall Plan created a deeper rift between the two rivals. It encouraged restrictions on East-West trade, and helped revive West Germany, thereby arousing Moscow's fears of its nemesis. A European Recovery Program was sorely needed, but how it was presented and shaped by the United States had something to do with why it became a divisive element. Finally, the Marshall Plan gave way increasingly to military aid. In 1951 the Economic Cooperation Administration was submerged in the Mutual Security Administration and by 1952 80 percent of American aid to Western Europe was military in nature.

## NATO and the Militarization of the Cold War

The military dimension had always been present in American foreign policy. Much of Greek-Turkish aid, for example, was military. In July, 1947, Congress passed the National Security Act, which streamlined the military establishment and created the Department of Defense (abolishing the Department of War), the National Security Council (NSC) to advise the President, and the Central Intelligence Agency (CIA) for spying and gathering information. On March 16, 1948 Britain, France, and the three Benelux nations, with American encouragement, signed the Brussels Treaty for collective defense. Recollections of the 1930s stirred people to assert that this time they would be ready for an aggressor. In June the Senate passed (64 to 4) Senator Vandenberg's moderate resolution applauding European efforts on behalf of collective security and suggesting American participation.

After his victory in the election of 1948, Truman summarized American foreign policy in his Inaugural Address of January 20, 1949. Articulating simple juxtapositions of "communism" and "democracy," the President listed four central points. First, he endorsed the United Nations. Second, he applauded the European Recovery Program. Third, he announced that the United States was planning a North Atlantic defense pact. And fourth, "we must embark on a bold new program" of technical assistance for "underdeveloped areas," a reference to the Point Four Program, to be launched in 1950.[57] Dean Acheson became secretary of state that month and guided complicated negotiations on the defense pact. On April 4, 1949 the North Atlantic Treaty was signed in Washington by the five

**Dean Acheson (1893–1971).** Graduate of Yale and Harvard, wealthy lawyer, and government administrator, this man, as he put it, "was always a conservative." Polished if not stuffy, self-confident if not cocky, Acheson called his critics "primitives." He served as secretary of state for 1949–1953 and helped design NATO. (Portrait by Gardner Cox, National Portrait Gallery, Smithsonian Institution, Gift of Covington and Burling)

Brussels Treaty countries of Britain, France, Belgium, the Netherlands, and Luxembourg, as well as by Denmark, Iceland, Italy, Norway, Portugal, Canada, and the United States (Greece and Turkey joined in 1952 and West Germany in 1954). Article 5 provided "that an armed attack against one or more . . . shall be considered an attack against them all."[58]

Acheson anticipated heated debate at home. After all, the United States had not participated in a European alliance since the days of George Washington, and by 1949 an entangling alliance for some Americans was the equivalent of, if not worse than, original sin. Furthermore, no Russian military attack seemed imminent. Article 5, said critics, meant that the United States was creating a Pearl Harbor in every NATO country, drawing America into a war even if it did not want to go. "Mr. Republican" Senator Robert Taft of Ohio recoiled from NATO, considering it a threat to Russia, a provocative act that would eventually force the United States to send military aid to Europe, and a stimulant to an arms race. Taft noted that the President could commit American troops almost at will without constitutional restraint. Some dissenters thought that the Truman Administration skirted questions on the precise nature of the Soviet threat: was it military, political, or ideological? Other critics from both the left and right thought that the United States was overextending itself, draining its resources—in short, weakening rather than strengthening its position.

The critics made little impact. Fear was rampant and the urge to join the crusade compelling. The times were unusual; tradition had to give way. The outcome in the Senate was a foregone conclusion. James Reston of the *New York Times* reported that "there seems to be ignorance about specific parts of the treaty, indifference or a certain fatalistic approach to the future, combined with an acceptance of the idea of 'doing something' about the Russians."[59] Vandenberg endorsed NATO as a healthy reversal of the Neutrality Acts, which, he said, had encouraged Hitler. When asked in Senate hearings whether the United States planned to send substantial numbers of American troops to Europe to stand in the way of a potential Soviet attack, Secretary Acheson replied "no." It was not clear, then, what difference NATO meant in actual military terms. Soviet divisions far outnumbered those of Western Europe, and the United States possessed the atomic bomb. If Washington did not plan to dispatch troops to Europe, then the military balance remained the same. Basically NATO was a question of giving Europe not arms, but the will to resist, the confidence to thwart internal subversion. Such confidence would also encourage economic recovery under the Marshall Plan. "People could not go ahead and make investments for the future," Harriman recalled, "without some sense of security."[60] NATO also stood as a warning, a deterrent, to the Soviets after the Czech coup. It would serve as a "trip wire." NATO was created for other reasons as well. Acheson wanted to rearm West Germany, and NATO would permit the United States to undertake that revival of German power while reassuring Western Europeans. NATO was also a way of knitting the Western nations more tightly into an American sphere of influence, heading off any tendencies toward neutralism or appeasement in the Western camp, as Harriman put it.

On July 21, 1949 the Senate ratified the NATO Treaty by a handsome 82 to 13 margin. Truman, who had had an enduring respect for the military ever since his own Battery "D" days in World War I, signed the treaty two days later. That day he also sent the Mutual Defense Assistance Bill to Congress bearing a request for a one-year appropriation of $1.5 billion for European military aid. Critics complained that that amount was hardly sufficient to build European forces up to adequate defensive strength, but enough to start an arms race by alarming Russia. The Truman Administration admitted that this request was just a first step in a long-term military program. Containment had taken a distinct turn to military means. The stakes became bigger. In January, 1950, after the Soviets exploded an atomic device, Truman ordered speedier development of a hydrogen bomb, and began serious thinking about integrating West German units into a large European army.

On January 30, 1950 the President asked the State and Defense departments to review American defense policy. Eventually tagged National Security Council Paper Number 68 (NSC-68), the report of June predicted a future of indefinite tension and Communist aggression (China had become Communist in the fall of 1949, feeding notions of a giant international conspiracy). NSC-68 recommended a bold military building program. Advisers contemplated about fifty billion dollars a year for the defense budget. By comparison, in fiscal year 1947, security expenditures were $14.4 billion; in 1948, $11.7 billion; in 1949, $12.9 billion; and in 1950, $13 billion. NSC-68 ultimately committed the United States to the unilateral defense of what became known as the "free world." The secret report, glossing over complexities, postulated that "communism" orchestrated the world's troubles. Ignored were the indigenous nationalist movements that challenged colonial masters. The "threat" had been exaggerated and seldom defined during the push for NATO; NSC-68 simplified the threat as monolithic communism. NSC-68 further implied that the United States could accomplish the task of creating world order. What Lippmann had warned against when he criticized the Truman Doctrine became reality: globalism, or the "world policeman," became an accurate depiction of American foreign policy after NSC-68. Worried about how to "sell" the document to the public, the Administration kept it secret. It could be implemented only if a crisis stirred Americans up enough to pay the high military bills. "We were sweating over it, and then—with regard to NSC-68—thank God Korea came along."[61]

## American Answers for Asia: The Restoration of Japan and the Chinese Civil War

At the end of World War II Asia entered a major process of reconstitution. In Indochina, Burma, and Indonesia the old imperial system was crumbling. Japan was defeated and occupied. Korea, formerly dominated by Japan, was divided along the thirty-eighth parallel by Russia and the United States. China was still rocked by its long civil war. The colonial powers, recognizing their diminished position, looked to the United States to help them salvage what they could. The Pacific Ocean, they agreed quite reluctantly, would become an American sphere of influence. The ingredients for tremendous Asian conflict existed in substantial quantities: nationalists, retreating imperialists, civil war, occupied countries, and a new and enlarged American and Soviet presence. Who came out best in the reconstruction of Asia depended upon who had the most power.

If the Soviets ran some of the Eastern European countries, the Supreme Commander for the Allied Powers, General Douglas MacArthur, ran Japan. Unlike Germany, Japan was not divided into zones. Depite the establishment of a Far

Eastern Advisory Commission with Soviet membership, the United States made its supremacy stick and rejected Soviet requests for shared power. The United States also assumed power over Micronesia (the Marianas, Marshalls, and Carolines), Okinawa, Iwo Jima, and more then a hundred other Pacific outposts. As if to demonstrate the point, on July 7, 1946, an atomic bomb was tested on the Marshall Island of Bikini. To avoid the charge of imperial land grabbing, the United States had the United Nations place Micronesia under an American trusteeship. In 1949 MacArthur declared that "now the Pacific had become an Anglo-Saxon lake and our line of defense runs through the chain of islands fringing the coast of Asia."[62]

Although occupation officials planned at first to "reform" Japan, they gradually shifted to a revitalization program as the Cold War progressed and it appeared evident that Communist Mao Tse-tung would win in China. Japan would become a pro-American bastion. During 1947–1950 labor unions were restricted, the reparations program curtailed, production controls in war-related industries relaxed, the antitrust program suspended, Communists barred from government and university positions, and former Japanese leaders reinstated. George F. Kennan helped tailor the rebuilding program in early 1948. Japan and Germany, Kennan later recalled, were "two of our most important pawns on the chessboard of world politics."[63]

The restoration of Japan carried international ramifications. Russia constantly complained, through the ineffective Far Eastern Advisory Commission, about American unilateralism. Finally, in April, 1950, after years of Soviet objection and Defense Department foot-dragging, the United States proceeded without Soviet participation to negotiate a peace treaty with Japan. At that time John Foster Dulles, chief Republican adviser on foreign policy and a skillful negotiator, joined the State Department with the assignment to arrange a settlement with Tokyo. In September, 1951, the United States and fifty other nations signed Dulles' Japanese peace treaty, which restored Japanese sovereignty, gave the United States a base on Okinawa, and permitted the retention of foreign troops in Japan. The Soviet Union refused to sign. A separate Japanese-American security pact was also effected, insuring the presence of American troops and planes on Japanese soil. When the Senate ratified Dulles' handiwork in 1952, the occupation officially terminated. Japan, which a decade earlier bombed Pearl Harbor and earned American opprobrium as a "beast," had become a pivotal element in the postwar American sphere of influence and culturally quite "Americanized."

Americans wanted China within their sphere of influence too. For decades they had preached the Open Door, dreamed of vast Chinese markets and Christian havens, considered China a special friend, if not client, of the United States, and, during World War II, anticipated the elevation of China to great power status. Americans held postwar dreams for a pro-American China, but the Chinese themselves would have it otherwise. Washington underestimated the depth of the Chinese civil war and overestimated the political viability of Generalissimo Chiang Kai-shek, who fell from power in 1949. The United States for the period 1945–1949 became a counterrevolutionary force in a revolutionary country. Something had gone wrong in America's dream. Critics began to point the finger. How could the powerful United States "lose" China? they asked. Unwilling to acknowledge that the problem of China was *Chinese*, they searched for answers in the United States. Vicious recriminations helped launch a domestic search for *American* villains who had "sold out" China.

American postwar goals, at least as understood in Washington, were a united non-Communist country under Chiang, trade with the United States, China as a keeper of the balance of power in Asia, and an American ally. At the end of the war, to fulfill these hopes, American troops took positions in northern China, including Peking and Tientsin. They transported Chiang's soldiers to Manchuria in a race to beat the Communists there. Hundreds of American military officers advised the Nationalist armed forces. The Soviets, following their pledge at Yalta, signed a treaty of friendship with Chiang's regime in August, 1945. Moscow seemed to be abandoning the Chinese Communists of Mao Tse-tung and Chou En-lai. The Soviets preferred a divided, weak China that would pose no threat along the 4,500 miles of the Sino-Soviet border. Mao was too independent-minded, too "Titoist" for the Soviet taste. Stalin said the "Chinese Communists are

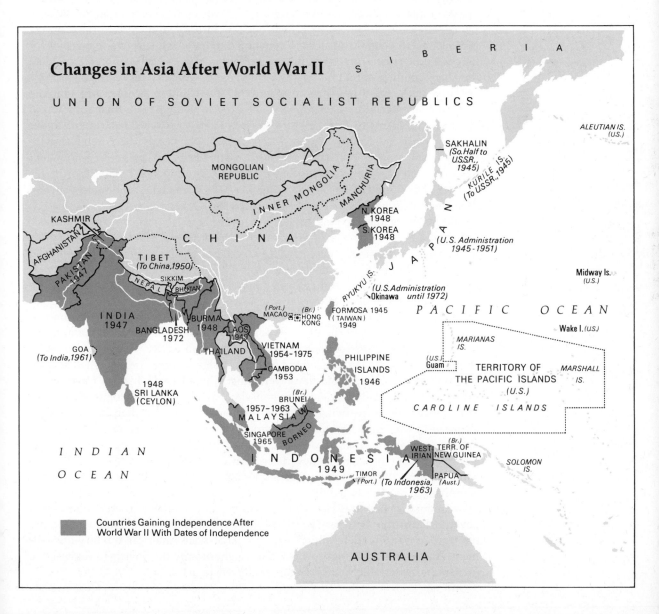

**Changes in Asia After World War II**

Countries Gaining Independence After World War II With Dates of Independence not real Communists. They are 'margarine' Communists."[64] American Foreign Service Officers like John Paton Davies and John S. Service reported from China that relations between Moscow and Mao were tenuous and that the Communists would probably defeat Chiang without much help from Russia, despite the presence of Soviet troops in Manchuria.

American Ambassador Patrick J. Hurley, who, it was said, could strut sitting down, saw an opportunity. If Russia was jilting the Chinese Communists, Hurley reasoned, then Chiang might be able to defeat Mao. The swashbuckling ambassador managed to bring Mao and Chiang together for talks in the fall of 1945, but Chiang proved to be an obstructionist, unwilling to make any concessions, confident that the United States was backing him, and the talks failed. In November Hurley, with his typical blast-furnace approach, resigned and charged that Foreign Service officers had subverted his efforts by favoring Mao and Chou, or "Mouse Dung" and "Joe N. Lie" as he called them.[65] Hurley's vituperative attack on the professional diplomats satisfied the conspiracy-minded who needed scapegoats for the American frustration over China. The "China experts" had not preferred Mao; they had simply reported the truth about Chiang—that he was corrupt, reactionary, and unlikely to gain the allegiance of the Chinese people, and that the Communists would thus gain support. The experts would pay for their accuracy; in the early 1950s many of them were ousted from the State Department under pressure from red-baiting Senator Joseph McCarthy. If only the Foreign Service Officers had supported Chiang, bellowed Hurley and McCarthy, then he would have won. History knows few more masterful distortions of reality.

After the Hurley debacle, in December, 1945, Truman sent the "Marshall Mission" to China. Headed by highly respected General George C. Marshall, it sought to unite the factions under a non-Communist government. The basic fallacy, again, was that such a task could be accomplished. It testified to a shallow understanding of the Chinese civil war. Yet Marshall arranged a cease-fire in January, 1946. The Communists, apparently trying to avoid a bloody confrontation, saw a coalition government as a nonviolent route to power. About the same time, the Soviets pulled out of Manchuria, after having seized and exported great quantities of equipment as war booty, leaving the area to superior Communist forces. By the end of April, 1946, 90 percent of Manchuria rested in Communist hands. Chiang's headstrong effort, against American advice, to storm into Manchuria to challenge Mao, spelled the end of Marshall's cease-fire. Marshall and the 1,000 American military and naval personnel who advised Chiang's forces could not restrain the overconfident Generalissimo, while Chinese Communists protested that they were being killed by American arms. A chagrined Marshall returned to the United States in January, 1947, to become secretary of state.

Uncertain about what to do next, but hopeful of preventing a Communist victory, Truman dispatched a new delegation. The "Wedemeyer Mission" went to China in July, 1947. General Albert C. Wedemeyer criticized the disarray of the Nationalists, but concluded that China, like Greece, needed an aid program to end the Communist menace. He also suggested that a United Nations commission govern Manchuria. Secretary Marshall vetoed both proposals. China was simply not worth a war of undetermined length or large-scale American military involvement. And a United Nations role in China might prompt the Soviets to suggest one for Greece, where the United States preferred to act alone.

Still not knowing what to do, and unwilling to concede that the Communists might be satisfying Chinese needs, Marshall intervened further by releasing undelivered Lend-Lease goods to Chiang. In the autumn of 1947 he offered the Nationalists arms and ammunition and authorized the Army Advisory Group to train Chinese combat troops on Formosa. In part to answer critics who asked why Greece should be saved from communism but not China—who, in short, insisted that the Truman Administration follow the logic of its own containment doctrine—the White House asked Congress in early 1948 for $570 million in China aid. In April Congress authorized $400 million in the China Aid Act. It was just enough to antagonize further the advancing Communists and far too little to save Chiang. Many congressmen saw it as a postponement of American decision, a gesture to a dying regime. "China aid," Vandenberg claimed, "is like sticking your finger in the lake and looking for the hole."[66] Senator Tom Connally thought it a waste of money, "just giving the beggar at the corner a dime."[67]

Indeed, despite the extension of $2.8 billion in American aid between V-J Day and early 1950, despite advisers and missions, the United States could not halt the Communist march. A recalcitrant Chiang permitted inflation to run rampant, rejected popular land reforms, launched risky military expeditions, helped his cohorts raid the Chinese treasury, and generally forfeited the support of the Chinese people. Poor morale spawned massive defections from his army. About one half of United States military aid fell into Communist hands. Ironically, in this way, the Communists got more aid from the United States than from Russia.

## Communist China and American Nonrecognition

In June, 1949, Mao Tse-tung indicated that he was "leaning to one side," choosing between imperialism and socialism.[68] This declaration should not have surprised Washington, which since 1945 had set itself against Mao and had heard Mao's denunciations of American intervention. But to jittery Americans in the thick of the Cold War, it appeared that China had become a puppet of the Soviet Union, because, the simple notion went, Moscow ultimately directed all Communists. Despite Marshall's admonition that he could find no evidence of Soviet intervention, such thinking became popular. Indeed, in August, 1949, Secretary of State Dean Acheson (who replaced Marshall in January) issued the famous *China White Paper*, which began with the statement that "the Communist regime serves not [Chinese] interests but those of Soviet Russia."[69] It was a grand assumption worthy of some of Acheson's best Cold War generalizations. As historian Akira Iriye has written: "Since the documents in the *White Paper* did not warrant the assertion that the Soviet Union had systematically sought to extend its power and influence in China, Acheson must have come to such a sweeping conclusion through the medium of Cold-War visions."[70] The documents in fact showed that there was little the United States could have done, because there was little that Chiang was willing to do. In December, 1949, Chiang finally fled with the Chinese treasury to the island of Formosa (Taiwan). The Communist People's Republic of China, established on October 1, took power on the mainland.

The Truman Administration had a difficult time explaining the "fall" of China. Critics like publisher Henry R. Luce of *Time* magazine, Republican congressmen, and missionaries charged that Truman had "lost" China, as if it had once "belonged" to the United States. Senator Styles Bridges and Congressman Walter Judd headed an informal, noisy, and influential "China Lobby," which for years had

**"The Open Door."** The Communists, led by Mao Tse-tung, defeated the crumbling forces of Chiang Kai-shek in 1949, opening a door that the United States had tried to keep closed. (*The Reporter,* 1950. Copyright 1950 by Fortnightly Publishing Co. Inc.)

advocated American military involvement in the Chinese civil war. They asked: If the essence of American foreign policy was the containment of communism without geographical limit, as stated in the Truman Doctrine and the "X" article, why did not the United States intervene in China? If Greece, why not China? Truman and his advisers never gave a systematic answer, although at different times they said that China was too large, that a land war in Asia was unthinkable, that Chiang, unlike the Greek government, was unmanageable, that the Greek question was an immediate crisis, that there was no evidence of foreign influence in China, and that the monetary costs were prohibitive. The Truman Administration conceded that the containment doctrine was sound, but argued that the Administration had done the best it could to apply containment in China to stem the Communists. Not good enough, the critics easily shot back.

The United States' failure in China was not due to insufficient aid or lack of concern; rather, more fundamental, American leaders never understood the dynamic force of a peasant society ripe for change and the real appeal the land-reforming Communists had among the Chinese people. Americans never marshaled the courage to admit their mistake in clinging to Chiang. The United States' backing of the unpopular Chiang proved foolhardy because, as historian Barbara Tuchman has noted, "there is little virtue in a client being anti-Communist if he is at the same time rotting from within."[71]

After Mao's victory over Chiang, the United States refused to recognize the People's Republic of China. Behind the nonrecognition policy lay mounting Sino-American animosities. In June of 1949 Communist leaders asked American Ambassador J. Leighton Stuart to meet with them. The Truman Administration vetoed a conference, fearing howls from the pro-Chiang "China Lobby." The Communists had not ingratiated themselves with Washington. They rudely reminded Americans of their imperialist past, including military participation in the Boxer Rebellion, support for Japan's seizure of Shantung in 1919, and naval gunboat patrols on Chinese rivers in the 1920s and 1930s. They confiscated American property and harassed Americans. American Consul General at Mukden Angus Ward was kept under house arrest from November, 1947, to October, 1949, when he was formally tried, convicted of spying, and expelled from China.

From December of 1949 through February of 1950, Mao negotiated with the Soviets in Moscow and signed a treaty of friendship and alliance. Fearful of a revived Japan and of the American presence in Asia, Mao needed an ally. Stalin was hesitant, wary of a Chinese Tito and a strong China. Although the talks were often acrimonious, because the Soviets wanted to retain their spoils won at Yalta, the United States looked upon the result as evidence that communism was a cohesive monolith. The treaty provided for the withdrawal of Soviet troops from Port Arthur, the transfer of Soviet interests in railroads to China, Soviet commercial rights in Sinkiang, and recognition of Russian control of Outer Mongolia. What is striking is the inconsequential foreign aid Russia promised and the clash of traditional Russian-Chinese national interests. Yet Americans largely ignored the schism, stressed Sino-Soviet ideological affinity, and denounced the treaty as further evidence of the Soviet conquest of China. State Department officer Louis J. Halle later wrote that some American diplomats were quite cognizant of the "long record of conflict between Mao and Moscow. They were, however, intimidated into silence, or if they tried to speak out their careers and reputations were ruined by accusations of treason."[72] The "Chi Commies," as State Department telegrams tagged the new Chinese leaders, would not be recognized. The nonrecognition policy was born in failure, misinterpretation, and exaggeration, for it set the United States firmly against the largest (650 million people) and ultimately most influential nation in Asia. Assistant Secretary of State Dean Rusk facilely summarized the rigid American position in early 1951: "The Peiping regime may be a colonial Russian government—a Slavic Manchukuo on a large scale. It is not the Government of China. It does not pass the first test. It is not Chinese."[73]

## Legacies of the Early Cold War

"We thought we could do anything," noted an American writer who recalled the end of the Second World War. "We were heirs to a smiling and victorious confidence."[74] Indeed, Americans in 1945 were flushed with a sense of power; the British, the Russians, and many other foreign observers noted it with some apprehension. This confidence contributed to America's zealous pursuit of its goals in the postwar period, as did American ideology and economic needs. Shorn of their ignoble "isolationism," impatient to throw off the failures of the depression decade, and committed to a world of peace and prosperity on their terms, Americans were outraged when the Soviet Union, nursing its own sense of growth, challenged the American mission and opportunity. In their frustration to explain how the grand ideals of the Allies had deteriorated to the bickering of the Cold War, Americans—leaders and common folk alike—often adopted superficial assumptions and a diplomatic style befitting the bully on a streetcorner.

"After World War II," Senator J. William Fulbright remembered, "we were sold on the idea that Stalin was out to dominate the world. I didn't have the knowledge or the foresight to make a judgment at that time. . . . Henry Wallace sensed it, he

**"Uncle Sam's World Wide Umbrella."** As the donor of large amounts of foreign aid, as the chief partner in military alliances, and as the professor of the containment doctrine, the United States undertook new global responsibilities after World War II. (*The Reporter,* 1950. Copyright 1950 by Fortnightly Publishing Co. Inc.)

had a feeling about it, but he was ridiculed for being a visionary, an appeaser, unrealistic."[75] As Fulbright suggested, a popular, largely untested idea captivated many Americans in the early Cold War: the Soviet Union had launched a crusade to communize the world. Certainly there were appearances to feed such a notion. Austere, intransigent, and ruthless, Stalin became in American eyes an obstructionist. Soviet diplomatic machinations were alarming, and simple-minded Communist ideology and propaganda offended the ear. The Soviet diplomatic style was rude, with threats as common as compromises.

But the hard evidence for the assumption that the Soviet Union was following a path of global aggression did not exist. Americans embraced soothing simplicity rather than sophisticated analysis. So they thought that revolutions and civil wars were Moscow-directed. They supported, however reluctantly, the restoration of European imperialism in Asia. They exaggerated the Communist menace—seeing blacks and whites where greys abounded. They articulated what later was called a "domino theory"—if one country falls to communism, others will be tipped in the same direction, like a row of dominoes. They did not believe that Soviet behavior could be explained in part as a response to external factors, such as American behavior; influenced by Kennan's arguments, they posited a mechanistic view that an internal imperative, the need to maintain the totalitarian system and Communist ideology, compelled nasty Soviet actions. Americans reacted; the Soviets acted. Americans defended; the Soviets aggressed. The Soviets certainly practiced an uncooperative diplomacy, but the Truman Administration too often cast a very complex international environment as a simple contest between "good guys" and "bad guys." Analysts would later identify such thinking as the Cold War mentality. George F. Kennan himself later concluded that Americans, especially military planners, exaggerated Soviet behavior and created "the image of the totally inhuman and totally malevolent adversary" and "reconjured [it] daily, week after week, month after month, year after year, until it takes on every feature of flesh and blood and becomes the daily companion of those who cultivate it, so that any attempt on anyone's part to deny its reality appears as an act of treason or frivolity."[76]

American diplomats in the early Cold War years pursued a self-conscious, expansionist, often unilateral, foreign policy. In a world recently ravaged by war, American businessmen and government officials cooperated to expand American foreign trade. By 1947 the United States accounted for one-third of the world's exports. The Americans exploited opportunities such as Middle Eastern oil and tapped the raw materials of the so-called Third World, importing manganese ore from Brazil and India, for example. The United States continued to preach the Open Door policy to help spur this trade and facilitate the investment of $12 billion abroad by 1950, but other nations complained that they could not compete and that therefore the Open Door was really an invitation to American domination. Stalin thought the "Open Door policy as dangerous to a nation as foreign military invasion."[77] The foreign aid program of the postwar years was designed in part to keep trade and investments flowing; American products could not be purchased unless foreigners had dollars to spend on them. One of the chief legacies of the Truman period, then, was the establishment of foreign aid as a major tool of American diplomacy—a way of curbing revolution, thwarting communism, and stimulating the American economy. Americans got in the habit of thinking that dollars could buy diplomatic friends and economic security.

The containment doctrine became the commanding principle of American Cold War foreign policy. When Americans were in doubt, the containment doctrine told them what to do. There were enough successes, enough "lessons," that it became fixed as a cure-all. "Like medieval theologians," Fulbright has noted, "we had a philosophy that explained everything to us in advance, and everything that did not fit could be readily identified as a fraud or a lie or an illusion. . . . The perniciousness of the anti-Communist ideology of the Truman Doctrine arises not from any patent falsehood but from its distortion and simplification of reality, from its universalization and its elevation to the status of a revealed truth."[78] Throughout the 1950s, 1960s, and well into the 1970s, Americans applied the historical lessons of the 1940s, and thereby failed to define precisely the "threat," placed few geographical limits on containment, and increasingly adopted military methods.

Another legacy of the early Cold War affected the American political process. The Truman Administration, sometimes using scare tactics, shaped the thinking of the "foreign policy public." Most foreign policy debates centered on how much to spend, not whether to spend. Congress sometimes proved obstinate, but on the

**Dollar and Atomic Diplomacy.** In this Soviet view of American foreign policy Truman wields the atomic bomb and the money bag. Note Winston S. Churchill on the right. (*Krokodil,* U.S.S.R.)

whole Truman got what he wanted. It seemed the contest with the Communists was too important to leave to the people, because, as historian Thomas A. Bailey reasoned, "the masses are notoriously short-sighted and generally cannot see danger until it is at their throats." A President may have to deceive them. Concluded Bailey, in an unabashed endorsement of the practice in 1948: "Deception of the people may in fact become increasingly necessary, unless we are willing to give our leaders in Washington a free hand. . . . [T]he yielding of some of our democratic control of foreign affairs is the price that we may have to pay for greater physical security."[79]

Bipartisanship also helped the President control the making of foreign policy. Americans had to speak with unity. As bipartisan leader Vandenberg proudly concluded, "our Government did not splinter. It did not default. It was strong in the presence of its adversaries."[80] Unfortunately bipartisanship meant too often that legislation was superficially analyzed, that debate was pro forma, that alternative policies were lightly dismissed, and that Congress permitted the President considerable freedom in foreign policy, abdicating its own responsibilities. Acheson bluntly remarked: "Bipartisan foreign policy is the ideal for the executive because you cannot run this damned country any other way except by fixing the whole organization so it doesn't work the way it is supposed to work. Now the way to do that is to say politics stops at the seaboard—and anyone who denies that postulate is a son-of-a-bitch and a crook and not a true patriot. Now if people will swallow that, then you're off to the races."[81]

People swallowed it. Debate—the testing of assumptions—became shallow. Critics were isolated as enemies of the state, appeasers, Communist sympathizers, or just muddleheaded idealists. During the 1948 presidential campaign, in a choice example of "red-baiting," Truman deliberately attempted to link Wallace and the Communists in the American mind. Timid congressmen, afraid of recrimination if they did not join the crusade, and constantly handed alarmist faits accomplis by the President, fell into line. Critics ventured forth in fear with their questions and sometimes at great cost to political careers. Although McCarthyism was just around the corner, it was the Truman Administration that, in 1947, instituted a federal employee loyalty program to identify and ferret out suspected subversives. Definitions of disloyalty were imprecise, and too often criticism was taken for subversion. The lifeblood of a democratic system—debate, free inquiry, tolerance of dissenting views—deteriorated during the Cold War.

Finally, one of the significant legacies of the early Cold War for the United States was Washington's disdain for diplomacy as a means of solving disputes and avoiding confrontations. Walter Lippmann sensed this attitude when he pointed out the shortcoming of the containment doctrine in 1947. There seemed to be little faith in negotiations with the Soviet Union. Truman and Stalin never met again after Potsdam. Each side in the Cold War glared angrily at the other over the barricades, mental and physical, that they constructed after World War II. Both sides became convinced of their absolute rightness, and missed opportunities for diplomatic give-and-take.

## Further Reading for the Period 1945–1950

For general studies of the Cold War see some of the works mentioned in Chapter 11 and the following: Stephen Ambrose, *Rise to Globalism* (1976), Richard Barnet, *Roots of War* (1972), Louis Halle, *The Cold War as History* (1967), Richard Kirkendall, ed., *The Truman Period as a Research Field* (1974), Gabriel and Joyce Kolko, *The Limits of Power* (1972), Walter LaFeber, *America, Russia, and the Cold War* (1976), Ernest R. May, "*Lessons*" *of the Past* (1973), Philip Mosely, *The Kremlin and World Politics* (1960), Thomas G. Paterson, ed., *Containment and the Cold War* (1973), Arthur M. Schlesinger, Jr., *The Imperial Presidency* (1973), Marshall D. Shulman, *Stalin's Foreign Policy Reappraised* (1963), Ronald Steel, *Pax Americana* (1967), Robert Tucker, *The Radical Left and American Foreign Policy* (1971), and Adam Ulam, *The Rivals* (1971) and *Expansion and Coexistence: The History of Soviet Foreign Policy, 1917–1973* (1974).

Biographical studies include John Blum, ed., *The Price of Vision: The Diary of Henry A. Wallace* (1973), Isaac Deutscher, *Stalin* (1967), Milovan Djilas, *Conversations with Stalin* (1962), Robert H. Ferrell, *George C. Marshall* (1966), the essays on Truman, Acheson, and Kennan by John L. Gaddis, Robert H. Ferrell and David McLellan, and Thomas G. Paterson, in Frank Merli and Theodore A. Wilson, eds., *Makers of American Diplomacy* (1974), W. Averell Harriman and Elie Abel, *Special Envoy to Churchill and Stalin, 1941–1946* (1975), Richard Kirkendall, "Harry S Truman," in Morton Borden, ed., *America's Eleven Greatest Presidents* (1971), David McLellan, *Dean Acheson* (1976), Gaddis Smith, *Dean Acheson* (1972), and Richard Walton, *Henry Wallace, Harry Truman and the Cold War* (1976). Short biographies of leading decisionmakers are located in John A. Garraty, ed., *Encyclopedia of American Biography* (1974).

For the origins of the Cold War, including economic diplomacy, consult Barton J. Bernstein, ed., *Politics and Policies of the Truman Administration* (1970), Thomas Campbell, *Masquerade Peace: America's UN Policy* (1973), Lynn Etheridge Davis, *The Cold War Begins* (1974), Herbert Feis, *From Trust to Terror* (1970), John L. Gaddis, *The United States and the Origins of the Cold War* (1972), Lloyd Gardner, *Architects of Illusion* (1970), Richard Gardner, *Sterling-Dollar Diplomacy* (1969), George Herring, *Aid to Russia, 1941–1946* (1973), Gabriel Kolko, *The Politics of War* (1968), and Thomas G. Paterson, *Soviet-American Confrontation* (1973) and ed., *Cold War Critics* (1971).

The atomic bomb and its impact on diplomacy are discussed in Gar Alperovitz, *Atomic Diplomacy* (1965), Barton J. Bernstein, ed., *The Atomic Bomb* (1975), Herbert Feis, *The Atomic Bomb and the End of World War II* (1966), Richard Hewlett and Oscar Anderson, *The New World* (1962), Lisle Rose, *After Yalta* (1973), and Martin Sherwin, *A World Destroyed* (1975). The H-bomb decision is treated in Herbert F. York, *The Advisors: Oppenheimer, Teller, and the Superbomb* (1975).

For the question of postwar Germany, see Stephen Ambrose, *Eisenhower and Berlin, 1945* (1967), John Gimbel, *The American Occupation of Germany* (1968) and *The Origins of the Marshall Plan* (1976), Warren Kimball, *Swords or Ploughshares? The Morgenthau Plan for Defeated Nazi Germany, 1943–1946* (1976), Bruce Kuklick, *American Policy and the Division of Germany* (1972), and Jean Smith, *The Defense of Berlin* (1963).

For the Truman Doctrine, Marshall Plan, NATO, and containment, consult Richard Barnet, *Intervention and Revolution* (1972), Richard Freeland, *The Truman Doctrine and the Origins of McCarthyism* (1971), John O. Iatrides, *Revolt in Athens* (1972), Joseph Jones, *The Fifteen Weeks* (1955), Robert Osgood, *NATO: The Entangling Alliance* (1962), Thomas G. Paterson, ed., *Containment and the Cold War* (1973), Harry Price, *The Marshall Plan and Its Meaning* (1955), and Stephen Xydis, *Greece and the Great Powers* (1963).

Diplomatic problems in Asia are treated in Russell Buhite, *Patrick J. Hurley and*

*American Foreign Policy* (1973), Warren Cohen, *American's Response to China* (1971), Herbert Feis, *The China Tangle* (1953), Edward Friedman and Mark Selden, eds., *America's Asia* (1971), Gary Hess, *America Encounters India, 1941-1947* (1971), Akira Iriye, *The Cold War in Asia* (1974), George Kahin and John Lewis, *The United States and Vietnam* (1969), Ross Koen, *The China Lobby in American Politics* (1974), Tang Tsou, *America's Failure in China, 1941-1950* (1963), and Paul Varg, *The Closing of the Door: Sino-American Relations, 1936-1947* (1973).

For domestic politics, anticommunism, interest groups, and public opinion in the early Cold War period, see Robert A. Divine, *Foreign Policy and U.S. Presidential Elections, 1940-1960* (1974), Robert Griffith, *The Politics of Fear: Joseph R. McCarthy and the Senate* (1970), Robert Griffith and Athan Theoharis, ed., *The Specter: Original Essays on the Cold War and McCarthyism* (1974), Alonzo Hamby, *Beyond the New Deal* (1973), Earl Latham, *The Communist Controversy in Washington* (1966), Richard Neustadt, *Presidential Power* (1960), Ronald Radosh, *American Labor and U.S. Foreign Policy* (1969), John Snetsinger, *Truman, the Jewish Vote, and the Creation of Israel* (1974), Athan Theoharis, *Seeds of Repression* (1971) and *The Yalta Myths* (1970), H. Bradford Westerfield, *Foreign Policy and Party Politics* (1955), and Lawrence Wittner, *Rebels Against War: The American Peace Movement, 1941-1960* (1974).

For representative essays and an extensive list of other works, see Thomas G. Paterson, ed., *The Origins of the Cold War* (1974). Also see the following notes.

## Notes to Chapter 12

1. Quoted in Hanson W. Baldwin, "Hiroshima Decision," in New York Times, *Hiroshima Plus 20* (New York: Delacorte Press, 1965), p. 41.
2. Quoted in John Toland, *The Rising Sun* (New York: Random House, 1970), p. 780.
3. Quoted in William L. Laurence, *Dawn Over Zero: The Story of the Atomic Bomb* (New York: Alfred A. Knopf, 1946), pp. 219, 221.
4. Michihiko Hachiya, *Hiroshima Diary* (Chapel Hill: University of North Carolina Press, 1955; trans. by Warner Wells), p. 6.
5. Harry S Truman, *Memoirs* (Garden City, N.Y.: Doubleday, 1955-56; 2 vols.), I, 421.
6. William D. Leahy, *I Was There* (New York: Whittlesey House, McGraw-Hill, 1950), p. 441.
7. Quoted in Richard Barnet, *Roots of War* (Baltimore: Penguin Books, 1973), p. 46.
8. Quoted in Barton J. Bernstein, "Roosevelt, Truman and the Atomic Bomb, 1941-1945: A Reinterpretation," *Political Science Quarterly,* XC (Spring, 1975), 61.
9. Truman, *Memoirs,* I, 416.
10. Quoted in Martin J. Sherwin, *A World Destroyed: The Atomic Bomb and the Grand Alliance* (New York: Alfred A. Knopf, 1975), p. 224.
11. Harry S Truman to Eleanor Roosevelt, December 12, 1948, Box 4560, Eleanor Roosevelt Papers, Franklin D. Roosevelt Library, Hyde Park, New York.
12. U.S. Department of State, *Foreign Relations of the United States, 1946, VI* (Washington: Government Printing Office, 1969), 707.
13. Jeanette P. Nichols, "Dollar Strength as a Liability in United States Diplomacy," *Proceedings of the American Philosophical Society,* III (February 17, 1967), 47.

14. Truman quoted in Thomas G. Paterson, *Soviet-American Confrontation: Postwar Reconstruction and the Origins of the Cold War* (Baltimore: The Johns Hopkins University Press, 1973), p. ix; Earl of Halifax to Mr. Bevin, August 9, 1945, AN2560/22/45, Foreign Office Correspondence, Public Record Office, London, England.
15. Gaddis Smith, *Dean Acheson* (New York: Cooper Square Publishers, 1972), p. 416.
16. Minutes on the Political Situation in the United States, August 20-21, 1945, AN2505/4/45, Foreign Office Correspondence, Public Record Office.
17. Bert Cochran, *Harry Truman and the Crisis Presidency* (New York: Funk and Wagnalls, 1973), p. 232.
18. Quoted in John L. Gaddis, *The United States and the Origins of the Cold War* (New York: Columbia University Press, 1972), p. 205.
19. Quoted in John L. Gaddis, "Harry S Truman and the Origins of Containment," in Frank Merli and Theodore Wilson, eds., *Makers of American Diplomacy* (New York: Charles Scribner's Sons, 1974), p. 500.
20. U.S. Department of State, *Foreign Relations of the United States, Yalta* (Washington, D.C.: Government Printing Office, 1955), p. 669.
21. Quoted in Lloyd C. Gardner, *Economic Aspects of New Deal Diplomacy* (Madison: University of Wisconsin Press, 1964), p. 308.
22. Quoted in Barton J. Bernstein, "American Foreign Policy and the Origins of the Cold War," in Bernstein, ed., *Politics and Policies of the Truman Administration* (Chicago: Quadrangle Books, 1970), p. 36.

23. Quoted in Lisle Rose, *After Yalta* (New York: Charles Scribner's Sons, 1973), pp. 123–124.

24. Henry L. Stimson and McGeorge Bundy, *On Active Service in Peace and War* (New York: Harper & Brothers, 1948), p. 644.

25. Walter Millis, ed., *The Forrestal Diaries* (New York: The Viking Press, 1951), p. 96.

26. U.S. Department of State, *Foreign Relations, 1946* (Washington, D.C.: Government Printing Office, 1969), VII, 223.

27. Quoted in Paterson, *Soviet-American Confrontation*, pp. 129–130.

28. Truman, *Memoirs*, I, 552.

29. *Foreign Relations, 1946*, VI (Washington, D.C.: Government Printing Office, 1969), 706.

30. George F. Kennan, *Memoirs, 1925–1950* (Boston: Little, Brown, 1967), p. 294.

31. *Congressional Record*, 79th Cong., 2nd sess., XCII, A1145–1146.

32. Quoted in Gaddis, *United States and Origins of the Cold War*, p. 309.

33. *Ibid.*, p. 315.

34. *New York Times*, March 14, 1946 (*Pravda* interview).

35. Quoted in Paterson, *Soviet-American Confrontation*, p. 182.

36. *Vital Speeches*, XII (October 1, 1946), 738–741.

37. Quoted in William Hillman, *Mr. President* (New York: Farrar, Straus and Young, 1952), p. 128.

38. *Foreign Relations, 1944*, IV, 951.

39. Paraphrase by Colonel Bernard Bernstein of the President's meeting with him, in U.S. Congress, Senate, Judiciary Committee, 90th Cong., 1st sess., *Morgenthau Diary (Germany)* (Washington, D.C.: Government Printing Office, 1967; 2 vols.), II, 1555.

40. W. Averell Harriman, "Certain Factors Underlying Our Relations with the Soviet Union," November 14, 1945, W. Averell Harriman Papers (in his possession).

41. Quoted in Thomas G. Paterson, ed., *The Origins of the Cold War* (Lexington, Mass.: D. C. Heath, 1974; 2nd ed.), p. 34.

42. Quoted in Paterson, *Soviet-American Confrontation*, p. 235.

43. *Public Papers of the Presidents, Truman, 1947* (Washington, D.C.: Government Printing Office, 1963), pp. 176–180.

44. Joseph Jones, "Memorandum for the File," March 12, 1947, Box 1, Joseph Jones Papers, Harry S Truman Library, Independence, Missouri.

45. Quoted in John O. Iatrides, *Revolt in Athens* (Princeton: Princeton University Press, 1972), p. 208.

46. "The Truman Doctrine," *New Republic*, CXVI (March 24, 1947), 5.

47. *Congressional Record*, XCIII (April 22, 1947), 3772–3773.

48. *Foreign Relations, Yalta*, p. 903.

49. *Ibid., 1946*, VII, 895.

50. "Record of Meeting at the Kremlin, Moscow, 9th October, 1944, at 10 P.M.," Premier 3, 434/4, Prime Minister's Office Records, Public Record Office.

51. Richard Barnet, *Intervention and Revolution* (New York: New American Library, 1968), p. 121.

52. "X," "The Sources of Soviet Conduct," *Foreign Affairs*, XXV (July, 1947), reprinted in Thomas G. Paterson, ed., *Containment and the Cold War* (Reading, Mass.: Addison-Wesley, 1973), pp. 18–33.

53. Lippmann quoted *ibid.*, pp. 41–51.

54. *Department of State Bulletin*, XVI (July 15, 1947), 1159–1160.

55. Quoted in Paterson, *Soviet-American Confrontation*, p. 214.

56. Quoted in Richard D. McKinzie and Theodore A. Wilson, "The Marshall Plan in Historical Perspective" (unpublished paper delivered at annual meeting of the American Historical Association, 1972), p. 8.

57. *Public Papers of the President, Truman, 1949* (Washington: Government Printing Office, 1964), p. 114.

58. *Department of State Bulletin*, XX (March 20, 1949), 340.

59. *New York Times*, May 19, 1949.

60. W. Averell Harriman in "Princeton Seminar," October 10–11, 1953, Box 65, Dean Acheson Papers, Harry S Truman Library.

61. Edward W. Barrett, *ibid.*

62. Quoted in John W. Dower, "Occupied Japan and the American Lake, 1945–1950," in Edward Friedman and Mark Selden, eds., *America's Asia* (New York: Vintage Books, 1971), pp. 146, 170.

63. Kennan, *Memoirs, 1925–1950*, p. 369.

64. Quoted in Herbert Feis, *The China Tangle* (New York: Atheneum, 1965), p. 140.

65. Quoted in Robert A. Hart, *The Eccentric Tradition: American Diplomacy in the Far East* (New York: Charles Scribner's Sons, 1976), p. 156.

66. Quoted in Norman Graebner, *The New Isolationism* (New York: Ronald Press, 1956), p. 14.

67. Quoted in Ernest R. May, *The Truman Administration and China, 1945–1949* (Philadelphia: J. B. Lippincott Company, 1975), p. 83.

68. Quoted in Warren I. Cohen, *America's Response to China* (New York: John Wiley & Sons, 1971), p. 199.

69. U.S. Department of State, *United States Relations with China* (Washington, D.C.: Department of State, 1949), p. xvii.

70. Akira Iriye, *The Cold War in Asia* (Englewood Cliffs, N.J.: Prentice Hall, 1974), p. 170.

71. Barbara Tuchman, "The United States and China," *Colorado Quarterly*, XXI (Summer, 1972), 12.

72. Louis J. Halle, "After Vietnam—Another Witch Hunt?" *New York Times Magazine*, June 6, 1971, p. 44.

73. *Department of State Bulletin*, XXIV (May 28, 1951), 847.

74. L. E. Sissman, "Missing the Forties," *Atlantic Monthly*, CCXXXII (October, 1973), 35.

75. Quoted in Daniel Yergin, "Fulbright's Last Frustration," *New York Times Magazine*, November 24, 1974, p. 87.

76. George F. Kennan, "The United States and the Soviet Union, 1917–1976," *Foreign Affairs*, LIV (July, 1976), 682.

77. Quoted in W. Averell Harriman and Elie Abel, *Special Envoy to Churchill and Stalin, 1941–1946* (New York: Random House, 1975), p. 528.

78. J. William Fulbright, "Reflections: In Thrall to Fear," *The New Yorker*, XLVII (January 8, 1972), 43.

79. Thomas A. Bailey, *The Man in the Street: The Impact of American Public Opinion on Foreign Policy* (New York: Macmillan, 1948), p. 13.

80. Arthur H. Vandenberg, Jr., ed., *The Private Papers of Senator Vandenberg* (Boston: Houghton Mifflin, 1952), pp. 550–551.

81. Quoted in Theodore A. Wilson and Richard D. McKinzie, "White House versus Congress: Conflict or Collusion? The Marshall Plan as a Case Study" (unpublished paper delivered to the annual meeting of the Organization of American Historians, 1973), p. 2.

**Blair House Meeting.** Attorney General J. Howard McGrath, President Harry S Truman, and Secretary of Defense Louis Johnson break for lunch on June 27, 1950, after discussing the Korean crisis at Blair House, across the street from the White House. (Harry S Truman Library)

# 13 Something Old, Something New: Global Confrontations, 1950–1961

## Diplomatic Crossroad: American Troops to Korea, 1950

American Ambassador to South Korea John J. Muccio was awakened by a telephone call at 8:00 A.M. "Brace yourself for a shock," his chief deputy said, "the Communists are hitting all along the front!"[1] Muccio dressed hurriedly and rushed out to check the alarming reports. United Press correspondent Jack James, also in Seoul, alertly did the same and earned himself a rare scoop. At 9:50 A.M. he cabled the UP in the United States that North Korean troops had crossed the thirty-eighth parallel. About the same time Muccio cabled Washington about "an all-out offensive."[2]

At 4 A.M. that rainy Sunday morning of June 25, 1950, some 75,000 troops of the Democratic People's Republic of Korea (North Korea) bolted across the thirty-eighth parallel, the boundary drawn after World War II by the United States and Russia which cut Korea into North and South. North Korean units attacked along a 150-mile front with heavy artillery and a spearhead of well-armored tanks that followed the valley roads into the South. The Russian-made tanks rumbled along, seemingly invulnerable to South Korean resistance. South Korean forces quickly collapsed in a rout. General Douglas MacArthur remembered that the North Korean army "struck like a cobra."[3]

James's cable beat Muccio's to the United States, over 7,000 miles away, by a few minutes. It was a hot, humid Saturday evening (June 24) in Washington, D.C., thirteen hours behind Seoul time. The UP called the Department of State to verify James's report. Dumbfounded officers had no information. They phoned Assistant Secretary of State Dean Rusk, then dining with journalist Joseph Alsop in the Georgetown section of Washington. Rusk left the Alsop party about the same time that Muccio's cable reached the State Department. It was decoded. The time was now after 10:00 P.M. Secretary of State Dean Acheson, resting at his Maryland farm just outside the capital, had begun reading himself to sleep when his official phone rang. He got the bad news. A burst of calls soon ricocheted around the Washington area, as official after official was roused. General

J. Lawton Collins, the army chief of staff, heard early morning pounding on the door of his Chesapeake Bay cottage, and immediately recalled a similar incident years before when an aide suddenly awakened him to announce the attack on Pearl Harbor. He was soon racing toward Washington.

Acheson and State Department officials agreed that the United Nations Organization should be notified and an emergency session of the Security Council convened. It was a natural first step, for the United States dominated that body, Korean issues had been handled there before, the principle of collective security in the face of aggression seemed at issue, and they did not know what else to do. At 11:20 P.M. Acheson rang up the President, at home in Independence, Missouri, with his family. "Mr. President, I have very serious news."[4] Acheson told Truman that there was little to do at this point, so he should remain in Missouri, get a good night's sleep, and come to Washington the next day, Sunday, June 25. State Department personnel worked through the night drafting a Security Council resolution that charged North Korea with a "breach of the peace."[5] Meetings in the Pentagon and the State Department debated courses of action. An evacuation of Americans in Seoul was ordered.

President Truman boarded his plane early Sunday afternoon for the trip to the capital. An aide told one reporter: "The boss is going to hit those fellows [Communists] hard."[6] The President stood low in the opinion polls at the time, in large part because he was being charged by Senator Joseph McCarthy of Wisconsin with softness toward communism. Former State Department official Alger Hiss, to right-wing critics the epitome of the "sell-out" spy, had been convicted of perjury in January, and China had "fallen" just a few months before. Bold action now would disarm the President's critics. As Truman sat alone in the airplane *Independence,* he pondered history. He frequently drew lessons from the past and they usually came easily to him. Korea was the American Rhineland, he thought. It was the 1930s all over again. "Communism was acting in Korea just as Hitler, Mussolini, and the Japanese had acted ten, fifteen, and twenty years earlier."[7] There would be no appeasement this time. While he was thinking somewhere over the Midwest, the Security Council passed America's resolution of condemnation of North Korea. Except for Yugoslavia's abstention, all the members present voted "yes." The Soviet delegation, which could have cast a veto to kill the measure, was surprisingly absent, still boycotting the United Nations over its refusal to seat the new Communist government in China.

A stern, short-tempered Truman, familiar bow tie firmly in place, deplaned in Washington and headed for a dinner meeting of top officials at Blair House, that elegant federal style building on Pennsylvania Avenue, then being used as a residence during the renovation of the White House. After a chicken dinner (including hearts of lettuce with Russian dressing!) the conferees began the weighty task of meeting the Korean crisis. All assumed without question that Russia had engineered the attack, using North Korean stooge forces to probe for a soft spot in the American containment shield. Here was a test of American will and power. Worse still, they speculated, the thrust in Korea might be only one component of a worldwide Communist assault. Would Yugoslavia be next? Iran? Formosa? Indochina? The Philippines? Japan? Germany? The State Department cabled overseas posts: "Possible that Korea is only the first [of a] series of coordinated actions on part of Soviets. Maintain utmost vigilance."[8] Historical references to World War II marked the discussion at Blair House. The pull of the past helped shape military decisions in this new crisis. Aggression had to be halted. Truman ordered General MacArthur in Japan to send arms and equipment to the South Koreans and to use American war planes to attack the North Korean spearhead. Further, he sent the Seventh Fleet into the waters between the Chinese mainland and Formosa to squelch any potential outbreak of trouble there.

The nation stirred Monday morning, June 26, with the news of the Korean crisis. In the White House a resolute Truman pointed a finger at Korea on the globe: "This is the Greece of the Far East. If we are tough enough now there won't be any next step."[9] He told a senator that "I'm not going to tremble like a psychopath before the Russians."[10] Although Truman received widespread bi-partisan support for his decisions, some conservative Republicans seized the moment to indulge in McCarthyite recriminations. Senator William E. Jenner of Indiana, one of the emotional, cliché-ridden, anti-Communist tramplers of civil liberties in the postwar period, waxed splenetic: "The front paging of the present plight of Korea is a grim reminder that the Russian bear is sprawled across the Eurasian continent, biding its time, digesting its prey, and digging itself in for a long and cruel international winter. The Korean debacle also reminds us that the same sell-out-to-Stalin statesmen, who turned Russia loose, are still in the saddle, riding herd on the American people."[11]

By Monday evening South Korea was clearly sinking, with Seoul about to fall. At 9:00 P.M. another Blair House conference convened. Truman learned that a North Korean plane had been shot down and remarked that he "hoped it was not the last."[12] Again, recollections of the 1930s punctuated the discussion, as diplo-mats and military leaders vowed to avoid the mistakes of the past by drawing the line against perceived aggression. They believed, too, that the reputation of the United States was at stake. If it did not back its word—its principle of contain-ment—its image would be tarnished and its power diminished. As Acheson put it later: "To back away from this challenge, in view of our capacity for meeting it, would be highly destructive of the power and prestige of the United States. By prestige I mean the shadow cast by power, which is of great deterrent impor-tance."[13] Korea, then, was a supreme test, a symbol, part of a larger whole, a link in a Cold War chain of events. To falter was to forfeit world leadership. American leaders decided to take firm action: United States aircraft and vessels were ordered into full-scale action below the thirty-eighth parallel; Formosa was declared off limits to the mainland Chinese; and military aid was to be sent to Indochina and the Philippines.

Truman did not ask Congress for a declaration of war or a resolution of support. He simply informed key congressmen about the choices he had made as Com-mander-in-Chief and justified them bluntly: "We've got to stop [the] USSR now."[14] This was war by the executive branch. Critics would soon label it "Mr. Truman's War." On Tuesday, June 27, Americans applauded Truman's response with a sense of relief reminiscent of the day after Pearl Harbor. The United Nations passed another United States-sponsored resolution urging mem-bers to aid South Korea. Thus the United Nations approved actions the United States had already taken. Nevertheless, Seoul fell as the American embassy staff burned secret documents in a farewell bonfire. Truman recalled his thinking that day: "If . . . the threat to South Korea was met firmly and successfully, it would add to our successes in Iran, Berlin, and Greece a fourth success in opposition to the aggressive moves of the Communists."[15]

The news of the continued North Korean push into the South sparked talk on June 28 and 29 of sending American troops. Presidential supporters cited historical precedent to counter criticism that Truman had bypassed the congressional right to declare wars: Jefferson had ordered action against the Barbary pirates and McKinley had sent troops into China during the Boxer Rebellion without prior congressional sanction. On the twenty-ninth, Truman ordered American pilots to attack above the thirty-eighth parallel. On Friday, June 30, after visiting the war front, MacArthur asked Truman to send American soldiers to Korea. The President soon gave the order. The risk of global war was great, but American leaders

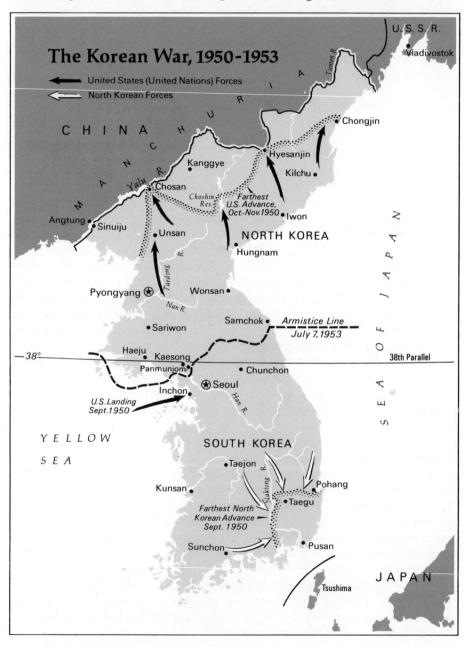

**The Korean War, 1950–1953**

⟵ United States (United Nations) Forces
⟵ North Korean Forces

believed that Russia would not directly enter the fray. Amid reports that the North Korean surge was pushing the South Koreans into a small area at the bottom of the peninsula, the Pusan perimeter, Truman left Washington for a weekend yacht cruise on the Chesapeake. He had made his tough decisions, and, as was characteristic of him, he would not brood over them. The nation mobilized, readying itself for an undeclared but initially popular war against communism. Truman tagged it a "police action." The decision to send American troops to Korea, Truman said in his "Farewell Address" in 1953, "was the most important in my time as President of the United States."[16]

## The Korean War and the Cold War

The Korean War lasted thirty-seven months. What began as an American attempt to contain the North Korean onslaught soon became an effort to "liberate" the North from the Communist camp. Until September 15, 1950, the war went badly for the United States, South Korea, and the small numbers of troops offered by allies, all functioning nominally under United Nations auspices. On that day, General MacArthur launched a brilliant amphibious assault at Inchon, several hundred miles behind the North Korean lines. American troops quickly cut through to Seoul. Farther south the American Eighth Army broke out of the Pusan bridgehead. Trapped North Korean soldiers were cut off from supplies. The Inchon victory, General Maxwell Taylor recalled, had an "intoxicating effect" on American leaders.[17] The Truman Administration, envisioning a major Cold War victory, decided to unite the two Koreas by crossing the thirty-eighth parallel in force.

Once Truman decided to push beyond the parallel to the Chinese and Russian borders to wipe out North Korea, the war aims and the consequences of American intervention in Korea were drastically altered. The Chinese had been surprised by the outbreak of the Korean War in June, and the American push to the Yalu River posed a direct threat to their security. Mao Tse-tung and Chou En-lai, in noisy public speeches and quiet warnings passed through India, fumed that Peking would not permit Americans to touch the Chinese border. American officials believed, without adequate intelligence, that China would not enter the war, if only because Russia would restrain its "puppet" regime and because Chinese forces were small and poorly organized. MacArthur told Truman on October 15, "We are no longer fearful of their [Chinese] intervention. . . . They have no air force . . . [and] if the Chinese tried to get down to Pyongyang there would be the greatest slaughter."[18] It was a grand miscalculation. "The advance to the Yalu," scholar David McLellan has written, "is a prime example of an American propensity to take the righteousness of its actions for granted and to ignore the objective reality which its behavior represents to others."[19]

It was in October that United States forces crossed the thirty-eighth parallel, and they nearly reached the Yalu by the end of the month. Bridges over the Yalu, vital links between China and North Korea, were bombed. Suddenly, on October 26, Chinese "volunteer" soldiers hit back. After fierce fighting, however, they retreated—perhaps China's signal that it did not wish to engage in full-scale war, but that it took American military action near its borders seriously. The signal was ignored. Hence, on November 26, two days after MacArthur announced a major new offensive intended to bring American soldiers home by Christmas, Chinese forces, at least 200,000 in number, swept down upon MacArthur's unsuspecting

**Douglas MacArthur (1880–1964).** Familiar corncob pipe between set teeth, the West Point graduate commanded American forces in Asia during the Second World War, directed the postwar occupation of Japan, and headed the "United Nations" effort in Korea until he was dramatically relieved of duty by the President in April, 1951. The testy MacArthur did not suffer well those who disagreed with him. (Library of Congress)

armies. Within weeks Chinese and North Korean soldiers engulfed the North. MacArthur asked Washington, without success, to approve a massive air strike against China. The United Nations soon branded China an "aggressor." Truman hinted at a news conference that the United States might use the atomic bomb, whereupon the agitated British Prime Minister Clement Attlee quickly flew to Washington to protest that the United States should seek negotiations, not a military solution, to end the war.

By March of 1951 MacArthur had managed to shove Communist forces back across the thirty-eighth parallel. The fighting stabilized at roughly the prewar boundary. Truman thought of negotiations at this point, but MacArthur grew restless, hell-bent on reversing earlier defeats and slashing the North on behalf of the crusade against international communism. He also grew reckless, accustomed as he was to independent decisionmaking. Truman would not let him attack China proper or use Nationalist Chinese forces in Korea, so the general with the Napoleonic ego began to make public statements suggesting that his Commander-in-Chief was an appeaser. To Congressman Joseph Martin, he wrote, in a letter made public in April, 1951: "There is no substitute for victory."[20] Asia, not Europe, argued the general, was the key to defeating Communist aggression. Later he would say that the President had lost his nerve in Korea. On April 11 Truman, backed strongly by the Joint Chiefs of Staff, fired MacArthur for insubordination and for sabotaging chances for a ceasefire by crossing the thirty-eighth parallel again.

The vain general, who had so badly miscalculated Chinese reactions, returned home to ticker-tape parades. In a televised address that left many in tears, he told Congress on April 19 that the war had to be expanded. He closed with the now famous words: "Old soldiers never die; they just fade away."[21] Congressional hearings featuring the old hero revealed that many Americans shared Mac-Arthur's frustrations over military restraint. Americans were used to winning wars; Truman was now talking about something alien—a "limited war," localized and without atomic weapons. One critical soldier wrote home: "We need somebody who will . . . give Russia an ultimatum, slap down a few dissenters . . . , jump into the driver's seat, put the gas to the floor and a hand on the horn, and let her roll so that everyone will see we mean business. Certainly we'll scrape a few fenders, may even lose one or two, but it won't stop us."[22] Senator McCarthy spewed his venom, too. The President, he declared on the Senate floor, "is a rather sinister monster of many heads and many tentacles, a monster conceived in the Kremlin, and then given birth to by Acheson . . . , and then nurtured into Frankenstein proportions by the Hiss crowd, who still run the State Department."[23]

Truman and Acheson replied to the charges of appeasement, and talk of impeachment, by pointing to the risk of world war. Acheson compared MacArthur and other opponents to the farmer who "goes out every morning and pulls up all his crops to see how they have been doing during the night."[24] The Chairman of the Joint Chiefs of Staff, General Omar Bradley, answered critics of the Administration. As much an anti-Communist as the next man, he pointed out that an enlargement of the war would by no means guarantee victory, that it might bring Russia in, and that the United States would lose angry allies in other parts of the world. He rejected the idea of a "showdown" with Soviet communism in Korea, for it would be "the wrong war, at the wrong place, at the wrong time, and with the wrong enemy."[25] In short, Russia was still enemy number one and Europe the primary strategic area. MacArthur faded away, but Truman and the Democrats suffered politically under their tarnished image.

Peace talks began at Panmunjom in July of 1951. They made little headway and

**Battle in the United Nations.** Dean Acheson squares off with Soviet diplomat Andrei Vishinsky in the arena of the United Nations over the Korean War and a multitude of other squabbles. Vishinsky was famous for his jabs and Acheson for his eloquent and stubborn defenses. (*United Nations World,* 1952)

the fighting continued. In June, 1952, American aircraft blasted the large hydro-electric plants along the Yalu. During the 1952 presidential campaign, Republican candidate Dwight D. Eisenhower pledged, if elected, to go to Korea to find a way to end the conflict. He was elected, in good part because of American frustration with the inconclusive nature of the war. And he went to Korea, but found no easy solution. The most serious difference between Chinese and American negotiators was the disposition of prisoners of war (POWs). Thousands of Chinese and North Korean soldiers, encouraged by a "re-education" program in the South, refused repatriation. A few hundred captives in the North, having undergone Communist "brainwashing," elected to remain above the thirty-eighth parallel. The usual international practice was to return all prisoners, but Truman and Eisenhower wanted to liberate their POWs from Communist rule by keeping them in the South.

In early 1953 Eisenhower put pressure on the Chinese to settle the question. He threatened to widen the war. Secretary of State John Foster Dulles hinted that atomic weapons might be employed in Korea. And Washington "unleashed" Chiang Kai-shek to attack the mainland; Nationalist bombing raids in fact followed. The March death of Stalin, combined with these actions, probably helped bring the peace talks to a conclusion. New Soviet policies were more flexible, and Moscow urged Peking to settle the prisoner question.

On July 27, 1953, the adversaries signed an armistice. They agreed to turn over the POW issue to a committee of neutral nations (ultimately the POWs stayed where they chose—including twenty-one Americans in North Korea). The conferees drew a new boundary line close to the thirty-eighth parallel, which gained South Korea 1,500 square miles of territory. The agreement also provided for a demilitarized zone between the two Koreas. The "Korean Conflict," as it was tagged in the document, thus ended with at least one million South Koreans and over a million North Koreans and Chinese dead. The United States lost 33,000 dead and 105,000 wounded, and spent about twenty billion dollars. The United States supplied over 80 percent of the naval power and over 90 percent of the air support, as well as half the combat troops, in this "United Nations" effort. There were no victors—no dancing, cheering crowds in Times Square. The Cold War persisted. "We have won an armistice on a single battleground—not peace in the world," said Eisenhower. "We may not now relax our guard nor cease our quest."[26]

The Korean War has left many questions, most of which cannot be answered definitively until that distant day when Chinese and Soviet government archives are opened to historians. Speculations abound. Did Russia launch the Korean War? We just do not know for sure. There are plausible reasons why Moscow might have induced its client North Korean government to attack. Since Secretary Acheson had indicated in a speech before the National Press Club on January 12, 1950, that, although South Korea was an area of vital concern to the United States, it lay outside the American defense perimeter, perhaps Stalin thought the United States would not defend the South. The joint chiefs of staff had earlier decided that South Korea was strategically unimportant and indefensible. American economic and military aid to South Korea before the war was miniscule. Maybe Stalin gambled on a quick victory.

The "gamble thesis" raises a more fundamental question: What did Russia hope to gain? Perhaps Moscow could reaffirm its leadership of the Communist world,

**Dean Acheson (1893–1971).** He, like the President, assumed that Russia had initiated the Korean War and urged resolute American reaction. The new crisis, coming after his National Press Club speech of January 12, 1950, and other foreign policy woes such as Mao's recent victory in China, emboldened some of his critics to ask once again for his resignation. (*The Reporter,* 1952. Copyright 1952 by Fortnightly Publishing Co. Inc.)

then being challenged by the new Chinese regime. Also, Russia could perhaps block the movement toward a separate Japanese peace treaty, which it saw as a long-term threat to Soviet security. Third, it could unite Korea and gain strength in Asia. Other questions, however, leave doubts about Soviet intentions. Why was the Soviet delegate absent from the United Nations at such a crucial time, especially if the Soviets were planning an attack? More important, why did Russia give such inadequate aid to the North Koreans and Chinese during the war, and especially fail to give an added push when the North Koreans could have defeated the South Koreans and Americans at Pusan, before the success at Inchon? Why, when it had launched a European movement for peaceful coexistence, would Moscow torpedo that effort by provoking war in Asia? Some scholars suggest that the North Koreans, armed heavily by the Soviets, took matters in their own hands in June and launched an attack that surprised the Russians almost as much as the Americans.

This hypothesis derives plausibility from the long-standing civil war between the Northern Communists led by Kim Il-sung and the politicians in the South grouped around Syngman Rhee. Both leaders sought national unification and both looked to foreign sources for material aid. Kim drew large amounts from the Soviet Union; Rhee tapped the United States. In February of 1950, the American Congress authorized $60 million in economic aid for Seoul; in March it voted $10,970,000 in military assistance; and on June 5 it granted another $100 million in economic aid. (An American Military Advisory Group remained active in the South, although American troops departed in July, 1949.) North Korea, fearing a military build-up below the thirty-eighth parallel, may have decided to attack the South before all of this aid could take effect. Also, in May elections, Rhee lost control of the South Korean National Assembly. Kim may have thought he had to strike before Rhee could stabilize his precarious position through his usual repressive measures. For months before June, skirmishes along the border were common as units of both sides crossed the parallel. Some scholars speculate that Rhee himself may have provoked the Northern assault by attacking, on the morning of June 25, the town of Haeju, five miles inside North Korea. As historian Edmund S. Wehrle has suggested, perhaps "both the United States and Russia may merely have found themselves suddenly committed to support the abrupt actions of unruly satellites."[27]

If we do not know for certain how the war began, or why, we *can* measure its consequences. At home in the United States, it meant the repudiation of the Democrats in 1952 and the election of a Republican administration, both made possible by popular exasperation with the stalemate in Korea. It wounded bipartisanship and fueled McCarthyism. It helped set off a "great debate" in the early 1950s over whether Europe or Asia was more important in the campaign against communism and whether the United States was overcommitted around the globe. Truman's handling of the American response to the Korean War also confirmed presidential supremacy in foreign policy; he neither consulted Congress nor asked for a declaration of war. Acheson did not wish to invite hearings which might produce that "one more question in cross-examination which destroys you, as a lawyer. We had complete acceptance of the President's policy by everybody on both sides of both houses of Congress." He did not wish to answer "ponderous questions" that might have "muddled up" Truman's policy.[28] As historian Arthur Schlesinger, Jr. has concluded, Truman "dramatically and dangerously enlarged the power of future Presidents to take the nation into major war." Furthermore, the "Constitution could not easily sustain the weight of the indiscriminate globalism to which the Korean War gave birth."[29]

Indeed, the United States thereafter placed itself against nationalist movements, interpreted as components of an international Communist plot: it gave aid to the French in Indochina, and intervened in the Chinese civil war by aiding Chiang on Formosa. Between 1953 and 1972 South Korea itself received $5.5 billion in foreign aid from the United States. The Korean War also poisoned Sino-American relations. Washington continued to refuse to recognize Mao's government, and China, which had ignobly forced United States troops to retreat and had denied them a victory, became a chief villain in the Cold War melodrama written by Americans. At the same time, the United States became the principal foreign devil for Peking. The Korean War also demonstrated how easily the United States could manhandle the United Nations Organization, which dutifully passed American resolutions, and it further strengthened the simple notions of a Communist monolith and suggested that limited wars could alter Communist behavior. Exaggerations became legion. President Truman proclaimed on October 4, 1952, that "We are fighting in Korea so we won't have to fight in Wichita, or in Chicago, or in New Orleans, or on San Francisco Bay."[30]

The Truman Administration utilized the Korean War to fulfill other goals as well. As Acheson noted, the dispatch of troops to Korea "removed the recommendations of NSC-68 from the realm of theory and made them immediate budget issues."[31] He made the most of the opportunity. The Defense Department budget for fiscal year 1951 shot up to $48 billion; in 1952 it reached $60 billion. The United States acquired bases in Saudi Arabia and Morocco, among other places. Negotiations began with Fascist Spain, eventually leading to an air base there. The American nuclear stockpile grew rapidly in 1950–1951, reaching at least 750 warheads by the latter year, up from about 100–150 in 1948. The United States Army increased by 50 percent, to 3.5 million men. Two new divisions were sent to Europe, making a total of six there. The hydrogen bomb was developed by March, 1951. A new jet bomber, the B-52, made its maiden flight a year later. Plans were initiated for the rearmament of West Germany. Added to the incorporation of Japan into the American camp, this military expansion was awesome. The Cold War rested on a dangerously militarized footing. George F. Kennan opposed the decision to develop the H-bomb, because he feared that "we would come to think of our security as embraced solely in the mathematics of whatever power of destruction we could evolve, and we would forget our security lies still very largely in our ability to address ourselves to the positive and constructive problem of world affairs to create confidence in other people."[32]

## The Foreign Policy of Dwight D. Eisenhower

The stalemated Korean War and the "loss" of China provided Republicans with considerable political ammunition in the 1952 presidential campaign. Bipartisanship was shelved, because the political stakes—removing the Democratic party from its twenty-year hold on the White House—were high. Although Republican candidate General Dwight D. Eisenhower conducted a smiling, moderate campaign, his party's right wing attacked vehemently. The Truman Administration,

**Richard M. Nixon (1913—).** Before he was elected vice-president in 1952, Nixon graduated from Whittier College, took a law degree from Duke University, served in Congress (1946–1951), and represented California as senator (1951–1953). An anti-Communist alarmist who often used excessive language to score debating points, Nixon was, said Adlai Stevenson, "McCarthy in a white collar." Nixon lost a bid for the presidency in 1960, but miraculously returned in 1968 and served in the White House until 1974 when, plagued by the "Watergate" political corruption he had spawned, he became the first President to resign. (*The Reporter,* 1960. Copyright 1960 by The Reporter Magazine Co.)

which had launched containment, gotten "tough" with the Soviets, and established an internal security system, now somehow had become soft on communism. Vice-presidential candidate Richard M. Nixon, already famous for his anti-Communist zeal as a senator, charged that Democratic candidate Adlai E. Stevenson was a graduate of "Dean Acheson's cowardly College of Communist Containment."[33] The Republican party platform, written by John Foster Dulles, loaded invective on the Truman Administration for ineptly squandering American power and for practicing "appeasement."

The containment doctrine became a target of abuse. Republicans called it "negative, futile, and immoral."[34] It had failed because it was too defensive. Dulles proposed "liberation" as a replacement. By that he meant lifting the Communist yoke from Eastern Europe. He was never precise about how to do this; he often merely advocated a propaganda program to arouse Eastern Europeans against their Soviet masters. Democrats retorted that meddling in Eastern Europe would do those people little good because the Soviets would crush them—an assumption the Democrats themselves had rejected during the first years of the Cold War.

"Liberation" did not decide the election of 1952, but the political rhyme "I like Ike" may have. Eisenhower was a sincere, modest, wholesome, and honest person, whose simple rhetoric and homespun illustrations made him attractive to millions. He was also a professional military man and, since the Cold War seemed to be increasingly a military matter, he seemed better qualified for the job than Adlai Stevenson. Although no less a Cold Warrior than Eisenhower, the Democratic governor of Illinois was tainted by his association with the unpopular Truman Administration. Stevenson became the scapegoat for America's Cold War frustrations. Eisenhower's "I shall go to Korea" statement of October 24 helped insure his election with 55 percent of the popular vote.[35]

## Makers of American Foreign Policy from 1950 to 1961

| *Presidents* | *Secretaries of State* |
|---|---|
| Harry S Truman, 1945–1953 | Dean G. Acheson, 1949–1953 |
| Dwight D. Eisenhower, 1953–1961 | John Foster Dulles, 1953–1959 |
| | Christian A. Herter, 1959–1961 |

The lean, happy Ike, arms often raised high forming a large "V" for victory, was a skillful politician. The first Republican President since Hoover, Eisenhower appeared, but was not, simple-minded. His language was so commonplace that reporters listening to his speeches ridiculed his "five-star generalities"; one remarked that "he just crossed the thirty-eighth platitude."[36] He certainly lacked a surefootedness for grammar. His utterances often displayed mangled syntax and Eisenhowerese colloquialisms that produced dizziness in his listeners. How this idiosyncratic style affected foreign diplomats and negotiations is not clear, but it may have fed popular ideas and Democratic grumblings that Eisenhower lacked a grasp of tough realities.

Born in Texas and raised in Abilene, Kansas, Eisenhower graduated from West Point and led an obscure military life until appointed the supreme allied commander in Europe during the Second World War. After the war he served as president of Columbia University and as NATO commander. He liked fishing and golfing, and most of his companions in sport were members of the business elite. Eisenhower admired business leaders and their financial success, and even more than Truman, he appointed a great number to high office in agencies shaping foreign policy. Representatives of business, finance, and law held 76 percent of such posts under Eisenhower, whereas the figure for Truman had been 43 percent. These businessmen tended to look upon the world as something to be managed. They were conservative advocates of "private enterprise" in a world increasingly turning toward revolution and socialism.

Eisenhower and his advisers saw capitalist development as a deterrent to communism, and like the "peace and prosperity" ideologues of Truman days, they venerated foreign trade. As Eisenhower told his Cabinet, there was "no instrument in diplomacy quite as powerful as trade."[37] Eisenhower appointed a Commission on Foreign Economic Policy in 1953, and it urged a more liberal trade policy through tariff reduction. To achieve this goal he extended the reciprocal trade agreements program, expanded the lending authority of the Export-Import Bank, and relaxed controls on trade with Eastern European nations. Total American exports expanded from $15 billion in 1952 to $20 billion in 1960. The Eisenhower Administration favored trade over foreign aid as a vehicle for combating Communist exploitation of economic dislocations abroad. The character of the foreign aid program shifted from "economic" to "military" assistance under Eisenhower. This emphasis carried benefits for a President interested in balancing the budget. Military aid constituted sound economics, said the President, because it cost less to maintain a Greek soldier than an American one. Throughout the 1950s the United States spent over three billion dollars a year in military assistance overseas under the Mutual Security program. Eisenhower also added a new program in 1954, later called "Food for Peace," wherein the United States disposed of its agricultural surplus overseas. In ten years this program accounted for $12.2 billion in farm exports. And in 1959, after years of ignoring ardent Latin American requests, the United States established the Inter-American Development Bank to spur hemispheric economic projects.

Unlike Truman and Acheson, Eisenhower at least seemed willing to negotiate with the Soviets. Stalin's death in March, 1953 removed one of the original Cold War villains, and in April Eisenhower seized the opportunity to deliver a stirring address titled "The Chance for Peace." The President berated the Soviets for disrupting the postwar world, but he also invited more friendly relations, noted that "an era ended with the death of Joseph Stalin," and revealed his discomfort with militarism. "Every gun that is made, every warship launched, every rocket fired signifies, in the final sense, a theft from those who hunger and are not fed. . . . The cost of one modern heavy bomber is this: a modern brick school in more than 30 cities."[38] Thereafter he often urged disarmament and a reduction in the military methods used to implement the containment doctrine. In 1954 he vetoed the suggestion of Dulles and Nixon that the United States send troops to Indochina to forestall a Vietnamese victory over the French. In 1955 and 1960 Eisenhower negotiated with the Soviets at summit meetings, reestablishing a practice abandoned by Truman. When asked during the Berlin crisis of 1959 if he would use nuclear weapons, he said "destruction is not a good police force. You don't throw hand grenades around streets to police the streets so that people won't be molested by thugs."[39] And in his "Farewell Address" of 1961 Eisenhower

**Dwight D. Eisenhower (1890–1969).** Graduate of the United States Military Academy, Supreme Commander in Europe during World War II, and President of Columbia University (1948–1951), smiling "Ike" touched the American imagination in the 1950s—"the bland leading the bland," quipped one humorist. (Dwight D. Eisenhower Library)

warned against a "military-industrial complex"—the powerful lobby of the military establishment and the defense industry—which threatened peace, American liberties, and democratic processes. Eisenhower was an uneasy Cold Warrior, a military man uncomfortable with militarism.

Ike's peace initiatives fizzled and his antimilitarist sentiments were seldom acted upon. Eisenhower ended up espousing and applying the containment doctrine, acting under the lessons learned in the 1940s. He sent troops to Lebanon and helped organize native military units to invade Guatemala and Cuba; his Central Intelligence Agency tried, but failed, to overthrow the Indonesian government in 1958. By 1959 one million Americans were stationed overseas in forty-two countries. By 1960 the Defense Department controlled 35 million acres of land at home and abroad. Defense budgets reached $35–40 million each year, although Eisenhower kept restrictions on them because he feared the United States would spend itself into weakness. Defense expenditures ate up one-half of the 1960 United States budget. New alliances—the Southeast Asia Treaty Organization and Baghdad pact—were formed, revealing in part the American penchant for thinking that an international Communist conspiracy existed. Eisenhower may have wanted to relax tensions with the Soviets and the Chinese, but his foreign policy ultimately did little to achieve relaxation.

## Secretary John Foster Dulles and McCarthyism

Secretary of State John Foster Dulles (1953–1959) was a more inflexible Cold Warrior than Eisenhower, but the President, dominating their relationship, tempered some of the secretary's militance. Dulles seemed groomed for the post. His grandfather, John W. Foster, had served as secretary of state in 1892–1893 and the grandson had more than once trooped behind him in foreign capitals. Tutelage from a father who was a Presbyterian minister, education at Princeton and George Washington Law School, service as a negotiator on reparations at the Paris Peace Conference at Versailles, membership in the prestigious Wall Street firm of Sullivan and Cromwell, and worldwide activity on behalf of the Federal Council of Churches gave Dulles a varied, cosmopolitan experience before World War II. After the war he helped promote bipartisanship. In 1952 he vigorously assailed the very policies of the Truman Administration he had helped to shape, but he later admitted that his desire to elect Eisenhower had promoted this political gambit.

Dulles was forceful, ambitious, sharp, self-righteous—a mixture of moral idealism and hard-nosed realism. Indeed, he pursued ideals through the exercise of power. As he told a journalist, the United States "is almost the only country strong enough and powerful enough to be moral."[40] Because he was a dull, flat speaker, he preferred "personal diplomacy"—face-to-face negotiations with foreign diplomats. He despised compromise. Like Acheson, who called Soviet peace initiatives "Trojan doves," Dulles would rather lecture to than negotiate with Communists.

**John Foster Dulles (1888–1959).** Chief formulator of the "liberation" idea, Dulles was not "one of these amiable persons," remarked one of his law colleagues on Wall Street. He helped scuttle "bipartisanship" and gave Cold War rhetoric a shrill and self-righteous quality. (*The Reporter,* 1956. Copyright 1956 by The Reporter Magazine Co. Inc.)

He read Soviet initiatives for a reduction of tension as Communist traps. Scholar Adam Ulam has mused: "If Moscow proposed a joint declaration in favor of motherhood, this would have called forth position papers from the State Department's Policy Planning Council, somber warnings from Senator [William] Knowland, and eventually a declaration that while the United States welcomed this recognition of the sanctity of family life on the part of the Russians, it would require clear indication that the USSR did not mean to derogate the status of fatherhood."[41] Winston Churchill once remarked that Dulles was the only bull he knew who carried his own china shop with him. Others said, with some exaggeration, that he was a card-carrying Christian who pictured the Cold War as a Biblical contest between good and evil, between atheistic communism and Western Christianity. Dulles thought with much more sophistication and for him moral pronouncements served to counter simplistic Soviet ideological appeals. Still, foreigners thought his incantations were rigid and hardly conducive to fruitful diplomacy. One European newspaper depicted Dulles as the "conscience and straightjacket of the free world."[42] The Soviets respected Dulles as a formidable negotiator but they probably also remembered an old Russian proverb: "A bellowing cow gives little milk."[43] Dulles was not, however, a rigid ideologue. He was a practitioner of power who employed a variety of tools: moral appeals, foreign aid, trade, military training of foreign armies, overseas bases, a ballistic missile program, subversion of governments, and alliances. At least, as Soviet Premier Nikita S. Khrushchev later commented, Dulles "knew how far he could push us, and he never pushed us too far."[44]

The Eisenhower-Dulles team gave catchy phrases to its foreign policy. "Liberation" was one. Another was "massive retaliation," meaning that any adversary who stepped across the line could expect to be bombed or "nuked" into oblivion by nuclear weapons. Massive retaliation comforted those people frustrated by the "limited war" in Korea. The "new look" was Eisenhower's program for the military: emphasis on atomic armaments and the Air Force—or, in one of the most gruesome phrases of the 1950s, "more bang for the buck." "Brinkmanship" meant not backing down in a crisis by being willing to go to the brink of war. In 1954 Eisenhower uttered the "'falling domino' principle": "You have a row of dominoes set up, you knock over the first one, and what will happen to the last one is the certainty that it will go over very quickly."[45] The President was explaining that if one country in Asia fell to the Communists, others would fall in rapid succession. The 1957 "Eisenhower Doctrine" read that the United States would intervene in the Middle East if any government threatened by a Communist takeover requested aid. This was another containment "stop" sign; indeed most of these policies or concepts were actually Truman reruns or elaborations of policies set earlier.

Eisenhower once said that "sometimes Foster is just too worried about being accused of sounding like Truman and Acheson."[46] Dulles had watched the harassment of Acheson by Republican right-wingers in endless congressional hearings. They boldly charged Acheson with softness toward communism. Dulles decided to avoid a similar fate by striking his anti-Communist colors early and by permitting McCarthyites to intimidate and demoralize professional Foreign Service Officers in the State Department, an institution that Senator Joseph McCarthy believed harbored Communists or their sympathizers. Dulles demanded "positive loyalty," by which he apparently meant correct thinking, from State Department personnel and appointed an ex-FBI man and McCarthy henchman, Scott McLeod,

**Joseph McCarthy (1909–1957).** The notorious senator from Wisconsin used the "big lie" as a tool for advancing his political career. He charged without evidence that the State Department was infested with Communists. He castigated former secretaries Marshall and Acheson. Graduate of Marquette University, judge, Marine, and Republican, the demagogic senator was once known as the "Pepsi-Cola Kid" for protecting the interests of that company. The Senate censured him in December, 1954. (*The Reporter*, 1951. Copyright 1951 by Fortnightly Publishing Co. Inc.)

the chief security officer. McLeod's distaste for Democrats and "New Dealers" soon manifested itself in witch-hunting tactics that confused criticism with treason. "The quiet reign of terror," Townsend Hoopes has written, "burned its deadly way through the State Department for nearly two years, immolating along the way the careers of several hundred officers and employees."[47] It included the equivalent of book burning, for in early 1953 Dulles ordered books authored by "Communists, fellow travellers, et cetera" to be removed from the libraries of American overseas information centers.[48] Who was an "et cetera"? Bureaucrats gave the broadest interpretation and tossed out the books of such people as Bert Andrews (Washington bureau chief of the *New York Herald Tribune*), Joseph Davies (former ambassador to Russia), Walter White (deceased former head of the NAACP), and historian Foster Rhea Dulles, the secretary of state's own cousin.

One of the more prominent and tragic cases was that of Foreign Service Officer John Carter Vincent, an independent-minded "China hand" who during World War II reported from China that Chiang Kai-shek was destined to lose.

McCarthyites took this to mean that Vincent plotted to defeat Chiang. A State Department Loyalty Board cleared Vincent, but the Civil Service Loyalty Review Board declared by a vote of 3 to 2 that his loyalty to the United States was in doubt. Dulles at first rejected that decision. But, seeking to satiate the extreme anti-Communists, he forced Vincent out by questioning his "standards" as an officer. Dulles once asked Vincent if he had read Stalin's *Problems of Leninism*. Vincent said he had not and Dulles replied that Vincent would not have advocated the China policies he did if he had read it. Ross Terrill has commented that "since Stalin failed in China no less than Truman, one may wonder whether Stalin read his own book."[49] Another China specialist, John Paton Davies, was fired even though nine security reviews cleared him. By 1961, State Department Asian specialist James C. Thomson, Jr. has concluded, the purged Bureau of Far Eastern Affairs "was notorious for its rigidity and its resistance to policy change" and "dominated by Cold Warriors and staffed largely by the cowed."[50] President Eisenhower never halted Dulles' disembowelment of the State Department.

**"I Hear There's Something Wrong With Your Morale."** Secretary Dulles launched a regretful purge of Foreign Service Officers to satisfy the right wing of the Republican party. (*Herblock's Here and Now,* 1955)

After Stalin's death, Eisenhower tried to encourage changes in Soviet foreign policy through his "Chance for Peace" speech, wherein he asked "what is the Soviet Union ready to do?"[51] The early signs for improved Soviet-American relations seemed auspicious. Moscow helped end the deadlock over Korea, opened diplomatic relations with Yugoslavia and Greece, abandoned territorial claims against Turkey, toned down its anti-American rhetoric, and launched a "peace offensive." Although the Soviet crushing of an East Berlin riot in June reminded Americans of the past, the freeing of Stalinist victims from forced labor camps conversely suggested that Stalin's heirs were not replicas of their long-time master.

Soviet leaders scrambled for position in the succession crisis. Gradually Nikita S. Khrushchev, son of a farmer, and for years the Communist party boss of the Ukraine, climbed to the top of the Kremlin hierarchy and eased out Stalin's apparent favorite Georgi Malenkov. By September, 1953, Khrushchev was first secretary of the Central Committee of the party; five years later he took the title "Premier." Portly and amiable, Khrushchev was an impulsive, competitive person of coarse speech. Eisenhower did not care for the man. Khrushchev, the President concluded, was not a statesman, "but rather a powerful, skillful, ruthless, and highly ambitious politician." Worse, he was "blinded by his dedication to the Marxist theory of world revolution and Communist domination."[52] Vice-President Nixon described the Soviet leader as a "bare knuckle slugger who had gouged, kneed, and kicked."[53] On his part, Khrushchev thought Eisenhower "a good man, but he wasn't very tough."[54]

Both Eisenhower and Khrushchev concentrated their attention on Europe, still troubled by large armies, hostile blocs, Germany, and divided Berlin—all reminders of the unresolved problems bequeathed by World War II. Because of European squabbles the United States and the Soviet Union were spending billions for large military systems. The Soviets stressed the development of ballistic missiles, while Americans emphasized intercontinental bombers under the concept of "massive retaliation." By 1955, American bombers capable of dropping atomic devices on Russia numbered 1,350; the Soviets had 350 in the same category. Soviet ground forces outnumbered their American counterparts by a 2–1 margin. An expert on Soviet affairs, Zbigniew Brzezinski, has written that the United States "now seemed to have both the capacity to inflict very heavy damage on the Soviet Union and to significantly impede any Soviet effort to seize Western Europe."[55] In one attempt to expand this capacity, Dulles sponsored the European Defense Community (EDC) as a plan to integrate European forces, including West German units. When the French balked, he warned them that the United States would undertake an "agonizing reappraisal." Paris called his bluff and rejected EDC. The secretary had to settle for an enlarged Western European Union in late 1954 and West German membership in NATO in May, 1955. Nineteen fifty-five was a banner year for ringing Communist nations with military alliances: SEATO went into effect, the American defense treaty with Nationalist China became active, the Baghdad Treaty was signed, and West Germany joined NATO. To counter an expanded NATO in 1955, the Soviets formed their own military organization, the Warsaw Pact of Eastern European nations.

The two giants, then, continued their military posturing. But they seemed more willing to reach accommodations, however minimal. The Cold War cost too many dollars and rubles, so both sides wanted to trim their military expenditures. Diplomacy returned to Soviet-American relations. On May 15, 1955 Russia and the United States signed an accord to end their ten-year joint occupation of Austria and to create an independent, neutral Austria. Although Dulles soon bragged that the Austrian State Treaty symbolized a Soviet retreat, a victory for his "liberation" policy, he did not drop his guard. He suspected Soviet trickery and warned about new dangers: "the wolf has put on a new set of sheep's clothing, and while it is better to have a sheep's clothing on than a bear's clothing on, because sheep don't have claws, I think the policy remains the same."[56]

Throughout 1954–1955, from several corners of the globe, came calls for a summit meeting of the great powers. Winston Churchill made an eloquent plea and Democrats in Congress urged negotiations. Eisenhower was cautious in the face of Dulles' long list of reasons why Americans should not meet with the Soviets: a summit conference would permit them to use propaganda on a grand scale; it would let them appear equal to Americans; a summit might encourage neutralism, for other countries would fear less and align less; it would be best to wait until the West German military was larger; the Soviets would not bargain seriously because totalitarianism depended upon an outside enemy. Eisenhower overruled him, for the President thought that one could not speak of Soviet intentions without testing them in discussions. Making the best of this setback, Dulles advised the President to avoid social settings where he might be photographed with Soviet officials. If that was difficult, Eisenhower should maintain "an austere countenance on occasions where photographing together is inevitable."[57]

Russia, the United States, Britain, and France met in Geneva from July 18 to 23, 1955. Just before leaving for that beautiful city where diplomats historically seek international peace, Eisenhower and Dulles assured congressmen that "Geneva was not going to be another Yalta."[58] The reference was timely, for early in 1955 Dulles had engineered the publication of the secret *Yalta Papers* in an abortive attempt to embarrass the Democrats. Geneva was certainly no Yalta, because the Big Four struck no concrete agreements. Everybody was trying to impress, to score points for prestige. Even evangelist Billy Graham journeyed to the city of John Calvin and preached to a throng of 35,000. Reporters and photographers flocked around smiling dignitaries. Eisenhower ignored Dulles' advice and behaved in his usual amiable manner. The Russians were sensitive to appearances; Khrushchev,

**Nikita S. Khrushchev (1894–1971).** The short, stocky Soviet Premier who succeeded Stalin could wear either memorable smiles or scowls. He denounced the former dictator in a "de-Staliniza-tion" speech in 1956 and contributed to a short-lived thaw in the Cold War during the decade. He fell from power in 1964. (*The Reporter,* 1956. Copyright 1956 by the Reporter Magazine Co.)

for example, was embarrassed because the Russians flew into Geneva in a two-engine plane, whereas Eisenhower and Dulles disembarked from a more imposing four-motor aircraft. Khrushchev, the peasant of little schooling, was also aware that he was being tested by graduates of West Point, Eton, Oxford, and the Sorbonne. "Would we be able to represent our country competently?" Khrushchev thought before Geneva. His answer afterward: "We had established ourselves as able to hold our own in the international arena."[59]

American officials believed before Geneva that they would have the upper hand in bargaining. As Ike told a press conference, the United States was approaching negotiations "from a greater position of strength than we ever had before."[60] Dulles said before Geneva that the Russians were economically weak and on the verge of collapse. That drew a heated rebuttal from Khrushchev. At the conference itself, East and West split over the issues of German reunification, European security, and arms control. Correspondent James Reston reported, the conferees "disagreed so nicely."[61] Each side wanted to unite Germany but to set the terms. Americans sought a unified Germany which could join NATO. Both sides favored arms control, but parted over methods. Eisenhower dramatically presented his "open skies" proposal, wherein Russia and the United States would exchange maps and submit their military installations to aerial inspection to insure compliance with control agreements. On this American propaganda ploy designed to counter pre-Geneva Soviet appeals for disarmament, Eisenhower later remarked: "We knew the Soviets wouldn't accept it. We were sure of that, but we took a look and thought it was a good move."[62] Indeed, secrecy was one of Russia's deterrents, keeping Americans guessing on whether the inferior Soviets were catching up in airborne striking power. That secrecy ended in 1956 when the United States unilaterally instituted a version of the "open skies" proposal: reconnaisance flights of high altitude U-2 planes over the Soviet Union.

When Eisenhower returned home, he applauded a "new spirit of conciliation and cooperation" and assured Americans that he had not penned any secret agreements.[63] Geneva was largely a ceremonial affair. Russia did recognize West Germany in 1955, and that fall Khrushchev indicated he endorsed "détente." Yet, he went on: "if anybody thinks that for this reason we shall forget about Marx, Engels, and Lenin, he is mistaken. This will happen when shrimps learn to whistle."[64] About all that came out of the summit were cultural exchanges. One "cultural" consequence of Geneva was Vice-President Nixon's 1959 trip to Russia, where at a display of American products in a Moscow exhibition, he engaged Khrushchev in the "kitchen debate" on the disputed merits of capitalism. And journalist I. F. Stone wrote in 1955 about the visits of Communists to the Kiwanis Club of Des Moines, Iowa, and about the excursions of American farmers to the fields of Kharkov: "Nothing is more deadly for the war spirit than the discovery that the enemy, too, is human."[65]

Disillusionment followed Geneva because differences remained great. Russia still wanted Germany removed from NATO and NATO expunged from Europe. The United States still wanted Russia excluded from Eastern Europe and the indefinite perpetuation of American nuclear superiority. "Well, I think," said Dulles on the last day of the conference, "it is a little premature to talk about the 'era of good feelings.'"[66] Former diplomat W. Averell Harriman, a partisan Democrat, charged that the "free world was psychologically disarmed" by the "spirit of Geneva," which was actually a Soviet "smokescreen" for further aggres-

**Preparation for the "Kitchen Debate."** Khrushchev and Vice-President Richard M. Nixon sip Pepsi-Cola at the American National Exhibition in Moscow in July, 1959, just before their "kitchen debate" over the comparative virtues of capitalism and socialism. (PepsiCo, Inc.)

sion.[67] Harriman's extreme conclusion underestimated the degree to which Dulles was perpetuating the Cold War diplomacy that Harriman himself had helped launch in the 1940s.

The Cold War thaw of 1955 marked a brief interlude in the Soviet-American confrontation in Europe. It did signal that neither Moscow nor Washington had the power to force significant changes in European alignments. Nobody liked this seeming permanence of Cold War lines in Europe, but neither side wanted to risk war to alter the status quo. After Geneva, Eisenhower appeared bored with his job and contemplated not seeking re-election in 1956. That possibility almost became reality when he was felled in September, 1955 by a coronary thrombosis after playing twenty-seven holes of golf. But within months he recovered and won a substantial victory over Democratic candidate Adlai Stevenson, who had charged that the Eisenhower Administration was losing the Cold War to the Soviets.

In February, 1956, Khrushchev, once the loyal follower of Stalin and supporter of the bloody purges of the 1930s, delivered a momentous speech to the Twentieth Party Congress. He denounced Stalin for domestic crimes, initiated a "de-Stalinization" program, endorsed "peaceful coexistence," and suggested that the Kremlin would now recognize different brands of communism. In the Communist nations of Eastern Europe, this apparent acceptance of Titoism emboldened erstwhile victims of Stalinism to challenge Stalinist politicians in office. "Polycentrism" in the Communist world became an irresistible force: ideological affinity, yes, but Moscow's domination, no. The abolition of the Cominform in April seemed to demonstrate Moscow's new tolerance for diversity. Young people and intellectuals soon insisted on self-determination. In Poland, for example, a labor dispute in mid-1956 ballooned into national resistance to Soviet tutelage. After using force to put down riots, Russia compromised with Polish nationalism by reluctantly accepting as the Polish Communist party chairman Wladyslaw Gomulka, heretofore denied influence because Stalin thought him too "Titoist". The United States, which had been giving aid to Tito himself for years, soon offered Poland economic assistance. Any crack in the Communist edifice was encouraged by the Eisenhower Administration. "Our hearts go out" to the Poles, the President declared.[68] Also the Central Intelligence Agency began to train, in West Germany, para-military units composed of East Europeans who might intervene in uprisings in Poland, Rumania, and Hungary.

Revolt erupted next in Hungary. Young revolutionaries marched and fought in the streets of Budapest. A new government, backed by local revolutionary councils throughout Hungary, took a drastic step when it announced that Hungary was pulling out of the Warsaw Pact and thereby becoming neutral in the Cold War. Khrushchev looked upon neutrals in Eastern Europe much as Dulles looked upon them elsewhere—with utter disdain. Russia began to move troops into Hungary and on November 4 crushed the resistance with brute force. The courageous hand-to-tank combat of underarmed students and workers in the streets of Budapest stirred global sympathy. The West would have scored some propaganda points against Russia had not British, French, and Israeli troops invaded Egypt shortly before the Soviets smashed the Hungarian Revolution. The West now had to share the moral revulsion against aggression. The simultaneous Suez and Hungarian crises demonstrated how much the Cold War antagonists feared losing their spheres of influence.

The Polish and Hungarian rebellions seemed to satisfy Dulles' dream of "liberation." The Eisenhower Administration had been encouraging discontent in Eastern Europe through the Voice of America and the CIA-financed Radio Free

**"I'll Be Glad to Restore Peace to the Middle East, Too."** The ugly Soviet suppression of the Hungarian rebellion of 1956 prompted this telling cartoon by Herblock. (*Herblock's Special for Today,* 1958)

**Propaganda Balloons for Eastern Europe.** Although the United States did not send troops or military supplies to Hungary during the 1956 uprising there, in the 1950s the Free Europe Committee floated message-filled balloons across the ''iron curtain'' from West Germany to stir up unrest with Soviet rule. (Franklin D. Roosevelt Library)

Europe, which beamed anti-Soviet propaganda broadcasts into the Soviet sphere. Dulles hinted that nations which split from the Soviet orbit would receive American foreign aid. In 1953, Congress had passed the first annual Captive Peoples' Resolution as a spur to self-determination in Eastern Europe. Three years later the secretary of state hailed the Hungarian tumult as evidence of the ''weakness of Soviet imperialism. . . . The captive peoples should never have reason to doubt that they have in us a sincere and dedicated friend who shares their aspirations.''[69] In the midst of the crisis, on November 2, Dulles suffered severe abdominal pains from the cancer that would eventually kill him in 1959. Following surgery he was incapacitated for weeks and did not manage the American response to the Hungarian Revolution. Even had he been healthy, however, it is doubtful American policy would have been different. Although Hungarian dissidents appealed for some kind of American intervention and expected it, Washington was ''boxed,'' as one official put it.[70]

The United States simply lacked the means to direct or influence events in the Soviet sphere, short of full-scale war. ''Poor fellows, poor fellows,'' Eisenhower told a journalist. ''I think about them all the time. I wish there were some way of helping them.''[71] ''Liberation'' was exposed for the hollow and misleading generality it had always been. The Eisenhower Administration lowered immigration barriers to permit over 20,000 Hungarian refugees to enter the United States and introduced a resolution condemning Soviet force in the General Assembly of the United Nations. That was all Americans could do. Still, Eastern Europeans themselves had succeeded in forcing the Soviets to make some compromises with nationalism, thereby reducing Soviet authority in the region, the brutal crushing of the Hungarian uprising notwithstanding.

## From *Sputnik* to U-2

In 1956–57, the United States seemed on the defensive and the Soviets on the offensive. Washington's adjustment to this appearance took the now familiar military course. The United States hastened to patch up its crumbling European alliance, rocked by American disapproval of British-French military actions in the Middle East. Thus NATO was reinvigorated and American intermediate range ballistic missiles were placed in Britain. Still, the French became bogged down in a colonial war in Algeria and had to transfer many of their NATO contingents to Africa. An economic recession in the United States in 1957 further sapped Western vitality. The United States and its allies were by no means weak or insecure, but their unity and confidence were waning.

Communists grew pompous in the face of the apparent Western malaise. "The East Wind Prevails Over the West Wind," asserted Mao Tse-tung.[72] On October 4, 1957 it appeared so. That day the Russians launched into outer space the world's first man-made satellite, *Sputnik.* Two months earlier the Soviets had fired the first intercontinental ballistic missile (ICBM). These achievements in rocketry shocked Americans into the realization that the Soviets had surpassed them in missile development. Never comfortable in second place, Americans chastised Eisenhower for apparently letting American power and prestige slip; the Democrats in particular sensed political advantage and publicly attacked the Administration. "The idea of *them* [Democrats] charging *me* with not being interested in *defense!*" General Eisenhower snapped. "Damn it, I've spent my whole life being concerned with defense of our country."[73] Although the "United States still had a substantial lead in strategic weapons," as historian Stephen Ambrose has noted, prominent Americans began to speak of a "bomber gap" and "missile gap."[74] A Ford Foundation Commission study, the "Gaither Report," fed popular fears about the same time that the Soviets were outstripping the United States both militarily and economically. Like NSC-68 in 1950, the "Gaither Report" in 1957 urged a large American military buildup. The Eisenhower Administration knew that *Sputnik* had not undermined American security, because since 1956 American U-2 spy planes, flying at high altitude with sensitive instruments, had been gathering intelligence data on Soviet military capabilities. Yet, as the British ambassador reported, *Sputnik* stunned official Washington: "The Russian success in launching the satellite has been something equivalent to Pearl Harbor. The American cocksureness is shaken."[75]

Presidential Assistant Sherman Adams bantered that the United States was not interested in scoring in an outer-space basketball game. When in November another *Sputnik* circled the globe, this time with a dog aboard, someone quipped that next the Russians would orbit cows—hence: the herd shot 'round the world. The Eisenhower Administration, of course, took the missile matter seriously. The President accelerated the American ballistic missile program. He ordered the dispersal of Strategic Air Command bombers and continued U-2 flights. In

January, 1958, rocket scientists, many of them former Germans like Werner von Braun brought to the United States at the end of World War II, successfully launched an American satellite named Explorer I. In July, the National Aeronautics and Space Administration (NASA) was created; its expensive operations culminated in 1969 in the landing of Americans on the moon. America's educational system was given a jolt by *Sputnik*, too. Why wasn't "Johnny" keeping up with "Ivan"? Many answered that Russian schools offered superior instruction in mathematics and science. The National Defense Education Act (NDEA), passed in September, 1958, provided for federal aid to finance new educational programs in the sciences, mathematics, and foreign languages. Soviet-American competition helped make education a Cold War phenomenon. One university president declared in the 1960s that the nation's colleges and universities had become "bastions of our defense, as essential as . . . supersonic bombers."[76]

The continued militarization of the Cold War and the new emphasis on missile development alarmed George F. Kennan, an earlier architect of the containment doctrine. In November and December of 1957 Kennan delivered the "Reith Lectures" in London, vaguely calling for the "disengagement" of foreign troops from Eastern Europe and Germany, restrictions on nuclear weapons in that area, and a unified, nonaligned Germany. The ideas were neither his alone, nor new. Earlier in the year, for example, Polish Foreign Minister Adam Rapacki advocated a "denuclearized zone" in Central and Eastern Europe.[77] The "Rapacki Plan" seemed a sensible way to reduce the atomic arms race, but the Eisenhower Administration, despite its own appeals for disarmament, did not pursue the proposal. In the fall of 1957 Kennan tried to keep the idea alive through his

**American Missiles.** President Eisenhower accelerated the United States missile program in the late 1950s. These warheads stood awesomely in West Germany. (Cornell Capa, Magnum Photos)

eloquent lectures widely broadcast over BBC radio. Also, in order to reduce Moscow's security fears, he wanted to remove Germany from the Cold War and thereby permit a withdrawal of Soviet troops from Eastern Europe. He was critical, too, of the Eisenhower Administration's strengthening of NATO, which he labeled a "military fixation" at a time when diplomacy was needed.[78]

Kennan's suggestions were greeted with unalloyed hostility by leading Americans. Former Secretary of State Dean Acheson spared Eisenhower and Dulles the task of debating "disengagement". "Next to the Lincoln Memorial in moonlight," columnist James Reston wrote, "the sight of Mr. Dean G. Acheson blowing his top is without doubt the most impressive view in the capital."[79] Acheson warned against a new American isolationism. Should Kennan's plan be realized, he scolded, Russia might reintroduce troops into Eastern Europe, threaten Western Europe, and actually sign an anti-American military pact with the new united Germany. The Russians simply could not be trusted. A rearmed West Germany must remain in the American camp. More soberly, German-born Henry A. Kissinger, a Harvard political scientist, argued that a German defense line had to be held against a potentially aggressive Russia. In his *Nuclear Weapons and Foreign Policy* (1957), Kissinger also criticized Dulles' concept of "massive retaliation" and appealed instead for a mobile, tactical missile system tied to flexible fighting units so that conventional wars would not ignite nuclear annihilation. Kennan answered Acheson and Kissinger, both committed to the military Cold War in Europe, that the United States would never know Russia's intentions unless it negotiated. He spoke of new "realities" in Europe which made the 1950s different from the 1940s. Walter Lippmann, who had criticized Kennan's containment in 1947, stood with him in 1957. People like Acheson and Kissinger, Lippman complained, are "like old soldiers trying to relive the battles in which they won their fame and glory. . . . Their preoccupation with their own past history is preventing them from dealing with the new phase of the Cold War."[80]

The "disengagement" debate had hardly subsided before a crisis over Berlin demonstrated the importance of Kennan's suggestions for defusing European issues. West Berlin, 110 miles inside Communist East Germany, was a bone in the Russian throat, as Khrushchev put it. Approximately three million East German defectors, many of them skilled workers, had used West Berlin as an escape route since 1949. For Americans and their allies, including the West German government of Konrad Adenauer, the city was an espionage and propaganda center for activities directed eastward. West Berlin's prosperity, induced by billions of dollars in American aid, glittered next to somber East Berlin. Washington heated Soviet tempers by bragging about economic success in West Berlin and applauding the East German exodus. The United States also insisted that the two Germanies be united under free elections and refused to recognize the East German government. Finally, the continued rearmament of West Germany, including American planes capable of dropping nuclear bombs, alarmed Russia, which had endorsed the Rapacki Plan.

In November of 1958 the Soviet Union boldly issued an ultimatum to solve the German "problem" through negotiations. Within six months, warned Khrushchev, unless East-West talks on Germany had begun, Russia would sign a peace treaty with East Germany, thereby ending the occupation agreements still in effect from World War II and turning East Berlin over to the East German regime. He recommended that Berlin be converted to a "free city" without foreign troops.

"**Braggers.**" In this Japanese cartoon Khrushchev and Eisenhower brag about their missiles during the serious arms race of the 1950s. (Nasu, courtesy of the State Historical Society of Missouri)

Washington was clearly worried, because it did not recognize East Germany and therefore would not negotiate with it. To deal with it would be to accept the Soviet position that there were two Germanies. Such an acceptance would in turn call into question the post-World War II occupation rights and hence the American presence within West Berlin itself. Unwilling to accept anything less than a united Germany tied to NATO, the United States was not eager to negotiate "disengagement" with the Russians. Dulles called the Russians reckless and braced himself for an episode in brinkmanship. Dean Acheson and Army Chief of Staff Maxwell Taylor urged the President to test Soviet intentions by sending American military units through the corridors to West Berlin. Eisenhower rejected such inflammatory advice and stalled. Privately Eisenhower said that "in this gamble, we are not going to be betting white chips, building up the pot gradually and fearfully. Khrushchev should know that when we decide to act, our whole stack will be in the pot."[81] Khrushchev wanted to talk, not fight. He backed away from his ultimatum and agreed to a foreign ministers conference for May, 1959, which proved inconclusive, a trip of September, 1959 to the United States to speak with Eisenhower, and ultimately a Paris summit meeting in May, 1960.

Khrushchev's tour of the United States in September, 1959 was a real spectacle. Eisenhower personally welcomed him, hoping to "soften up the Soviet leader even a little bit. Except for the Austrian peace treaty, we haven't made a chip in the granite in seven years."[82] Dulles had died of cancer in April, so Eisenhower was more in the forefront of diplomacy now. Khrushchev and his party began a national tour. The Premier inspected an IBM plant, fell in love with the city of San Francisco, cuddled babies just like an American politician, and visited a Hollywood movie set where he was offended by the bare legs exposed in a cancan dance—a sign to him of the decadence of Western capitalism. He was annoyed that proper security arrangements could not be made for a trip to Disneyland. He seemed, in brief, altogether human. He plugged "peaceful coexistence" and said that his earlier statement that "we will bury capitalism" should not be taken in a literal or military sense. "I say it again—I've almost worn my tongue thin repeating it—you may live under capitalism and we will live under socialism and build communism. The one whose system proves better will win. We will not bury you, nor will you bury us."[83] Khrushchev reminded Americans that they had sent troops into the Russian civil war during the World War I period, and they reminded him that they had also sent relief aid in the early 1920s. After ten days on the road, the Soviet Premier went to Camp David, that quiet, secluded presidential retreat near the Catoctin Mountains in Maryland. For two days the two leaders exchanged war stories and discussed the question of Berlin in a relaxed atmosphere. Eisenhower would not agree to a new summit meeting until Khrushchev abandoned his Berlin ultimatum. The Premier agreed to do so. Although the President and Premier were no closer to a German settlement, observers identified a "Spirit of Camp David"—a willingness on both sides to talk their way to détente.

In 1959–1960 Eisenhower himself made a number of foreign trips in a deliberate effort to conduct "personal diplomacy." His new vigor and determination to ease tensions suggested that Ike had been previously restrained by Dulles' intransigence. Just before Khrushchev's visit to the United States, the President had flown to London, Paris, and Bonn for talks with European leaders. In December he traveled 22,000 miles to eleven nations in Europe, Asia, and North Africa. Among his hosts were Pope John XXIII, neutralist Prime Minister Jawaharlal Nehru of India, where a million people in New Delhi hailed Eisenhower as the "Prince of Peace," and Francisco Franco, the dictator who had authorized American air bases on Spanish soil. It was a "goodwill" tour of little apparent diplomatic value. In February, 1960, he toured Latin America for two weeks and encountered a mixed

**Camp David, 1959.** Eisenhower and Khrushchev discussed Berlin in a relaxed manner at the Maryland presidential retreat, but the "Spirit of Camp David" soon evaporated. (Dwight D. Eisenhower Library)

reception. And then he departed for the Paris summit meeting in May. There the "goodwill" ended.

Two weeks before that summit meeting, on May 1, 1960, an American airplane carrying high-powered cameras and other reconnaisance instruments was shot down over Sverdlovsk in the Ural Mountains, 1,200 miles within the Soviet Union. The U-2 intelligence plane was part of a CIA operation and was flying from a base in Turkey to one in Norway. Although such flights had been conducted for four years and the Soviets had learned about them, this was the first time that Soviet firepower had been able to reach the high altitude craft. Evidently pilot Francis Gary Powers' U-2 had engine trouble and dropped several thousand feet before being shot down. He parachuted and was captured immediately, unable or unwilling to take his CIA-issued death potion. CIA officials in the United States knew only that a plane was missing. NASA, used as "cover," announced routinely on May 3 that a "research airplane" studying weather patterns over Turkey had apparently crashed. Two days later Khrushchev cryptically announced that an American airplane had been shot down over Russia after it had violated Soviet air space. Thereafter, the Eisenhower Administration bungled badly. The State Department issued a fabricated statement that a weather plane piloted by a "civilian" had probably strayed over Russian territory by mistake. On May 6 Premier Khrushchev exploded that story by displaying photographs of the uninjured pilot, his spy equipment, and his pictures of Soviet military installations. Then the State Department lamely admitted that the plane was "probably" on an intelligence operation. No longer able to keep the truth hidden, Eisenhower decided to speak out. "I felt anything but apologetic," he recalled.[84] The President took responsibility for the U-2 reconnaisance flights and said they were necessary to avoid another Pearl Harbor. With such logic, Emmet John Hughes has noted, the Administration transformed "an unthinkable falsehood into a sovereign right."[85] This was the dramatic background to the summit meeting of May, which was supposed to deal with Berlin. At Paris Khrushchev denounced American aggression, demanded an apology for the U-2 flights, and stalked out of the conference. Soviet-American hostility, despite years of "personal diplomacy" and "thaws," was as intense as ever in 1960.

## The Containment of China

The Chinese Communists were not unhappy with this deterioration in Soviet-American relations. From the mid-1950s onward, Peking openly condemned Moscow's concept of "peaceful coexistence" and any movement toward a Soviet-American rapprochement. China opposed summit meetings and criticized Khrushchev's timidity in not sending troops to Lebanon in 1958 to drive out American soldiers. The *People's Daily* chastised Khrushchev for "yielding to evil" and "coddling wrong."[86] Peking believed that the Soviets refused Chinese requests for assistance in nuclear development because of this "coddling" of the capitalist adversary. Some Western observers have suggested that Khrushchev seized upon the U-2 incident to wreck the Paris summit so as to demonstrate that Moscow could still be uncompromising with the capitalist West and to deflate Chinese criticism of Russian "appeasement." In any case, a Communist détente with the United States in the 1950s was anathema to Chinese leaders, who recognized the deep roots of the Sino-American antagonism: American aid before 1949 to Chiang;

**Mao Tse-tung (1893–1976).** Chief of the Communist party in "Red China," father of the successful Communist Revolution, and radical philosopher-poet, Mao brooked no tolerance for the "imperialist" United States. Yet he helped launch Sino-American détente before his death. (*The Reporter,* 1956. Copyright 1956 by The Reporter Magazine Co.)

Chinese harassment of Americans; Washington's nonrecognition policy; bitter Chinese denunciations of American "imperialism"; the Sino-Soviet Treaty of 1950; American blockage of Chinese membership in the United Nations; continuing American support for Chiang on Formosa; and the Chinese-American military confrontation in Korea.

In early 1953, President Eisenhower "unleashed" Chiang Kai-shek by announcing that the Seventh Fleet would no longer block his attempts to attack the mainland. Chiang actually lacked the resources for a major fight, but the decision alarmed Peking, especially after Nationalist bombing raids began to hit coastal regions. Throughout the 1950s Chiang pledged a return to China. He received an annual average of over $250 million in American economic and military assistance. The Seventh Fleet remained in the Formosa Straits, prompting the Communists to protest that it was as if China stationed vessels between Hawaii and the United States. By the late 1950s, as well, China was ringed by American bases and armed forces stretching from Japan to South Korea. In 1954 the United States had created SEATO, an alliance of the United States, France, Britain, Australia, New Zealand, Thailand, Pakistan, and the Philippines, pledged to assist one another when their "peace and safety" were threatened. The new pact was essentially aimed at "Red China" and Peking's support, on behalf of international communism, of nationalist revolution in Indochina. In December, 1954, Taiwan and the United States signed a mutual defense treaty. The following year Congress, by an overwhelming vote of 83–3 in the Senate and 410–3 in the House, gave the President authority in the "Formosa Resolution" to use American troops if necessary to defend Taiwan and adjoining islands. The United States in 1957 placed on Taiwan missiles capable of firing nuclear warheads.

Washington also resisted cultural or economic contacts with China. American officials forbade American journalists to accept China's 1956 invitation to visit the mainland. The State Department even banned the shipment of a panda bear to the United States, because the animal had been born in China. At the 1954 Geneva Conference on Indochina (see next chapter), Chinese and American diplomats barely mixed. At one point Foreign Minister Chou En-lai approached Secretary of State John Foster Dulles intending to shake hands, but Dulles, afraid that photographers would record this contaminating event, brusquely shunned Chou's outstretched hand by turning his back. The United States also imposed a trade embargo on China, hoping that that would weaken the Peking government.

In 1954–1955 a major dispute brought the two nations to the brink. In early 1955 Dulles advised the President, "there is at least an even chance that the United States will have to go to war."[87] Two tiny islands triggered the confrontation. Quemoy and Matsu, only a few miles off the Chinese mainland, were heavily fortified islands occupied by about 60,000 Nationalist troops. They served as bases for Nationalist commando raids against China as well as defensive posts for Formosa. In mid-1954 China announced its intention to "liberate" Formosa, not a serious threat because the People's Republic lacked the amphibious equipment required for such a venture. But in September its shore batteries began to bombard Quemoy and Matsu. Eisenhower elected to defend the islands, not because they were important to United States security (they were not) or because they were important to Formosa's security (it is doubtful they were), but because they stood as symbols of American toughness in the face of the Communist menace.

China had the legal case for possession on its side, but that did not matter.

According to Vice-President Richard Nixon, American policy "was formulated on the principle that we should stand ready to call international Communism's bluff on any pot, large or small. If we let them know that we will defend freedom when the stakes are small, the Soviets are not encouraged to threaten freedom where the stakes are higher." Indeed, "that is why the two small islands . . . are so important in the poker game of world politics."[88] Congress gave Eisenhower a blank check in the "Formosa Resolution" and waited anxiously. Lacking nuclear weapons and any guarantees of support from Russia, China defused the crisis by offering to open discussions. Beginning in 1955 at Geneva, and after 1958 in Warsaw, Chinese and American officials quietly talked at the ambassadorial level about Taiwan, trade, and other topics. These limited discussions constituted the only sensible, civil element in Chinese-American relations.

In 1958, Quemoy and Matsu again became a flash point when more shells from the mainland hit the fortified islands, where Chiang had built up his forces, reaching 100,000 by 1958. During the new crisis Eisenhower ordered American airlifts to these troops and Seventh Fleet escorts for Nationalist supply ships. He stated in a televised address in September that abandoning the offshore islands would constitute a "Western Pacific Munich." "If history teaches us anything, appeasement would make it more likely that we would have to fight a major war."[89] Critics retorted that the islands were not worth American blood or the risk of nuclear war. America's European allies protested against a wastage of American resources over Quemoy and Matsu. Peking was unabashed: "Supported by the United States, the Chiang Kai-shek clique has for long been using coastal islands such as Quemoy . . . and Matsu . . . as advance bases for conducting all sorts of harassing and disruptive activities. . . . The Chinese Government has every right to deal resolute blows and take necessary military action against Chiang Kai-shek's troops entrenched on the coastal island[s]."[90] Eisenhower and Dulles stepped back from the brink and hinted to China that a mutual de-escalation would be welcomed. Peking suspended bombardment for a week and the United States suspended the escorting of Nationalist vessels. Dulles persuaded Chiang to remove some troops from the islands, and Peking announced that it would bomb Quemoy and Matsu only on alternate days. It was a strange way to conduct war, but the arrangement eased tension. "Who would have thought when we fired a few shots at Quemoy and Matsu," Mao asked, "that it would stir up such an earth-shattering storm?"[91]

## The New Challenge: Nationalism and the Third World

In the period 1946–1960, thirty-seven new nations emerged from colonial status in Asia, Africa, and the Middle East. In 1958, twenty-eight prolonged guerrilla insurgencies were under way. Eighteen countries became independent in 1960 alone. Revolutions and the collapse of empires thus claimed a central place in international affairs. These great changes occurred in the "Third World"—the "underdeveloped" or "developing" countries that were largely nonwhite, located in the southern half of the globe, and mostly nonindustrialized. In a somewhat derogatory term, the industrialized West called them "backward" nations. Once the Cold War lines were fairly firm in Europe, the Soviet-American confrontation shifted to the Third World. The stakes were high. These countries were rich in raw materials and had for decades served the needs of the industrial nations. In 1959

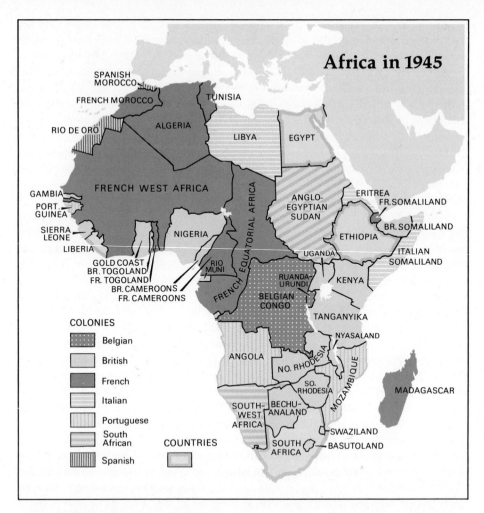

**Africa in 1945**

SPANISH MOROCCO
FRENCH MOROCCO
TUNISIA
RIO DE ORO
ALGERIA
LIBYA
EGYPT
GAMBIA
PORT. GUINEA
FRENCH WEST AFRICA
ERITREA
FR. SOMALILAND
ANGLO-EGYPTIAN SUDAN
BR. SOMALILAND
SIERRA LEONE
LIBERIA
NIGERIA
ETHIOPIA
ITALIAN SOMALILAND
GOLD COAST
BR. TOGOLAND
FR. TOGOLAND
BR. CAMEROONS
FR. CAMEROONS
RIO MUNI
FRENCH EQUATORIAL AFRICA
UGANDA
RUANDA-URUNDI
KENYA
BELGIAN CONGO
TANGANYIKA
NYASALAND
ANGOLA
NO. RHODESIA
SO. RHODESIA
MOZAMBIQUE
MADAGASCAR
SOUTH-WEST AFRICA
BECHU-ANALAND
SWAZILAND
SOUTH AFRICA
BASUTOLAND

COLONIES
Belgian
British
French
Italian
Portuguese
South African
Spanish
COUNTRIES

over one-third of American direct private investments abroad were in the Third World. Underdeveloped nations also bought manufactured goods and provided strategic sites for air and naval bases.

The volatile conditions in these "emerging" nations did not permit easy management by outsiders. Many of their leaders were anticolonial revolutionaries who established leftist, undemocratic regimes. Long exploited, they were poor countries, eager for economic improvement without foreign ownership. Nationalism was intense, politics unstable. Many of these developing nations declared themselves "uncommitted" or "neutral" in the Cold War, and both Washington and Moscow faced strong odds against trying to bring upstarts into their respective camps. However, in longer-established Third World nations, particularly in Latin America, in an effort to beat back rebel challenges, the United States continued to support governments controlled by military, political, or economic elites.

The Eisenhower Administration and its successors fared poorly. American leaders did not deal with the new nationalism as a force in itself, but as part of the Cold War struggle. They confused "nationalism" and "neutralism" with "communism" and assumed that much of the trouble in the Third World was inspired by Moscow. "Yet to blame the danger of these [explosions] on the presence of

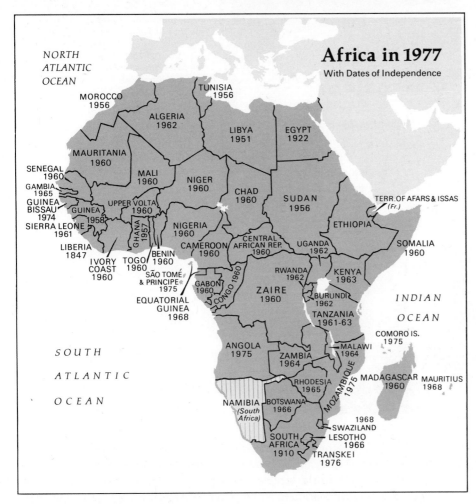

**Africa in 1977**

With Dates of Independence

NORTH
ATLANTIC
OCEAN

TUNISIA
1956

MOROCCO
1956

ALGERIA
1962

LIBYA
1951

EGYPT
1922

MAURITANIA
1960

SENEGAL
1960

GAMBIA
1965

GUINEA
BISSAU
1974

GUINEA
1958

SIERRA LEONE
1961

LIBERIA
1847

IVORY
COAST
1960

MALI
1960

UPPER VOLTA
1960

TOGO
1960

BENIN
1960

GHANA
1957

NIGER
1960

CHAD
1960

SUDAN
1956

TERR. OF AFARS & ISSAS
(Fr.)

ETHIOPIA

NIGERIA
1960

CAMEROON
1960

CENTRAL
AFRICAN REP.
1960

UGANDA
1962

SOMALIA
1960

SÃO TOMÉ
& PRINCIPE
1975

EQUATORIAL
GUINEA
1968

GABON
1960

CONGO 1960

ZAIRE
1960

RWANDA
1962

BURUNDI
1962

KENYA
1963

TANZANIA
1961-63

INDIAN

OCEAN

COMORO IS.
1975

SOUTH

ATLANTIC

OCEAN

ANGOLA
1975

ZAMBIA
1964

MALAWI
1964

MOZAMBIQUE 1975

MADAGASCAR
1960

MAURITIUS
1968

NAMIBIA
(South
Africa)

BOTSWANA
1966

RHODESIA
1965

1968
SWAZILAND

SOUTH
AFRICA
1910

LESOTHO
1966

TRANSKEI
1976

Communists," one scholar has written, "is like blaming the inherent danger in a huge mass of exposed combustible materials on the possible presence of arsonists."[92] The Eisenhower-Dulles team tried to apply the venerable containment doctrine to these regions in a futile effort to curb the new challenge.

America's great wealth proved a handicap. Americans were known as the "People of Plenty," to borrow the title of a 1954 book by historian David M. Potter. Foreigners both envied and resented America's unmatched abundance; many wanted to be like Americans, and grew indignant over the difficulty of becoming so. The image of the "Ugly American" exacerbated foreign resentment. In 1958 William J. Lederer and Eugene Burdick wrote a novel with that title to underscore the reasons why the United States had a tarnished reputation in the Third World. They noted, among other problems, that Americans abroad flaunted their wealth and that American diplomats often isolated themselves from the poor countryside by living lavishly in a "Golden Ghetto."[93] The authors appealed for Foreign Service Officers who spoke the language of the host country and would live, without accustomed comfort, among the "people." In this way, they argued rather superficially, the United States would win the struggle against communism.

American racism, symbolized by Jim Crow practices, also handicapped the

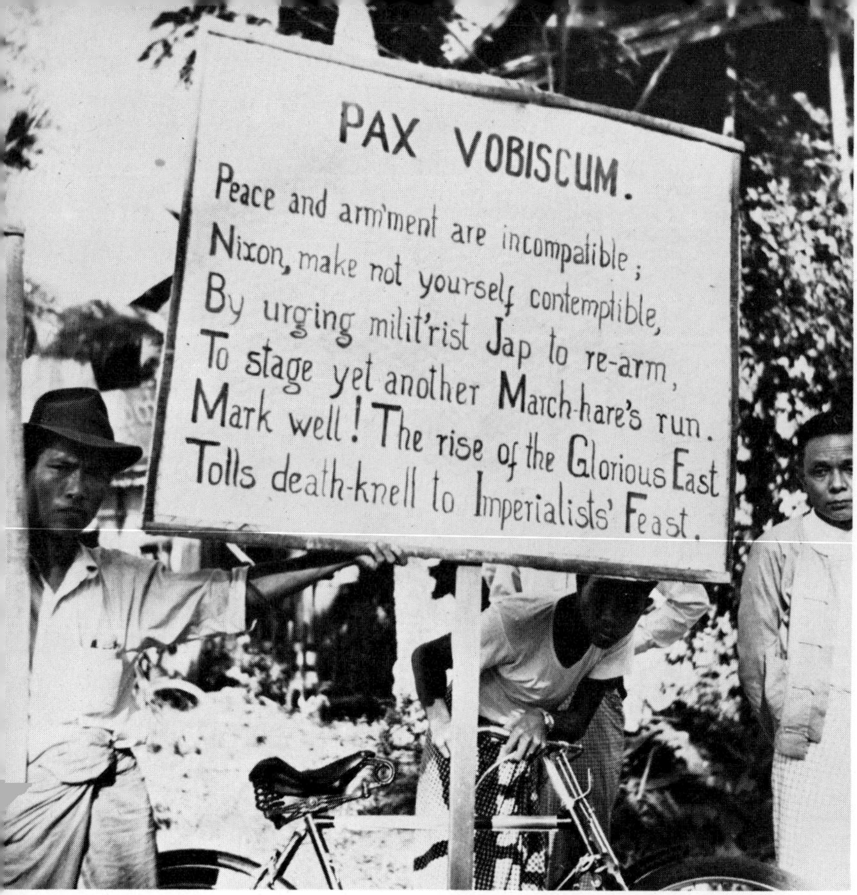
PAX VOBISCUM.
Peace and arm'ment are incompatible;
Nixon, make not yourself contemptible,
By urging milit'rist Jap to re-arm,
To stage yet another March-hare's run.
Mark well! The rise of the Glorious East
Tolls death-knell to Imperialists' Feast.

**Anti-Imperialist Protest.** During his tour of Asia in 1953, Vice-President Nixon was greeted with this nationalist sign of disapproval. (Department of State, National Archives)

United States. In December, 1952, when the attorney general asked the Supreme Court to strike down segregation in public schools, his brief read that "it is in the context of the present world struggle between freedom and tyranny that the problem of racial discrimination must be viewed." American segregation, in short, "furnished grist for the Communist propaganda mills."[94] He was right. In 1955 the Indian ambassador was refused service in an airport restaurant in Texas because of his dark skin. In 1957, on Route 40 leading into Washington, the finance minister of Ghana was denied food at a Howard Johnson's. President Eisenhower tried to assuage the insult by inviting him to breakfast at the White House. In the same year, when Eisenhower sent federal troops to Little Rock, Arkansas to escort black children to school in the midst of ugly white protest, the President criticized that state for a "tremendous disservice . . . to the nation in the eyes of the world."[95] With Soviet propaganda in the Third World mocking the blatant contradiction between America's professed principles and actual practice, the Voice of America and the State Department struggled to create a more favorable image.

Americans professed a revolutionary tradition ("the Spirit of '76") and often said they identified with the revolutionary aspirations of others. "We ourselves are the first colony in modern times to have won independence," Dulles proclaimed in 1954. "We have a natural sympathy with those everywhere who would follow our example."[96] But something was out of kilter between that tradition and American foreign policy in the post-World War II period. Professor K. E. Boulding suggested that the American attitude toward revolution "is a compound feeling of both love and hate, affectionate regard for the infants toddling in our early footsteps and unresolved guilt about our own breakaway."[97] Basically, Americans had become satiated, propertied representatives of the status quo. Revolution was no longer in America's national interest because it challenged an established order that guaranteed Americans both a prominent position in international relations and an affluent society. Mr. Dooley had remarked at the start of the century: "A riv'lution can't be bound be th' rules iv th' game because it's again' the rules iv th' game."[98] Americans at mid-century adhered to the "rules."

The American Revolution itself had been a rebellion of limited social change—nothing like the wrenching social revolutions of the twentieth century. "The men who pushed the American Revolution were not nationalists compelled to spend years in the jails of the colonial power," historian Carl N. Degler has written, "but political leaders seeking only to continue their free governments as they knew them all their lives."[99] Many Americans had been soured by the bloody excesses of the French Revolution. In the 1830s Alexis de Tocqueville observed that "in no other country in the world is the love of property more active and more anxious than in the United States; nowhere does the majority display less inclination for those principles which threaten to alter, in whatever manner, the laws of property."[100] To Americans in the nineteenth century, a "proper" revolution was a limited one like their own. As early twentieth-century revolutions, like those in Mexico, China, and Russia, rocked international equilibrium, the United States increasingly found itself a target rather than a model of revolution. One government report put the problem frankly in 1945: "The United States leans toward propertied classes who place a premium on order and trade."[101] So it was during the Eisenhower years. In late 1960, when forty-three Afro-Asian states, led by India, sponsored a United Nations resolution proclaiming irresistible and necessary the process of liberation from colonialism, the United States abstained from voting, not wishing to offend colonial nations and Cold War friends like Portugal.

The Soviets, with their own brand of revolutionary past, had their troubles in the Third World, too. On the ideological level, both Marxism and the professed anticolonialism of the Soviet Union enjoyed wide appeal. In the mid-1950s Khrushchev toured India, Burma, and Afghanistan; and Russia, however inexpertly, launched a foreign aid offensive. It agreed, for example, to build a $91 million steel plant in India and the Aswan Dam in Egypt. Between 1954 and 1959 Indonesia received the equivalent of a quarter-billion dollars in Soviet aid. At the Bandung Conference of 1955, where twenty-nine "nonaligned" states representing about one-quarter of the world's population met to applaud "neutralism" and Russia's call for "peaceful coexistence," it became evident that the "free world" was less popular than the "Communist world" in the Third World. Yet the Soviet Union came up against nationalism, too, and gained few allies. Egypt's Gamal Abdal Nasser and India's Jawaharlal Nehru would not become Soviet clients. Khrushchev, during a 1955 trip in India, vehemently denounced the West, and the neutralist Indians resented this blatant effort to bring the Cold War into their country. Then, too, Arab nationalism, not Soviet communism, dominated the Middle East. And in Latin America, between 1945 and 1955, sixteen nations outlawed the Communist party. As historian Donald Dozer wrote in 1959, "Latin Americans can be depended upon to adopt a solidary opposition to Soviet and every other imperialism . . . in defense of their independence and their institutions."[102] The Soviets, like the Americans, could not tolerate or exploit independent nationalism. Nor did they have the economic resources to make good on many of their foreign aid promises. Finally, they could not explain away the giant contradiction between their rhetoric on self-determination and their brutal suppression of Eastern European countries.

American officials remained fearful, however, that Soviet-directed communism would exploit nationalistic sentiment and poverty in the Third World. Foreign aid was the primary United States tool for combating the perceived threat, although the Central Intelligence Agency took on increasing importance as a manipulator of Third World events, with the secretary of state's brother Allen W. Dulles as its director, 1953–1961. Whereas during the 1949–1952 period over three-quarters of total American economic assistance went to Europe, in the years 1953–1957 three-quarters flowed to developing countries. By 1961 over 90 percent of United States aid went to the Third World. But to Washington's distress, many of the recipients refused to choose sides in the Cold War. As Nasser asserted: "We will not be subjected—either by West or East."[103] Such nonalignment naturally drew fire from Americans seeking political returns from foreign aid. To Dulles, it seemed, neutralism was but a deceitful stage on the way to communism. So he declared it an "immoral and shortsighted conception."[104] With such negative statements the United States faced the prevalent nationalist currents and earned itself the title of the New Rome—a counterrevolutionary in a revolutionary world.

## Tests in the Middle East and Latin America

America's troubles with the Third World are illustrated by two complex crises in the Middle East and Latin America. In 1952 Nasser led young Egyptian army officers against King Farouk, their vulgar, pro-Western ruler, who fled to Europe with his harem and his wealth. As head of state, Nasser initiated land reform and pledged to eliminate British control of the Suez Canal. A 1954 agreement, reluctantly signed by London, provided for a phased withdrawal. To maintain western influence in the Middle East, the United States tried in 1955 to rally nations to its side by promoting the Baghdad Pact, a military alliance of Britain, Turkey, Iran, Iraq, and Pakistan. Iran had been won over in 1953 when the United States, through the intervention of the CIA and a cut-off of foreign aid, helped overthrow Iranian nationalist Mohammed Mossadegh, who had attempted to nationalize foreign oil interests. American companies produced about 50 percent of the region's oil. Israel, the Jewish state Truman had quickly recognized after its creation in May, 1948, was drawn closer to the United States by foreign aid totaling $374 million from 1952 to 1961. Yet bitter Arab-Israeli conflict thwarted American hopes for order in the Middle East. After the Israelis raided the Gaza Strip in 1955 and exposed Egypt's military weakness, Cairo signed an arms agreement with Czechoslovakia. Heretofore Western nations had monopolized arms sales in the Middle East.

Despite his dislike for Nasser's independent spirit, Dulles decided to employ foreign aid to draw him toward the West. In December, 1955, the secretary offered to fund Nasser's dream of the Aswan Dam on the Nile, a potential source of electrical power and irrigation. During the next year the World Bank worked out the details of the $1.3 billion project, involving British, American, and World Bank monies. About the same time Egypt joined an anti-Israeli military alliance with

Saudi Arabia, Syria, and Yemen. Anger from vocal Jewish-Americans swept down on Washington and southern congressmen asked why the United States should support a project that would permit Egypt to produce competitive cotton. Eisenhower and Dulles, who disapproved of Nasser's neutralism and who may have thought that the Czech arms deal signified Egyptian alignment with the Soviets, grew less interested in the dam. Cairo had, not long before, recognized the People's Republic of China, and this also annoyed Washington. Part of the Eisenhower Administration's thinking can be gleaned from a rhetorical question Dulles asked: "Do nations which play both sides get better treatment than nations which are stalwart and work with us?"[105] Some American officials actually thought the arms deal was a bluff because the Soviets lacked adequate military supplies to fulfill it. Dulles' abrupt withdrawal of the Aswan Dam offer in July, 1956 thus afforded an opportunity not only to punish neutralism but to expose Soviet feet of clay.

**Gamal Abdal Nasser (1918–1970).** The bold Egyptian leader and advocate of Arab nationalism evicted the British from his country, but when he seized the Suez Canal, the British, joined by the French and Israelis, returned in arms. (*The Reporter,* 1956. Copyright 1956 by The Reporter Magazine Co.)

But American economic pressure backfired. Nasser quickly seized the Suez Canal, intent upon using its $25 million annual profit to help build the Aswan Dam. Without consulting Washington, the British and French huddled with Israel and planned a military operation. In late October and early November, 1956, British, French, and Israeli forces invaded Egypt and nearly captured the canal. Eisenhower was boiling mad, especially furious that his wartime friend Anthony Eden, now Prime Minister, would proceed without informing him. To make matters worse, Dulles had just entered the hospital for treatment of his cancer. Eisenhower publicly upbraided the British and French for taking military action that might draw the Soviets into the Middle East and that took the spotlight off simultaneous Soviet brutalities in Hungary. To force the European and Israeli offenders out, American officials introduced a United Nations resolution calling for withdrawal and a cutback of oil shipments to the invaders. By late December the troops departed, leaving a United Nations peacekeeping unit, which returned the canal, now clogged with sunken ships, to Egypt.

The Suez crisis produced mixed results for America. Although the United States retained its oil holdings and Middle Eastern friends, it alienated the leading Arab nation, Egypt. By withdrawing the Aswan Dam offer, Washington opened the Middle Eastern door to Soviet influence, the very opposite of what the United States wanted; the Russians eventually built the dam. Relations with Britain and France were fractured. Although the United States stood against this abortive return of Victorian imperialism, it simultaneously snubbed nationalism and neutralism, and thereafter the United States became further ensnarled in the tumultuous politics of the Middle East. In 1957, for example, Saudi Arabia let the United States keep its air base at Dhahran in exchange for American military aid and a promise not to station Jewish-Americans at the base. That year Washington also issued the "Eisenhower Doctrine" and in 1958 sent 14,000 troops to Lebanon to head off a threatened coup by pro-Nasser Arabs. In the American ledger this was another Cold War "victory," but the phrase rang hollow.

Nationalism also tightened its grip on the United States' own sphere of influence, Latin America. Through the Rio Pact (a defensive military alliance formed in 1947), the Organization of American States (launched the following year but formally established in 1951 to help settle inter-American disputes), investments of $8.2 billion by 1959, economic assistance totaling $835 million for the period 1952–1961, and support to military dictators like Fulgencio Batista in Cuba, the United States perpetuated its hegemony over neighbors to the south. But many

Latin Americans were restless, and their nationalism, which had already challenged the United States in Mexico, became strident. Latin American poverty was stark; illiteracy rates were high; health care was inadequate; a population explosion was under way; productivity showed miniscule growth; profits from raw materials like sugar and oil flowed through American companies to the United States; and Washington had taken the region for granted. However, as the Cold War shifted to the Third World, Washington grew wary of Latin American discontent. American anticommunists joined long-standing economic interests to revitalize United States attention to its client states. Dulles told a congressional committee in 1953 that "if we don't look out, we will wake up some morning and read in the newspapers that there happened in South America the same kind of thing that happened in China in 1949."[106] To prevent such a debacle in Latin America, the United States was willing to use force, the Good Neighbor policy notwithstanding.

Guatemala became a test case in 1954. Three years before, leftist Jacobo Arbenz Guzman had been elected President. His primary goal was land reform, in a country where 2 percent of the population owned 70 percent of the land. The influential United Fruit Company, a huge banana exporter and the largest landowner in Guatemala, had 234,000 acres of its uncultivated land expropriated by the Arbenz government in early 1953. Arbenz offered to compensate the company, using the value of the land as declared by the company itself for Guatemalan tax purposes ($600,000). United Fruit quickly demanded over $15 million and received backing from the State Department. Exploiting American anticommunism to save its properties, United Fruit began an extensive propaganda effort in the United States. The message: Communism threatened Latin America. Arbenz consulted with Communist leaders in planning his social program, but few Communists held offices and the Arbenz government had minimal ties with the Soviet Union. The Eisenhower Administration nevertheless joined United Fruit in the simplistic and inaccurate depiction. Ambassador to Guatemala John E. Peurifoy, already experienced in the 1940s in the Greek civil war, reported that Arbenz "thought like a Communist and talked like a Communist, and if not actually one, would do until one came along."[107]

The United States thereupon subverted the Guatemalan government. In early 1954 an unenthusiastic Organization of American States declared, by a vote of 17–1, that the domination of any American state by the "international communist movement" would constitute a threat to the hemisphere.[108] The Guatemalan foreign minister called the action "the internationalization of McCarthyism."[109] Washington also cut off technical assistance funds to Guatemala. About the same time, the Central Intelligence Agency began covert activities, dubbed "Operation el Diablo," in cooperation with Colonel Carlos Castillo Armas, a Guatemalan willing to accept American counsel. In Honduras and on an island off Nicaragua, the CIA trained Castillo's mercenary troops. Arbenz turned to the Soviet Union for help, after being refused weapons from the United States and Western Europe. In May of 1954 the Swedish freighter *Alfhem* sailed to Guatemala laden with two thousand tons of rifles and machine guns made in Czechoslovakia. Although the United States followed the ship closely, the *Alfhem* was permitted to unload its wares. The CIA began to airlift material into Guatemala, dropping arms near United Fruit facilities. On June 18 Castillo attacked from Honduras as American planes manned by CIA pilots bombed Guatemala City. Abandoned by his army,

Arbenz went into exile. Castillo took power, returned United Fruit lands, and jailed political dissidents. In 1957 Castillo was assassinated but the new regime remained in the American camp. Indeed, it provided training sites for Cuban exiles being readied by the CIA for a planned attack upon Cuba—an invasion to subvert the government of another Latin American nationalist, Fidel Castro.

The 1954 United States intervention in Guatemala evoked a chorus of international boos. Now where was the Good Neighbor pledge of nonintervention? British Prime Minister Clement Atlee bluntly told the House of Commons: "The fact is that this was a plain act of aggression, and one cannot take one line on aggression in Asia and another line in Central America."[110] Latin Americans in particular, more fearful of United States intervention than of Communist activities, protested their neighbor's subversive operations and economic supremacy. Their discontent surfaced angrily and most dramatically in April–May, 1958, when Vice-President Richard M. Nixon went south on a "goodwill" tour of eight countries.

In Montevideo, Uruguay, anti-Yankee pickets mingled with the cheering crowds when Nixon motored through the city. Determined to counter what he considered Communist agitation, Nixon stopped at the University of the Republic and engaged students in an emotional debate on American foreign policy. Nixon claimed a rhetorical "victory" over the Communists, and went on to Peru, where

**Rioters Stone Nixon in Venezuela.** His car surrounded by hostile Venezuelan protesters, Vice-President Nixon experienced a grueling outbreak of anti-Americanism in May, 1958. He was forced to leave Caracas ahead of schedule, his experience highlighting problems in Latin America for the United States. (United Press International)

anti-American sentiment welled up at San Marcos University. Nixon pondered whether to visit the institution. American Ambassador Theodore Achilles urged him to go: "One characteristic common throughout this hemisphere is that people admire courage. They have contempt for fear. That is why the bullfight is a favorite sport here." Nixon decided not to run from a "bunch of Communist thugs."[111] He was stoned and spat upon. He then headed for Caracas.

In Venezuela all hell broke loose. Earlier in 1958 the ruthless dictatorship of Marcos Perez Jimenez ("P.J.") had been overthrown by a military junta. "P.J." had been a special friend of the United States during his seven-year rule. In 1954 the United States had decorated him with the Legion of Merit. In 1955 Dulles had told a Senate committee that Venezuela "has adopted the kind of policies which we think that other countries of South America should adopt. Namely, they have adopted policies which provide in Venezuela a climate which is attractive to foreign capital to come in."[112] When Jimenez was driven from Caracas and the Eisenhower Administration provided asylum for him and his hated chief of police, Venezuelan bitterness toward the United States deepened. Into this volatile environment stepped Nixon, emboldened by his earlier ventures among shouting students. His motorcade in Caracas was halted by hostile crowds and blockades; demonstrators stoned his car, shattering windows. They smashed fenders, rocked the automobile, and threatened the vice-president's life. A Secret Service agent drew his pistol: "Let's get some of these sons-of-bitches."[113] Before shooting broke out, however, Nixon's car somehow sped away. Eisenhower dispatched two airborne infantry companies to the Caribbean, but Nixon left Venezuela without further trouble. His toughness under stress gained him public admiration in the United States. "A national defeat," noted one chagrined journalist, "has been parlayed into a personal political triumph."[114]

After Nixon's trip, Washington stuck to its policy of hegemony but began to spend more money below the border. Nixon's recommendations to the President largely stressed the ways in which the United States might better influence its southern neighbors. For example, he suggested that American officials "must do a more effective job of reaching the opinion-makers of Latin America." Next, in what reads like a contradiction: "We must develop an economic program for Latin America which is distinctively its own." He further advised that the United States "should not appear to give dictators, of either the right or the left, the same moral approval that we gave to leaders who were trying to build free and democratic institutions."[115] He urged more military aid to Latin America to halt communism, more United States courage in the face of adversity, and more sensitivity about ways of providing aid so as not to offend Latin American pride. Nixon essentially advocated a change in public relations, not in policy. The shallowness of his proposals helped reveal why the United States was troubled in its response to Third World nationalism. Third World leaders were calling for self-determination, equality among nations, and ownership of their own raw materials. New United States "Madison Avenue" techniques, critics argued, would not alter those goals. The one positive program to emerge from the rethinking generated by Nixon's proposals was the Inter-American Development Bank, to which the United States granted a meager $500 million in 1959. Eisenhower still preferred the extension of private loans by American businessmen to the expenditure of public funds. Latin American leaders wanted the latter, and continued to complain that Washington ignored their dire needs.

**Space-Age Toy Shop.** Children at a Christmas-decorated window marvel at toy models of military weaponry and destructive gadgetry created to wage the cold war in the 1950s. Adults played with the real things. (A. Kovarsky, Swann Collection of Caricature and Cartoon)

## Holding the Line, 1950–1961

When the Eisenhower Administration gave way to the Democratic Administration of John F. Kennedy in January, 1961, it was holding the line—against nationalism, against revolution, against neutralism, against communism, against Soviet Russia, against China. Despite the catchy phrases of the Eisenhower-Dulles years, there had been no new departures in foreign policy. "Liberation" was "containment" by different means. The "Eisenhower Doctrine" was an extension of the "Truman Doctrine." Dulles' strictures against neutralism sounded very much like Truman's declaration that all nations must choose between two ways of life. The "domino theory" in Asia differed little from the Truman Administration's alarmist predictions that if Greece fell, the Middle East would fall and then Europe would be undermined. Eisenhower and Dulles reinforced the Truman-Acheson hostility to "Red China." Both administrations intervened, with different methods, in the Middle East. Both took Latin America for granted. Both had Berlin crises accentuate their determination to draw West Germany into Western Europe. Indeed, the continuity in American foreign policy from Truman through Eisenhower is conspicuous. America's Cold War institutions, its high defense budgets, its large and intransigent foreign affairs bureaucracy, its assumptions from the past—all ground on, largely resistant to change, perpetuating a momentum begun by Truman.

But the world had changed. In 1945 the United States sat atop the hierarchical structure of international relations. There were few restraints upon the exercise of its power. Americans confidently placed restraints on others. A bipolar world developed with lines fairly well drawn between the two camps. But as the Soviet Union and the United States built their economies and military forces toward a stalemate, particularly in Europe, the bonds of stability loosened elsewhere. Throughout the 1950s new nations claimed independence and threw off the shackles of colonialism. These new nations of the Third World did not wish to join sides in the Cold War. Even more troubling for the superpowers were the rebellions in their own spheres of influence. Latin America became less responsive to United States tutelage, and political turmoil and anti-Yankeeism ran rampant. The 1959 victory of nationalists in the Cuban Revolution symbolized the new challenge (see next chapter). Anti-American Japanese rioters forced Eisenhower to cancel a trip to Japan in 1960, and Europeans like Charles de Gaulle of France sought restrictions on United States influence. For the Soviets there were the Hungarian Revolution, growing discontent in Eastern Europe, and a challenge from China for leadership in the Communist camp. The crude display in November, 1960 of Khrushchev banging his shoe at the United Nations suggested to some that in their desperation the Soviets were going mad.

The bipolar world was becoming multipolar. Neither Russia nor America, tied to rigid policies and military programs basically defending the status quo, adjusted

**Khrushchev at the United Nations, 1960.** The Soviet Premier's temper flared into childish outbursts that rudely interrupted speakers. At one point, a devilish smirk on his face, he took off his shoe and banged it on the table. (United Nations)

**A Saddened "Ike."** The end of Eisenhower's Administration included cancellation of a trip to Japan because of anti-American riots, the U-2 crisis, and the breakup of the Geneva Conference. Just before leaving office, the still popular general warned Americans against a military-industrial complex. (*The Reporter,* 1960. Copyright 1960 by The Reporter Magazine Co.)

well to the new complexity. Although both professed an understanding of Third World needs and aspirations, both sought to place curbs on nationalism. After all, notwithstanding their propaganda, they wanted friends or allies, not a fulfillment of the principle of self-determination. The two antagonists, in their drive to accumulate friends through foreign aid and subversion, became vulnerable to cries for economic assistance from newly independent small nations. Washington often paid the dollars but gained few friends. Its basic antipathy toward revolutionary nationalism, socialism, the nationalization of land and industry, and neutralism created a formidable barrier between the United States and the Third World. Nor did military alliances like SEATO and CENTO, CIA activities in Iran and Guatemala, the training of counterrevolutionaries in South Vietnam (see next chapter), and the sending of troops to Lebanon reveal an American understanding of the new challenge.

If, as critics said, the Eisenhower Administration was unimaginative in dealing with the Third World, it also evinced little innovation in its relations with the Soviet Union or China. The arms race continued, evolving into a space race and missile race. Washington seemed only minimally interested in considering ideas for reducing tension in Central Europe and Germany, quickly rejecting the Rapacki

Plan and "disengagement" proposals. Surely the Soviet Union did not make accommodation easy on these issues, but as Kennan pointed out, diplomacy was hardly given a chance. For China there was nonrecognition, a tired policy that simply isolated the United States from one of the world's most important nations. Holding the line with Chiang Kai-shek on Formosa became an absurdity when many other Western nations recognized the Peking government and traded with it. By 1961 nonrecognition did not make sense, but it was fixed.

Perhaps the Eisenhower Administration could not easily break free from old policies and habits because of domestic political restrictions. McCarthyism did compel a blind anticommunism and did inhibit sophisticated analysis. But McCarthyism as a political force had begun to peter out by 1954. One of its offshoots in that year was the Bricker Amendment, a proposed addition to the Constitution limiting the President's authority to make executive agreements (as distinct from treaties) in foreign affairs. Senator John Bricker of Ohio said he wanted to prevent another Yalta; others recalled Truman's decision to send troops to Korea without congressional sanction. The Administration, joined by Cold Warriors from the Truman years, defeated this thrust against executive power, but by a narrow margin in a congressional vote. Eisenhower henceforth faced few domestic restraints on his foreign policy. The President remained a popular hero and Congress usually granted his requests. The "Formosa Resolution" of 1955, for example, passed 83–3 in the upper chamber and 410–3 in the lower body. The "Eisenhower Doctrine" of 1958 earned a 72–19 vote from the Senate and a 350–60 count in the House. The Cold War consensus shaped in the 1940s was still pervasive, not merely the property of McCarthyites. The Eisenhower Administration failed to devise new policies for new realities and to undertake negotiations with its myriad adversaries, not only because of the emotional restraints of such forces as Joe McCarthy and the China Lobby, but because of its own assumptions.

In the election of 1960, the Democrats charged not that the Cold War should be abandoned, but rather that it should be won. They differed from Eisenhower in the methods with which to continue the old fight and to reverse the United States' declining position in the Third World. "Indeed, although their accents and rhythms were different," Townsend Hoopes has concluded, "the fervent anti-Communist absolutes of John Foster Dulles were embedded in the very bone structure of John Fitzgerald Kennedy's inaugural address."[116]

In studying the Eisenhower-Dulles record, it is tempting to balance each negative with a positive. But that attempt would be misleading. Eisenhower did negotiate with the Soviets and did warn Americans against a "military-industrial complex." The Austrian State Treaty was effected. Eisenhower kept more militant types like Dulles and Nixon in check and tried to limit military spending. He did avoid a full-scale intervention in Indochina in 1954 (see next chapter). He was sometimes victimized by accident—such as the U-2's losing altitude over Russia. The Soviets were often intransigent, and comparative American power was bound to slip as Russia recovered from World War II. And with the rise of new nations, power was bound to disperse. Yet whatever its positive intentions, the Eisenhower Administration's achievements in diplomacy were few. The "Spirit of Camp David" evaporated. In the end, Eisenhower settled "for the half-solace of a series of truces."[117] Holding the line defensively and unimaginatively against ever growing challenges, Washington did not consider whether the line might be partially erased to accommodate new configurations.

For general studies of the Cold War, which cover this period, see the works mentioned in the first paragraph of the "Further Reading" section in Chapter 14.

The Korean War is discussed in Frank Baldwin, ed., *Without Parallel* (1975), Ronald J. Caridi, *The Korean War and American Politics* (1969), Glenn D. Paige, *The Korean Decision* (1968), David Rees, *Korea: The Limited War* (1964), Robert R. Simmons, *The Strained Alliance* (1975), John W. Spanier, *The Truman-MacArthur Controversy* (1959), and Allen Whiting, *China Crosses the Yalu* (1960).

For studies of Eisenhower, Dulles, their foreign policy, and their times, see Charles Alexander, *Holding the Line* (1975), Edward Crankshaw, *Khrushchev* (1966), Louis Gerson, *John Foster Dulles* (1968), Richard Goold-Adams, *The Time of Power: A Reappraisal of John Foster Dulles* (1962), Norman Graebner, *The New Isolationism* (1956), Michael Guhin, *John Foster Dulles* (1972), Townsend Hoopes, *The Devil and John Foster Dulles* (1973), Emmet J. Hughes, *The Ordeal of Power* (1963), George F. Kennan, *Russia, the Atom, and the West* (1958), Peter Lyon, *Eisenhower: Portrait of the Hero* (1974), Herbert S. Parmet, "Power and Reality: John Foster Dulles and Political Diplomacy," in Frank Merli and Theodore Wilson, eds., *Makers of American Diplomacy* (1975) and *Eisenhower and the American Crusades* (1972), James Patterson, *Mr. Republican* (1972) (on Robert A. Taft), and I. F. Stone, *The Haunted Fifties* (1963).

For specific issues and crises, including the Third World, see Stanley D. Bachrack, *The Committee of One Million: "China Lobby" Politics, 1953–1971* (1976), Samuel Baily, *The United States and the Development of South America, 1945–1975* (1977). John C. Campbell, *Successful Negotiation: Trieste 1954* (1976), Donald Dozer, *Are We Good Neighbors?* (1959), J. C. Hurewitz, *Soviet-American Rivalry in the Middle East* (1969), Ramon Ruiz, *Cuba: Making of a Revolution* (1968), Nadav Safran, *From War to War: The Arab-Israeli Confrontation, 1948–1967* (1969), Edmund Stillman and William Pfaff, *The New Politics* (1961), Hugh Thomas, *The Suez Affair* (1966), and Kenneth T. Young, *Negotiating with the Chinese Communists: The United States Experience, 1953–1967* (1968).

For short biographies of major figures in the 1950s, see John A. Garraty, ed., *Encyclopedia of American Biography* (1974). For other works, see E. David Cronon and Theodore D. Rosenof, eds., *The Second World War and the Atomic Age 1940–1973* (1975), Wilton B. Fowler, *American Diplomatic History Since 1890* (1975), and the following notes.

## Notes to Chapter 13

1. Quoted in Glenn D. Paige, *The Korean Decision* (New York: The Free Press, 1968), p. 82.
2. Glenn D. Paige, ed., *1950: Truman's Decision* (New York: Chelsea House Publishers, 1970), p. 49.
3. Quoted in David Rees, *Korea: The Limited War* (London: Macmillan, 1964), p. 36.
4. Harry S. Truman, *Memoirs* (Garden City: Doubleday, 1955–1956; 2 vols.), II, 332.
5. Paige, *1950*, p. 63.
6. Quoted in Paige, *Korean Decision*, p. 114.
7. Truman, *Memoirs*, II, 333.
8. Quoted in Paige, *Korean Decision*, p. 134.
9. Quoted in Beverly Smith, "The White House Story: Why We Went to War in Korea," *Saturday Evening Post*, CCXXIV (November 10, 1951), 80.
10. Quoted in Paige, *Korean Decision*, p. 149.
11. *Congressional Record*, XCVI (June 26, 1950), 9188.
12. Memorandum of Conversation, "Korean Situation," June 26, 1950, Department of State Records (Decimal File), Washington, D.C.
13. Dean Acheson, *Present at the Creation* (New York: W. W. Norton, 1969), p. 405.

14. "Meeting with Congressional Leaders," notes of George Elsey, June 27, 1950, Box 71, George Elsey Papers, Harry S. Truman Library, Independence, Missouri.

15. Truman, *Memoirs, II,* 340.

16. *Public Papers of the Presidents, Harry S. Truman, 1952–1953* (Washington, D.C.: Government Printing Office, 1966), p. 1200.

17. Maxwell Taylor, *Swords and Plowshares* (New York: W.W. Norton, 1972), p. 134.

18. Quoted in Martin Lichterman, "To the Yalu and Back," in Harold Stein, ed., *American Civil-Military Decisions* (Birmingham: University of Alabama Press, 1963), p. 598.

19. David S. McLellan, "Dean Acheson and the Korean War," *Political Science Quarterly,* LXXXIII (March, 1968), 39.

20. United States Senate, Committee on Armed Services and Committee on Foreign Relations, *Military Situation in the Far East* (Hearings), 82nd Cong., 1st Sess. (Washington, D.C.: Government Printing Office, 1951; 5 parts), Part 5, p. 3182 (letter of March 20, 1951).

21. *Congressional Record, XCVII* (April 19, 1951), 4125.

22. Senate, *Military Situation,* Part 4, p. 3089 (letter of May 24, 1951).

23. *Congressional Record, XCVII* (April 24, 1951), 4261.

24. *Department of State Bulletin, XXIII* (November 27, 1950), 839.

25. Senate, *Military Situation,* Part 2, p. 732.

26. *Public Papers of the Presidents, Dwight D. Eisenhower, 1953* (Washington, D.C.: Government Printing Office, 1960), p. 147.

27. Edmund S. Wehrle and Donald F. Lach, *International Politics in East Asia Since World War II* (New York: Praeger Publishers, 1975), p. 90.

28. "Princeton Seminar," February 13–14, 1954, Box 66, Dean Acheson Papers, Harry S. Truman Library.

29. Arthur M. Schlesinger, Jr., *The Imperial Presidency* (New York: Popular Library, 1973), pp. 138, 168.

30. *Public Papers, Truman, 1952–1953,* p. 708.

31. Acheson, *Present at the Creation,* p. 420.

32. Quoted in Lloyd Gardner, *Architects of Illusion* (Chicago: Quadrangle Books, 1970), p. 230.

33. Quoted in Barton J. Bernstein, "Election of 1952," in Arthur M. Schlesinger, Jr. and Fred L. Israel, eds., *History of American Presidential Elections* (New York: Chelsea House Publishers, 1971; 4 vols.), IV, 3246.

34. *Ibid.,* p. 3284.

35. Quoted in Robert A. Divine, *Foreign Policy and U.S. Presidential Elections: 1952–1960* (New York: New Viewpoints, 1974), p. 74.

36. Quoted *ibid.,* p. 28 and in Bernstein, "Election of 1952," p. 3241.

37. Notes of Sherman Adams on Cabinet meeting of January 12, 1953, Box 7, Sherman Adams Papers, Dartmouth College Library.

38. *Public Papers of the Presidents, Dwight D. Eisenhower, 1953* (Washington: Government Printing Office, 1960), pp. 182–183.

39. *Ibid., 1959* (Washington: Government Printing Office, 1960), p. 252.

40. Quoted in Herbert S. Parmet, "Power and Reality: John Foster Dulles and Political Diplomacy," in Frank Merli and Theodore Wilson, eds., *Makers of American Diplomacy* (New York: Charles Scribner's Sons, 1974), p. 593.

41. Adam Ulam, *The Rivals* (New York: Viking Press, 1971), p. 230.

42. Quoted in Townsend Hoopes, *The Devil and John Foster Dulles* (Boston: Atlantic, Little, Brown, 1973), p. 492.

43. Quoted in Adam Ulam, *Expansion and Coexistence* (New York: Frederick A. Praeger Publishers, 1974; 2nd ed.), p. 545.

44. Nikita S. Khrushchev, *Khrushchev Remembers* (New York: Bantam Books, 1971; trans. by Strobe Talbott), p. 435.

45. *Public Papers of the Presidents, Eisenhower, 1954* (Washington: Government Printing Office, 1960), p. 383.

46. Quoted in Emmett John Hughes, *The Ordeal of Power* (New York: Dell, 1964 [c. 1962]), p. 98.

47. Hoopes, *Devil and John Foster Dulles,* p. 158.

48. Quoted in Earl Latham, *The Communist Controversy in Washington* (New York: Atheneum, 1969), p. 338.

49. Ross Terrill, "When America 'Lost' China: The Case of John Carter Vincent," *Atlantic Monthly, CCXXIV* (November, 1969), 79.

50. James C. Thomson, Jr., "On the Making of U.S. China Policy, 1961–9: A Study in Bureaucratic Politics," *China Quarterly,* No. 50 (April–June, 1972), p. 222.

51. *Public Papers, Eisenhower, 1953,* p. 187.

52. Dwight D. Eisenhower, *The White House Years: Mandate for Change, 1953–1956* (Garden City, New York: Doubleday, 1963), p. 522.

53. Richard M. Nixon, *Six Crises* (Garden City, New York: Doubleday, 1962), p. 258.

54. Khrushchev, *Khrushchev Remembers,* p. 434.

55. Zbigniew Brzezinski, "The Competitive Relationship," in Charles Gati, ed., *Caging the Bear* (Indianapolis: Bobbs-Merrill, 1974), p. 168.

56. Quoted in Walter LaFeber, *America, Russia, and the Cold War, 1945–1975* (New York: John Wiley and Sons, 1976: 3rd ed.), p. 183.

57. Quoted in Hoopes, *Devil and John Foster Dulles,* p. 295.

58. Sherman Adams, *Firsthand Report* (New York: Popular Library, 1962 [1961]), p. 177.

59. Khrushchev, *Khrushchev Remembers,* pp. 430, 438.

60. *Public Papers of the Presidents, Eisenhower, 1955* (Washington: Government Printing Office, 1959), p. 507.

61. *New York Times,* July 24, 1955.

62. Quoted in Herbert S. Parmet, *Eisenhower and the American Crusades* (New York: Macmillan, 1972), p. 406.

63. *Public Papers, Eisenhower, 1955,* p. 730.

64. Quoted in Denis Healey, "'When Shrimps Learn to Whistle': Thoughts After Geneva," *International Affairs, XXXII* (January, 1956), 2.

65. I. F. Stone, *The Haunted Fifties* (New York: Random House, 1963), p. 104.

66. Quoted in Hoopes, *Devil and John Foster Dulles,* p. 300.

67. Averell Harriman, "The Soviet Challenge and the American Policy," *Atlantic Monthly, CXCVII* (April, 1956), 45.

68. Dwight D. Eisenhower, *The White House Years: Waging Peace, 1956–1961* (Garden City, New York: Doubleday, 1965), p. 60.

69. *Department of State Bulletin, XXV* (November 5, 1956), 697.

70. Robert Murphy quoted in LaFeber, *America, Russia, and the Cold War,* p. 193.

71. Quoted in Charles C. Alexander, *Holding the Line: The Eisenhower Era, 1952–1961* (Bloomington, Indiana: Indiana University Press, 1975), p. 180.

72. Quoted in Brzezinski, "The Competitive Relationship," p. 171.

73. Quoted in Hughes, *Ordeal of Power,* p. 216.

74. Stephen Ambrose, *Rise to Globalism* (Baltimore: Penguin Books, 1976; rev. ed.), p. 257.

75. Quoted in Harold Macmillan, *Riding the Storm, 1956–1959* (New York: Harper & Row, 1971), p. 320.

76. Quoted in Richard Barnet, *Roots of War* (Baltimore: Penguin Books, 1973 [c. 1972]), p. 43.

77. Noble Frankland and Royal Institute of International Affairs, *Documents on International Affairs, 1957* (London: Oxford University Press, 1960), p. 157.

78. Quoted in Thomas G. Paterson, ed., *Containment and the Cold War* (Reading, Mass.: Addison-Wesley, 1973), p. 114.

79. *New York Times Book Review,* March 2, 1958, p. 26.

80. Quoted in Paterson, *Containment and the Cold War,* p. 116.

81. Quoted in Hoopes, *Devil and John Foster Dulles,* p. 470.

82. Eisenhower, *Waging Peace,* p. 432.

83. *Khrushchev in America* (New York: Crosscurrents Press, 1960), p. 120.

84. Eisenhower, *Waging Peace,* p. 550.

85. Hughes, *Ordeal of Power,* p. 261.

86. Quoted in Edward Crankshaw, *The New Cold War: Moscow v. Peking* (Baltimore: Penguin Books, 1965 [c. 1963]), p. 81.

87. Quoted in Eisenhower, *Mandate for Change,* p. 477.

88. Nixon, *Six Crises,* p. 273.

89. *Public Papers, Eisenhower, 1958* (Washington, D.C.: Government Printing Office, 1959), p. 697.

90. Quoted in Melvin Gurtov, "The Taiwan Strait Crisis Revisited: Politics and Foreign Policy in Chinese Motives," *Modern China, II* (January, 1976), 79.

91. Quoted in John Gittings, "New Light on Mao: His View of the World," *China Quarterly,* No. 60 (December, 1974), p. 755.

92. Robert L. Heilbroner, "Making a Rational Foreign Policy Now," *Harper's Magazine, CCXXXVII* (September, 1968), 65.

93. William J. Lederer and Eugene Burdick, *The Ugly American* (New York: Fawcett Publications, 1958), p. 234.

94. C. Vann Woodward, *The Strange Career of Jim Crow* (New York: Oxford University Press, 1974; 3rd ed.), p. 132.

95. *Public Papers, Eisenhower, 1957* (Washington, D.C.: Government Printing Office, 1957), p. 694.

96. *Department of State Bulletin, XXX* (June 21, 1954), 936.

97. Kenneth E. Boulding, "The U.S. and Revolution," in *The U.S. and Revolution* (Santa Barbara, California: Center for the Study of Democratic Institutions, 1961), p. 4.

98. Finley Peter Dunne, *Dissertations of Mr. Dooley* (New York: Harper and Brothers, 1906), p. 130.

99. Carl N. Degler, "The American Past: An Unsuspected Obstacle in Foreign Affairs," *American Scholar, XXXII* (Spring, 1963), 194.

100. Alexis de Tocqueville, *Democracy in America,* edited by Richard D. Heffner (New York: New American Library, 1956), p. 267.

101. State, War, and Navy Coordinating Committee, "Political and Military Problems in the Far East; the Policy of the United States with Respect to the Soviet Union in the Far East," November 29, 1945, James F. Byrnes Papers, Clemson University Library (from the notes of James Gormly).

102. Donald Dozer, *Are We Good Neighbors?* (Gainesville: University of Florida Press, 1959), p. 353.

103. Quoted in Edmund Stillman and William Pfaff, *The New Politics* (New York: Harper and Row, Publishers, 1961), p. 127.

104. *Department of State Bulletin, XXXIV* (June 18, 1956), 1000.

105. Quoted in Hoopes, *Devil and John Foster Dulles,* p. 337.

106. Quoted in LaFeber, *America, Russia, and the Cold War,* p. 159.

107. Quoted in Eisenhower, *White House Years: Mandate for Change,* p. 422.

108. Quoted in Dozer, *Are We Good Neighbors?,* p. 340.

109. Quoted in Philip B. Taylor, "The Guatemalan Affair: A Critique of U.S. Foreign Policy," *American Political Science Review, L* (September, 1956), 791.

110. *Ibid.,* p. 804.

111. Nixon, *Six Crises,* pp. 198–199.

112. U.S. Senate, Committee on Finance, *Trade Agreements Extension* (Hearings), 84th Cong., 1st Sess. (1955), Part 4, p. 2049.

113. Quoted in Nixon, *Six Crises,* p. 219.

114. James Reston quoted in J. Fred Rippy, "The Hazards of Dale Carnegie Diplomacy," *Inter-American Economic Affairs, XII* (Summer, 1958), 35.

115. Quoted in Nixon, *Six Crises,* pp. 229–230.

116. Hoopes, *Devil and John Foster Dulles,* p. 505.

117. Hughes, *Ordeal of Power,* p. 299.

**The United States Embassy in Saigon.** American soldiers inspect the outer wall of the embassy compound, blasted open by Viet Cong commandos in one of the first attacks of the Tet offensive of early 1968. (Dick Swanson, Time-Life Picture Agency, © Time, Inc.)

# 14 Bearing the Burden: The Vietnam Years, 1961–1969

## Diplomatic Crossroad: The Tet Offensive in Vietnam, 1968

"They're coming in! They're coming in! VC in the compound," the young MP shouted into his radio.[1] Seconds later he and another guard were gunned down by attacking Viet Cong commandos. Moments before, about 3:00 A.M. that January 30, 1968, the compound of the American Embassy in Saigon, South Vietnam, was quiet, the only noise coming from the whirring air conditioners and the fireworks exploding nearby in celebration of the Lunar New Year, or Tet. Only a few Americans were guarding the grounds. Completed in 1967 at a cost of $2.6 million, the six-story embassy building was protected by shatterproof Plexiglas windows, a concrete sun shield covering the entire structure, and an eight-foot high, thick outer wall. Topped by a helicopter pad, the fortified building was an imposing reminder of the American presence in Southeast Asia. One critical Vietnamese thought it "the symbol of America's power to stay, to destroy, to change a whole way of life, to propose and dispose at will."[2]

At 2:45 A.M. a Renault taxi cab and Peugeot truck moved without lights into the early morning darkness from a repair shop a few blocks from the embassy. About fifteen Viet Cong passengers leaped from their vehicles and fired at two embassy MP's. The stunned Americans fired back and hastily bolted the heavy steel gate to the compound. Soon a huge explosion blew a three-foot hole in the wall. The VC scrambled through, firing automatic rifles at the two MP's, who managed to radio for help before they died. The invaders then unleashed their antitank guns and rockets, transported into Saigon weeks before under shipments of tomatoes and firewood. The thick teakwood embassy doors took a direct hit, sending the United States seal crashing to the ground. Inside, a skeleton crew of Central Intelligence Agency and Foreign Service officials felt it was "like being in a telephone booth in the *Titanic* while the ship was going down."[3] A few blocks away, Ambassador Ellsworth Bunker was awakened and whisked away to a secret hiding place for protection. The news of the attack spread quickly across

Saigon. Flash bulletins reached the United States. In Washington, where it was afternoon, presidential adviser Walt W. Rostow immediately labeled the Viet Cong assault on the embassy a "grandstand" play.[4] Few American leaders could believe that "Bunker's bunker" had been invaded. After all, on January 17, in his State of the Union message, President Lyndon B. Johnson himself had said that most of South Vietnam was "secure," and the embassy seemed the most secure of any site.

In Saigon's dim morning light, American soldiers counterattacked. MPs used a jeep to knock down the steel gate and paratroopers landed by helicopter on the roof. By 9:15 A.M. the compound was "secure" and General William "Westy" Westmoreland arrived to survey the littered yard. He counted nineteen dead Vietnamese (four were friendly embassy employees), five dead Americans, and two Viet Cong prisoners, and thereupon, to the disbelief of those around him, declared an American victory. One reporter mumbled that the compound looked like a "butcher shop in Eden," and another mournfully described the "bodies twisted over the ornamental shrubbery and their blood pooling in the white gravel rocks of the embassy garden."[5]

The bold sally against the embassy was but one part of the well-coordinated, massive Tet offensive. Apparently conceived in Communist North Vietnam by General Vo Nguyen Giap, famous for his defeat of the French at Dienbienphu in 1954, the offensive was launched on January 30–31, 1968 by Viet Cong and North Vietnamese soldiers. "The map of South Vietnam," scholar Peter Poole has written, "was lit up like a pinball machine by separate enemy attacks."[6] The forays struck thirty-six of the forty-four provincial capitals, over a hundred other villages, the gigantic Tan Son Nhut airbase, and numerous sites in Saigon. The Communist forces attacked when about half of the South Vietnamese Army (ARVN) was on leave for the Tet holiday, for in the past each side had observed a truce during the New Year celebrations. The VC and North Vietnamese hoped to seize the cities, foment a general sympathetic uprising, force ARVN and American forces to move to the cities—leaving a vacuum in the countryside, and disrupt the governmental bureaucracy. The Viet Cong Order of the Day prophesized "the greatest battle ever fought throughout the history of our country. It will bring forth worldwide changes, but will also require many sacrifices."[7] Secretary of State Dean Rusk remarked shortly after the assaults that the Tet offensive "may well be the climactic period of the struggle in Southeast Asia."[8] General Westmoreland somberly compared it to Pearl Harbor.

After Tet the "mighty U.S. suddenly seemed as impotent as a beached whale."[9] Yet the ARVN and American armies struck back "with the fury of a blinded giant," according to Pulitzer Prize-winning journalist Frances Fitzgerald. "Forced to fight in the cities, they bombed, shelled, and strafed the most populous districts as if they saw no distinction between them and the jungle."[10] Americans at home watched the counterattacks every night on color television and many were appalled by the bloodshed. To dislodge the VC from Hué, South Vietnam's old imperial capital and third largest city, American and ARVN forces used everything from nausea gas to rockets. "Nothing I had seen during the Second World War in the Pacific [and] during the Korean War" matched the "destruction and despair" in Hué, recalled journalist Robert Shaplen.[11] After three weeks of fighting, the VC fled this old religious center of architectural beauty. Over 100,000 of the city's 145,000 people became refugees, and 4,000 civilians were killed—some by Viet Cong, most by American bombings.

In the northwest corner of South Vietnam several thousand American soldiers bravely resisted a siege of their two-square-mile hillside at Khe Sanh, which, according to Westmoreland, "served to lure North Vietnamese to their deaths."[12] Hundreds of Americans died during the first months of 1968, as enemy rockets zeroed in on the strategic but vulnerable base. American B-52s countered by dropping tons of bombs on the surrounding area. By the end of March, remembered a colonel, "the jungle had become literally a desert—vast stretches of scarred, bare earth with hardly a tree standing, a landscape of splinters and bomb craters."[13] Some observers predicted an American Dienbienphu, but American soldiers held their ground and the Communist troops never launched a major assault at Khe Sanh. Still, to many Americans, the sight of pinned-down GIs represented a new defensive posture for the United States in Vietnam.

The provincial capital of Ben Tre symbolized the costs of the Tet offensive. To ferret out the VC, American and ARVN forces leveled Ben Tre, killing a thousand civilians. In unforgettable words, an American officer declared that "it became necessary to destroy the town to save it."[14] That statement joined one newsreel to sear American memory. The NBC *Huntley-Brinkley News* program of February 1 showed a brief film clip of the national police chief of South Vietnam pointing a pistol at the head of a suspected VC. As reporter John Chancellor narrated "rough justice on a Saigon street," General Nguyen Ngoc pulled the trigger and blasted the young man. The 52 seconds of footage, said an NBC producer, was the "rawest, roughest film anyone had ever seen."[15]

The Johnson Administration, having said that the war was showing steady progress for the South Vietnamese and that a Communist offensive had been expected, suffered an ever-growing "credibility gap" with the American people. January was a bad month for Lyndon B. Johnson. On the twenty-third the North Koreans captured the American spy ship *Pueblo* and its entire crew off the Korean coast. The international balance of payments for the United States, Johnson learned, was running at an adverse annual rate of seven billion dollars. A B-52 with four H-bombs aboard was lost in Greenland. And Senator Eugene McCarthy, a "dove" on Vietnam, was gaining political stature as a challenger to Johnson's renomination to the presidency. Johnson quickly labeled the Tet attacks a "complete failure," thereby setting off a national debate about the consequences of the offensive.[16]

Some critics pointed to the wrenching costs of Tet. By mid-March one-eighth of the South Vietnamese people were embittered refugees in their own country. Over forty thousand Viet Cong were killed. Over a thousand American and two thousand ARVN forces died. The Communists had gone "for broke," thought Westmoreland.[17] One critic, Senator Robert Kennedy, soon also to declare himself a candidate against Johnson for the Democratic presidential nomination, said "it is as if James Madison [had claimed] victory in 1812 because the British only burned Washington instead of annexing it to the British Empire."[18] "Victory" and "defeat" seemed hollow words to describe the Vietnamese carnage. "Perhaps failure," wrote a columnist in the *Wall Street Journal*, "is anything short of total success."[19] Most agreed that the losers were the Vietnamese civilians. Questions were raised, too, about what the United States would do next, especially in light of official public statements that the Tet offensive was only a minor setback, if one at all. "What will we do with the initiative when we regain it?" asked the *Washington Post*.[20] Senator Stuart Symington quizzed Secretary Rusk: "It is clear what we are losing, but what do we win if we win?"[21] On the televised program *Face the Nation*, after Secretary of Defense Robert McNamara recited the Tet figures for dead VC, a reporter asked him: "Isn't there something Orwellian about it, that the more we kill, the stronger they get?"[22]

As a Texan who often remembered the Alamo, President Johnson decried the

**Rough Justice on a Saigon Street.** The South Vietnamese national police chief executes a suspected Viet Cong guerrilla in the street during the early tense days of the Tet offensive, 1968. Associated Press photographer Eddie Adams caught the moment of impact in this shocking picture, as did an NBC television crewman. (Wide World Photos)

"chorus of defeatism."[23] He authorized 10,500 more troops for Vietnam, gave hawkish speeches against quitting under fire, and flamboyantly toured some American military bases. He aroused his defenders. "Don't be discouraged by the croakers," advised historian Allan Nevins.[24] Columnist Joseph Alsop told him to call up the military reserves; the President would be "feckless, foolish, and derelict in his duty" if he did not.[25] Journalist William Shannon, remembering the 1944 Battle of the Bulge, told his readers that "we must be patient and stoical, not fluttering foolishly with every enemy thrust and parry."[26] The President was nevertheless worried. He conceded that the Viet Cong had scored a "psychological victory," and privately Westmoreland admitted that the VC had dealt South Vietnam a "severe blow."[27] Although the VC had not generated a national rebellion, had failed to hold the cities, and had suffered huge casualties, they had freed thousands of prisoners, disrupted the South Vietnamese governmental structure, crippled the American "pacification" program in the countryside, gained more influence in rural areas, heaped monstrous refugee and reconstruction problems on the Saigon regime, and proved that they were capable of massive assaults—in short, that it was difficult for either side to assume it could "win."

In late February Johnson ordered the new Secretary of Defense, Clark Clifford, a former Truman adviser, to undertake a major review of Vietnam policy, after General Westmoreland suggested that 206,000 more American troops join the more than 500,000 already there. The generals, including Joint Chiefs of Staff Chairman Earle G. Wheeler, one student of Tet has written, "hoped that Clifford would be a *tabula rasa* on which they could write their plan."[28] They planned a major new ARVN-American offensive. Within the Pentagon, formerly timid dissenters began to gain Clifford's ear, as they pleaded for de-escalation of the violence. Vietnam could not be saved by destroying it, advisers like Under Secretary of the Air Force Townsend Hoopes and Deputy Secretary of Defense Paul Nitze counseled. Furthermore, Vietnam was draining America's resources from its more serious confrontation with the key enemy, the Soviet Union. Priorities had to be put straight. In early March, too, Rusk began to speak with the President about halting the bombing of North Vietnam as an inducement to peace talks. In the New Hampshire Democratic primary on March 12, McCarthy made a surprisingly strong showing against the President, by polling 42 percent of the vote to Johnson's 49 percent. Johnson also talked with the quintessential Cold Warrior about Vietnam. Dean Acheson, as usual, was blunt: "With all due respect, the Joint Chiefs of Staff don't know what they're talking about."[29] Clifford found that out when he fired a series of questions at the generals. He was dismayed that they did not know how long the fighting would continue or how many more men would be required. "All I had was the statement, given with too little self-assurance to be comforting," Clifford recalled, "that if we persisted for an indeterminate length of time, the enemy would choose not to go on."[30] Clifford's review committee, the *Ad Hoc* Task Force on Vietnam, recommended in early March a step-up in bombing North Vietnam and the deployment of 20,000 additional American troops, but Clifford expressed private doubts to the President. Later in the month, another advisory body, the "Wise Men," or Senior Informal Advisory Group on Vietnam made up of several Truman era diplomats and generals, among others, told the President that victory was impossible. "The President was visibly shocked by the magnitude of the defection," Hoopes later noted.[31] Indeed, he began to dream he was Woodrow Wilson paralyzed from the neck down.

**Lyndon B. Johnson (1908–1973).**
The troubled and exhausted President writes his television speech of March 31, 1968 in the Cabinet Room of the White House. In removing himself as a candidate from the presidential race and initiating Vietnam peace talks, LBJ ended a political career of supreme energy and influence. (Wide World Photos)

On March 31 Johnson spoke on prime time television. "We are prepared to move immediately toward peace through negotiations," he announced. Although the United States was sending another 13,500 men to South Vietnam and more military aid to ARVN, he reported that American airplanes would halt their bombing of a major portion of North Vietnam. "Even this limited bombing of the North could come to an early end—if our restraint is matched in Hanoi [the North Vietnamese capital]."[32] The President spoke again about the alarming disparity in the American balance of payments, and he asked Congress to pass a higher tax bill to pay for a proposed increase in aid to South Vietnam of $5.1 billion over the next two years. His conciliatory message appealed for peace talks. Then, to the amazement of viewers and even some of his advisers, Johnson said he would not seek re-election. Tet had claimed a political casualty. On April 3 the North Vietnamese agreed to bargain at the conference table. Discussions began on May 14. The fighting and talking—and dying—would go on for several ghastly years more, but there would never again be anything to match the horror of Tet, 1968. Out of the sacrifices of Hué, Saigon, Khe Sanh, and Ben Tre had come a belated and grudging willingness to try diplomacy.

## Indochina: War and Diplomacy Before 1961

The tragic Tet offensive was a conspicuous but not an unusual experience in Vietnamese history. Before the 1960s that history was marked by centuries of resistance to foreigners—Chinese, French, Japanese, and Americans. In 1867 France colonized Vietnam and soon began to exploit the country's raw materials, as well as those of Laos and Cambodia, which became protectorates in 1883 and part of French Indochina in the 1890s. Rice, rubber, tin, and tungsten were taken from the Indochinese Peninsula to European markets. France constructed a haughty and repressive imperial government and monopolized land holdings, while over

**Ho Chi Minh (1890–1971).** The Vietnamese nationalist and Communist who led his nation's battle against foreign intruders for decades was considered a tool of Moscow-oriented communism by Washington officials. (*The Reporter,* 1950. Copyright 1950 by Fortnightly Publishing Co., Inc.)

80 percent of the Vietnamese people existed as poor, rural peasants. From 1867 onward the embittered Vietnamese, in varying degrees of intensity, battled their French overlords.

The most famous nationalist leader in the twentieth century was Ho Chi Minh, born in 1890 to a low-level government employee. Later described as a "small man, with a face the color of tea, a beard the color of rice, a piercing look beneath a forehead crowned by a somewhat absurd lock of hair," Ho traveled to Europe and at the time of World War I took up with other Vietnamese to plead for independence.[33] In Paris, Ho sent a memorandum to the Big Four leaders at the Versailles Conference, but his upstart anticolonial ideas, despite their deliberate reference to Woodrow Wilson's principle of self-determination, went unnoticed by the conferees. Because the Communists seemed to be the only political force vigorously denouncing colonialism, Ho and other nationalists joined the Communist party and throughout the twenties and thirties lived and agitated in China and Russia. In 1930–1931 the French brutally suppressed a Vietnamese peasant rebellion, killing 10,000 and deporting another 50,000. "It is safe to say," scholar Joseph Buttinger has concluded, "that if the French had chosen a less disastrous approach to the land question and employed all available means for eliminating rural poverty, the Communist movement in Vietnam would never have gained its extraordinary strength."[34]

In 1940–41 the rampaging Japanese took over Vietnam, but left collaborating French officials in charge. Vietnamese nationalists, including Ho's Communists, went underground, used China as a base, and in 1941 organized the Viet Minh, a coalition of nationalist groups led by the Communist party. In the final days of World War II, Viet Minh guerrillas tangled with Japanese troops, liberated some northern provinces, and worked with the United States Office of Strategic Services (OSS). An OSS interpreter recalled that Ho "would talk about American ideals and how he was sure America would be on his side" in the postwar period.[35] Ho sent formal messages to Washington, depicted himself as the George Washington of his country, and often mentioned the American Declaration of Independence and the Atlantic Charter. On August 29, 1945 the Viet Minh organized the Democratic Republic of Vietnam (DRV) and established headquarters in Hanoi. Vietnam seemed closer to independence than ever before.

During the Second World War, the United States warily watched events in Vietnam, but hardly considered them of great significance. In the fall of 1944 State Department officials told the President that Indochina and Southeast Asia were "potentially important markets for American exports. They lie athwart the southwestern approaches to the Pacific Ocean and have important bearing on our security and the security of the Philippines."[36] Roosevelt, eager to break up the despised French empire, spoke vaguely about placing Indochina under international trusteeship. The British, protective of their own empire, protested that such a policy would mark a bad precedent. State Department officials, often out of touch with the President, wanted to restore French power in Indochina as a counterweight against potential Russian influence. Ambassador to Russia W. Averell Harriman predicted that the Soviet Union would become a "world bully" and "reach into China and the Pacific."[37]

Roosevelt never formulated precise plans for Indochina. A combination of British, United States State Department, and French pressures undermined the trusteeship idea, and the President only faintly objected. At Yalta he decided not to discuss Indochina with an aroused Winston Churchill. The President thought it "better to keep quiet just now."[38] "Above all," historian Walter LaFeber has written, "American officials, including Roosevelt, wanted an orderly, nonrevolutionary Southeast Asia open to Western interests."[39] Such an objective, once the trusteeship notion was discarded, could not be achieved through a Viet Minh government. So the French, with British military help and American tolerance, returned to Vietnam. They were not welcomed. Abandoned by the United States, receiving no support from Russia, and now facing French forces, the Viet Minh accepted a compromise with France in March, 1946: DRV status as a "free state" in the French Union and French military occupation of northern Vietnam. It soon became clear that Paris intended to re-establish its former grip. Viet Minh and French soldiers clashed in December. One French bombardment of Haiphong killed several thousand civilians. The Viet Minh responded with guerrilla terror. For the next eight years Vietnam was wracked by bloody combat, with the French holding the cities and the Viet Minh the countryside.

Indochina, Truman Administration adviser Clark Clifford later recalled, was seen at first as a "French problem."[40] To win Paris' favor for its postwar policies in Europe, Washington acquiesced in the re-establishment of French colonialism in Vietnam. Although in the early postwar months Ho Chi Minh had sent a number of letters to Washington requesting economic assistance and support for independence, he never received replies. As the Cold War heated up in 1946–1947, Ho's Moscow "training" became a topic of American discussion. By late 1946 the Department of State considered him an "agent of international communism," although some State Department officers dissented and pointed out that Vietnamese leaders were nationalists, not servants of Moscow. Some commentators saw Ho as an Asian Tito. It did not matter, because Secretary Dean Acheson settled the question in 1949: Ho was an "outright Commie."[41] That year the French

installed Bao Dai, who had served the Japanese in World War II, as their Vietnamese leader. In February, 1950, Washington recognized this French puppet.

Mao's victory in China and the outbreak of the Korean War stirred considerable
American interest in Indochina. Seeing that area as another Cold War battleground, rather than as a localized, indigenous nationalist rebellion against European imperialism, the Truman Administration extended foreign aid to help the
beleaguered French. In 1950 Washington sent $150 million in aid and a contingent
of military advisers to Vietnam. In the period 1945–1954 the United States
supplied two billion of the five billion dollars that Paris spent to keep Vietnam
within the French empire. In 1954 United States aid covered 78 percent of the cost
of the war, and over three hundred Americans were assigned to Vietnam as part of
the Military Assistance Advisory Group—all to no avail. In the spring of 1954, at
Dienbienphu, a fortress where the besieged French had chosen to stand or fall, Viet
Minh forces moved toward a major, symbolic victory. The Eisenhower Administration was divided on a response. Vice-President Richard M. Nixon and Secretary
of State John Foster Dulles urged the despatch of American troops and bombers;
Army Chief of Staff Matthew Ridgway opposed large-scale intervention. In April
President Dwight D. Eisenhower uttered the "falling domino" theory to explain
American interest in Southeast Asia and sounded out the Congress and Britain
about an American, or joint, military operation. The replies were timid; Vietnam
could not be saved for France by military action. When the French forces at
Dienbienphu surrendered on May 7, Washington was leaning against military
intervention.

A few days earlier, on April 26, 1954, representatives from France, Russia,
Britain, China, the United States, Bao Dai's Vietnam, the DRV, Laos, and Cambodia met in Geneva to discuss the morass in Vietnam. If war would not work,
thought the Western powers, perhaps diplomacy would halt the deterioration of
the once-glorious French stature in Asia. But the French themselves upset American hopes. A new government, led by Pierre Mendès-France, pledged to end the
war quickly. With Ho's Viet Minh in control of two-thirds of Vietnam, the
conferees signed the Geneva Accords in July. The Viet Minh, now assured that
their military successes had led to political victory, accepted the accords: temporary partition of Vietnam at the seventeenth parallel; French withdrawal to below
that latitude; neither North nor South Vietnam to sign military alliances or permit
foreign bases on Vietnamese soil; national elections to be held in 1956; unification
of the country after elections; and elections also in neighboring strife-torn Laos and
Cambodia, the other territories in French Indochina. The United States, however,
refused to sign the agreements. The National Security Council found the Geneva
settlement a "disaster" that represented a "major forward stride of Communism
which may lead to the loss of Southeast Asia."[42] Quite an exaggeration, but
apparently the United States believed that Communist China, which had sent
some aid to the Viet Minh, would use Vietnam as a base for expansion. As French
reporter Bernard Fall, longtime Vietnam watcher, has noted, the "struggle now
began to rebuild a truncated land into a viable non-Communist Vietnamese
state."[43]

In October a smiling Ho Chi Minh returned to Hanoi, still the "frail, stooped
wisp of a man whose classic endurance of body and soul were almost visible
aspects of his being."[44] In early 1955 he warned his followers in language quite

different from that of a decade before that "we must be vigilant . . . against the plans of the imperialistic Americans who are seeking to intervene in Indochina, to incite their lackeys, to sabotage the armistice accords, and to cause war."[45] He could not have known, of course, that much of this would in fact occur; at that very time Washington was designing its strategy to establish a new regime in South Vietnam. Not about to "mourn the past," as Dulles remarked, the United States moved deliberately.[46] It created the Southeast Asia Treaty Organization in September, 1954 to protect Cambodia and Laos from Communist aggression and South Vietnam from the Viet Minh. SEATO violated the spirit of the Geneva Accords by specifying protection over the southern half of Vietnam—now treated, it seemed, as a separate state. After the creation of SEATO the seventeenth parallel seemed less a provisional and more a permanent line.

In the South, the United States backed the new government of Prime Minister Ngo Dinh Diem, a non-Communist Vietnamese nationalist and Catholic who had spent a number of years in the United States before the Geneva Conference and who had gradually undermined the authority of Bao Dai. An enlarged group of American advisers, in violation of Geneva, began to train a South Vietnamese army, and millions in American military and economic assistance flowed to Diem's government. In mid-1955 the government in the North invited preliminary talks to plan the national election scheduled by Geneva for 1956. Diem refused, and the Eisenhower Administration, convinced that Ho would win an election, publicly endorsed the cancellation of the electoral provisions of the Geneva Accords, thereby dealing a setback to unification. In 1955 Diem held his own referendum in the South. That blatant fraud gave him 98.2 percent of the vote. In Saigon, his backers vigorously stuffed the ballot boxes so that 605,000 votes emerged from 450,000 registered voters.

The two Vietnams went their separate ways, with the North receiving aid from both Russia and China, but cautiously avoiding dependence on either by deftly shifting intimacy from one to the other. Diem received American aid of about $300

**Eisenhower, Ngo Dinh Diem (1901–1963), and Dulles.** The South Vietnamese nationalist Diem, from a mandarin and Catholic family, spent time in exile in the United States before returning to his country as Premier (1954–1963). His police state rule did not seem to upset President Eisenhower or Secretary Dulles in May, 1957 when they met with Diem in Washington. (Dwight D. Eisenhower Library)

million a year, but true to the Vietnamese tradition of resisting foreign influence, he ignored American advice on the need for political and economic reforms. He also placed family members in profitable positions, permitting corruption. Americans supported Diem's suppression of those Viet Minh remaining in the South, but not his crude methods. In 1956 he jailed 20,000 to 30,000 suspected Communists in "re-education" camps. Angry Southern rebels, ignoring Hanoi's advice to practice restraint, desperately retaliated by killing village teachers, policemen, and government officials in a reign of terror. Exploiting widespread rural support and general anti-Diem dissent, the Viet Minh organized the National Liberation Front in December, 1960. Hanoi, for the first time since Geneva playing a direct but timid role in the South, encouraged this Communist-dominated political group. Diem labeled the front the "Viet Cong," meaning Vietnamese Communists, to discredit it.

Although Washington and Saigon would later claim that the new Vietnamese war was initiated by aggression from the North, most scholars agree that the Viet Cong sprang from the peculiar, repressive environment of the South, at first received more spiritual than material help from the North, and engaged Diem in a *civil war*. Because of Cold War conditioning and an awareness of the economic and strategic value of the Indochinese Peninsula, however, American officials did not view the new conflict as a *Vietnamese* question. Rather, they depicted it as a great power confrontation between Russia or China and the United States. Senator John F. Kennedy said in 1956 that Diem's Vietnam was the "cornerstone of the Free World in Southeast Asia, the keystone to the arch, the finger in the dike."[47] In 1961 Kennedy became President of the United States.

### "Action Intellectuals" and the Foreign Policy of John F. Kennedy

The 1960 presidential election was a contest between two Cold Warriors with distinctively different styles. Republican Richard M. Nixon seemed bland and tied to the shopworn phrases of the 1950s. Democratic candidate John F. Kennedy, who beat Nixon by a narrow margin, aroused support through the slogan: "I think it's time America started moving again."[48] Both Nixon and Kennedy were part of the "containment generation" of people who matured politically in the 1940s and imbibed the popular lessons of World War II and the Cold War. Historian Robert Divine has concluded that Kennedy "sincerely believed in the cold war shibboleths that men like Dean Acheson and John Foster Dulles had been voicing for a decade and a half."[49] Both Nixon and Kennedy had been elected to Congress in 1946 and heard President Truman enunciate the "Truman Doctrine" the following year. In 1960, Kennedy charged that the Eisenhower-Nixon Administration had failed to enter the new battleground of the Cold War, the Third World, thus consigning it to communism without a fight. With the U-2 affair, the noisy demise of the Paris summit meeting, an adverse balance of payments, cancellation of a presidential visit to Japan, and crises in Cuba, the Congo, and Indochina all as the immediate backdrop, Kennedy and many Americans believed that Russia (or communism) was winning the Cold War. "I think there is a danger that history will make a judgment," Kennedy stated in August of 1960, "that these were the days when the tide began to run out for the United States. These were the times when the communist tide began to pour in."[50] The next month his words smacked of John

**John F. Kennedy (1917–1963).** The thirty-fifth President graduated from Harvard, ran a PT boat in World War II, and represented Massachusetts in the House (1947–1953) and Senate (1953–1961). His book *Profiles in Courage* (1957) won a Pulitzer Prize. (*The Reporter*, 1962. Copyright 1962 by The Reporter Magazine Co.)

Foster Dulles himself when he described the Cold War as a "struggle for supremacy between two conflicting ideologies: Freedom under God versus ruthless, godless tyranny."[51] Kennedy pledged to move the Cold War from stalemate and potential Communist victory to American triumph.

Kennedy said he did not mind being called Truman with a Harvard accent. Born in 1917 to wealthy, Catholic, politically active parents, John Fitzgerald Kennedy graduated from Harvard College and served with honor in World War II. In 1940, at the time his father was ambassador to Great Britain, his senior thesis was published as *Why England Slept*, with the theme that England should have demonstrated a willingness to use force in resisting Nazi aggression, rather than embracing weakness. For Kennedy's generation, the Munich agreement became the "Munich syndrome" or appeasement lesson. During the Cuban Missile Crisis, Kennedy tapped that historical legacy for a policy rationale: "The 1930s taught us a clear lesson: aggressive conduct, if allowed to go unchecked and unchallenged, ultimately leads to war."[52] He also remembered the experience of the 1940s. As presidential assistant and grand theorist Walt Whitman Rostow reported, the "first charge of the Kennedy Administration in 1961—somewhat like the challenge faced by the Truman Administration in 1947— was to turn back the Communist offensive."[53] History both tugged at the Kennedy advisers and pushed them.

So did the distinctive style and personality of the young President. "All at once you had something exciting," recalled a student campaigner in comparing the Eisenhower and Kennedy days. "You had a young guy who had kids, and who liked to play football on his front lawn. He was a real human being. He was talking about pumping some new life into the country . . . just giving the whole country a real shakedown and a new image. . . . Everything they did showed that America was alive and active. . . . To run a country it takes more than just mechanics. It takes a psychology."[54] Call it psychology, charisma, charm, image, mystique, or cult, Kennedy had it. Photogenic and quick-witted, he became a television star. Observers marveled at his speed-reading abilities. Decrying softness in the American people, he challenged their egoes by launching a physical fitness program. Handsome, articulate, ingratiating, dynamic, energetic, competitive, athletic, cultured, bright, self-confident, cool, analytical, mathematical, zealous— these were the traits universally ascribed to the President. People often listened not to what he said, but to how he said it, and he usually said it with verve and conviction. He simply overwhelmed. Dean Rusk remembered him as an "incandescent man. He was on fire, and he set people around him on fire."[55] For historian-politician and presidential assistant Arthur M. Schlesinger, Jr., JFK had "enormous confidence in his own luck," and "everyone around him thought he had the Midas touch and could not lose."[56]

Style and personality are usually important to the conduct of diplomacy; how we behave obviously affects how others read us and respond to us, and our personal characteristics and needs generate measurable behavior. Many of his friends have commented that John F. Kennedy was driven by a desire for power, because power ensured winning. Furthermore, he personalized issues, converting them into tests of will. Diplomacy became a matter of crises and races. His father, Joseph P. Kennedy, demanded excellence. As political scientist James Barber has pointed out, old Joe "pressed his children hard to compete, never to be satisfied with anything but first place. The point was not just to try; the point was to win."[57] John developed a thirst for victory and a self-image as the vigorous man. Aroused in the

**Arthur M. Schlesinger, Jr. (1917—) and Kennedy.** The distinguished historian-politician became a special assistant to the President in 1961 and helped plan policies for Latin America. His partisan defense of JFK, *A Thousand Days* (1965), won a Pulitzer Prize. (John F. Kennedy Library)

campaign of 1960 by the stings of anti-Catholic bias, by misplaced right-wing charges that he was soft on communism, and by his narrow victory over Nixon, Kennedy, once in office, seemed eager to prove his toughness. He took up challenges with zest and soon Americans watched for box scores on the missile race, the arms race, and the space race. Kennedy and his advisers, it seems, thought that Premier Nikita Khrushchev and the Russians were testing them as men. In early 1961, when they discussed the possibility of a summit meeting with Khrushchev, Kennedy asserted that "I have to show him that we can be as tough as he is. . . . I'll have to sit down with him, and let him see who he's dealing with."[58] John F. Kennedy and his aides feared to be thought fearful.

With these psychic needs and with their high intellectual talents, the Kennedy officials came to Washington, "swashbuckling" and suffering from "auto-intoxication," commented one observer.[59] Cocky, thinking themselves the "right" people, they were, as skeptical Under Secretary of State Chester Bowles later

**Robert Strange McNamara (1916—).** Kennedy's mathematically minded secretary of defense was infatuated with charts. Graduate of the University of California, Berkeley and a Ford Motor executive, McNamara applied dollar-saving efficiency methods to his department and served as war minister for the Vietnamese conflict. In 1968 he became president of the World Bank. (*The Reporter,* 1967. Copyright 1967 by The Reporter Magazine Co.)

complained, "sort of looking for a chance to prove their muscle." They were "full of belligerence."[60] Schlesinger captured the mood: "Euphoria reigned; we thought for a moment that the world was plastic and the future unlimited."[61] Kennedy's alarmist Inaugural Address reflected the new spirit. Its swollen Cold War language was matched only by its pompous phrasing: "the torch has been passed to a new generation." He paid homage to historical memories when he noted that his generation had been "tempered by war" and "disciplined by a hard and bitter peace." Then came those moving, but in hindsight rather frightening words: "Let every nation know that we shall pay any price, bear any burden, meet any hardship, support any friend, oppose any foe to assure the survival and the success of liberty."[62] No halfway measures here. Kennedy and his assistants, impatient and tough, thought they could lick anything—or anyone.

The Kennedy people considered themselves "can-do" types, who with rationality and careful calculation could revive an ailing nation and world. Theodore H. White tagged them "the Action Intellectuals."[63] "Management" became one of the catchwords of the time. With adequate data, and they had an inordinate faith in data, they were certain they could succeed. When an heretical White House assistant attempted to persuade Secretary of Defense Robert McNamara, the "whiz kid" from the Ford Motor Company, that the Vietnam venture was doomed, the efficiency-minded McNamara shot back: "Where is your data? Give me something I can put in the computer. Don't give me your poetry."[64] There were dangers in a heavy reliance on quantified information. "Ah, *les statistiques*," said a Vietnamese general to an American official. "We Vietnamese can give him [McNamara] all he wants. If you want them to go up, they will go up. If you want them to go down, they will go down."[65] Nonetheless, with its faith in formulas and the computer, the Kennedy "can-do" team brought a freshness to American foreign policy, if not in

**Makers of American Foreign Policy from 1961 to 1969**

| Presidents | Secretaries of State |
| --- | --- |
| John F. Kennedy, 1961–1963<br>Lyndon B. Johnson, 1963–1969 | Dean Rusk, 1961–1969 |

substance, at least in slogans: "The Grand Design" for Europe; the "New Africa" policy; "Flexible Response" for the military; the "Alliance for Progress" for Latin America; and the "New Frontier" at home.

Kennedy's Secretary of State, Dean Rusk, was somewhat uneasy with the crusading "action intellectuals," but he was a loyal member of the team. A Rhodes Scholar, Rusk had been a military intelligence officer in Asia during World War II, a political science instructor, an assistant secretary of state under Truman, and in the 1950s president of the Rockefeller Foundation. Truman warhorses Robert Lovett and Dean Acheson enthusiastically recommended Rusk to Kennedy, who liked Rusk's quiet, modest, and unflappable manner. The President wanted to design his own foreign policy and did not desire a secretary of state who was too independent-minded or outspoken. The relatively unknown Rusk fit the bill. "The gentle, gracious Rusk," presidential assistant Theodore C. Sorenson later noted, "deferred almost too amiably to White House initiatives and interference."[66] A native of Georgia and the son of a Presbyterian minister, Rusk formed his world view in the 1930s and 1940s. The containment doctrine especially guided him. Somebody scratched graffiti in a State Department telephone booth: "Dean Rusk is a recorded announcement."[67] He often compared Ho Chi Minh and Mao Tse-tung to Hitler, Vietnam to Greece in 1947, and peace protesters to the appeasers of Nazi Germany; he warned against Asian Munichs. Rusk was also enamored with military solutions—he took an unusual eight years of ROTC in high school and college—and usually endorsed Pentagon policy recommendations. The secretary loyally served for eight years. Lyndon Johnson especially liked him: "He has the compassion of a preacher and the courage of a Georgia cracker. When you're going in with the Marines, he's the kind you want at your side."[68]

**Dean Rusk (1909–).** After graduating from Davidson College, Rusk went on to Oxford as a Rhodes Scholar. He taught political science at Mills College in the 1930s, served in World War II, then entered the State Department. In 1952 he became president of the Rockefeller Foundation, expanding its philanthropic activities in the Third World. He was selected as secretary of state in 1961 and served until 1969. (Lyndon B. Johnson Library)

**U.S.S. *Sam Rayburn.*** Laid down in 1962 and launched the next year, this Polaris submarine with sixteen missile tubes and a missile range of 2,875 miles became part of a large Kennedy-inspired military buildup. The first Polaris submarine was commissioned in 1959. (U.S. Navy, Naval Photographic Center)

## Building Arms and Nations Under Kennedy

One of the Kennedy Administration's top priorities was military expansion. During the presidential campaign of 1960 Kennedy charged that the Eisenhower Administration was losing the Cold War by tolerating a "missile gap" favorable to Russia. The charge was part politics, part exaggeration by the military establishment, part frustrating symbol of the post-Sputnik shock, and part guesswork based upon conflicting sets of intelligence estimates. Democrats, led by Senator Stuart Symington, declared that the Soviets would have a 3-1 edge in Intercontinental Ballistic Missiles (ICBMs) by 1962. Eisenhower, who had warned in 1959 against the "feverish building of vast armaments to meet glibly predicted moments of so-called 'maximum peril,'" knew the charge was nonsense;[69] U-2 intelligence flights revealed that the Soviets were not undertaking a massive missile program. The United States was in fact immensely superior.

Once in office, Kennedy and McNamara learned how wrong they were, but, frightened by Moscow's belligerence and by revolutionary movements in the Third World, they initiated a massive American military expansion program. Soon they bragged about American nuclear supremacy. They called their overall defense strategy "flexible response," providing a method for every conceivable kind of war.

The Special Forces or Green Berets would conduct counterinsurgency against wars of national liberation; conventional forces would handle limited wars; more and better missiles would deter war or serve as primary weapons in nuclear war; at home, bomb or fallout shelters would protect Americans under a civil defense plan; and, when required, the United States would participate in collective security arrangements through the United Nations. In 1961 Kennedy increased the defense budget by 15 percent. Obviously not paying attention to Eisenhower's Farewell Address, he enlarged the Army, Air Force, Navy, and missile arsenal. By 1963 the United States had 275 major bases in 31 nations; 65 countries were "hosting" United States forces, and the American military was training soldiers in 72 countries. Also, one and a quarter million military-related American personnel were stationed overseas. In 1961, the United States had 63 ICBM's; by 1963 that figure had jumped to 424. During 1961–1963, NATO's nuclear firing power increased 60 percent. This tremendous military spurt goaded the Soviets, who alarmed Americans in September, 1961, by resuming atmospheric nuclear testing and by exploding a monster bomb of 50 megatons the next month. The irony of the arms race was that the more missiles Americans acquired, the more vulnerable they became, as the Russians tried to keep up by also building more. Although Kennedy established the United States Arms Control and Disarmament Agency, his heavy military emphasis tended to discourage disarmament and to play down diplomatic solutions to crises. His one diplomatic achievement in this area was the Nuclear Test Ban Treaty of 1963, in which the United States and Russia agreed to halt atmospheric but not underground tests.

Kennedy met with Khrushchev at Vienna in June, 1961, to discuss a test ban treaty, Berlin, and Laos. Khrushchev's style, Kennedy was warned, ranged from "cherubic to choleric."[70] Kennedy sought to prove his toughness at Vienna, to show the Russians that they "must not crowd him too much."[71] At the conference Khrushchev began a war of nerves by insisting that Berlin become a "free city," thereby ending Western occupation; if the United States did not negotiate the question, he threatened, Russia would sign a separate treaty with East Germany. "If Khrushchev wants to rub my nose in the dirt, it's all over," snapped Kennedy. "That son of a bitch won't pay any attention to words. He has to see you move."[72]

**"The Purpose of the Meeting Is to Take Measurements."** Nikita S. Khrushchev and John F. Kennedy convened at the summit in Vienna in June, 1961 and sized one another up. (Parrish, Chicago Tribune–New York News Syndicate, Inc.)

Still, some presidential advisers told Kennedy that he probably had not rebutted the Premier vigorously enough at Vienna and that Khrushchev may have left the meeting thinking that he had out-dueled the young President. Kennedy vowed it would never happen again.

Eschewing negotiations over Berlin, the President decided to force the issue. Some of his assistants thought he should try diplomacy, but Kennedy listened to Dean Acheson. That ardent Cold Warrior seemed to welcome a confrontation by daring the Russians. Echoing Acheson's sentiments, Kennedy announced on July 25 that Berlin was "the great testing place of Western courage and will." He asked Congress for a $3.2 billion addition to the regular defense budget and authority to call up military reservists. He frightened Americans by also requesting $207 million to begin a civil defense, fall-out shelter program—"in the event of an attack."[73] His exaggerated, alarmist language helped turn a Soviet-American issue into a major crisis. On August 13 the Soviets suddenly put up a barbed wire barricade, followed by an ugly concrete block barrier, between the two Berlins. The Berlin Wall became a tragic symbol of Soviet repression, and finally shut off the exodus of immigrants that Khrushchev had so often protested. Washington could not knock the wall down, so it sent a contingent of troops along the access road through East Germany to West Berlin without incident. In September Kennedy finally invited Soviet-American talks. The crisis passed, and critics asked if it had been necessary. Yet Berlin remained a Soviet-American tension point. Kennedy traveled there in June of 1963 to underscore the American will to stay, and electrified a mass rally with emotional words: *Ich bin ein Berliner* (I am a Berliner)."[74]

**The Berlin Wall.** East German soldiers replace barbed wire with concrete slabs at the ugly Berlin Wall erected by the Soviets in 1961 to stop the flow of refugees to West Berlin. (United Press International)

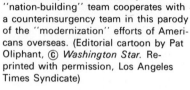

"Could You Point Out the Ground You've Taken? We're Here to Secure and Develop it Economically." A "nation-building" team cooperates with a counterinsurgency team in this parody of the "modernization" efforts of Americans overseas. (Editorial cartoon by Pat Oliphant, © *Washington Star*. Reprinted with permission, Los Angeles Times Syndicate)

As Kennedy dealt with the old sores of the Cold War, he also attended to events in the Third World, the region he thought most vulnerable to revolution and communism and at the same time most susceptible to American influence. His governing concept was "nation building." The Kennedy team understood the force of nationalism in the Third World; rather than flatly oppose it, the "action intellectuals" sought to use or channel it. Through "modernization," or what the Kennedy team called "peaceful revolution" or "middle-class revolution," Third World nations would be helped through the stormy times of economic infancy to economic and hence political maturity.[75] The hope was that evolutionary, controlled, economic development would insure non-Communist political stability. "Modern societies must be built," one of the chief theoreticians of the concept, Walt W. Rostow, declared, "and we are prepared to help build them."[76] Kennedy liked to quote Mao's statement that "guerrillas are like fish, and the people are the water in which fish swim. If the temperature of the water is right, the fish will thrive and multiply."[77] Kennedy sought to affect the temperature of the water through modernization, and counterinsurgency became his means. Whether or not Khrushchev had given his January, 1961 proclamation that Russia would support movements of national liberation, the Kennedy team would probably have undertaken counterinsurgency operations to defeat the destabilizing insurgencies. These movements might permit Communist exploitation and check traditional United States economic expansion. Counterinsurgency took several forms, all reflecting the "can-do" philosophy: the training of native police forces and bureaucrats, flood control, transportation and communications, and community action projects. Most dramatic were the American Special Forces units, or Green Berets. Kennedy personally elevated their status in the military and supervised their choice of equipment. It was assumed, for example, that they would apply America's finest technology in Vietnam to succeed where the French had failed.

Besides enlarging counterinsurgency forces and continuing and extending foreign aid, the Kennedy Administration created the Peace Corps to assist in "nation building." Established by executive order in 1961, this volunteer group of mostly young Americans numbered 5,000 by early 1963 and 10,000 a year later. They went into developing nations as teachers, agricultural advisers, and technicians. The Peace Corps, although certainly a self-interested arm of American foreign policy, blunted some of the sharper edges of poverty and hardship. Hundreds of dedicated individuals worked to improve living conditions, in stark contrast to the destructive presence of the United States military in Indochina at the same time. Peace Corps monuments—irrigation systems, water pumps, larger crops—arose throughout Latin America and Africa, but the corps's humanitarian

**AN ANSWER TO THE LIBERAL ARTS GRADUATE WHO ASKS:**
**What Can I Do in the Peace Corps?**

**Peace Corps Pamphlet.** One of the instruments of "nation building," and Kennedy's pet project, the Peace Corps attracted young graduates of American universities for service in developing countries. Thousands of humane individuals, including some middle-aged and elderly Americans, took up the call. (The Peace Corps)

efforts fell far short of resolving the Third World's profound squalor or winning many friends to American foreign policy.

The Kennedy Administration also embarked upon the "Alliance for Progress" in Latin America to head off revolution. Launched at the Punta del Este meeting of the Organization of American States in August, 1961, the alliance envisioned spending $20 billion in private and public United States funds during the next decade. In return, the Latin Americans promised land and tax reforms, housing projects, and health improvements. Launched with great fanfare, the alliance soon sputtered. American businessmen did not invest as expected; the State Department dragged its feet in bureaucratic lethargy; Latin American nationalists disliked United States control; elites resisted reforms and pocketed American money; the gap between rich and poor widened; middle-class Latin Americans, whom Washington counted upon, proved to be selfish; and the United States abandoned its requirement that political democracy accompany economic change. In Colombia dams were built but needed land reforms were ignored. When the United States cut off aid to Haiti and Peru because of their repressive regimes, some Latin American governments protested American "intervention." What the alliance produced, complained critics, was a better grade of dictator. One of the architects of the alliance, Arthur M. Schlesinger, Jr., had told the President in early 1961 that Latin America was "set for miracles."[78] The "miracles" never materialized, and for all its sincere intentions to improve living conditions, the *Alianza para el Progreso* became in the last analysis another form of interference to maintain United States hegemony in the hemisphere. By the mid-1960s, under the leadership of staunchly conservative diplomat Thomas Mann, the alliance had turned its resources to military purposes, such as internal security forces. Cuba's Fidel Castro thought the alliance "a politically wise concept put forth to hold back the tide of revolution." It did not work, he pointed out, "because those in charge of seeing that the agrarian reform was implemented in Latin America were the very owners of the lands."[79]

The difficulties of "nation building" were also revealed dramatically in the Congo (now called Zaire), which was granted hurried independence from Belgium in mid-1960. Civil war quickly erupted. Backed by American and European cobalt and copper interests, Moise Tshombe tried to detach Katanga Province from the new central government headed by Patrice Lumumba. The United States, fearing Communist penetration of the volatile former colony, helped a United Nations mission quell the Katanga insurrection. Secretary Rusk prophetically worried about the consequences of the United States intervention. "What are the prudent and practical limitations on our traditional view of colonialism?" he asked privately. "One or two more Congo's—and we've had it."[80] Although Lumumba died in 1961, by early 1963 the central Congolese government had defeated Tshombe. About a year later, however, a major leftist revolt supported by Russia, Communist China, and Ghana, broke out. With the United Nations forces gone, the CIA soon bolstered former enemy Tshombe as the new leader of the central government, and with direct American aid, including military advisers, he recruited white mercenaries. The rebels responded by terrorizing white foreigners. In November of 1964, a small force of Belgian paratroopers dropped from American aircraft into the Congo to rescue Belgian and American citizens. Although there had never been a serious "Communist threat" in the Congo, the Kennedy Administration was reading Cold War lessons and thus thrust itself into the shaky politics of Africa. American Ambassador to Guinea William Attwood noted that leading African nationalists felt humiliated by the American and foreign intervention in the Congo, because "the white man with a gun, the old plunderer who had enslaved his ancestors, was back again, doing what he pleased, when he pleased, where he pleased. And there wasn't a damn thing Africa could do about it, except yell rape."[81] Attwood exaggerated, but he did identify the chief source of resistance to American "nation building"—nationalism itself.

## Cuba and the Bay of Pigs

Africa counted as a sideshow compared to Latin America, formerly a secure American sphere of influence. Cuba claimed center stage. On July 26, 1953, a young lawyer and Cuban nationalist, Fidel Castro, attempted to overthrow the harsh American-backed regime of Fulgencio Batista. Beaten back, Castro fled to Mexico; he returned to Cuba in 1956 but failed again. This time he escaped into the mountains, where for three years he augmented his guerrilla forces and sporadically fought Batista's American-supplied army. In early 1959 the cigar-smoking, bearded rebel seized Havana and initiated social and economic programs designed to reduce the extensive United States interests that had developed since 1898 and had come to dominate Cuba's sugar, mining, and utilities industries. The new Havana government confiscated American property, and, knowing that he alienated the United States by this action, Castro began to look to Russia for help. Cuba and Russia struck a trade agreement in early 1960, and Castro increasingly used simplistic Communist language to explain the Cuban revolution. Historians debate when this authoritarian nationalist committed himself to "communism," but two elements in his thought seem consistent: socialism and nationalistic anti-Americanism. Often citing the abhorred Platt Amendment, which Cubans

**Fidel Castro (1926—).**
This persevering Cuban revolutionary finally overcame American-backed Fulgencio Batista in 1959 and created a strong-arm government that the United States refused to recognize. (*The Reporter,* 1962. Copyright 1962 by The Reporter Magazine Co.)

called a yoke of colonialism, Castro determined that the only path to liberation from United States economic exploitation was public, rather than private, ownership of productive facilities. "This revolution may be like a watermelon," one American businessman remarked. "The more they slice it, the redder it gets."[82]

Castro's angry mixture of nationalism and communism and strong-arm tactics, including execution without fair trial, antagonized Washington, which had hesitantly supported Batista almost to the last. When the American Society of Newspaper Editors invited Castro to the United States for a speech in April, 1959, President Eisenhower refused to meet with him. Instead he departed for Augusta, Georgia to play golf on his favorite course. One conclusion seemed clear in Washington: Castro had to be squashed. In March, 1960, Eisenhower ordered the CIA to train Cuban exiles in Guatemala for a potential invasion of their former homeland. And in July the United States drastically reduced imports of Cuban sugar, hoping thereby to stagger the Cuban economy. Castro replied by seizing American-owned sugar mills. The Russians, meanwhile, were declaring the Monroe Doctrine dead. Eisenhower began to protest this seeming attempt by "international communism to intervene in the affairs of the Western Hemisphere."[83] Just before leaving office Eisenhower broke off diplomatic relations with Cuba. To Castro, courtship with Moscow seemed to provide protection against hostile "Yanquis." Anti-Castro American Ambassador to Cuba Philip W. Bonsal frankly admitted that Castro's "thrust in 1959 was radically and exclusively nationalistic; it became oriented toward dependence on the Soviet Union only when the United States, by its actions in the spring of 1960, gave the Russians no choice other than to come to Castro's rescue."[84] When Eisenhower undertook a "goodwill" tour of Latin America in early 1960 he was disconcerted to read a placard in a Rio de Janeiro crowd: "We like Ike; We like Fidel too."[85]

During the 1960 presidential campaign, candidate Kennedy hammered on the issue of Cuba. He called Castro a "source of maximum danger" and lambasted Eisenhower and Nixon for permitting a "communist satellite" to spring up on "our very doorstep." Kennedy called for a "serious offensive" against Cuba: "we do not intend to be pushed around any longer and in particular do not intend to be pushed out of our naval base at Guantánamo, or denied fair compensation for American property he has seized."[86] Critics complained that he was inviting an American Hungary in the western hemisphere. Just before leaving office in January, 1961, Eisenhower advised the incoming President to accelerate the exile training program. Kennedy seemed a willing recipient of such counsel.

Cuba was hardly a puppet of Russia or a threat to American security in 1961. "The Castro regime is a thorn in the flesh," Senator J. William Fulbright argued, "but it is not a dagger in the heart."[87] Still, ignoring America's own contribution to Castro's anti-Americanism, Kennedy defined it as a test of will, a new Cold War battleground, and he decided to remove the Cuban irritation. The CIA assured him that it could deliver another Guatemala, just like 1954—or even better. The CIA predicted that the Cuban people would rise up against their Communist masters. CIA agents pinpointed Cochinos Bay, the "Bay of Pigs," as the invasion site and organized a Cuban Revolutionary Council to take office after the successful expedition. Kennedy was uneasy with the plan, not so much because it meant a blatant violation of Cuban sovereignty, but because, even though it was a covert operation and the American military was not *directly* involved, the mission might generate criticism at home and abroad or even fail. To help counter complaints,

Kennedy put Arthur M. Schlesinger, Jr. to work writing a justification or "White Paper." The Kennedy Administration never attempted to open talks with the Castro government, and it never consulted Congress on what amounted to war with Cuba.

In mid-April, 1961, 1,400 CIA-trained commandos departed from Guatemala for Cuba. They met early resistance from Castro's militia, no sympathetic insurrection occurred, and within two days the invasion had become a fiasco. Like his brother John, Attorney General Robert Kennedy found defeat difficult to accept. "We just could not sit and take it"; Moscow might think Americans "paper tigers." Walt Rostow, sensitive to Kennedy *machismo*, reassured him that "we would have ample opportunity to prove we were not paper tigers in Berlin, Southeast Asia, and elsewhere."[88] After the disaster President Kennedy, who had vetoed American air support for the invasion, blamed the CIA and joint chiefs of staff for faulty intelligence and sloppy execution. He never questioned his policy of attempting to overthrow a sovereign government, only the methods for doing it. Hardly sobered by the Bay of Pigs setback, Kennedy announced the lesson learned: "let the record show that our restraint is not inexhaustible." He vowed a "relentless struggle in every corner of the globe" with communism.[89] During the next several years, the United States imposed an economic blockade on Cuba, ousted the island nation from the Organization of American States, refused to recognize Castro, directed United States Information Agency propaganda at the Havana regime, continued aid to anti-Castro forces in Miami, Florida, and even sponsored assassination plots on Castro's life. For their part, the Cubans attempted to stimulate revolution and anti-Americanism in other nations through such daring rebels as Ché Guevara, who finally died at the hands of CIA-directed Bolivian soldiers in 1967. The Bay of

**"Cuban Fiasco."** The Bay of Pigs expedition to Cuba in 1961 did not turn out as American intelligence officials and the President had hoped. (Roy Justus, *Minneapolis Star*)

Pigs, or "Battle of Giron Beach," was etched like the Platt Amendment on the Cuban mind. An official Cuban tourist map of the 1970s described Giron Beach as the site of "the first defeat of imperialism in America."[90]

## The Cuban Missile Crisis

The Kennedy Administration's preoccupation with Castro's Cuba helped precipitate one of the Cold War's momentous crises. The Cuban Missile Crisis of October, 1962, as Nikita Khrushchev remarked, was a time when "the smell of burning hung in the air."[91] Walt Whitman Rostow thought it the Gettysburg of the Cold War. On October 14 a U-2 reconnaisance plane photographed some intermediate-range missile sites under construction in Cuba. After gathering more data, American officials informed the President on October 16 that the Soviet Union had indeed placed missiles in Cuba. Kennedy created an Executive Committee of the National Security Council (Ex Comm), consisting of his "action intellectuals" and experienced diplomats from the Truman years. Besides McNamara, brother Robert, McGeorge Bundy, Maxwell Taylor, and Theodore Sorenson, there were Dean Acheson, Paul Nitze, and Robert Lovett, among others. Dean Rusk participated little in the exhausting, sometimes panicky, always vigorous, marathon meetings of Ex Comm. Kennedy had instructed them to find a way to remove the missiles. Something had to be done.

The Soviet installation of missiles was a reckless decision. Moscow's motivation is not altogether clear, although Khrushchev probably did not want a nuclear confrontation. Khrushchev himself has written that after the Bay of Pigs invasion the Soviets and Cubans predicted that the United States would strike again, an act that had to be prevented. "If the United States had not been bent on liquidating the Cuban revolution," Fidel Castro has said, "there would not have been an October crisis."[92] Russia was already committed, through large shipments of arms, to the maintenance of Cuban sovereignty and did not wish to "lose" Cuba. "We had to think up some way of confronting America with more than words," Khrushchev recalled. Then, too, the Russian leader, noting the presence of threatening American missiles in Turkey, reasoned that missiles in Cuba would teach Americans "just what it feels like to have enemy missiles pointing at you; we'd be doing nothing more than giving them a little of their own medicine."[93] Analysts have also suggested that Moscow was actually trying to force negotiations over Berlin and removal of the missiles from Turkey. Another explanation derives from debate within the Kremlin, wherein some Russian hawks disapproved Khrushchev's "peaceful coexistence" and worried about the Chinese challenge to Soviet preeminence among Communists. Khrushchev may have thought he needed a Cold War triumph to disarm his Kremlin critics and to demonstrate to Peking and other Communist capitals that Russia would take serious measures to defend an ally. Maybe he wanted what some observers called a nuclear "quick-fix"—the appearance of nuclear parity. It is difficult to believe that the Russians thought they could have installed the missiles without being detected. Ship after ship, loaded with components and technicians, conspicuously docked in Cuba. When the U-2 flights spotted the missiles, some sat uncamouflaged at their sites, thereby easily photographed. Khrushchev certainly knew about U-2s. Maybe he expected detection and then an offer from Kennedy to negotiate their removal, in conjunction with other issues like Berlin and Turkey. If so, Khrushchev grossly miscalculated and helped initiate a frightening crisis.

Kennedy and the Ex Comm initially gave little attention to negotiations to remove the missiles, and hardly probed for Soviet motivation. They feared that prolonged diplomacy would give Russian technicians enough time to make the missiles operational. Ex Comm discussions centered on questions of a military response. Several alternatives were discussed and rejected. Dean Acheson, among others, favored an air strike. Robert Kennedy listened and passed a note to his brother: "I now know how Tojo felt when he was planning Pearl Harbor."[94] Bobby said that he did not want his brother to become a Tojo. Anyway, Air Force officials reported they could not guarantee one hundred percent success; some missiles might remain in place for firing against the United States. Russians might also be killed. The joint chiefs of staff recommended a full-scale military invasion, a successful Bay of Pigs with American soldiers, thus getting rid of both the missiles and Castro. Although alluring, such a scheme could mean a prolonged war with Cuba, heavy American casualties, and a Soviet retaliatory attack upon Berlin. A private overture to Castro was ruled out, as was the suggestion that the issue be given to the United Nations. Ambassador to the United Nations Adlai Stevenson's proposal that the United States offer to trade the missiles in Turkey for those in Cuba met open derision. The Ex Comm members, tired and irritable, finally decided upon a naval blockade or "quarantine" of arms shipments to Cuba. Some members warned that such an action might prompt the Soviets to blockade Berlin and that the main problem, the removal of the missiles, would remain unsolved.

**Soviet Missile Site at San Cristobal, Cuba.** This low-level photograph was taken in October, 1962, when Soviet technicians were busily trying to assemble the various missile components. (U.S. Air Force)

The "quarantine," pushed ardently by McNamara, constituted a compromise between armed warfare and doing nothing and left open options for further escalation.

Kennedy, recalling the lessons of the 1930s and refusing to approach Moscow for talks, went on national television on October 22 and set off a war of nerves with Moscow. He announced a blockade, soon endorsed by a compliant Organization of American States, and insisted that Khrushchev "halt and eliminate this clandestine, reckless and provocative threat to world peace."[95] Over 180 American ships patrolled the Caribbean, and the American naval base on Cuba, Guantánamo, was reinforced. A B-52 bomber force loaded with nuclear bombs took to the skies. On October 24, Soviet vessels sailed toward the blockade. "It looks really mean, doesn't it," remarked the President as he awaited a collision.[96] But the Russian ships stopped. Secretary General of the United Nations U Thant urged talks; Khrushchev quickly called for a summit meeting. Kennedy replied that the missiles had to be removed first. The hours passed without a flare-up, but the tension was electric. On October 26 a Soviet agent contacted correspondent John Scali of the American Broadcasting Company and offered to disengage the missiles if the United States promised publicly not to invade Cuba in the future. Later Dean Rusk told Scali, "remember when you report this—that eyeball to eyeball, they blinked first."[97] Then came a long letter from Khrushchev stating much the same offer, but still insisting that the missiles were defensive, not offensive.

The next day, October 27, the crisis accelerated. FBI agents learned that Soviet officials in New York City were burning documents, perhaps a sign that war loomed. A U-2 plane was shot down over Cuba. Work continued with greater speed at the Cuban missile sites to make them operational. Also, another Khrushchev letter arrived in Washington on the 27th. The Premier raised the stakes: Russia would withdraw the missiles from Cuba if the United States removed its missiles from Turkey. Kennedy exploded at his advisers, because he had ordered the removal of the strategically vulnerable and obsolete Jupiter missiles from Turkey some months before. Nothing had been done, but Kennedy was not now interested in a swap. Robert Kennedy suggested that the President ignore the last letter and answer the first. JFK thereupon endorsed Khrushchev's first proposal: removal of the missiles in Cuba in exchange for a public American pledge to respect Cuba's territorial integrity. On the 28th Khrushchev agreed to these terms. Kennedy had thrown down the gauntlet and Khrushchev, fortunately, had not picked it up. The crisis was over. "Khrushchev, that complex, humane gambler-bandit," Walt Rostow later concluded, "did not stop until he felt the knife on his skin."[98]

Although congressmen and popular opinion applauded Kennedy's "finest hour," critics asked if the crisis was necessary. They questioned Kennedy's willingness to risk nuclear war, his disdain for private negotiations, and his resort to public confrontation. Ex Comm advisers and former ambassadors to Russia Charles Bohlen and Llewellyn Thompson urged private talks upon the President. Walter Lippmann on October 25 wrote a widely read column asking why, when the President met privately in the White House with Soviet Foreign Minister Andrei Gromyko on October 18, Kennedy did not show the Russian diplomat the U-2 photographs and seek a diplomatic solution then and there. The President could have warned him that the United States would go public with its demand for removal if the Soviets did not act posthaste. Public statements on television were not calculated to defuse a serious crisis. Yet Kennedy issued a public ultimatum, leaving Khrushchev little chance to repudiate his mistake or to save face, usually the very stuff of effective diplomacy. Kennedy risked the lives of millions of Americans and Russians in a scary gamble that the Soviets would back down. The members of the Ex Comm were bright and dedicated, Robert Kennedy recalled, but "if six of them had been President of the U.S., I think that the world might have been blown up."[99] "We were in luck," John Kenneth Galbraith later commented, "but success in a lottery is no argument for lotteries."[100]

Why Kennedy chose to ignore the possibilities of negotiations remains a topic of considerable debate. As most Ex Comm members noted, it does not appear that the Soviet missiles in Cuba, forty-two in number, altered the strategic balance of power. The medium-range weapons did not diminish America's overwhelming nuclear superiority. It would have been suicidal for the Russians to use the missiles in Cuba. Yet, as Sorenson concluded, the balance would have been "altered *in appearance;* and in matters of national will and world leadership, as the President said later, such appearances contribute to reality."[101] Regardless of strategic importance, then, the Kennedy people thought the very placement of missiles a diminution of American credibility and a direct challenge to American hegemony in Latin America. It was a matter of prestige, another test of will. Most observers have agreed that something had to be done to remove the weapons. But why a public confrontation? Put another way, American security was not threatened, but the Administration of John F. Kennedy may have been. Congressional elections were scheduled for early November and the Republicans were harping, before the missile crisis, about Kennedy's failure at the Bay of Pigs and his seeming irresolution over Cuba. Public toughness against the Soviets over the Cuban missiles would disarm his critics and protect his Administration's foreign policy from a hostile Congress. Politics seemed to demand a bold stance. Then, too, there was the style and psyche of the "action intellectuals" who craved a victory, especially after the Bay of Pigs, the Vienna summit experience, and the Berlin Wall. Adolf A. Berle, one of Kennedy's leading advisers on Latin America, recorded in his diary: "This [Cuban Missile Crisis] is reprise on the Bay of Pigs business and this time there will be no charges that somebody weakened at the crucial moment."[102]

No weakness indeed—but an alarming example of brinkmanship. Afterward Kennedy seemed more willing to avoid crises and to entertain ideas of arms control. The 1963 Test Ban Treaty was one result, as was the installation of the "hot line," a direct telephone link between the White House and Kremlin. Yet, as scholar James Nathan has argued, "force and toughness became enshrined as instruments of policy." Some of the lessons the Kennedy advisers drew from the crisis encouraged military solutions to diplomatic problems because of their belief, Nathan has written, "that success in international crisis was largely a matter of national guts; that the opponent would yield to superior force; that presidential control of forces can be 'suitable' . . . , and that crisis management and execution are too dangerous and events move too rapidly for anything but the tightest secrecy."[103] The Russians read different lessons. They had been humiliated publicly. They had been shown to be inferior in nuclear power. The Chinese rubbed salt in the wound and exacerbated the bitter Sino-Soviet split by demeaning the Russians for having capitulated. Khrushchev would fall from power in 1964, but even before his ouster, Moscow determined to enter the nuclear arms race on a massive scale. As one Soviet leader remarked: "Never will we be caught like this again."[104]

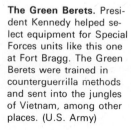

**The Green Berets.** President Kennedy helped select equipment for Special Forces units like this one at Fort Bragg. The Green Berets were trained in counterguerrilla methods and sent into the jungles of Vietnam, among other places. (U.S. Army)

The Kennedyites prided themselves on their success as managers, but the legacy of the Cuban Missile Crisis meant an intensified arms race with the Soviets, alienation of America's allies (especially France), and an arrogant belief in the efficacy of American answers to world problems through the exercise of United States power.

## Indochina Still: The Kennedy Escalation and Legacy, 1961–1963

Continued unrest in Laos and Vietnam placed those Asian trouble spots high on the "action intellectuals'" list for the remedial magic of counterinsurgency and nation building. Rostow saw an opportunity to use "our unexploited counterguerrilla assets"—helicopters and Special Forces units. "In Knute Rockne's old phrase," he told President Kennedy, "we are not saving them for the Junior Prom."[105] The landlocked agricultural nation of Laos, wracked by civil war, seemed to provide a testing ground. Granted independence at Geneva in 1954, Laos chose neutralism in the Cold War when nationalist leader Souvanna Phouma organized a coalition government of neutralists and the pro-Communist Pathet Lao in 1957. The Eisenhower Administration opposed the neutralist government and initiated a major military aid program to build up the rightist and corrupt Laotian army; by 1961, $300 million had been spent. The money helped only slightly to improve the army's desire or ability to fight, but it did disrupt the Laotian economy through inflation and graft. In 1958 CIA-funded rightists helped displace Souvanna and shape a pro-American government without Pathet Lao participation. Washington soon dispatched military advisers to the new but shaky regime.

Souvanna Phouma returned to power after a coup in August, 1960, but the United States undermined him by again equipping rightist forces. Seeking a counterweight to American influence, Souvanna received assistance from Moscow and North Vietnam. But in December he fled his country. "The Americans say I am a Communist," he sighed. "All this is heartbreaking. How can they think I am a Communist? I am looking for a way to keep Laos non-Communist."[106] Unwilling to accept neutralism, the United States had helped convert a civil war into a big power confrontation. For Eisenhower the problem was simple: "the fall of Laos to Communism would mean the subsequent fall—like a tumbling row of dominoes—of its still-free neighbors, Cambodia and South Vietnam and, in all probability, Thailand and Burma. Such a chain of events would open the way to Communist seizure of all Southeast Asia."[107] The neutralists and the Pathet Lao, it appeared to Eisenhower, were simply part of a global Communist conspiracy.

The incoming Kennedy Administration did not perceive the Laotian problem much differently, although Kennedy was miffed over having to deal with it. In a rephrasing of the "domino theory," adviser Arthur M. Schlesinger, Jr. later explained that "If Laos was not precisely a dagger pointed at the heart of Kansas, it was very plainly a gateway to Southeast Asia."[108] In March Kennedy blotched the historical record by blaming the Pathet Lao for preventing the creation of a neutral Laos. As conspicuous Soviet aid flowed to the Pathet Lao, Kennedy determined to halt the imminent collapse of the pro-American government. He ordered the Seventh Fleet into the South China Sea, alerted American forces in Okinawa, and moved 500 Marines with helicopters into Thailand a short distance from the Laotian capital. Then the Bay of Pigs disaster struck. Fearing to appear weak with one arm tied down in Cuba, Kennedy flexed the other in Laos. The President instructed the several hundred American military advisers in Laos, heretofore involved in covert operations, to discard their civilian clothes and dress in more ostentatious military uniforms as a symbol of American resolve. The Soviets wanted no fight in Laos. In April, 1961 they endorsed Kennedy's appeal for a cease-fire. But the Soviets were unable to control the independent-minded Pathet Lao, who battled on. Kennedy asked the joint chiefs of staff if an American military expedition could succeed. The military experts demurred. However, "if we are given the right to use nuclear weapons," remarked JCS Chairman General Lyman L. Lemnitzer, "we can guarantee victory."[109] Somebody in the room incredulously suggested the President ask the general what he meant by "victory." Kennedy adjourned the meeting, wondering what to do.

The answer came in Geneva, where a conference on Laos began in May, 1961. Although it took deft diplomatic pressure from W. Averell Harriman, continued bloodshed in Laos, and hard bargaining lasting until June, 1962, the major powers did sign a Laotian agreement. Laos would be neutral; it could not enter military alliances or permit foreign military bases on its soil. Souvanna Phouma headed the new government. Bernard Fall, veteran observer of Southeast Asia, measured the results of the United States involvement in Laos by looking at the difference between the neutralist government of the 1950s that the United States had subverted and that of 1962: "Instead of two communists in Cabinet positions, there would be four now; instead of having to deal with 1,500 poorly armed Pathet Lao fighters, there were close to 10,000 now well-armed with new Soviet weapons."[110] Still, peace did not come to that ravaged land. In late 1962, in clear violation of the agreement it had just signed, Washington secretly began arms shipments to Souvanna's government, which increasingly turned to the right. The pretext was the presence of small numbers of North Vietnamese soldiers in the north, but it seems evident that Washington had not given up its goal of building a sturdy pro-American outpost in Indochina. Unbeknownst to the American people, the United States began in 1964 secret bombing raids against Pathet Lao forces, after a right-wing coup had diminished Souvanna's authority. By then Laos' major problem was that it lay too close to Vietnam, where American intervention had also escalated under Kennedy.

"This is the worst one we've got, isn't it," Kennedy asked Rostow. "You know, Eisenhower never mentioned it. He talked at length about Laos, but never uttered the word Vietnam."[111] For the next decade Vietnam would indeed become America's "worst one." Some Kennedy watchers have suggested that his intervention in Vietnam and his bold action in the Cuban missile crisis stemmed from his reaction to the criticism of the joint chiefs of staff and such hawks as columnist Joseph Alsop that he had weakened over Laos, and that, in turn, his success in the missile episode further emboldened him in Vietnam. Whatever the relationship of events, Kennedy shared America's antirevolutionary and expansionist attitudes. Early in his Administration he decided to apply counterinsurgency methods in Vietnam to gain a triumph over communism. Washington soon kept a "box score" on counterinsurgency efforts. Vietnam was beset by a nasty civil war between the National Liberation Front and the Diem regime. The Kennedy advisers considered the conservative, vain Premier Ngo Dinh Diem a liability, but as Vice-President Lyndon B. Johnson put it privately—after having publicly annointed Diem the Winston Churchill of Asia—"Sh--, man, he's the only boy we got out there."[112]

Kennedy was cautious about Vietnam, hardly wanting to tie American fate to a faltering Diem or to tread the disastrous path already traveled by the French. He said he did not want to launch a white man's war in Asia and that Asians had to fight their own battles. But because he accepted the "domino theory," interpreted all Communists as part of an international conspiracy, thought that China lay behind the Vietnamese turmoil, and believed that "nation building" promised success, he expanded the American presence. "We have a very simple policy in Vietnam," Kennedy told a news conference in September, 1963. "We want the war to be won, the Communists to be contained, and the Americans to go home."[113] Asked that year if he would reduce aid to South Vietnam, the President replied that he would not. "Strongly in our mind is what happened in the case of China at the end of World War II, where China was lost. . . . We don't want that."[114] In January, 1961, Kennedy authorized $28.4 million to enlarge the South Vietnamese army and another $12.7 million to improve the civil guard. In May he sent Vice-President Johnson to Saigon. That veteran Texas politician stated the problem in extreme terms: either "help these countries . . . or throw in the towel in the area and pull back our defenses to San Francisco and a 'Fortress America.'"[115] That month Kennedy also ordered 400 Special Forces soldiers and another 100 military "advisers" to South Vietnam. Meanwhile the Viet Cong captured more territory and accelerated the violence through a bloody campaign of assassinations of village chiefs. In October a United States intelligence report indicated that 80–90 percent of the 17,000 Viet Cong in South Vietnam were recruited in the South, and hence were not from North Vietnam, and that most of their supplies were also Southern. Although this estimate exploded the theory of advisers like Walt Rostow that the Vietnamese crisis was a case of aggression by North Vietnam, the report apparently made only a slight impact on Kennedy.

The President was, however, troubled by conflicting viewpoints, so in October he dispatched two hawks, General Maxwell Taylor and Walt Rostow, to South Vietnam to study the war firsthand. Diem naturally asked for more American military aid, and when Taylor returned to Washington he urged the President to send American combat troops. Rusk questioned such advice, arguing that Diem must first reform his conservative government; and the intelligence agencies suggested that sending such military assistance would likely arouse a North Vietnamese counterresponse. McNamara and the joint chiefs of staff supported Taylor and Rostow. Conscious that his decision violated the Geneva Accords but unwilling to say so publicly, Kennedy authorized in November a large increase in American forces or "advisers" in South Vietnam. By the end of 1961 there were 2,600; at the start of the year the figure had been about 900. During 1962 the figure jumped to 11,000, and at the time of Kennedy's death in November, 1963 the number had reached 16,700. American troops, helicopter units, minesweepers, and air reconnaisance aircraft went into action. In 1962, 109 Americans died and in 1963, 489. A "strategic hamlet" program was initiated to fortify villages and isolate them from Viet Cong influence. This population control through barbed wire, however, proved disruptive and unpopular with villagers and permitted the Viet Cong to appear as Robin Hoods. Then, too, many of the American weapons actually ended up in Viet Cong hands. From New Delhi, a doubting Ambassador John Kenneth Galbraith asked the President a telling question: "Incidentally, who is the man in your administration who decides what countries are strategic? I would like to have his name and address and ask him what is so important about this real estate in the space age. What strength do we gain from alliance with an incompetent government and a people who are largely indifferent to their own salvation?"[116] To allay such questioning, the Administration issued optimistic statements. In February of 1963 Rusk announced that the "momentum of the Communist drive has been stopped."[117]

In May, 1963 the difficulties of "nation building" were exposed when South Vietnamese troops attacked protesting and unarmed Buddhists in Hué, massacring nine. The incident erupted after Diem, a Catholic, had banned the flying of

**A Suicide in Protest, Saigon.** Quang Duc, a Buddhist monk aged seventy-three, set his gasoline-drenched yellow robes afire in June, 1963, at a main intersection in Saigon to protest Diem's restrictions on Buddhists. (Wide World Photos)

Buddhist flags. Vietnam was a nominally Buddhist country governed by Catholics; the remnants of French colonialism were evidenced in various privileges, including education, for Catholics. Although the Buddhist demonstrations were a vehicle for the expression of long-standing nationalist sentiments, Diem soon equated Buddhism with communism. The Viet Cong were actually as surprised as Diem with the Buddhist uprising. On June 10 a Buddhist monk sat in a Saigon street, poured fuel over his body, and immolated himself. The appalling sight led Diem's callous sister-in-law Madame Nhu to chortle about "Buddhist barbecues." During the late summer and fall the protest spread; so did Diem's military tactics, including an attack upon Hué's pagoda. Also, thousands of students were arrested, including the children of many of Diem's own civil and military officers. Kennedy publicly chastised Diem and exerted pressure by reducing aid. Senior South Vietnamese generals, now aware that Diem was no longer in American favor, asked American officials how they would respond to a coup d'état. The new Ambassador, Henry Cabot Lodge, unsuccessful Republican vice-presidential candidate in 1960, was ready to dump Diem in order to get on with the war, but officials in Washington were divided. McNamara sent a new study mission. Marine General Victor H. Krulak and State Department officer Joseph Mendenhall took a hurried tour; Krulak reported that the war was going well despite the Buddhist squabble, and Mendenhall argued that the Vietnamese were more displeased with Diem than with the Viet Cong. A puzzled Kennedy commented: "Were you two gentlemen in the same country?"[118]

Washington continued cool relations with Diem, who proved more and more resistant to American advice. In early October the Vietnamese generals informed the CIA that they were going to overthrow the recalcitrant premier. Lodge did not discourage them from the undertaking, a signal the generals fully appreciated. The White House was less eager than Lodge for the coup, fearing a failure. On November 1 the generals surrounded the Saigon palace with troops, took Diem prisoner, and murdered him. The assassination shocked Kennedy. "I had not seen him so depressed since the Bay of Pigs," Schlesinger recalled.[119] A few weeks later, on November 22, Kennedy himself was assassinated in Dallas. Some observers have suggested that after the presidential election of 1964, when he no longer suffered political vulnerability and was less fearful of right-wing charges of softness on communism, Kennedy would have withdrawn from Vietnam. We can never know for sure. We know only what he *did* for his 1,000 days in office.

The Kennedy legacy defies easy analysis. The "ifs" persist. Kennedy's apologists have asked historians to judge him not so much by his accomplishments, admittedly less than sterling, but rather by his intentions, for, they have argued, had he not been removed from his appointed journey so tragically in 1963, his good intentions would have reached fruition. Others have recommended that students ignore Kennedy's inflated and monolithic Cold War rhetoric, because it was mere political verbiage. Also, there were ambiguities in his actions. He sent soldiers to Vietnam to wage war and Peace Corps volunteers to Latin America to grow food; he combined a compassionate idealism with traditional anti-Communist fervor; he had serious doubts about the escalation of the Cold War and military intervention in the Third World, yet he escalated and intervened. In June, 1963, in a high-minded speech at American University, the President expressed his uneasiness with large weapons expenditures, called for a re-examination of American Cold War attitudes, suggested that conflict with Russia was not inevitable, and appealed

**Radicals in Venezuela.** Surrounded by posters of revolutionary heroes Ché Guevara and Ho Chi Minh, leftists march in Venezuela for ''people's liberation.'' Despite Kennedy's Alliance for Progress and Peace Corps in Latin America, persistent, rebellious anti-Americanism ricocheted back to Washington. Ché, whose intense eyes dominate the photograph, was killed in Bolivia by American-supported troops in 1967. (François Chalais, Camera Press, London)

for disarmament. Still, as George F. Kennan has noted, "one speech is not enough."[120] Nor was Kennedy willing to reverse the nonrecognition policy toward China or restore the standing of the "China hands" so maligned by Dulles and McCarthy in the early 1950s. The Sino-Soviet split did not impress him: "A dispute over how to bury the West is no ground for Western rejoicing."[121]

The ambitious "nation-building" thrust proved faulty, in large part because it was so interventionist in the affairs of other peoples. In trying to be the "world's social worker," wrote critic John McDermott, the United States practiced "welfare imperialism."[122] The nation-building concept did not pay proper attention to complexities—the multitude of indigenous forces, the varied traditions of other cultures, the entrenched position of native elites, and the persuasive appeals of the insurgent left. Americans discovered in the 1960s that economic growth and democracy did not necessarily go hand in hand, that a middle class could be selfish (if one existed at all), that some nations had no tradition of liberal politics, that not all insurgencies are Communist, and that rebels, closer to their nation's pulse, believe deeply in their cause. The nation-building concept also overestimated America's power to shape other nations. It assumed that soldiers from Connecticut, Iowa, North Carolina, and California could manage "natives" abroad, much as they had done in the Philippines or in Latin America through much of the twentieth century. Unable to force reform on others, Americans often violated their principles by supporting the elite or military or by trying to topple regimes. The concept assumed too that the United States had an obligation to cope with insurgencies everywhere. It made few distinctions between key and peripheral areas. It did not define the "threat" carefully. It tried to do too much; it was globalism gone rampant. The concept, furthermore, possessed a procapitalist, private-enterprise bias, while in the Third World, "private" development was traditionally identified with imperialist exploitation and hence was unpopular.

The Kennedy foreign policy did not assess the strain that would be placed on America's resources and endurance in its long-term global role as policeman, teacher, and social worker. In other words, the Kennedy team tended to take for granted the American people and the constitutional system, including congressional prerogatives in policymaking, as they centralized foreign policy in the White House. Overall, then, the revered, clinical concepts of the Kennedy Administration came up against a host of realities at home and abroad. The Administration often neglected diplomacy, sometimes turning to it only after inflaming crises through military responses. The Kennedy team was reluctant to do little or nothing, or to get out of the way of the profound, even inexorable, movement toward national liberation in the Third World. Several years after Kennedy's death, the *Wall Street Journal* reflected on the diplomatic record of the Kennedy years: "too much vigor and too little restraint, too much grace and too little earthiness, too much eloquence and too little thoughtfulness . . . , too much flexibility and too little patience, too much brilliance and too little common sense."[123]

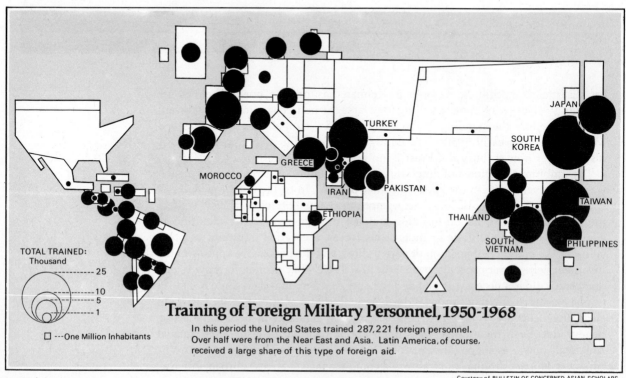

**Training of Foreign Military Personnel, 1950-1968**

In this period the United States trained 287,221 foreign personnel.
Over half were from the Near East and Asia. Latin America, of course,
received a large share of this type of foreign aid.

TOTAL TRAINED:
Thousand
— 25
— 10
— 5
— 1

□ ---One Million Inhabitants

Courtesy of BULLETIN OF CONCERNED ASIAN SCHOLARS

**Lyndon B. Johnson (1908–1973) and Hubert H. Humphrey (1911—).** Vice-President Hubert H. Humphrey of Minnesota does as the Texan does on the LBJ Ranch, 1964. Elected to the Senate in 1949, Humphrey was noted for civil rights and social reform legislation before he joined Johnson on the 1964 Democratic ticket. In 1968, troubled by the tragedy in Vietnam, he ran for the presidency against Richard M. Nixon, but lost a close election. (Lyndon B. Johnson Library. Photo by Staughton)

## No More Munichs, No More Cubas: The Foreign Policy of Lyndon B. Johnson

The presidential transition from John F. Kennedy to Lyndon B. Johnson (LBJ) was smooth. Johnson kept on many of Kennedy's foreign policy advisers. McNamara stayed until early 1968; Rusk remained until the end; when McGeorge Bundy stepped down in 1966 as adviser on national security affairs, Walt Rostow left the State Department to take on that assignment and to become one of LBJ's most ardent supporters. Others resigned. If Johnson lacked Kennedy's zeal for "nation building," he had his own brand of international reform, derived from a sensitivity to the ugliness of poverty. Influenced by his New Deal reform years, he talked about building Tennessee Valley Authorities abroad. "I want to leave the footprints of America there [Vietnam]. I want them to say, 'This is what the Americans left—schools and hospitals and dams. . . .' We can turn the Mekong [River area] into a Tennessee Valley."[124] He shared the Cold War assumptions of most Americans, repeatedly citing the "lessons" of Munich, Greece, China, and Korea, and adding some Texas history of his own. "Just like the Alamo," Johnson remarked about Vietnam, "somebody damn well needed to go to their aid."[125]

Johnson was a political maestro from the poor, dusty hill territory of Texas between Fort Worth and San Antonio. "It is unrelenting country," his gracious and well-respected wife Lady Bird commented, "and Lyndon is unrelenting, too."[126] In explaining his energy, an aide said Johnson had "extra glands."[127] He gulped his meals and drove his Lincoln Continental at breakneck speed over his Texas ranch, wildly dodging cattle. An incessant talker, he usually talked about himself and his accomplishments. His friends and enemies alike witnessed his inflated ego and moody rages. Once, talking with reporters, he lashed out: "Why do you come and ask me, the leader of the Western world, a chicken-sh-- question like that?"[128] He often exaggerated. Critics became "rattlebrains" and "Nervous Nellies" and Vietnam a "raggedy-ass fourth-rate country."[129] On the Communist menace: "[If] we don't stop the Reds in South Vietnam, tomorrow they will be in Hawaii, and next they will be in San Francisco."[130] And he once said about the Organization of American States: "It couldn't pour piss out of a boot if the instructions were written on the heel."[131] A "credibility gap" dogged his Administration, not so much because he told barefaced lies, but because he embellished the actual record with exaggerations and trite analogies in a drawl that sometimes made him appear to be stupid. He was not. His mind was quick and retentive, although very much a captive of the past. "He is purely and aggressively American"—a British journalist claimed—"the first uninhibited product of the American frontier to take over since Andrew Jackson."[132]

Johnson's foreign policy was marked by military responses, hurried decisions, spread-eagle patriotism, hyperbolic rhetoric, overreaction, stubbornness, and intolerance for dissenting views. He seemed to thrive on crises, those times when, as he put it, he was "like a jackrabbit hunkered up in a storm."[133] The many crises were not due solely to the Texan's style or personality, however. A general international phenomenon that caused a slippage of American authority—the diffusion of world power—helps explain the tumult of the 1960s. That is, in that decade blocs were breaking up, NATO members were demanding more independence from Washington, and the Third World, on the rise since the decade before, commanded more autonomy in world affairs. In responding to these changes, the United States clung to the past, still thinking that Uncle Sam could direct events through the exertion of arms and aid. The articulate Chairman of the Senate Foreign Relations Committee, J. William Fulbright of Arkansas, thought Americans suffered under an "arrogance of power" that left the United States by the end of the 1960s a "crippled giant."[134]

During Johnson's five years in office Vietnam consumed his energies, his ambitions, his reputation. He left relations with Russia and China much as he had found them—calmer after the Cuban Missile Crisis, but still strained and based upon military competition. He met with Soviet Premier Aleksei Kosygin in Glassboro, New Jersey in 1967, but the proclaimed "spirit of Glassboro" proved superficial. That year the Johnson Administration asked Congress for the construction of a controversial antiballistic missile system (ABM), a new set of "defensive" weapons to maintain a posture of massive retaliation or deterrence, not just against Russia but against the nuclear-armed Chinese as well. The Soviets already had a limited ABM system and American generals wanted one too. They argued that the United States would not be able to knock Soviet missiles out in wartime, leaving Americans vulnerable to attack; and, because by the late 1960s the Soviets had achieved near nuclear parity with the United States, the Pentagon called again for nuclear superiority. The heated debate over further enlargement of the arms race via the ABM was still fuming when Johnson left office. There was little serious talk about nuclear disarmament, although Russia, the United States, and over fifty other nations signed a nuclear nonproliferation treaty in 1968 (ratified in 1969), a pledge not to spread nuclear weapons to other nations. Unfortunately neither France nor China agreed, and the menacing nuclear weapons still stood in the United States, Great Britain, and Russia. Nonsigner India joined the elite nuclear weapons circle in 1974, demonstrating again the diffusion of power.

In Latin America, smoldering nationalism, the frequency of military coups, and Castro's irritating survival helped define Johnson's policies, which smacked of Roosevelt's Big Stick. Johnson put Assistant Secretary of State Thomas C. Mann in charge of the Alliance for Progress and it soon withered away from neglect. Mann also issued his "Mann Doctrine," a simple declaration that the United States was more interested in supporting anti-Communist governments through economic assistance than in opposing military regimes—a negation of Kennedy's fading hope that democracy would accompany economic growth. In 1964 Washington quickly recognized the new military junta in Brazil, and when Panamanians rioted against American control of the Canal Zone, Johnson employed strong language in telling the President of Panama that the United States would not tolerate insults to the American flag. In 1965, fearing another Cuba, Johnson sent more than 20,000 American soldiers into the Dominican Republic. The trouble had started when, in late 1962, after the assassination of dictator Rafael Trujillo the year before, radical reformer Juan Bosch was elected President of the economically depressed Caribbean country. Ten months later a military coup ousted him. But in April, 1965, pro-Bosch rebels launched a new civil war against the military regime. Johnson and his advisers, with trigger-finger quickness and with very fragmentary evidence, assumed that the revolt was Communist or "Castroite" or nearly so. They ordered an American invasion. "This was a democratic revolution smashed by the leading democracy of the world," a chagrined Bosch declared.[135]

The President also took the opportunity to declare the "Johnson Doctrine." Henceforth, he announced, the United States would unilaterally prevent any Communist government from taking office in the hemisphere, would insist on peaceful change, and would defend "free" nations. Thus, while the United States positioned troops around the globe to prevent others from establishing spheres of influence, it attempted to maintain its own traditional sphere in Latin America. (In 1968, after the Soviets had ruthlessly invaded rebellious Czechoslovakia, the Kremlin issued rationalizations which sounded much like those of Johnson in 1965.) The American inability to distinguish between nationalism and communism, critics noted, meant that the United States was forfeiting the support of leftist reformers in the Third World. As Senator Fulbright, who opposed the Dominican venture, complained: "we have made ourselves the prisoners of the Latin American oligarchs who are engaged in a vain attempt to preserve the status quo—reactionaries who habitually use the term communist very loosely, in part . . . in a calculated effort to scare the United States into supporting their selfish and discredited aims."[136] As for the exaggerated Communist threat in Latin America, the words of a familiar verse seemed to fit:

> As I was going up the stair,
> I met a man who wasn't there.
> He wasn't there again today.
> I wish to God he'd go away!

"Now I am the most denounced man in the world," Johnson stated publicly after the Dominican intervention.[137] An abundance of anti-Americanism, with the President singled out as an impulsive Texan, did flash across the world. But the criticism was directed more against American actions in Vietnam than against those in Latin America. Soon after Diem's death, the National Liberation Front, Secretary General U Thant of the United Nations, France, and many concerned Americans called for a coalition government in Saigon and neutralism or neutralization. It seemed a propitious time for negotiations. Yet President Johnson announced in December, 1963, that the United States sought "victory," because the "neutralization of South Vietnam would only be another name for a Communist take-over."[138] In February, 1964, the American-advised South Vietnamese began covert commando raids and sabotage missions into North Vietnam. Air strikes hit Laos, through which some supplies flowed south. Still, the war did not go well for the American-backed Saigon regime. By April the Viet Cong controlled 42 percent of the villages, compared with 34 percent for the Saigon government; 24 percent were classified "neutral." During the 1964 presidential campaign, Republican candidate Barry Goldwater urged an attack upon Ho Chi Minh's North Vietnam to reverse the trend, an idea already expressed in Saigon by Prime Minister (and General) Nguyen Khanh and endorsed by Walt Rostow and General Maxwell Taylor inside Washington. Johnson, however, scored Goldwater for dangerous warmongering and pledged he would not send American boys to fight in Vietnam.

On August 4, 1964, in the dark of evening, the United States destroyers *Maddox* and *C. Turner Joy* apparently tangled with some North Vietnamese torpedo boats in the Gulf of Tonkin. Although the alleged offenders fled and neither American ship endured damage, the Johnson Administration exploited the issue to enlarge the war. That very night, the President went on television to announce retaliatory air strikes against North Vietnamese targets, including a major oil depot near Vinh. "The challenge that we face in Southeast Asia today is the same challenge that we have faced with courage and that we have met with strength in Greece and Turkey, in Berlin and Korea, in Lebanon and in Cuba," Johnson said the next day when he sent a resolution to Congress.[139] The "Tonkin Gulf Resolution" passed on August 7 without much debate and by huge margins, 466–0 in the House and 88–2 in the Senate. Only Senators Ernest Gruening of Alaska and Wayne Morse of Oregon dissented. The resolution authorized the President to "take all necessary measures to repel any armed attack against the forces of the United States and to prevent further aggression."[140] This open-ended language placed considerable warmaking power in the hands of the President. For Johnson, the resolution "was like Grandma's nightshirt—it covered everything."[141] Belatedly regretting in 1970 this concession to the "imperial presidency," the Senate repealed it.[142]

Controversy surrounds the Tonkin Gulf incident. For example, North Vietnam admitted attacking the *Maddox* on August 2, but not 4, in retaliation for the *Maddox*'s participation in offensive actions against North Vietnam. The *Maddox* itself may or may not have been directly involved in these forays, but it plied waters recently frequented by South Vietnamese raiders attacking North Vietnamese islands. At one point the *Maddox* had ventured within four miles of the targeted islands. The August 2 attack on the *Maddox* was a serious one in which

**Wayne L. Morse (1900–1974).** An independent-minded maverick politician from Oregon, Morse was one of only two senators to vote against the Tonkin Gulf Resolution of 1964. An early critic of American intervention in Vietnam and an impassioned orator, Senator Morse was never afraid to ask a bold question or to state provocative opinions. He served in the Senate from 1945 to 1969 and sat on the Foreign Relations Committee. (*The Reporter,* 1956. Copyright 1956 by The Reporter Magazine Co.)

two torpedoes were fired at the American ship. Hanoi claimed there was no attack whatsoever two days later. The best that can be gleaned from the contradictory evidence is that the captain of the *Maddox* thought he had been attacked that cloudy night of August 4. Uncertainty or not, Johnson reacted quickly. The war in Vietnam was on its way to becoming Americanized.

After the Tonkin Gulf affair, American officials drew up plans for bombing raids on North Vietnam, and after Johnson's overwhelming victory in the November elections, those plans took on importance. In early December Johnson approved in principle bombing raids against North Vietnam and stepped-up bombing of Laos. The American people were not informed of this critical shift in warmaking, but they did watch with growing apprehension the political instability in Saigon, where generals vied for political power and the Buddhists marched for a negotiated peace and neutralism. On February 7, 1965, after a Viet Cong attack upon the American airfield at Pleiku in which nine Americans died, Johnson ordered retaliatory air strikes against North Vietnam. Within hours of the decision of February 7, forty-nine carrier-based American jets dropped bombs above the seventeenth parallel. By March the United States had undertaken a sustained bombing program—"Operation Rolling Thunder." Johnson argued that escalated violence was necessary to protect the American soldiers already there. The very American presence, it now seemed, justified a larger American presence. Uncle Sam, charged some critics, was moving step by step into a quagmire. Johnson had never gone to Congress for a declaration of war, but the President had no doubts about the containment of international communism dating from the 1940s: "Let no one think for a moment that retreat from Viet-Nam would bring an end to conflict. The battle would be renewed in one country and then another. . . . We must say in Southeast Asia—as we did in Europe—in the words of the Bible: 'Hitherto shalt thou come, but no further.'"[143]

With the argument that he had to provide security for Americans in South Vietnam, Johnson also moved more and more ground troops into that troubled land, sending them first to Da Nang, a large American air base. By the end of 1965, United States forces in South Vietnam numbered 184,314; a year later they totaled 385,000. "I don't want to save my face, I just want to save my ass," Johnson was reported to have said as proof of his desire to avoid a large Asian war. A doubter asked: "Does he conceive of that portion of himself as extending all the way to Southeast Asia?"[144] In 1966 American bombers hit oil depots in the North, and by midyear 70 percent of the North's storage capacity had been destroyed. Predictably, Hanoi increased its flow of arms and men into the South, the heavy bombing apparently having had little impact in undercutting either the Viet Cong and North Vietnamese commitment or their ability to resist. During 1965–1968 the United States lost six billion dollars worth of aircraft, or 800 planes, over North Vietnam. General William Westmoreland kept asking for more troops, and Johnson grew restless about the escalation. "When we add divisions, can't the enemy add divisions?" he asked in April, 1967. "If so, where does it all end?"[145] Yet the President approved more. By the start of 1968 American forces totaled 535,000. The peak level of 542,000 was reached in February, 1969. "I deeply believe we *are* quarantining aggressors over there," Johnson remarked, "just like the smallpox." Citing simple historical precedent, he went on: "Just like FDR and Hitler, just like Wilson and the Kaiser. . . . What I learned as a boy in my teens and in college about World War I was that it was our lack of strength and failure to show stamina that got us into that war." For Johnson, history was repeating itself; once again "aggression" would be stopped.[146]

In this period of escalation, 1965–1968, the bloodshed and dislocation were awesome. In "search and destroy" missions under a strategy of "attrition," American and South Vietnamese forces bombed and destroyed villages that harbored suspected Viet Cong, the "Charlie." Tens of thousands of civilians died, many from fiery napalm attacks. "It gets completely impersonal," explained an American air officer. "After you've done it for a while you forget that there are people down there."[147] Refugees grew in number as "pacification" camps became overcrowded.

**Viet Cong Tunnel.** One of the reasons for the frustration of American efforts to defeat the elusive Viet Cong is illustrated in this United States Army depiction of a "typical" VC tunnel. Living off the land and under it, the black-clad guerrillas defied superior American military power. (U.S. Army)

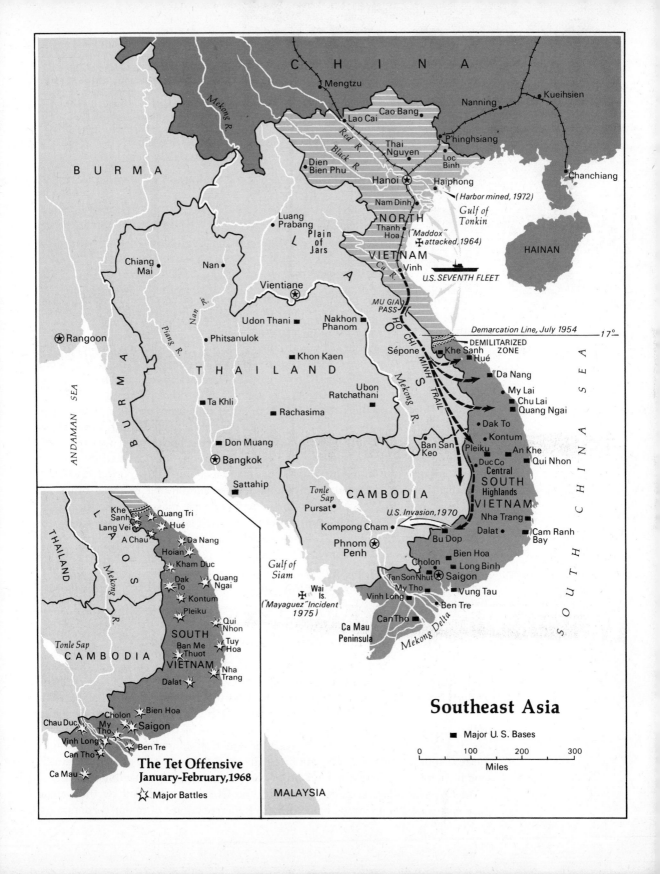

# Southeast Asia

■ Major U.S. Bases

0    100    200    300

Miles

## The Tet Offensive
### January–February, 1968

☆ Major Battles

*( Harbor mined, 1972 )*

*("Maddox" attacked, 1964)*

U.S. SEVENTH FLEET

*Demarcation Line, July 1954* — 17°

DEMILITARIZED ZONE

U.S. Invasion, 1970

Wai Is.
*("Mayaguez" Incident 1975)*

**Flight to Safety in South Vietnam.** With bombs about to rain from American aircraft on their village of Qui Nhon, which apparently harbored Viet Cong snipers, this family flees across a river. Kyoichi Sawada won a Pulitzer Prize for this photograph of 1965. (United Press International, photo by Kyoichi Sawada)

By the end of 1967, as many as four million people, or 25 percent of the population, were refugees. The United States and Saigon, according to two students of the Vietnamese war, "were building up large islands of hostile peasants," many of whom turned sympathetically toward the Viet Cong.[148] Defoliation missions using chemical sprays laid waste the countryside in an effort to expose Viet Cong hideouts and to deny "Charlie" cover; crops were destroyed with herbicides to deny the "enemy" food. In Saigon, the regimes of Generals Nguyen Cao Ky and Nguyen Thieu had jailed about 20,000 political dissenters by 1968. The United States was not alone responsible for the ugly terror that visited South Vietnam, for the Viet Cong and North Vietnamese were shooting back, but it was the overwhelming American fire power and clearing operations that inflicted this horror, much of it televised into American homes every evening. In the period 1965–1973 American aircraft dropped bombs in Indochina amounting to three times the explosives used in World War II. To many Americans, massacres like that at My Lai on March 16, 1968, where an American Army platoon commanded by Lieutenant William Calley shot to death scores of helpless women and children, or "gooks," represented a depravity unbecoming a civilized nation. As was so often true of Washington's manipulation of news and the military's coverup of unfavorable reports, the story of the My Lai massacre did not become public until twenty months later.

## Political Dissent and Peace Efforts: Shedding the Burden

As the war escalated, critics in the United States became more outspoken. Students and faculty at universities began to hold "teach-ins" in 1965, beginning with the University of Michigan in March. Hundreds refused military draft calls and went to jail or fled to Canada. The protest songs of Bob Dylan and Joan Baez inspired rallies. Many protested the expenditure of billions of dollars in Vietnam when social maladjustments at home begged for attention. Johnson tried a "guns-and-butter" approach in the 1960s, but more and more was spent on guns for Vietnam and his reformist "Great Society" programs suffered. The liberal-minded National Student Association, secretly funded by the CIA, was upstaged by the radical Students for a Democratic Society (SDS). Representatives of major corporations, such as Dow Chemical, a maker of napalm, were beset by sit-ins when they attempted to recruit employees on campus. In early 1967, 300,000 demonstrators marched in New York City and in November 100,000 surrounded the Pentagon. They were often vitriolic and impolite, shouting down prowar speakers or government spokesmen with "Hey, hey, LBJ, how many kids did you kill today?"

More reserved, prominent intellectuals, like linguist Noam Chomsky, political scientist Hans Morgenthau, Jr., and a disaffected Arthur M. Schlesinger, Jr., called for withdrawal from Vietnam. Businessmen, lawyers, and clergymen, too, organized into antiwar groups. Widely watched television commentators like CBS's Walter Cronkite increasingly editorialized the evening news with an antiwar bias. The critics' arguments were multifaceted: the war cost too much and weakened needed reform at home; America's youth was dying—30,000 by 1968; inflation and a worsening balance of payments were weakening the economy; the ghastly bloodshed was immoral; the war damaged relations with allies and foes alike; the war could not be won; the President was usurping power and undermining the constitutional system of checks and balances; and domestic America was being ripped apart by dissension. Widely respected historian Henry Steele Commager placed the Vietnamese revolt in a larger context when he told a Senate committee that the rebellion "is against two or three hundreds of years of exploitation and of imperialism. . . . And by what seems to me a most unfair, but perfectly understandable process, a great many of the antagonisms against the European West are focused on us."[149] America had stepped into a traditional struggle over which it could not exert control. Above all else, the critics argued, the United States had succumbed to a debilitating globalism of anticommunism, overcommitment, and overextension. In short, some critics complained about how the war was being conducted, whereas others, more searching, criticized globalism itself.

**Antiwar Newsletter.** Growing numbers of Americans in the 1960s marched in protest against war and segregation, as the front page of this antiwar newsletter noted. (University of Connecticut Library)

The growing public disaffection with the war encouraged dissenters in the House and Senate. Senator J. William Fulbright and some of his colleagues had had lingering doubts about the Tonkin Gulf Resolution. Fulbright decided in 1965 that America was "losing its perspective on what exactly is within the realm of its power and what is beyond it."[150] In February, 1966 his Senate Foreign Relations Committee conducted publicly televised hearings. Administration spokesmen defended the war, citing the traditional need to contain communism. Critical senators, however, kept asking what it was the United States was containing in Vietnam. The Soviet Union? China? North Vietnam? The Viet Cong? Wars of national liberation? Communism? Revolution? It was a frustrating set of possibilities. Secretary Rusk settled on China as the main culprit, especially after Chinese leader Lin Piao declared in 1965 that China would encourage wars of national liberation in the Third World. American leaders interpreted this, incorrectly, to mean that China would initiate them. "It is on this spot," as Rostow once asserted, "that we have to break the liberation war—Chinese type. If we don't break it here we shall have to face it again in Thailand, Venezuela, elsewhere. Vietnam is a clear testing ground for our policy in the world."[151] Although China was North Vietnam's chief supplier of arms until the mid-1960s, the Soviet Union took over that costly role in an attempt to match American armaments and curry favor in Hanoi. Generally overlooked in the search to find the enemy was the fundamental fact that the conflict in South Vietnam grew from indigenous roots—that it was a civil war. The important Fulbright hearings touched on that fact, but the surprise testimony came from the poised and persuasive figure of George F. Kennan. The father of containment insisted that the containment doctrine, designed for a stable

**The Vietnam Hearings, 1966.** As Chairman of the Senate Foreign Relations Committee, J. William Fulbright (on the right) held numerous "educational" hearings to ask government officials like Defense Secretary Robert McNamara (on the left) to explain why the United States fought in Vietnam. Here the two adversaries ham it up nose to nose. Earlier Harry S Truman ridiculed the Rhodes Scholar and former president of the University of Arkansas as "Senator Halfbright." (Wide World Photos, courtesy of University of Arkansas Library)

European nation-state context in the 1940s, was not applicable in Asia. Facile analogies with the 1940s did not face the new realities of the 1960s. He urged a gradual withdrawal from Vietnam. So did Senator Eugene McCarthy of Minnesota, who declared in late 1967 that he would attempt to unseat President Johnson for the 1968 Democratic nomination.

The Johnson Administration lashed back at this apparent defection from the Cold War consensus, citing polls showing that most Americans would not tolerate a Viet Cong victory. Yet doubters grew within its own ranks. "Increasingly," observed Johnson adviser and Princeton historian Eric F. Goldman, "he was seeing himself as the lonely, traduced figure limned against history resolutely doing right, grimly awaiting the verdict of the future."[152] Rostow tried to reassure Johnson with statistical charts showing the "enemy's" heavy loss of life and property, but overarching reality could not be ignored: the United States, with a gross national product 325 times as great as that of North Vietnam, the United States, the most heavily industrialized, most militarily powerful, richest nation on earth, could not subdue rural Vietnam. Nor could Johnson, the supreme politician, ignore the burgeoning dissent inside and outside his Administration. McNamara's growing disenchantment and 1967 decision to resign both shocked and angered the President. White House national security adviser McGeorge Bundy, Under Secretary of State George Ball, and close political adviser Bill Moyers had departed already. The President took petulant verbal potshots at them for leaving his team and for having questioned his quest for victory in Vietnam with their appeals for a stop to the bombing. In 1967–1968 it was evident that winning was an elusive goal; Johnson seemed determined at least not to lose. He would stick it out, it appeared, like Davy Crockett at the Alamo.

His critics said that opportunities for peaceful negotiations should be seized. Throughout the 1965–1968 escalation period, international groups, including the United Nations and the Vatican, reached for peace. In 1965, through Italy, Hanoi offered a peace plan resembling the 1954 Geneva agreements. For the month of January, 1966, Johnson halted the bombing of North Vietnam while American diplomats encouraged mediation in foreign capitals. During the bombing pause the United States increased its troop strength in South Vietnam. America's peace offensive hinged on tremendous obstacles to negotiations. The United States would not talk until North Vietnam ceased its "aggression." The National Liberation Front would not be recognized as a political force in the South. Hanoi, increasingly speaking for the Viet Cong, would not negotiate until a permanent bombing halt was instituted and until the NLF was granted political status. Assistant Secretary of Defense John McNaughton, another "hawk" rapidly becoming a "dove," concluded that the United States was in essence demanding "capitulation by a Communist force that is far from beaten."[153] A promising start toward a negotiated settlement through a Polish representative, in December, 1966, was tragically crippled when American bombers stepped up air strikes around Hanoi to pressure the "enemy" to come to the conference table on American terms. Hanoi thereupon scuttled the Polish peace initiative. Another bombing pause came in February, 1967, in part induced by McNamara's argument

**Antiwar Buttons.** Opponents of the Vietnam War demonstrated their protest in a panoply of buttons urging withdrawal and peace. (Division of Political History, Smithsonian Institution)

**Harvard Strike, 1969.**
The clenched fist and
V-shaped fingers became
symbols of the antiwar
movement. (*Old Mole*,
1969, University of Con-
necticut Library)

that the bombing was not seriously impeding the flow of arms and soldiers into the South, much of it on bicycles over narrow, jungle paths (the "Ho Chi Minh Trail"), or undermining Northern morale. Former State Department official and critic George Ball commented that the United States "is using a hammer to kill a mosquito."[154] Johnson in his "San Antonio formula" of 1967, insisted on an end to "infiltration" before suspending bombing or beginning to negotiate. But, as Clark Clifford wrote two years later, "the North Vietnamese had more than 100,000 men in the South. It was totally unrealistic to expect them to abandon their men by not replacing casualties, and by failing to provide them with clothing, food, munitions, and other supplies. We could never expect them to accept an offer of negotiations on those conditions."[155] After each pause, the bombing was intensified.

And then the Tet offensive of early 1968 wrought its havoc; the trend of military escalation and Johnson's political career were wrenched out of shape; the bombing was scaled down, and the peace talks finally began in Paris. In November, Richard M. Nixon defeated Vice-President Hubert Humphrey for the presidency. Back in Texas in January, 1969, Lady Bird Johnson remarked that "the coach has turned back into a pumpkin and the mice have all run away."[156] In 1961 John F. Kennedy had asked Americans to "pay any price" and "bear any burden." Many refused. The new Nixon Administration would then be faced with the task of halting the decline of American power and maintaining American interests abroad while at the same time mollifying the evident discontent with globalism. As Americans asked, "How could Vietnam happen?" and received such answers from critics as mindless anticommunism, the domino theory, the momentum of containment, the arrogance of power, presidential hubris, economic expansion and the military-industrial complex, bureaucratic politics, an inadvertent and ignorant walk into a quagmire, racist views of "inferior" Asians, welfare imperialism, right-wing domestic political pressure, insensitivity to morality, and a failure to understand an alien culture, the incoming Administration was asking, "How can the United States get out?"

## Further Reading for the Period 1961–1969

Several works cited in chapters 12 and 13 treat this period in diplomatic history. General studies of the foreign policy of these years include Richard J. Barnet, *Intervention and Revolution* (1972), Theodore Draper, *Abuse of Power* (1967), David Halberstam, *The Best and the Brightest* (1972), Jim Heath, *Decade of Disillusionment* (1975), Robert A. Packman, *Liberal America and the Third World* (1973), Walt W. Rostow, *Diffusion of Power* (1972), and Franz Schurmann, *Logic of World Power* (1974).

John F. Kennedy's strife-torn diplomatic years are discussed in Graham Allison, *Essence of Decision* (1971) (on the missile crisis), Herbert Dinerstein, *The Making of a Missile Crisis: October 1962* (1976), Robert A. Divine, "The Education of John F. Kennedy," in Frank Merli and Theodore A. Wilson, eds., *Makers of American Diplomacy* (1974), Louise FitzSimons, *The Kennedy Doctrine* (1972), Roger Hilsman, *To Move a Nation* (1967), Jerome Levinson and Juan de Onís, *The Alliance That Lost Its Way* (1970), James Nathan, "The Missile Crisis," *World Politics* (1975), David Nunnerly, *President Kennedy and Britain* (1972), Jack Schick, *The Berlin Crisis, 1958–1962* (1974), Arthur M. Schlesinger, Jr., *A Thousand Days* (1965), Robert M. Slusser, *The Berlin Crisis of 1961* (1972), Richard Walton, *Cold War and Counterrevolution*

(1972), and Stephen Weissman, *American Foreign Policy in the Congo, 1960–1964* (1974).

Lyndon B. Johnson and his diplomacy are scrutinized in Philip Geyelin, *Lyndon B. Johnson and the World* (1966), Eric Goldman, *The Tragedy of Lyndon Johnson* (1968), Doris Kearns, *Lyndon Johnson and the American Dream* (1976), and Robert Sellen, "Old Assumptions versus New Realities: Lyndon Johnson and Foreign Policy," *International Journal* (1973).

For the long, agonizing wars in Indochina, see Joseph Buttinger, *Vietnam: A Political History* (1970), Chester Cooper, *The Lost Crusade* (1970), Bernard Fall, *The Two Vietnams* (1967), Frances Fitzgerald, *Fire in the Lake* (1972), Townsend Hoopes, *The Limits of Intervention* (1969), George M. Kahin and J. W. Lewis, *The United States in Vietnam* (1969), New York Times, *Pentagon Papers* (1971), Douglas Pike, *The Viet Cong* (1966), Peter Poole, *The United States and Indochina from FDR to Nixon* (1973), and Robert Shaplen, *Time Out of Hand: Revolution and Reaction in Southeast Asia* (1970).

For bibliographical lists see E. David Cronon and Theodore D. Rosennof, eds., *The Second World War and the Atomic Age, 1940–1973* (1975) and Milton Leitenberg and Richard D. Burns, eds., *The Vietnam Conflict* (1973).

For brief studies of prominent individuals, see John A. Garraty, ed., *Encyclopedia of American Biography* (1974). Also see the following notes.

## Notes to Chapter 14

1. Quoted in Joseph L. Dees, "The Viet Cong Attack that Failed," *Department of State News Letter*, No. 85 (May, 1968), p. 22.
2. Tran-van Dinh, "Six Hours that Changed the Vietnam Situation: The New Year Siege of the Saigon Embassy," *Christian Century*, LXXXV (March 6, 1968), 289.
3. Don Oberdorfer, *Tet!* (Garden City, New York: Doubleday, 1971), p. 25.
4. Quoted *ibid.*, p. 18.
5. Quoted *ibid.*, p. 33, and in Frances Fitzgerald, *Fire in the Lake: The Vietnamese and the Americans in Vietnam* (New York: Vintage Books, 1972), p. 518.
6. Peter A. Poole, *The United States and Indochina from FDR to Nixon* (Hinsdale, Ill.: The Dryden Press, 1973), p. 177.
7. Quoted in Robert Shaplen, *Time Out of Hand: Revolution and Reaction in Southeast Asia* (New York: Harper Colophon Books, 1970; rev. ed.), p. 408.
8. *Department of State Bulletin*, LVIII (March 4, 1968), 304.
9. *Time*, XLI (February 9, 1968), 15.
10. Fitzgerald, *Fire in the Lake*, p. 524.
11. Shaplen, *Time Out of Hand*, p. 416.
12. William C. Westmoreland, *A Soldier Reports* (Garden City, N.Y.: Doubleday, 1976), p. 348.
13. Quoted in Townsend Hoopes, *The Limits of Intervention* (New York: David McKay, 1969), p. 213.
14. Quoted in George McTurnan Kahin and John W. Lewis, *The United States in Vietnam* (New York: Dell, 1969; rev. ed.), p. 373.
15. Quoted in George A. Bailey and Lawrence W. Lichty,

"Rough Justice on a Saigon Street: A Gatekeeper Study of NBC's Tet Execution Film," *Journalism Quarterly*, XLIX (Summer, 1972), 222.
16. *Public Papers of the Presidents: Lyndon B. Johnson, 1968* (Washington: Government Printing Office, 1970), p. 152.
17. Westmoreland, *A Soldier Reports*, p. 311.
18. Quoted in *Newsweek*, LXXI (February 19, 1968), 24.
19. Ward Just, "That Long Night at the U.S. Embassy," *Wall Street Journal*, February 19, 1968, p. 20.
20. *Washington Post*, March 6, 1968.
21. U.S. Senate, Foreign Relations Committee, *Foreign Assistance Act of 1968—Part 1—Vietnam* (Washington: Government Printing Office, 1968), p. 100.
22. *Department of State Bulletin*, LVIII (February 26, 1968), 261.
23. Lyndon B. Johnson, *The Vantage Point: Perspectives of the Presidency, 1963–1969* (New York: Holt, Rinehart and Winston, 1971), p. 384.
24. Quoted in *Public Papers, Johnson, 1968*, p. 287.
25. Quoted in Hoopes, *Limits of Intervention*, p. 149.
26. William V. Shannon, "Viet Cong Escalation," *Commonweal*, LXXXVII (February 23, 1968), 613.
27. Quoted in Marvin Kalb and Elie Abel, *Roots of Involvement* (New York: W. W. Norton, 1971), p. 211.
28. John B. Henry II, "February, 1968," *Foreign Policy*, No. 4 (Fall, 1971), p. 19.
29. Quoted in Kalb and Abel, *Roots of Involvement*, p. 235.
30. Clark M. Clifford, "A Viet Nam Reappraisal," *Foreign Affairs*, XLVII (July, 1969), 612.
31. Hoopes, *Limits of Intervention*, p. 217.

32. *Public Papers, Johnson, 1968*, p. 470.

33. Jean Lacouture, *Ho Chi Minh: A Political Biography* (New York: Vintage Books, [1967], 1968), p. 3.

34. Joseph Buttinger, *Vietnam: A Dragon Embattled* (New York: Frederick A. Praeger, 1967; 2 vols.), I, 174–175.

35. Quoted in U.S. Senate, Committee on Foreign Relations, *The United States and Vietnam: 1944–1947* (Washington: Government Printing Office, 1972), p. 3.

36. Quoted in Christopher Thorne, "Indochina and Anglo-American Relations, 1942–1945," *Pacific Historical Review, XLIV* (February, 1976), 93.

37. Quoted in Walter LaFeber, "Roosevelt, Churchill, and Indochina: 1942–45," *American Historical Review, LXXX* (December, 1975), 1289.

38. Quoted in Gary R. Hess, "Franklin Roosevelt and Indochina," *Journal of American History, LIX* (September, 1972), 364.

39. LaFeber, "Roosevelt, Churchill, and Indochina," p. 1295.

40. Clifford, "Viet Nam Reappraisal," p. 603.

41. Quoted in U.S. Senate, *United States and Vietnam: 1944–1947*, pp. 18, 21.

42. Quoted in New York Times, *The Pentagon Papers* (New York: Bantam Books, 1971), p. 14.

43. Bernard Fall, *The Two Viet-Nams* (New York: Frederick A. Praeger, 1967; 2nd ed.), p. 233.

44. Robert Shaplen, *The Lost Revolution* (New York: Harper and Row, 1965), p. 98.

45. Quoted *ibid.*

46. Quoted in Kahin and Lewis, *United States in Vietnam*, p. 61.

47. Quoted in Robert A. Divine, "The Education of John F. Kennedy," in Frank Merli and Theodore Wilson, eds., *Makers of American Diplomacy* (New York: Charles Scribner's Sons, 1974), p. 623.

48. Quoted in Theodore C. Sorensen, *Kennedy* (New York: Harper and Row, 1965), p. 199.

49. Divine, "Education of John F. Kennedy," p. 621.

50. *New York Times*, August 25, 1960.

51. Quoted in Richard J. Walton, *Cold War and Counterrevolution: The Foreign Policy of John F. Kennedy* (Baltimore: Penguin Books, [1972], 1973, p. 9.

52. *Public Papers, John F. Kennedy, 1962* (Washington: Government Printing Office, 1963), p. 807.

53. Walt W. Rostow, "The Third Round," *Foreign Affairs, XLII* (October, 1963), 5–6.

54. Don Ferguson in Peter Joseph, *Good Times: An Oral History of America in the Nineteen Sixties* (New York: William Morrow, 1974), p. 4.

55. *Ibid.*, p. 54.

56. Arthur M. Schlesinger, Jr., *A Thousand Days: John F. Kennedy in the White House* (Boston: Houghton Mifflin, 1965), p. 259.

57. James Barber, *The Presidential Character* (Englewood Cliffs, N.J.: Prentice-Hall, 1972), p. 298.

58. Quoted in Kenneth P. O'Donnell and David F. Powers, *"Johnny, We Hardly Knew Ye": Memoirs of John Fitzgerald Kennedy* (Boston: Little, Brown, 1972), p. 287.

59. Midge Decter, "Kennedyism," *Commentary, XLIX* (January, 1970), 21.

60. Oral History Interview by Chester Bowles, pp. 49, 90, John F. Kennedy Library, Massachusetts.

61. Schlesinger, *A Thousand Days*, p. 217.

62. *Public Papers, Kennedy, 1961* (Washington: Government Printing Office, 1962), pp. 1–3.

63. Theodore H. White, "The Action Intellectuals," *Life, LXII* (June, 1967), 43.

64. Quoted in David Halberstam, "The Programming of Robert McNamara," *Harper's Magazine, CCXLII* (February, 1971), 62.

65. Quoted in Roger Hilsman, *To Move a Nation: The Politics of Foreign Policy in the Administration of John F. Kennedy* (Garden City, N.Y.: Doubleday, 1967), p. 523.

66. Sorensen, *Kennedy*, p. 270.

67. Quoted in David Halberstam, *The Best and the Brightest* (Greenwich, Conn.: Fawcett Publications, 1973), p. 770.

68. "Memorandum of Conversation with President Johnson," by Max Frankel, July 8, 1965, Box 1, "Black Notebooks," Arthur Krock Papers, Princeton University Library, Princeton, New Jersey.

69. *Public Papers, Dwight D. Eisenhower, 1959* (Washington: Government Printing Office, 1960), p. 8.

70. "Biographic Briefing Book," June, 1961, Box 126, President's Office File, John F. Kennedy Papers, Kennedy Library.

71. Schlesinger, *A Thousand Days*, p. 348.

72. Quoted *ibid.*, p. 391.

73. *Public Papers, Kennedy, 1961*, pp. 534, 536.

74. *Ibid.*, *1963* (Washington: Government Printing Office, 1964), p. 524.

75. Memorandum by Arthur M. Schlesinger, Jr., [1961], Box 121, President's Office File, John F. Kennedy Papers, Kennedy Library.

76. Marcus G. Raskin and Bernard B. Fall, eds., *The Viet-Nam Reader* (New York: Vintage Books, 1967; rev. ed.), p. 113.

77. Quoted in Seyom Brown, *The Faces of Power* (New York: Columbia University Press, 1968), p. 164.

78. Memorandum by Arthur M. Schlesinger, Jr., [1961], Box 121, President's Office File, John F. Kennedy Papers, Kennedy Library.

79. Quoted in Frank Mankiewicz and Kirby Jones, *With Fidel: A Portrait of Castro and Cuba* (New York: Ballantine Books, 1975), p. 175.

80. Dean Rusk to G. Mennen Williams, January 8, 1962, Box 29, Records of G. Mennen Williams, Department of State Records, National Archives, Washington, D.C.

81. William Attwood, *The Reds and the Blacks: A Personal Adventure* (New York: Harper & Row, 1967), p. 219.

82. Quoted in Walter LaFeber, ed., *America in the Cold War* (New York: John Wiley & Sons, 1969), p. 139.

83. *Public Papers, Eisenhower, 1960–61* (Washington: Government Printing Office, 1961), p. 567.

84. Philip W. Bonsal, *Cuba, Castro, and the United States* (Pittsburgh: University of Pittsburgh Press, 1971), p. 67.

85. Dwight D. Eisenhower, *The White House Years: Waging Peace, 1956–1961* (Garden City, N.Y.: Doubleday, 1965), p. 527.

86. Quoted in Walton, *Cold War and Counterrevolution*, pp. 36–37.

87. Quoted in Schlesinger, *A Thousand Days*, p. 251.

88. Walt W. Rostow, *The Diffusion of Power* (New York: Macmillan, 1972), pp. 210–211.

89. *Public Papers, Kennedy, 1961*, pp. 304–306.

90. Quoted in Stanley Meisler, "Reports and Comment: Cuba," *Atlantic Monthly*, CCXXXVI (September, 1975), 4.

91. Quoted in Hilsman, *To Move a Nation*, p. 157.

92. Quoted in Mankiewicz and Jones, *With Fidel*, p. 150.

93. Nikita S. Khrushchev, *Khrushchev Remembers* (New York: Bantam Books, 1971; trans. by Strobe Talbott), pp. 546–547.

94. Robert F. Kennedy, *Thirteen Days: A Memoir of the Cuban Missile Crisis* (New York: W. W. Norton, 1969), p. 31.

95. *Public Papers, Kennedy, 1962*, p. 808.

96. Quoted in Kennedy, *Thirteen Days*, p. 67.

97. Quoted in Hilsman, *To Move a Nation*, p. 219.

98. Rostow, *Diffusion of Power*, p. 297.

99. Quoted in Ronald Steel, "Endgame," *New York Review of Books*, March 13, 1969, p. 22.

100. John Kenneth Galbraith, "The Plain Lessons of a Bad Decade," *Foreign Policy*, No. 1 (Winter, 1970–71), 32.

101. Sorensen, *Kennedy*, p. 678.

102. Adolf A. Berle, *Navigating the Rapids, 1918–1971: From the Papers of Adolf A. Berle* (New York: Harcourt Brace Jovanovich, 1973), p. 774.

103. James A. Nathan, "The Missile Crisis: His Finest Hour Now," *World Politics*, XXVII (January, 1975), 269, 280–281.

104. Quoted *ibid.*, p. 274.

105. Memorandum for the President by Walt W. Rostow, March 29, 1961, Box 193, National Security Files, Kennedy Papers, Kennedy Library.

106. Quoted in Schlesinger, *A Thousand Days*, p. 330.

107. Eisenhower, *White House Years: Waging Peace*, p. 607.

108. Schlesinger, *A Thousand Days*, p. 324.

109. Quoted *ibid.*, p. 338.

110. Bernard Fall, *Anatomy of a Crisis: The Laotian Crisis of 1960–1961* (Garden City, N. Y.: Doubleday, 1969), p. 229.

111. Quoted in Rostow, *Diffusion of Power*, p. 265.

112. Quoted in Halberstam, *Best and the Brightest*, p. 167.

113. *Public Papers, Kennedy, 1963*, p. 673.

114. *Ibid.*, p. 659.

115. New York Times, *Pentagon Papers*, p. 129.

116. John Kenneth Galbraith, *Ambassador's Journal: A Personal Account of the Kennedy Years* (Boston: Houghton Mifflin, 1969), p. 311 (March 2, 1962).

117. U.S. Senate, *Foreign Assistance Act of 1968—Part I—Vietnam*, p. 218.

118. Quoted in John Mecklin, *Mission in Torment* (Garden City, N.Y.: Doubleday, 1965), p. 208.

119. Schlesinger, *A Thousand Days*, p. 997.

120. Quoted in Louise FitzSimons, *The Kennedy Doctrine* (New York: Random House, 1972), p. 15.

121. Quoted in Jim F. Heath, *Decade of Disillusionment: The Kennedy-Johnson Years* (Bloomington: Indiana University Press, 1975), p. 137.

122. John McDermott, "Welfare Imperialism in Vietnam," *The Nation*, CCIII (July 25, 1966), 85.

123. *Wall Street Journal*, January 21, 1971.

124. Quoted in Heath, *Decade*, p. 186.

125. Quoted in Barber, *Presidential Character*, pp. 51–52.

126. Quoted in Robert W. Sellen, "Old Assumptions versus New Realities: Lyndon Johnson and Foreign Policy," *International Journal*, XXVIII (Spring, 1973), 206.

127. Quoted in Hugh Sidey, *A Very Personal Presidency* (New York: Atheneum, 1968), p. 187.

128. Quoted in Barber, *Presidential Character*, p. 84.

129. Quoted in Eric F. Goldman, *The Tragedy of Lyndon Johnson* (New York: Alfred A. Knopf, 1969), pp. 484, 499; Halberstam, "Programming of Robert McNamara," p. 64.

130. Quoted in Philip Geyelin, *Lyndon B. Johnson and the World* (New York: Frederick A. Praeger, 1966), p. 20.

131. Quoted in Goldman, *Tragedy*, p. 382.

132. Quoted in Geyelin, *Lyndon B. Johnson*, p. 22.

133. Quoted in Barber, *Presidential Character*, p. 87.

134. J. William Fulbright, *The Arrogance of Power* (New York: Vintage Books, 1966) and *The Crippled Giant* (New York: Vintage Books, 1972).

135. Quoted in *Newsweek*, LXV (May 17, 1965), 52.

136. Fulbright, *Arrogance of Power*, pp. 91–92.

137. *Public Papers, Lyndon B. Johnson, 1965* (Washington: Government Printing Office, 1966; 2 vols.), I, 480.

138. Quoted in Kahin and Lewis, *United States and Vietnam*, p. 152.

139. *Public Papers, Lyndon Johnson, 1963–1964* (Washington: Government Printing Office, 1965; 2 vols.), II, 930.

140. *Congressional Record*, CX (August 7, 1964), 18471.

141. Quoted in Robert A. Divine, *Since 1945: Politics and Diplomacy in Recent American History* (New York: John Wiley and Sons, 1975), p. 148.

142. Arthur M. Schlesinger, *The Imperial Presidency* (New York: Popular Library, 1973).

143. *Department of State Bulletin*, LII (April 26, 1965), 607.

144. Quoted in Robert L. Beisner, "1898 and 1968: The Anti-Imperialists and the Doves," *Political Science Quarterly*, LXXXV (June, 1970), 197–198.

145. Quoted in New York Times, *Pentagon Papers*, p. 567.

146. Quoted in Doris Kearns, *Lyndon Johnson and the American Dream* (New York: Harper and Row, Publishers, 1976), p. 329.

147. Quoted in Jonathan Mirsky, "The Root of Resistance," *The Nation*, CCVII (August 5, 1968), 90.

148. Kahin and Lewis, *United States and Vietnam*, p. 370.

149. U.S. Senate, Committee on Foreign Relations, *Changing American Attitudes Toward Foreign Policy* (hearings), 90th Cong., 1st Sess. (February 20, 1967), p. 25.

150. Quoted in Heath, *Decade*, p. 249.

151. Quoted in Stephen Ambrose, *Rise to Globalism* (Baltimore: Penguin Books, 1976; rev. ed.), p. 313.

152. Goldman, *Tragedy*, p. 511.

153. Quoted in Donald F. Lach and Edmund S. Wehrle, *International Politics in East Asia Since World War II* (New York: Praeger Publishers, 1975), p. 338.

154. George W. Ball, *The Discipline of Power* (Boston: Little, Brown, 1968), p. 321.

155. Clifford, "Viet Nam Reappraisal," p. 608.

156. Quoted in Johnson, *Vantage Point*, p. 568.

**At the Great Wall, 1972.**
President Richard M.
Nixon and Patricia Nixon
visited the Great Wall during their momentous trip
to China in February.
(White House)

# 15 The Diffusion of World Power: American Foreign Policy Since 1969

## Diplomatic Crossroad: Richard M. Nixon to China, 1972

The President's chief security officer aboard the aircraft radioed an American agent at the Peking airport below: "What about the crowd?" The answer came back: "There is no crowd." The disbelieving officer asked: "Did you say, 'No crowd'?"[1] Indeed, when President Richard M. Nixon's blue and silver jet, the *Spirit of '76,* touched down on the Chinese runway that wintry morning of February 21, 1972, the reception was decidedly restrained and spartan. Apparently the Chinese wanted observers to think the United States was more eager than the People's Republic of China for this dramatic meeting. Usually the Chinese greeted visiting dignitaries at the Capital Airport with cheering schoolchildren waving flags. "A vast silence" welcomed Nixon.[2] When the President emerged from the plane he rather awkwardly kept his arms to his sides, difficult for one who habitually waved his hands high when departing an aircraft. At the foot of the stairs stood trim seventy-three-year-old Premier Chou En-lai in grey overcoat, a veteran Communist who had served Chairman Mao Tse-tung as key administrator since the success of the Chinese Revolution in 1949. An American aide complained that "Chou had a faint come-to-me smile and I was afraid they were going to portray the President as a supplicant."[3]

Nixon and Chou formally shook hands—the very gesture that Secretary John Foster Dulles had spurned at Geneva in 1954. The Premier noticed Henry A. Kissinger and purred, "Ah, old friend."[4] The television cameras whirred, sending back to the United States, via satellite, picture postcards of the historic encounter. The ceremony was brief, with no speeches. The People's Liberation Army Band played the American national anthem and "The March of the Volunteers," the Chinese anthem. A large banner hung at the airport: "Make trouble, fail; make trouble again, fail again; make trouble until doom: that is the logic of the imperialists and reactionaries."[5] Chou and Nixon left quickly for the eighteen-mile trip to Peking, passing a grey landscape of communes, their caretakers indoors to escape the freezing temperatures. Pictures of Mao and political signs hung everywhere. "Serve the people" seemed a popular slogan. The Chinese apparently painted over one poster which had read: "We must Defeat the U.S. Aggressors and All Their Running Dogs Wherever They May Be."[6]

Nixon's "journey for peace" marked a dramatic event in diplomatic history.[7] At the time, neither China nor the United States formally recognized the other. Since 1949 they had engaged in numerous crises and considerable name-calling. Each tagged the other an "aggressor"; each had created an image of the other as the demon monster incapable of rational action. Washington maintained diplomatic relations with Chiang Kai-shek's creation, the Republic of China on Taiwan, which Peking considered a rebellious province. In early 1969, however, newly inaugurated President Nixon instructed his Assistant for National Security Affairs, Henry A. Kissinger, to restudy relations with Peking. The United States soon urged a reopening in Warsaw of Sino-American talks, suspended since early 1968 because of China's protests over American warfare in Vietnam. Those Warsaw talks started again in early 1970. The year before, the United States had relaxed trade and travel restrictions and tamed Seventh Fleet operations in the Taiwan Straits. Quietly the Nixon Administration dropped the pejorative phrasing "Red China," and Chou hinted that China would "open" its "door" to the United States.[8] Suddenly, in April of 1971, an American table tennis team competing in Japan received and accepted an invitation from Peking to visit China. Quips about "Ping-Pong diplomacy" did not detract from the seriousness of the invitation. Kissinger made contact with Chinese officials through Pakistan and secretly flew to Peking on July 9. On July 15, President Nixon captured headlines and confused analysts when he announced that he would go to China to "seek the normalization of relations"[9] Although his speech did not explain the turnaround, it was like a "home run," said one admirer. The ambassador to the United States from Taiwan called it a "shabby deal."[10] Nixon himself thought it comparable to a moonshot. In October the United States stood aside to permit the United Nations to seat the People's Republic of China and oust Taiwan. Stunned Cold Warriors asked how one of their own could betray the past and sit down with the detested Chinese Communists. A conservative journalist later grumbled: "He [the President] would toast Alger Hiss tonight, if he could find him."[11]

Richard M. Nixon, who as a congressman had hounded alleged spy Alger Hiss in the days of McCarthyism, most assuredly would not have gone that far in repudiating the past. Still, world politics had changed since the 1950s. The trip of 20,395 miles, Nixon said, "will signal the end of a sterile and barren interlude in the relationship between two great peoples."[12] That comment in itself explained much. The absence of formal relations with the most populous nation in the world served no useful diplomatic purpose. Opened relations, however, promised a number of advantages. First, because of the gaping Sino-Soviet split, American recognition of China would keep Moscow wondering what Washington intended and conceivably might permit the United States to play off the antagonistic Communist nations against one another. As one journalist put it: "The President is in the position of the lovely maiden courted by two ardent swains [China and Russia], each of whom is aware of the other but each of whom is uncertain of what happens when the young lady is alone with his rival."[13] And the great China market once again loomed large in American imaginations. With the American economy sagging in the early 1970s, trade with China seemed to beckon as

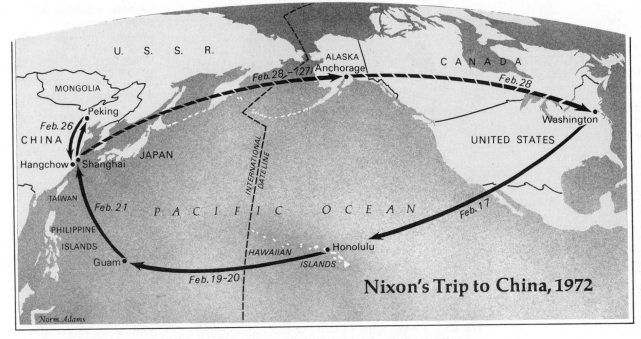

**Nixon's Trip to China, 1972**

possible relief. Another explanation can be found in China's possession of nuclear weapons. Peking had not yet been brought into international antiproliferation arrangements. Without Chinese participation, nuclear arms control agreements were ultimately feeble. Then, too, American recognition of China might encourage Peking to reduce its aid to North Vietnam and to urge a political settlement upon Hanoi.

The China trip also promised profits in American politics. Some commentators spoke of "The Peking Primary."[14] Antiwar Democratic Senator George McGovern had launched a conspicuous campaign against the Nixon Administration's continued intervention in Vietnam, and in March New Hampshire voters would go to

**Marco Polo.** Political cartoonist Ray Osrin portrayed two reasons for the Nixon journey to China, 1972. (Ray Osrin in *The Cleveland Plain Dealer*)

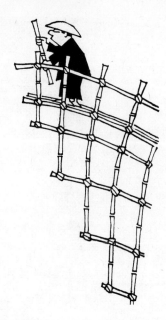

**"A Brick, A Bamboo, A
Brick, A Bamboo . . ."**
China and the United
States began building
bridges toward one
another in the late 1960s
and early 1970s. (Pierre,
*Aux Ecoutes*)

the polls in the first presidential primary of 1972. "Look," Kissinger remarked
frankly, "it wasn't just a matter of this summit—[Nixon's] political ass was on the
line."[15] Liberal-left Americans had been calling for relations with China for years,
and Democrats soon fell over one another to applaud the Nixon journey. At the
same time, the right wing of the Republican party could hardly charge that Nixon,
the proven anti-Communist, was soft on communism. Finally, overarching all
explanations was the place of the China journey in the general Nixon-Kissinger
policy of "détente"—the relaxation of international tensions to protect American
global interests. "Do we talk about our differences, or do we fight about our
differences?" asked the President.[16]

The Chinese had their own reasons for inviting Nixon. The United States no
longer ranked as the greatest threat to China. In the immediate years preceding the
Nixon trip, Sino-Soviet relations had seriously deteriorated. Military skirmishes on
the shared border erupted in 1969 and many Chinese, recalling the brutal Russian
invasion of Czechoslovakia in 1968, feared a Soviet attack. The Soviet Union
constructed an air base in Mongolia; the Chinese dug air-raid shelters and tunnel
networks. Sino-American ties, then, might strengthen China by deterring the
Soviets. "The principle of using barbarians to control barbarians," Asian specialist
James C. Thomson, Jr. noted, "is hardly new to Chinese geopolitics."[17] China also
feared a revived Japan, and a Sino-American rapprochement might unsettle Japan,
keeping it off guard and cautious. Or it might, as it did, lead to the opening of
Sino-Japanese relations, thereby further strengthening China against Russia.
Furthermore, China was interested in trade and in reducing the American commitment to the regime on Taiwan. The reception on February 21, 1972, then,
although chilly, did not unduly alarm American diplomats, because the trip itself
represented profound and enduring questions of national security for both China
and the United States.

On the flight from the United States to China, Nixon, Kissinger, and their aides
studied lengthy black notebooks about Chinese politics, culture, and diplomacy.
The planes, reported the *New York Times*, were "air-borne universities."[18] The

President also practiced with chopsticks and learned to say *Ni hau* ("How are you?"). Making this excursion with him was a press corps of eighty-seven, heavy with television newspeople, and a presidential party numbering thirty-seven, including Secretary of State William Rogers, upstaged as always by Kissinger. The American delegation also carried with it American champagne, cigarettes, and Milton and Matilda, two North American musk oxen coveted by the Peking Zoo. The Chinese reciprocated with Hsing-Hsing and Ling-Ling, two giant panda bears destined for the Washington Zoo. Americans carried specially printed souvenir matchbooks and wore flags in their lapels. All in all, the Nixon journey was a carefully staged diplomatic performance, which the President made sure ran on prime-time evening television screens back home.

The President had hardly settled into his guesthouse when he received a telephone call. Mao requested a meeting at the chairman's residence. Soon seated in overstuffed chairs in a room cluttered with books, Nixon, Kissinger, Mao, and Chou talked vigorously for about an hour, with "Nancy" Tang Wen-sheng, a Radcliffe graduate and Chinese citizen, serving as interpreter. Secretary Rogers had not been invited. Seventy-eight-year-old Mao was an imposing figure, to the Chinese almost godlike as the leader of the Long March and father of the People's Republic. "He has the quality of being at the center wherever he stood," remarked Kissinger. "It moved with him wherever he moved."[19] Chou too impressed. Always polite, the crew-cut, bushy-eyebrowed Chou was tireless and affable. Born into a well-to-do Mandarin family, he spoke English, Russian, French, and Japanese as well as Chinese. A skillful negotiator with a sharp memory, he handled the day-to-day diplomatic chores and never sought the limelight. Chou had met with American officials in Chungking during the war and bargained with General George C. Marshall during the abortive Marshall mission to China in the 1940s. American diplomats greatly respected him. In turn Chou had lofty words for Nixon's chief adviser: "Kissinger? There is a man who knows the language of both worlds—his own and ours."[20]

In the evening of February 21, 1972, in the Great Hall of the People, Chou hosted a massive banquet of 800 guests who were served, among other delicacies, shark's fin. Sipping glasses of *mao tai,* a potent 150 proof rice liquor, Nixon and Chou, Americans and Chinese, generously toasted one another. Chou applauded the "positive move" toward formal relations.[21] Nixon became effusive. As a Chinese military band somewhat stiltingly played "Home on the Range," the President uttered *"kan pei"* ("bottoms up") and remarked: "Never have I heard American music played better in a foreign land." He continued with exaggerations: "What we do here can change the world." Tearing a page from Chinese Communist history, he called for a "long march together." And he even quoted Mao himself: "Seize the day, seize the hour." "This is the hour," proclaimed the President.[22]

On Tuesday, February 22, Nixon and Chou conferred for much of the afternoon. Newspeople could learn little, began to grumble about the secrecy surrounding the talks, and thus toured Peking and reported on the Chinese life-style—clean streets, gauze masks to prevent infectious diseases, acupuncture techniques for surgery, anti-imperialist banners, expertise in table tennis, regimented schools, puritanical social habits, irrigation systems, the improvement in nutrition and health since 1949, Mao's photographs plastered on village walls, thousands of bicycles on Peking's streets, the monotony of blue dress, tree-lined avenues, and the pioneering and diligent character of the Chinese. Flamboyant conservative and fervent anti-Communist William Buckley did not appreciate the comments of a Nixon aide who found the journalist in a souvenir store: "Doing a little trading with the enemy, Bill?"[23] Although Buckley resisted new attitudes, images did change quickly. After years of thinking the Chinese were a bestial enemy, Americans soon considered them human, loving and suffering like the rest of mankind. Whereas in the 1960s Americans used words like "ignorant, warlike, treacherous, and sly" to describe the "Red Chinese," in 1972 they described them as "hard-working, intelligent, progressive, artistic, and practical."[24] As for Chinese images, in an unusual issue, the *Peking Daily* of February 22 carried pictures of Nixon's meeting with Mao. No longer was the American the demonic traducer. Any friend of Mao's became a friend of China's.

That evening a touch of the past was portrayed in *The Red Detachment of Women*, a ballet drama about a young Chinese woman who joins the Communist party and slays the tyrant. More meetings and more entertainment followed. On February 24 the presidential party visited the Great Wall, where Nixon, television cameras in place, uttered a memorable banality: "I think that you would have to conclude that this is a great wall. . . . As we look at this wall, we do not want walls of any kind between peoples."[25] On his way back to the airport Nixon passed a children's park; twenty-five years before, under Chiang, it had been a golf course for foreigners fronted by a sign: "No Chinese Allowed."

On February 27, after much Sino-American bickering, a joint communiqué was issued, but a weary Kissinger proved extremely evasive in elaborating upon its meaning. One State Department official said there had been "no pulling of punches" in the discussions.[26] Nixon later commented that he "talked cold turkey" with Chou.[27] Before he traveled to China, the President had stated that "we do not expect instant solutions to deep-seated differences," and he depicted the talks as a "dialogue" rather than "negotiations," a "launching of a process."[28] The joint communiqué suggested in fact that the Chinese and Americans had agreed to disagree. The Americans stated that they wanted peace in Asia, with "social progress for all peoples . . . free of outside pressure or intervention." The com-

**Meeting with Chou.** Secretary of State William Rogers, President Nixon, and Premier Chou En-lai during one of their meetings in February, 1972. Rogers was a policy implementer rather than formulator. (Department of State *Newsletter*)

**Peking Ball Park.** This advertisement, titled "Yankees come here," reads: "The way things are going in China, hot dogs will be sold right along with egg rolls." Mao, of course, neither donned a New York Yankees uniform, nor carried a baseball bat, nor blasted a home run over the Great Wall, but in the flush times of Sino-American relations after Nixon's trip, exaggerations like this one proliferated. (Lucy Gould, *Parade.* Courtesy of Frankfurt Communications, Inc., New York)

muniqué noted that these words applied to Vietnam, from which the United States hoped to withdraw after a negotiated settlement. The United States, furthermore, would maintain friendly relations with South Korea and Japan. The Chinese stated in the joint communiqué that they would continue to support "the struggles of all oppressed people" against large nations which attempt to "bully" the small. All foreign troops should be withdrawn from Asia, especially Vietnam. Both parties agreed that "neither should seek hegemony in the Asia-Pacific region and each is opposed to efforts by any other country or group of countries to establish such hegemony," an apparent slap at Russia.[29]

Then came the "murderously tough problem" of Taiwan, which the United States still recognized as the official government of China.[30] In the joint communiqué, the Chinese stated that Taiwan was the "crucial question obstructing the normalization of relations between China and the United States." The United States should withdraw its military forces from the island. There is only one China. The American response was equivocal, calling for "a peaceful settlement of the Taiwan question by the Chinese themselves."[31] But the United States would reduce its military installations on Taiwan. Finally, both sides appealed for increased cultural and commercial contacts. On the seventh day of his China trip, February 28, the President bid farewell at Shanghai to his gracious Chinese hosts, declaring with trite hyperbole that "this was the week that changed the world."[32]

## Nixon-Kissinger Foreign Policy and Détente

President Richard M. Nixon liked the "big play" in his quest for the "title of peacemaker."[33] The Nixon presidency, 1969–1974, witnessed striking diplomatic changes, heralded by some as the "Great Nixon Turnaround."[34] Few expected the once truculent Cold Warrior to negotiate with Communists or to thaw the Cold War through a policy of "détente." Nixon urged the American people to accept both Soviet Russia and the People's Republic of China as legitimate nations with which the United States could negotiate. Gone was the once popular idea of an international and monolithic Communist conspiracy. Americans would still confuse nationalism with communism, but the multipolar world was accepted as reality. Détente in fact became a new way of containing nationalism and revolution. That is, as Dr. Henry A. Kissinger (national security affairs adviser, 1969–1973, and secretary of state, 1973–1977) interpreted the configuration of world affairs, there were five power centers: Russia, America, China, Japan, the Common Market nations of Western Europe. Each had a responsibility to keep order in its region and not to intrude in areas dominated by the others. In this way, small nations could no longer play off one great power against another and could not count on outside help. In essence, the scheme presumed to grant the United States more freedom and flexibility in its diplomacy toward Latin America and the same for Russia in Eastern Europe. This five-way balance of power would also permit the United States to contain both Russia and China at the same time by having them contain each other. The Sino-Soviet split was a reality Americans now recognized and welcomed. Détente was also a cheaper way of pursuing the containment doctrine; it did not require as many interventions or weapons expenditures (Nixon reduced the armed forces from 3.5 million in 1968 to 2.3 million in 1973 and ended the draft). Détente permitted serious discussions of Soviet-American arms control, evidenced in the Strategic Arms Limitation Talks (SALT) at Helsinki, which in 1972 produced curbs on defensive nuclear weapons and an interim agreement on offensive weapons systems. The 1975 Helsinki accords accepted the inviolability of European borders, thereby confirming the boundaries of Eastern Europe outlined three decades earlier.

Détente simply made common sense. The Cold War was costing too much, nonrecognition of China had proven a failure, and the Congress, aroused over Vietnam, was demanding a more limited role for the United States overseas. At a time when American foreign trade needed a boost to eliminate a billion-dollar balance of payments deficit and to overcome challenges from Japan, détente promised new markets. Soon massive grain shipments would flow to Russia, and American businessmen would flock to Peking in revived pursuit of the great China market dream. Détente was thus happily seized upon as a convenient and necessary step toward world stability. As Nixon put it, the "five great economic superpowers will determine the economic future, and, because economic power will be the key to other kinds of power, [they will determine] the future of the world in other ways in the last of this century."[35] Détente was premised, however, on a shaky point: Third World nations would stay in their place and the great powers could manage affairs. Kissinger would spend much of his time trying to keep the scheme glued together, endangered as it constantly was by violent conflicts in Asia, Africa, and the Middle East, and by economic challenges from OPEC (Organization of Petroleum Exporting Countries). Détente was also hostage at times to terrorists and airborne hijacking guerrillas, who continually disrupted political agreements. To disarm critics of this new brand of globalism and to discredit advocates of a retrenchment from overcommitment and empire like Walter Lippmann, J. William Fulbright, and George F. Kennan, the Nixon Administration conjured up exaggerated images of "neo-isolationism" and then denounced it as a withdrawal from world responsibility reminiscent of the fateful 1930s. Détente did not mean an end to globalism, but a change in tactics. "[Woodrow] Wilson had the greatest vision of America's world role," Nixon concluded. "But he wasn't practical enough."[36]

Richard Milhous Nixon was extremely self-conscious about his own future place in history and secretly taped conversations in the White House so that his legacy would be remembered accurately. Ultimately this quest for historical stature via the tape recorder ended his presidency. The White House maneuverings during "Watergate," that affair of massive political corruption at home, were dutifully recorded. When made public by court order, the tapes inspired an impeachment process that Nixon, caught in numerous barefaced lies, himself terminated by resigning from the presidency on August 8, 1974. Nixon had frankly considered himself a "sovereign" who could break laws to protect national security.[37] The "Watergate" corruption included the wiretapping of telephones of foreign policy advisers and newsmen. The exposure of such illegal behavior weakened the White House's position in the on-going struggle with Congress over policymaking, and stripped the sacred garb from the phrase "national security," which Nixon had invoked to keep the tapes secret for months. Yet the political scandal did not basically interrupt the Nixon-Kissinger foreign policy. Gerald Ford, a hardworking, honest, but lackluster former congressman from Michigan, succeeded Nixon, continued détente, and retained Henry Kissinger.

An ambitious Harvard political scientist of German-Jewish ancestry, with an Old World accent, the very influential Kissinger had escaped from Nazism in 1938.

**"Some Chicken, Some Egg."** Henry A. Kissinger (1923—) received his doctorate in 1954 from Harvard, where he taught until Nixon appointed him national security affairs adviser in 1969. An architect of détente, the German-born political scientist also undertook extensive travel to trouble spots like the Middle East and Africa to conduct personal negotiations. Critics on the left compared him to "Dr. Strangelove," the slightly deranged fictional character in the movie by that name who perpetrated a nuclear holocaust. Critics on the right thought Kissinger too conciliatory to the dreaded Communists. (*The Economist*, London, 1975)

| *Presidents* | *Secretaries of State* |
| --- | --- |
| Richard M. Nixon, 1969–1974 | William P. Rogers, 1969–1973 |
| Gerald Ford, 1974–1977 | Henry A. Kissinger, 1973–1977 |
| James Carter, 1977— | Cyrus A. Vance, 1977— |

He spent much of his academic life advising politicians and Pentagon officials. In the 1950s, in his book *Nuclear Weapons and Foreign Policy* (1957), he criticized "massive retaliation" for limiting American choices and rejected Kennan's "disengagement" proposals. He also wrote a book on the Congress of Vienna of 1815, extolling the conservative balance-of-power techniques Austria's Prince Metternich used to curb revolution. Considered a pragmatist rather than an ideologue, Kissinger acted as the architect of the détente policy under Nixon. (For 1969–1973, the secretary of state was actually William P. Rogers, a quiet, evenhanded man often overshadowed and embarrassed by Kissinger's mastery of foreign policy-making.) Reflective, charming, witty, seldom rattled, never giddy, energetic, overlabored in style, and persistent, Kissinger became the most traveled secretary of state in American history, in what critics identified as "personal diplomacy." Indeed, he distrusted and bypassed the bureaucracy, and many of his agreements were based on the word of gentlemen or on the perpetuation in office of foreign leaders he had befriended. The danger remained that a change in leadership might undo Kissinger's personally fashioned agreements. During his tenure as a White House adviser, Kissinger did not have to appear before congressional committees; he left that chore to an ill-equipped Rogers, as Nixon declared the shield of "executive privilege" for his assistant. But once Kissinger entered the State Department, congressmen began to criticize what a senator called "one-man authoritarianism."[38] Kissinger fought back and launched a campaign for continued presidential supremacy and secrecy in foreign affairs. "What the hell is an Establishment for, if it's not to support the President?" Kissinger responded when confronted with a growing disenchantment over executive authority in policy-making among academicians, businessmen, and lawyers, many of whom had frequented the halls of the Council on Foreign Relations or written for its prestigious journal *Foreign Affairs*.[39] Still, emboldened in part by the apparent vulnerability of the presidency during the "Watergate" crisis of 1973–1974, Congress passed the limited War Powers Act (1973), wherein the President could commit American forces abroad for sixty days, but after that period would need to request congressional approval. Congress also made cuts in or ordered restrictions on foreign aid, to Turkey, Cambodia, South Vietnam, and Angola, for example.

Kissinger, despite these intragovernmental tussles, was a popular secretary of state, in part because of his coolheaded handling of doubters and patient diplomatic bargaining in the Middle East. He was the only member of the Nixon team to enjoy good press relations, occasionally "leaking" secret information to reporters to generate favorable newspaper stories. Kissinger also cultivated a "swinger" image until his marriage in 1974. He visited nightclubs arm-in-arm with attractive women, including Hollywood star Jill St. John, and seemed to thrive on the public twittering about his smiling approval of a belly-dancer, a moment captured by a photographer. The secretary remarked that "I've always acted alone. Americans admire this enormously. Americans admire the cowboy leading the caravan alone astride his horse. . . . This romantic, surprising character suits me." In negotiations, "my playboy reputation has been and still is useful, because it has helped and helps to reassure people, to show them I'm not a museum piece."[40] Although Kissinger was widely respected, his popularity suffered from his wiretapping of aides and journalists, his loyalty to a deceitful President in the basest days of the "Watergate" blot, his endorsement of Nixon's virtual suspension of civil liberties to silence critics, his support for CIA efforts to undermine the constitutionally elected government of Salvador Allende in Chile (1973), his promotion of massive arms sales abroad to win "friends," and his approval of a new, utterly inhumane bombing of North Vietnam. Nonetheless, in 1973 he was awarded the Nobel Peace Prize for his negotiation of a Vietnamese settlement permitting American withdrawal. An admirer once approached him at a Washington gathering and said, "Dr. Kissinger, I want to thank you for saving the world." The secretary replied, "You're welcome."[41] Generally, observers thought Kissinger a better tactical negotiator than strategist.

Kissinger's secret negotiations prepared the way for the stunning Nixon expedition to Peking in 1972. This venture produced the vague Shanghai communiqué and an exchange of "liaison" representatives in 1973. One nasty result of the Sino-American détente was American backing in 1972 for an ally of China's, Pakistan, in its futile but ruthless attempt to crush a secessionist rebellion in East Pakistan (Bangladesh) supported by India, an enemy of China's. The old adage that "the enemy [China] of my enemy [Russia] is my friend" seemed to apply. Another result manifested itself in trade relations. In 1973 United States exports to China reached $700 million and giant companies like Boeing, Radio Corporation of America, and Monsanto Chemical signed contracts. One hundred American businessmen participated in the Spring, 1973 Canton Fair. One State Department official believed, furthermore, that "trade fosters habits and attitudes of adaptation, accommodation and agreement which, hopefully, will be carried over into political and security relationships."[42] Whether the Sino-American détente would persist remained an open question in the late 1970s, especially after the deaths of Chou En-lai and Mao Tse-tung.

Moscow worried about this American rapprochement with an adversary of the Soviets. Peking in turn had to be concerned when the Nixon-Kissinger team journeyed to Russia in May of 1972. At the Moscow summit, Russia and America agreed to cooperate in space exploration (a joint space venture was launched in 1975), to improve trade relations (grain sales to Russia followed), to restrict the deployment of antiballistic missiles (ABMs), to suspend the building of ICBM's, and to set a ceiling on missile-launching submarines. The final drafting of the complex arms agreements was left to the technical staffs at the SALT talks in Helsinki. After SALT, although Russia retained superiority in the total number of missiles, the United States held nuclear parity because many of its missiles were fitted with multiple warheads, each targeted for a different site (MIRVs). The two behemoths possessed enough nuclear power to destroy the other several times ("overkill"). And with orbiting space satellites providing surveillance, neither power could easily conceal its missile tests or war preparations. The conferees also discussed Vietnam; they concluded that small nations should not interfere with détente. Satisfied with the summit, Kissinger reflected that "I don't think our relationships will ever be the same."[43] One by-product of détente was a 1972 accord between the two Germanies. Largely the work of West German Chancellor Willy Brandt, the agreement virtually recognized the permanent division of Germany and eased travel between the two Berlins. Russia also promised not to impede access to West Berlin. The "German problem" had finally found a solution. The Berlin Wall still stood as a reminder of bitter Cold War days, but it had been hurdled.

## Over at Last: Exit from Vietnam

"What we are doing now with China is so great, so historic, the word 'Vietnam' will be only a footnote when it is written in history," Kissinger declared in 1971.[44] That prognostication will certainly prove absurd, but once the Nixon Administration embarked upon détente, Vietnam as a problem in the great balance of power scheme took on less significance. Vietnam became, in the words of a senior White House official, simply a "cruel side show."[45] Indeed, one of the offshoots of détente was the Soviet and Chinese aloofness when the United States resumed massive bombing of the North. Leaders in Moscow, Peking, and Washington were willing to write off Vietnam as a bad investment. The question was under what terms the United States could withdraw from the war and achieve a "peace with honor," to use Nixon's constant refrain. During the presidential campaign of 1968, Nixon repeatedly but imprecisely claimed he had a plan for ending the bloodshed in Vietnam. When pressed he usually begged off from specifics and simply recalled that Eisenhower had ended the Korean War shortly after taking office. Ultimately his program for "peace" included toughness at the Paris conference, renewed bombing of the North, and "Vietnamization"—building up South Vietnamese military forces to do the fighting formerly done by Americans. The President in 1969 also declared the rather fuzzy, seemingly restrictive "Nixon Doctrine"—the United States would assist only those Asian nations that helped themselves. Since he also rejected the containment of China as a rationale for the American presence in Vietnam, it was not clear to many critics why the United States did not pull out of the nearly destroyed territory "lock, stock and barrel," as Senate majority leader Mike Mansfield demanded.[46] Washington did begin to remove American troops, cutting the number to 474,000 in January, 1970, and to 139,000 by the end of 1971.

In Paris the talks stalled over the scheduling of troop withdrawals by North Vietnam and the United States from the South and over the postwar political arrangement. Meanwhile the fighting continued, accelerated by a Viet Cong offensive beginning February, 1969. In April, 1970, the Nixon Administration stunned the world by launching an offensive operation against Cambodia to interdict supply routes and drive North Vietnamese soldiers from their Cambodian sanctuary. Demonstrations rocked the United States over this bold enlargement of the war. At Kent State University in Ohio and Jackson State College in Mississippi, demonstrators were beaten back by rifles, and the sight of unarmed students lying dead on campuses horrified Americans. The Senate, in another attempt to reduce the power of the "imperial presidency" by the Cooper-Church Amendment to a military bill, voted to forbid the further expenditure of funds for fighting in Cambodia. Still, Cambodia had become a new battleground in Indochina. Laos, at

**"We Demand: Strike!"** The thrust into Cambodia in 1970 prompted a new wave of domestic protests, including a demand from the radical Boston paper *Old Mole* that students go on strike. Many universities temporarily suspended classes to discuss the costly war. (*Old Mole,* 1970, University of Connecticut Library)

the same time, received increased American military and CIA advice and suffered bombing missions, as well as a South Vietnamese invasion in February of 1971.

To put further pressure on North Vietnam, Nixon gradually resumed and extended bombing raids, calling them "protective reaction strikes."[47] In November, 1970, a massive bombing campaign was directed at the North. Nixon warned that further raids would follow unless the North Vietnamese stopped shooting at American reconnaisance planes flying over the North. Hanoi's Defense Minister Vo Nguyen Giap defiantly replied that North Vietnam was "a sovereign independent country, and no sovereign independent country will allow its enemy to spy freely upon it."[48] In the spring of 1972, American planes dropped mines into Haiphong harbor to curb the movement of supply ships. For Nixon it was important to end the war before the 1972 presidential election, because he was being challenged by Democratic Senator George McGovern, who pledged to end the war immediately upon taking office. Just a few days before the election, Kissinger said peace was at hand, but South Vietnam scuttled the agreement. After Nixon's electoral landslide, the bombing of the North intensified, and in December, 1972,

Nixon unleashed a devastating attack of two hundred B-52s to cripple the North Vietnamese economy and to persuade South Vietnam that the United States could be tough. Bombs smashed water supplies, textile factories, and hospitals in Hanoi and Haiphong. Fifty-foot craters gashed the cities. Earlier one magazine writer had asked, why? His answer: "We seek prestige. We seek respect. We seek credibility. We seek honor. *That* is why. And in the course of all this seeking, all this bombing, our souls have withered. Day by day, we are turning into monsters. For a hundred reasons, and for no reason whatever, we are blowing men, women, and children to bits with our bombs, and we can't feel a thing."[49]

Hanoi evacuated huge numbers of people to the countryside and managed to shoot down over thirty American bombers. The destruction and counterdestruction shocked both Hanoi and Washington into talking more intently about a political settlement. Actually, Henry Kissinger had been meeting secretly off and on with North Vietnam's chief negotiator Le Duc Tho since mid-1969. South Vietnam was seldom consulted. Through the spring and summer of 1972 Kissinger and Le Duc Tho huddled, even as the United States continued to attack the North. The United States, besides bombing heavily, made an important political concession: a cease-fire in place rather than the withdrawal of all North Vietnamese from the South. On January 27, 1973 a Vietnam cease-fire agreement was finally signed. The United States consented to withdraw its armed forces from South Vietnam within sixty days. Both sides agreed to exchange prisoners of war. An International

**"Une Grande, une Immense Majorité Silencieuse."** President Nixon said that he was devising his policies to suit the majority of Americans who remained silent during the vocal protests of the 1960s and early 1970s. In this harsh sketch, Vazquez de Sola translated Nixon's "silent majority" into war dead. (Swann Collection of Caricature and Cartoon)

Commission of Control and Supervision would oversee the cease-fire. The political terms were confused, providing eventually for a coalition council to hold democratic elections in the South. Although many civilian American advisers remained in the South after the 1973 accord, the American military was removed. Yet neither the Viet Cong–North Vietnamese nor the Saigon government undertook serious bargaining, so the bloody fighting continued.

On April 29, 1975 the Saigon government surrendered; the victorious Viet Cong entered Saigon shouting *Giai phong* ("liberation"). As the remaining Americans and thousands of Vietnamese escaped in a hasty evacuation by air and sea, Saigon was renamed Ho Chi Minh City. It was an undignified exit after over twenty years of American effort. Cambodia and Laos also were soon governed by nationalist Communists. Since 1950 the United States had spent at least $155 billion in Southeast Asia. The Vietnam War, the longest of all American wars, would cost taxpayers in the future over $200 billion in veterans' benefits. Over 56,000 American servicemen died in Vietnam. A "footnote" the war was not.

## Vietnam Reflections

Americans reached for lessons after the Vietnam debacle, but the debate took place largely among the intellectual and governmental elite. Most Americans were more relieved than inquisitive about the consequences of the war. They switched off the war like a TV set. Mention of Vietnam, for example, was extremely rare in the 1976 presidential campaign. Hawkish commentators feared that the defeat in Vietnam would weaken America's credibility elsewhere, as the nation's ill-defined "enemies" exploited Washington's setback. Nixon's Secretary of Defense James Schlesinger regretted that the military had had too many restraints placed upon it during the war. Next time, he advised, the United States should bomb the enemy's cities, the heart of its military power. Generals Maxwell Taylor and William Westmoreland lamented that they could have won the war if only the American people had not succumbed to a "failure of will" during the trying days of the Tet offensive and forced American retrenchment. Just let the military do its job next time, unencumbered by public or congressional pressure. In short, the use of massive military force in Vietnam was not wrong; the mistake was in not applying it adequately. "As a reaffirmation of our determination to regain our former high estate," concluded Taylor, "an increased military budget would be a convincing action which all observers would understand."[50] To others, Vietnam was the wrong terrain on which to battle communism; the struggle would continue, but the United States would choose the next site with strategic advantages on its side and use aerial and naval power rather than troops. For President Ford, the collapse of the American-supported regimes in Southeast Asia simply confirmed the validity of the "domino theory."

A former architect of American intervention in Indochina and later president of the philanthropic Ford Foundation, McGeorge Bundy, explained that the Vietnam War was unique, and America's sour experience there should not govern responses to future crises. Arthur M. Schlesinger, Jr. allowed that the United States had stepped inadvertently deeper and deeper into a quagmire without really knowing what it wanted or what it was getting into. The war, then, was basically an accident. One school of political scientists, with Harvard's Graham Allison as a leading spokesman, used what they called a "bureaucratic model" to interpret

**Vietnam Refrain.**
Presidents Eisenhower
through Ford kept talking
about victory in Vietnam,
but kept losing the war.
Finally, in 1975, the
United States departed
from Indochina. (Mike
Peters, *Dayton Daily
News,* 1975)

events; they suggested that it is difficult to blame individuals, because of the impersonal, oversized bureaucracy that resists change, follows standard operating procedure, and becomes rutted in traditional channels. The bureaucracy in Washington, according to this view, took on a momentum of its own that no one seemed able to control. Still other observers blamed the Vietnam disaster on strong presidents like Johnson, who actually controlled the bureaucracy through appointments, an overpowering personality, and a pervasive ideology, or who simply bypassed the bureaucracy. This viewpoint implied that a change in presidents would permit a reformation in foreign policy. Some commentators noted that the Vietnam War's causes and consequences exposed the "imperial presidency" and the executive abuses in the constitutional system, and optimistically concluded that in the future Congress might command a more competitive position in the making of foreign policy.

Other opinions differed radically. Vietnam was not unique, inadvertent, accidental, presidential, or bureaucratic, but rather a prime example of American global expansionism and arrogance, encouraged by a zealous belief that the United States, through superior power and ideals could and should manage events almost everywhere. In mid-May, 1975, for example, when a few Cambodian naval patrol boats having no instructions from the central government and thinking that they were protecting their territorial waters, seized the American merchant ship *Mayaguez,* Washington bypassed diplomatic channels and responded with a show of force. American Marines landed on islands off the Cambodian coast, American warships attacked and sank Cambodian gunboats, and American bombers struck an air base and a petroleum depot near Sihanoukville. The ship was recaptured and American hawks, reeling from the recent expulsion from Vietnam, applauded this firmness and resolve as evidence that the United States remained a virile power. The *Mayaguez* affair was a matter of self-defense, said the Ford Administration. But critics replied that the excessive military response and the public boasting about clobbering a much weaker nation suggested that the United States had learned too little from the debacle in Vietnam.

The Vietnam War, said other critics, revealed the shortcomings of the rigid containment doctrine, which had failed to make distinctions between peripheral and vital areas, and which, according to poet Archibald MacLeish, "put us in bed with every anti-Communist we could find."[51] Analyst Edmund Stillman put it this way: "Freedom *is* divisible. Some places are worthy of defense. Some are not. Some are capable of being defended. Some are not. And some places are not free, were not free, and quite possibly never will be free."[52] Ronald Steel, long a critic of *Pax Americana,* commented in a similar vein that the "elementary rule of playing power politics is that you win some and lose some, but that you should never confuse knights and bishops with pawns."[53]

In one of the most searching evaluations, Richard J. Barnet of the Institute for Policy Studies in Washington, D.C., wrote in his impressive book *Roots of War* (1972), that the "Vietnam War was certainly a mistake. But it was not an accident. . . . The Vietnam War has had a unique result not because American policy has been fundamentally different from what it was when the American military effort smashed the Greek guerrilla movement in 1949 or suppressed the Dominican revolution in 1965 but because the Vietnamese exacted a price for American victory that the United States was unwilling to pay." He predicted more Vietnams unless the American people examined "those drives within our society that impel us toward destruction": the concentration of power in the national security bureaucracy; the capitalist economy and its business creed, which has sought influence abroad to maintain the American standard of living; and the vulnerability of the public to manipulation by foreign policy leaders.[54]

Historian Henry Steele Commager, who like other humanists was sickened by the immorality of using napalm, bombing civilians, the murders at My Lai, and other atrocities, wondered why "we find it so hard to accept this elementary lesson of history, that some wars are so deeply immoral that they must be lost, that the war in Vietnam was one of these wars, and that those who resist it are the truest patriots."[55] To some, then, defeat became a victory for humane values. Yet skeptics pointed out that the American people as a whole and probably many leaders had not really understood what their exercise of power did to others abroad. They still clung to notions of superiority and self-righteousness that blinded them to their own crimes. They protested the outrageous sabotage by Arab terrorists, but supported the callous American bombings and destruction of entire villages in Vietnam. They complained bitterly when Venezuela and other Third World nations took control of their own natural resources, yet forgot that the United States had baldly exploited those resources for decades. Americans still practiced the double standard, and still believed themselves somehow exceptional. But, as conservative sociologist Daniel Bell sadly suggested, "there is no longer a Manifest Destiny or mission. We have not been immune to the corruption of power. We have not been the exception."[56]

"Neo-isolationism" became a respectable term by the mid-1970s. "Compared to people who thought they could run the universe," remarked Walter Lippmann, "I *am* a neo-isolationist and proud of it."[57] Never again, predicted spokespeople for this school of thought, would the United States undertake unrestrained globalism. Never again would a President, without a declaration of war, send American soldiers into foreign fields. Interventions would be more selective and largely nonmilitary. The United States would have to find other methods than the

**"Uncle Sam."** Famous cartoonist Bill Mauldin pictured a hard-pressed Uncle Sam in the mid-1970s, especially after the United States' hasty withdrawal from and defeat in Vietnam. (Copyright © 1975 Bill Mauldin, *Chicago Sun-Times.* Reproduced by courtesy of Bill Mauldin)

bludgeon to exert influence. Commitments would be limited. Yet, asked pessimists, who would define the commitments, and would America's economic, strategic, and psychic needs permit anything but continued interventionism? Instead of Vietnams, there would be Chiles, with the United States employing covert means to undermine sovereign governments. Clark Clifford, however, thought otherwise. "I believe we are a better country today because we went through this experience." It was costly, he admitted, but it took a catastrophe like Vietnam to awaken Americans to the limits of their power. "We were too spread out. That was part of the reason that we got into Vietnam. . . . I think, I hope, we have learned now."[58] His comment was conspicuously tinged with doubt.

## The Middle East, Latin America, and Africa

Middle Eastern rivalries sorely tested détente. After the 1956 Suez crisis, Soviet Russia and the United States armed Egypt and Israel respectively. In June, 1967, after years of growing friction and months of threats and counterthreats, Israel attacked Egypt and Syria, joined temporarily as the United Arab Republic. In the Six-Day War, the Israelis, using American-supplied weapons, scored a devastating victory by capturing the ancient city of Jerusalem from Jordan, the Golan Heights from Syria, and the entire Sinai Peninsula including the eastern bank of the Suez Canal from Egypt. Half of the Arab states broke diplomatic relations with Washington and Soviet vessels were permitted access to Arab ports. With pressure from American Jews, the United States sold fifty F-4 Phantom jets to Israel in December of 1967. By the time Nixon and Kissinger entered office in early 1969, the Middle East, said the President, was a "powder keg."[59] Washington began talks with Moscow to defuse conflict in the region, but no arrangements could be made so long as the Egyptians refused to negotiate until Israeli forces had departed occupied territory. The Soviets in early 1970 further contributed to tension when they began to send sophisticated antiaircraft weapons and thousands of troops to Egypt. On their part, some two million Palestinian Arabs, half of them refugees ousted from their lands in 1948 when Israel was created as a nation, began to organize

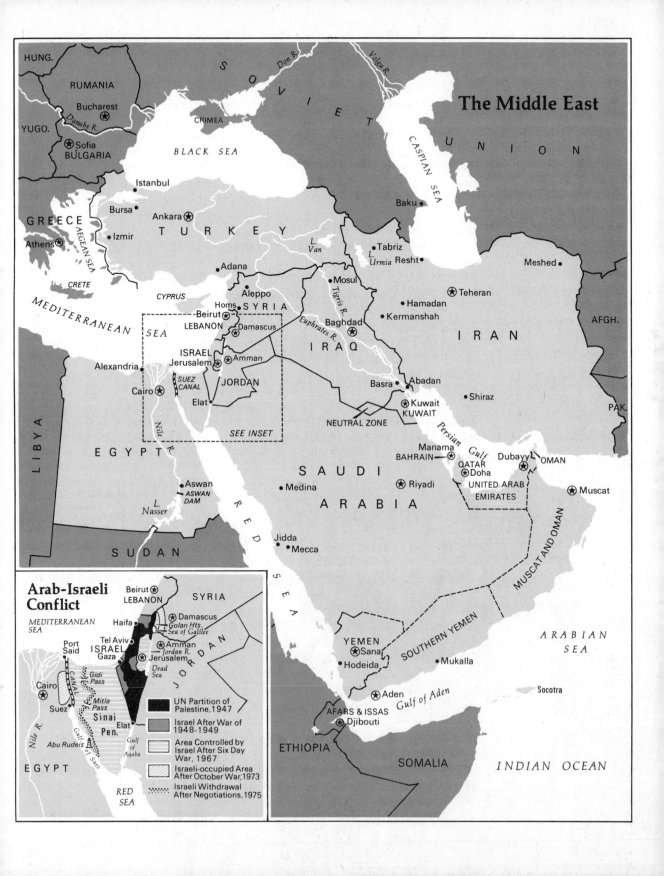

# The Middle East

HUNG.
RUMANIA
• Bucharest
YUGO.
☆ Sofia
BULGARIA
Danube R.

GREECE
Athens ☆
AEGEAN SEA
CRETE

MEDITERRANEAN SEA

SOVIET UNION

Don R.
Volga R.
CRIMEA
BLACK SEA

CASPIAN SEA
• Baku

Istanbul
Bursa •
Ankara ☆
• Izmir
T U R K E Y
• Adana
CYPRUS

L. Van
• Tabriz
L. Urmia  Resht •
• Meshed

• Mosul
Tigris R.
☆ Teheran
AFGH.

Homs •  S Y R I A
Beirut ☆
LEBANON  • Damascus
Euphrates R.
• Hamadan
• Kermanshah
I R A N

ISRAEL
Jerusalem ☆  ☆ Amman
JORDAN
Baghdad
I R A Q

Alexandria •
Cairo ☆
SUEZ CANAL
Nile R.
• Elat
SEE INSET

Basra •  • Abadan
☆ Kuwait
KUWAIT
Persian Gulf
• Shiraz
PAK.

NEUTRAL ZONE

LIBYA
E G Y P T

• Aswan
ASWAN DAM
L. Nasser

S U D A N

RED SEA

S A U D I
A R A B I A

• Medina

• Jidda
• Mecca

☆ Riyadi

Manama
BAHRAIN ☆  Dubayy L
QATAR
☆ Doha
UNITED ARAB
EMIRATES

OMAN
☆ Muscat

MUSCAT AND OMAN

YEMEN
☆ Sana
• Hodeida

SOUTHERN YEMEN

• Mukalla

ARABIAN SEA

☆ Aden
Gulf of Aden
Socotra

AFARS & ISSAS
☆ Djibouti
ETHIOPIA
SOMALIA
INDIAN OCEAN

## Arab-Israeli Conflict

MEDITERRANEAN SEA

Beirut ☆
LEBANON  SYRIA
Haifa •
☆ Damascus
Golan Hts.
Sea of Galilee
Tel Aviv •
ISRAEL
Gaza
Port Said
☆ Amman
Jordan R.
Jerusalem ☆
Dead Sea
JORDAN

Cairo ☆
Suez
CANAL
Gidi Pass
Mitla Pass
Sinai Pen.
Elat
Gulf of Aqaba

Nile R.
Abu Rudeis
Gulf of Suez

E G Y P T

RED SEA

■ UN Partition of Palestine, 1947
■ Israel After War of 1948-1949
□ Area Controlled by Israel After Six Day War, 1967
▨ Israeli-occupied Area After October War, 1973
⋯ Israeli Withdrawal After Negotiations, 1975

more effectively as the Palestine Liberation Organization (PLO). The PLO soon battled Jordanian troops armed by the United States; Palestinian terrorists hijacked airliners and, in 1972, murdered Israeli athletes at the Olympic Games in Munich.

After Nasser died in September, 1970, his successor, Anwar al-Sadat, vowed a new war against Israel and became angry with the Soviets when his requests for more arms were denied. Moscow was then developing détente with the United States and did not wish to jeopardize that great power plan. Egypt felt abandoned, and in the summer of 1972 abruptly expelled several thousand Soviet technicians and military advisers. In early October, 1973, Egyptian and Syrian forces struck Israel, gaining back some of their lost land. During this so-called "Yom Kippur War," Soviet ships laden with military equipment steamed toward Egypt. Washington, caught up in its "Watergate" political crisis (Vice-President Spiro Agnew resigned, after evidence surfaced that he had been involved years before in a Maryland payoff scheme), promised to replace all of Israel's destroyed planes and tanks. A huge American airlift began. The "Middle East may become in time what the Balkans were in Europe before 1914," a tired Kissinger commented.[60] To avoid a great power confrontation, he arranged a cease-fire. Nevertheless, both Russia and America put their armed forces on alert. Détente had not worked.

The secretary of state next, in November of 1973, launched his "shuttle diplomacy," flying back and forth between Middle Eastern capitals in search of a peaceful settlement. Not only did the Arab-Israeli imbroglio threaten to cripple détente; it also threatened the American economy. Oil-rich Arab states like Saudi Arabia, which through the last three decades had supplied Western nations with very inexpensive petroleum, now imposed for five months an embargo on petroleum shipments to the United States and others, and more than quadrupled the price of crude oil for Western Europe and Japan. The United States, which had been obtaining between 10 and 15 percent of its oil from the Middle East, suffered

**Golda Meir (1898—), Nixon, and Kissinger.** In 1973, the Prime Minister of Israel gets a pointer from the President in Washington, as the secretary of state prepares for his "shuttle diplomacy" in the Middle East. (Department of State *Newsletter*)

an "energy crisis" in 1974, as gasoline prices at the pumps spun upward and frustrated drivers lined up, sometimes for hours, hoping to fuel their automobiles. With impressive stamina and patience, Kissinger bargained in Cairo and Tel Aviv intermittently for two years. Egypt's President Sadat was soon calling Kissinger his friend and brother—"Dr. Henry, you are my favorite magician."[61] Washington also pressured Israel. Finally, on September 1, 1975, Egypt and Israel initialed a Kissinger-designed agreement wherein Israel would pull back from part of the Sinai, a buffer zone would be created, and American technicians would be placed in "early warning" stations to detect military activities. Vague promises of United States military aid to both Egypt and Israel were tendered.

Problems remained. The homeless Palestinian Arabs, who essentially constituted a nation, were still suffering in refugee camps and demanding their lands from Israel. The Israeli government began to entrench itself in occupied territories, building industries, farms, and housing developments for Israelis. Jordan still demanded the West Bank. Syrian-Israeli hostility persisted. A bloody civil war broke out in Lebanon, which prompted Syria to send in troops in 1976. Sophisticated American weapons continued to be shipped to both the Arabs and Israelis after the October war, and Sadat warned that military conflict could erupt again. Egypt's economy remained unstable, promoting political unrest. In March, 1976, Sadat, needing American technology and mediation, angrily denounced Russia. "I still say that 99 percent of the cards in the game are in America's hands whether the Soviet Union likes it or not," Sadat asserted.[62] In April, he canceled the Soviet Navy's right to use Egypt's ports. American policy in the Middle East looked more like "containment" than détente.

Troubles in the Middle East, extrication from Indochina, and the emphasis on détente did not mean that Latin America was ignored. Latin American military officers still trained in the United States, arms flowed to military regimes, the Organization of American States could usually be counted upon to do Washington's bidding, and inter-American trade remained large. In the early 1970s about one-third of Latin American exports went to the United States and about two-fifths of the region's imports came from the United States. In 1976, Latin American countries supplied 34 percent of the United States' petroleum imports, 68 percent of its coffee, 57 percent of its sugar, 47 percent of its copper, and 98 percent of its bauxite. In that year United States direct investments in its southern neighbors totaled about $17 billion. Despite these strong ties, Latin American governments increasingly flung challenges at Washington. Mexico, always a thorny competitor, refused to honor the economic blockade of Cuba and strongly criticized the Dominican intervention of 1965. Panama continued to demand control of the canal, and although a 1974 treaty with the United States promised Panamanian authority some day, negotiations stalled. Peru and Ecuador engaged the United States in a "tuna war" when they declared a 200-mile territorial limit and began seizing American fishing vessels in their coastal waters. Peru also nationalized an Exxon oil subsidiary and other foreign properties.

Chile, Venezuela, and Cuba presented special problems. In 1970 the Central Intelligence Agency unsuccessfully used bribe money in Chile in an attempt to prevent the election of Marxist President Salvador Allende. Fearing, in traditional Cold War terms, the emergence of a Communist regime, President Nixon ordered the CIA to "make the economy scream."[63] Thereupon CIA covert operations included pressure on American companies like International Telephone and

**"You're Like a Bunch of . . . of . . . of . . . CAPITALISTS!!"** The oil embargo by the OPEC nations in 1974 produced anger among Americans who found that gasoline stations ran out of the vital fuel or that what they could buy had been drastically raised in price. Venezuela and the Arab nations replied that they were only doing what the developed nations had done to them for decades. (Dennis Renault, *Sacramento Bee*)

Telegraph to halt credit and the shipment of spare parts in order to create economic chaos within Chile and thereby weaken Allende. The United States government also subsidized newspapers critical of the constitutionally elected Chilean leader, supported para-military groups, and encouraged military officers to undertake a coup. Although Washington cut off economic aid to the beleaguered South American nation, it continued to send arms in order to retain contact with the Chilean military establishment. In 1973 Allende was overthrown by a military junta, satisfying Nixon and Kissinger in their policy of "destabilization." The new government suspended freedom of speech and press, jailed dissenters, and killed thousands. A brutal dictatorship replaced a constitutional democracy. In 1976, President-elect Jimmy Carter, who throughout the presidential campaign had criticized the repressive Chilean regime and America's support for it, indicated that the United States in the future would be "more demanding in the moral character of our national affairs."[64]

Venezuela was a founding member in 1960 of the Organization of Petroleum Exporting Countries (OPEC) and through this institution cooperated with the Arabs in raising oil prices. Caracas also nationalized American oil companies in 1976 and opened diplomatic relations with Castro's Cuba the year before. Pressure from Venezuela, Mexico, and others in the OAS compelled the United States reluctantly to permit a lifting of the economic blockade from Cuba in 1975.

Washington itself made timid gestures toward improved Cuban-American relations, when it permitted some Americans to travel to Cuba in the early 1970s and in 1972 signed a hijacking treaty with Havana to discourage terrorism of the airways. But the participation of Cuban troops in the civil war in Angola led President Ford in the mid-1970s to criticize Cuba and stall improvements in relations.

In Latin America the United States probably came to fear communism less and the evolution of a nonaligned bloc more. Kissinger had tried in early 1976 to patch up the growing anti-Americanism with a trip to the region. He spoke of "a more open relationship . . . which now turns not on the memories of an earlier age of tutelage, on pretensions by us to hegemony, or on national inequality, but on mutual respect, common interests, and cooperative problem solving."[65] He constantly applauded the "interdependence" of the United States and Latin America. Yet critics complained that the United States showed no willingness to relinquish its sphere of influence. President Ford's public announcement, after revelations of clandestine CIA activities in Chile, that the United States would continue to "destabilize" Latin American governments when it was in the United States' national interest to do so suggested that the new American policy toward Latin America had not altogether shed "memories of an earlier age of tutelage."

Events in Africa caused Americans to devise new policies for that continent. In 1974–1975 the United States assisted with clandestine military aid two factions in the Angolan civil war, which had flared up after Portugal abruptly granted independence to its African colony. South Africa joined the United States in an effort to defeat a faction backed by the Soviet Union and Cuba. Cuba sent several thousand troops to Angola, arousing vehement American charges that communism was gaining a foothold in Africa. "Africa is of immense size, strategically located," Kissinger told a Senate committee. "The interdependence of America and our allies with Africa is increasingly obvious. Africa is a continent of vast resources. We depend on Africa for many key products: cobalt, chrome, oil, cocoa, manganese, platinum, diamonds, aluminum, and others."[66] By 1976, American investors had placed $3.68 billion in Africa. But 40 percent of this figure, or $1.5 billion, was invested in the Republic of South Africa, a white-ruled nation that practiced the repressive segregationist policy of *apartheid* against the black majority. That economic linkage, combined with continued American trade in chrome with the white racist regime of Rhodesia, aroused bitterness in most black African governments. To help forestall further deterioration in its African position, the United States had intervened in the Angolan civil war. It proved a tragic blunder.

American critics, fearing another Vietnam, sprang into debate when the news leaked out in 1975 about secret involvement in Angola. Congress, which had not been consulted, cut off military funds for the Angolan venture. Ford thereupon upbraided the legislators for shirking America's international responsibilities: "I believe," he asserted, "that resistance to Soviet expansion by military means must be a fundamental element of United States foreign policy."[67] That sounded very much like the old containment doctrine without limits. Ford did not discuss some salient facts: the United States had been funneling military aid into Angola before it became independent and before Soviet and Cuban interference. Opponents of American intervention argued that the United States should refrain from participation in a civil war, that it was supporting the losing side, that its alignment with white South Africa was seriously alienating black Africa, that America's national interest was minimally threatened by Angolan events, and that further aid would likely prove unsuccessful.

Ford and Kissinger, however, depicted Angola as another Cold War test of will. Kissinger told a senatorial opponent of military aid, "you may be right in African terms but I'm thinking globally."[68] Indeed, Washington and Moscow had once again helped convert a civil war into a global power confrontation. The short-sightedness of that approach was spelled out by the President of Tanzania in early 1976: "frankly when we are dealing with our friends, whether it is the Soviet Union or China or the United States, we must refuse to judge African issues from *their* perspective. We must judge these issues from *our own* perspective."[69] In early 1976 the Soviet-endorsed faction won the civil war. Russia and Cuba continued their military assistance. In March, Ford and Kissinger, in essence noting the frailty of détente, denounced Soviet "adventurism" in Angola. Ford stopped using the expression détente and replaced it with "peace through strength." The State Department suspended Soviet-American negotiations on some minor issues as warnings to Moscow "that we will not tolerate another similar Soviet venture."[70]

The ill-fated Angolan experience forced Washington to try other courses of action. Huge arms shipments left American ports for Kenya, Ethiopia, and Zaire to counter Soviet shipments of military hardware to Somalia, Uganda, and Angola. Washington also spurred new investments to curry African favor. Bethlehem Steel, for example, invested several millions to develop titanium deposits in Sierra Leone, and Kaiser Aluminum expanded its bauxite operation in Ghana. The outbreak of violence in Rhodesia, where the white minority that was only four percent of the population clung to power against large-scale black resistance, prompted Kissinger to visit Africa in early 1976. Thereupon he pressed South Africa to abandon *apartheid* and announced dramatically that the United States placed itself squarely on the side of black Africans in their quest for majority rule. "Africa's problems," Kissinger reported, "must be for Africans to solve."[71] Why had the United States changed course? "To avoid a race war . . . , to do all we can to prevent foreign intervention," and *"to prevent the radicalization of Africa."*[72] Hence, one element remained constant in American policy toward the Third World: antiradicalism, or counterrevolution.

## The Interdependent World Economy

In the early 1970s a global recession disrupted the world economy. "History has shown that international political stability requires international economic stability," Kissinger commented in 1975, in what seemed a virtual paraphrase of Cordell Hull four decades earlier.[73] Worldwide inflation, spurred in part by large American expenditures in the Vietnam War, raised the cost of industrial goods for developing nations and weakened the international monetary system, forcing the United States itself to devalue the dollar in 1971. The high price of oil hit poor and rich nations alike, while the price of other commodities, like copper, slumped, causing devastating recessions in countries dependent upon the export of one product. Protectionist barriers increased and further impeded world trade. Economists began to talk about the "Fourth World"—poor, less developed countries (LDCs) that lacked profitmaking raw materials and relied heavily on imports of food.

Disease, malnutrition, a rapid birth rate and falling death rate, an insufficient number of physicians to promote birth control among suspicious and traditional peoples, limited farm acreage, fertilizer shortages, shrinking fish supplies because of overharvesting, maldistributed wealth, high unemployment, and droughts condemned millions to daily hunger. In Africa famines struck mercilessly, and at least 10,000 people a day died from malnutrition. In 1976 the world population reached four billion. Scientists thought it might double in just thirty-five years. The rate of agricultural production was barely keeping pace with the population increase. Estimates were that between 460 million and 1.03 billion people were eating less than the number of calories required to sustain ordinary physical activity. There was a hopeful sign by the late 1970s: a slower growth in the world birth rate due to sterilization programs, the expanded use of contraceptives, and abortion.

"Food. Like the weather, which affects it so much, everybody talks about it. Some people, who lack it, agonize over it and die from its absence. Starvation and malnutrition still kill millions each year," wrote one student of the food crisis in the Third and Fourth Worlds. "Others, who may possess it in abundance but foresee its absence on an enormous scale, perhaps within a decade, theorize about

**Famine in Chad, Africa.** Drought-stricken Chad was only one of many poor nations that suffered in the world hunger crisis of the 1970s, wherein millions died. (CARE, New York)

it."[74] A World Food Conference in 1974 demonstrated concern, but offered few plans. Large agricultural producers like the United States did undertake to share their foodstuffs, but few Americans were willing to reduce their wasteful consumption rates to help feed a hungry world. Anyway, there was not enough American food for all the world's hungry. By continuing to practice marketplace economics in the distribution of their surplus food, such as large grain shipments to the dollar-paying Russians, Americans, in essence, made choices about which people would die. To humanists it seemed utterly incomprehensible that in 1974 Americans used more fertilizer on lawns and golf courses than did all the farmers in India on their vast lands. Nor were the oil barons of the Third World willing to help much. Instead, they pocketed billions in profits from inflated oil prices, which Fourth World nations also had to pay, spent "petro-dollars" on huge military establishments—the United States sold $10 billion in arms to Iran during 1972–1976—and invested in American companies *in* the United States. The Shah of Iran even established a million-dollar academic chair in petroleum engineering at the University of Southern California. When Americans complained about the high cost of oil, the Shah brusquely replied, "it's a solution you of the West have wished on yourselves. . . . You've increased the price of wheat you sell us by 300 percent. . . . You buy our crude oil and sell it back to us, refined as petrochemicals at a hundred times the price you've paid us. . . . It's only fair that, from now on, you should pay more for oil."[75] In part, the halfhearted American response to the food crisis was determined by the fact that over half of American trade was with the "First World" of Japan, Canada, and Western Europe, and about two-thirds of American overseas investments were located in Canada and Western Europe. In short, America's primary economic stakes were not in the Third or Fourth Worlds, and indeed, American businessmen increasingly looked away from those areas in favor of less risky investment climates.

"The division of the planet between rich and poor," Kissinger warned, "could become as grim as the darkest days of the cold war."[76] To blunt the impact of this schism, Kissinger recommended in 1976 the establishment of a new International Resources Bank financed by the oil-rich and industrial nations, with a capital fund of one billion dollars. But poor nations were not satisfied; they wanted raw materials prices pegged to what they paid for manufactured goods. Nations exporting raw materials threatened to form commodity cartels modeled on OPEC and sharply increase prices. Many nations, including the United States in 1976, declared 200-mile fishing limits and competition began for control of seabed minerals. Kissinger, in another attempt to create world order, appealed for a new "law of the sea" to protect the traditional principle of freedom of the seas.

The United States was deeply entwined in global economic issues and was ardently defending its stakes. It exported over 20 percent of its farm products and about 10 percent of its manufactured goods in the mid-1970s. Large American firms, like Coca-Cola, Gillette, and IBM, earned over half of their profits abroad. The United States accounted for about one-seventh of the world's exports and about a third of the world's total goods and services. In 1975 American direct investments abroad totaled $133.2 billion. American industry also needed raw materials imports: 75 percent of America's tin, 91 percent of its chrome, 99 percent of its manganese, and 64 percent of its zinc consumed in 1975 came from foreign sources. "America's prosperity," Kissinger pointed out, "could not continue in a chaotic world economy."[77] OPEC's control of foreign oil actually sparked serious

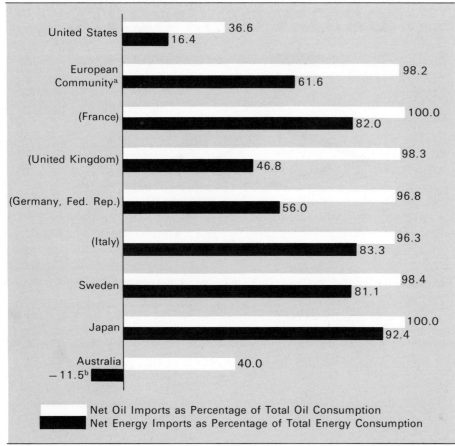

**Dependence of Developed Countries on Imported Energy, 1973***
(percentages)

United States — 36.6 / 16.4

European Community[a] — 98.2 / 61.6

(France) — 100.0 / 82.0

(United Kingdom) — 98.3 / 46.8

(Germany, Fed. Rep.) — 96.8 / 56.0

(Italy) — 96.3 / 83.3

Sweden — 98.4 / 81.1

Japan — 100.0 / 92.4

Australia — 40.0 / −11.5[b]

☐ Net Oil Imports as Percentage of Total Oil Consumption
■ Net Energy Imports as Percentage of Total Energy Consumption

*Source: Roger D. Hansen and the staff of the Overseas Development Council, *The U.S. and World Development: Agenda for Action, 1976* (New York: Praeger Publishers, Inc., 1976), p. B-11. Quoted from Committee for Economic Development, Research and Policy Committee, *International Economic Consequences of High-Priced Energy: A Statement on National Policy,* September 1975 (New York), p. 77.

[a]Belgium, Denmark, France, Fed. Rep. of Germany, Ireland, Italy, Luxembourg, Netherlands, and United Kingdom.
[b]Net energy exporter.

discussion in leading American magazines about a possible invasion of the Middle East to seize the oil wells. Washington also started a petroleum conservation program to reduce American dependence on foreign supplies, yet by 1976 the United States still satisfied 40 percent of its petroleum needs through imports. Five years earlier the United States had suffered a trade deficit for the first time in several decades. Further trouble surfaced in the mid-1970s when congressional committees revealed that leading American multinational corporations, including Lockheed Aircraft and Exxon Oil, had spent millions of dollars to bribe politicians in Italy and Japan, among others, and had disguised those bribes in their American reports. With expropriations (85 unsettled cases were pending by 1975) also causing upheavals, American businessmen appeared defensive in the world economy.

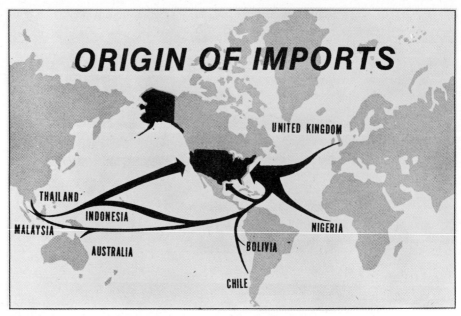

**Tin Imports.** The United States in the 1970s relied heavily upon imports of strategic raw materials to maintain its economic health and defense. Tin imports in 1975, for example, equaled 75 percent of total American consumption of that soft, crystalline, silvery-white metal. Malaysia, Thailand, and Bolivia were America's primary suppliers of tin. The Department of the Navy prepared this map to emphasize the nation's foreign dependence and the role of the Navy in protecting American "lifelines" to mineral sources. (U. S. Department of the Navy, *U. S. Life Lines,* 1974)

The multinational corporation seemed to promise them some advantage, and also posed a unique problem. In Argentina, for example, American-owned automobile subsidiaries received orders from Cuba, still on the American blockade list. Argentina protested that the United States was determining *Argentine* national interest by prohibiting the parent companies, and hence the Argentine subsidiaries, from trading with Cuba. In 1974 Washington backed down and permitted the sales; thus a multinational corporation, owned in the United States, stood at odds with American foreign policy. Multinationals, by exporting United States technology, were also possibly weakening the American trade balance and the American economy by reducing the United States' competitive position. Were the multinationals beholden to the laws and policies of any nation, or were they in essence extranational forces? Ten of the top twelve multinationals in the mid-1970s were American, including General Motors, Exxon, and Ford Motor. As economic powers, they ranked above most of the world's nations. These imperial giants intervened in the politics of other nations (International Telephone and Telegraph worked to prevent Allende's election in Chile), changed local tastes and customs through standardized products, moved factories from country to country seeking cheaper labor and higher profits (many went to Taiwan), and set, or as critics said "fixed", world prices on key commodities. Multinationals vied with governments as primary actors in the international system, and their proponents predicted that they would create the "One World" that Wendell Willkie espoused in the 1940s. "The men who run the global corporations," concluded two critical students of the subject in 1974, "are the first in history with the organization, technology, money, and ideology to make a credible try at managing the world as an integrated unit."[78] Whether they succeeded or not would depend upon whether national governments—in short, the nationalism that has always resisted empires—could bring them under control.

## Dangers to American Power

As the United States moved toward its two hundredth birthday, Kissinger summarized its international position. "We have become the engineer of the global economy, the rock of security for those who share our values, the creative force in building international institutions, and the pioneer in science and technology." He concluded that "we cannot solve every problem, but few solutions are possible without us."[79] Yet in the bicentennial year of celebration the United States was beleaguered, its global power apparently having crested. Kissinger had undertaken détente with the Soviets in part to preserve and conserve American power. He hoped that Russia and China would balance each other off and isolate Third World trouble spots through big power agreement. By the mid-1970s, however, détente was troubled, and it appeared that Kissinger had oversold the policy's healing powers.

American power faced numerous challenges in the 1970s, evident in the decline of the dollar as a diplomatic tool, the determination of OPEC and Third World nations to gain control over their own raw materials, the redistribution of the world's wealth with America holding a smaller share, the apparent nuclear parity with Russia, and the international proliferation of nuclear weapons. The latter challenge grew from the spread of nuclear technology to generate energy—in 1976 twenty-one countries had nuclear power reactors—which thereby threatened to expand nuclear weaponry. One byproduct of nuclear power production is plutonium, a fissionable material that can be utilized to produce nuclear weapons. India, for example, used American technical advice and a nuclear reactor obtained in Canada to explode a nuclear bomb in 1974. The United States "Atoms for Peace" program initiated in 1953 for nuclear cooperation and the exportation of American nuclear technology had become, it appeared, "atoms for sale."

America's international "friends" were less content to follow America's lead. Latin America no longer served as a compliant sphere of influence, and America's alliance system limped into the late 1970s. Japan and Western Europe were more independent-minded. Resentful Canadian nationalists placed restrictions on large American investments. "Living next to you is in some ways like sleeping with an elephant," said Canadian Prime Minister Pierre Trudeau. "No matter how friendly and even-tempered is the beast, if I can call it that, one is affected by every twitch and grunt."[80] Greece and Turkey, squabbling over Cyprus, threatened NATO's cohesion, already loosened by DeGaulle's assaults in the 1960s. SEATO was phased out; Thailand terminated American rights to air bases and went "neutral." In Italy in 1976, notwithstanding Kissinger's protests, Communists gained a sizable electoral vote. "The image we have of America now," said the young mayor of Anzio, Italy in 1976, "is the guy with money, ready with his fists, whose clothes don't look too well on him, however expensive they are, whose power of riches, industry, agriculture—even capacity for self-criticism and self-flagellation—have lost intimate meaning for us. You aren't our promised land anymore."[81] By contradicting their own best ideals of democracy and fair play—a contradiction evidenced by massive "Watergate" corruption, business bribery abroad, devastation of Vietnam, and covert CIA activities—Americans began to forfeit one of their international strengths: respect.

In the period 1945–1966, the United States usually had a two-thirds majority on its side on issues in the General Assembly of the United Nations. And because America's friends constituted a majority of the Security Council, the United States often got its way in that body without having to use the embarrassing veto. With the birth of numerous new states in the 1960s, and their entrance into the United Nations, however, American power declined markedly. The United Nations broke free from American domination. Third and Fourth World nations by the early 1970s held a majority of votes in the General Assembly, and in the Security Council the United States had to resort to the veto time and again. Many annoyed Americans urged a cutback in American monetary contributions to the United Nations or outright withdrawal from the institution; Kissinger made it clear that the United States would reduce its foreign aid to countries that voted against United States proposals. And in 1975–1976 colorful, volatile Ambassador Daniel Patrick Moynihan decided to stick it out and to match every extreme anti-American statement with similar language for America's detractors. "There is blood in the water and the sharks grow frenzied," he remarked.[82] The General Assembly, he charged, had become a "theater of the absurd." Once, when the Saudi Arabian Ambassador was berating the United States from the podium, Moynihan started to leave the hall. The speaker called out, "Come back, sit down, perhaps you will learn something."[83] It is doubtful that Moynihan learned anything, but he sat through the rest of the speech leering at the Saudi. On another occasion, the chief delegate from Kuwait identified historical changes in the United Nations Organization. The developing nations, he said, were ending the "supremacy of a certain group that used to roam the building like serene falcons in an uninhabited forest."[84]

**"United Nations."** Uncle Sam, once the master of the organization, found in the 1960s and 1970s that his power had slipped; indeed, he began to complain about the "tyranny" of the UN majority. (Tony Auth, *The Philadelphia Inquirer,* 1971)

**The Rich and Poor Countries**: A Comparison, 1960 and 1972*
(percentages)

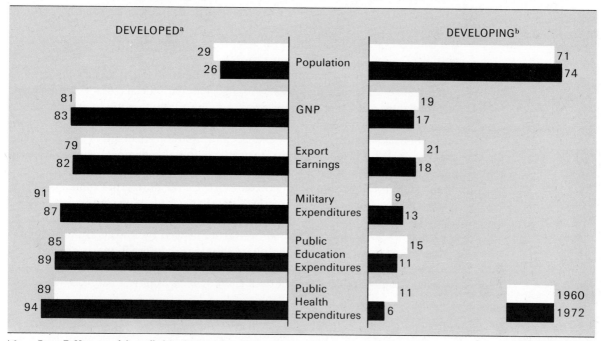

* *Source:* Roger D. Hansen and the staff of the Overseas Development Council, *The U.S. and World Development: Agenda for Action, 1976* (New York: Praeger Publishers, Inc., 1976), p. A-9. Based on Ruth Leger Sivard, *World Military and Social Expenditures, 1974,* published under the auspices of the Institute for World Order (New York), pp. 6 and 17; export figures from *International Trade, 1973–74* (Geneva: General Agreement on Tariffs and Trade, 1974), Publication Sales No. GATT/1974-4, Table E.

[a]Includes North America, USSR, most European countries, Oceania, Israel, Japan, and South Africa.
[b]Includes Latin America, a few southern European countries, Asia (except Israel and Japan), and Africa (except South Africa).

One critic of détente, charging that it was a detriment to American security, has quoted Henry A. Kissinger as saying that the United States "has passed its historic high point like so many earlier civilizations" and that the American people "lack stamina to stay the course against the Russians who are 'Sparta to our Athens.'"[85] The United States in the 1970s, however, remained a major world power, and, as Kissinger said elsewhere, few solutions were possible without American participation. The "industrial democracies" accounted for 65 percent of the world's production and 70 percent of its commerce. Economic power—including the power to sell or deny food—remained. "America's comeback," wrote the German magazine *Stern,* "is a question of when, not of if."[86] During the presidential campaign of 1976, Kissinger, under heavy attack from Republican right-winger Ronald Reagan and Democratic candidate Jimmy Carter, kept asserting that "America remains the most powerful nation in the world."[87] Venerable columnist James Reston called the campaign "The Great Nondebate" in foreign policy.[88]

The 1976 election of Jimmy Carter over Republican candidate Gerald Ford did not signal significant changes in American foreign policy. Carter frequently applauded the precedents of Harry S Truman and John F. Kennedy and appointed as his Secretary of State Cyrus Vance. A veteran diplomat of the 1960s, who served as deputy defense secretary (1964–1967) and assisted W. Averell Harriman as a negotiator in the unsuccessful Paris talks over Vietnam in 1968, West Virginia-born Vance was schooled at Yale University and became a prominent New York lawyer before joining the Defense Department in 1961. Once a strong supporter of American intervention in Vietnam, he said in 1977 that he learned the lesson that the United States cannot "prop up a series of regimes that lacked popular support."[89] The low-keyed, fifty-nine year old Vance was anything but a Kissinger in style. The new secretary of state possessed demonstrated negotiating skill and his quiet manner and credentials as a former govenment official reassured Americans and foreigners alike that the transition from one administration to another would not create fissures in American foreign relations. Carter's appointment of Polish-born political scientist Zbigniew Brzezinski (pronounced Zbig-NYEFF Breh-JIN-skee) as his White House national security adviser also demonstrated attachment to past policies. Recognized as an unreconstructed Cold Warrior, Brzezinski was a bright and prolific writer who had counseled Carter during the campaign. "U.S. foreign policy is like an aircraft carrier," Brzezinski said. "You simply don't send it into a 180-degree turn; at most you move it a few degrees to port or starboard."[90]

President Carter, indicating that he was influenced by lessons from the recent past, pledged he would seek nonmilitary solutions to international problems, curb the covert activities of the CIA, cooperate with Congress, reduce secrecy in the making of foreign policy, and cut back United States arms sales abroad, which had

**The Carter Foreign Policy Team.** Secretary of State Cyrus Vance (at head of table) and (to the right) President Jimmy Carter, National Security Affairs Adviser Zbigniew Brzezinski, and Vice-President Walter Mondale confer with diplomats from South Africa in 1977. (White House)

totaled $20 billion in 1976. He promised that the United States would not sup-
ply foreign aid to repressive governments that tread on human rights and he
appointed a black American, Congressman Andrew Young, as ambassador to the
United Nations to demonstrate the President's sympathy for emerging nationalism
and self-determination in the Third World. Doubters wondered if the Carter
Administration could shed tired, antirevolutionary assumptions and the habit and
apparent need for interventionism. In the future Washington certainly faced the
root test of a sophisticated diplomacy: whether or not it had the imagination and
flexibility to deal pragmatically with, and make concessions to, what the United
States does not have within its power to direct or to dominate—aspirations of
people in the Third and Fourth Worlds, the former colonial areas, to make their
own national choices, to control their own natural resources, and to be treated with
human dignity. As French President Charles DeGaulle once commented: "One
should avoid being caught between the dog and the lamp post."[91] One trait was
certain to characterize America's adjustments to a less powerful position. An
imperial power does not relinquish its domain and commanding status without
wrenching dislocations and reluctance—witness the Spanish, Dutch, Portuguese,
French, and British imperial death throes. Uncle Sam, tattered and torn in the
1970s, sensed the cresting of his power but still clung to the legacies of the past.

## Further Reading for the Period Since 1969

General studies that discuss this period and the conspicuous figures of Nixon and
Kissinger include Henry Brandon, *The Retreat of American Power* (1973), Lloyd C.
Gardner, ed., *The Great Nixon Turnaround* (1973), Stephen Graubard, *Kissinger:
Portrait of a Mind* (1973), Alan M. Jones, Jr., *U.S. Foreign Policy in a Changing World*
(1973), Bernard and Marvin Kalb, *Kissinger* (1974), Walter LaFeber, *America, Russia,
and the Cold War* (1976), David Landau, *Kissinger: Uses of Power* (1972), Robert E.
Osgood et al., *Retreat From Empire* (1973), Richard Rosecrance, ed., *America as an
Ordinary Country* (1976), Michael Roskin, "An American Metternich: Henry A.
Kissinger and the Global Balance of Power," in Frank Merli and Theodore Wilson,
eds., *Makers of American Diplomacy* (1974), Arthur M. Schlesinger, Jr., *The Imperial
Presidency* (1973), John Stoessinger, *Henry Kissinger: The Anguish of Power* (1976), and
Garry Wills, *Nixon Agonistes* (1970). Brief biographies appear in John A. Garraty,
ed., *Encyclopedia of American Biography* (1974).

Specific issues and areas are discussed in Charles F. Barnaby and Ronald
Huisken, *Arms Uncontrolled* (1975), Richard J. Barnet and Ronald Müller, *The Global
Reach: The Power of the Multinational Corporations* (1974), Edward Friedland, Paul
Seabury, and Aaron Wildavsky, *The Great Détente Disaster: Oil and the Decline of
American Foreign Policy* (1975), Alexander L. George and Richard Smoke, *Deterrence in
American Foreign Policy* (1975), Jon Glassman, *Arms for the Arabs* (1976), Melvin
Gurtov, *The United States Against the Third World* (1974), Gene T. Hsiao, ed.,
*Sino-American Détente and Its Policy Implications* (1974), Roger Kanet, ed., *The Soviet
Union and the Developing Nations* (1976), Anthony Lake, ed., *The Vietnam Legacy* (1976)
and *The "Tar Baby" Option: American Policy Toward Southern Rhodesia* (1976), Zuhayr
Mikdashi, *The International Politics of Natural Resources* (1976), Theodore H. Moran,
*Multinational Corporations and the Politics of Dependence: Copper in Chile* (1975), William
and Paul Paddock, *Time of Famines: America and the World Food Crisis* (1976), Barbara

Rogers, *White Wealth and Black Poverty: American Investments in Southern Africa* (1976), Edward R. F. Sheehan, *The Arabs, Israelis, and Kissinger* (1976), Robert W. Stookey, *America and the Arab States* (1975), and Franklin Tugwell, *The Politics of Oil In Venezuela* (1975).

Also consult the following magazines and journals for relevant articles on the issues of this period: *Foreign Policy, Foreign Affairs, International Journal, The Nation, Political Science Quarterly,* and *World Politics.* Also see the following notes.

## Notes to Chapter 15

1. Quoted in Marvin Kalb and Bernard Kalb, *Kissinger* (Boston: Little, Brown, 1974), p. 266.

2. Hugh Sidey in *Life, LXXII* (March 3, 1972), 12.

3. *Newsweek, LXXIX* (March 6, 1972), 15.

4. Quoted in Kalb and Kalb, *Kissinger,* p. 267.

5. Joseph Kraft, *The Chinese Difference* (New York: Saturday Review Press, 1973), p. 19.

6. *Newsweek, LXXIX* (February 28, 1972), 13.

7. *Department of State Bulletin, LXVI* (March 6, 1972), 290.

8. Quoted in Edgar Snow, *The Lost Revolution* (New York: Random House, 1972), p. 160.

9. *Public Papers of the Presidents, Richard M. Nixon, 1971* (Washington: Government Printing Office, 1972), p. 819.

10. Quoted in Frank van der Linden, *Nixon's Quest for Peace* (Washington–New York: Robert B. Luce, 1972), pp. 145–146.

11. Quoted in Lloyd C. Gardner, ed., *The Great Nixon Turnaround* (New York: New Viewpoints, 1973), p. 1.

12. *Department of State Bulletin, LXVI* (March 13, 1972), 315.

13. Harry Schwartz, "The Asian Triangle," *New York Times,* February 21, 1972.

14. Tom Wicker, "The Peking Primary," *ibid.,* February 24, 1972.

15. Quoted in William L. Safire, *Before the Fall: An Inside View of the Pre-Watergate White House* (Garden City, N.Y.: Doubleday, 1975), p. 452.

16. *Public Papers, Nixon, 1971,* p. 1121.

17. James C. Thomson, Jr., "China's New Diplomacy: A Symposium (II)," *Problems of Communism, XXI* (January–February, 1972), 49.

18. *New York Times,* February 21, 1972.

19. Quoted in Henry Brandon, *The Retreat of American Power* (New York: Dell, 1972), p. 190.

20. Quoted in Snow, *Lost Revolution,* p. 183.

21. Quoted in *Peking Review,* Nos. 7–8 (February 25, 1972), 8.

22. *Department of State Bulletin, LXVI* (March 20, 1972), 421.

23. Quoted in Safire, *Before the Fall,* p. 12.

24. George Gallup, "U.S. Image of Red China Shows Favorable Change," *Hartford Courant,* March 12, 1972.

25. *Department of State Bulletin, LXVI* (March 20, 1972), 422.

26. *Ibid.,* p. 424.

27. Quoted in van der Linden, *Nixon's Quest,* p. 162.

28. *Department of State Bulletin, LXVI* (March 6, 1972), 290 and (March 13, 1972), 331.

29. *Ibid., LXVI* (March 20, 1972), 436–437.

30. Kissinger quoted in Theodore H. White, *The Making of the President, 1972* (New York: Atheneum, 1973), p. x.

31. *Department of State Bulletin, LXVI* (March 20, 1972), 437–438.

32. Quoted in *New York Times,* February 28, 1972.

33. Quoted in Safire, *Before the Fall,* p. 102 and *Department of State Bulletin, LX* (February 10, 1969), 121.

34. Gardner, *The Great Nixon Turnaround.*

35. *Public Papers, Nixon, 1971,* p. 806.

36. Quoted in Garry Wills, *Nixon Agonistes: The Crisis of the Self-Made Man* (Boston: Houghton Mifflin, 1970), p. 20.

37. *New York Times,* March 12, 1976.

38. Quoted in Leslie H. Gelb, "Kissinger and Congress," *ibid.,* February 22, 1975.

39. Quoted in J. Garry Clifford, "Change and Continuity in American Foreign Policy Since 1930," in James T. Patterson, ed., *Paths to the Present* (Minneapolis: Burgess, 1975), p. 137.

40. "An Interview with Oriana Fallaci: Kissinger," *New Republic, CLXVII* (December 16, 1972), 21–22.

41. Quoted in Kalb and Kalb, *Kissinger,* p. 13.

42. Quoted in Jerome A. Cohen, "Implications of the Détente for Sino-American Trade," in Gene T. Hsiao, ed., *Sino-American Détente and Its Policy Implications* (New York: Praeger, 1974), p. 71.

43. Quoted in Kalb and Kalb, *Kissinger,* p. 334.

44. Quoted in Michael Roskin, "An American Metternich: Henry A. Kissinger and the Global Balance of Power," in Frank J. Merli and Theodore A. Wilson, eds., *Makers of American Diplomacy* (New York: Charles Scribner's, 1974), p. 698.

45. Quoted in Tad Szulc, "How Kissinger Did It: Behind the Vietnam Cease-Fire Agreement," *Foreign Policy,* No. 15 (Summer, 1974), p. 35.

46. Quoted in Stanley Millet, ed., *South Vietnam: U.S.-Communist Confrontation in Southeast Asia, 1969* (New York: Facts on File, 1973–1974; 7 vols), IV, 64.

47. *Ibid., 1970, V,* 100.

48. *Ibid.,* p. 107.

49. "The Talk of the Town," *The New Yorker, XLVIII* (September 23, 1972).

50. Quoted in *New York Times,* July 31, 1976.

51. Archibald MacLeish, "Now Let Us Address the Main Question: Bicentennial of What?" *ibid.,* July 3, 1976.

52. Edmund Stillman, in "America Now: A Failure of Nerve?" *Commentary, LX* (July, 1975), 83.

53. Ronald Steel, *ibid.,* p. 79.

54. Richard J. Barnet, *Roots of War* (Baltimore: Penguin Books, 1972), pp. 7–9.

55. Henry Steele Commager, "The Defeat of America," *New York Review of Books,* October 5, 1972, p. 13.

56. Daniel Bell, "The End of American Exceptionalism," *Public Interest,* No. 41 (Fall, 1975), 205.

57. Quoted in Ronald Steel, "The Power and the Glory," *New York Review of Books*, May 31, 1973, p. 29.

58. *Bill Moyer's Journal*, "A Conversation with Clark Clifford— Vietnam and Its Aftermath," April 10, 1975 (New York: Educational Broadcasting Corporation, 1975).

59. Quoted in Robert W. Stookey, *America and the Arab States* (New York: John Wiley and Sons, 1975), p. 221.

60. Quoted in Kalb and Kalb, *Kissinger*, p. 473.

61. Quoted in Edward R. F. Sheehan, "How Kissinger Did It: Step by Step in the Middle East," *Foreign Policy*, No. 22 (Spring, 1976), p. 48.

62. Quoted in *New York Times*, March 15, 1976.

63. Quoted in U.S. Senate, Staff Report of Select Committee to Study Governmental Operations with Respect to Intelligence Activities, *Covert Action in Chile, 1963–1973* (Washington, D.C.: U.S. Government Printing Office, 1975), p. 33.

64. U.S. Senate, Committee on Foreign Relations, *Meeting With President-Elect Carter* (Washington, D.C.: Government Printing Office, 1976), p. 16.

65. *Department of State Bulletin*, LXXIV (March 22, 1976), 357.

66. *Ibid.*, LXXIV (June 7, 1976), 713.

67. Quoted in Tom Wicker, "Mr. Ford and Angola," *New York Times*, January 30, 1976.

68. Quoted in Tom Wicker, "How Not to Think Globally," *ibid.*, March 14, 1976.

69. Quoted in Michael T. Kaufman, "Communist Giants Are Using Africa as an Arena," *ibid.*, March 7, 1976. Italics added.

70. Quoted in *Hartford Courant*, March 17, 1976.

71. *Department of State Bulletin*, LXXIV (June 7, 1976), 714.

72. *Ibid.*, LXXV (July 12, 1976), 46. Italics added.

73. *Ibid.*, LXXII (June 2, 1975), 713.

74. Lawrence Van Gelder, "Response Loses Its Urgency," *New York Times*, January 25, 1976.

75. *Ibid.*, December 12, 1973.

76. *Department of State Bulletin*, LXXIII (September 22, 1975), 425.

77. *Ibid.*, LXXII (June 2, 1975), 713.

78. Richard J. Barnet and Ronald E. Müller, *The Global Reach: The Power of the Multinational Corporations* (New York: Simon and Schuster, 1974), p. 13.

79. *Department of State Bulletin*, LXXIII (October 6, 1975), 493.

80. Quoted in Ivo D. Duchacek, *Nations and Men: An Introduction to International Politics* (Hinsdale, Ill.: The Dryden Press, 1975; 3rd ed.), p. 146.

81. Quoted in Claire Sterling, "The View From Anzio: They Do Not Love Us," *New York Times Magazine*, July 4, 1976, p. 138.

82. Quoted in Zbigniew Brzezinski, "America in a Hostile World," *Foreign Policy*, No. 23 (Summer, 1976), p. 81.

83. Quoted in *Time*, CVII (January 26, 1976), 27.

84. Quoted in *New York Times*, December 8, 1974.

85. From notes of retired Admiral Elmo R. Zumwalt, *ibid.*, March 17, 1976.

86. *Ibid.*, April 9, 1976.

87. *Department of State Bulletin*, LXXIV (April 12, 1976), 458.

88. *New York Times*, April 16, 1976.

89. Quoted in *Washington Post*, January 12, 1977.

90. Quoted in *Newsweek*, LXXXVIII (December 27, 1976), 19.

91. Quoted in Thomas H. Etzold, "Interdependence 1976?" *Diplomatic History*, I (Winter, 1977), 43.

# Appendix

## Makers of American Foreign Policy

| Presidents | Secretaries of State | Chairmen of the Senate Foreign Relations Committee |
|---|---|---|
| George Washington (1789–1797) | Thomas Jefferson (1790–1793) | |
| | Edmund Randolph (1794–1795) | |
| | Timothy Pickering (1795–1800) | |
| John Adams (1797–1801) | Timothy Pickering (1795–1800) | |
| | John Marshall (1800–1801) | |
| Thomas Jefferson (1801–1809) | James Madison (1801–1809) | |
| James Madison (1809–1817) | Robert Smith (1809–1811) | James Barbour (1816–1818) |
| | James Monroe (1811–1817) | |
| James Monroe (1817–1825) | John Quincy Adams (1817–1825) | James Barbour (1816–1818) |
| | | Nathaniel Macon (1818–1819) |
| | | James Brown (1819–1820) |
| | | James Barbour (1820–1821) |
| | | Rufus King (1821–1822) |
| | | James Barbour (1822–1825) |
| John Quincy Adams (1825–1829) | Henry Clay (1825–1829) | Nathaniel Macon (1825–1826) |
| | | Nathan Sanford (1826–1827) |
| | | Nathaniel Macon (1827–1828) |
| | | Littleton W. Tazewell (1828–1832) |
| Andrew Jackson (1829–1837) | Martin Van Buren (1829–1831) | Littleton W. Tazewell (1828–1832) |
| | Edward Livingston (1831–1833) | John Forsyth (1832–1833) |
| | Louis McLane (1833–1834) | William Wilkins (1833–1834) |
| | John Forsyth (1834–1841) | Henry Clay (1834–1836) |
| | | James Buchanan (1836–1841) |
| Martin Van Buren (1837–1841) | John Forsyth (1834–1841) | James Buchanan (1836–1841) |
| William H. Harrison (1841) | Daniel Webster (1841–1843) | William C. Rives (1841–1842) |
| John Tyler (1841–1845) | Daniel Webster (1841–1843) | William C. Rives (1841–1842) |
| | Abel P. Upshur (1843–1844) | William S. Archer (1842–1845) |
| | John C. Calhoun (1844–1845) | |
| James K. Polk (1845–1849) | James Buchanan (1845–1849) | William Allen (1845–1846) |
| | | Ambrose H. Sevier (1846–1848) |
| | | Edward A. Hannegan (1848–1849) |
| | | Thomas H. Benton (1849) |
| Zachary Taylor (1849–1850) | John M. Clayton (1849–1850) | William R. King (1849–1850) |
| Millard Fillmore (1850–1853) | Daniel Webster (1850–1852) | Henry S. Foote (1850–1851) |
| | Edward Everett (1852–1853) | James M. Mason (1851–1861) |
| Franklin Pierce (1853–1857) | William L. Marcy (1853–1857) | James M. Mason (1851–1861) |

# Makers of American Foreign Policy

| Presidents | Secretaries of State | Chairmen of the Senate Foreign Relations Committee |
|---|---|---|
| James Buchanan (1857–1861) | Lewis Cass (1857–1860) | James M. Mason (1851–1861) |
| | Jeremiah S. Black (1860–1861) | |
| Abraham Lincoln (1861–1865) | William H. Seward (1861–1869) | Charles Sumner (1861–1871) |
| Andrew Johnson (1865–1869) | William H. Seward (1861–1869) | Charles Sumner (1861–1871) |
| Ulysses S. Grant (1869–1877) | Elihu B. Washburne (1869) | Charles Sumner (1861–1871) |
| | Hamilton Fish (1869–1877) | Simon Cameron (1871–1877) |
| Rutherford B. Hayes (1877–1881) | William M. Evarts (1877–1881) | Hannibal Hamlin (1877–1879) |
| | | William W. Eaton (1879–1881) |
| James A. Garfield (1881) | James G. Blaine (1881) | Ambrose E. Burnside (1881) |
| | | George F. Edmunds (1881) |
| Chester A. Arthur (1881–1885) | Frederick T. Freylinghuysen (1881–1885) | William Windon (1881–1883) |
| | | John F. Miller (1883–1887) |
| | Thomas F. Bayard (1885–1889) | John F. Miller (1883–1887) |
| Grover Cleveland (1885–1889) | | John Sherman (1887–1893) |
| | James G. Blaine (1889–1892) | John Sherman (1887–1893) |
| Benjamin Harrison (1889–1893) | John W. Foster (1892–1893) | |
| | Walter Q. Gresham (1893–1895) | John T. Morgan (1893–1895) |
| Grover Cleveland (1893–1897) | Richard Olney (1895–1897) | John Sherman (1895–1897) |
| | John Sherman (1897–1898) | William P. Frye (1897) |
| William McKinley (1897–1901) | William R. Day (1898) | Cushman K. Davis (1897–1901) |
| | John Hay (1898–1905) | |
| | John Hay (1898–1905) | William P. Frye (1901) |
| Theodore Roosevelt (1901–1909) | Elihu Root (1905–1909) | Shelby M. Cullom (1901–1913) |
| | Robert Bacon (1909) | |
| | Philander C. Knox (1909–1913) | Shelby M. Cullom (1901–1913) |
| William Howard Taft (1909–1913) | William Jennings Bryan (1913–1915) | Augustus O. Bacon (1913–1915) |
| Woodrow Wilson (1913–1921) | Robert Lansing (1915–1920) | William J. Stone (1915–1919) |
| | Bainbridge Colby (1920–1921) | |
| | Charles E. Hughes (1921–1925) | Henry Cabot Lodge (1919–1924) |
| | Charles E. Hughes (1921–1925) | Henry Cabot Lodge (1919–1924) |
| Warren G. Harding (1921–1923) | Frank B. Kellogg (1925–1929) | Henry Cabot Lodge (1919–1924) |
| Calvin Coolidge (1923–1929) | Henry L. Stimson (1929–1933) | William E. Borah (1925–1933) |
| | Cordell Hull (1933–1944) | William E. Borah (1925–1933) |
| Herbert C. Hoover (1929–1933) | Edward R. Stettinius, Jr. | Key Pittman (1933–1941) |
| Franklin D. Roosevelt (1933–1945) | (1944–1945) | Walter F. George (1941) |
| | | Tom Connally (1941–1947) |

# Makers of American Foreign Policy

| Presidents | Secretaries of State | Chairmen of the Senate Foreign Relations Committee | Secretaries of Defense |
|---|---|---|---|
| Harry S Truman (1945–1953) | Edward R. Stettinius, Jr. (1944–1945) | Tom Connally (1941–1947) | James V. Forrestal (1947–1949) |
| | James F. Byrnes (1945–1947) | Arthur H. Vandenberg (1947–1949) | Louis A. Johnson (1949–1950) |
| | George C. Marshall (1947–1949) | Tom Connally (1949–1953) | George C. Marshall (1950–1951) |
| | Dean G. Acheson (1949–1953) | | Robert A. Lovett (1951–1953) |
| Dwight D. Eisenhower (1953–1961) | John F. Dulles (1953–1959) | Alexander Wiley (1953–1955) | Charles E. Wilson (1953–1957) |
| | Christian A. Herter (1959–1961) | Walter F. George (1955–1957) | Neil H. McElroy (1957–1959) |
| | | Theodore F. Green (1957–1959) | Thomas S. Gates, Jr. (1959–1961) |
| | | J. W. Fulbright (1959–1975) | |
| John F. Kennedy (1961–1963) | Dean Rusk (1961–1969) | J. W. Fulbright (1959–1975) | Robert S. McNamara (1961–1968) |
| Lyndon B. Johnson (1963–1969) | Dean Rusk (1961–1969) | J. W. Fulbright (1959–1975) | Robert S. McNamara (1961–1968) |
| | | | Clark M. Clifford (1968–1969) |
| Richard M. Nixon (1969–1974) | William P. Rogers (1969–1973) | J. W. Fulbright (1959–1975) | Melvin R. Laird (1969–1973) |
| | Henry A. Kissinger (1973–1977) | | Elliot L. Richardson (1973) |
| | | | James R. Schlesinger (1973–1976) |
| Gerald R. Ford (1974–1977) | Henry A. Kissinger (1973–1977) | J. W. Fulbright (1959–1975) | James R. Schlesinger (1973–1976) |
| | | John Sparkman (1975—) | Donald Rumsfeld (1976–1977) |
| James Carter (1977—) | Cyrus A. Vance (1977—) | John Sparkman (1975—) | Harold Brown (1977—) |

# Index